THE MACARTHUR NEW TESTAMENT COMMENTARY

1 CORINTHIANS

John MacArthur, Jr.

MOODY PRESS/CHICAGO

To my professors at Talbot Theological Seminary
who encouraged and educated me in the science and
art of biblical exposition

All Scripture quotations in this book are from *The New American Standard Bible,* © 1960, 1962, 1963, 1968, 1971, 1972, 1973, 1975, and 1977 by The Lockman Foundation, and are used by permission.

Library of Congress Cataloging in Publication Data

MacArthur, John F.
First Corinthians.

(The MacArthur New Testament commentary)
Bibliography: p.
Includes index.
1. Bible. N.T. Corinthians, 1st—Commentaries.
I. Title. II. Series: MacArthur, John F. MacArthur
New Testament commentary.
BS2675.3.M29 1984   227'.207   84-20795
ISBN 0-8024-0754-4

3 4 5 6 7 Printing/RR/Year 89 88 87 86 85

Printed in the United States of America

Contents

Preface

It continues to be a rewarding divine communion for me to preach expositionally through the New Testament. My goal is always to have deep fellowship with the Lord in the understanding of His Word, and out of that experience to explain to His people what a passage means. In the words of Nehemiah 8:8, I strive "to give the sense" of it so they may truly hear God speak and, in so doing, may respond to Him.

Obviously, God's people need to understand Him, which demands knowing His Word of truth (2 Tim. 2:15) and allowing that Word to dwell in us richly (Col. 3:16). The dominant thrust of my ministry, therefore, is to help make God's living Word alive to His people. It is a refreshing adventure.

This New Testament commentary series reflects this objective of explaining and applying Scripture. Some commentaries are primarily linguistic, others are mostly theological, and some are mainly homiletical. This one is basically explanatory, or expository. It is not linguistically technical, but deals with lingistics when this seems helpful to proper interpretation. It is not theologically expansive, but focuses on the major doctrines in each text and on how they relate to the whole of Scripture. It is not primarily homiletical, though each unit of thought is generally treated as one chapter, with a clear outline and logical flow of thought. Most truths are illustrated and applied with other Scripture. After establishing the context of a passage, I have tried to follow closely the writer's development and reasoning.

My prayer is that each reader will fully understand what the Holy Spirit is saying through this part of His Word, so that His revelation may lodge in the minds of believers and bring greater obedience and faithfulness—to the glory of our great God.

Introduction

Today Corinth is a small town with little significance other than historical. But in New Testament times it was a thriving, prosperous, and strategically located city.

Greece is divided geographically into two parts. The southern part, the Peloponnesus, is attached to the northern by a very narrow, four-mile-wide isthmus. On the western side was the Gulf of Corinth and the port city of Lechaeum. On the eastern side was the Saronic Gulf and the port city of Cenchreae. In the middle of the isthmus, to the south, is Corinth, situated on a commanding plateau. In ancient times all north and south overland traffic, including that to and from Athens, had to pass through Corinth.

Sea travel around the Peloponnesus was both time-consuming and dangerous. It was so treacherous that mariners had the saying "A sailor never takes a journey around Malea [the cape at the south end of the peninsula] until he first writes his will." Most captains, therefore, chose to carry their ships overland on skids or rollers across the narrow isthmus, directly past Corinth. This procedure was quicker, more economical, and much safer than sailing 250 miles around the peninsula. In fact, the isthmus came to be known as *dialcos,* which means "the place of dragging across." Corinth benefited from traffic in all directions and consequently became a major trade center.

Today a canal—envisioned by Perisander in the sixth century B.C., begun by the Roman emperor Nero in the first century A.D., but not completed until the end of the nineteenth century—connects the two gulfs across the isthmus, greatly facilitating maritime travel.

Corinth was also successful as an entertainment center. The two great athletic festivals of that day were the Olympian and the Isthmian games, and Corinth was host city for the latter—named after and played on the Isthmus of Corinth.

Corinth had been destroyed by the Romans in 146 B.C. and then rebuilt by Julius Caesar a hundred years later. At first it was a Roman colony, largely populated by Romans, and eventually became the capital of the Roman province of Achaia. Because of its location it soon became again a major trade center, with the resulting cosmopolitan population. It was made up of Greeks, Roman officials and businessmen, and Near Eastern peoples, including many Jews.

Like most Greek cities, Corinth had an acropolis (literally, "high city"), called Acrocorinth, which was used as a place of defense and for pagan worship. From its top on a clear day Athens can be seen, some forty-five miles away. Situated on a 2,000-foot high granite mound, Acrocorinth was large enough to hold all the population of Corinth and of its surrounding farmlands in time of siege. It also held a famous temple to Aphrodite, goddess of love. The temple normally housed some one thousand priestesses, ritual prostitutes, who each night would come down into Corinth and ply their trade among the many foreign travelers and the local men.

Even to the pagan world the city was known for its moral corruption, so much so that in classical Greek *corinthiazesthai* ("to behave like a Corinthian") came to represent gross immorality and drunken debauchery. The name of the city became synonymous with moral depravity. In this letter to the church there, Paul lists some of the city's characteristic sins—fornication (*porneia,* from which comes our term pornography), idolatry, adultery, effeminacy, homosexuality, stealing, covetousness, drunkenness, reviling (abusive speech), and swindling (6:9-10).

Some of the Corinthian believers had been guilty of practicing those sins before their conversion and had been cleansed (6:11). Others in the church, however, were still living immorally, some involved in sins worse than those—sins that Paul reminds them even pagan Gentiles did not commit, such as incest (5:1).

FOUNDING OF THE CHURCH AT CORINTH

Paul first came to Corinth on his second missionary journey. He had been preaching and working in Macedonian/Greek cities for some time. From Philippi (where he first ministered in Europe), he had gone to Thessalonica, Berea, Athens, and then Corinth (Acts 16:11–18:1).

Upon arriving in Corinth he met Aquila and Priscilla, Jews who had been driven out of Rome, and who were, like himself, tentmakers. He stayed with them for a while and began to preach regularly in the synagogue every Sabbath. Silas and Timothy joined him from Macedonia, and, as Paul's preaching intensified, so did resistance to his message. Soon, however, many Corinthians, including Jews, began to believe in Christ. Even Crispus, leader of the synagogue, along with his household, trusted in the Lord (Acts 18:8).

Paul continued to minister in Corinth for one and a half years (Acts 18:11). Jewish opposition became so strong that he was brought before a Roman tribunal. Since the charges were purely religious, however, the proconsul, Gallio, refused to hear the case. After staying a while longer, Paul left Corinth with Priscilla and Aquila and went to Ephesus. Leaving his friends there, he returned to Palestine (Acts 18:12-22).

The second leader of the Corinthian church was Apollos. An eloquent Jewish convert from Alexandria, Apollos had come to Ephesus and begun preaching while Aquila and Priscilla were there. Although "he was mighty in the Scriptures," he had some doctrinal deficiencies, which Aquila and Priscilla were instrumental in correcting. When he wanted to preach in Achaia, the Ephesian church not only encouraged him but gave him a letter of commendation, and he began ministering in Corinth as its next pastor (Acts 18:24–19:1).

Some time between Paul's leaving Corinth and his writing what we call First Corinthians, Paul had written the church another letter (1 Cor. 5:9), commonly referred to as the lost epistle. It too was corrective in nature.

Church Problems

The Corinthian church had many serious problems, one of which was factionalism. After Apollos had ministered in Corinth for a time, some of the believers developed a special loyalty to him. Friction began to develop between them and those whose loyalty was to Paul. Others were loyal to Peter (Cephas, his Aramaic name) and still another group identified itself as belonging only to Christ. The apostle strongly rebuked all of them for quarreling and having such unspiritual divisions (1:10-13; 3:1-9).

Their most serious problem, however, was in not detaching themselves from the worldly ways of the society around them. They could not understand, and perhaps did not want to understand, the principle of "Do not love the world, nor the things in the world" (1 John 2:15). They could not get "decorinthianized." In his previous lost letter, Paul specifically had warned them "not to associate with immoral people" (1 Cor. 5:9). Some of the Christians thought he meant for them not to associate with unbelievers who were immoral. But the sexually corrupt, the covetous, swindling, and idolatrous people to whom Paul referred were fellow church members who refused to give up, or had fallen back into, the debauched life-style of Corinth (5:9-11). The faithful believers were not to associate with such as those. Such wicked brethren were, in fact, to be put out of the fellowship in order to purify the church (5:13).

Like many Christians today, the Corinthian believers had great difficulty in not mimicking the unbelieving and corrupt society around them. They usually managed to stay a little higher than the world morally, but they were moving downward, in the same direction as the world. They wanted to be in God's kingdom while keeping one foot in the kingdom of this world. They wanted to have the blessings of the new life but hang on to the pleasures of the old. They wanted to have what they thought was the best of both worlds, but Paul plainly warned them that that was impossible (6:9-10).

The Corinthians had gotten the principles confused. They continued to associate with openly and arrogantly sinful church members, with whom they should have broken fellowship. And, on the other hand, they mimicked, but refused to associate with, their unbelieving neighbors, to whom they should have been witnessing.

Yet they lacked no spiritual resources (1:5-7) and had great potential for spiritual power and blessing. Paul longed to see that potential realized. Such was the church to whom Paul wrote.

Brief Outline of First Corinthians

Calling and benefits of sainthood (1:1-9)
Errors and problems in the church (1:10–16:4) regarding:
      Unity (1:10–3:23)
      Servanthood (4:1-21)
      Morality (5:1–6:20)
      Marriage (7:1-40)
      Liberty (8:1–11:1)
      Men and women in the church (11:2-16)
      The Lord's Supper (11:17-34)
      Spiritual gifts (12–14)
      The resurrection (15)
      Stewardship (16:1-4)
Personal plans and greetings (16:5-24)

Called to Be Saints
(1:1-3)

1

Paul, called as an apostle of Jesus Christ by the will of God, and Sosthenes our brother, to the church of God which is at Corinth, to those who have been sanctified in Christ Jesus, saints by calling, with all who in every place call upon the name of our Lord Jesus Christ, their Lord and ours: Grace to you and peace from God our Father and the Lord Jesus Christ. (1:1-3)

Rather than placing their names at the end of a letter, as is the modern custom, ancient Greeks put their names at the beginning, allowing readers to immediately identify the author. In a joint letter, the names of the others involved in sending the message were also given. **Paul** always gave his name at the beginning of his letters and frequently named other church leaders who, in some degree or other, joined him in writing. In 1 Corinthians he mentions **Sosthenes,** and in 2 Corinthians, Timothy (2 Cor. 1:1; cf. Phil. 1:1; Col. 1:1; 1 Thess. 1:1; 2 Thess. 1:1; Philem. 1).

Next was given the name of the addressee, the person or persons to whom the letter was sent, which for the present letter was **the church of God which is at Corinth.** Then words of greeting or blessing were often given, as in v. 3. Paul used such a threefold salutation in all of his New Testament letters.

Paul also generally referred to himself as **an apostle,** not for the purpose of identity—that is to distinguish himself from other Pauls in the church or simply to

1

inform his readers of his office—but to indicate at the very beginning that he was writing first of all as an emissary of the Lord. His apostleship established his authority. Even in his letters to Timothy, his close associate and "true child in the faith" (1 Tim. 1:2), Paul calls attention to his apostleship (1 Tim. 1:1; 2 Tim. 1:1). Only in Philippians, the Thessalonian letters, and Philemon does he not mention his apostleship in his opening words.

His description of himself as **an apostle of Jesus Christ by the will of God** was not a reflection of pride or self-glory. He was not flaunting his position of authority, as some speakers and writers often do with their titles, degrees, and accomplishments. Self-glory was the furthest thing from Paul's intent. Later in this same epistle he refers to himself as "the least of the apostles, who am not fit to be called an apostle, because I persecuted the church of God" (15:9).

Sometimes, however, it is important to establish one's right to speak authoritatively on a subject. A person, for instance, who has no medical degree or training or experience would never get a hearing at a conference on medicine. A person's credentials give some indication as to whether or not what he has to say should be taken seriously. Paul did not mention his apostleship in order to gain honor as an individual but to gain respect as a teacher of God's Word. He was not an apostle by his own appointment, or even by the church's appointment, but by God's appointment—**by the will of God**. At the outset he wanted to establish that what he had to say was said with God's own authority. Since his message was so corrective, this was of great necessity.

FIVE REASONS FOR PAUL'S ASSERTING HIS APOSTLESHIP

I believe there are perhaps five reasons why Paul, unlike the other apostolic writers, was so careful to assert his apostleship in his letters. First of all, he was not a part of the twelve. He had not been called by Jesus during His earthly ministry to be one of the inner circle of disciples who accompanied Him "beginning with the baptism of John, until the day that He was taken up from us" (Acts 1:22). Of that original group, one (Judas) was disqualified and was later replaced by Matthias (Acts 1:21-26)—who, though identified by casting lots, was chosen by God (v. 24). With the selection of Matthias the apostolic ranks were again complete. Beginning at Pentecost the apostles were clearly the authoritative voice of the gospel. When Peter gave his message at that time, he did so "taking his stand with the eleven" (Acts 2:14; cf. v. 37), and the infant church in Jerusalem devoted itself to "the apostles' teaching" (v. 42). The apostles were the Lord's supreme earthly representatives, and they preached and taught with His authority. With Christ as the "corner stone," the apostles were the foundation of the church (Eph. 2:20).

As far as we know, however, Paul never saw or heard Jesus during that time. Paul was first known to the church as a bitter enemy and persecutor, "breathing threats and murder against the disciples of the Lord" (Acts 9:1; cf. 8:1). He not only had not chosen to be a follower of Christ but had chosen to oppose Christ's followers with all his might. Even after his conversion there was no way he could retroactively become one of the twelve. Yet he declared himself to be an apostle, based on the same foundational qualifications as those of the twelve. He, too, had seen the resurrected Christ (Acts 9:3-6, 17; 22:11-15; 1 Cor. 9:1; 15:8) and he, too, in unique revelations, had been specifically chosen by the Lord to be an apostle (1 Cor. 1:1). He was concerned to establish the fact that he was equal to the twelve as a foundational teacher of revealed truth.

Second, I believe that he emphasized his apostleship because of his dealings with detractors and false teachers, by whom he was continually being challenged and harassed. The Judaizers were particularly strong and persistent in opposing Paul's authority and doctrine and in questioning his motives. Even some who claimed to be his friends resisted his leadership and questioned his teaching. Such ridicule and persecution Paul considered to be badges of apostleship. "For," he said, "I think, God has exhibited us apostles last of all, as men condemned to death; because we have become a spectacle to the world, both to angels and to men" (4:9). In spite of denials, Paul's teaching was true and reliable, for he was a divinely-called apostle of Jesus Christ.

Third, Paul emphasized his apostleship because of his relationship to Christ. This emphasis was for the benefit of fellow believers. The Christians in Jerusalem, especially, had not been sure about the genuineness of Paul's faith. Having known him, or known of him, as Saul of Tarsus, the fierce persecutor of the church, they had difficulty believing that he could now be a reliable Christian leader, much less an apostle (Acts 9:26). Their fears were, of course, also fed by the accusations and detractions of the false teachers. It was not hard to believe the worst about him. Christians in other places also had misgivings. Legalistic Judaizers, for example, had confused many Christians in Galatia both about the gospel (Gal. 1:6; 3:1-5) and about Paul's authority in teaching it (1:11–2:10). He therefore carefully reminded the Corinthian church of his full apostolic authority in writing this letter to them, pointing out that, when he had ministered among them, he did so in God's power and wisdom (1 Cor. 2:1-7).

Fourth, Paul emphasized his apostleship to point up his special relationship to the church in Corinth itself, which was "a seal of [his] apostleship in the Lord" (9:2). They, of all people, should recognize his special calling and position. Their very existence as a body of believers was a proof of his right to address them with divine authority. He had been the instrument God used to bring them to salvation.

Fifth, Paul emphasized his apostleship in order to show his special relationship to God as His emissary. He was **an apostle of Jesus Christ by the will of God.** He was saying, in effect, "What I say to you is delegated by God. I am His apostle, and my message to you is God's message to you."

When the Jewish supreme court, the Sanhedrin, was asked to arbitrate a serious dispute or to give an interpretation regarding Jewish law or tradition, they would send their decision by an *apostolos* to the parties involved, who were often represented through a synagogue. As far as the message was concerned, the *apostolos* possessed the full authority of the Sanhedrin. He did not speak for himself, but for the Sanhedrin. Yet he was more than a messenger. He was an emissary, an envoy, an ambassador. Paul was God's envoy, God's ambassador (cf. 2 Cor. 5:20; Eph. 6:20), God's *apostolos*. While among them he had not preached his own message to the Corinthians, but God's message. He was not now writing his own message to them, but God's message.

In light of the twelve, in light of false teachers, and in light of his relationship to Christ, to the Corinthian church, and to God the Father, Paul was fully an apostle. He was careful to establish the legitimacy of his apostleship in order to establish the legitimacy of his message.

The Purposes and Responsibilities of the Apostles

Apostles were chosen by God to work in the founding and forming of the church, after which time apostleship ceased. When all the apostles had died, the office of apostle no longer existed. They were selected, sent, and empowered by God for that period in the history of the church, which was over when their lives were over. As the human founders and foundation of the church, the apostles had particular purposes and responsibilities.

First, as eyewitnesses, they were to preach the gospel—the true, complete, and authoritative gospel of Christ's substitutionary atonement by His death and resurrection and of salvation by faith in Him (1 Cor. 1:17-18; cf. 9:14). Their teaching was equivalent to Christ's teaching. As will be developed in a later chapter, there is no distinction, as some interpreters maintain, between what Paul (or Peter or James or John) teaches in the New Testament and what God teaches. Paul's statement in 1 Corinthians 7:12 ("I say, not the Lord"), for example, simply indicates that Jesus, during His earthly ministry, gave no specific teaching on the subject being discussed (that of a believer's remaining with an unbelieving spouse). As an apostle, Paul was qualified to teach in behalf of Christ, and his teaching was as authoritative as if spoken from Jesus' own lips.

The apostles also were to be devoted to prayer and to ministering the word (Acts 6:4) and to equipping believers for service in order to build up Christ's Body (Eph. 4:11-12). Finally, they were to evidence their apostleship by performing miracles (2 Cor. 12:12).

Sosthenes our brother may have been Paul's amanuensis, or secretary, at the time this letter was written. The fact that his name is included in the greeting, however, indicates that he not only penned the letter but fully agreed with Paul about its message.

This is no doubt the same Sosthenes mentioned in Acts 18, one who knew the Corinthian situation well. He had been a leader of the synagogue at Corinth, probably replacing Crispus, the former leader who had become a believer (Acts 18:8). On one occasion Sosthenes was beaten for his involvement in bringing Paul before the civil court at Corinth (Acts 18:12-17). Some ancient manuscripts of the text report that the Jews beat him and other manuscripts report that the Greeks beat him. If by the Jews, it no doubt was because he represented them so poorly at court. If by the Greeks, it was because they resented his taking up their court time with a matter that concerned only Jewish religion.

Now, however, Paul could refer to Sosthenes as "our brother," indicating that some time after the incident just mentioned—and perhaps partly because of it—this former opponent of the gospel, like Paul himself, had become a Christian. Having likely been converted under Paul's preaching and having worked with the apostle for perhaps a year or more in Corinth, Sosthenes was known and respected by the Corinthian believers whom he now joined Paul in writing.

SAINTHOOD

To the church of God which is at Corinth, to those who have been sanctified in Christ Jesus, saints by calling, with all who in every place call upon the name of our Lord Jesus Christ, their Lord and ours. (1:2)

The church to whom Paul was writing was not the church of the Corinthians but **the church of God** which was located at Corinth. The church is a body of people who belong not to themselves or to any leader or group but to God. Believers, whether pastors, officers, or ordinary members in the church, together compose Christ's earthly Body and all are called to be stewards of it (Eph. 4:11-13). We are not our own, individually or collectively, but have all been bought with the price of Christ's blood (1 Cor. 6:20).

POSITION AND PRACTICE

All believers **have been sanctified in Christ Jesus** and are **saints by calling.** A saint, as the term is used in the New Testament, is not a specially pious or self-sacrificing Christian who has been canonized by an ecclesiastical council. The Greek word translated **saint** is *hagios,* meaning "set apart one," or "holy one." The Corinthian believers *were* holy in God's sight, regardless of their sinful living and distorted doctrine. They were saints because they had **been sanctified** (from *hagiazō*), set apart from sin, *made* holy **in Christ Jesus.** According to Scripture, every true believer in Jesus Christ—whether faithful or unfaithful, well known or unknown, leader or follower—is a set apart person, a holy person, a saint. In the biblical sense, the most obscure believer today is just as much a saint as the apostle Paul. This is the believer's position in Christ.

Holiness, in that positional sense, is not a matter of good works, of holy living. As Christians we should live holy lives, but holy living does not make us holy. To the extent our living is holy, it is because, in Christ, we already *are* holy and have the counsel and power of His Holy Spirit. We are holy because the Sanctifier (the One who makes holy) has already sanctified us in response to our trust in Him (Heb. 2:11). Christ's work, not our own, makes us holy. We are "saints by calling." That refers to the efficacious call of God to salvation (1:24, 26).

Like all believers, the Corinthians were **saints** because God called them to be saints (cf. Gal. 1:6; Eph. 4:1, 4; Col. 3:15; 1 Tim. 6:12; 1 Pet. 2:9, 21; 3:9; 2 Pet. 1:3; Jude

1). "We have been sanctified through the offering of the body of Jesus Christ once for all" (Heb. 10:10; cf. v. 14). By His own sacrificial work on the cross, Jesus Christ sanctifies those who believe in Him. He sets them apart (the root meaning of *hagiazō*) for Himself, cleanses them, and perfects them. God provides holiness through His Son. Man's part is to claim holiness, to claim sainthood, by faith in the Son (Acts 26:18). We have a new nature, the divine nature, and have escaped the corruptions of the world, possessing all things related to life and godliness (2 Pet. 1:3-4).

Paul's declaring all the Corinthian believers to be saints was quite a declaration in light of the things—very evident from the rest of this letter—that characterized their living. The Corinthian church was far from being saintly in the sense in which the term is often used. They were particularly worldly and immoral, yet in his opening words Paul stressed that every one of them who had truly believed in Jesus Christ was saved and was a saint. Not only are all saints saved, but all the saved are saints. Every believer has the right to call himself a saint. None of us is worthy of the title, but God has declared us to be saints because of our trust in His Son. Our practice, our behavior in our humanness, needs to be conformed to our "saintly" new divine nature.

Paul seems to have been especially determined to make that truth clear to the Corinthians. Virtually the entire letter of 1 Corinthians, beginning with 1:10, deals with wrong doctrine and wrong behavior. It seems that nearly every serious doctrinal and moral error imaginable could be found within that congregation. Yet Paul begins the letter by calling them saints. In practice they were gross sinners, but in position they were pure saints. We should note that there were, no doubt, some in the church who were not saints at all, who were unbelievers (16:22).

It is important for every Christian to keep in mind the great difference between his position and his practice, his standing and his state. God sees us as righteous, because He sees us through His righteous Son, who has taken our place, and because He has planted in us a righteous new nature. Without keeping this important and encouraging truth in mind, it is impossible to clearly understand 1 Corinthians or any other part of the New Testament.

Presidents do not always act presidentially, diplomats do not always act diplomatically, kings do not always act kingly—but they are still presidents, diplomats, and kings. Christians do not always act like Christians, but they are still Christians.

Some years ago a young boy, whose father was a pastor, was put in jail for stealing some merchandise from a department store. His father happened to be playing golf with some of the church leaders at the time and received a call while on the golf course to come down to the jail to get his son. Thinking it was a mistake, the pastor took the other men with him to the police station, where embarrassment abounded. The deepest impression of the incident left on the boy's mind was made by the repeated reminders he received from those men, and from many others afterward, about who his father was. "Having a father like yours," they would ask, "how could you have done what you did?" Yet as humiliating and painful as the experience was, the boy knew he was still his father's son. He had not acted like a son of his father should have acted, but he was still a son.

As Christians one of the strongest rebukes we can have when we sin is to be reminded of who our Father is. And reminding ourselves of whose we are should be one of our strongest deterrents to sin. Remembering our position can compel us to improve our practice.

Further, Paul increased the Corinthians' sense of responsibility by reminding them that they were linked in spiritual life to **all who in every place call upon the name of our Lord Jesus Christ, their Lord and ours.** This is added to heighten their sense of identity and responsibility with all "who have received a faith of the same kind as ours" (2 Pet. 1:1).

Before Paul took the Corinthians to task for their failures as Christians, he carefully and lovingly reminded them that they *were* Christians. They belonged to God and to each other in a far-reaching fellowship. That in itself should have been a rebuke to them and no doubt pierced the consciences of those who were at all spiritually sensitive. In 1:2-9 he summarizes their position and their blessings as believers in Jesus Christ, as children of God, as saints. "Look at what you are! Look at what you have!" Only then does he say, "Now I exhort you, brethren" (1:10).

Grace to you and peace from God our Father and the Lord Jesus Christ. (1:3)

Paul used a common form of Christian greeting (cf. Rom. 1:7; Gal. 1:3; Eph. 1:2; 1 Pet. 1:2; 2 John 3; Rev. 1:4; etc.). **Grace** is favor, and **peace** is one of its fruits. Peace (Greek *eirēnē*) was used as the equivalent of the Hebrew *shālôm*, still the most common Jewish greeting today. The peace of which Paul speaks here is "the peace of God, which surpasses all comprehension" (Phil. 4:7). It is the peace that only Christians can have, for only Christ can give it (John 14:27). The world does not have and cannot give that kind of peace. The greeting "grace and peace" is appropriate only for believer to believer, because it speaks of blessings that only they possess.

The Benefits of Being a Saint (1:4-9)

2

I thank my God always concerning you, for the grace of God which was given you in Christ Jesus, that in everything you were enriched in Him, in all speech and all knowledge, even as the testimony concerning Christ was confirmed in you, so that you are not lacking in any gift, awaiting eagerly the revelation of our Lord Jesus Christ, who shall also confirm you to the end, blameless in the day of our Lord Jesus Christ. God is faithful, through whom you were called into fellowship with His Son, Jesus Christ our Lord. (1:4-9)

As discussed in the previous chapter, Paul always used the word *saint* to refer to Christians—not to dead ones but to living ones, not to a few but to all. I think it must have been his favorite word for Christians, because he used it some sixty times in his letters. In the very opening words of this letter (1:2) Paul assured the believers in Corinth, immoral and unfaithful as many of them were, that they were all saints—along with everyone else who calls on the name of the Lord Jesus Christ.

The main thrust of the letter is exhortation for pure, godly living. But Paul's foundation for this exhortation is the fact of the believers' sainthood, their having been sanctified by Christ because of their trust in Him. Because they have been declared holy and have been given a holy nature, he pleads, they should act holy. The indicative "you are" is the basis for the imperative "you ought," a basic principle taught

9

throughout the New Testament. As the apostle would write to the Philippian believers a few years later, it is God's plan that "He who began a good work in you will perfect it until the day of Christ Jesus" (Phil. 1:6) and that the supreme purpose of those who are *in* Christ should be to be *like* Christ—to have His mind, His attitude, His way of thinking and living (2:5; cf. 1 John 2:6).

After Jesus had forgiven the woman taken in adultery, His parting words to her were, "From now on sin no more" (John 8:11). He was commanding a woman who had been living a vile life as a prostitute, and who had been caught in the very act of adultery, to forsake her sinful living. To ask her to change her ways so radically had to assume that she had experienced a change not only in her position but in her heart and mind, in the very nature of her life. It is obvious, though John does not mention it explicitly, that the woman had trusted in Christ and that she was saved. Jesus' instructions to cease sinning, given to anyone but a believer, would have been a mockery, since they could not possibly have been obeyed. Jesus had granted the woman a new life, and now He exhorted her to follow a new way of living. First He said, "Neither do I condemn you." Only then did He say, "Go on your way. From now on sin no more." The Lord was saying to her, "From now on I hold no sin against you. You are holy in My eyes, in God's eyes. Go and live a holy life."

That same truth is proclaimed throughout the New Testament. As Christians we are not condemned but are declared holy. Our sins are forgiven, set aside forever. And since our new nature in Christ is holy, our living should also be holy. "Therefore consider the members of your earthly body as dead to immorality, impurity, passion, evil desire, and greed, which amounts to idolatry," Paul teaches (Col. 3:5). In other words, our orientation to the world, our sinful and fleshly desires, are to be done away with and considered as no longer existing—because we "have died and [our] life is hidden with Christ in God" (3:3). A few verses later the apostle explains that the reason lying should be forsaken is that "the old self with its evil practices" has been laid aside and we have "put on the new self who is being renewed to a true knowledge according to the image of the One who created him" (3:9-10). Because we have come into a unique relationship with God through Christ, those things have no legitimate part in our lives. Unholy things have no place in a holy life. We are not to lie, or steal, or covet, or commit any other sin—because all sin is inconsistent with who we are in Jesus Christ. The new person is conformed to the image of Christ. Because He is holy, we are holy, we are saints. Because we are in Christ, we should act like Christ. We should never think anything He would not think, say anything He would not say, or do anything He would not do. Because He is holy our lives should be holy. That is the foundation of Christian living.

Paul takes the first nine verses of 1 Corinthians to show believers who they are—saints, holy ones, sanctified ones. The rest of the letter is built on this foundation. "You *are* holy; therefore *act* holy. Live a life commensurate with who you are."

In 1:4-9 Paul summarizes the benefits of believing in Christ, of being a saint. The benefits have three dimensions. Some are past, given the moment we accept Christ as Savior and Lord. Others are present, worked out as we live our lives in Him. Still others are future, to be experienced only when we go to be with Him in heaven. In the past there is grace, in the present there are gifts, and for the future there are guarantees. Our past is already taken care of, our present is provided for, and our future is assured.

PAST BENEFITS OF GRACE

I thank my God always concerning you, for the grace of God which was given you in Christ Jesus . . . even as the testimony concerning Christ was confirmed in you. (1:4, 6)

The first benefit of being a saint is the grace of salvation. Both **which was given** and **was confirmed** in the Greek are in the aorist tense, indicating action completed at a particular, definite point of time. At the moment a person trusts in Jesus Christ, he receives God's grace and the testimony of Christ is confirmed in him. Once we are in Christ the grace of God is ours. Paul is grateful [**I thank my God always concerning you**] for those who have received the grace of salvation. His passion was to see people redeemed, and his joy was greatest when that happened. Keeping a proper perspective, his thanks is directed Godward.

Grace (*charis*) was a common Christian greeting, which Paul had just used in the previous verse in his salutation. The basic meaning of the word is "favor," but in regard to God's saving men through His Son it always has the special and distinct sense of undeserved and unrepayable kindness or mercy given to sinners. It is supermagnanimous giving, giving that is totally undeserved and unmerited. It need not, in fact cannot, be repaid. God's saving grace is free and unearned.

In order to understand the true meaning and significance of God's grace we need to understand three things that cannot coexist with grace: guilt, human obligation, and human merit.

GRACE CANNOT COEXIST WITH GUILT

First of all, grace cannot coexist with guilt. Grace provides for the alleviation of guilt. God cannot say, "I am gracious and I give you salvation, but one false move and I'll take it away." That would not be a gracious gift, but a qualified, legal gift that could be taken away whenever we fell short of God's requirements. Grace would not be grace if God said, "I will save you if you don't sin." If we could keep from sinning we would not need grace, because we would merit salvation, we would deserve it. If grace were given and then later withheld in the least degree because of sin, it would not be the grace taught in Scripture. Grace involves unmerited, undeserved, and permanent forgiveness. Grace can operate only where there is sin. Without need of forgiveness there is no need of grace.

Man can neither escape from nor atone for his own sin. He is guilty and helpless in himself. Because God is holy and just He cannot ignore sin. It must be punished, and its penalty is death (Rom. 6:23). Yet this same verse that declares sin's penalty also declares the way of its removal, its atonement: "The free gift of God is eternal life in Christ Jesus our Lord." By His work on the cross, Christ fulfilled the demands of God's justice by taking the penalty of our sins upon Himself. In this was God's supreme provision of grace. When Jesus Christ became guilty for our sin, the price was paid in His death. And once God sovereignly acts in grace to forgive a person's sin because of trust in His Son's work, that person is totally and forever free of guilt. He stands in grace, which is continually dispensed to him (Rom. 5:1-3). All guilt is removed and can never return. Grace is God's gift that completely and permanently overrules guilt.

I have talked with Christians who are so absolutely distraught with guilt that they no longer are able to cope with life. They cannot accept the reality of forgiveness. They have long before trusted Christ as Savior and understood the truth of grace theologically and theoretically. But they do not understand it practically. This is often because they fail to separate the feelings of guilt that result from sin from the ultimate condemnation of the guilty. Sin not only produces feelings of guilt but real guilt, for we *are* guilty for the sins we commit. Yet that is the very guilt that Christ bore on the cross and that God's grace in Christ removes. We feel it, we may be chastened for it (Heb. 12:3-11), but we will never be condemned by it. The pain that follows sin is not a mark of condemnation or rejection by God, but is a reminder that we have sinned and should also be a deterrent to further sin.

To have the benefit of being a saint but not be able to experience its full blessing because of doubting is tragic. Still some Christians apparently cannot believe that God could be so completely gracious. Yet incomplete or temporary grace would not be grace. Of course we cannot earn it. Of course we can never deserve it. Of course we can never repay it. That is what makes grace grace.

What greater motivation for becoming a Christian could an unbeliever have, and what greater consolation could a believer have, than to know that in Christ all sins—past, present, and future—are forgiven forever? In Christ all guilt and all penalty are permanently removed. In Him we will stand totally guiltless and holy for the rest of eternity. When God saves, He ultimately takes away all sin, all guilt, all punishment. That is grace.

GRACE CANNOT COEXIST WITH HUMAN OBLIGATION

Second, grace cannot coexist with human obligation. We are not to say, "Well, God was gracious to me and He saved me, and now I have to pay Him back." Grace is a free gift, not a loan. Grace makes us totally indebted to God, but because the cost is so great we cannot repay it, and because His grace is so great we need not repay it. In other words, we are completely indebted, but we have no debt. We cannot pay for our salvation either before or after we are saved.

In discussing the relationship of faith and works to God's grace, Paul writes, "Now to the one who works, his wage is not reckoned as a favor [*charis,* grace], but as what is due" (Rom. 4:4). If we were able at any time or in any way to earn God's forgiveness, it would be our due. We would earn it and God would owe it to us. We may thank our employer for getting our paycheck to us on time and for paying us willingly and gladly, but we do not thank him simply for paying us. If we have worked for it as we should, we deserve the money and he is obligated to pay it. In paying his employees what they have earned, an employer is not being gracious but simply honest and just. And if for any reason he will not pay for work done, his employee can demand his money, because by right it belongs to the worker.

But grace does not operate on the principle of works, of earning. It is the giving of that which has not been earned or deserved. In relation to God's gift through His Son, it cannot be earned or deserved. Money can be given or it can be earned. But God's grace can only be given.

How could we pay for what is priceless? To offer God the greatest love and devotion and obedience and service we have could not approach paying for what He offers us in Jesus Christ. To do so would be like offering a few pennies to pay the national debt. Beside God's grace our very best works are even more of a pittance.

What makes the message of Christ such good news is that we do not need to pay for salvation. By itself, the truth that we cannot earn salvation would be bad news, the very worst of news, because it would leave man entirely hopeless. But grace makes it good news, the very greatest of news, because grace has made it unnecessary to pay for salvation. Our sinful limitations make it impossible; God's abundant grace makes it unnecessary. God in Christ has paid for it; we have only to receive it through Him.

We owe God our highest love, our deepest devotion, and our greatest service as expressions of our gratitude and because all we have and are belong to Him—but not because these are able in the least way to buy or repay His gift of love and mercy to us. We love Him; but we are only able to love Him because first "He loved us and sent His Son to be the propitiation for our sins" (1 John 4:10). We owe Him everything out of gratitude; we owe Him nothing out of obligation.

GRACE CANNOT COEXIST WITH HUMAN MERIT

Third, grace cannot coexist with human merit. Grace is not offered simply to "good" people. In relation to each other, some people obviously are morally better than others. But in relation to God's righteousness, our very best is "like a filthy garment" (Isa. 64:6). A person's goodness, in relation to other people and certainly in relation to God, is not considered in God's grace. Merit, like guilt and obligation, has no part in grace. Jesus, speaking to the religious and moral Jewish leaders, shocked them with the fact that tax collectors (traitors to their own people and usually dishonest) and prostitutes (the lowest members of that society) would enter the kingdom of God before those religious leaders (Matt. 21:31-32). Luke 18:9-14 gives the classic account of a morally good man condemned to hell and a morally bad man headed for heaven.

For centuries Israel believed that God had chosen them as His special covenant people because they were better than others. They firmly believed this, in spite of the fact that God had told them otherwise at the very beginning. "The Lord did not set His love on you nor choose you because you were more in number than any of the peoples, for you were the fewest of all peoples, but because the Lord loved you and kept the oath which He swore to your forefathers" (Deut. 7:7-8).

Paul points out that, though the Jews had many blessings and many advantages, especially as recipients of God's special revelation of Himself, they were not chosen because they were deserving. In many ways they were especially undeserving (Rom. 2:17–3:20). To Gentiles he gave the same warning. They were no better, "for we have already charged that both Jews and Greeks are all under sin" (3:9). Among ourselves we can distinguish between those who are humanly better and those who are worse, but before God every person *spiritually* stands the same—sinful and condemned in regard to his own merit, his own righteousness. "There is no distinction; for all have sinned and fall short of the glory of God" (3:22-23). Even in himself—in fact especially in himself—Paul recognized no righteousness, no merit before God. In his own eyes he was the foremost of sinners (1 Tim. 1:15) and "the very least of all saints" (Eph. 3:8).

But again God's grace turns bad news into good. Because of His grace we do not *need* to merit salvation. Paul was eternally grateful **for the grace of God which was given . . . in Christ Jesus.**

In recent years we have been able, through magazines, newspapers, and television, to see vividly the terrible plight and anguish of people in such places as Cambodia, Afghanistan, Central America, and the Middle East. The sensitive Christian who lives in a free, peaceful country cannot help asking, "Why, Lord, have you given me so much? Why am I free to live peacefully, free to worship where and as I choose, free to work, free to raise my family as I think best, free to have fellowship with other believers?" We know it is not because we are more deserving of blessing. We are blessed because of God's grace and for no other reason.

THREE REASONS FOR GOD'S GRACE

God has three reasons, three motives, for being gracious to us. First, He provides salvation in order that those who are saved may produce good works. Good works touch and help the lives of others, including telling them of God's grace in Jesus Christ. Paul tells the Ephesians, "For we are His workmanship, created in Christ Jesus for good works, which God prepared beforehand, that we should walk in them" (Eph. 2:10). In another letter he instructs Titus that Christ "gave Himself for us, that He might redeem us from every lawless deed and purify for Himself a people for His own possession, zealous for good deeds" (Titus 2:14). Later in the epistle he explains, "This is a trustworthy statement; and concerning these things I want you to speak confidently, so that those who have believed God may be careful to engage in good deeds. These things are good and profitable for men" (3:8). God saved us to do good works because good works benefit men. God wants His children to touch all the world with their goodness, made possible through His Son.

Second, saving grace is meant to bring blessing to believers. "But God, being rich in mercy, because of His great love with which He loved us, . . . made us alive together with Christ, . . . in order that in the ages to come He might show the surpassing riches of His grace in kindness toward us in Christ Jesus" (Eph. 2:4-7). God graciously saves us in order that He can pour out His great blessings on us forever.

Third, and most importantly, God saves us through grace in order to glorify Himself. Grace is given "in order that the manifold wisdom of God might now be made known through the church" and that "to Him be the glory in the church and in Christ Jesus to all generations forever and ever" (Eph. 3:10, 21). Jesus taught that the primary purpose for letting our light shine before men, made possible by our salvation, is to "glorify [our] Father who is in heaven" (Matt. 5:16). Jesus' own primary purpose in going to the cross, which made our salvation possible, was to glorify His Father and to be glorified Himself (John 12:28; 17:1, 4-5). God's glory is clearly on display in the gracious and powerful work of salvation.

The Lord's gracious salvation is given in order for the saved to bring blessing to other men through good works, to bring blessing to believers themselves, and above all to bring glory to Himself. He is gracious for the world's sake, for His children's sake, and for His own sake.

even as the testimony concerning Christ was confirmed in you. (1:6)

We receive God's grace when the testimony of Christ is confirmed—that is, settled, made steadfast and solid—in us. **Testimony** is the Greek *marturion,* meaning "witness," as it is sometimes translated (see Acts 1:8). It is from this term that we get the English *martyr.* Christ's witness is settled and confirmed in us when we trust in Him as Lord and Savior. At that moment, and forever after that moment, we stand in God's grace.

In the New Testament *marturion* is most commonly used in relation to the gospel, and first of all to its proclamation. The Holy Spirit empowered the apostles, and continues to empower all Christ's disciples, to be His witnesses (Acts 1:8). Paul's own calling centered in his "solemnly testifying to both Jews and Greeks of repentance toward God and faith in our Lord Jesus Christ" (Acts 20:21; cf. v. 24), whether his testimony was accepted or not (22:18). The Lord assured Paul that he would not die until his testimony for Him was complete, the final witness being in Rome (23:11).

The context indicates that the deepest meaning of *marturion* (or *marturia*), however, is in its representing the gospel itself, not merely its proclamation. The testimony of which Paul counseled Timothy not to be ashamed was the "testimony of our Lord" (2 Tim. 1:8), that is, the gospel of the Lord. John tells us that "the witness is this, that God has given us eternal life, and this life is in His Son" (1 John 5:11). The greatest testimony is not about the message of salvation but *is* the message of salvation. It is not when we hear the testimony about Christ, but when we *have* **the testimony concerning Christ . . . confirmed** in us, that we become partakers of God's grace.

In 1 Corinthians 1:4, then, we see the divine offer of grace, and in 1:6 the positive human response to grace. When a person in faith accepts God's offer, grace becomes operative. All sin is forgiven and all guilt is removed, forever. At that time

God begins to pour out the superabundance of His blessings and riches on His new child, and He will not stop throughout all eternity. That is the extent of God's grace.

PRESENT BENEFITS OF GRACE

That in everything you were enriched in Him, in all speech and all knowledge, . . . so that you are not lacking in any gift. (1:5, 7a)

The first benefits of grace for the believer are established in the past, totally completed when we trust in Christ. Other benefits are present, a continuing treasury of riches given throughout our earthly lives. In Christ we are continually **enriched** in everything. A key word in verse 5 is **in**. We are enriched **in everything . . . in Him**. The *in Him* qualifies the *in everything*. That is, we have everything that Christ has to give, and He gives everything we need—though many times not everything we want. God's "divine power has granted to us everything pertaining to life and godliness" (2 Pet. 1:3), which is all a believer needs and should be all he wants. In Jesus Christ we "have been made complete" (Col. 2:10). "All things belong to [us]" (1 Cor. 3:21).

Among the most important of the things we have in Christ are **all speech and all knowledge.** Again the *all* is qualified. We have all the speech and knowledge necessary to accomplish all God wants us to do. We will always be able to say everything God wants us to say and to know everything He wants us to know. His will is concurrent with His enablement.

ALL SPEECH

The particular **speech** in mind here is that of telling God's truth. God gives *every* believer the capacity to speak for Him. We do not all have eloquence, an impressive vocabulary, or a captivating personality. But we all have the necessary God-given ability, the same capability and the same capacity, to speak for Him in the unique way that He wants us to speak.

Besides lack of holiness, I believe the most common failure of Christians is in not speaking for their Lord. The most frequent excuses are "I don't know what to say" or "I don't know how to say it" or "I just don't think I can do it." Paul shatters these excuses. We are **enriched in Him, in all speech and all knowledge.** Witnessing is no more optional for "ordinary" believers than for the apostles. "You *shall* receive power when the Holy Spirit has come upon you; and you *shall* be My witnesses" (Acts 1:8). We can witness and we must witness. We have no excuses for not giving testimony to Christ. We *can* speak; we *can* testify, just as those of the early church testified. Those saints prayed, "Grant that Thy bond-servants may speak Thy word with all confidence" (Acts 4:29). God was quick to answer and provide, and "they were all filled with the Holy Spirit, and began to speak the word of God with boldness" (v. 31). As believers, we too have the Holy Spirit, and He will enable us, like them, to speak for the Lord with confidence and boldness.

Though every believer has access to bold witnessing, it is obvious that we do not all take advantage of it. Confident and faithful witnessing not only requires God's empowering but our willingness. Paul asked the Ephesian church, "Pray on my behalf, that utterance may be given to me in the opening of my mouth, to make known with boldness the mystery of the gospel" (Eph. 6:19). Like an arctic river in deep winter, our mouths are frozen. It is so easy to talk ourselves out of talking to others about the gospel.

When some Christians lead a person to the Lord, they are more amazed that God actually used them than that the miracle of the new birth took place. They are shocked that *they* are able to witness effectively.

As a young ministerial student I was sent out to preach to the crowds at the bus depot. After about two weeks I decided that this was not very effective, because of the many distractions. People waiting in a ticket line or getting on or off a bus were not the most attentive. So I started to walk up and down the street speaking to people individually and found this approach to be much more fruitful. One day as another student and I were out witnessing, we came upon two fellows on their way to a YMCA dance and we each picked one of them to talk with. After briefly presenting the gospel to my nervous listener, I asked him if he wanted to confess Jesus as Lord and receive Him into his life—to which he replied, "Yes." At first I was more surprised than pleased. The Lord had really used me to bring someone to Himself! What a blessing that always is.

Many years later, after much training and experience in proclaiming the gospel, a man approached me outside the church one day and said, "I'm Jewish and I want to know how to be Christian." All I needed to do was to tell him. After we had looked at Scripture and prayed together, he received the Lord. Even when we confidently expect the Lord to use us, it is still no less amazing and wonderful when He does. Whether we are experienced or inexperienced, our willingness to witness is the key to God's using us.

When we are willing to open our mouths to speak for Him, we can be sure that He will give us the right thing to say. It is not that we put our minds in neutral but that we submit our minds to Him to use as He sees fit and to empower as He has promised. We need to be prepared, in knowledge of God's Word, in prayer, in cleansing, and even in witnessing techniques. We are to "be diligent to present [ourselves] approved to God as a workman who does not need to be ashamed, handling accurately the word of truth" (2 Tim. 2:15) and we are always to be "ready to make a defense to everyone who asks [us] to give an account for the hope that is in [us]" (1 Pet. 3:15). We are to be patient, diligent, and gentle in our presenting the faith (2 Tim. 2:24-25). But with all our study and faithfulness and prayer, only God's Spirit can bring a person to Himself.

ALL KNOWLEDGE

Despite His empowering, God does not expect us to speak from a vacuum. With provision of all speech necessary He also provides **all knowledge** necessary. It is not that we know everything, even about the gospel. Now we know only "in part" (1 Cor. 13:12). But we are given everything we need to know to speak effectively for the Lord. God has given us enough revelation and will give us enough understanding to speak His truth to the world. We have His Word and we have His Spirit to interpret it. "Things which eye has not seen and ear has not heard, and which have not entered the heart of man, all that God has prepared for those who love Him. For to us God revealed them through the Spirit; for the Spirit searches all things, even the depths of God" (1 Cor. 2:9). Such things are not knowable or acceptable to the natural man, "for they are foolishness to him, and he cannot understand them, because they are spiritually appraised" (v. 14). God hides "these things from the wise and intelligent and [reveals] them to babes" (Matt. 11:25). Only to believers does He give "the light of the knowledge of the glory of God in the face of Christ" (2 Cor. 4:6).

It is necessary to claim and to use the knowledge God provides for us in order for it to be effective in our witnessing. In Christ we know God, His Spirit, His truth, His revelation, and His power. Yet Paul prayed for the Ephesians that God would give them "a spirit of wisdom and of revelation in the knowledge of Him" (Eph. 1:17). Likewise he prayed for the Colossian church that they would "be filled with the knowledge of His will in all spiritual wisdom and understanding, . . . bearing fruit in every good work and increasing in the knowledge of God" (Col. 1:9-10). We must internalize the knowledge God gives in order to make it truly ours.

God has given us all speech, but we must open our mouths in order to use it. God has given us all knowledge, but we must appropriate it. Just as we were graciously saved, we are also graciously gifted. God has made us fit for the kingdom, "qualified us to share in the inheritance of the saints in light" (Col. 1:12).

ALL GIFTS

Paul moves from the specific provisions of speech and knowledge to God's general provision of all gifts that a believer needs to serve Him. A Christian is never **lacking in any gift** that he needs to live a full and faithful life.

Not lacking is in the present tense and is therefore still referring to present benefits of believing. In light of the corruption in the Corinthian church, it may seem strange that Paul would state categorically that they lacked nothing. Unlike the Thessalonian and Philippian churches, the Corinthian church was exceptionally lacking in spiritual maturity and in moral purity. But they were not lacking, Paul says, in any spiritual gift. They did not have the same spiritual maturity and moral character as believers in those other churches, but they had all of the same resources.

Paul was speaking of God's provisions, not their use of His provisions. God had already provided them with everything and continued to provide them with everything, despite the fact that they were so unfaithful and perverse in using His gifts and in being thankful for them. (And they sought gifts they did not have, as we see in 1 Cor. 14.) The apostle seemed to be emphasizing two things in this statement. First, the believers in Corinth, as believers everywhere, did not need to look for, and should not try to look for, additional special blessings or gifts. God has already provided every spiritual gift His children need or may have. Second, believers should claim and begin to use the gifts that the Lord has given them. The Corinthians lacked no gifts, only the willingness to use them.

The word **gift** is the Greek *charisma,* which is specifically a gift of grace, derived from the term for grace (*charis*) used in verses 3-4. The gifts of which they had no lack were gifts provided by "the grace of God which was given you in Christ Jesus" (1:4). The particular blessings of speech and knowledge seem to refer primarily to presenting the gospel to the world; the general gifts of verse 7 seem to refer primarily to ministering to fellow believers. God's resources dispensed to the churches are adequate to reach the world and adequate to build the church.

Our English word *charismatic* comes from the plural (*charismata*) of the term used here, and refers to the endowment by God of gracious gifts to His people to minister to His church. It does not refer to the endowment of special, extraordinary gifts to those who are supposedly more spiritual or more advanced in the faith, as maintained by many in what is generally known as the charismatic movement. God endows all believers with *charismata,* although, as with His other blessings, these gifts are often ignored or misused.

As believers we all have spiritual gifts, given since the Lord redeemed us, and we have them as fully as we need them and can have them. Because of indifference or ignorance it may take years to recognize them and many more years to develop them, but we already possess them. Many of us, like the Corinthians (1 Cor. 12:1), are ignorant of our spiritual gifts and even of the fact that we possess them. We need to recognize that we have spiritual gifts and we need to identify them and use them. We need to know whether we have the gift of teaching, preaching, exhortation, administration, helps, giving, or whatever it may be. And we then must be responsive to the Spirit as He uses us to minister with the gifts He has given us.

We are born spiritually just as we were born physically, with everything complete and intact. We do not add arms or legs or organs as we mature physically. These grow and develop, but they are not added. Likewise when we are born spiritually, we are undeveloped but complete. We need spiritual food and exercise in order to grow, but we do not need and we will not be given additional "spiritual parts." If we do not grow, or if we regress, it is not because we lack God's resources but only because we do not use them. When a Christian falls into sin, laziness, ineffective service, or impurity it is not because he lacks anything from the Lord. It is because he is not appropriating what he has. In Christ we "have been made complete" (Col. 2:10). We already have been given everything we need for spiritual health, vitality, growth, and reproduction. A Christian can never say, "I need this spiritual blessing, or that spiritual gift or ability." We need nothing else from God. God has been abundantly faithful; He has given us everything. Failure is never on God's side, but always on ours. The only lack, the only shortcoming, is in our commitment to use our divine resources.

FUTURE BENEFITS OF GRACE

Awaiting eagerly the revelation of our Lord Jesus Christ, who shall also confirm you to the end, blameless in the day of our Lord Jesus Christ. God is

faithful, through whom you were called into fellowship with His Son, Jesus Christ our Lord. (1:7b-9)

God's grace not only provides past and present benefits, but also future benefits. God has saved us by His grace; He presently empowers us with gifts of His grace; and He guarantees the final fulfillment of His grace. The best is yet to come. The faithful believer cannot help being eschatological. We are grateful for past grace, we seek to be responsible in using present grace, but our greatest joy is looking forward to future grace. We watch, we wait, and we hope for the Lord's next coming, His final coming. We have work to do on earth, gifts to employ for the Lord. And as long as He has work for us here, it "is more necessary" for us to remain. But to enter the future life, to be forever with Christ "is very much better" (Phil. 1:23-24) because our true home, our true citizenship is in heaven (3:20). We are constantly feeling the tug of that world to come. We are **awaiting eagerly the revelation of our Lord Jesus Christ.** We are looking for Jesus to come. We are confident He is coming, and we know it could be soon.

The Greek word *apekdechomenous* (**awaiting eagerly**) means to wait with eager anticipation and also with activity. It is not idle, passive waiting, as when sitting on a street corner waiting for a bus. It involves working while we wait and watch and hope. We know that God takes care of His own. We wait eagerly, but not anxiously. We live in a hopeless world, and often we cannot help grieving for it, as Jesus grieved over Jerusalem (Luke 13:34). But the world's hopelessness does not steal our hope. We can say with Paul, "I know whom I have believed and I am convinced that He is able to guard what I have entrusted to Him until that day" (2 Tim. 1:12). It is that very day which is **the revelation of our Lord Jesus Christ.** The **revelation** refers to His manifestation without the veil of humanity He wore in His incarnation. At His next coming He will be fully revealed in blazing splendor.

We look for the coming of our Lord for at least five reasons.

IT MEANS CHRIST'S EXALTATION

The **revelation of our Lord Jesus Christ** will bring His long-due and eternally deserved exaltation. He will finally be crowned "Lord of lords and King of kings" (Rev. 17:14). He has been generally neglected, humiliated, despised, and rejected for 2,000 years since His first coming. His second coming will end that, for then "every knee [will] bow, of those who are in heaven, and on earth, and under the earth" (Phil. 2:10). He will not come the second time as sin-bearer (Heb. 9:28), but in His full glory and honor and majesty (Rev. 4:11; 5:12).

IT MEANS SATAN'S DEFEAT

The Lord's return will bring Satan's final defeat, humiliation, and punishment, which he deserves, just as Christ deserves and will then receive exaltation. Satan will no longer be "the ruler of the world" (John 14:30) or "the prince of the power of the air" (Eph. 2:2). He will be bound for a thousand years, released for a little while, then chained and thrown into the lake of fire for all eternity (Rev. 19:20; 20:10).

IT MEANS JUSTICE FOR THE MARTYRS

The Lord's return will bring retribution against all who have persecuted and afflicted God's faithful people. In his vision of the seal judgments, John "saw underneath the altar the souls of those who had been slain because of the word of God, and because of the testimony which they had maintained; and they cried out with a loud voice, saying, 'How long, O Lord, holy and true, wilt Thou refrain from judging and avenging our blood on those who dwell on the earth?'" (Rev. 6:9-10). Vengeance belongs to the Lord (Deut. 32:35; Rom. 12:19), and when the Son returns, God will take that vengeance—long deserved and long delayed. "For after all it is only just for God to repay with affliction those who afflict you, and to give relief to you who are afflicted and to us as well when the Lord Jesus shall be revealed from heaven with His mighty angels in flaming fire" (2 Thess. 1:6-7). They fully deserve it.

IT MEANS THE DEATH OF CHRIST REJECTORS

Christ's return will bring the death of all who have rejected Him. "When the Lord Jesus shall be revealed from heaven with His mighty angels in flaming fire," He will deal out "retribution to those who do not know God and to those who do not obey the gospel of our Lord Jesus. And these will pay the penalty of eternal destruction, away from the presence of the Lord and from the glory of His power" (2 Thess. 1:7-9). The Lord is coming to judge those who have hated and rejected Him, for they deserve it.

IT MEANS HEAVEN FOR THOSE WHO BELIEVE

For all who have believed in the Lord Jesus Christ, His coming will mean heaven for all eternity. Unlike Satan's defeat, justice for the martyrs, and death for Christ rejectors, our gift of heaven will be totally undeserved. That is because we are under God's grace. In ourselves we deserve the same fate as they; but in Christ we are granted forgiveness, redemption, holiness, and life everlasting in the presence of the unfading glory of our Lord.

When Christ returns He will **confirm,** or establish, us as **blameless** before His heavenly Father. When we enter heaven we will not have all our sins and shortcomings flashed before us for everyone to see, as we sometimes hear in popular theology. Christ will affirm before the eternal throne of God that we are now counted blameless. Only then will we be confirmed blameless, made blameless, actually *be* blameless—settled and secured in blamelessness for all eternity.

When the day of the Lord Jesus Christ comes, He is going to present to the Father "the church in all her glory, having no spot or wrinkle or any such thing; but that she should be holy and blameless" (Eph. 5:26-27). The bride will be forever "a pure virgin" (2 Cor. 11:2).

We are sure of this grace—past, present, and future—because **God is faithful**. The Greek order is inverted ("faithful is God"), because that form is more emphatic. God is faithful to His sovereign will—**through whom you were called**. When God calls someone to salvation, He is faithful to that call. Thus our future glory at Christ's appearing is certain, for whom "He called, these He also justified; and whom He justified, these He also glorified" (Rom. 8:30). It is helpful to note that in Paul's epistles the call of God is always seen as an effective call that produces salvation.

We are saved because God wanted us saved, and we stay saved because God does not change His mind about that desire. We had no part in God's original desire to call us, and we can do nothing to change it. If He called us when we were lost and wretched, He surely will not cease to be faithful to that call now that we have come **into fellowship with His Son**. The word *koinonia* (**fellowship**) also means partnership, oneness. We are secured to glory by being one with God's beloved Son. We entered the kingdom by grace and we will be kept in the kingdom by grace.

Paul's prayer for the Thessalonian church was, "May the God of peace Himself sanctify you entirely; and may your spirit and soul and body be preserved complete, without blame at the coming of our Lord Jesus Christ" (1 Thess. 5:23). It was a prayer that he knew with all certainty would be answered, a prayer not of request but of acknowledgement, as is clear from the following verse: "Faithful is He who calls you, and He also will bring it to pass."

Splits and Quarrels in the Church (1:10-17)

Now I exhort you, brethren, by the name of our Lord Jesus Christ, that you all agree, and there be no divisions among you, but you be made complete in the same mind and in the same judgment. For I have been informed concerning you, my brethren, by Chloe's people, that there are quarrels among you. Now I mean this, that each one of you is saying, "I am of Paul," and "I of Apollos," and "I of Cephas," and "I of Christ." Has Christ been divided? Paul was not crucified for you, was he? Or were you baptized in the name of Paul? I thank God that I baptized none of you except Crispus and Gaius, that no man should say you were baptized in my name. Now I did baptize also the household of Stephanas; beyond that, I do not know whether I baptized any other. For Christ did not send me to baptize, but to preach the gospel, not in cleverness of speech, that the cross of Christ should not be made void. (1:10-17)

One of the main reasons that cults in our day have had such an impact on the world is their unity. Disharmony is not tolerated. Though misguided, misused, and often totalitarian, such unity is attractive to many people who are tired of religious uncertainty, ambiguity, and confusion.

Few of us who have attended church for a number of years have not been in or known of a congregation where there was a split or at least serious quarreling. The problem has existed in the church from New Testament times. The Corinthian believers fell short of the Lord's standards in many ways, and the first thing for which Paul called them to task was quarreling.

Quarrels are a part of life. We grow up in them and around them. Infants are quick to express displeasure when they are not given something they want or when something they like is taken away. Little children cry, fight, and throw tantrums because they cannot have their own ways. We argue and fight over a rattle, then a toy, then a football, then a position on the football team or in the cheerleading squad, then in business, the PTA, or politics. Friends fight, husbands and wives fight, businesses fight, cities fight, even nations fight—sometimes to the point of war. And the source of all the fighting is the same: man's depraved, egoistic, selfish nature.

Scripture teaches nothing more clearly than the truth that man is basically and naturally sinful, and that the heart of his sinfulness is self-will. From birth to death the natural inclination of every person is to look out for "number one"—to be, to do, and to have what he wants. Even believers are continually tempted to fall back into lives of self-will, self-interest, and general self-centeredness. At the heart of sin is the ego, the "I." Self-centeredness is the root of man's depravity, the depravity into which every person since Adam and Eve, except Jesus Christ, has been born. Even Christians are still sinners—justified, but still sinful in themselves. And when that sin is allowed to have its way in our flesh, conflict is inevitable. When two or more people are bent on having their own ways, they will soon be quarreling and arguing, because their interests, concerns, and priorities sooner or later will conflict. There cannot possibly be harmony in a group, even a group of believers, whose desires, goals, purposes, and ideals are generated by their egos.

Writing to fellow Christians, James asks, "What is the source of quarrels and conflicts among you? Is not the source your pleasures that wage war in your members? You lust and do not have; so you commit murder. And you are envious and cannot obtain; so you fight and quarrel" (James 4:1-2). The cause for all conflicts, quarrels, and fighting is selfish desire.

Tragically—though it is forbidden by God, is totally out of character with our redeemed natures, and is in complete opposition to everything our Lord prayed for and intended for His church—fighting does occur among believers, among those who are called to be one in the Lord Jesus Christ.

What the Lord laments and opposes, Satan applauds and fosters. Few things demoralize, discourage, and weaken a church as much as bickering, backbiting, and fighting among its members. And few things so effectively undermine its testimony before the world.

Quarreling is a reality in the church because selfishness and other sins are realities in the church. Because of quarreling the Father is dishonored, the Son is disgraced, His people are demoralized and discredited, and the world is turned off and confirmed in unbelief. Fractured fellowship robs Christians of joy and effectiveness, robs God of glory, and robs the world of the true testimony of the gospel. A high price for an ego trip!

Among the Corinthian church's many sins and shortcomings, quarreling is the one that Paul chose to deal with first. In unity lies the joy of Christian ministry and the credibility of Christian testimony. In His high priestly prayer the Lord prayed repeatedly that His church would be one (John 17:11, 21-23). The implication of the oneness of nature and communion with God for which He prayed for His disciples was a "fleshed out" oneness in life. Immediately after Pentecost the newly empowered believers were in perfect harmony with each other—sharing, rejoicing, worshiping, and witnessing together, "day by day continuing with one mind in the temple . . . praising God, and having favor with all the people. And the Lord was adding to their number day by day those who were being saved" (Acts 2:46-47). Their unity bore great fruit in their ministry to each other, in their witness to the world, and in their pleasing and glorifying God.

The first need of the Corinthian church was for that sort of harmony. It is also the need of many churches today. With this discussion, Paul moves into the exhortation and instruction that occupies the rest of the epistle.

In verses 10-17 he deals with four basic areas that relate to unity: the *plea* for doctrinal agreement, the *parties* that were loyal to men, the *principle* of oneness in Christ, and the *priority* of preaching.

THE PLEA: DOCTRINAL AGREEMENT

Now I exhort you, brethren, by the name of our Lord Jesus Christ, that you all agree, and there be no divisions among you, but you be made complete in the same mind and in the same judgment. (1:10)

Exhort comes from the Greek *parakaleō,* the verb root of *paraklētos,* the "Helper" (or Comforter) of John 14:16, 26; 15:26; 16:7 and the "Advocate" of 1 John 2:1. The basic meaning is that of coming alongside someone in order to help. Paul wanted to come alongside his Corinthian brothers and sisters in order to help correct their sins and shortcomings. He used the same word in writing Philemon. After noting that he had the right to order Philemon to forgive the slave Onesimus and send him back to Paul, the apostle says, "Yet for love's sake I appeal [*parakaleō*]to you" (Philem. 9; cf. 10).

Likewise he appealed to the Corinthians. He had been careful to establish his apostolic authority in the opening words of the letter. But now he appeals to them as **brothers.** In so doing he moderates the harshness, without minimizing the seriousness, of the rebuke. They are his brothers and each other's brothers, and should act in harmony as brothers.

They had all been "called into fellowship with His Son, Jesus Christ" (1:9) and are now being lovingly exhorted **by the name of our Lord Jesus Christ** to **agree,** to eliminate **divisions,** and to **be made complete in the same mind and in the same judgment.** Because they were one in fellowship with their Lord, they should be one in fellowship with each other. Their unity in Jesus Christ was the basis for Paul's appeal for unity among themselves. As in many of Paul's letters, believers' identity with Christ is the pad from which he launches his call to holy living.

Christ's **name** represents all that He is, His character and His will. To pray "in Jesus' name" is not to expect God to bow to our wishes or demands simply because we use that phrase. To pray in His name is to pray in accordance with His Word and His will. Jesus said to pray, saying, "Hallowed be Thy name. . . . Thy will be done" (Matt. 6:9-10). Christ's Word, which perfectly reflects His character and His will, forms the supreme basis for all Christian behavior. What we think, say, and do is right or wrong not primarily because of its effect on us or on others but because it does or does not conform to Christ and bring honor to Him. Our behavior as believers has its most direct relationship to Jesus Christ. When we sin or complain or quarrel, we harm the church and its leaders and our fellow believers. We also put a barrier between unbelievers and the gospel. But worst of all, we bring dishonor to our Lord.

When the Ephesian elders came to Miletus to meet Paul on his way to Jerusalem, he admonished them to "be on guard for yourselves and for all the flock, among which the Holy Spirit has made you overseers, to shepherd the church of God which He purchased with His own blood" (Acts 20:28). He was saying to them, "Don't lose sight of Whose you are and Whose they are. You all belong to Jesus Christ and are precious to Him. You are overseers on the Lord's behalf."

The emphasis in this passage, written to a local church, is on the unity of the local assembly of believers, not on the mystical unity of the universal church—as is the emphasis, for example, in Ephesians, which was a general letter without local reference. Nor is Paul talking about denominational unity. He is saying that there should be unity within the local congregation, that **you should all agree.**

That seems to be an impossible standard. Yet the Lord Himself commanded His followers to "be perfect, as your heavenly Father is perfect" (Matt. 5:48), and what could be more humanly impossible than that? In the name and power of Christ that standard is possible. So is this one. God does not give His standards on the basis of human ability but on the basis of divine provision. He does not accommodate them to human limitations, much less to human inclinations and desires. No matter how impossible the idea may seem, all believers in a local church are to be in agreement about the things of God.

In the Greek, **that you all agree** is literally, "that you all speak the same thing," as in the King James Version. Nothing is more confusing to new Christians, or to unbelievers who are considering the claims of Christ, than to hear supposedly mature and informed Christians tell conflicting things about the gospel, the Bible, or Christian living. And few things are more devastating to a church than everyone having his own ideas and interpretations about the faith, or of the congregation being divided into various factions, each with its own views.

For a local church to be spiritually healthy, harmonious, and effective, there must, above all, be doctrinal unity. The teaching of the church should not be a smorgasbord from which members can pick and choose. Nor should there be various groups, each with its own distinctives and leaders. Even if the groups get along with each other and tolerate each other's views, doctrinal confusion and spiritual weakness are inevitable. Unfortunately some churches today, and even some seminaries, have just that sort of doctrinal and ethical selectivity. They often have unity on a social and organizational level—but doctrinally, ethically, and spiritually they are confused and confusing. They hold to no certainties, including the certainties and absolutes of Scripture. They have no lasting or binding commitments. One does not make permanent commitments to temporary beliefs. Many people, of course, including some professing Christians, do not *want* absolutes in doctrine or ethics, simply because absolute truths and standards demand absolute acceptance and obedience.

As far as God's truth is concerned, there cannot be two conflicting views that are right. Obviously, we cannot know dogmatically what is not fully or clearly revealed (Deut. 29:29). But God is not confused or self-contradictory. He does not disagree with Himself, and His Word does not disagree with itself. Consequently Paul insists that the Corinthians, and all believers, have doctrinal unity—not just *any* doctrinal unity, but unity that is clearly and completely based on God's Word. He appeals to them **in the name of our Lord Jesus Christ.** That is, there must be agreement in Him, in His will, in His Word.

Many of the factions in the Corinthian church, as in some parts of the church today, had unity within their own groups but not unity with other believers in Jesus Christ. Paul's call for agreement was not agreement on just any basis but agreement in God's revealed truth, given by and consummated in Jesus Christ and completed through the teaching of His apostles. "Let us therefore, as many as are perfect, have this attitude; and if in anything you have a different attitude, God will reveal that also to you; however, let us keep living by that same standard to which we have attained" (Phil. 3:15-16). The standard was the apostolic doctrine which Paul personally had related to them and exemplified among them (v. 17), just as the teaching he had given the Corinthians was as "an apostle of Jesus Christ by the will of God" and "in demonstration of the Spirit and of power" (1 Cor. 1:1; 2:4).

The word **divisions** translates the Greek *schismata,* from which we get *schism.* In the physical sense the meaning is "to tear or rip," that is, to separate, as in Matthew 9:16 ("tear"). Metaphorically it means to have a difference of opinion, a division of judgment, a dissension. Once when Jesus was preaching in Jerusalem the people listening to Him could not agree on who He was. Some thought He was the great prophet, some that He was the Christ, and some that He was just an ordinary man making extraordinary claims. Consequently, John reports, "There arose a division [*schisma*] in the multitude because of Him" (John 7:43). Still today there are divisions because of disagreements as to who Christ is, even among those who go by His name.

The most serious divisions a church can have are those involving doctrine. In closing his letter to the Romans Paul warned, "Now I urge you, brethren, keep your eye on those who cause dissensions and hindrances contrary to the teaching which you learned, and turn away from them" (Rom. 16:17). Those who teach anything contrary to Scripture are not serving Christ but themselves and their own interests. In matters on which Scripture is not explicit there is room for difference of opinion. But in the clear teachings of the Bible there is no room for difference, because to differ with Scripture is to differ with God. On those things a church must agree.

I believe there are even some things, though not specifically taught in Scripture, about which the church should be of one mind when the elders and pastors have come to agreement on it. Otherwise there will be confusion in the local church and often division and factions. Members will tend to line up with the teachers and leaders with whom they agree, and they will soon become like the Corinthians, who were of Paul, Apollos, Peter, or Christ (1 Cor. 1:12). There was no doctrinal disagreement among those teachers; the division was one of personality or style preference on the part of the Corinthians—a popularity contest. Because Paul ranked them with the other factions, we know that even those claiming to be loyal only to Christ were really loyal only to their own opinions.

I also believe there must be agreement in the decision-making process of the local church leadership and that their decisions should be accepted and followed by other church members, especially by those, such as teachers, who are in positions of responsibility and influence. These decisions do not, of course, have the same authority as Scripture. But if they are consistent with what Scripture teaches and are sought in prayer, they should be followed by everyone in the church for the sake of harmony and unity. A good word for those who seek unity in the leadership of the church's life and practice is found in Philippians 1:27, where Paul exhorts believers to stand "firm in one spirit, with one mind striving together for the faith of the gospel."

Obviously the key to unity in doctrine and decisions is having godly leaders who are united themselves in the will of the Spirit. Men who are not close to the Lord and well-taught in His Word cannot possibly recognize or agree on sound doctrine or make sound decisions. Without knowing God's Word they cannot perceive error, even when they want to. The only sure way to identify a counterfeit bill is to compare it with one known to be genuine. Only Scripture-taught, Spirit-led men are able to guide a church into the unity of truth and protect it from error. If a church does not have that kind of men, no form of leadership will work spiritually. Such men are God's men and they represent Jesus Christ. Christ rules the church through them, and their decisions should be agreed with and followed. Such men are able to lead the church in the unity of faith and practice which the New Testament consistently demands (cf. Heb. 13:7). They are able to guide a congregation in being complete in the same mind and in the same judgment. But if they are not united, the people will not be either.

Made complete is the Greek *katartizō,* used in classical Greek as well as in the New Testament to speak of mending such things as nets, bones, dislocated joints, broken utensils, and torn garments. The basic meaning is to put back together, to make one again something that was broken or separated. Christians are to be **made complete** ("perfectly joined together," KJV), both internally (**in the same mind**) and externally (**in the same judgment**). In our individual minds and among ourselves we are to be one in beliefs, standards, attitudes, and principles of spiritual living.

The epistles have nothing to say about the role of the congregation in church government, but a great deal to say about the role of its leadership. "We request of you, brethren, that you appreciate those who diligently labor among you, and have charge over you in the Lord and give you instruction, and that you esteem them very highly in love because of their work" (1 Thess. 5:12-13). Only when its leadership is right can a congregation be right. They will never be perfect or infallible, but godly men are Christ's instruments for leading and shepherding His people. They have the right to lead the congregation and to make decisions for them in the Lord, and they are to be respected, loved, and followed in the Lord. "Obey your leaders," we read in Hebrews, "and submit to them; for they keep watch over your souls, as those who will give an account. Let them do this with joy and not with grief, for this would be unprofitable for you" (13:17).

God's people are to follow, not quibble with and question, godly leaders who are one in mind as to God's Word and will. In God's order a congregation is to be under the rule of its leaders just as children are to be under the rule of their parents. That is God's way.

Being of **the same mind and . . . the same judgment** rules out grudging or hypocritical unity. Unity must be genuine. We are not simply to speak the same thing, while keeping our disagreements and objections to ourselves, making a pretense of unity. Unity that is not of the same mind and judgment is not true unity. Hypocrites will add to a congregation's size but they will take away from its effectiveness. A member who strongly disagrees with his church leadership and policy, not to mention doctrine, cannot be happy or productive in His own Christian life or be of any positive service to the congregation.

It is not that believers are to be carbon copies of each other. God has made us individual and unique. But we are to be of the same opinion in regard to Christian doctrine, standards, and basic life-style. The apostles themselves were different from one another in personality, temperament, ability, and gifts; but they were of one mind in doctrine and church policy. When differences of understanding and interpretation arose, the first order of business was to reconcile those differences. Ego had no place, only the will of God.

When, for example, the Judaizing controversy became serious in Antioch, "the brethren determined that Paul and Barnabas and certain others of them should go up to Jerusalem to the apostles and elders concerning this issue" (Acts 15:2). At what has come to be called the Jerusalem Council the issue was discussed, prayed about, and settled; and the decision was put in letter form to be circulated among the churches involved (vv. 6-30). It was not an arbitrary ruling made by a group of influential and persuasive men. It was a decision made by godly apostles and elders in accordance with God's revealed will and under the guidance of the Holy Spirit. Those leaders were able to say of their decision, "For it seemed good to the Holy Spirit and to us" (v. 28). We can be sure that many of the Judaizers were not convinced or pleased, for the problem continued to plague the early church for many years. But for faithful believers the issue was settled and "they rejoiced because of its encouragement" (v. 31). That is why the qualifications for elders are spiritual (1 Tim. 3:1ff.; Titus 1:5ff.).

Pastoral elders should make decisions on the basis of unanimous agreement. Not even a three-fourths vote should carry a motion. No decision should be made without total one-mindedness, no matter how long that takes. Because the Holy Spirit has but one will, and because a church must be in complete harmony with His will, the leaders must be in complete harmony with each other in that will. The congregation then is to submit to the elders because it has confidence that the elders' decisions are made under the Spirit's direction and power. Because they believe the elders are one in the Spirit, the congregation is then determined to be one with the elders. There may be struggle in coming to this kind of unity, as there was in Corinth—but it is here mandated by the Spirit Himself through Paul.

Unity has always been God's way for His people and a source of blessing to them. "Behold, how good and how pleasant it is for brothers to dwell together in unity" (Ps. 133:1). At the end of the great discourse on Christian liberty in his letter to the Romans, Paul prayed, "Now may the God who gives perseverance and encouragement grant you to be of the same mind with one another according to Christ Jesus; that with one accord you may with one voice glorify the God and Father of our Lord Jesus Christ. Wherefore, accept one another, just as Christ also accepted us to the glory of God" (15:5-7). Since Christ is of one mind about us we should be of one mind with and about each other. Luke reports that shortly after Pentecost "the congregation of those who believed were of one heart and soul" (Acts 4:32). Paul encouraged the Philippians to make his "joy complete by being of the same mind, maintaining the same love, united in spirit, intent on one purpose" (2:2). Among God's wonderful gifts to His people are oneness in mind, love, accord, voice, purpose, and spirit.

The *purpose* of unity first of all is to glorify God. Unity will always bless a congregation and be a joy to its leaders (Heb. 13:17), but its primary aim is God's glory. Just as Christ accepted us to the glory of God, we accept each other and the rule of our leaders to His glory. We should always, therefore, be "diligent to preserve the unity of the Spirit in the bond of peace" (Eph. 4:3).

The *source* of unity is the Lord Himself. We are called to preserve it and we are able to destroy it, but we are not able to create it. The unity of the church is already established by the Holy Spirit. We can only keep it or harm it. It is kept by doing "nothing from selfishness or empty conceit," but with humility counting others better than ourselves (Phil. 2:3). If an issue arises that we feel needs attention, we should carefully and lovingly present our views to those involved or to those in authority, but without pride or contention. Vanity and self-will are almost always the causes of divisions and factions in a congregation – and in every other group. We keep unity by not insisting on our own way, by avoiding squabbles and bickering, and by putting the interests of our Lord and of His people above all else.

THE PARTIES: LOYALTY TO MEN

For I have been informed concerning you, my brethren, by Chloe's people, that there are quarrels among you. Now I mean this, that each one of you is saying, "I am of Paul," and "I of Apollos," and "I of Cephas," and "I of Christ." (1:11-12)

Paul had ministered in Corinth for a year and a half. He then sent Apollos to be the second pastor. Apparently a group of Jews in the church had been saved under

Peter's (Cephas's) ministry. Parties soon developed in the names of each of those men. Paul learned of the factions through Chloe, probably a prominent person in the Corinthian church who had written or come to visit Paul in Ephesus. The first two groups each had their favorite former pastor, the third had a strong loyalty to Peter, and the fourth, probably the most pious and self-righteous, seemed to think they had a special claim on Christ. They had the right name but it is clear from Paul's accusation that they did not have the right spirit. Perhaps like some "Christ only" groups today they felt they had no need for human instructors—despite the Lord's specific provision for and appointment of human preachers, teachers, and other leaders in His church (1 Cor. 1:1; 12:28; Eph. 4:11; 2 Tim. 1:11; etc.).

Each group was vocal in its opinions and had its own shibboleth, its own slogan of identity and implied superiority. **"I am of Paul," "I of Apollos," "I of Cephas," and "I of Christ."** These were the great teachers of the early years, around whom people gathered and through whom they were given the saving message. People clung to the man who had evangelized and taught them, and then pitted their group against the groups loyal to the other leaders. Often, as with the Corinthian church, leaders about whom such factions center are not responsible for the division. Many times they are not even aware of it. When, however, leaders do know of and even encourage groups that have a special loyalty to them, those leaders are doubly guilty. They not only participate in factionalism but allow it to center on themselves.

The inevitable result of such party spirit is contention, quarrels, wrangling, and disputes—a divided church. It is natural to have special affection for the person who led us to Christ, for a pastor who has fed us from the Word for many years, for a capable Sunday school teacher, or for an elder or deacon who has counseled and consoled us. But such affection becomes misguided and carnal when it is allowed to segregate us from others in the church or to decrease our loyalty to the other leaders. It then becomes a self-centered, self-willed exclusiveness that is the antithesis of unity.

Spirituality produces humility and unity; carnality produces pride and division. The only cure for quarreling and division is renewed spirituality. In my experience the most effective means of correcting a contentious, factious person is to share with him selected Scripture passages on carnality and its evidences, to confront him directly with the cause of his sin.

THE PRINCIPLE: ONENESS IN CHRIST

Has Christ been divided? Paul was not crucified for you, was he? Or were you baptized in the name of Paul? (1:13)

The central principle of Paul's argument is that believers are one in Christ and should never do anything that disrupts or destroys that unity. No human leader, no matter how gifted and effective, should have the loyalty that belongs only to the Lord. Paul began his letter by establishing his authority as an apostle. But he wanted no part of the faction named for him. He had never been **crucified** for anyone. No one was ever **baptized** in his name. His authority had been delegated to him and was not his own, and his purpose was to bring men to Christ, not to himself.

A Christian church that is divided is a contradiction. "One who joins himself to the Lord is one spirit with Him" (1 Cor. 6:17). "For even as the body is one and yet has many members, and all the members of the body, though they are many, are one body, so also is Christ. For by one Spirit we were all baptized into one body, whether Jews or Greeks, whether slaves or free, and we were all made to drink of one Spirit" (12:12-13). "We, who are many, are one body in Christ, and individually members one of another" (Rom. 12:5). "There is one body and one Spirit, just as also you were called in one hope of your calling; one Lord, one faith, one baptism, one God and Father of all who is over all and through all and in all" (Eph. 4:4-6). To be divided in Christ's Body is a violation of our redeemed nature and is in direct opposition to our Lord's will. In His longest recorded prayer, Jesus interceded for those who were His and who would be His. Included was His beautiful appeal for their unity, "that they may all be one; even as Thou, Father, art in Me, and I in Thee, that they also may be in Us; that the world may believe that Thou didst send Me. And the glory which Thou hast given Me I have given to them; that they may be one, just as We are one" (John 17:21-22).

When the Lord's people quarrel and dispute and fight, they reflect against the Lord before the world, they weaken His church, and worst of all they grieve and put to shame the One who bought them—who died to make them one in Him. The Father is one, the Son is one, the Spirit is one, and the church is one.

THE PRIORITY: PREACHING THE GOSPEL

I thank God that I baptized none of you except Crispus and Gaius, that no man should say you were baptized in my name. Now I did baptize also the household of Stephanas; beyond that, I do not know whether I baptized any other. For Christ did not send me to baptize, but to preach the gospel, not in cleverness of speech, that the cross of Christ should not be made void. (1:14-17)

Crispus was the leader of the synagogue in Corinth when Paul first ministered there and was converted under the apostle's preaching. His conversion led to that of many others in the city (Acts 18:8). Since the letter to the Romans was written from Corinth, this **Gaius** was probably the Corinthian "host" to whom Paul refers in Romans 16:23. The apostle was grateful that he had personally baptized only those two and a few others.

Jesus did not baptize anyone personally (John 4:2). To have been baptized by the Lord Himself would have brought almost irresistible temptation to pride and would have tended to set such people apart, whether they wanted to be or not. As an apostle, Paul faced a similar danger. But he also had another: the danger of creating his own cult; and so he declared, **I thank God . . . that no man should say you were baptized in my name.**

As already mentioned, it is not wrong to have special affection for certain persons, such as the one who baptized us, especially if we were converted under his ministry. But it is quite wrong to take special pride in that fact or pride in any close relationship to a Christian leader. Paul was not flattered that a group in Corinth was claiming special allegiance to him. He was distraught and ashamed at the idea, as he had already said: "Paul was not crucified for you, was he? Or were you baptized in the name of Paul?" (1:13). "How could you even think of showing a loyalty to me," he was saying, "that belongs only to the Lord Jesus Christ?" He wanted no cult built around himself or around any other church leader.

Paul was not certain of the exact number he had baptized in Corinth. **Now I did baptize also the household of Stephanas; beyond that, I do not know whether I baptized any other.** This comment gives an interesting insight into the inspiration of Scripture. As an apostle writing the Word of God, Paul made no errors; but he was not omniscient. God protected His apostles from error in order to protect His Word from error. But Paul did not know everything about God or even about himself, and was careful never to make such a claim. He knew what God revealed—things he had no way of knowing on his own. What he could know on his own, he was prone to forget. He was one of us.

Another reason for Paul's baptizing so few converts was that his primary calling lay elsewhere. **For Christ did not send me to baptize, but to preach the gospel, not in cleverness of speech, that the cross of Christ should not be made void.** He was not sent to start a cult of people baptized by him. Jesus had personally commissioned him: "For this purpose I have appeared to you, to appoint you a minister and a witness not only to the things which you have seen, but also to the things in which I will appear to you; delivering you from the Jewish people and from the Gentiles, to whom I am sending you, to open their eyes so that they may turn from darkness to light and from the dominion of Satan to God, in order that they may receive forgiveness of sins and an inheritance among those who have been sanctified by faith in Me" (Acts 26:16-18). His calling was to preach the gospel and bring men to oneness in Christ, not in baptizing to create a faction around himself.

As we each have the right priority in our lives, we too will be determined to serve the Lord in truth and in unity, not living in the carnality and confusion of dissension and division.

The Foolishness of God—part 1 (1:18-25)

4

For the word of the cross is to those who are perishing foolishness, but to us who are being saved it is the power of God. For it is written, "I will destroy the wisdom of the wise, and the cleverness of the clever I will set aside." Where is the wise man? Where is the scribe? Where is the debater of this age? Has not God made foolish the wisdom of the world? For since in the wisdom of God the world through its wisdom did not come to know God, God was well-pleased through the foolishness of the message preached to save those who believe. For indeed Jews ask for signs, and Greeks search for wisdom; but we preach Christ crucified, to Jews a stumbling block, and to Gentiles foolishness, but to those who are the called, both Jews and Greeks, Christ the power of God and the wisdom of God. Because the foolishness of God is wiser than men, and the weakness of God is stronger than men. (1:18-25)

First Corinthians 1:18–2:5 continues to deal with the problem of division in the church, focusing on what Paul calls the "foolishness of God" (v. 25). It is a contrast between the foolishness of men, which they think is wisdom, and the wisdom of God, which they think is foolishness. It is a contrast between God's true wisdom and man's supposed wisdom, between God's supposed foolishness and man's true foolishness.

The Inferiority of Human Wisdom

The ancient Greeks were in love with philosophy, around which their culture was built. They had perhaps as many as fifty identifiable philosophical parties or movements, which vied for acceptance and influence. Each had its views of man's origin, significance, destiny, and relationship to the gods—of which they had many. Some of the philosophies had detailed schemes for the religious, political, social, economic, and educational ordering of society. The Greeks were in love with human wisdom. They believed that philosophy (*philosophia*, "love of wisdom") was all-important. Philosophy provided a view, invented by man, of the meaning of life, values, relationships, purpose, and destiny. Thus there were as many philosophies as there were philosophers, and people tended to line up behind their favorite. They widely disagreed as to which philosophy was the truest and most reliable, and, inevitably, many factions developed, each with its own leaders and adherents. Without an absolute standard for truth, ideas of right and wrong were based entirely on human opinion.

Unfortunately many of the Corinthian converts carried their spirit of philosophical factionalism into the church. Some of them still held onto beliefs of their former pagan philosophy. They were divided not only regarding Christian leaders (1:12) but also regarding philosophical viewpoints. They could not get over their love for human wisdom. They had trusted in Christ and recognized their redemption by grace through the cross, but they wanted to add human wisdom to what He had done for them.

Although it is true that men have recognized much that is true about life, a Christian has no need of human philosophy. It is unnecessary and, more often than not, misleading. Where it happens to be right it will agree with Scripture, and is therefore unnecessary. Where it is wrong it will disagree with Scripture, and is therefore misleading. It has nothing necessary or reliable to offer. By nature it is speculation, based on man's limited and fallible insights and understanding. It is always unreliable and always divisive. "See to it that no one takes you captive through philosophy and empty deception, according to the tradition of men, according to the elementary principles of the world, rather than according to Christ" (Col. 2:8).

The general intent of what Paul is saying to the philosophically oriented Corinthians can be stated like this: "Since you have become Christians, have been filled by God's Spirit, and recognize the Scriptures as His Word, you have no more need for philosophy. It did not help you when you were unbelievers and it will certainly not help you now that you believe. Give it up. It has nothing to offer but confusion and division. You are now united around God's supreme revelation in Jesus Christ. Don't be misled and split by human speculations."

Society in our own day still is enamored of various philosophies. These are not usually expressed in philosophical systems such as the Greeks had, but they are nevertheless human ways of understanding life's meaning and values and of understanding them. The world today, just as in Paul's day, is caught up in the admiration and worship of human opinion, human wisdom, and human desires and aspirations. Men are continually trying to figure out on their own what life is all about—where it came from, where it is going, what it signifies (if anything), and what can and should be done about it (if anything). Modern man has made gods of education and human opinion. Although human ideas are constantly changing, appearing and disappearing, being tried and found wanting, conflicting with and contradicting each other, men continue to put faith in them. As long as they reject divine authority, they have no other option.

Just as in Paul's time, the church today has not escaped the problem. We ourselves can fall prey to current trends in human thought. Some Christians frantically look almost everywhere but to God and His Word for values, meaning, guidance, and help. Or they add human ideas and insights *to* Scripture or try to "baptize" human ideas and insights *with* Scripture. We sometimes are more concerned about human opinion than about God's Word—"using" Scripture, but not fully believing, trusting, and obeying it.

Paul had begun to attack the problem earlier in the chapter: "For Christ did not send me to baptize, but to preach the gospel, not in cleverness of speech, that the cross of Christ should not be made void" (1:17). "Cleverness of speech" (*sophia logou*) means literally "wisdom of words" or "wisdom of doctrine." Paul came to preach God's Word (which is the gospel), not men's words (which are *sophia logou*). From 1:18 through the end of chapter 3, he continues to show the superiority of the former over the latter. In that passage he uses *sophia* (wisdom) 13 times—sometimes referring to God's true wisdom (as in 1:24, 30; 2:6-7) and sometimes to man's presumed wisdom (as in 1:17, 19, 22; 2:4-5). God's Word is the only true wisdom and is all the wisdom that is reliable and needed. All truth that God intends us to have and that we need is there. It needs no addition of human wisdom, which always falls short of His Word and most often contradicts or distorts it. Scripture stands alone—reliable, sufficient, and complete.

Human wisdom, epitomized in philosophy, has always been a threat to revelation. Martyn Lloyd-Jones has commented, "The whole drift toward modernism that has blighted the church of God and nearly destroyed its living gospel may be traced to an hour when men began to turn from revelation to philosophy." But the trust in human wisdom that we call modernism is hardly modern. It began with Adam and Eve, when they set their own judgment above God's, and was in full bloom in Paul's day. Whenever human wisdom, whether a definite philosophical system or not, gets mixed with divine revelation, revelation loses.

The Bible, for example, affirms that its first five books were written by Moses. In many places in Scripture those books are referred to as "the law of Moses," using "law" in its broadest sense. Beginning in the late 18th century, however, and coming to a peak about a hundred years later, rationalist scholars developed the "documentary hypothesis." They did not agree on all details, but the main idea was that the Pentateuch (the first five books) was written by a number of different men over a considerable period of time. Some of those men strongly affirmed that sophisticated codes of law did not even exist in Moses' day and that he could not possibly have written *any* of the Pentateuch. (Incidentally, archaeology has long since proved that law was highly developed in the Near East centuries before Moses.) Some parts of the Pentateuch, they maintained, were not written or finally edited until after the Babylonian Exile. They divided those Bible books into various subparts—called J, E, D, and P (representing the supposed Jahwist, Elohist, Deuteronomist, and Priestly sources of the parts).

Behind that theory was the presupposition that only what is understandable to the human mind (rational) is true and reliable. Also behind it was the specific notion of evolution, then coming into vogue among many intellectuals. They reasoned that, because man and his ideas evolve, those parts of the Pentateuch that reflect more "primitive" stories and beliefs were obviously written earlier than those that are more "advanced." Later editors, or redactors, put it all together in its present form. They taught that monotheism (belief in one God) had not evolved as a theory of deity early in the Pentateuch period, so that part of Scripture must be dated later. Thus philosophy became the judge of biblical authority—and Scripture was declared unreliable.

The most difficult part of the Pentateuch for rationalists to accept is its account of creation. There is no room in evolution for the immediate and full-grown type of creation described in Genesis 1–2. Some scholars, trying to allow for some sort of creation as well as some sort of evolution, hold that God got it all started by creating the raw elements, or perhaps primitive forms of life, and that evolution then took over, with God interjecting the soul at the proper time. But such "theistic evolution" or "progressive creationism" also contradicts Scripture. It imposes a philosophy and process on creation that the literal interpretation of Scripture does not allow. Again revelation was forced to bow to human ego.

Psychology is another form of human wisdom that frequently contradicts or is used to modify or "enhance" God's Word. It is not a true or exact science but is basically philosophical. It seeks to understand and modify man's inner workings—his mind, emotions, and spirit—by human observations and theories. But every form of psychology has an underlying, preconceived philosophy that colors, and to a great extent predetermines, its methods and its interpretation of findings. Like every other form of philosophy, it sees man and the world through the lens of human reason and understanding. By its very nature, psychology could never discover and understand sin, because sin is offense against God—whose nature and will are totally outside psychology's scope. Psychology may understand men's offending men and try to deal with a person's *feeling* of sin and guilt. But human reason and wisdom cannot possibly identify, much less determine, what sin against God is or give a remedy for any of it. Only God's Word can identify sin and only His forgiveness can remove it. Because sin is offense against God, only God can determine what sin is or provide forgiveness for it. The Bible is clear that the heart of all man's problems—physical, mental, social, economic, and spiritual—is sin. And a true understanding of sin is completely out of psychology's realm. But Christ not only can remove guilt feelings; He can remove the guilt itself—in fact, the sin itself.

Even some theologians (whose name means "student or studier of God") try to improve on God's Word by their own understandings. Because his own philosophy did not allow for the miraculous, the very influential German theologian Rudolph Bultmann, for example, decided to "demythologize" the Bible—to identify the supposed myths and to consider only what remained to be God's Word. That is, he decided in advance what God's Word could and could not be. He relied on his own wisdom to determine God's wisdom. In doing so he tried to make God in his own human image. When man tries on his own to determine what God is like, what His will is, and what He can and cannot do, the creature merely creates an imaginary god, an idol in his own image and to his own egoistic satisfaction. When human philosophy is in any way imposed upon God's revelation, revelation loses.

Without exception, man's wisdom elevates himself and lowers God. It always, no matter how seemingly sincere and objective and scholarly, caters to man's self-will, pride, fleshly inclinations, and independence. Those are the basic characteristics of the natural man, and they always direct and determine the natural man's thinking, desires, and conclusions. The reason men love complex, elaborate philosophies and religions is because these appeal to human ego. They offer the challenge of understanding and doing something complex and difficult. For the same reason some men scoff at the gospel. It calls on them to do nothing—it allows them to do nothing—but accept in simple faith what God has done. The cross crushes man's sin and crushes man's pride. It also offers deliverance from sin and deliverance from pride.

In his own wisdom man inevitably exchanges the truth of God for a lie and worships the creature rather than the Creator (Rom. 1:25). Man's wisdom is founded in his own will and it is always directed toward the fulfilling of his own will. Consequently it is always against God's wisdom and God's will. Human wisdom ("cleverness of speech") will always make God's wisdom ("the gospel" and "the cross of Christ") void (1 Cor. 1:17).

Men have, of course, made remarkable discoveries and accomplished amazing feats over the centuries, especially in the last fifty years or so. Science and technology have developed countless products, machines, instruments, medicines, and procedures that have made great contributions to human welfare.

It is also true that becoming a Christian does not give us all the answers to everything—certainly not in the areas of science, electronics, math, or any other field of strictly human learning. Many nonbelievers are more educated, brilliant, talented, and experienced than many believers. If we want our car fixed we go to the best mechanic we can find, even if he is not a Christian. If we need an operation we go to the best surgeon. If we want to get an education we try to go the school that has the best faculty in the field in which we want to study.

As long as they are used properly and wisely, medicine and technology and science and all such fields of human learning and achievement can be of great value. Christians should thank God for them.

But if we want answers to what life is about—answers about where we came from, where we are going, and why we are here, about what is right and what is wrong—then human learning cannot help us. If we want to know the ultimate meaning and purpose of human life, and the source of happiness, joy, fulfillment, and peace, we have to look beyond what even the best human minds can discover. Man's attempts to find such answers on his own are doomed to fail. He does not have the resources even to find the answers about himself, much less about God. In regard to the most important truths—those about human nature, sin, God, morality and ethics, the spirit world, the transformation and future of human life—philosophy is bankrupt.

The Superiority of God's Wisdom

For the word of the cross is to those who are perishing foolishness, but to us who are being saved it is the power of God. (1:18)

When man elevates his own wisdom he automatically attempts to lower God's wisdom, which looks to him like foolishness, because it conflicts with his own thinking. That God would take human form, be crucified, and raised in order to provide for man's forgiveness of sin and entrance into heaven is an idea far too simple, foolish, and humbling for the natural man to accept. That one man (even the Son of God) could die on a piece of wood on a nondescript hill in a nondescript part of the world and thereby determine the destiny of every person who has ever lived seems stupid. It allows no place for man's merit, man's attainment, man's understanding, or man's pride. This **word of the cross** is **foolishness** (*moria,* from which we get *moron*). It is moronic, absolute nonsense, to unbelievers who rely on their own wisdom—**to those who are perishing**. That phrase is a graphic description of Christ rejectors, who are in the process of being destroyed in eternal judgment.

Word in verse 18 is from the same Greek term (*logos*) as "speech" in verse 17. Paul is contrasting man's word, which reflects man's wisdom, and God's Word, which reflects God's wisdom. Consequently **the word of the cross** includes the entire gospel message and work, God's plan and provision for man's redemption. In its fullest sense it is God's total revelation, for His revelation centers in the cross. God's whole redemption story and His whole redemption process seem foolish to unbelievers. And because Christ's work on the cross is the pinnacle of God's revealed Word and work, to reject the cross is to reject His revelation, and to perish.

When Paul first came to Corinth he continued to face the maelstrom of philosophies with which he had contended in Athens (Acts 17:18-21). But he had "determined to know nothing among [them] except Jesus Christ, and Him crucified" (1 Cor. 2:2). The response of some in Corinth was the same as that of some in Athens: "When they heard of the resurrection of the dead, [they] began to sneer" (Acts 17:32). But Paul did not change his message to suit his hearers. The Corinthians, like the Athenians and most other Greeks, had more than enough philosophy. They did not need Paul's opinions added to their own, and the apostle was determined not to give them his opinions but **the word of the cross.** He would give them nothing but God's profoundly simple, but historical and objective, truth—not another man's complex and subjective speculations.

Human wisdom cannot understand the cross. Peter, for example, did not understand the cross when he first heard Jesus speak of it. In fact Peter took Jesus "aside and began to rebuke Him, saying, 'God forbid it, Lord! This shall never happen to You'" (Matt. 16:22). Peter's own understanding about the Messiah had no place for the cross. He thought the Messiah would soon set up an earthly kingdom and that everything would be pleasant for His followers. But Peter's wisdom was contrary to God's wisdom, and anything contrary to God's wisdom works for Satan. Jesus' reply to His disciple was quick and sharp: "Get behind Me, Satan! You are a stumbling block to Me; for you are not setting your mind on God's interests, but man's" (v. 23). When the soldiers came to the garden to arrest Jesus, Peter still did not understand. He still tried to interfere with God's plan. Drawing his sword, he cut off a slave's ear—for which Jesus again rebuked him (John 18:10-11). Only after the resurrection and ascension did Peter understand and accept the cross (Acts 2:23-24; 3:13-15). He now had God's Spirit and God's wisdom, and no longer relied on his own. Years later he would write, "He Himself bore our sins in His body on the cross, that we might die to sin and live to righteousness; for by His wounds you were healed" (1 Pet. 2:24).

To the natural mind, whether Jewish or Gentile, the cross is offensive and unacceptable. **But to us who are being saved it is the power of God.** All men are either in the process of being saved (salvation present is not complete until the redemption of the body—Rom. 8:23; 13:11) or of being destroyed. One's view of the cross determines which.

Paul proceeds (1:19–2:5) to give five reasons why God's wisdom is superior to man's: its permanence, its power, its paradox, its purpose, and its presentation.

THE PERMANENCE OF GOD'S WISDOM

For it is written, "I will destroy the wisdom of the wise, and the cleverness of the clever I will set aside." Where is the wise man? Where is the scribe? Where is the debater of this age? Has not God made foolish the wisdom of the world? (1:19-20)

Paul uses a quotation from Isaiah 29:14 to emphasize that the wisdom of men will be destroyed. Isaiah's teaching will have its ultimate fulfillment in the last days, when all men's philosophies and objections to the gospel will be swept away. Christ will reign unopposed and unobstructed as Lord of lords and King of kings (Rev. 17:14), and all of man's wisdom will become ashes.

But the prophecy also had a more immediate significance and fulfillment, which serves to illustrate its future and ultimate fulfillment. When Isaiah made the prophecy, Sennacherib, the king of Assyria, was planning to conquer Judah. The Lord told His prophet not to worry or fear, because the king's plan would fail. But it would not fail because of the strength of Judah's army or because of the strategy of King Hezekiah and his advisors. "The wisdom of their wise men [would] perish, and the discernment of their discerning men [would] be concealed" (Isa. 29:14). Judah would be saved solely by God's power, with no human help. He destroyed 185,000 men of the Assyrian army with just one angel (37:36). The full account is given in 2 Kings 17.

God continually told Israel that He would fight for her. All she had to do was trust and obey. That is why, when Israel went into battle, a choir singing the Lord's praises often preceded the army.

Men are all inclined to try to solve their problems and fight their battles by their own ingenuity and in their own power. But human ingenuity and power only get in God's way. Men's own efforts hinder God in His work rather than help Him. "There is a way which seems right to a man," Solomon tells us, "but its end is the way of death" (Prov. 14:12). One of the things that keeps many people away from Christ, away from the Bible, and away from salvation is their disagreement with the gospel. It just does not fit their way of thinking. Even when they know their own philosophy or their own religion is shaky, they often would rather put their heads in the sand and hope for the best than simply take God at His word. This is the willful ignorance of unbelief described by Paul in Romans 1:18-23. Pretending to be wise, such men are fools.

Jeremiah asked, "The wise men are put to shame, they are dismayed and caught; behold, they have rejected the word of the Lord, and what kind of wisdom do they have?" (8:9). If men reject God's revelation, what truth is left, what sort of wisdom do they have? It "is not that which comes down from above, but is earthly, natural, demonic" (James 3:15). Being earthly, it never gets beyond what man can see, touch, and measure. Being natural, it is based on human desires and standards. Being demonic, its real source is Satan. That is human wisdom. "But the wisdom from above," James goes on to say, "is first pure, then peaceable, gentle, reasonable, full of mercy and good fruits, unwavering, without hypocrisy" (3:17).

Where is the wise man? Where is the scribe? Where is the debater of this age? Has not God made foolish the wisdom of the world? (1:20)

This verse specifically teaches that human wisdom not only is unreliable but impermanent. To continue that thought, Paul asks several questions, really one question in three parts. In slightly different form they each ask, "Where are all the smart people that have the answers?" How much closer to peace is man than he was a century ago—or a millennium ago? How much closer are we to eliminating poverty, hunger, ignorance, crime, and immorality than men were in Paul's day? Our advances in knowledge and technology and communication have not really advanced us. It is from among those who are intelligent and clever that the worst exploiters, deceivers, and oppressors come. We are more educated than our forefathers but we are not more moral. We have more means of helping each other but we are not less selfish. We have more means of communication but we do not understand each other any better. We have more psychology and education, and more crime and more war. We have not changed, except in finding more ways to express and excuse our human nature. Throughout history human wisdom has never basically changed and has never solved the basic problems of man.

In asking about **the wise man** Paul paraphrased Isaiah, who wrote, "Well then, where are your wise men?" (Isa. 19:12). The prophet was referring to the wise men of Egypt—the soothsayers, mediums, and wizards—who always promised but never produced good counsel. "They have led Egypt astray in all that it does, as a drunken man staggers in his vomit" (v. 14). **The scribe** probably referred to the Assyrians, who sent scribes along with their soldiers to record the booty taken in battle. But God would see to it that they had nothing to record, nothing to count or to weigh (Isa. 33:18).

The debater of this age does not seem to have a counterpart in the Old Testament. **Debater** was a very Greek word (*suzētētēs*) and referred to arguing about philosophy, of which Greeks were so fond. "Where is the debater now?" Paul asks almost sarcastically. "Where have all the clever arguments and impressive rhetoric brought you? Are you better off because of them—or simply more self-satisfied and complacent? Don't you see that all the wisdom of your wise men, your scribes, and your debaters is folly?" Nothing really changes. Life has the same problems; men have the same struggles.

Could the apostle have written anything more appropriate for our own day? Where have our great thinkers—our philosophers, sociologists, psychologists, economists, scientists, and statesmen—brought us? Never before has mankind been so fearful of self-destruction or been so self-consciously perplexed, confused, and corrupt. Modern human wisdom has failed just as ancient human wisdom failed, except that its failures come faster and spread farther. The outer life improves in a material way, while the inner life seems to have correspondingly less meaning. The real issues are not solved.

Human wisdom sometimes sees the immediate cause of a problem but it does not see the root, which always is sin. It may see that selfishness is a cause of injustice, but it has no way to remove selfishness. It may see that hatred causes misery and pain and destruction, but it has no cure for hatred. It can see plainly that man does not get along with man, but does not see that the real cause is that man does not get along with God. Human wisdom *cannot* see because it *will not* see. As long as it looks on God's wisdom as foolishness, its own wisdom will be foolish. In other words, human wisdom itself is a basic part of the problem.

Peace, joy, hope, harmony, brotherhood, and every other aspiration of man is out of his reach as long as he follows his own way in trying to achieve them. He who sees the cross as folly is doomed to his own folly.

THE POWER OF GOD'S WISDOM

For since in the wisdom of God the world through its wisdom did not come to know God, God was well-pleased through the foolishness of the message preached to save those who believe. For indeed Jews ask for signs, and Greeks search for wisdom; but we preach Christ crucified, to Jews a stumbling block, and to Gentiles foolishness, but to those who are the called, both Jews and Greeks, Christ the power of God and the wisdom of God.

Because the foolishness of God is wiser than men, and the weakness of God is stronger than men. (1:21-25)

With all their supposed wisdom men have never been able to know God, much less come to a personal relationship with Him. Man's increase in knowledge and philosophies tends to increase his problems, not solve them. Hatred increases, misunderstanding increases, conflicts and wars increase, drunkenness increases, crime increases, mental breakdowns increase, family problems increase. They increase not only in numbers, but also in extent and in severity. The more man looks to himself and depends on himself, the worse his situation becomes. As his dependence on his wisdom increases, so do his problems.

This is God's plan, as the words **in the wisdom of God** indicate. God wisely established it this way, that man could not come to know Him by the wisdom of the world. Man cannot solve his problems because he will not recognize their source, which is sin, or their solution, which is salvation. Man's own sinful nature is the cause of his problems, and he cannot change his nature. Even if human wisdom could recognize the problem it does not have the power to change it. But God has the power. **God was well-pleased through the foolishness of the message preached to save those who believe.** He chose to use that which the world's wisdom counts as moronic, as **foolishness,** to save those of the world who would simply **believe.** Believing implies complete assent to all the truth of the saving gospel. For those who will exchange their wisdom for His, God offers transformation, regeneration, new birth and new life through the power of the cross of Jesus Christ, His Son. This "foolishness" is man's only hope.

When human wisdom recognizes its own bankruptcy and a man turns in faith to Jesus Christ, whose saving work is **the message preached,** he can exchange poverty for riches, sin for righteousness, despair for hope, death for life. The simplicity of the gospel gives what the complexity of human wisdom promises but never delivers. "Let no man deceive himself. If any man among you thinks that he is wise in this age, let him become foolish that he may become wise" (3:18). When we come down (in the world's eyes) to the cross, God will raise us up to eternal life.

Even though surrounded by evidences of God's wisdom men choose to trust their own. They "suppress the truth in unrighteousness, because that which is known about God is evident within them; for God made it evident to them. For since the creation of the world His invisible attributes, His eternal power and divine nature, have been clearly seen, being understood through what has been made, so that they are without excuse" (Rom. 1:18-20). The wisdom of men is totally indicted. Their wisdom is not merely ignorant of God's wisdom but is scornful of it. Their ignorance is willful, because they refuse to recognize that which is "evident," that which can be "clearly seen."

Every time a person looks at a mountain he should think of God's greatness. Every time he sees a sunset he should think of God's glory. Every time he sees a new life come into the world he should see God's creative hand at work. Yet an astronomer can look through his telescope and see a hundred thousand stars, and not see God's greatness. A natural scientist can look through his microscope and see intricacies of life beyond description, yet not see God's creation. A nuclear physicist can produce a thousand megatons of destruction, yet not recognize God's power.

When Paul came to Athens he noticed a shrine inscribed: "To an unknown God." He proceeded to declare to those around him on Mars Hill (the Areopagus), "What therefore you worship in ignorance, this I proclaim to you" (Acts 17:23). With all their learning and philosophies and debating they had come to recognize countless gods—but not the true God. They made for themselves many gods, but the God who had made them they did not know. **The world through its wisdom did not come to know God.**

God does not *expect* men to come to Him through their own wisdom; He knows they cannot. But they can come to Him through *His* wisdom. **God was well-pleased through the foolishness of the message preached to save those who believe.** The phrase **message preached** is one word in the Greek (*kērugmatos*) and can also be translated "proclamation." It does not refer to the act of declaring a message but to the content of the message. The content of God's message is the gospel, "the word of the cross" and "the power of God" (v. 18). The content, in fact, is Jesus Christ Himself, who is "the power of God and the wisdom of God" (v. 24).

Paul is not talking about foolish preaching, of which there has always been more than enough. He is talking about the preaching of that which is foolish in the world's eyes—the simple, unadorned, uncomplicated truth of the cross of Jesus Christ that allows no place for man's wisdom or man's work or man's glory. The wisdom and work and glory are all God's. But the blessing they give can be man's.

It is not through philosophy, intellectual understanding, or human wisdom that salvation comes, but through believing. God saves only **those who believe.** Men cannot "figure out" salvation; they can only accept it in faith.

For indeed Jews ask for signs, and Greeks search for wisdom; but we preach Christ crucified, to Jews a stumbling block, and to Gentiles foolishness. (1:22-23)

Unbelief is always the basic reason for not accepting God's will and God's way, but unbelief is expressed in various ways. The **Jews** wanted supernatural **signs** before they would believe the gospel. The Gentiles, represented by **Greeks,** wanted proof through human **wisdom,** through ideas they could propound and could debate.

Desire for proof most frequently is an evasion, an excuse for not believing. Jesus performed miracle after miracle in the heartland of Judaism, most of them in public. Yet most of those who witnessed the miracles, the supernatural signs, did not believe in Him. A man whom Jesus healed in Jerusalem had been blind from birth and was a well-known beggar in the city. After he was healed, however, some of his neighbors refused to believe he was the same person, even though he told them himself (John 9:9). The man was taken before the Pharisees, to whom he gave his testimony of miraculous healing. They too refused to believe the **sign,** even with the additional witness of the man's parents. The Pharisees believed in the supernatural, but only in the supernatural that fit their own scheme of understanding.

At another time, a group of scribes and Pharisees came to Jesus, demanding a sign from Him to prove He was of God. Knowing their insincerity and hypocrisy, Jesus refused to give them a sign—at least of the kind they wanted. He told them, "An evil and adulterous generation craves for a sign; and yet no sign shall be given to it but the sign of Jonah the prophet," which represented His crucifixion and resurrection (Matt. 12:38-40). As events proved, most of the Jews did not believe even that greatest of all signs when it was given.

Most of the Jews of Jesus' and Paul's day could not accept the idea of a crucified Messiah. That was a **stumbling block** to them (cf. Rom. 9:31-33). To them He was to come in earthly power and splendor and establish an earthly throne and kingdom. Such clear messianic teachings as those found in Psalm 22 and Isaiah 53 were either explained away or ignored. Scripture that did not conform to their preconceived notions was simply reinterpreted or sidestepped.

The **Greeks,** on the other hand, wanted intellectual proof, something they could mull over and figure out with their own minds. They too were insincere. As Paul had discovered in Athens, the Greek philosophers there were not interested in discovering truth, especially not truth about God. They were interested only in hearing and arguing about exciting new ideas and problems (Acts 17:21). They had no interest in seeking out eternal truth to believe and accept and follow. The **wisdom** they sought was not divine and eternal wisdom, but human and temporary wisdom. The wisdom they sought, as illustrated by the Athenian philosophers, was not divine truth but intellectual novelty.

Like the Jews, they also had preconceived ideas about what a god could and could not, or would and would not, do. Greeks generally believed that all matter was evil and that everything spiritual was good. It was therefore inconceivable to them that a god *could* come to earth as a man. It was even more inconceivable that he would *want to.* To them the gods were indifferent to men. They were totally apathetic to things that transpired on earth.

The second-century philosopher Celsus, who made a career out of attacking Christianity, wrote, "God is good and beautiful and happy, and if in that which is most beautiful and best, if then he descends to man it involves change for him, and a change from good to bad, from beautiful to ugly, from happiness to unhappiness, from what is best to what is worst, and God would never accept such a change." The idea of the incarnation, not to mention the crucifixion, was utter folly to Greek thinking. To those rationalists nothing could be more absurd than the idea of an incarnate God giving Himself to be crucified in order to secure salvation, holiness, and eternal life for a fallen world.

The two groups Paul mentions here are representative of all of unbelieving mankind. Whether, like the typical Jew, they demand proof by a supernatural sign or, like the typical Greek, they want proof by natural wisdom, unbelievers will find an excuse for rejecting the gospel.

Paul very much believed in the supernatural; and he was, by any standard, highly intelligent. He was both a supernaturalist and a rationalist in the best senses. But above all he was a believer, a believer in God. The gospel is both supernatural and sensible. But it cannot be discovered through supernatural signs or appropriated through natural wisdom apart from a willing heart. It will save only those who believe.

Paul would only preach Christ crucified, the only true sign and the only true wisdom. Those who will not believe that sign or accept that wisdom will not accept God. To those who seek other signs the cross is a **stumbling block,** and to those who seek other wisdom it is **foolishness.**

The only message a Christian has to tell is the message of the cross—of God the Son becoming man, of His dying to pay the penalty for our sins, and of His being raised from the dead in order to raise us to life.

But to those who are the called, both Jews and Greeks, Christ the power of God and the wisdom of God. Because the foolishness of God is wiser than men, and the weakness of God is stronger than men. (1:24-25)

Paul makes clear that he had been using the terms **Jews** and **Greeks** in a general way to represent *unbelieving* Jews and Gentiles. God's called people also include **both Jews and Greeks.** For those who believe in His Son, the crucified **Christ** is both **the power of God and the wisdom of God.** He who is a stumbling block to the unbelieving Jew is Savior of the believing, and the One who is foolishness to the unbelieving Gentile is Redeemer to the believing.

In mentioning God's **foolishness** and **weakness** the apostle is, of course, speaking from the unbeliever's point of view. Ironically, and tragically, the very part of God's plan and work that seems most ridiculous and useless from man's natural standpoint actually exhibits His *greatest* power and *greatest* wisdom.

Paul is also saying that, even if God could possess any sort of foolishness, it would be **wiser** than man's greatest wisdom. And if God were able to have any weakness, it would be **stronger** than the greatest strength men could muster.

God's power is real power, power that means something and accomplishes something. It is not *of* men but it is offered *for* men. It is the power of salvation from sin, of deliverance from Satan, of life in God's very presence for all eternity.

The Foolishness of
God—part 2 (1:26–2:5)

For consider your calling, brethren, that there were not many wise according to the flesh, not many mighty, not many noble; but God has chosen the foolish things of the world to shame the wise, and God has chosen the weak things of the world to shame the things which are strong, and the base things of the world and the despised, God has chosen, the things that are not, that He might nullify the things that are, that no man should boast before God. But by His doing you are in Christ Jesus, who became to us wisdom from God, and righteousness and sanctification, and redemption, that, just as it is written, "Let him who boasts, boast in the Lord." And when I came to you, brethren, I did not come with superiority of speech or of wisdom, proclaiming to you the testimony of God. For I determined to know nothing among you except Jesus Christ, and Him crucified. And I was with you in weakness and in fear and in much trembling. And my message and my preaching were not in persuasive words of wisdom, but in demonstration of the Spirit and of power, that your faith should not rest on the wisdom of men, but on the power of God. (1:26–2:5)

THE SUPERIORITY OF GOD'S WISDOM (continued)

THE PARADOX OF GOD'S WISDOM

Paul possibly went over the membership of the Corinthian church in his mind as he wrote verse 26. He reminded them that they had very few who were famous, wealthy, highly educated, powerful, or influential when they believed in the Lord Jesus Christ. It is likely that, when they became Christians, they lost a great deal of the prestige, influence, and income they did have. **Consider your calling, brethren,** he says. Paul always uses the term *calling* to refer to the saving call of God, the effectual call that results in redemption. "You know what sort of persons you were when God called you out of darkness. You know that He did not accept you as His child because you were brilliant or wealthy or intelligent or powerful. If you were any of these things," he says, "you were saved in spite of them not because of them. If anything they were stumbling blocks that hindered you, obstacles between you and God's grace." He implies that they should be *glad* that **not many** were **wise according to the flesh** or **mighty** or **noble.** Such things often keep people from the sense of need that leads to salvation. If more of them had been **wise, mighty,** or **noble,** it is likely that fewer of them would have been saved.

God is not looking for Phi Beta Kappas to save and to do His work. Nor is He looking for millionaires or famous athletes or entertainers or statesmen. His salvation is open to them just as surely as to others, but only on the same basis of faith. The very things that put them ahead in the world may actually put them behind with God. It is the feeling of inadequacy that makes people aware that they have need, and often draws them to the gospel.

Jesus prayed on one occasion, "I praise Thee, O Father, Lord of heaven and earth, that Thou didst hide these things from the wise and intelligent and didst reveal them to babes" (Matt. 11:25). As the context makes clear, this prayer was spoken publicly as a part of His preaching to the crowds. He was addressing His hearers as much as His Father when He prayed these words. He wanted them to know that God wanted only their faith and nothing else. He was also warning that "the wise and intelligent" were at a disadvantage as far as spiritual life and understanding are concerned. It is not that they could not accept and believe, but that pride in and dependence on their accomplishments and abilities could keep them from the kingdom. Weakness and insufficiency are the climate in which God's strength is made manifest.

God's wisdom is a kind of paradox. In human thinking, strength is strength, weakness is weakness, and intelligence is intelligence. But in God's economy some of the seemingly strongest things are the weakest, some of the seemingly weakest things are the strongest, and some of the seemingly wisest things are the most foolish. The paradox is not by accident but by God's design.

A simple, uneducated, untalented, and clumsy believer who has trusted in Jesus Christ as Savior and who faithfully and humbly follows His Lord is immeasurably wiser than the brilliant Ph.D. who scoffs at the gospel. The simple believer knows forgiveness, love, grace, life, hope, God's Word—God Himself. He can see eternity. The unbelieving Ph.D., on the other hand, knows nothing beyond his books, his own mind, and his own experience. He sees nothing beyond this life, and he cannot be considered anything but foolish.

We are often tempted to think that it would be wonderful if such-and-such a great athlete—or brilliant scientist, popular entertainer, or world leader—would become a Christian. But Jesus did not think this way when He chose His disciples. Some were probably well known in their local circles and perhaps a few of them were well off financially. But He did not choose them for their wealth or influence, and in His training of them He did not try to capitalize on any such things. None of them had anything so great that he was not ready to leave it to follow Christ.

In A.D. 178 the philosopher Celsus mockingly wrote of Christians:

> Let no cultured person draw near, none wise and none sensible, for all that kind of thing we count evil; but if any man is ignorant, if any man is wanting in sense and culture, if anybody is a fool, let him come boldly [to become a Christian]. . . . We see them in their own houses, wool dresses, cobblers, the worst, the vulgarest, the most uneducated persons. . . . They are like a swarm of bats or ants creeping out of their nest, or frogs holding a symposium around a swamp, or worms convening in mud.

That is also what much of the rest of the world of his day thought of Christians. The simplicity of the gospel and the humility of faithful believers is incomprehensible to the world; it seems to be abject foolishness. The Lord planned it that way. **God has chosen the foolish things of the world to shame the wise, and . . . has chosen the weak things of the world to shame the things which are strong, and the base things of the world and the despised, God has chosen, the things that are not, that He might nullify the things that are.** It is interesting to note that **the despised** means, in the root form, "to be considered as nothing." The Greek is in the perfect tense here, indicating that what was once despised will continue to be despised. So people who were thought to be nobodies in society would continue to be thought of as nobodies. The phrase **things that are not** translates the most contemptible expression in the Greek language. "Being" was everything to the Greeks, and to be called a nothing was the worst insult. The phrase may have been used of slaves.

The world measures greatness by many standards. At the top are intelligence, wealth, prestige, and position—things which God has determined to put at the bottom. God reveals the greatness of His power by demonstrating that it is the world's nobodies that are His somebodies.

According to God, the greatest man who ever lived, apart from Jesus Himself, was John the Baptist. He had no formal education, no training in a trade or profession, no money, no military rank, no political position, no social pedigree, no prestige, no impressive appearance or oratory. Yet Jesus said, "Truly, I say to you, among those born of women there has not arisen anyone greater than John the Baptist" (Matt. 11:11).

This man fit none of the world's standards but all of God's. And what he became was all to the credit of God's power.

THE PURPOSE OF GOD'S WISDOM

That no man should boast before God. But by His doing you are in Christ Jesus, who became to us wisdom from God, and righteousness and sanctification, and redemption, that, just as it is written, "Let him who boasts, boast in the Lord." (1:29-31)

The first and primary purpose of the wisdom of God that produces salvation is that He be glorified. **No man** will ever have a reason to **boast before God**. Foolish, weak, base man can do nothing for himself; God has done everything. "For by grace you have been saved through faith; and that not of yourselves, it is the gift of God; not as a result of works, that no one should boast. For we are His workmanship" (Eph. 2:8-10).

God also has a purpose for those who are saved. His purpose for His redeemed has many aspects, four of which are mentioned in verse 30. Because they **are in Christ Jesus,** they receive God's **wisdom, righteousness, sanctification,** and **redemption.**

First, believers are given God's **wisdom.** They not only are *saved* by God's wisdom rather than their own but are *given* God's wisdom to replace their own. The truly wise of this world are those whose wisdom is not of this world but is from the Lord. Christians can say, without pride or self-boasting, that they have become wise in Jesus Christ. They stand as a testimony for all time that God in His wisdom chose the sinful, the weak, and the unwise in order to make them righteous, strong, and wise. God grants them His wisdom that He might be glorified, that it might be clearly seen that the wisdom Christians have is not their own but is by His power and grace.

Men are saved not by their intelligence, accomplishments, or human wisdom. Those who trust in these will never receive God's salvation and life and wisdom—because these may be had only by humbly receiving what His Son has done on our behalf on the cross. Jesus said, "I am the way, and the truth, and the life; no one comes to the Father, but through Me" (John 14:6), and, on another occasion, "If you abide in My word, then you are truly disciples of Mine; and you shall know the truth, and the truth shall make you free" (8:31-32).

The wisdom received from God through Christ is both instant and progressive. In his next letter to the Corinthians, Paul wrote, "For God, who said, 'Light shall shine out of darkness,' is the One who has shone in our hearts to give the light of the knowledge of the glory of God in the face of Christ" (2 Cor. 4:6). The maker and giver of physical light is also the source and giver of spiritual light. The first thing a believer learns is knowledge of God's glory.

The glory of God signifies His majesty and His greatness. But in its fullest sense it represents all that God is—all of His attributes, His whole nature, the fullness of His divine being. We come to know personally the creator of the universe and the source of all life and all goodness.

Godly wisdom also has a progressive aspect. The God whom we have come to know through Christ we come to know better as we live by His Spirit. Paul prayed for the Ephesian believers to be given "a spirit of wisdom and of revelation in the knowledge of Him," that is, of Christ (Eph. 1:17). They already had the initial gift of God's wisdom, received when they first believed. But the apostle was concerned that they continue to grow in His wisdom and truth (cf. 2 Pet. 3:18).

Wisdom from God also has a future aspect. In this same prayer Paul asks, "that the eyes of your heart may be enlightened, so that you may know what is the hope of His calling, what are the riches of the glory of His inheritance in the saints" (v. 18). Both "hope" and "inheritance" suggest future fulfillment of wisdom and knowledge. God has given us wisdom, He is now giving us wisdom, and He will ultimately give us wisdom.

The person of the world cannot see or receive God's wisdom, the wisdom that could show him God Himself, His plan for the world and for His people, and the future eternity that He gives through His Son. And so men live only for the moment, for the now, having no idea where they came from, where they are going, or what they are doing here in the first place. Yet the simplest, most uneducated person who humbly places his life in Christ's hands is given the truth about all of these things. He knows what all the sages and philosophers of all time have never been able to discover or will ever be able to discover. He has God's wisdom as one of His Savior's precious gifts.

Second, believers receive God's **righteousness**. They are made right with God and they participate in His righteousness, His rightness. Rightness means to be as something or someone *should* be—right as opposed to wrong, good as opposed to evil, sinless as opposed to sinful. God is totally righteous because He is totally as He should be. He cannot vary from His rightness. When we trust His Son, He shares His Son's righteousness with us. "To the one who does not work, but believes in Him who justifies the ungodly, his faith is reckoned as righteousness" (Rom. 4:5). God "made Him who knew no sin to be sin on our behalf, that we might become the righteousness of God in Him" (2 Cor. 5:21). When God looks on a Christian He sees His Son and His Son's righteousness. When a person trusts in Christ, his unrighteousness is exchanged for Christ's righteousness, "that which is through faith in Christ, the righteousness which comes from God on the basis of faith" (Phil. 3:9). Man has never had any righteousness of his own and can never have any righteousness of his own, that is, which originates in him. The only righteousness he can have is that which God gives him through His Son. It is the only righteousness he needs, because it is perfect righteousness.

Third, believers receive God's **sanctification**. In Christ we are set apart, made holy. We are declared righteous in Christ and are made holy in Christ. When we receive Christ's nature we receive His incorruptible seed, the seed which is not, and cannot be, habitually corrupted by sin. With the flesh still present, we can slip into sin, but only intermittently. As we spiritually mature the frequency of sin decreases. The righteousness that is counted to us judicially also becomes ours in actuality—in holiness, in sanctification. We are given life in the Spirit and we begin to walk in the Spirit (Rom. 8:4-11). We begin to bear the fruit of the Spirit (Gal. 5:22-23) as we are being transformed into Christ's image (2 Cor. 3:18). Our new nature is "created in Christ Jesus for good works," for holiness (Eph. 2:10).

Fourth, believers receive God's **redemption.** To redeem means to buy back. God by Christ has purchased us from the power of sin. Christ "is given as a pledge of our inheritance, with a view to the redemption of God's own possession, to the praise of His glory" (Eph. 1:14). Peter reminds us that we "were not redeemed with perishable things like silver or gold . . . but with precious blood, as of a lamb unblemished and spotless, the blood of Christ" (1 Pet. 1:18-19).

That, just as it is written, "Let him who boasts, boast in the Lord." (1:31)

Although in Christ we have received God's wisdom, righteousness, sanctification, and redemption, we have no grounds for pride or boasting, because we did not deserve, earn, or produce any of them. Man's wisdom can produce none of those things. It can only produce pride, misunderstanding, strife, and division. As Jeremiah had written hundreds of years before Paul quoted him, **"Let him who boasts, boast in the Lord."** "May it never be," he wrote the Galatians, "that I should boast, except in the cross of our Lord Jesus Christ" (Gal. 6:14).

THE PRESENTATION OF GOD'S WISDOM

The party spirit in Corinth was the result of philosophy, of human wisdom. The Corinthians were fragmented in their beliefs and in their loyalties, because those were human beliefs and human loyalties. Paul reminded them that when he first came to Corinth and presented the gospel he did not do so with impressive words of human reasoning.

And when I came to you, brethren, I did not come with superiority of speech or of wisdom, proclaiming to you the testimony of God. For I determined to know nothing among you except Jesus Christ, and Him crucified. (2:1-2)

As we have noted, the gospel of God's wisdom, righteousness, sanctification, and redemption cannot be obtained through human wisdom. Here Paul demonstrates that it also is not to be presented through human wisdom. Paul did not come to Corinth as a philosopher but as a witness. He came **proclaiming . . . the testimony of God. Testimony** (*marturion*) means just that—a testimony or witness. A person can only testify to what he himself has seen or heard or experienced. A witness in a courtroom is to report only what he knows objectively, factually, and personally. He is not to speculate, guess, or deduce. Paul was a witness only to God's revelation, not to his own human understanding or reason or inclinations. God's revelation was everything; human wisdom was nothing.

We should not come to church to hear the pastor's opinions about politics, psychology, economics, or even religion. We should come to hear a word from the Lord *through* the pastor. God's Word edifies and unifies; human opinions confuse and divide.

Paul assured the Corinthians that he had not come to them with a lot of human verbiage and opinion. He presented them with the testimony of God and nothing else. Some years later he assured them again: "We have renounced the things hidden because of shame, not walking in craftiness or adulterating the word of God, but by the manifestation of truth commending ourselves to every man's conscience in the sight of God" (2 Cor. 4:2). The primary task, the *only* task, of the ministry is to manifest the truth of God.

Paul warned Timothy, "The Spirit explicitly says that in later times some will fall away from the faith, paying attention to deceitful spirits and doctrines of demons, by means of the hypocrisy of liars seared in their own conscience as with a branding iron" (1 Tim. 4:1-2). Timothy was to "give attention to the public reading of Scripture, to exhortation and teaching" (v. 13). That was his job. That is every preacher's job. Any other approach prostitutes the pulpit.

In his second letter to that young minister, Paul solemnly charged him "in the presence of God and of Christ Jesus" to "preach the word" (2 Tim. 4:1-2). I cannot comprehend how any man who calls himself a minister of God can do anything but preach the Word of God and be ready to do it "in season and out of season" (v. 2). Many congregations, however, do not *want* their pastors to preach only the Word. They "will not endure sound doctrine; but wanting to have their ears tickled, they will accumulate for themselves teachers in accordance to their own desires" (v. 3). As one commentator has observed, "In periods of unsettled faith, skepticism, and mere curious speculation in matters of religion, teachers of all kinds swarm like the flies in Egypt. The demand creates the supply. The hearers invite and shape their own preachers. If the people desire a calf to worship, a ministerial calf-maker is readily found." Some people, including some immature believers, will go from church to church looking for the right preacher. Unfortunately their idea of "right" preaching is not sound biblical exposition but interesting observations and suggestions based on the preacher's personal philosophy. They are not looking for a word from God to believe but for a word from man to consider.

When Paul had preached to the Corinthians, as when he had preached anywhere, he was **determined to know nothing among** his hearers **except Jesus Christ, and Him crucified.** He was not interested in discussing men's ideas or insights, his own or those of anyone else. He would proclaim nothing but Jesus Christ, the crucified, risen, and redeeming Jesus Christ. He did not preach Jesus simply as the perfect teacher or the perfect example or the perfect Man—though He was all of these. The foundation of all of his preaching was Jesus as the divine Savior.

Obviously the apostle was not saying that he preached or taught nothing but evangelistic messages, or that he expounded only those parts of Scripture that deal directly with Christ's atonement. He taught the full counsel of God, as his writings make clear (Acts 20:27). He ministered in Corinth for a year and a half, "teaching the word of God among [them]" (Acts 18:11). But it was, and still is, the cross of Jesus Christ that is the stumbling block or the foolishness to unbelievers (1 Cor. 1:23), and until a person accepts God's revelation in the cross, no other revelation matters. The preaching of the cross was so dominant in the early church that many Jews and Gentiles accused the Christians of worshiping a dead man. To help a person understand the gospel Paul would go to any length to explain and clarify the cross, but he would not say one word to modify or contradict it.

And I was with you in weakness and in fear and in much trembling. And my message and my preaching were not in persuasive words of wisdom, but in demonstration of the Spirit and of power, that your faith should not rest on the wisdom of men, but on the power of God. (2:3-5)

Weakness, fear, and **trembling** do not seem appropriate to Paul; and they were not appropriate in their usual senses. The **weakness** in which Paul had come to Corinth was the weakness of the gospel, which is really the power of God (1 Cor. 1:25, 27). And by **fear** and **trembling** I do not think he was referring to mental timidity or to physical shaking. He preached boldly, lived boldly, and counseled other believers to be bold in the things of the Lord (Acts 13:46; 19:8; Eph. 3:12; 6:19). He used the phrase "fear and trembling" in several other passages, each of which have to do with deep concern over an important, urgent issue (2 Cor. 7:15; Eph. 6:5; Phil. 2:12).

Paul came to Corinth after being beaten and imprisoned in Philippi, run out of Thessalonica and Berea, and scoffed at in Athens (Acts 16:22-24; 17:10, 13-14, 32). He came knowing that to be "Corinthianized" meant to be morally corrupt in the extreme. Corinth was the epitome of paganism and moral degeneracy. Though having every human reason to be discouraged and no doubt every temptation from Satan to compromise, Paul would not change his message. He was fearful and trembling only in the sense of being deeply anxious that the gospel somehow find root even in this most unpromising of places. He was not fearful for his own life or safety or of the gospel's having lost its power. He was fearful only of its being rejected, and of the terrible consequences of that rejection. Surely he also feared his own inadequacy and sin which could weaken his ministry (cf. 1 Cor. 9:16, 27).

Paul was especially determined, therefore, that his **message and . . . preaching were not in persuasive words of wisdom.** Human words of wisdom, no matter how impressive and persuasive, would have robbed the gospel of its power. He saw no place for calculated theatrics and techniques to manipulate response. Many have responded to an emotional appeal, without a true knowledge and conviction of God. Paul did not do that kind of preaching. He surely would have gotten a wider and more receptive hearing, but his hearers would have been left in their sins and without a Savior. Some have said that the great preacher Jonathan Edwards read his sermons so that he would not be guilty of using human persuasive techniques to gain a response. He wanted only the message to bring the results.

Paul had great natural abilities, but he did not rely on them. Even the human words and wisdom of an apostle could not save a person. He did not want his hearers to identify with his own wisdom, which could give them only another philosophy, but with God's wisdom in Jesus Christ, which could give them eternal life.

I remember a pastor's saying to me one day after the morning service, "Do you see that man over there? He is one of my converts." He then explained, "Not the Lord's, but mine." The man had become a disciple of the pastor but not a disciple of Christ.

John Stott has written, "It seems that the only preaching God honors through which His wisdom and power are expressed is the preaching of a man who is willing in himself to be both the weakling and the fool."

The unbelieving Corinthians, as all unbelievers, had needed the demonstration of the Spirit and of power, and that is what Paul had brought them. That is all that he had preached and practiced among them. Only God's Spirit and power could deliver them from sin and bring them to Himself. He did not want them to have a new philosophy but new life.

Charles Spurgeon said:

> The power that is in the Gospel does not lie in the eloquence of the preacher, otherwise men would be the converters of souls, nor does it lie in the preacher's learning, otherwise it would consist in the wisdom of men. We might preach until our tongues rotted, till we would exhaust our lungs and die, but never a soul would be converted unless the Holy Spirit be with the Word of God to give it the power to convert the soul.

If the Corinthians had come to have faith in **the wisdom of men**, even in Paul's wisdom, they might have changed intellectually, but they would not have changed spiritually. They would still have been spiritually dead, and Paul would not have been able to write to them as saints and brothers (1:2, 10). He had not come with his own message but had come simply as a channel of God's message. Only the message of God brings with it **the power of God.**

The church should not have divisions based on philosophy any more than it should have divisions based on individuals. We are to be united around God's wisdom, not human wisdom. We are one in Jesus Christ and should be one in His Word and power, and in the fellowship of those who are His.

Understanding the Wisdom of God

(2:6-16)

Yet we do speak wisdom among those who are mature; a wisdom, however, not of this age, nor of the rulers of this age, who are passing away; but we speak God's wisdom in a mystery, the hidden wisdom, which God predestined before the ages to our glory; the wisdom which none of the rulers of this age has understood; for if they had understood it, they would not have crucified the Lord of glory; but just as it is written, "Things which eye has not seen and ear has not heard, and which have not entered the heart of man, all that God has prepared for those who love Him." For to us God revealed them through the Spirit; for the Spirit searches all things, even the depths of God. For who among men knows the thoughts of a man except the spirit of the man, which is in him? Even so the thoughts of God no one knows except the Spirit of God. Now we have received, not the spirit of the world, but the Spirit who is from God, that we might know the things freely given to us by God, which things we also speak, not in words taught by human wisdom, but in those taught by the Spirit, combining spiritual thoughts with spiritual words. But a natural man does not accept the things of the Spirit of God; for they are foolishness to him, and he cannot understand them, because they are spiritually appraised. But he who is spiritual appraises all things, yet he himself is appraised by no man. For who has known the mind of the Lord, that he should instruct Him? But we have the mind of Christ. (2:6-16)

This section continues to deal with the problem of disunity in the church at Corinth and in particular with the continued allegiance to human philosophies and leaders that contributed to the disunity. Human wisdom was keeping believers from divine wisdom, and from spiritual growth and unity.

Yet, Paul said, **we do speak wisdom among those who are mature.** Whereas false, human wisdom is a great hindrance to the gospel, true, divine wisdom flows *from* the gospel. To believers, "to those who are the called," Christ is "the power of God and the wisdom of God" (1:24). **Mature** (*teleios*) can mean "perfect" (KJV) or "complete," but can also refer to a person who has full membership in a group, one who is fully initiated. Here Paul uses this term in the same way it is used in other forms by the writer of Hebrews (6:1; 10:14) to refer to salvation. **Those who are mature** are those who are redeemed and are completely trusting in Jesus Christ. The apostle is not saying that he speaks God's wisdom only when he is with believers who are advanced in the faith, but only when he is among believers who are truly in the faith—the saved. True believers are the only ones among whom the gospel can be wisdom. To all others it is a stumbling block or foolishness (1:23). Obviously some Christians are better taught in and more obedient to God's wisdom than are others. But for every Christian, "in all wisdom and insight He made known to us the mystery of His will, according to His kind intention which He purposed in Him" (Eph. 1:8-9). While the Christ rejectors hear his message as foolishness, to believers it is wisdom—the wisdom of God.

In 1 Corinthians 2:6-16 Paul emphasizes two points: (1) true wisdom is not humanly discovered and (2) true wisdom is divinely revealed.

True Wisdom Is Not Humanly Discovered

It is impossible for a lesser creature to understand a more advanced one. How can anything understand something more complex and advanced than itself? For a flea to understand a dog it would have to be at least as advanced as a dog. For a dog to understand a man it would have to be at least as advanced as a man. How much greater distance is there between Creator and creature. Men can imagine what God might be like, and people have plenty of ideas about Him. Almost everyone has an opinion as to what God is or is not like, or as to whether He even exists. But man's opinions are irrelevant, because they can never be more than speculations. By his own resources the creature cannot possibly comprehend his Creator.

God's wisdom, the truth about Him and His message for man, is **a wisdom, however, not of this age, nor of the rulers of this age. Age** (*aiōnos*) refers to a period of time, a historic age. Paul was speaking not only of the particular historical period in which he lived, but of all periods of history. All human wisdom is **passing away.** It is empty, futile, and comes to naught. Even **the rulers** (*archontōn*, meaning leading men, or men of authority) cannot claim it or even relate to it.

Paul repeats the assertion that he is indeed speaking wisdom: **but we speak God's wisdom . . . the hidden wisdom.** The natural man does not know and understand it, and considers it foolishness, because it is **wisdom in a mystery, the hidden wisdom.** **Mystery** (*mustērion*) does not refer to something strange and puzzling but to that which is held secret. God intentionally holds His wisdom a secret from natural man and his earthly wisdom (cf. Matt. 11:25; 13:10-13).

But to His people, His called and perfected ones, **God predestined before the ages** to give His wisdom through His Son **to our glory.** Before time began, our heavenly Father determined to give us His saving wisdom that would lead ultimately to our eternal glorification (Rom. 8:18).

The wisdom which none of the rulers of this age has understood; for if they had understood it, they would not have crucified the Lord of glory. (2:8)

The crucifixion is proof that **the rulers of this age** did not have God's wisdom. Had they **understood it, they would not have crucified the Lord of glory.** Neither the leaders of the Jews, to whom the gospel was a stumbling block, nor the leaders of the Gentiles, to whom it was foolishness, understood God's divine wisdom. In their ignorance of God, their willing ignorance, they executed His Son. Paul's own testimony demonstrates that ignorance (1 Tim. 1:12-13). That is the outcome of human wisdom. In the world's eyes, Jesus was anything but glorious; but in God's eyes He is the very **Lord of glory.** Yet all of the

things which eye has not seen and ear has not heard, and which have not entered the heart of man, all that God has prepared for those who love Him. (2:9-10)

That free quotation from Isaiah 64:4 and 65:17 is often memorized. But it is also frequently misapplied. Paul is not referring to the wonders of heaven, but to the wisdom God has prepared for believers. His point is that the natural eyes, ears, and hearts of men cannot know or comprehend His wisdom. It is **prepared** only **for those who love Him.**

Neither externally nor internally, objectively nor subjectively, can man discover God. His external searching is empirical, experimental—represented by seeing and hearing. God's truth is not observable by the **eye** or the **ear,** no matter how many sophisticated instruments we may use.

We are just as helpless in trying to discover His truth subjectively, through our minds (**heart**). Rationalism cannot reason out God's truth. Man's two greatest human resources, empiricism and rationalism, his observation and his reason, are equally useless in discovering divine truth. They will always, in fact, eventually turn men against divine truth. Ultimately they lead men to crucify Christ.

But God's truth, God's plan, God's wisdom, is not hidden from His children. **All** *that* **God has prepared for those who love Him.**

True Wisdom Is Divinely Revealed

It is as unnecessary as it is impossible for man to discover God's truth on his own. What man cannot find God has given. Man cannot come to God on his own; but God has come to him. The Holy Spirit has invaded man's closed box and shown him God—through revelation, inspiration, and illumination.

BY REVELATION

For to us God revealed them through the Spirit; for the Spirit searches all things, even the depths of God. For who among men knows the thoughts of a man except the spirit of the man, which is in him? Even so the thoughts of God no one knows except the Spirit of God. (2:10-11)

The Holy Spirit is the Trinity's agent of transmission and communication. The first step of His transmission of God's truth is *revelation*. As a member of the Godhead, **the Spirit** knows the mind of God perfectly. God has used angels for many amazing and wonderful services to man. But He did not entrust the revelation of the New Covenant to an angel. The truths of His Word **God revealed through the Spirit.** The Holy Spirit is the divine author of Scripture. He used many human agents, but the message is entirely His. The revelation is God's pure Word.

To illustrate the Holy Spirit's unique qualification for revealing the Word, Paul compares the Spirit's knowledge of God's mind to a human being's knowledge of his own mind. No person can know another person as well as he knows himself. Even husbands and wives who have lived together for dozens of years, and have freely shared their thoughts and dreams and problems and joys, never come to know their mates as intimately as they know themselves. Our innermost **thoughts,** the deep recesses of our hearts and minds, are known only to ourselves.

In a similar way, only God's own Spirit can know Him intimately. And, wonder of wonders, it is **the Spirit of God,** the One who intimately knows **the depths of God** and **the thoughts of God,** whom God has sent to reveal His own wisdom to those who believe—**to us.**

BY INSPIRATION

Now we have received, not the spirit of the world, but the Spirit who is from God, that we might know the things freely given to us by God, which things we also speak, not in words taught by human wisdom, but in those taught by the Spirit, combining spiritual thoughts with spiritual words. (2:12-13)

The process of the Spirit's transmission of God's truth is called *inspiration*. His truth cannot be discovered by man; it can only be **received.** In order to be received, something must first be offered. God's truth can be received because is it **freely given.**

The Spirit who is from God, not **the spirit of the world** (that is, human wisdom) has brought God's Word—which comprises **the things freely given to us by God.** The Bible is the Spirit's vehicle for bringing God's revelation.

The **we's** and the **us** of verses 12-13 (as in vv. 6-7, 10) do not refer to Christians in general but to Paul himself. God's Word is for all believers, but was *revealed* only to the apostles and the other writers of Scripture. Only those men properly can be said to have been *inspired*. The promise of John 14:26 ("But the Helper, the Holy Spirit . . . will teach you all things, and bring to your remembrance all that I said to you") is for the benefit of all believers, but was given only to the apostles. Paul and the other writers of Scripture did not record their own ideas and interpretations. They recorded what God *gave* them and only what He gave them. **We have received . . . that we might know.** The Spirit used words that the human writers knew and used, but He selected them and arranged them in precisely the order that He wanted. The Bible, therefore, not only is God's Word but God's words.

It is not simply the "Word behind the words" that is from God, as many liberal and neoorthodox interpreters maintain. "*All* Scripture is inspired by God [lit., 'God-breathed']" (2 Tim. 3:16). *Scripture* means "writings," and refers specifically to what God's chosen men wrote by His revelation and inspiration, not to *everything* they said and wrote. It refers, as Paul explains, to **the things freely given to us by God,** to the "God-breathed" words they recorded.

When Jesus responded to Satan's first temptation in the wilderness, He said (quoting from Deut. 8:3), "Man shall not live on bread alone, but on every word that proceeds out of the mouth of God" (Matt. 4:4). God gave His own Word in His own words. "*Every* word that proceeds out the mouth of God" is revealed, inspired, and authoritative. **Which things we also speak, not in *words* taught by human wisdom, but in those taught by the Spirit, combining spiritual thoughts with spiritual *words.***

BY ILLUMINATION

But a natural man does not accept the things of the Spirit of God; for they are foolishness to him, and he cannot understand them, because they are spiritually appraised. But he who is spiritual appraises all things, yet he himself is appraised by no man. For who has known the mind of the Lord, that he should instruct Him? But we have the mind of Christ. (2:14-16)

The third step in the Spirit's transmission of God's truth is that of *illumination*. It is possible to read the Bible—even many different copies and versions of the Bible—and yet not understand it. It is possible to study the Bible for many years, memorizing much of it, and still not understand it. The scribes and Pharisees of Jesus' day were highly trained in the Old Testament, yet they missed its central message. They completely failed to recognize the promised Messiah when He came and lived among them (John 5:37-39). They did not believe Jesus because they did not truly believe Moses, the great lawgiver in whom they placed their hope (vv. 45-47). They did **not accept the things of the Spirit of God** because those things seemed to be **foolishness**. Because those men did not belong to God, they **could not understand them, because they are spiritually appraised**. Those scribes and Pharisees, like everyone who rejects God, lived only in the realm of the **natural man**. They had no means and had no desire to understand the spiritual nature of God's Word.

The **natural man** cannot know or understand **the things of the Spirit of God** because they can only be **spiritually appraised. Spiritual** is in opposition to **natural**, and thus refers to the inner capacity of the redeemed to grasp God's truth. God's Word is spiritually evaluated, spiritually discerned, spiritually understood—and the natural man is spiritually dead.

The psalmist understood the need for God's illumination of His Word. He prayed, "Open my eyes, that I may behold wonderful things from Thy law" (Ps. 119:18). He did not need the Lord's help to read His Word, but he knew he needed His help to understand it.

Martin Luther said, "The Bible cannot be understood simply by study or talent; you must count only on the influence of the Holy Spirit."

John Calvin wrote: "The testimony of the Spirit is superior to reason. For . . . these words will not obtain full credit in the hearts of men until they are sealed by the inward testimony of the Spirit."

Someone else has suggested that the best man can do on his own is to "gnaw the bark of Scripture without getting to the wood."

God must open the eyes of our understanding before we can truly know and rightly interpret His truth. His truth is available only to those with a regenerate spirit and in whom His Spirit dwells, for only the Spirit can illumine Scripture. Just as the physically blind cannot see the sun, the spiritually blind cannot see the Son. Both lack proper illumination. Martin Luther said, "Man is like a pillar of salt, like Lot's wife—he is like a log or a stone, he is like a lifeless statue which uses neither eyes nor mouth, neither senses nor heart—unless he is enlightened, converted and regenerated by the Holy Spirit."

He who is spiritual, on the other hand, **appraises all things**. The believer has a resident Truth Teacher to enlighten him about all the things of God about which he needs to know. "As for you," John wrote, "the anointing which you received from Him abides in you, and you have no need for anyone to teach you; but as His anointing teaches you about all things, and is true and is not a lie, and just as it has taught you, you abide in Him" (1 John 2:27). The Holy Spirit takes God's Word, the Word which He has revealed and inspired, and illuminates it for those in whom He dwells.

Unlike God's revelation and inspiration, which were given to the biblical writers, His illumination is for *all* Christians. We all can rightly appraise the Word when we rely on the Giver of the Word.

Because the natural man cannot rightly appraise God's Word he cannot rightly appraise God's people, either. **He who is spiritual . . . himself is appraised by no man.** It is just as impossible for the world to understand faithful Christians as it is for them to understand God Himself and His Word. They *try* to appraise believers, of course, but they are always wrong. They may accurately evaluate our faults, shortcomings, and our living that is inconsistent with our faith. But they cannot accurately evaluate our faith. If the gospel itself is a stumbling block and foolishness to them, so is faith based on the gospel.

The person in Christ will be misunderstood and mistreated just as Christ was misunderstood and mistreated (John 15:20). The world will laugh at us, mock us, and, in many places of the world still today, even kill us. The world crucified Christ and it will crucify His followers.

Paul asks, **Who has known the mind of the Lord?** What natural man thinks God's thoughts? None. Unbelievers frequently want to correct believers, to argue about the truths we believe and follow. But when they contradict scriptural teaching, they are not arguing with us but with God, whose thoughts they do not understand. They are trying to **instruct Him.** What folly.

As Christians, however, God instructs us. We are able to understand **all things** of His Word because **we have the mind of Christ.** Christ thinks God's thoughts, understands God's wisdom. We have His **mind** (*nous*). This term is translated "understanding" in 14:14, 15, 19. Its usage here may best be understood from its use in Luke 24:45 of Jesus' revelation to the disciples on the road to Emmaus: "Then He opened their minds to understand the Scriptures."

The doctrine of illumination does not mean we can know and understand everything (Deut. 29:29), that we do not need human teachers (Eph. 4:11-12), or that study is not hard work (2 Tim. 2:15). It does mean that Scripture can be understood by every Christian who is diligent and obedient.

Carnal Christians
(3:1-9)

7

And I, brethren, could not speak to you as to spiritual men, but as to men of flesh, as to babes in Christ. I gave you milk to drink, not solid food; for you were not yet able to receive it. Indeed, even now you are not yet able, for you are still fleshly. For since there is jealousy and strife among you, are you not fleshly, and are you not walking like mere men? For when one says, "I am of Paul," and another, "I am of Apollos," are you not mere men? What then is Apollos? And what is Paul? Servants through whom you believed, even as the Lord gave opportunity to each one. I planted, Apollos watered, but God was causing the growth. So then neither the one who plants nor the one who waters is anything, but God who causes the growth. Now he who plants and he who waters are one; but each will receive his own reward according to his own labor. For we are God's fellow workers; you are God's field, God's building. (3:1-9)

In his book *The New Life* Michael Green reports that a friend of his came to him and explained his new-found Christian life in words something like these: "It is rather like a cyclist who, when he is climbing a long hill, thinks he will be able to freewheel down the other side. It is not until he reaches the top that he sees that his task has only just started and that the road winds on with even steeper hills than the one he has just climbed."

Many Christians have come to the same conclusion. Faithful Christian living becomes increasingly more difficult and more demanding. It is the furthest thing from a downhill ride. Christ does solve all of our important problems. He does bring peace, joy, meaning, purpose, and many other blessings of which the unbeliever knows nothing. But the Christian life is not easy. In many ways living is far more demanding than before we were saved.

How is this so? How—when we have God's own Spirit within us, the mind of Christ, and the power of God—could it become more difficult to do what is right, to do what our Lord wants us to do? There are two reasons: the world and the flesh. The first is outside us, the second is inside us. They are Satan's supreme instruments in tempting believers and keeping them from faithfulness and victory.

The promise of the New Covenant in Christ is the promise of a new spirit and a new heart (Ezek. 36:25-27). When a person becomes a Christian he also becomes a new creation, with a new nature, a new inner being, and a favorable disposition toward God—none of which a person can have apart from Christ (2 Pet. 1:4; 2 Cor. 5:17). From that point, until the Lord takes him to be with Himself, he is swimming upstream. Like a salmon returning to spawn, he discovers that gravity and the current are continually against him. His new heart drives him in an entirely different direction from that of the world around him.

The church has often thought of worldliness only in terms of dancing, alcoholic drinking, and the like. But worldliness is much deeper than bad habits; it is an orientation, a way of thinking and believing. Basically it is buying the world's philosophies, buying human wisdom. It is looking to the world—to human leaders, to influential and popular people, to neighbors, associates, and fellow students—for our standards, attitudes, and meaning. Worldliness is accepting the world's definitions, the world's measuring sticks, the world's goals.

The second great obstacle Christians face is the flesh. In fact, it is the flesh that produces the bridge the world uses to reach us. When we are given Christ's divine nature, our flesh is not removed. That will not occur until we are glorified (Rom. 8:18-25). Until then the flesh continually resists and opposes the new heart. Paul tells about the struggle in his own life:

> For that which I am doing, I do not understand; for I am not practicing what I would like to do, but I am doing the very thing I hate. . . . For the good that I wish, I do not do; but I practice the very evil that I do not wish. . . . For I joyfully concur with the law of God in the inner man, but I see a different law in the members of my body, waging war against the law of my mind. (Rom. 7:15, 19, 22-23)

When we were born physically we inherited from Adam the flesh with its propensity to sin. When we were born spiritually and given a new spirit, a new heart, God broke the back of sin, crippled its ability, and paid its penalty. But the tendency to evil remains. The one word that best characterizes the flesh, our humanness, our Adamic nature, is *selfish*. The sin of Adam, like the sin of the tempter when he fell (Isa.

14:13), centered on setting his own will and interests against God's; and that has been the center of sin ever since.

The world and the flesh are closely related. They are used by the same power, Satan, and they serve the same purpose, evil. They complement each other and are often hard to distinguish. But it is not necessary to precisely distinguish between them, because both of them are spiritual enemies, and both must be fought with the same weapons—God's Word and God's Spirit.

Our ultimate triumph over the world and the flesh is certain, but our continued struggle with them in this life is also certain. We will win the ultimate battle, but can lose a lot of skirmishes along the way.

The Corinthian believers had an especially hard struggle against those twin enemies, a struggle which they seldom won. They would not break with the world or break with the flesh and were continually succumbing to both. Consequently they fell into one serious sin after another. Almost all of this epistle has to do with identifying and correcting those sins.

The sin of division was closely related to numerous other sins. Sins are always interrelated. There is no such thing as an isolated sin. One sin leads to another, and the second reinforces the first. Every sin is a combination of sins, and a sinning believer cannot confine the evil to one dimension.

From 1:18 through 2:16 Paul points out that the Corinthians were divided because of worldliness, because of their continued love for human wisdom. In 3:1-9 the apostle shows them that they also were divided because of the flesh, because of their continued yielding to the evil in their humanness. He shows the cause, the symptoms, and the cure.

THE CAUSE OF DIVISION: THE FLESH

And I, brethren, could not speak to you as to spiritual men, but as to men of flesh, as to babes in Christ. I gave you milk to drink, not solid food; for you were not yet able to receive it. Indeed, even now you are not yet able, for you are still fleshly. (3:1-3a)

The cause of division in the church was more than an external, worldly influence. It was also internal, fleshly. The Corinthians had succumbed to the pressures of the world, but they were also succumbing to the pressures and enticements of their own flesh.

Before Paul chastises them for their immature sinfulness, he reminds them again that he is speaking to them as **brethren,** as fellow believers. That is a term of recognition and of love. It reminded his brothers in Christ that they were still saved, that their sinning, terrible and inexcusable as it was, did not forfeit their salvation. He did not try to diminish the seriousness of their sins, but he did try to diminish or prevent any discouragement that his rebuke might otherwise have caused. He stood with them as a brother, not over them as a judge.

But Paul could not speak to the Corinthian believers as **spiritual men.** They had come through the door of faith but had gone no farther. Most of them had received Jesus Christ years earlier but were acting as if they had just been born again. They were still **babes in Christ.**

The New Testament uses the word *spiritual* in a number of ways. In a neutral sense it simply means the realm of spiritual things, in contrast to the realm of the physical. When applied to men, however, it is used of their relationship to God in one of two ways: positionally or practically. Unbelievers are totally unspiritual in both senses. They possess neither a new spirit nor the Holy Spirit. Their position is natural and their practice is natural. Believers, on the other hand, are totally spiritual in the positional sense, because they have been given a new inner being that loves God and is indwelt by His Holy Spirit. But practically, believers can also be unspiritual.

In 2:14-15 Paul contrasts believers and unbelievers, and his use of "spiritual" in that context refers, therefore, to positional spirituality. The "natural man" (v. 14) is the unsaved; "he who is spiritual" (v. 15) is the saved. In the positional sense, there is no such thing as an unspiritual Christian or a partially spiritual Christian. In this sense every believer is equal. This *spiritual* is a synonym for possessing the life of God in the soul, or as we saw in 2:16, having the mind of Christ.

A positionally spiritual person is one with a new heart, indwelt by and controlled by the Holy Spirit. "You are not in the flesh but in the Spirit, if indeed the Spirit of God dwells in you. But if anyone does not have the Spirit of Christ, he does not belong to Him" (Rom. 8:9; cf. v. 14). When we trust in Jesus Christ, His Spirit takes charge of our lives and remains in charge until we die. He will control us to His own ultimate ends, whether we submit or not. "We know that God causes all things to work together for good to those who love God, to those who are called according to His purpose" (Rom. 8:28). Our resistance and disobedience can cause many unnecessary detours, delays, and heartaches, but He *will* accomplish His work in us. "He who began a good work in you will perfect it until the day of Christ Jesus" (Phil. 1:6).

Practically, however, believers may be anything but spiritual. Such were the Corinthian Christians. Paul addressed them as brethren, but he made it clear that he had to speak to them on the lowest possible spiritual level. He had to speak to them as if they were **men of flesh.**

Men of flesh (*sarkinos*) is literally "fleshy ones." In this context it refers to man's fallen humanness, his Adamic self—his bodily desires that manifest re-belliousness toward God, his glorying in himself, and his proneness to sin. As mentioned above, the flesh is not eradicated when we are saved. It no longer can ultimately dominate or destroy us, but it can still greatly influence us. That is why we yearn for the redemption of the body (Rom. 8:23). Glorification, in one sense, will be less of a change than justification. Justification was transformation of the inner being; glorification is the elimination of the outer being, which bears the curse.

So a Christian is not characterized by sin; it no longer represents his basic nature. But he is still able to sin, and his sin is just as sinful as the sin of an unbeliever. Sin is sin. When a Christian sins, he is being practically unspiritual, living on the same practical level as an unbeliever. Consequently Paul is compelled to speak to the

Corinthian believers much as if they were unbelievers.

Perhaps somewhat to soften the rebuke, he also compares them to **babes in Christ**. It was far from a compliment, but it did recognize that they truly belonged to Christ.

The Corinthian believers were spiritually ignorant. Paul had ministered to them for eighteen months, and after that they were pastored by the highly-gifted Apollos. Some of them were acquainted with Peter and others apparently had even heard Jesus preach (1:12). Like the "babes" of Hebrews 5:13, they had no excuse for not being mature. Yet they were exactly the opposite. They were not babes because they were newly redeemed, but because they were inexcusably immature.

The Corinthians were not unintelligent. Their problem was not low IQ or lack of teaching. They were not ignorant of the faith because they were dumb, but because they were fleshly. The cause was not mental but spiritual. Because they refused to give up their worldly ways and their carnal desires, they became what James calls forgetful hearers (James 1:25). A person who does not use information will lose it; and spiritual truth is no exception. Spiritual truths that we ignore and neglect will become less and less remembered and meaningful (cf. 2 Pet. 1:12-13). Nothing causes us to ignore God's truth more than not living it. A sinning Christian is uncomfortable in the light of God's truth. He either turns from his fleshly behavior or he begins to block out God's light. Only when we put aside "malice and all guile and hypocrisy and envy and all slander"—that is, the flesh—are we able to "long for the pure milk of the word" and "grow in respect to salvation" (1 Pet. 2:1-2).

I gave you milk to drink, not solid food; for you were not yet able to receive it. Indeed, even now you are not yet able, for you are still fleshly. (3:2-3a)

When Paul first preached to the Corinthians he taught the more easily digestible elementary truths of doctrine, the **milk**. But now, some five years later, they still needed to be fed milk. They could not yet spiritually digest **solid food**.

Like many Christians today, the Corinthians seemed quite content to stay on milk. Some congregations do not *want* the pastor to get "too deep." Their fleshly habits are not much threatened if, for instance, the preacher sticks primarily to evangelistic messages. Evangelism is the cutting edge of the church's mission, but it is for unbelievers, not believers. Or the congregation wants Scripture to be preached so superficially that their sin is not exposed, much less rebuked and corrected.

There is no difference at all between the truths of a spiritual milk diet and a spiritual solid food diet, except in detail and depth. All doctrine may have both milk and meat elements. It is not that we are to be continually learning new doctrines in order to grow, but that we are to be learning more about the doctrines we have known for years. A new Christian might explain the atonement, for example, as, "Christ died for my sins." A long-time student of the Word, on the other hand, would go into such things as regeneration, justification, substitution, and propitiation. One explanation would not be truer than the other; but the first would be **milk** and the second, **solid food.**

For a Christian preacher or teacher to give only milk week after week, year after year, is a crime against the Word of God and the Holy Spirit! It cannot be done without neglecting much of the Word and without neglecting the leading and empowering of the Holy Spirit, the supreme Teacher and Illuminator. It is also a terrible disservice to those who hear, whether or not they are satisfied with having only milk. The appetite must be created.

Nothing is more precious or wonderful than a little baby. But a twenty-year-old with the mind of an infant is heartbreaking. A baby who acts like a baby is a joy; but an adult who acts like a baby is a tragedy. It doubtlessly grieved the Holy Spirit, as it grieved Paul, that the Christians in Corinth had never gotten out of their spiritual infancy. This tragedy is immensely worse than that of the physically or mentally retarded, who have no responsibility for their conditions. Spiritual retardation, however, is always primarily our own doing. We may not have the best human preacher or teacher, but every believer has the perfect Teacher within, who longs to instruct him in the things of God (cf. 1 John 2:20, 27). If we do not grow spiritually, the reason is always that we are **still fleshly.**

The believer's growth times are those times when he walks in the Spirit (Gal. 5:16-17). It is essential to understand that carnality is not an absolute state in which a believer exists (Rom. 8:4-14), but a behavior pattern he chooses one moment at a time. To say it another way, a Christian is not fleshly in the sense of being, but in the sense of behaving.

THE SYMPTOMS OF DIVISION: JEALOUSY AND STRIFE

For since there is jealousy and strife among you, are you not fleshly, and are you not walking like mere men? For when one says, "I am of Paul," and another, "I am of Apollos," are you not mere men? (3:3b-4)

Immature, fleshly Christians are never the result of deficient spiritual genes or of a spiritual birth defect. They are the way they are by their own choices. One of the worst and most disappointing problems the church can have is a congregation full of babes, Christians who are not growing because they seek to fulfill fleshly appetites.

Because self-centeredness is at the heart of fleshly behavior, **jealousy and strife** are always found in an immature congregation. Jealousy is the attitude, and strife is the action that results from it. One is the inner emotional condition, the other the outward expression of selfishness.

Those two problems, however, are merely representative of the many symptoms of the flesh. Sinful desire is like cancer; it has many forms and affects many parts of the church in many ways—all of them destructive. Carnality is a general evil that has many manifestations. It will corrupt morals, weaken personal relationships, produce doubt about God and His Word, destroy prayer life, and provide fertile ground for heresy. It will attack right doctrine and right living, right belief and right practice.

Jealousy and strife are not the least of the symptoms of fleshly living. Those sins are more destructive than many Christians seem to think. They are far from being petty sins, because, among other things, they cause division in the church, Christ's body, for whom He gave His life. They are among the surest marks of fallen humanness, just as unity is one of the surest marks of divine transformation.

Jealousy is a severe form of selfishness, begrudging someone else what we wish were ours. And selfishness is one of the most obvious characteristics of babyhood. An infant's life is almost totally self-centered and selfish. Its whole concern is with its own comfort, hunger, attention, sleep. It is typical of a young child to be self-centered, but it should not be typical of an adult, especially a Christian adult. It is spiritually infantile to be jealous of and to cause strife among fellow believers, and it betrays a fleshly perspective.

Division can only occur where there is selfishness. Fleshly, immature people cooperate only with those leaders and fellow believers with whom they happen to agree or who personally appeal to them or will flatter them. Factions cannot help resulting where there is jealousy and strife, or any other form of carnality. When a congregation develops loyalties around individuals, it is a sure symptom of spiritual immaturity and trouble. It was sinful for factions to develop around **Paul** and **Apollos,** and it is sinful for divisive factions to develop around any leader in the church today. **Are you not walking like mere men?** is another way of saying, "You are thinking and behaving in a fleshly way."

The Cure for Divisions: Glorifying God

What then is Apollos? And what is Paul? Servants through whom you believed, even as the Lord gave opportunity to each one. I planted, Apollos watered, but God was causing the growth. So then neither the one who plants nor the one who waters is anything, but God who causes the growth. Now he who plants and he who waters are one; but each will receive his own reward according to his own labor. For we are God's fellow workers; you are God's field, God's building. (3:5-9)

The cure for division is turning away from self and setting our eyes on the one God whom we all glorify. When our attention is focused on our Lord, as it always should be, there will be no time and no occasion for division. When our attention is on Him it cannot be on ourselves or on human leaders or human factions.

Apollos and **Paul** were simply the **servants through whom you believed.** They were the instruments, not the source, of salvation. As Paul had reminded them earlier, he had not died for them and they were not baptized in his name (1:13). The same was true, of course, for Apollos and Peter, as it is true for all other ministers of the Lord of all time. All Christians, including even such men as those, whom the Lord used so mightily, are but His **servants** (*diakonoi*), or ministers (KJV). It is not the same word (*doulos*) often translated "servant, slave, or bond-servant" (7:21-23; Rom. 1:1; etc.), but simply meant a menial worker of any sort, free or slave. It was often used of a table waiter or what we would now call a busboy.

Paul was saying in effect, "No one builds a movement around a waiter or busboy, or erects monuments to them. Apollos and I are just waiters or busboys whom the Lord used as servants to bring you food. You do not please us by trying to honor us. Your honor, your glory, is misplaced. You are acting like the world, like **mere men**. Build your monuments, give your praise to the One who prepared the spiritual food we delivered."

The world honors and tries to immortalize great men because men are the highest thing it knows. The world cannot see beyond itself. But Christians know God—the Creator, the Sustainer, the Savior, the Lord of the universe, and the Source of all things. He alone is worthy of honor. We are but His servants, His instruments. If an artist is to be honored, you do not make a statue of his brush or his palette. It makes no more sense for Christians to glorify men, even a Paul or an Apollos, who are only brushes or palettes in the Master's hands. Such are to be esteemed and loved for their work (1 Thess. 5:12-13), but not revered or set against each other.

Those men had their God-appointed work to do. Using agricultural metaphors, Paul acknowledged that he had **planted** and that **Apollos watered**. They had done their work well and faithfully. But the real work was the Lord's. **God was causing the growth.** No man, not even the best farmer or the best horticulturist, can give physical life or growth to a plant. How much less can anyone, even an apostle, give spiritual life or growth to a person. The most that men can do in either case is to prepare and water the soil and to plant the seeds. The rest is up to God. **Neither the one who plants nor the one who waters is anything, but God who causes the growth.** The human instrument is not **anything** but a tool. All the honor for the accomplishment goes to God.

Paul here mentions only two types of ministry, represented by planting and watering. His principle, however, applies to every type of ministry. In our eyes, some Christian work is more glamorous, or seems more important or more significant than other work. But if God has called a person to a work, that is the most important ministry he can have. All of God's work is important. To glorify one kind of Christian work above another is just as carnal and divisive as to glorify one leader above another.

Our Lord's parable in Matthew 20:1-16 demonstrates the equality of our ministries in the day of rewards. Jesus gave the parable as a corrective to the disciples' feeling that they were more worthy than others (19:27-30). We will all equally inherit the promised eternal life, with all its blessings. That is the sameness of future glory.

He who plants and he who waters are one. All of God's workers are one in Him, and to Him all glory should go. Recognition of our oneness in the Lord is the sure and only remedy for divisiveness. It leaves no place for the flesh and its jealousy, strife, and division.

God does not fail to recognize the faithful work of His servants. **Each will receive his own reward according to his own labor.** God will "give their reward to [His] bond-servants the prophets and to the saints and to those who fear [His] name, the small and the great" (Rev. 11:18). That is the uniqueness of future glory.

God rewards on the basis of **labor,** not success or results. A missionary may work faithfully for 40 years and see only a handful of converts. Another may work far fewer years and see far more converts. Jeremiah was one of God's most faithful and dedicated prophets, yet he saw little result of his ministry. He was ridiculed, persecuted, and generally rejected along with the message he preached. Jonah, on the other hand, was petty and unwilling, yet through him God won the entire city of Nineveh in one brief campaign. Our usefulness and effectiveness are purely by God's grace (cf. 1 Cor. 15:10).

It is appropriate that God's faithful servants be appreciated and encouraged while they are on earth. But they are not to be glorified, set apart, or made the center of special groups or movements.

Paul and Apollos were but **God's fellow workers.** It was not their own ministry that they worked in, but His. What divine companionship! It was *God's* church in Corinth, not Paul's or Apollos's or Peter's. The believers there were **God's field, God's building,** and His alone. And the glory for any good work done there, or anywhere, is also His alone.

The Judgment of Believers' Works

(3:10-17)

According to the grace of God which was given to me, as a wise master builder I laid a foundation, and another is building upon it. But let each man be careful how he builds upon it. For no man can lay a foundation other than the one which is laid, which is Jesus Christ. Now if any man builds upon the foundation with gold, silver, precious stones, wood, hay, straw, each man's work will become evident; for the day will show it, because it is to be revealed with fire; and the fire itself will test the quality of each man's work. If any man's work which he has built upon it remains, he shall receive a reward. If any man's work is burned up, he shall suffer loss; but he himself shall be saved, yet so as through fire.

Do you not know that you are a temple of God, and that the Spirit of God dwells in you? If any man destroys the temple of God, God will destroy him, for the temple of God is holy, and that is what you are. (3:10-17)

This passage continues Paul's discussion (1:10–3:23) of divisions within the Corinthian church. But its more immediate background is the Lord's second coming. Paul shows how worldly and fleshly behavior, and the spiritual division it causes, affects the rewards the Lord will give when He returns. Moving ahead, he discusses the paradox of rewards, with their sureness (since all of us are equally undeserving) and their uniqueness (in that each of us is rewarded individually). Paul affirms both truths, while waiting for glory to bring final resolution to the paradox.

The Lord's coming to reward His own was one of Paul's greatest motivations. In a sense, everything the apostle did was motivated by that truth. His objective, within the supreme objective of glorifying his God and Savior, was to prepare himself to stand before the Lord and be able to hear Him say, "Well done, good and faithful slave" (Matt. 25:21, 23). He wrote the Philippians, "One thing I do: forgetting what lies behind and reaching forward to what lies ahead, I press on toward the goal for the prize of the upward call of God in Christ Jesus" (Phil. 3:13-14). It was not that he wanted glory or honor for himself, or wanted to prove himself better than other Christians, showing them up in Christian service. He wanted the Lord's highest reward because that would be the most pleasing to the Lord Himself, and would most graphically demonstrate his grateful love.

In his second letter to Corinth, Paul mentions three specific motivations he had for doing his best for Christ. First, he wanted to please his Lord: "We have as our ambition," he said, "whether at home or absent, to be pleasing to Him" (2 Cor. 5:9). Second, Christ's great love controlled everything he did (v. 14); his whole ministry was directed by his love of God. And third, he knew that Christ's work was complete, that "He died for all" (v. 15), and that therefore the ministry of the gospel would *always* be effective; it could not fail. Jesus Christ had already finished all the work that would ever have to be done for people to be saved.

Paul was not one to do things halfway. When he ran a race or fought a fight, he did so to win—to win the imperishable wreath of His Lord's reward (1 Cor. 9:24-27). He was not competing with other believers, but against his own weakness, weariness, and sin. Though the particular words had not yet been written, Paul always had before him the knowledge that, "Behold, I [Jesus] am coming quickly, and My reward is with Me, to render to every man according to what he has done" (Rev. 22:12).

In speaking about believers' rewards, Paul was not talking about our judging works or about God's judging sin. Because all believers will "stand before the judgment seat of God," each of us giving an "account of himself to God," we have no right to judge the work of other believers (Rom. 14:10-12). We do not even know what rewards we will receive for ourselves, much less what another will receive. Both favorable and unfavorable judging are excluded. We do not even have the necessary insight to judge unbelievers in the church, who are tares among the wheat (cf. Matt. 13:24-30). Obviously, we are to rebuke sin and confront the sinning brother (Matt. 18:15-19; 1 Cor. 5:1-13), but that is because we can *see* such sin. Judging motives and the worthiness of reward is for God, who alone knows the heart.

It is as wrong to highly elevate a person as it is to degrade him. Paul already had warned twice in this letter against such worldly elevation of Christian leaders, including himself (1 Cor. 1:12-13; 3:4-9). We do not know enough about another's heart and motives and faithfulness—in fact, not enough about our own—to know what rewards are or are not deserved. We should not "go on passing judgment before the time, but wait until the Lord comes who will both bring to light the things hidden in the darkness and disclose the motives of men's hearts; and then each man's praise will come to him from God" (1 Cor. 4:5).

The subject here is not God's judgment on sin, either. The "judgment seat" before which all believers will one day stand (Rom. 14:10; 2 Cor. 5:10) is the Greek *bēma,* a tribunal. But both of those passages make it clear that the judgment at that place and that time will not be to dispense condemnation for sin but reward for good works, and that it involves only believers. Christ judged sin on the cross, and because we stand in Him we will never be condemned for our sins; He was condemned for us (1 Cor. 15:3; Gal. 1:4; 1 Pet. 2:24; etc.). He took the penalty of *all* our sins upon Himself (Col. 2:13; 1 John 2:12). God has no more charges against those who trust in His Son, those who are His elect, and will allow no one else to bring charges against them (Rom. 8:31-34). "There is therefore now no condemnation for those who are in Christ Jesus" (Rom. 8:1). As we will see later, "each man's praise will come to him from God" (1 Cor. 4:5).

In 1 Corinthians 3:10-17 Paul changes the analogy from agriculture to architecture. He had been speaking of his own planting, of Apollos's watering, and of God's giving the growth (vv. 6-8). At the end of verse 9 he makes a transition in his metaphors: "You are God's field, God's building."

Using the figure of a building, Paul discusses five aspects of the work of the Lord's people on earth: the master builder, the foundation, the materials, the test, and the workmen.

The Master Builder: Paul

According to the grace of God which was given to me, as a wise master builder I laid a foundation, and another is building upon it. But let each man be careful how he builds upon it. (3:10)

Paul himself was the **master builder** of the Corinthian project. **Master builder** is one word (*architektōn*) in the Greek, and, as can be guessed, is the term from which we get *architect.* But the word in Paul's day carried the idea of builder as well as designer. He was a combination architect and general contractor.

As an apostle, Paul's specialty was foundations. Over the years since his conversion, Paul had been used by the Lord to establish and instruct many churches across Asia Minor and in Macedonia and Greece. But lest some think he was bragging, he began by making it clear that his calling and his effectiveness were only by **the grace of God** that **was given to** him. That he was a good, **wise** builder was God's doing, not his own. He had already declared that "neither the one who plants nor the one who waters is anything, but God who causes the growth" (3:7). The same truth applied to those who laid foundations and those who built upon them. A few years later he would tell the believers in Rome, "I will not presume to speak of anything except what Christ has accomplished through me" (Rom. 15:18). His great success as an apostolic foundation layer was due entirely to God. "By the grace of God I am what I am, and His grace toward me did not prove vain; but I labored even more than all of them, yet not I, but the grace of God with me" (1 Cor. 15:10). He labored and strived by God's power (Col. 1:29) and claimed no cause to boast, except in His Lord (1 Cor. 1:31). He did not choose to be a builder, much less make himself a builder. He "was *made* a minister, according to the gift of God's grace" and considered himself to be "the very least of all saints" (Eph. 3:7-8). He encouraged people not to laud him (1 Cor. 9:15-16), but rather to pray for him (Eph. 6:19).

In the eighteen months he had worked among the Corinthians (Acts 18:11) he had faithfully preached and taught the gospel and nothing else (1 Cor. 2:2). In that he showed himself to be a **wise master builder. Wise** (*sophos*) in this context has to do not only with spiritual wisdom but also with practical wisdom, with skill. Paul knew why he had been sent to Corinth. He was sent to build the foundation of the church there, and that is what he carefully and skillfully did. He had the right motive, the right message, and the right power.

He also had the right approach; he was a master strategist. Though he was primarily the apostle to the Gentiles (Acts 9:15), Paul went to the synagogue to preach first, because the gospel is first of all for the Jews (Rom. 1:16). He also knew that the Jews would listen to him as one of themselves, and that those who were converted could help him reach the Gentiles. The Jews were his best open door, as well as a passion of his heart (cf. Rom. 9:1-3; 10:1). After winning converts in the synagogue, and often being thrown out, he would begin preaching and ministering among the Gentiles in the community (Acts 17:1-4; 18:4-7). He carefully and diligently planned and laid a solid foundation. The footings were deep and would last.

The foundation is only the first part of the building process. Paul's task was to lay the proper foundation of the gospel, to establish the doctrines and principles for belief and practice revealed to him by God (1 Cor. 2:12-13). It was the task of laying down the mysteries of the New Covenant (cf. Eph. 3:1-9). After he left, **another** began **building upon it.** In the case of Ephesus, that person was Timothy (1 Tim. 1:3). In the case of Corinth, it was Apollos. Paul was not jealous of those who followed him in ministry. He knew that, as one who laid foundations, he would have to be followed by other builders. Most of the Corinthians, for example, had been baptized by later pastors. Paul was glad for that, because it gave less excuse for the Corinthians to develop earthly loyalties to him (1:14-15).

He was quite concerned, however, that those who built upon the foundation he had laid would work as faithfully and well as he had worked. **Let each man be careful how he builds upon it.** The Greek form of the verb **builds** is the present active indicative, which stresses continual action. All believers go on through their lives and through history building on Jesus Christ.

Each man primarily refers to evangelists, pastors, and teachers, who have continued to build on the foundation laid by the apostles. These are given special and the most direct responsibility for teaching Christian doctrine. Paul later instructs Timothy that men who build should be faithful and capable (2 Tim. 2:2).

But the context makes it clear that a broader and more inclusive application is also in mind. The numerous references to "each man" and "any man" (vv. 10-18) indicate that the principle applies to every believer. All of us, by what we say and do, to some extent teach the gospel. No Christian has the right to be careless in representing the Lord and His Word. Every believer is to be a careful builder. We all have the same responsibility.

The Foundation: Jesus Christ

For no man can lay a foundation other than the one which is laid, which is Jesus Christ. (3:11)

Paul was a master builder whose primary task, as an apostle, was to lay the foundation of the Christian gospel. But he did not design the foundation; he only laid it. The only foundation of biblical Christianity is **Jesus Christ.** The foundation is not New Testament ethics, many of which are found in other religions. Nor is it in the history, traditions, and decisions of churches and church leaders through the centuries. It is Jesus Christ and Him alone. In a sense, it is all of Scripture, for all of Scripture is both from and about Jesus Christ. The Old Testament predicted and prepared for His incarnation. The gospels tell the history of His earthly ministry, and Acts the history of His church in its early years. The epistles are commentaries on His message and work, and the book of Revelation is the final testimony of His reigning and imminent return. What Jesus said of the Old Testament is even truer, if this were possible, of the New: "You search the Scriptures . . . and it is these that bear witness of Me" (John 5:39).

Some builders have tried to make the foundation of Christianity to be church tradition, others the moral teachings of the human Jesus, others ethical humanism, and still others some form of pseudo-scientism or simply sentimental love and good works. But the only foundation of the church and of Christian living is Jesus Christ. Without that foundation no spiritual building will be of God or will stand.

After the lame man had been healed at the Temple gate and the crowds there were marveling at it, Peter gave them an impromptu sermon. He explained in some detail how Jesus was the One on whom the Old Testament focused and was the only One through whom they could be saved and have eternal life. The priests and Sadducees then had Peter and John arrested and put in jail. On the next day the two men were brought before the high priest and a large group of other priestly leaders and commanded to explain their preaching and the healing. Peter continued his message of the previous day, telling them that it was by Jesus of Nazareth, the One whom they had crucified, that God raised the crippled man, and that this same Jesus, the Stone whom they had rejected, was the cornerstone of God's kingdom (Acts 3:1–4:12). He was saying that those Jewish leaders could not accept the gospel of the kingdom because they refused to accept the very center, the very foundation, of the kingdom— the Lord Jesus Christ.

Those presumed builders of Israel, of God's chosen people, tried to erect a religious system of tradition and works, but they had no foundation. They built their religious house on sand (Matt. 7:24-27). The foundation had been revealed in their

Scriptures for centuries—by Isaiah and other prophets—but they rejected it, as Peter reminds us again (1 Pet. 2:6-8). Every human philosophy, religious system, and code of ethics is doomed to failure and destruction, because it has no foundation. There is only one foundation, and, no matter how he may try, **no man can lay a foundation other than the one which is laid, which is Jesus Christ.** God's kingdom is built on Jesus Christ, and every individual life ("each man," v. 10) that pleases God must be carefully built on that foundation.

THE MATERIALS: BELIEVERS' WORKS

Now if any man builds upon the foundation with gold, silver, precious stones, wood, hay, straw. (3:12)

Ancient buildings were often built with precious metals and jewels. No Christian need worry about the **foundation** of his faith. That is the marble and granite of the person and work of Christ, secure and stable and perfect. Our concern should be that, whatever we build on this foundation, we build with the best of materials. There is only one foundation, but there are many types of materials for erecting the spiritual edifice. As long as believers are alive, they *are* building. They are building some sort of life, some sort of church, some sort of Christian fellowship and service. It may be a beautiful structure or a hovel, it may be by intention or by neglect, but it cannot help being something.

From the earliest history of the church in Acts and the epistles, and from the accounts of the seven churches of Revelation 2–3 through today, it has been obvious that Christians and the congregations they form are vastly different. From the beginning there have been **gold** Christians and **wood** Christians, **silver** churches and **hay** churches, **precious stone** endeavors and those that are **straw**—in every degree and combination.

The building materials mentioned in verse 12 are in two categories, each listed in descending order of value. The first category—**gold, silver, precious stones**—clearly represents high-quality materials. The second—**wood, hay, straw**—just as clearly represents inferior materials. Gold signifies the greatest faithfulness, the most skillful and careful work done for the Lord. Straw signifies the opposite, the least, the leftovers.

The materials do not represent wealth, talents, or opportunity. Nor do they represent spiritual gifts, all of which are good and are given to each believer by the Lord as He sees fit (1 Cor. 12:11). The materials represent believers' responses to what they have—how well they serve the Lord with what He has given them. In other words, they represent our works. We cannot be saved by good works or stay saved by good works. But every Christian has been "created in Christ Jesus for good works, which God prepared beforehand, that we should walk in them" (Eph. 2:10) and is to bear "fruit in every good work" (Col. 1:10). Works are not the source of the Christian life, but they are the marks of it.

Every Christian is a builder, and every Christian builds with some sort of materials. God wants us to build only with the best materials, because only the best materials are worthy of Him, are the most effective, and will last.

It is important to note that these first three materials are equally valuable. There is no grading, since some precious stones (such as pearls) were, in the ancient world, considered to be more valuable than gold, and silver could be used for things that gold could not. Things with different functions can be equally precious (cf. Matt. 13:23).

Only the Lord can determine which works are high quality and which are low. It is not the believer's role to grade Christians and the work they do. The point Paul is making is that our purpose should always be to serve the Lord with the best He has given us and with full dependence on Him. He alone determines the ultimate value of each man's work.

If Christ Himself is the foundation of our lives, He should also be the center of the work we build on the foundation. That is, the work we do should be truly His work, not just external activity or religious busy work. It is easy to become deeply involved in all sorts of church programs and activities and projects that are hay work. They are not bad programs or projects, but they are trivial. The **wood, hay,** and **straw** are not sinful things, but inferior things. Each can be useful in building something. Even hay or grass may be used to make a roof in some cases, and straw is often used in bricks and plaster. But when tested by fire, all three of the second group of materials will burn up.

Paul may have had a similar thought in mind in 2 Timothy 2:20-21, where he says, "Now in a large house there are not only gold and silver vessels, but also vessels of wood and of earthenware, and some to honor and some to dishonor. Therefore, if a man cleanses himself from these things, he will be a vessel for honor, sanctified, useful to the Master, prepared for every good work."

We build for the Lord, and use the various materials for the Lord, in three basic ways: by our motives, by our conduct, and by our service.

First, we build by our *motives*. Why we do a thing is as important as what we are doing. A campaign of neighborhood visitation done because of compulsion is wood, but visiting the same people in love to win them to the Lord is gold. Singing a solo in church and being concerned about how the people like our voice is hay, but singing to glorify the Lord is silver. Giving generously out of duty or pressure from men is straw, but giving generously with joy to extend the gospel and to serve others in the Lord's name is a precious stone. Work that on the outside looks like gold to us may be hay in God's eyes. He knows "the motives of men's hearts" (1 Cor. 4:5).

Second, we build by our *conduct*. "For we must all appear before the judgment seat of Christ, that each one may be recompensed for his deeds in the body, according to what he has done, whether good or bad" (2 Cor. 5:10). "Bad" (*phaulos*) is here best understood as "worthless." It produces no gain. Our conduct, therefore, can be "good" (*agathos,* "inherently good in quality"), evil, or just useless—like **wood, hay** and **straw** when tested by fire. So things we do can also be gold or wood, silver or hay, precious stone or straw.

Third, we build by our *service*. The way we use the spiritual gifts God has given us, the way we minister in His name, is of supreme importance in our building for Him. In Christ's service, we must seek to be those vessels "for honor, sanctified, useful to the Master."

Some years ago a young man told me he was leaving a certain ministry. The reason he gave was: "I wasn't doing what I do best. I was using my abilities but not my spiritual gifts." There was nothing wrong with the work he had been doing. In fact, for another person it could be gold. But for him it was wood, hay, or straw, because he was doing what others thought he should do rather than what the Lord had particularly gifted and called him to do.

THE TEST: BY FIRE

Each man's work will become evident; for the day will show it, because it is to be revealed with fire; and the fire itself will test the quality of each man's work. (3:13)

A new building is usually checked out carefully before it is occupied or used. Cities, counties, and states have codes that require buildings to meet certain standards. God has strict standards for what we build for Him in and with our lives. When Christ returns, every believer's work will be tested as to **quality. Fire** is the symbol of testing. Just as it purifies metal, so will the fire of God's discernment burn up the dross and leave what is pure and valuable (cf. Job 23:10; Zech. 13:9; 1 Pet. 1:17; Rev. 3:18).

As the following verses (14-15) make clear, that will not be a time of punishment but a time of reward. Even the one who has built with wood, hay, or straw will not be condemned; but his reward will correspond to the **quality** of his building materials. When wood, hay, or straw come in contact with fire they are burned up. Nothing is left but cinders. They cannot stand the test. Gold, silver, and precious stones, however, do not burn. They will stand the test, and they will bring great reward.

THE WORKMEN: ALL BELIEVERS

If any man's work which he has built upon it remains, he shall receive a reward. If any man's work is burned up, he shall suffer loss; but he himself shall be saved, yet so as through fire.

Do you not know that you are a temple of God, and that the Spirit of God dwells in you? If any man destroys the temple of God, God will destroy him, for the temple of God is holy, and that is what you are. (3:14-17)

Two types of workmen correspond to the two categories of materials: the valuable and the useless, the constructive and the worthless. Still another type of workman does not build at all, but destroys.

CONSTRUCTIVE WORKMEN

Believers who have right motives, proper conduct, and effective service build with gold, silver, and precious stones. They do constructive work for the Lord and will receive corresponding rewards. **He shall receive a reward.** That simple and hopeful promise is the message of eternal joy and glory. Whatever our service to God's glory, He will reward.

When a pastor preaches sound, solid doctrine he is building constructively. When a teacher teaches the Word consistently and fully, he is building with good materials. When a person with the gift of helps spends himself serving others in the Lord's name, he is building with materials that will endure testing and will bring great reward. When a believer's life is holy, submissive, and worshipful, he is living a life built with precious materials.

The Lord's rewards for His faithful followers are varied and wonderful, as unique as each believer, and all of them are imperishable (1 Cor. 9:25). The New Testament often refers to them as crowns. For those who are faithful until Jesus comes and who look forward to that day there will be "the crown of righteousness" (2 Tim. 4:7-8). For faithful soulwinners there will be a "crown of exultation" (1 Thess. 2:19-20). For faithful pastors there will be "the unfading crown of glory" (1 Pet. 5:4). For all who love the Lord there will be "the crown of life" (James 1:12). These represent the future eternal blessedness God has promised to give His people.

WORTHLESS WORKMEN

Many humanly impressive and seemingly beautiful and worthwhile works that Christians do in the Lord's name will not stand the test in "that day." Many acclaimed Christian leaders and workers will find their work consumed by God's testing fire. It "will become evident" (v. 13) that the materials used were wood, hay, and straw. The great works will turn out not to have been great, and the apparently productive lives will turn out not to have been so productive. The workmen will not lose their salvation, but they will lose a portion of any reward they might be expecting. They **shall be saved, yet so as through fire.** The thought here is of a person who runs through flames without being burned, but who has the smell of smoke on him—barely escaping! In the day of rewards, the useless and evil things will be burned away, but salvation will not be forfeited.

It is easy to fool ourselves into thinking that anything we do in the Lord's name is in His service, just as long as we are sincere, hardworking, and well meaning. But what looks to us like gold may turn out to be straw, because we have not judged our materials by the standards of God's Word—pure motives, holy conduct, and selfless service.

We should be careful not to waste our opportunities by building with worthless materials, for if we do we will become worthless workmen. Paul warned the Colossians, "Let no one keep defrauding you of your prize by delighting in self-abasement and the worship of the angels, taking his stand on visions he has seen, inflated without cause by his fleshly mind" (Col. 2:18). When we rely on human wisdom, or even supernatural visions, rather than God's Word, we are carnal, following a "fleshly mind." We can be sure that any doctrine or principle or practice developed from such fleshly sources will at best be worthless.

DESTRUCTIVE WORKMEN

The third group of workmen obviously is made up of unbelievers, because God will never **destroy** those He has redeemed and given eternal life. It is composed of evil, unsaved people who attack God's people and God's work. That destructive group can work either from within or without the church, destroying what God has built up.

Every believer is **a temple of God**, indwelt by **the Spirit of God**. Consequently the church itself is a temple of God, a composite temple composed of all God's elect. Like each individual Christian, it **is holy**, and God jealously guards that which is holy. Under the Old Testament any person, other than the high priest on the Day of Atonement, who dared to enter the Holy of Holies would drop dead on the spot. He would not need to be put to death by the people; God would strike Him dead. Even less does God look kindly upon those who threaten or defile His holy people (cf. Matt. 18:6-10).

The day of rewards is coming. It is coming as soon as Jesus returns, for He will bring His rewards with Him (Rev. 22:12). If we are still living on earth then, there will be no time left for preparing. If we go to be with the Lord before that time, there will be no opportunity to prepare after we die. The only time we have for doing the Lord's work that brings reward is now.

How to Eliminate Division (3:18-23)

Let no man deceive himself. If any man among you thinks that he is wise in this age, let him become foolish that he may become wise. For the wisdom of this world is foolishness before God. For it is written, "He is the one who catches the wise in their craftiness"; and again, "The Lord knows the reasonings of the wise, that they are useless." So then let no one boast in men. For all things belong to you, whether Paul or Apollos or Cephas or the world or life or death or things present or things to come; all things belong to you, and you belong to Christ; and Christ belongs to God. (3:18-23)

This passage follows the problem Paul has already carefully delineated, that of division and disunity. Typical of Paul, the solution to the problem is found in correct thinking. To gain and maintain unity in the church, we must have the proper view of ourselves, of others, of our possessions, and of our Possessor.

THE PROPER VIEW OF OURSELVES

Let no man deceive himself. If any man among you thinks that he is wise in this age, let him become foolish that he may become wise. For the wisdom of this world is foolishness before God. For it is written, "He is the one who

catches the wise in their craftiness"; and again, "The Lord knows the reasonings of the wise, that they are useless." (3:18-20)

Much division in the church would be eliminated if individuals were not so impressed with their own wisdom. A person who thinks that he is wise in this age— that is, wise in contemporary human wisdom—does nothing but **deceive himself.** Anyone who is so self-deceived ought to **become foolish** (*mōros*), that is, identify with those who recognize that human wisdom, including our own, is mere **foolishness** (*mōria*) without God. Those two Greek terms are from the same root from which we get *moron*. Human wisdom is moronic in the Lord's sight, **before God.** Unity in the church can never come without recognizing human wisdom to be what God declares it to be: **foolish.** And unity can never come without Christians becoming foolish in the world's eyes by conforming to God's wisdom.

The human wisdom that is foolish is in the area of spiritual truth. Paul is not talking about such things as business, mathematics, science, or mechanics. We can be quite knowledgeable about those things without any special enlightenment from God. Where human wisdom becomes foolish and useless is in matters concerning God, salvation, and spiritual truth. Human wisdom has no way of discovering and understanding divine things.

Even Christians, therefore, do not have a right to their own opinions about the things God has revealed. When Christians start expressing and following their own ideas about the gospel, the church, and Christian living, the saints cannot help becoming divided. Christians are no wiser in their flesh than are unbelievers. The first step in a Christian's becoming truly wise is to recognize that his own human wisdom is **foolishness,** a reflection of **the wisdom of this world,** which **is foolishness before God.** It is the product of intellectual pride and is the enemy of God's revelation.

The church must create an atmosphere in which the Word of God is honored and submitted to, in which human opinion is never used to judge or qualify revelation. As far as the things of God are concerned, Christians must be totally under the teaching of Scripture and the illumination of the Holy Spirit. Only then can we be open to God's wisdom and truly **become wise.** Common commitment to the Word of God is the basic unifier.

Where the Word of God is not set up as the supreme authority, division is inevitable. Such happens even in evangelical churches, when pastors and other leaders begin substituting their own ideas for the truths of Scripture. The substitution is seldom intentional, but it will always happen when the Bible is neglected. A Bible that is not studied carefully cannot be followed carefully. And where it is not followed there will be division, because there will be no common ground for beliefs and practices. When the truth of Scripture is not the sole authority, men's varied opinions become the authority.

Some people are not satisfied unless they can express their opinion on virtually everything. Some are not happy unless they take the opposite side from the majority. Intellectual pride cannot be content to listen and admire; it must always speak up and criticize. By its very nature, it must always try to win out in an issue. It cannot stand opposition or contradiction. It must justify itself at any cost and is exclusive. It looks down its nose at all who disagree.

Pride is always at the heart of human wisdom, **the wisdom of this world, which is foolishness before God.** It is difficult to teach a person who thinks he knows everything. The Roman rhetorician Quintilian said of some of his students, "They would doubtlessly have become excellent scholars if they had not been so fully persuaded of their own scholarship." A well-known Arab proverb goes: "He who knows not, and knows not that he knows not, is a fool. Shun him. He who knows not, and knows that he knows not, is simple. Teach him."

If a congregation were to have ten men with doctorates who were only nominal in their commitment to the Lord and to His Word, and ten other men who had only finished high school but who were completely sold out to the Lord and steeped in His Word, it should not be hard to decide which ten were most qualified to lead the church. By God's standards it would be no contest. Having members who are highly talented and trained can be of considerable help to a church, but only if those who possess such abilities are submitted to the truths and standards of Scripture. Christ will rule and unify His church if He is given pure channels committed to His Word through whom to mediate that rule.

When believers look to psychology alone, instead of to God's Word, for answers to personal or marital or moral problems, spiritual disaster results. When Christian businessmen look to popular methods of expediency alone, rather than to the principles of Scripture, to determine business ethics, their spiritual life and testimony are undermined. In science and technology men have made great advances, for which we should be glad and from which we can profit. But in regard to the things of God and His plan and will for men, human ideas and understanding stand completely empty and helpless.

The liberal Bible scholars and theologians of the late 19th and early 20th centuries were brilliant men, highly learned in many areas. They often disagreed with one another on doctrines and interpretations, but the one belief in which they were unanimous was that the Bible was essentially a human book. Because they considered it to be primarily human, though perhaps influenced by divine guidance of some sort, they felt perfectly free to reject or modify whatever part of Scripture did not fit their own understanding. Because they did not believe that writing had been developed by Moses' time, they concluded that he could not have written the Pentateuch. Because they did not believe in supernatural predictions, they did not believe that the man Daniel could possibly have written the book of Daniel, which tells of events hundreds of years after he lived. When Scripture reported that God said or did something that was contrary to their self-invented view of God, they denied that He said or did it. In the name of intellectualism they decimated God's Word, leaving only that which suited their personal biases. They also decimated a great part of His church, causing unimaginable confusion, doubt, unbelief, and spiritual division. The legacy of those men is still polluting seminaries, colleges, and churches throughout the world.

The person who elevates his own wisdom will always have a low view of Scripture. But the more important truth is that God knows the value of that person's own wisdom. It is foolishness, stupid, totally unreliable and useless. Eventually God will trip up those who oppose His Word. **He is the one who catches the wise in their craftiness.** Like Haman, they hang on their own gallows (Esther 7:7-10). Their cunning plans turn to condemn them as God catches them in their own trap. He **knows the reasonings of the wise, that they are useless.**

Human philosophy is totally inadequate to bring men to God, to show them how to be saved or how to live. It will always become entrapped in its own schemes, and entrap those who trust in it. The one who trusts in human understanding does not have the right understanding of himself. He does not see that his spiritual opinions, ideas, and **reasonings** are **useless** (*mataios*), vain and empty.

The proper view of ourselves, the godly and true view, is that apart from divine truth we are fools with empty thoughts. Recognizing this truth opens the door to true wisdom and closes the door to division.

THE PROPER VIEW OF OTHERS

So then let no one boast in men. For all things belong to you, whether Paul or Apollos or Cephas. (3:21-22a)

A second requirement for overcoming church division is having the right view of others. Paul had spoken strongly against special loyalties to church leaders (1:12-14; 3:4-9), the same three leaders he mentions here. But now the emphasis is different. Although those men should not have been specially elevated or revered, they were sources of great help and blessing. They were sent to the Corinthians by the Lord, and therefore should have been listened to and respected. They were God's teachers. They taught the same truths from God and were meant by God to be sources of unity, not division.

The divisions that developed around them were based on the people's attraction to their individual styles and personalities, their personal appeal to various Corinthians. Church members began to **boast** of Paul or Peter (Cephas) or Apollos, giving honor to one over the other—and the church became divided.

Parenthetically, it should be added that sometimes certain leaders *should* be respected over others. A pastor who carefully preaches God's Word and lives a life consistent with his preaching deserves to be respected and followed. One who is careless in preaching and living, on the other hand, does not deserve to be respected or followed. In both cases our response should be based on the leader's faithfulness to the Word, not on his personality or style. If he is faithful he is worthy of esteem (1 Thess. 5:12-13).

Some years ago I spoke at a conference attended by people from a wide variety of churches, Protestant and Catholic, liberal and evangelical. The series of messages was on Christian ethics, with Hebrews 13 as the text. When I began explaining "Obey your leaders, and submit to them; for they keep watch over your souls," I received some interesting responses. Many of the people found it hard to justify the idea of obeying and submitting to their pastors—and for good reason. The pastors did not believe the Bible to be the Word of God, and their lives were consistent with that unbelief. I pointed out that Hebrews teaches submission to *godly* leaders, to those who are faithful to Scripture both in teaching and in living (Heb. 13:7, 17).

The Corinthians were fortunate to have had the ministry of at least three outstanding men of God, two of them apostles. Peter probably did not serve personally in Corinth, but some of the Corinthians had benefited from his ministry. Each of those men had special gifts and abilities that God used to teach and lead the believers. That variety of leadership should have enriched the church, not divided it.

Christians can learn from many good teachers and leaders today—through radio, television, books, magazines, tapes, conferences, and other means. To the extent that the leaders are scriptural and godly, they will spiritually unite those to whom they minister. Our first responsibility is to our local church, and our spiritual submission should first of all be to our own pastors. But no pastor should be jealous of the spiritual blessing that someone else may be giving to members of his congregation. This was Paul's spirit even in the very adverse circumstances he reported in Philippians 1:12-18.

The point Paul makes in 3:22a is that we should rejoice in and profit from *all* the faithful leaders God sends us, **whether Paul or Apollos or Cephas.** If the Corinthians had been careful to understand and follow what all three of those men *taught,* rather than, for instance, how they looked or spoke, the church would have been united, not divided. Their view of others had to be corrected.

THE PROPER VIEW OF POSSESSIONS

or the world or life or death or things present or things to come; all things belong to you. (3:22b)

A third requirement for overcoming division is having the right view of our possessions.

This phrase (v. 22b) continues the list of the "all things" that belong to us (v. 21). Not only are all godly leaders ours, but everything else from God is ours as well. As believers we are "heirs of God and fellow heirs with Christ" (Rom 8:17). We have even inherited Christ's glory, bequeathed to us by our Lord Himself (John 17:22). "We know that God causes all things to work together for good to those who love God, to those who are called according to His purpose" (Rom. 8:28).

The world or life or death or things present or things to come is totally inclusive. Paul begins and ends this declaration with **all things belong to you** (cf. 21b). In Christ, *all* things are for our sakes and for God's glory (2 Cor. 4:15).

Specifically, **the world** (*kosmos*) is ours, even now. His main point is that, in the millennial kingdom and throughout eternity in the new heavens and new earth, we will possess the earth in a richer way (Matt.5:5; Rev. 21). But even now the universe is a possession of God's people. It is ours. Our heavenly Father made it for us. It is still in the grip of the evil one (1 John 5:19), but it will someday and forever belong to us, not to him.

Joseph Parker reports an interesting story about his first pastorate:

> I began my ministry in Banbury, and my upper window looked over the vast estate of a wealthy man. It was I, really, who inherited that estate. Oh, I did not own a foot of it, but it was all mine. The owner came down to see it once a year, but I walked its miles day after day.

When we fully inherit the world, with Jesus on the throne, it will be perfect, and even more ours. In the meanwhile, this present world already belongs to us, with its wonders and glories, imperfections and disappointments. The believer can appreciate the world as no unbeliever can. We know where it came from, why it was made, why we are on it, and what its final destiny will be. We can sing with certainty as well as joy, "This is my Father's world." And we are His heirs.

All **life** is ours; but from the context it is clear that Paul is primarily referring to spiritual life, eternal life. In Christ we have new life, a quality of life that will never tarnish, diminish, or be lost. God's own life is in us now. Through Christ, God abides in us (John 14:23), and we share His nature and His life (cf. 2 Pet. 1:3-4).

Even **death** is ours. The great enemy of mankind has been overcome. Christ has conquered death, and through Him we have conquered death (cf.1 Cor. 15:54-57). Unless we are raptured, we will have to pass through death; but we will pass through it as its master not its slave. All death can do to the believer is deliver him to Jesus. It brings us into the eternal presence of our Savior. That is why Paul could say with such joy, "For to me, to live is Christ, and to die is gain" (Phil. 1:21). Whether he remained on earth for a while longer or went to be with the Lord, he could not lose. For Christians, death can only make things better. To stay here and finish the work Christ has given us to do may be "more necessary," but "to depart and be with Christ . . . is very much better" (Phil. 1:23-24). For God's people, this present life is good, but death—which ushers us into eternal life—is better.

Things present are ours. That encompasses everything we have or experience in this life. It is, in fact, a synonym for this life. It includes the good and the bad, the pleasant and the painful, the joys and the disappointments, the health and the sickness, the contentment and the grief. In God's hands it all serves us and makes us spiritually richer. "In all these things we overwhelmingly conquer through Him who loved us"; and because nothing "shall be able to separate us from the love of God, which is in Christ Jesus our Lord," nothing can cause us any real harm (Rom. 8:37-39). God causes *all* things to be working together for our good (v. 28).

Things to come are ours. The reference here is not primarily, if at all, to the future of our present lives. That is included under **things present**, meaning everything we will experience on earth. The things that are to come are heavenly blessings, of which we now have only a glimpse. Yet they will be the greatest blessings of all. These somewhat overlapping terms crisscross the reality that everything is for us to share equally as heirs of God's glories. So why should we divide ourselves into factions? No man is the source of any of this inheritance, so there is no reason to "boast in men" (v. 21a).

THE PROPER VIEW OF OUR POSSESSOR

and you belong to Christ; and Christ belongs to God. (3:23)

By far the most important requirement for overcoming division is having the right view of our Possessor, Jesus Christ. He is Himself the source of spiritual unity and the source for healing division. It is in taking our eyes off Him that division begins, and it is in putting our eyes back on Him that division ends. "The one who joins himself to the Lord is one spirit with Him" (1 Cor. 6:17). Believers all belong to the same Lord, and are thus one with each other. Therefore anything that denies our oneness with each other denies our oneness in Him (cf. Phil. 2:1-4).

The greatest possible motive for maintaining the unity of the Spirit and for avoiding church division is knowing that we **belong to Christ** and that **Christ belongs to God**. Because we all belong to Him, we all belong to each other.

In His high priestly prayer, our Lord wonderfully enriches His teaching on unity. Speaking of believers, He says, "For they are Thine; and all things that are Mine are Thine, and Thine are Mine, . . . that they all may be one; even as Thou, Father, art in Me, and I in Thee, that they also may be in Us, . . . that they may be one, just as We are one; I in them, and Thou in Me, that they may be perfected in unity" (John 9:9-10, 21-23).

We are tied together in an eternal oneness with God the Father and Jesus Christ, and thus with each other in them. How can men who are so much one, be divided? It begins with failure to understand the reality of our spiritual unity in the One who is our Possessor. With a common Possessor and possessions, common leaders and teachers, and common dependence on Scripture, there should be no cause for factions and disunity.

True Servants of Christ (4:1-5)

10

Let a man regard us in this manner, as servants of Christ, and stewards of the mysteries of God. In this case, moreover, it is required of stewards that one be found trustworthy. But to me it is a very small thing that I should be examined by you, or by any human court; in fact, I do not even examine myself. I am conscious of nothing against myself, yet I am not by this acquitted; but the one who examines me is the Lord. Therefore do not go on passing judgment before the time, but wait until the Lord comes who will both bring to light the things hidden in the darkness and disclose the motives of men's hearts; and then each man's praise will come to him from God. (4:1-5)

A popular game played by many Christians is that of evaluating pastors. All kinds of criteria are used to determine who are the most successful, the most influential, the most gifted, the most effective. Some magazines periodically make surveys and write up extensive reports, carefully ranking the pastors by church membership, attendance at worship services, sizes of church staff and Sunday school, academic and honorary degrees, books and articles written, numbers of messages given at conferences and conventions, and so on. As popular as that practice may be, it is exceedingly offensive to God.

First Corinthians 4:1-5 focuses on the true nature and marks of God's ministers. It sets forth the basic guidelines and standards by which ministers are to minister and be evaluated. It deals with what the congregation's attitude toward the minister should be and what the minister's attitude toward himself should be. In short, it puts the minister of God in God's perspective. Paul makes it clear that popularity, personality, degrees, and numbers play no role in the Lord's perspective—and that they should play no role in ours.

The main point of the passage here still concerns the divisions over different ministers. The message is that servants of God should not be ranked at all, by others or by themselves. All who are true to Scripture in their preaching and living should be treated equally. Where there is sound doctrine and personal holiness there is no justification for ranking God's servants. (Romans 16:17 and 1 Timothy 5:20, however, point out that where those two essentials are missing, there must be evaluation and confrontation.)

To help us understand God's purpose for His servants, Paul gives three characteristics of the true minister, the true servant of Christ: his identity, his requirements, and his evaluation.

The Identity of the Minister

Let a man regard us in this manner, as servants of Christ, and stewards of the mysteries of God. (4:1)

Us refers back to 3:22, indicating Paul, Apollos, Cephas, and, by extension, all other "fellow-workers" (cf. v. 9). **A man** is a nonspecific reference that first of all applies to Christians. That is, "Let all Christians **regard us in this manner.**" But in a wider sense it may also refer to unbelievers—not only to how the world should regard God's ministers, but also to how the church should portray God's ministers before the world. An unbeliever cannot understand the things of God, because they are spiritually discerned or appraised (2:14). But Christians should not parade worldly standards of the ministry before unbelievers any more than they should parade those standards among themselves. We have no right to use worldly criteria—such as popularity, personality, degrees, and numbers—to make the gospel seem more appealing. We should not try to make the world see God's humble messengers as anything but what He has ordained them to be: **servants of Christ, and stewards of the mysteries of God.**

SERVANTS OF CHRIST

Servants (*hupēretēs*) means literally, "under rowers," originally indicating the lowest galley slaves, the ones rowing on the bottom tier of a ship. They were the most menial, unenvied, and despised of slaves. From that meaning the term came to refer to subordinates of any sort, to those under the authority of another.

Christian ministers are first and above all else **servants of Christ.** In everything they are subordinate and subject to Him. They are called to serve men in Christ's name; but they cannot serve men rightly unless they serve their Lord rightly. And they cannot serve Him rightly unless they see themselves rightly: as His underslaves, His menial servants.

To look first of all at men's needs is to fail men as well as to fail the Lord. A minister who becomes so occupied with counseling and helping his congregation and community that he spends little time in the Word is unable to meet those people's deepest needs, because he has neglected his greatest resource for correctly knowing and adequately meeting those needs. That usually leads to compromising God's truth for the sake of peoples' desires. Before all else he must be a servant of Jesus Christ, "serving the Lord with all humility" (Acts 20:19). Then, and only then, can he best serve people.

Paul, though an apostle, considered himself to be a *hupēretēs,* a galley slave, of his Lord, and he wanted everyone else to consider him, and all of God's ministers, as that. Galley slaves were not exalted one above the other. They had a common rank, the lowest. They had the hardest labor, the cruelest punishment, the least appreciation, and in general the most hopeless existence of all slaves. As Paul had already written, "What then is Apollos? And what is Paul? Servants [*diakonoi*] through whom you believed, even as the Lord gave opportunity to each one" (3:5). A minister of Christ can be useful only as the Lord gives opportunity and power: "So then neither the one who plants nor the one who waters is anything, but God who causes the growth" (3:7).

Luke speaks of the "servants [*hupēretēs*] of the Word" who handed down eyewitness accounts of Jesus' teaching and ministry (Luke 1:2). To serve Christ is to serve His Word, which is the revelation of His will. A servant of Christ must also be a servant, a galley slave, of Scripture. His function is to obey God's commands as revealed in His Word.

Later in the epistle Paul says, "For if I preach the gospel, I have nothing to boast of, for I am under compulsion; for woe is me if I do not preach the gospel" (1 Cor. 9:16). His preaching the gospel was no cause for boasting or praise; he was only doing his duty, just as his Master had commanded (Luke 17:10). It had not been Paul's idea even to become a Christian, much less to preach the gospel. Before the Lord abruptly confronted him on the Damascus road, Paul (then Saul) was the furthest possible from serving Christ (Acts 9:1-6).

In his second letter to Corinth Paul describes in some detail what the life of a minister of God is like. He can expect affliction, hardship, distress, beatings, imprisonment, turmoil, sleeplessness, and hunger—as well as purity, knowledge, patience, kindness, the Holy Spirit, love, the word of truth, the power of God, and the weapons of righteousness (2 Cor. 6:4-7). God's servant sometimes appears as an enigma and a paradox:

> by glory and dishonor, by evil report and good report; regarded as deceivers and yet true; as unknown yet well-known, as dying yet behold, we live; as punished yet not put to death, as sorrowful yet always rejoicing, as poor yet making many rich, as having nothing yet possessing all things. (vv. 8-10)

The minister of God cannot depend on his appearance before other men. Their opinions vary and change, and are never reliable. A servant's obedience should be to his master alone, and his desire should be to please his master alone. Paul sought to do only that which the Lord called him to do. His calling was to preach the Word of God (Col. 1:25), to take the Word and give it out. In that he was faithful.

God's ministers are not called to be creative but obedient, not innovative but faithful.

STEWARDS OF GOD'S MYSTERIES

Ministers of the gospel are also **stewards of the mysteries of God.** The Greek (*oikonomos*) for **steward** literally means "house manager," a person placed in complete control of a household. The steward supervised the property, the fields and vineyards, the finances, the food, and the other servants on behalf of his master.

Peter speaks of all Christians being "good stewards of the manifold grace of God" (1 Pet. 4:10), but ministers are stewards in an especially important way. The minister "must be above reproach as God's steward" (Titus 1:7), because he is entrusted with proclaiming **the mysteries of God.**

As mentioned in a previous chapter, a mystery (*mustērion*), as used in the New Testament, is that which was hidden and can be known only by divine revelation. As a steward of God's mysteries, a minister is to take God's revealed Word and dispense it to God's household. He is to dispense all of God's Word, holding nothing back. Paul could tell the Ephesian elders, "I did not shrink from declaring to you anything that was profitable, and teaching you publicly and from house to house, solemnly testifying to both Jews and Greeks, . . . declaring to you the whole purpose of God" (Acts 20:20-21, 27). That which is profitable is "all Scripture" (2 Tim. 3:16). The reason so many Christians have spiritual malnutrition is that so many preachers dispense an unbalanced diet of biblical truth. What they preach may be scriptural, but they do not preach the full counsel, the whole purpose, of God.

Some years ago I read a magazine interview of a certain well-known pastor. The gist of his statement was:

> I decided that the pulpit was no longer to be a teaching platform but an instrument of spiritual therapy. I no longer preach sermons; I create experiences. I don't have time to write a systematic theology to give a solid theological basis for what I intuitively know. What I intuitively believe is right. Every sermon has to begin with the heart. If you ever hear me preaching a sermon against adultery, you'll know what my problem is. If you ever hear me preaching a sermon about the coming of Jesus Christ, you'll know that's where I am heartwise. It so happens I'm not hung up on either of those areas so I've never preached a sermon on either one. I could not in print or in public deny the virgin birth of Christ or the physical resurrection of Jesus Christ or the return of Christ. But when I have something I can't comprehend, I just don't deal with it.

That is the description of a totally corrupted and perverted ministry. Those who listen to that man are not hearing all God has to say. Rather than bringing men to God, he is standing between men and God. God's Word is explicit about adultery, the virgin birth of Jesus, and His second coming. God's ministers are not required to fully understand those truths, but to fully and faithfully proclaim them. Otherwise they will be "like many, peddling the word of God" (2 Cor. 2:17), selling a cheapened gospel and a cheapened Bible, made more palatable by removing essential truth. Acceptance of such a huckstered message may be damning.

"Therefore," said Paul, "since we have this ministry, . . . we have renounced the things hidden because of shame, not walking in craftiness or adulterating the word of God" (2 Cor. 4:1-2). The preacher or teacher who disregards certain Scripture texts, or twists them to support his own ideas and programs, adulterates the Word of God. The cults try to support their false doctrines by using Bible texts out of context and with interpretations that clearly contradict other texts. But the Bible is not a repository of prooftexts for men's opinions; it is the repository of God's truth—of which the minister of God is a steward. His concern should not be to please his hearers or to dispense his own views but to "be diligent to present [himself] approved to God as a workman who does not need to be ashamed, handling accurately the word of truth" (2 Tim.2:15).

A minister who does not study the Word cannot properly teach the Word. He cannot handle accurately that which he does not know. Under his care, as Milton observed, "The hungry sheep look up, and are not fed."

THE REQUIREMENT OF THE MINISTER

In this case, moreover, it is required of stewards that one be found trustworthy. (4:2)

By far the most important quality of a good steward is faithfulness, trustworthiness. He is entrusted with his master's household and possessions; and without faithfulness he will ruin both. Above all, God wants His ministers, His servant-**stewards**, to be **trustworthy**. God desires that His spiritual ministers be consistently obedient to His Word, unwavering in their commitment to be faithful. He does not require brilliance or cleverness or creativeness or popularity. He can use servants with those qualities, but only trustworthiness is absolutely essential. **It is required.**

Paul sent Timothy to minister to the Corinthians because that young man was "beloved and faithful" (1 Cor. 4:17). Paul knew that he was completely dependable to preach and teach God's Word. He did not have to worry about Timothy's adulterating the gospel or giving up in confusion. He was faithful to God's calling, just as Paul himself, "by the mercy of the Lord [was] trustworthy" (7:25). In the book of Colossians Paul mentions two other co-laborers who were outstanding in trustworthiness. Epaphras was a "beloved fellow bond-servant" and "a faithful servant of Christ" (1:7). Tychicus was a "beloved brother and faithful servant and fellow bond-servant in the Lord" (4:7).

Servanthood and stewardship are inseparable from faithfulness. An unfaithful servant or an untrustworthy steward is a self-contradiction. "Who then is the faithful and sensible slave whom his master put in charge of his household to give them their food at the proper time?" Jesus asked. "Blessed is that slave whom his master finds so doing when he comes" (Matt. 24:45-46). When the Lord returns, the only absolute requirement by which He will judge His servants is faithfulness: were they true to their Lord's commands?

God supplies His Word, His Spirit, His gifts, and His power. All that the minister can supply is his faithfulness in using those resources. The work is demanding but is basically simple: taking God's Word and feeding it faithfully to His people—dispensing the mysteries of God, proclaiming the hidden truths He has made known. There is to be no glory here, ranking one above the other. The best that any minister can be is faithful, which is just fulfilling the basic requirement.

THE EVALUATION OF THE MINISTER

But to me it is a very small thing that I should be examined by you, or by any human court; in fact, I do not even examine myself. I am conscious of nothing against myself, yet I am not by this acquitted; but the one who examines me is the Lord. (4:3-4)

Paul was not bragging or placing himself above other ministers or above any other Christian. What he said about his own attitude toward himself should be said by every minister and every Christian. It should be **a very small thing** to any of us when our ministry or our spiritual life is criticized or praised, whether by fellow Christians, **by any human court,** or any other of man's tribunals. We can benefit greatly from the counsel of a wise, spiritual friend, and sometimes even from the criticisms of unbelievers. But no human being is qualified to determine the legitimacy, quality, or faithfulness of our work for the Lord. We are not even qualified to determine those things for ourselves. Matters of outward sin are to be judged as 1 Timothy 5:19-21 indicates. But apart from the discipline of sinning servants, we can make no absolutely accurate judgment as to the faithfulness of heart, mind, and body of any servant of God.

Examined and **examine** are from *anakrinō*, which means "to investigate, question, evaluate." It does not mean to determine guilt or innocence, as the King James ("judged, judge") suggests. **Human court** (*anthrōpinēs hēmeras*) literally means "human day," that is, a day in a human court. No human being, or group of human beings, is qualified to examine and evaluate God's servants. No Christian, and in this context especially God's ministers, should be concerned about any such evaluation. Only God knows the truth.

OTHERS' EVALUATION

We should not be offended when people criticize us, or show false modesty when they praise us. We should simply say with Paul, "But we all, with unveiled face beholding as in a mirror the glory of the Lord, are being transformed into the same image from glory to glory" (2 Cor.3:18). Our focus is on our Lord Jesus Christ. We know that we are being transformed into His image because He says we are, not because of what we can see or what others can see.

A caring minister of Christ cannot be insensitive to the feelings, needs, and opinions of his people. He should not try to be. A sincere word of appreciation after a sermon is encouraging, and reflects spiritual concern and growth in the listener's life. A word of helpful criticism can be a needed corrective and even a blessing. But no minister can remain faithful to his calling if he lets his congregation, or any other human beings, decide how true his motives are or whether he is working within the Lord's will. Because their knowledge and understanding of the facts are imperfect, their criticisms and compliments are imperfect. In humility and love, God's minister must not allow himself to care about other people's evaluations of his ministry.

HIS OWN EVALUATION

Nor must he allow himself to care about his own evaluation of his ministry. All of us are naturally inclined to build ourselves up in our own minds. We all look into rose-colored mirrors. Even when we put ourselves down, especially in front of others, we often are simply appealing for recognition and flattery. The mature minister does not trust his own judgment in such things any more than he trusts the judgment of others. He agrees with Paul that his own evaluation may be as unreliable as that of anyone else.

Spiritual introspection is dangerous. Known sin must be faced and confessed, and known shortcomings are to be prayed about and worked on for improvement. But no Christian, no matter how advanced in the faith, is able to properly evaluate his own spiritual life. Before we know it, we will be ranking ourselves, classifying ourselves—and discover that a great deal of time is being spent in thinking of nothing but ourselves. The bias in our own favor and the tendency of the flesh toward self-justification make this a dangerous project.

Paul knew of no serious sin or deficiency in his own life. **I am conscious of nothing against myself** (cf. 2 Cor. 1:12). But he knew he could be wrong in that assessment; even as an apostle he could be wrong about his own heart. He, too, needed to remember to take heed when he stood, lest he should fall (1 Cor. 10:12). So he continued explaining to the Corinthians, **yet I am not by this acquitted.** But that did not let him matter either. He was not proud that he knew of nothing wrong, and he did not worry because he might be mistaken. His own evaluation, favorable or unfavorable, made no difference.

The only evaluation that makes a difference is the Lord's. **The one who examines me is the Lord.** Only His examination counts. Paul had long followed the counsel he gave to Timothy: "Be diligent to present yourself approved to God" (2 Tim. 2:15). He was not concerned about presenting himself to others for approval, or even to himself for approval, but only to His Lord.

A minister serves his people spiritually only when he is a faithful servant of Christ and steward of the mysteries of God. And God alone is the judge of the true spiritual value of that service.

GOD'S EVALUATION

Therefore do not go on passing judgment before the time, but wait until the Lord comes who will both bring to light the things hidden in the darkness and disclose the motives of men's hearts, and then each man's praise will come to him from God. (4:5)

God has a day planned when He **will both bring to light the things hidden in the darkness and disclose the motives of men's hearts.** Those two phrases refer to the attitudes of the inner man, which only God can see. Ultimate judgment of every kind, including the evaluation of His servants' ministries, will be by Him and in His time. God's people, including the ministers themselves, have no business **passing judgment before** [that] **time.** We see only the outside, the visible, and cannot know what is hidden in the recesses of the soul.

Because Paul speaks here of **each man's praise,** I do not believe **things hidden in the darkness** refers to sins or anything evil, but simply to things presently unknown to us. The passage emphasizes that every believer will have praise, no matter what his works and motives, because "There is therefore now no condemnation for those who are in Christ Jesus" (Rom. 8:1). All Christians will have some reward and some praise. Who will receive much and who will receive little only God knows. But once the wood, hay, and straw are burned away, the gold, silver, and precious stones will remain to be eternally rewarded.

We do know, however, that the rewards given will not be based on the degrees behind our name, the numbers we have preached to or witnessed to, the programs we have planned and directed, the books we have written, or even the number of converts won to Christ through us. It will be based on one thing alone: **the motives** (*boulē*, "secret thoughts") **of** [our] **hearts.**

One of the marvelous experiences we will have on that day will be to realize that many dear saints, completely unknown to the world and perhaps hardly known to fellow believers, will receive reward after reward after reward from the Lord's hands—because their works were of gold, silver, and precious stones. Their hearts will have been pure, their works will have been precious, and their rewards will be great.

Because God will reward according to **the motives of men's hearts,** our single purpose in life should be that, "whether, then [we] eat or drink or whatever [we] do, [we] do all to the glory of God" (1 Cor. 10:31). That motive should determine everything we think and do.

It is good when fellow Christians can speak well of us sincerely. It is good when our own conscience does not accuse us. But it will be wonderful beyond description if, on that day, our Lord can say of us, "Well done, good and faithful servant."

Paul's purpose here is to show that because all ministers are no more than servants and stewards, because neither we nor they can properly evaluate the value and worth of their ministry, and because God alone can and will give the proper estimate in a future reckoning day, it is not only destructive but ridiculous to cause divisions in the church by arguing over who is the most honored servant.

Conceit and Humility (4:6-13)

Now these things, brethren, I have figuratively applied to myself and Apollos for your sakes, that in us you might learn not to exceed what is written, in order that no one of you might become arrogant in behalf of one against the other. For who regards you as superior? And what do you have that you did not receive? But if you did receive it, why do you boast as if you had not received it? You are already filled, you have already become rich, you have become kings without us; and I would indeed that you had become kings so that we also might reign with you. For, I think, God has exhibited us apostles last of all, as men condemned to death; because we have become a spectacle to the world, both to angels and to men. We are fools for Christ's sake, but you are prudent in Christ; we are weak, but you are strong; you are distinguished, but we are without honor. To this present hour we are both hungry and thirsty, and are poorly clothed, and are roughly treated, and are homeless; and we toil, working with our own hands; when we are reviled, we bless; when we are persecuted, we endure; when we are slandered, we try to conciliate; we have become as the scum of the world, the dregs of all things, even until now. (4:6-13)

When Abraham was interceding to the Lord on behalf of Sodom he said,

"Now behold, I have ventured to speak to the Lord, although I am but dust and ashes" (Gen. 18:27). When Jacob was afraid that Esau was about to attack him, he prayed, "I am unworthy of all the lovingkindness and of all the faithfulness which Thou hast shown to Thy servant" (Gen. 32:10). When God commanded Moses to go before Pharaoh and demand the release of the Israelites, Moses replied, "Who am I, that I should go to Pharaoh, and that I should bring the sons of Israel out of Egypt?" (Ex. 3:11). In a similar way Gideon responded to God's call to deliver His people from Midian: "O Lord, how shall I deliver Israel? Behold, my family is the least in Manasseh, and I am the youngest in my father's house" (Judg. 6:15).

John the Baptist could not conceive of his baptizing Christ. "I have need to be baptized by You, and do You come to me?" (Matt. 3:14). The previous day John had told the crowds, "I baptize in water, but among you stands One whom you do not know. It is He who comes after me, the thong of whose sandal I am not worthy to untie" (John 1:26-27). Even self-confident Peter, after witnessing the miracle of the great catch of fish, "fell down at Jesus' feet, saying, 'Depart from me, for I am a sinful man, O Lord!'" (Luke 5:8). Paul served the Lord "with all humility" (Acts 20:19), acknowledging that "we are [not] adequate in ourselves to consider anything as coming from ourselves, but our adequacy is from God" (2 Cor. 3:5) and considering himself to be "the very least of all saints" (Eph. 3:8). God's choice people have always been humble.

In His incarnation Jesus Christ Himself gave the greatest example of humility. Paul speaks of Him as the One who, "although He existed in the form of God, did not regard equality with God a thing to be grasped, but emptied Himself, taking the form of a bond-servant, and being made in the likeness of men. And being found in appearance as a man, He humbled Himself by becoming obedient to the point of death, even death on a cross" (Phil. 2:6-8). Jesus even spoke of Himself as "gentle and humble in heart" (Matt. 11:29).

The Corinthian Christians, however, had not learned that virtue—not from the Old Testament saints or from Paul or even from the Lord Himself. Paul confronts the problem by contrasting the sin of their own conceit with the example of the apostles' humility.

THE CORINTHIANS' CONCEIT

Now these things, brethren, I have figuratively applied to myself and Apollos for your sakes, that in us you might learn not to exceed what is written, in order that no one of you might become arrogant in behalf of one against the other. For who regards you as superior? And what do you have that you did not receive? But if you did receive it, why do you boast as if you had not received it? You are already filled, you have already become rich, you have become kings without us; and I would indeed that you had become kings so that we also might reign with you. (4:6-8)

The Corinthians were proud and boastful. The cause of their factionalism—

with some claiming Paul, some Apollos, and some Cephas (1:12; 3:4, 22)—basically was pride. They were proud of their human wisdom and proud of their human leaders. It was that worldly, carnal pride that caused the serious divisions that plagued the church. Those leaders themselves were godly and humble servants of the Lord, and the Corinthians had much reason to be grateful for His having sent them such men. But instead of being grateful they were proud.

Throughout most of the letter thus far Paul had been teaching them not to exalt human wisdom and human leaders. **Now these things, brethren, I have figuratively applied to myself and Apollos for your sakes. These things** refers to the figures of farmers (3:6-9), builders (3:10-15), and servant-stewards (4:1-5), which refer to those who minister for the Lord. Paul tells his Corinthian **brethren** that he has applied these figures of speech and analogies to himself and Apollos. His reason is to begin to teach them not to exalt themselves, either: **that in us you might learn not to exceed what is written, in order that no one of you might become arrogant.** Paul (**myself**) and **Apollos** had been given as illustrations of what true ministers should be: humble servants and stewards (4:1). Servants are faithful and meek, not proud; stewards are trustworthy and submissive, not arrogant. Neither is any Christian to be.

God's faithful servants are to receive proper honor and respect. We are to "appreciate those who diligently labor among [us], and have charge over [us] in the Lord and give [us] instruction" (1 Thess. 5:12), and faithful elders should "be considered worthy of double honor, especially those who work hard at preaching and teaching" (1 Tim. 5:17). But they are to be honored only within such bounds of Scripture. Godly respect turns into ungodly exaltation when **we exceed what is written.** When loving gratitude and legitimate loyalty are contaminated with pride and conceit, Christ's church is fractured and weakened. What God intends as a means of unity Satan turns into a means of division.

The Corinthians had gone far beyond scriptural respect for ministers and had developed factions that were virtually sects. As is often the case, the leaders were exalted for the followers' own sakes, not for the leaders' sakes. The leaders were not a party to their glorification but were simply used as a focal point for the Corinthians' own pride. In fact, the humble example of their leaders was rejected; thus Paul had to remind them of his own humility and that of Apollos. The factions gave the Corinthians a means to **become arrogant in behalf of one against the other.**

When the Israelites were being delivered from Egypt, Moses was clearly the leader. Moses had stood before Pharaoh and demanded the release of his people. Through Moses the Lord had performed the great miracles that finally convinced Pharaoh to let them go. Moses was the undisputed head of his people. After the Lord sent a special anointing of his Spirit on seventy of the elders, two of them, Eldad and Medad, continued to prophesy in the camp after the others had stopped. When Moses was told what they were doing, his young assistant, Joshua, was annoyed and said, "'Moses, my lord, restrain them.' But Moses said to him, 'Are you jealous for my sake? Would that all the Lord's people were prophets, that the Lord would put His Spirit upon them!'" (Num. 11:28-29). Joshua's loyalty to Moses was misplaced. Misplaced loyalty, even to faithful men of God, inevitably brings hostility to others of God's servants. It causes envy, competition, and division.

Moses did not exalt himself and would not let others exalt him. That was the attitude of Paul and Apollos. "If we, as God's apostles and ministers, refuse to exalt ourselves or be exalted by you or anyone else," Paul was telling the Corinthians, "what reason do you have to exalt yourselves?" (An interesting comparison to this text can be made from Acts 14:8-18.)

The reason was arrogance. **Arrogant** (*phusioō*) literally means to "puff up" (KJV), inflate, blow up." The term was used metaphorically to indicate pride, which is having an inflated view of oneself. Paul uses that word four times to describe the Corinthian believers (see also 4:18, 19; 5:2) and three other times to warn them against pride (8:1; 13:4; 2 Cor. 12:20). The meaning of pride basically is "I'm for me." When everyone is pulling first of all for himself, fellowship and harmony are torn apart in the process.

A closely related sin is boasting. Pride must brag, but that is no more excusable than being arrogant. **Why do you boast?** Paul asked. Actually he asked the question in three parts. First, **For who regards you as superior?** "Why," he says, "do you think you are above other believers in the church? Why do you think your group is better than any other? You are made of the same stuff they are and have been redeemed by the same Lord. You are no better. You have nothing to boast of."

Second he asks, **And what do you have that you did not receive?** What does anyone have that, in one way or another, was not given to him? We did not give ourselves life, the food and care and protection we had as babies, an education, talents, the country we were born in, the opportunity to earn a living, the IQ we have, or anything else. No matter how hard we may have studied in school and worked at our business or profession, we would have nothing except for what the Lord and many others, by His providential hand, have given us.

Christians have been given even more. We have salvation, eternal life, God's presence within us, His Word, His spiritual gifts, His love, and countless other blessings for which we have done nothing and can do nothing. All those are gifts of God's grace. We have absolutely no good thing that we **did not receive** (cf. James 1:17; 1 Chron. 29:11-16). What does any person have to boast about?

If we have a good pastor, God gave him to us. If we have good parents, God gave them to us. If we live in a good country, God gave it to us. If we have a good mind or creative talent God gave it to us. We have no reason to boast either in people or possessions. Not only ministers, but all Christians, are but God's stewards. Everything we have is on loan from the Lord, entrusted to us for a while to use in serving Him.

The third question follows logically. **But if you did receive it, why do you boast as if you had not received it?** In other words, if they possessed only what someone else had given them, why were they boasting as if they had created the things themselves, or earned them? The whole foundation of their boasting was nothing more than a fabrication of their pride. Nothing is more self-deceitful than pride. We are inclined to believe almost anything about ourselves if it is favorable.

But Paul would not allow the Corinthians to remain self-deceived. He stripped away every excuse and broke down every defense. He loved them too much to allow Satan to so mislead and misuse them. The apostle was so concerned, and so determined that they would understand the seriousness of their sin, that he drove home his point with pointed sarcasm:

You are already filled, you have already become rich, you have become kings without us; and I would indeed that you had become kings so that we also might reign with you. (4:8)

To unmask their conceit he heaps on feigned praise. He tells the Corinthian believers they are great and wonderful. They are satiated with every good thing; they are wealthy; they are royal. They had it all. They had arrived. Except for the context, the Corinthians probably would have taken Paul's words in verse 8 at face value. That is exactly what they thought of themselves. Like the Laodiceans, they considered themselves to be rich and in need of nothing. Also like the Laodiceans, however, they were really "wretched and miserable and poor and blind and naked" (Rev. 3:17).

They were self-satisfied, and therefore were missing the blessing and satisfaction of those who "hunger and thirst for righteousness" (Matt. 5:6). They were not inclined to say with their former pastor, "Not that I have already obtained it, or have already become perfect" (Phil. 3:12), because, in their own mnds, they *had* obtained it. They already considered themselves to be reigning, as if their own Millennium had begun. **You have become kings without us.** Continuing the sarcasm, Paul suggested that they had received their crowns from Christ **without** (*chōris,* "without the agency of"; cf. John 1:3) assistance from him and Apollos, or from any of the other apostles.

At that point the sarcasm is modified, and Paul changes from reprimand to reflection. **I would indeed that you had become kings so that we also might reign with you.** Paul wished that it were really coronation time for all of them. If the Millennium had truly begun, they would have had true glory, shared with them by the Lord, and would truly be reigning with Him—and with Paul and Apollos. But that was not the case. The Corinthian believers were not reigning, and they had no cause at all to glory.

THE APOSTLE'S HUMILITY

For, I think, God has exhibited us apostles last of all, as men condemned to death; because we have become a spectacle to the world, both to angels and to men. We are fools for Christ's sake, but you are prudent in Christ; we are weak, but you are strong; you are distinguished, but we are without honor. To this present hour we are both hungry and thirsty, and are poorly clothed, and are roughly treated, and are homeless; and we toil, working with our own hands; when we are reviled, we bless; when we are persecuted, we endure; when we are slandered, we try to conciliate; we have become as the scum of

the world, the dregs of all things, even until now. (4:9-13)

The Father had allowed the Son to be sentenced to death and made a spectacle. Now **God has exhibited us apostles last of all, as men condemned to death.** To the world they were worthless teachers teaching worthless ideas, contributing nothing to mankind. The only thing they deserved was death. The imagery used here is of persons brought into the arena, condemned to die as criminals. The last ones brought out for slaughter were the grand finale. In this case, God brought the **apostles** out to be a spectacle in the sight of men in order to show His glory.

Verses 9-13 can be summarized by four words: spectacles, fools, sufferers, and scum. Those words describe Paul's condition in contrast to what the Corinthians considered their condition to be. They thought they had everything in themselves; he knew he had nothing in himself.

SPECTACLES

When a Roman general won a major victory it was celebrated by what was called a triumph. The general would enter the city in great military splendor, leading his officers and troops. Behind those would come a group of prisoners in chains, with the conquered king and his officers prominently displayed for all to see and mock. The prisoners were under the sentence of death and would be taken to the arena to fight wild beasts. That is the **spectacle** to which Paul refers. In the spiritual warfare he was fighting he was considered to be that sort of captive, that sort of conquered prisoner, **condemned to death.** James Moffatt translates, "God means us apostles to come in at the very end like doomed gladiators in the arena."

Shortly after His transfiguration Jesus told His disciples about His soon-coming arrest, death, and resurrection. They did not understand what He was talking about; but instead of asking Him to explain, they began to argue about which of them was greatest. When Jesus asked what they were discussing, they understandably were ashamed to reply.

> And sitting down, He called the twelve and said to them, "If anyone wants to be first, he shall be last of all, and servant of all." And taking a child, He set him before them, and taking him in His arms, He said to them, "Whoever receives one child like this in My name receives Me." (Mark 9:35-37)

The life of discipleship is the life of servanthood, and the life of servanthood is the life of humility—a life that so intimidates the world that it stands in danger of death (cf. John 10:2).

During the millennial kingdom the twelve apostles will reign with Christ on earth. They will "sit upon twelve thrones, judging the twelve tribes of Israel" (Matt. 19:28). But when they ministered on earth they did anything but rule. They became **a**

spectacle to the world, both to angels and to men. They were ridiculed, spit upon, imprisoned, beaten, mocked, an generally treated like criminals. Then they were last; but in Christ's coming kingdom they will be first.

FOOLS

Renewing the sarcasm, Paul says, **We are fools for Christ's sake, but you are prudent in Christ; we are weak, but you are strong; you are distinguished, but we are without honor.** "You still really think of the gospel as foolish and of its ministers as foolish. You are ashamed of being Christ's servant. You want glory, honor, and worldly recognition." The Corinthians still loved human wisdom. They were still tempted to look on preachers of the gospel as babblers, just as the Athenian philosophers had done (Acts 17:18). They could not bear to be **fools for Christ's sake,** and thought of themselves as **prudent, strong,** and **distinguished.**

SUFFERERS

The apostles not only were spectacles and fools but sufferers for Christ's sake. **To this present hour we are both hungry and thirsty, and are poorly clothed, and are roughly treated, and are homeless.** They lived in the lowest levels of society. While the Corinthian believers were living like kings, the apostles were living like slaves. The apostles had come to know firsthand the meaning of Jesus' words, "The foxes have holes, and the birds of the air have nests; but the Son of Man has nowhere to lay His head" (Matt. 8:20).

In his second letter to the Corinthians Paul cataloged his sufferings in the ministry:

> I [was] in far more labors, in far more imprisonments, beaten times without number, often in danger of death. Five times I received from the Jews thirty-nine lashes. Three times I was beaten with rods, once I was stoned, three times I was shipwrecked, a night and a day I have spent in the deep. I have been on frequent journeys, in dangers from rivers, dangers from robbers, dangers from my countrymen, dangers from the Gentiles, dangers in the city, dangers in the wilderness, dangers on the sea, dangers among false brethren; I have been in labor and hardship, through many sleepless nights, in hunger and thirst, often without food, in cold and exposure. Apart from such external things, there is the daily pressure upon me of concern for all the churches. (2 Cor. 11:23-28)

Paul also engaged in **toil** (*kopiaō,* "to work to the point of exhaustion") with his **own hands,** a kind of work considered by Greeks to be beneath their dignity. Manual work was for slaves. But Paul was not ashamed of any sort of treatment endured for His Lord or of any sort of work needed to be done for his Lord (cf. Acts 18:3; 20:34; 1 Thess. 2:9; 2 Thess. 3:8).

Nor was he resentful or bitter. **When we are reviled** (*loidoreō*, "to abuse with words"), **we bless; when we are persecuted, we endure; when we are slandered, we try to conciliate.** The apostles genuinely looked upon themselves as Christ's galley slaves and stewards. Their concern was to be humble and faithful. They had no time for resentment or jealousy. They knew that they were immeasurably better off than their persecutors. Knowing they would be first in the coming world, they were perfectly willing to be last in this world. This gave God the opportunity to demonstrate His power in their weakness.

SCUM

We have become as the scum of the world, the dregs of all things, even until now. It is clear from the following verse (14) that Paul was still contrasting himself and the other apostles with the Corinthians. They proudly saw themselves as being on top; the apostles humbly saw themselves as on the bottom.

Scum and **dregs** are synonyms and refer to scrapings or offscourings cleaned from a dirty dish or pot and then thrown away. The words were commonly used figuratively of the lowest, most degraded criminals, who often were sacrificed in pagan ceremonies. That is the way the world looked at the apostles. They were religious scum and dregs, and no better than the criminals like whom they were often treated.

It is not hard for believers to get along in the world as long as they keep the gospel to themselves. But if they preach, teach, and live God's full Word, the world takes great offense (cf. 2 Tim. 3:12). It resents being under the light of truth. Satan is the god of this world and the ruler of darkness. His kingdom cannot stand the light of the gospel and will persecute and destroy if possible those who stand for it and live in it. The world will attempt to scour off and throw away anyone who boldly proclaims the Word.

We are not scum and dregs in God's sight, but we are nevertheless servants and stewards. Therefore neither in the world's eyes nor in God's eyes do we have reason to boast in ourselves. That which the Lord loves in His servants, and that which eventually will bring them reward and glory, is a humble and obedient spirit. "Humble yourselves, therefore, under the mighty hand of God, that He may exalt you at the proper time" (1 Pet. 5:6).

Thus Paul brings to a climax the denunciation of the Corinthians' proud, divisive, and factious spirit.

Marks of a Spiritual Father (4:14-21)

12

I do not write these things to shame you, but to admonish you as my beloved children. For if you were to have countless tutors in Christ, yet you would not have many fathers; for in Christ Jesus I became your father through the gospel. I exhort you therefore, be imitators of me. For this reason I have sent to you Timothy, who is my beloved and faithful child in the Lord, and he will remind you of my ways which are in Christ, just as I teach everywhere in every church. Now some have become arrogant, as though I were not coming to you. But I will come to you soon, if the Lord wills, and I shall find out, not the words of those who are arrogant, but their power. For the kingdom of God does not consist in words, but in power. What do you desire? Shall I come to you with a rod or with love and a spirit of gentleness? (4:14-21)

In this epistle Paul has described the spiritual leader and teacher as a servant (3:5), a farmer (3:6), God's fellow worker (3:9), a builder (3:10), a galley slave ("servant," 4:1), and a steward (4:1). He now describes him as a spiritual father, using himself as the example.

The apostle has been stern, even to the point of sarcasm (4:8-10), in rebuking the Corinthians' sins. Now he tells them why he has been so harsh: he loves them as a father loves his children. He could not bear for them to be straying from God's Word and the fullness of the Christian life. He was their spiritual father and therefore doubly responsible for their spiritual welfare. He could say with John, "I have no greater joy than this, to hear of my children walking in the truth" (3 John 4; cf. Gal. 4:19; Phil. 1:23-27).

In 1 Corinthians 4:14-21 Paul presents by implication and pattern six characteristics of a faithful spiritual father: he admonishes, loves, begets, sets an example, teaches, and disciplines. He does not specifically label these characteristics or give them in chronological order or in order of importance. They are implied in what he says, and illustrate the various ways in which a faithful father is responsible for his children. They are elements necessary in an effective discipleship relation.

He Admonishes

I do not write these things to shame you, but to admonish you. (4:14a)

Paul was not being hard in his correction in order to **shame** the Corinthians, to make them cringe and cower. They had much to be ashamed of, and if they took the apostle's words to heart they could not have helped being ashamed. But it was not Paul's ultimate purpose to shame them. He would leave that to their own consciences. His purpose was to **admonish** them, exhort them, plead with them to repent and correct their ways. He did not want to destroy them but to reclaim them.

It is possible for a parent to correct a child in a way that tears down rather than builds up. In Ephesians Paul warns: "Fathers, do not provoke your children to anger; but bring them up in the discipline and instruction of the Lord" (Eph. 6:4). In the name of discipline, even Christian discipline, children can be provoked and abused in ways that leave permanent scars. They are often put down with criticism and punishment but seldom lifted up with admonition and encouragement.

Admonish (*noutheteō*) means literally "to put in mind," with the purpose of warning and reproving. It presupposes that something is wrong and its intention is to correct, to make right. Its purpose is to bring about a change—in belief, attitude, habit, life-style, or in whatever way is needed. In fact, it is a warning to change or incur judgment.

Eli was high priest at the tabernacle in Shiloh; but he was an irresponsible father. Only after he was very old did he question his sons' extremely sinful and wicked habits. At that point the sons, Hophni and Phinehas, were long grown and beyond his control. They abused the sacrificial offerings and committed fornication with the women who served at the tent of meeting. It seems that Eli was not even aware of what they were doing until told by some of the people. Scripture says that his own life and that of his sons ended tragically because he had not admonished them as a firm, caring, loving father. He had honored his sons above God, and in doing so he failed God and failed them (1 Sam. 2–4).

Failure to admonish spiritual children can be just as tragic. If we have spiritual responsibility over another believer, especially if we brought him to the Lord, there will be times when we *must* admonish. As a spiritual father we must lovingly criticize wrong beliefs or wrong behavior with the purpose of bringing correction and change (see Matt. 18:15-20; 1 Thess. 5:14). We must not browbeat or humiliate or judge self-righteously. A loving father does not do such things. But a loving father will always admonish, reprove, correct, and even discipline when necessary. He will do whatever he must that is right and proper for the welfare of his children. The tool for this is the Word of God, as indicated in 2 Timothy 3:16-17.

"You are witnesses," Paul told the Thessalonians, "and so is God, how devoutly and uprightly and blamelessly we behaved toward you believers; just as you know how we were exhorting and encouraging and imploring each one of you as a father would his own children, so that you may walk in a manner worthy of the God who calls you into His own kingdom and glory" (1 Thess. 2:10-12).

HE LOVES

as my beloved children. (4:14b)

Paul has referred to the Corinthians as his brothers several times (1:10; 2:1; 3:1), but now he calls them his children, which represents an even more intimate relationship. They are not merely children but **beloved children,** especially dear to their spiritual father. It is clear from what Paul has been saying to them that they were not obedient, morally upright, doctrinally sound, or mature. But they were loved.

Beloved is from the verb *agapaō,* which refers to the strongest kind of love, the deepest love. It is more than brotherly love (*philia*), a tender affection. It is a love that is determined and willful, having the one purpose of serving the object of love.

Some years later Paul again spoke of his great love for the Corinthians: "I will not be a burden to you; for I do not seek what is yours, but you; for children are not responsible to save up for their parents, but parents for their children. And I will most gladly spend and be expended for your souls" (2 Cor. 12:14-15). The Corinthians did little to deserve Paul's love, but they had it in full measure. His love for them gave everything and asked for nothing. It was self-sacrificing, far reaching, and lasting.

A loving father wants to *understand* his children as deeply as possible. He wants to know where they hurt so that he can help heal. He wants to know when they are afraid so he can help dispel their fears. He wants to know where they are weak so he can help strengthen them. He wants to know their needs so he can help meet them. Paul loved the Corinthians in that way. He loved them, understanding their situation and their needs.

A loving father is *gentle*. Jesus was "gentle and humble in heart" (Matt. 11:29), and Paul sought to treat the Corinthians with "the meekness and gentleness of Christ" (2 Cor. 10:1). Spiritual children, like natural children, grow slowly. They are not born mature and must be trained lovingly and gently, as well as carefully and sometimes sternly (cf. 1 Thess. 2:7-8).

A loving father is also *intense*. When those we love are in danger, we cannot help becoming concerned. When our children were small I worried about their running into the street. So I lectured and explained about the dangers of getting hit by a car. I would sometimes wake up in the night with a jolt, having dreamed of one of the children being run over. Love cannot help feeling intense concern and getting excited at times. The more our loved ones are threatened and endangered, the more intense our love becomes. We should have the same sort of concern for our spiritual loved ones, our children in the Lord. Paul's testimony to the Ephesian elders was that he tearfully admonished "night and day for a period of three years" out of love for his children in the faith (Acts 20:31).

HE BEGETS

For if you were to have countless tutors in Christ, yet you would not have many fathers; for in Christ Jesus I became your father through the gospel. (4:15)

As already mentioned, Paul is not discussing spiritual fatherhood chronologically. As in natural fatherhood, procreation must occur before there can be love or admonition. A child must be born before he can be cared for and trained.

Paul here illustrates the uniqueness of fatherhood. No child can have more than one natural father. In the spiritual realm as well, the Corinthians had **countless tutors** in Christ but only one spiritual **father.** Paul was the spiritual father of most of them. It is important to note here that he is not saying that he was the source of spiritual life (cf. Matt. 23:9, a reference to Jewish religious leaders who felt as though they were the true source of life), but was the tool God used.

Countless (*murios*) can represent the specific figure of ten thousand, as in the KJV, or simply a great, numberless amount. **Tutors** (*paidagōgos*) refers to home instructors, usually slaves, who were responsible for the basic training and moral upbringing of small children. They were not teachers in a formal sense but were more guardians and helpers.

The Corinthians, Paul tells them, could have had innumerable spiritual tutors of various sorts, and all of those may have been helpful to one degree or another. But he was uniquely their spiritual father.

A father, by definition, is a man who has children. He is the agent of God's creating a life. A man can be a man without having children and even a husband without having children. But he cannot be a father without having children. A Christian cannot be a spiritual father without being used by God to bring life to spiritual children.

Unfortunately, many Christians have never become spiritual fathers. They have never produced any spiritual offspring. They have never led a person to Christ and helped train him in the ways of God. A Christian is one who has been given new life in Christ, and one of the most important characteristics of life is reproduction. Yet many believers have never reproduced believers. In a sense they are contradictions to what a Christian is. Every believer should be a spiritual father, God's instrument for bringing new lives into His kingdom. That begins the discipling process.

Paul left spiritual progeny everywhere he visited and ministered. He had founded numerous churches in the province of Galatia, and when he wrote to them he addressed them not only as his brothers (Gal. 1:11;4:12) but also as his children (4:19). Paul called Timothy his "true child in the faith" (1 Tim. 1:2) and Titus his "true child in a common faith" (Titus (1:4). The runaway slave Onesimus was the apostle's "child, whom [he had] begotten in [his] imprisonment" (Philem. 10). Everywhere he went he led people to Christ, thereby becoming their spiritual father.

The apostle did not claim to have the power of spiritual procreation. **In Christ Jesus I became your father through the gospel.** The source of every spiritual birth is the power of God in Christ coupled with the Word of God. Only "that which is born of the Spirit is spirit" (John 3:6) and "In the exercise of [God's] will He brought us forth by the word of truth" (James 1:18).

But the Lord also has chosen to use human agents as His witnesses (Acts 1:8), to "make disciples of all the nations" (Matt. 28:19). Jesus commanded us to pray for "the Lord of the harvest to send out workers into His harvest" (Matt. 9:38). The fruit of the harvest is entirely in the Lord's hands, but He has called us to be His co-laborers in His fields. Charles Hodge said, "For though multitudes are converted by the Spirit through the Word without any ministerial intervention, just as grain springs up here and there without a husbandman, yet it is the ordinance of God that the harvest of souls should be gathered by workmen appointed for that purpose."

God's harvesters become the spiritual fathers of those they "reap" for the Lord.

He Sets an Example

I exhort you therefore, be imitators of me. For this reason I have sent to you Timothy, who is my beloved and faithful child in the Lord, and he will remind you of my ways which are in Christ. (4:16-17a)

Without a good example, a parent's teaching cannot be effective. A spiritual father must set the example for his spiritual children, as Paul was careful to do. With confidence, but without bragging, he could say, **be imitators of me.** He not only could say, "Do as I say," but also, "Do as I do." The Greek term is equivalent to our word *mimic* (cf. Matt. 23:3).

Often the hardest place to disciple is in the home. When we disciple those outside our families, they often see us only in ideal situations, where it is easy to act spiritual and mature. But our children see us in all of our moods, in all of our attitudes and actions. They know firsthand if we are living up to what we are trying to teach them. If we are not, most of our instruction and admonition will fall on deaf ears. Even if we sincerely love them, our children are more likely to follow what we do than what we say. Having godly children is required of an elder (1 Tim. 3:4-5) in part, at least, because that is good evidence that he himself is godly. Discipling is more than teaching right principles; it is also living those principles before the ones being discipled (cf. 1 Tim. 4:12).

Paul was so successful as a discipler that he could entrust his discipling to those he had discipled. **For this reason I have sent to you Timothy, who is my beloved and faithful child in the Lord, and he will remind you of my ways which are in Christ.** **For this reason** refers to the goal of making the Corinthians imitators of Paul. To accomplish that he sent Timothy. What a thought! Timothy was so like Paul that he could be sent as a Pauline model. The apostle had done such a complete work as a spiritual father to Timothy that he could send Timothy to continue discipling the Corinthians on his behalf. He was a replica. That is the epitome of raising spiritual children: being able to send them to work in our place. When we are Christlike, those we disciple will be more likely to become Christlike and be able to help others become Christlike. This obviously provides a potentially great multiplication of ministry. Paul loved Timothy and commended him as a faithful child who would bring back to mind the Christlike life pattern of Paul, because it was also his own life pattern.

He Teaches

just as I teach everywhere in every church. (4:17*b*)

We cannot believe truths we do not know or live principles we have never heard of. A major part of discipling is teaching the Word of God, telling and explaining its truths.

In the case of the Corinthian church, Paul had already taught them carefully for eighteen months (Acts 18:11). They had been thoroughly grounded in the Word. Timothy's job was to **remind** them of what Paul had taught and of the way he had lived among them. His discipling was a follow-up of the apostle's. Paul had taught the same truths **everywhere in every church,** indicating that he is referring to doctrine rather than some specific advice, and Timothy's job was to reinforce those great eternal truths by his own teaching and his own example.

It is not enough to be correct in what we teach; we must also be understandable. We must put aside our degrees, academic accomplishments, and theological jargon and simply speak the truth plainly and in love (Eph. 4:15). If we love those we witness to and disciple, our objective will not be to impress them with our learning but to help them with theirs. Bishop John Ryle was convinced that one of the keys to the 18th century revival in England was the simplicity of the preaching of such men as Wesley and Whitefield. He said, "They were not ashamed to crucify their style or sacrifice their reputation for learning. They carried out the maxim of Augustine, who said that a wooden key is not as beautiful as a gold one, but if it can open the door when the gold one cannot, it is far more useful." It is not sermonizing that is needed, nor homilies demonstrating cleverness, but sound, true doctrine out of Scripture to counter the wisdom of men (cf. 2:1-8).

Jesus' teaching not only was the supreme model of power and depth but of simplicity. The great crowds to whom He preached were composed mostly of common, uneducated folk. Yet they "enjoyed listening to Him," or, as in the King James Version, "the common people heard him gladly" (Mark 12:37).

He Disciplines

Now some have become arrogant, as though I were not coming to you. But I will come to you soon, if the Lord wills, and I shall find out, not the words of those who are arrogant, but their power. For the kingdom of God does not consist in words, but in power. What do you desire? Shall I come to you with a rod or with love and a spirit of gentleness? (4:18-21)

There are times when spiritual fathers, like natural fathers, have to discipline their children. When a Christian slips into wrong doctrine or wrong behavior he needs correction. He needs to be told in love, but with firmness, "Your testimony is not what it ought to be. You are not living by the Bible principles you have learned. You need to change." Such confrontations are never easy but they are often necessary.

Some of the Corinthians not only had slipped into sin but had **become arrogant** (*phusioō*, "to inflate, puff up, blow up") about it. Thinking they would probably never see Paul again, **as though** [he] **were not coming,** they thought they could get by with doing as they pleased. They may have been so arrogant as to think Paul would not dare to confront them. The church had a serious problem with pride and self-will, and when strong spiritual leadership was not in place, many believers easily slipped back into their old ways of thinking and behaving.

But contrary to what they hoped, Paul assured them that he planned to see them again and **soon.** He knew better than to make plans that were not subject to the Lord's change, and so added, **if the Lord wills.** More than once he had made plans for his ministry that he was not able to carry out. On the second missionary journey Paul, Silas, and Timothy "were trying to go into Bithynia, and the Spirit of Jesus did not permit them" (Acts 16:7). God's plan was for them to begin evangelizing farther west, into what we now know as Europe, and so they went to Macedonia instead of Bithynia. It is always presumptuous to make plans, even for the Lord's own work, that are not willingly open to His approval and change.

In spite of what they thought Paul might be afraid to do, if he went back to Corinth his first order of business would be to call the bluff of those who were blatant in their backsliding. He would soon discover **not the words of those who are arrogant, but their power.** He would not let their sinning go unchallenged. For their own sakes, as well as the gospel's, he could not fail to discipline them. An undisciplined child belongs to parents who do not deeply care about his welfare. Paul was too loving a spiritual father not to discipline. As he expected the Corinthians to follow his example, he would follow God's: "For whom the Lord loves He reproves, even as a father, the son in whom he delights" (Prov. 3:12; cf. Heb. 12:6; Rev. 3:19).

The arrogant backsliders talked a lot about their freedom and independence and rights, much as do many professing believers today who buy the world's philosophy and like to ape its ways. They no doubt thought they had good arguments for Paul in the event he showed up. But he would be checking their spiritual power, not their words, the inside not the outside. God's people should reflect God's **kingdom,** His rule and glory, which **does not consist in words, but in power.** This is a central principle of great importance. Faith that does not result in right living may have many words to support it, but it will have no power. A person's true spiritual character is not determined by the impressiveness of his words but by the power of his life (cf. Matt. 7:21-23).

Paul was hopeful that the erring Corinthians would repent of their arrogance and change before he returned. He gave them a choice. **What do you desire? Shall I come to you with a rod or with love and a spirit of gentleness?** Paul had made his own preference clear. He did not want to shame them, but to admonish them as children whom he loved dearly (v.14). That is the mark of every godly father.

If he needed to use a stick to shape them up, he would use one. He does not have in mind a literal stick to beat them with, but an attitude and spirit of strong, painful discipline. He would deal sternly with their pride, the sin God hates most. But if they responded favorably to his letter, he would treat them with restrained, patient kindness.

In his dealing with that wayward church that he loved so dearly, Paul demonstrates the elements for effective discipling of spiritual children.

Immorality in the Church (5:1-13)

13

It is actually reported that there is immorality among you, and immorality of such a kind as does not exist even among the Gentiles, that someone has his father's wife. And you have become arrogant, and have not mourned instead, in order that the one who had done this deed might be removed from your midst. For I, on my part, though absent in body but present in spirit, have already judged him who has so committed this, as though I were present. In the name of our Lord Jesus, when you are assembled, and I with you in spirit, with the power of our Lord Jesus, I have decided to deliver such a one to Satan for the destruction of his flesh, that his spirit may be saved in the day of the Lord Jesus. Your boasting is not good. Do you not know that a little leaven leavens the whole lump of dough? Clean out the old leaven, that you may be a new lump, just as you are in fact unleavened. For Christ our Passover also has been sacrificed. Let us therefore celebrate the feast, not with old leaven, nor with the leaven of malice and wickedness, but with the unleavened bread of sincerity and truth.

I wrote you in my letter not to associate with immoral people; I did not at all mean with the immoral people of this world, or with the covetous and swindlers, or with idolaters; for then you would have to go out of the world. But actually, I wrote to you not to associate with any so-called brother if he should be an immoral person, or covetous, or an idolater, or a reviler, or

121

a drunkard, or a swindler—not even to eat with such a one. For what have I
to do with judging outsiders? Do you not judge those who are within the
church? But those who are outside, God judges. Remove the wicked man
from among yourselves. (5:1-13)

The city of Corinth in Paul's day was like much of western society today.
People were strongly intent on having their own ways. In no regard were they more
intent than in regard to fulfilling physical lust. Sexual permissiveness was rampant;
and then, as now, the church was not unaffected.

All of 1 Corinthians 5 is devoted to the problem of immorality in the church,
much of it specifically to sexual immorality. As serious as the immorality itself was the
church's tolerance of it. Probably because of their philosophical orientation and their
love of human wisdom they rationalized the immoral behavior of their fellow
believers. In any case they were not inclined to take corrective measures. Even those
who were not involved in immorality had become arrogant about the matter (v. 2),
possibly citing their "freedom in Christ," as do many believers today. Apparently there
were many who arrogantly flaunted their vice in the church.

The chapter is not directed at the believers, or "so-called" believers (v. 11), who
were committing the sins but at the rest of the church who stood by doing nothing
about it—in fact, arrogantly *refusing* to do anything about it.

From 1:10 through 4:21 Paul has been dealing with the more philosophical
and psychological types of sin, the sins of intellect and attitude. The division in the
church was primarily caused by party spirit, seen in its numerous exclusive groups,
with each group considering itself to have the inside track on spirituality.

Chapter 5, however, focuses primarily on sins of the flesh. But those sins are
not unrelated to those of the mind or heart, because all sin is related. Sin in one area
always makes us more susceptible to sin in other areas. In our own day, the rise in
sexual sins and sins of violence closely parallel the rise in humanistic education and
amoral philosophy, and correspond to an increase in pride and self-satisfaction, and a
decreased concern for the things of God.

Paul's thrust in this chapter is for discipline of persistently sinning church
members. He presents the need, the method, the reason, and the sphere of the
discipline that should be imposed.

The Need for Discipline

It is actually reported that there is immorality among you, and immorality of
such a kind as does not exist even among the Gentiles, that someone has his
father's wife. And you have become arrogant, and have not mourned instead.
(5:1-2a)

The first things the Corinthians needed to see was the need for discipline.

Because they apparently had rationalized or minimized the immorality in their midst, they saw no need for discipline. Paul's first step was to show them that the immorality *was* immorality and that it was serious and should not be tolerated—something they already should have known. The fact that it was **actually reported that there is immorality among you,** indicates it was common information and should have been as shocking to them as it was to Paul.

The church had been carefully taught by Paul and other ministers. The Corinthian believers were well grounded in Christian doctrine and morals. They also had been told, in a previous, nonbiblical epistle from Paul, of the need for discipline of believers who persisted in sin. "I wrote you in my letter not to associate with immoral people" (v. 9). But sadly, the problems Paul addresses in this chapter were not new to the Corinthians, and were being tolerated by them.

The Corinthian church had a general reputation for immorality, and word of it had come to Paul more than once. As just mentioned, he had written them about it previously. But the particular problem he mentions first was **immorality of such a kind as does not exist even among the Gentiles, that someone has his father's wife.**

Immorality is the Greek *porneia,* from which we get *pornography,* and refers to any illicit sexual activity. In this case it was a form of incest, because a man was living with his father's wife, that is, his stepmother. The term **father's wife** indicates that the woman was not his natural mother but had married his father after his mother had died or been divorced.

That God considers such a relationship incestuous is clear from the Old Testament. Sexual relations between a man and his stepmother was in the same category as relations between him and his natural mother. Anyone guilty of those or other sexual "abominations" was to be cut off from his people (Lev. 18:7-8, 29; cf. Deut. 22:30), a reference to capital punishment. From Cicero and others we know that such incest was also strictly forbidden under Roman law. As Paul observes, it did **not exist even among the Gentiles.** A church member in Corinth was guilty of a sin that even his pagan neighbors did not practice or tolerate. The testimony of the church in Corinth was thereby severely hindered.

Three things about that particular relationship seem evident. First, the present tense **has** indicates that the sinful activity had been going on for some time and was still going on. It was not a one-time or short-term affair but was continuous and open. They may have been living together as if man and wife. Second, since adultery is not charged, the relationship between the son and his stepmother probably had caused her to be divorced from the father. At that time neither of them was legally married. Third, because Paul calls for no discipline of the woman, perhaps she was not a Christian. The man, therefore, being a believer, not only was immorally but unequally related to the woman (2 Cor. 6:14).

More shocking to Paul than the sin itself was the church's toleration of it. **And you have become arrogant, and have not mourned instead.** Nothing seemed to break through their pride and boasting (cf. 1:12; 3:3, 21; 4:6-7, 18). They were so self-satisfied and self-confident that they excused or rationalized the most wicked behavior within the congregation. Perhaps they looked on the incest as an expression of their Christian liberty, or perhaps they looked on their toleration of it as an expression of Christian love. In any case their arrogance blinded them to the clear truth of God's standards. Perhaps they felt so secure as members of a party attached to a great spiritual leader (Paul, Apollos, or Peter; see 1:12) that they thought they could sin without consequence.

They should have **mourned instead**. A church that does not mourn over sin, especially sin within its own fellowship, is on the edge of spiritual disaster. When we cease to be shocked by sin we lose a strong defense against it. Alexander Pope wrote:

> Vice is a monster of so frightful mien,
> As to be hated needs but to be seen;
> Yet seen too oft, familiar with her face,
> We first endure, then pity, then embrace.

That was the pattern followed by the church in Corinth. She arrogantly followed her own feelings and rationalizations rather than God's Word, and found herself ignoring, and perhaps even justifying, flagrant sin in her midst.

The church at Thyatira in many ways was a model church. It was strong in "love and faith and service and perseverance" and was growing in good deeds. But it was tolerating "the woman Jezebel, who calls herself a prophetess, and she teaches and leads My bond-servants astray, so that they commit acts of immorality" (Rev. 2:19-20). Someone in the church, claiming to speak for God, was actually leading the believers into immoral practices. Though rebuked, she refused to repent. Consequently she, and all who participated in immorality with her, became subject to God's severe judgment. The punishment was to be a warning to all Christians and a reminder of God's righteous standards for His people and of His knowing their minds and hearts (vv. 21-23). God takes the purity of His church seriously, and He commands His children to take it equally seriously.

Whenever sin is not repented of and cleansed, it increases and spreads its infection. When Paul wrote his next epistle to the church at Corinth he was still deeply concerned about its spiritual and moral condition. "I am afraid that when I come again my God may humiliate me before you, and I may mourn over many of those who have sinned in the past and not repented of the impurity, immorality and sensuality which they have practiced" (2 Cor. 12:21). Because the Corinthians refused to mourn, they caused Paul to mourn and the Holy Spirit to grieve (Eph. 4:30).

Christians are not to tolerate sin within the church any more than they are to tolerate it within their own lives. "But do not let immorality or any impurity or greed even be named among you, as is proper among saints. . . . And do not participate in the unfruitful deeds of darkness, but instead even expose them" (Eph. 5:3, 11). It is the responsibility of all church members, not simply the pastor and other leaders, to expose sinful practices in the fellowship. Without being self-righteous or prying, we are required to be continually on the lookout for any sort of immorality or sin that threatens the purity of our Lord's body, the church. We must recognize the need for identifying and cleansing sin within the church. When it is found we should be in spiritual mourning until it is cleansed.

THE METHOD OF DISCIPLINE

in order that the one who had done this deed might be removed from your midst. For I, on my part, though absent in body but present in spirit, have already judged him who has so committed this, as though I were present. In the name of our Lord Jesus, when you are assembled, and I with you in spirit, with the power of our Lord Jesus, I have decided to deliver such a one to Satan for the destruction of his flesh, that his spirit may be saved in the day of the Lord Jesus. (5:2b-5)

Paul makes clear the action that should have been taken to discipline the man who refused to repent of and forsake his blatant immorality. He should have been excommunicated, **removed from your midst.**

Jesus set forth the basic method of church discipline:

> And if your brother sins, go and reprove him in private; if he listens to you, you have won your brother. But if he does not listen to you, take one or two more with you, so that by the mouth of two or three witnesses every fact may be confirmed. And if he refuses to listen to them, tell it to the church; and if he refuses to listen even to the church, let him be to you as a Gentile and a tax-gatherer. (Matt. 18:15-17)

Discipline is not inconsistent with love. It is lack of discipline, in fact, that is inconsistent with love. "Those whom the Lord loves He disciplines, and He scourges every son whom He receives" (Heb. 12:6). The Lord disciplines his children because he loves them, and we will discipline our brothers and sisters in the Lord if we truly love Him and truly love them.

For I, on my part, though absent in body but present in spirit, have already judged him who has so committed this, as though I were present. Paul called on the Corinthian church to acknowledge with him the seriousness of the offense, to recognize the need for discipline, and to take appropriate action—as Paul had already done as if he were there. He is saying that he had in his inner spirit passed judgment on the sinning person and had affirmed the mandatory consequences.

The church was to come together **in the name of our Lord Jesus and with the power of our Lord Jesus.** That is, they were come together to do what they knew to be Christ's will in the matter, to do what He would do if He were there. They were aware of the principles Jesus had taught (Matt. 18), and the apostle calls on the people to apply those principles. As the Lord had instructed, the local congregation was responsible for the discipline. And when a local church acts in Jesus' **name,** that is according to His Word, they can be sure they are acting in His **power.** It is in the context of His teaching about church discipline that the Lord said, "Whatever you shall bind on earth shall be bound in heaven; and whatever you loose on earth shall be loosed in heaven" and "If two of you agree on earth about anything that they may ask, it shall be done for them by My Father who is in heaven. For where two or three have gathered together in My name, there I am in their midst" (Matt. 18:18-20). The Lord will always bless and empower what we truly do in His name. If we have followed His instruction to be sure that "every fact may be confirmed" (v. 16), we know that our decision about guilt or innocence (binding or loosing) will be in accordance with heaven's. When we meet in His name He is always with us—doing the discipline Himself (cf. Eph. 5:25-27). Never is the church more in harmony with heaven and operating in perfect accord with her Lord than when dealing with sin to maintain purity.

When the Corinthians were **assembled** to take disciplinary action Paul would be with them **in spirit.** The apostle had taught them as a pastor, was now writing them for the second time (1 Cor. 5:9), and intended to continue to give them his counsel and encouragement in doing the Lord's will—even when he could not be with them in person.

To put the offending believer out of their fellowship, to excommunicate him, would be **to deliver such a one to Satan for the destruction of his flesh.** Satan is the ruler of this world, and turning a believer over to Satan, therefore, thrusts the believer back into the world on his own, apart from the care and support of Christian fellowship. That person has forfeited his right to participation in the church of Jesus Christ, which He intends to keep pure at all costs. The word **deliver** (*paradidōmi*) is a strong term indicating the judicial act of sentencing, of handing over for punishment. The sentence passed on a sinning believer is to be given **to Satan.** Paul excommunicated Hymenaeus and Alexander because of their continued and unrepented blasphemy. They were Christian brothers, but he "delivered [them] over to Satan that they may be taught not to blaspheme" (1 Tim. 1:20).

The result of such discipline is **the destruction of the flesh. Destruction** (*olethros*) may refer even to death. It is used frequently in connection with divine judgment on sin. But Satan has no power over the spirits of believers. When Satan attacked Job, he was only allowed to harm that man of God physically. He could destroy his possessions and afflict his body, but he could not destroy his soul. The inner believer belongs entirely to Christ and we have the absolute assurance that he will **be saved in the day of the Lord Jesus.** But in the meanwhile the unrepentant believer may be turned over to suffer greatly at the hands of Satan.

Jesus made it clear that all suffering and affliction is not the direct result of sin—just as Job's was not. When the disciples assumed that the man born blind was being punished because of sin, Jesus replied, "It was neither that this man sinned, nor his parents; but it was in order that the works of God might be displayed in him" (John 9:2-3). Scripture is just as clear, however, that sickness may be the direct result of sin. Because some of the Corinthian Christians had abused and unworthily participated in the Lord's Supper, Paul told them, "For this reason many among you are weak and sick, and a number sleep" (1 Cor. 11:30). Physical weakness, sickness, and even death can result from persistent sinning. When Ananias and Saphira lied to the church about the proceeds from the sale of their property, they also lied to the Holy Spirit. Their wickedness caused them to die on the spot, "And great fear came upon the whole church, and upon all who heard of these things" (Acts 5:1-11). Because they were believers, the Lord took them to be with Himself, but He could not allow such wickedness to corrupt the church.

The **destruction of the flesh** indicates that the incestuous man in Corinth would eventually die unless he repented of his sin. We are not told of the specific affliction, disease, or circumstances, but his body was on the way to destruction in a special disciplinary way. If he kept sinning, his life would end before he otherwise would have died. He would go to heaven, because he was a believer; but he would go before he should have gone. To protect His church, the Lord would have to take him early. Since some believers hold so tightly to this life because they have such limited vision of heaven, such deadly discipline acts as a warning of what might happen to them because of sin.

Perhaps the man did repent. He may be the one spoken of in 2 Corinthians, whom Paul said should be forgiven and comforted and for whom they should reaffirm their love, "in order that no advantage be taken of us by Satan; for we are not ignorant of his schemes" (2:5-11). A disciplined brother is still a brother and is never to be despised, even when unrepentant (2 Thess. 3:14-15). And if he repents, he is to be forgiven and restored in love (Gal. 6:1-2).

The Reason for Discipline

Your boasting is not good. Do you not know that a little leaven leavens the whole lump of dough? Clean out the old leaven, that you may be a new lump, just as you are in fact unleavened. For Christ our Passover also has been sacrificed. Let us therefore celebrate the feast, not with old leaven, nor with the leaven of malice and wickedness, but with the unleavened bread of sincerity and truth. (5:6-8)

Discipline sometimes must be severe because the consequences of not disciplining are much worse. Sin is a spiritual malignancy and it will not long stay isolated. Unless removed it will spread its infection until the whole fellowship of believers is diseased.

The Corinthians could not face that truth, although they had been taught it long before. Their pride caused them to be forgetful and neglectful, and Paul tells them, **Your boasting is not good.** "Look where your arrogance and your boasting have brought you. Because you still love human wisdom and human recognition and the things of this world, you are completely blinded to the blatant sin that will destroy your church if you don't remove it." **Do you not know that a little leaven leavens the whole lump of dough?** In a more modern figure he was saying, "Don't you know that one rotten apple can spoil the whole barrel?"

God diagnoses spiritual health only by the standards of His righteousness. We can be highly gifted, highly blessed, highly successful, and highly respected—and also be highly sinful. That was the condition of the Corinthian church. The believers there had been under the ministry of Paul, Apollos, and Peter. They were "enriched in [Christ], in all speech and all knowledge," the "testimony concerning Christ was confirmed" in them, and they were "not lacking in any gift" (1:5-7). Yet they were proud, arrogant, boastful, and immoral—even tolerant of sins, including a sin that pagans condemned.

Similarly, the scribes and the Pharisees of Jesus' day were quite satisfied with themselves. They loved "the place of honor at banquets," the "respectful greetings in the market place," and "being called by men, Rabbi" (Matt. 23:6-7). They thought they deserved such recognition. But Jesus pronounced on them a long series of "woes," in which He pointed out sin after sin of which they were guilty. He characterized them as blind and hypocritical. Their unchecked pride completely blinded them to the most obvious of spiritual principles, and their arrogance caused them to live lives of continuous pretense. "You serpents, you brood of vipers," Jesus said, "how shall you escape the sentence of hell?" (vv. 13-33). But such pride is less offensive in the case of spiritual hypocrites like the Jews to whom our Lord spoke than it is in the assembly of believers.

A large congregation, an impressive Sunday school, active witnessing and visitation and counseling, and every other sort of good program give no protection or justification to a church that is not faithful in cleansing itself. When sin is willingly, or even neglectfully, allowed to go unchallenged and undisciplined, a larger church will be in danger of a larger malignancy.

In ancient times, when bread was about to be baked, a small piece of dough was pulled off and saved. That **little leaven,** or yeast, would then be allowed to ferment in water, and would later be kneaded into the next batch of fresh dough to make it rise.

Leaven in Paul's illustration, as throughout Scripture, represents influence. Usually it refers to the influence of evil, though in Matthew 13:33 it represents the good influence of the kingdom of heaven. In this case, however, evil influence is in view. **The whole lump of dough** is here the local church. If given opportunity, sin will permeate a whole church just as leaven permeates a whole loaf. Sin's nature is to ferment, corrupt, and spread.

For the Jews, leaven historically had also represented something bad from the past brought over into the present. When God was preparing Israel to leave Egypt He instructed His people to sprinkle lamb's blood on their doorposts and lintels so that, in the last of the ten plagues on Egypt, the angel of death would pass over and not slay their firstborn (Ex. 12:23). And when they baked bread in preparation for the trek out of Egypt, the Israelites were not allowed to add leaven. For one thing, they did not have time to knead the leaven into the dough and wait for it to rise, since "they could not delay" (v. 39). For another, bread represented sustenance of life, and the Passover and Exodus represented deliverance from the old life (in Egypt) and entrance into the new life (in the Promised Land). The leaven represented the old life—the way of Egypt, the way of the world—which was to be left entirely behind. Consequently, while they were traveling out of Egypt and during every subsequent Passover celebration, the Lord commanded that "nothing leavened shall be seen among you" (13:3, 7). Every bit of leaven was to be thrown out.

Christians likewise are to be separated from the old life. We are to bring none of it into the new life. **Clean out the old leaven, that you may be a new lump, just as you are in fact unleavened. For Christ our Passover also has been sacrificed. Clean out** is expressed with the use of a compound word (*ekkathairō,* "to purge or cleanse thoroughly") to emphasize the completeness of cleansing. As pictured in the Passover in Egypt, the sacrifice of Jesus Christ, God's perfect Passover Lamb, and the placing of His blood over us, completely separates us from the dominion of sin and the penalty of judgment. We, too, are to remove everything from the old life that would taint and permeate the new. As Israel was set free from Egypt as a result of the Passover and was to make a clean break with that oppressor, so the believer is to be totally separated from his old life, with its sinful attitudes, standards, and habits. Christ died to separate us from bondage to sin and give us a new bondage to righteousness (Rom. 6:19), which is the only true freedom.

David Brainerd, who spent his short adult life as a missionary to the American Indians, wrote in his diary:

> I never got away from Jesus, and him crucified, and I found that when my people were gripped by this great evangelical doctrine of Christ and him crucified, I had no need to give them instructions about morality. I found that one followed as the sure and inevitable fruit of the other. . . . I find my Indians begin to put on the garments of holiness and their common life begins to be sanctified even in small matters when they are possessed by the doctrine of Christ and him crucified.

One of the greatest protections from sin that we have as Christians is simply focusing on our Lord and on the sacrifice He made for us. To understand that His death for sin applied to us calls us away from sin and to a clean break with the old ways is to understand the sanctifying work of the cross (see Titus 2:11-14). It is impossible to be occupied with this truth and with sin at the same time.

The conclusion of Paul's point is that we are to continue to **celebrate the feast, not with old leaven, nor with the leaven of malice and wickedness, but with the unleavened bread of sincerity and truth.** The Old Testament Passover was celebrated but once a year, as a reminder of the deliverance from Egypt. The Christian's celebration should be continuous. Our every thought, every plan, every intention should be under Christ's control. The perfect **unleavened bread** He desires us to eat is that of **sincerity and truth. Sincerity** is the attitude of genuine honesty and integrity, from which **truth** results. In this context, those two words are synonyms for purity, the purity of the cleansed new life in Jesus Christ—which has no place for **the leaven,** the impurity, **of malice and wickedness. Malice** speaks of an evil nature or disposition. Wickedness is the act that manifests that evil disposition. We are called to celebrate our Passover in Christ not with an annual feast but with constant life devotion to purity and rejection of sin.

Discipline in the church assists in this celebration by removing impurities that will contaminate and corrupt it. It preserves Christ's Body from the permeation of evil.

THE SPHERE OF DISCIPLINE

I wrote you in my letter not to associate with immoral people; I did not at all mean with the immoral people of this world, or with the covetous and swindlers, or with idolaters; for then you would have to go out of the world. But actually, I wrote to you not to associate with any so-called brother if he should be an immoral person, or covetous, or an idolater, or a reviler, or a drunkard, or a swindler—not even to eat with such a one. For what have I to do with judging outsiders? Do you not judge those who are within the church? But those who are outside, God judges. Remove the wicked man from among yourselves. (5:9-13)

The discipline God commands His church to take against the unrepentant is to be of a certain kind and should be exercised within certain bounds. These verses indicate some types of offenses that require discipline and give further explanation as to how the discipline is to be carried out.

In a previous letter (see Introduction) Paul had commanded the Corinthian Christians **not to associate with immoral people. Associate with** translates *sunanamignumi,* which literally means "to mix up with." In this compound form it is more intense and means "to keep intimate, close company with."

Faithful believers are not to keep close company with any fellow believers who persistently practice serious sins such as those mentioned here. If the offenders will not listen to the counsel and warning of two or three other believers and not even of the whole church, they are to be put out of the fellowship. They should not be allowed to participate in any activities of the church—worship services, Sunday school, Bible studies, or even social events. Obviously, and most importantly, they should not be allowed to have any leadership role. They should be totally cut off both from individual and corporate fellowship with other Christians, including that of eating together (v. 11; cf. 2 Thess. 3:6-15).

No exceptions are made. Even if the unrepentant person is a close friend or family member, he is to be put out. If he is a true believer he will not lose his salvation because of the sin (v. 5), but he is to lose contact with fellow believers, in order not to corrupt them with his wickedness and to suffer the consequences of his sin. The pain of such isolation may drive the person to repentance.

A church that does not discipline a sinning member is like a person who has good reason to believe he has cancer but who refuses to go to a doctor—because he either does not want to face the problem or does not want to face the treatment. If he waits too long his whole body will be permeated with the disease and it will be too late for treatment to do any good. No church is healthy enough to resist contamination from persistent sin in its midst, any more than the healthiest and most nutritious bushel of apples can withstand contamination from even a single bad one. The only solution in both cases is separation.

The Corinthians had misinterpreted Paul's previous advice about associating with immoral people. **I did not at all mean with the immoral people of this world, or with the covetous and swindlers, or with idolaters; for then you would have to go out of the world,** he explained. Apparently the church had stopped having contact with unbelievers instead of with unrepentant believers. The apostle pointed out that to do so is impossible without leaving the planet. Besides, sin outside the church is not nearly as dangerous to the church as sin within its own membership. Perhaps their wrong response also reflected their wanting to tolerate sin in the church. And their treatment of the unsaved in the world may have indicated their spiritual arrogance.

It is the world to whom we are to witness, to whom we are called to bring the gospel. We are not to conform to the world (Rom. 12:2), but we must be in the world and have contact with unsaved people or we could never evangelize them. In His high priestly prayer, the Lord prayed, "I do not ask Thee to take them out of the world, but to keep them from the evil one. . . . As Thou didst send Me into the world, I also have sent them into the world" (John 17:15, 18). We are to "be blameless and innocent, children of God above reproach in the midst of a crooked and perverse generation, among whom [we] appear as lights in the world" (Phil. 2:15). God intends us to be in the world so we can be its salt and light (Matt. 5:13-16) and His witnesses to it (Acts 1:8).

It is the **so-called** [*onomazō,* "to bear the name of"] **brother** who is a threat to the spiritual welfare of a church and with whom we are **not to associate.** We cannot know who is and is not a true believer, but discipline is to be administered to **any** who professes to be a Christian. Since we cannot tell the difference, tares must be treated like wheat. Anyone who carries the name of Christ is subject to discipline.

Paul makes it clear that excommunication is not limited only to cases of extreme sin such as that of the incestuous brother who was living with his stepmother. It should be applied to any professing believer who is **an immoral person, or covetous, or an idolater, or a reviler, or a drunkard, or a swindler.**

Although true believers are recipients of a new nature—the divine nature, the life of God in their inner person, a new holy self—the flesh is still present and offers the potential for all kinds of sinning. The believer who refuses to appropriate the resources of his new life and yields to the flesh will fall into habitual patterns of evil such as those mentioned here. The Greek terms used here to indentify the sins are substantives, indicating *patterns* of behavior.

Can believers develop such patterns of sin? The answer is yes. In salvation the penalty of sin is paid and the dominion of sin is broken, so that subjection to it is not necessary, but voluntary. Believers who *choose sin* will develop sinful patterns unless they repent. In 6:9-11 Paul says such *unbelievers* do not enter the kingdom (salvation), and he assures the Corinthians that they are not like those people anymore. Yet in 6:8 he says that they are acting like them. The point is that in unbelievers there is an unbroken pattern of sinning that cannot be restrained. In believers that unbroken pattern is broken, the frequency and totality of sin is changed. Righteousness and goodness find a place and the life manifests virtue. Because of our humanness, however, sin will sometimes break the pattern of righteousness. If persisted in, it establishes a sinful pattern, interrupting the manifestations of holiness coming from the new nature. That is why there are so many commands and calls to obedience and to church discipline. The believer will never become totally sinful, but may be sinful enough at certain points in his life to be characterized as an unbeliever.

Paul's thought, as we combine this text with 6:9-11, is that believers can act like unbelievers, those who are shut out of the kingdom. We cannot tell wheat from tares, or know whether a **so-called brother** is genuine, for the very reason that Christians can fall into sinful patterns similar to those of unbelievers. Such sinful patterns make a believer indistinguishable from a nonbeliever to the world, to the church, and even to himself. All assurance is forfeited (cf. 2 Pet. 1:5-10; 1 John 2:5). It is essential to realize that in a true believer the flow of sin will not be uninterrupted, as in one who is unredeemed. There will be some fruit of righteousness, for the new nature *must* be manifest (John 15:1-8).

The Corinthian church had members who practiced all of those sins. An *immoral* member is the primary subject of 1 Corinthians 5. That some were *covetous* is implied in 10:24; and some were involved in *idolatry* (10:21-22). Apparently many of them were *revilers,* or slanderers, running down members of other parties (3:3-4) and likely to despise Timothy when he came to minister to them (16:11). They had *drunkards* (11:21) and they had *swindlers* (6:8). The whole epistle reminds us of the sinning capability of believers. All offenders were to be put out of the congregation unless they repented and changed. The rest of the believers were to withdraw from them in any social setting that implied acceptance, and were **not even to eat with such a one.**

We have no responsibility for **judging outsiders.** We are to witness to outsiders, but not judge them. We cannot chasten them, and no remedial steps will alter the sin of the ungodly. **Those who are outside, God judges.** But we do have a responsibility to **judge those who are within the church.** We must **remove the wicked man from among** [our]**selves.**

Discipline is difficult, painful, and often heartrending. It is not that we should not love the offenders, but that we should love Christ, His church, and His Word even more. Our love to the offenders is not to be sentimental tolerance but correcting love (cf. Prov. 27:6).

It is not that everyone in the church must be perfect, for that is impossible. Everyone falls into sin and has imperfections and shortcomings. The church is in some ways a hospital for those who know they are sick. They have trusted in Christ as Savior and they want to follow Him as Lord—to be what God wants them to be. It is not the ones who recognize their sin and hunger for righteousness who are to be put out of fellowship, but those who persistently and unrepentantly continue in a pattern of sin about which they have been counseled and warned. We should continue to love them and pray for them that they repent and return to a pure life. If they do repent we should gladly and joyfully "forgive and comfort" them and welcome them back into fellowship (2 Cor. 2:7).

Forbidden Lawsuits
(6:1-11)

14

Does any one of you, when he has a case against his neighbor, dare to go to law before the unrighteous, and not before the saints? Or do you not know that the saints will judge the world? And if the world is judged by you, are you not competent to constitute the smallest law courts? Do you not know that we shall judge angels? How much more, matters of this life? If then you have law courts dealing with matters of this life, do you appoint them as judges who are of no account in the church? I say this to your shame. Is it so, that there is not among you one wise man who will be able to decide between his brethren, but brother goes to law with brother, and that before unbelievers? Actually, then, it is already a defeat for you, that you have lawsuits with one another. Why not rather be wronged? Why not rather be defrauded? On the contrary, you yourselves wrong and defraud, and that your brethren. Or do you not know that the unrighteous shall not inherit the kingdom of God? Do not be deceived; neither fornicators, nor idolaters, nor adulterers, nor effeminate, nor homosexuals, nor thieves, nor the covetous, nor drunkards, nor revilers, nor swindlers, shall inherit the kingdom of God. And such were some of you; but you were washed, but you were sanctified, but you were justified in the name of the Lord Jesus Christ, and in the Spirit of our God. (6:1-11)

The Corinthian believers were so taken with human philosophy and so insistent on believing and doing what they wanted that they were divided, bickering, and exceptionally immoral. Their old ways of thinking and acting had reinvaded their lives, and the pattern of righteousness, the expression of the new inner man made after the divine nature, was so broken by sinning that it would have been difficult to have distinguished many of them from their pagan neighbors. This text reveals they were envious of fellow Christians, critical of fellow Christians, and took business and financial advantage of each other. They carried these things so far as to take each other to court—and secular, pagan courts at that. They hung out their dirty laundry for all the world to see.

The legal situation in Corinth probably was much as it was in Athens, where litigation was a part of everyday life. It had become a form of challenge and even entertainment. One ancient writer claimed that, in a manner of speaking, every Athenian was a lawyer. When a problem arose between two parties that they could not settle between themselves, the first recourse was private arbitration. Each party was assigned a disinterested private citizen as an arbitrator, and the two arbitrators, along with a neutral third person, would attempt to resolve the problem. If they failed, the case was turned over to a court of forty, who assigned a public arbitrator to each party. Interestingly, every citizen had to serve as a public arbitrator during the sixtieth year of his life. If public arbitration failed, the case went to a jury court, composed of from several hundred to several thousand jurors. Every citizen over thirty years of age was subject to serving as a juror. Either as a party to a lawsuit, as an arbitrator, or as a juror, most citizens regularly were involved in legal proceedings of one sort or another.

The Corinthian believers had been so used to arguing, disputing, and taking one another to court before they were saved that they carried those selfish attitudes and habits over into their new lives as Christians. That course not only was spiritually wrong but practically unnecessary.

For centuries Jews had settled all their disputes either privately or in a synagogue court. They refused to take their problems before a pagan court, believing that to do so would imply that God, through His own people using His own scriptural principles, was not competent to solve every problem. It was considered a form of blasphemy to go to court before Gentiles. Both Greek and Roman rulers had allowed the Jews to continue that practice, even outside Palestine. Under Roman law Jews could try virtually every offense and give almost any sentence, except that of death. As we know from Jesus' trial, the Sanhedrin was free to imprison and beat Jesus as they pleased, but they required the permission of Rome, represented by Pilate, in order to put Him to death.

Because Christians were considered by the Romans to be a Jewish sect, the Corinthian believers were probably free to settle their disputes among themselves. Possibly because they were not able to get as favorable settlements from their fellow Christians, however, many of them chose to sue each other in synagogues before Jewish judges, or in pagan public courts. Public litigation was a manifestation of their fleshly attitudes, one more piece of leaven (5:6-8) they had carried over into their new lives in Christ.

In confronting that evil in the Corinthian church, Paul mentions three areas of misunderstanding that those believers had. They misunderstood the true rank they had in relation to the world, the true attitude they should have had in relation to one another, and the true character they should have had in relation to God's standards of righteousness.

THE TRUE RANK OF CHRISTIANS

Does any one of you, when he has a case against his neighbor, dare to go to law before the unrighteous, and not before the saints? Or do you not know that the saints will judge the world? And if the world is judged by you, are you not competent to constitute the smallest law courts? Do you not know that we shall judge angels? How much more, matters of this life? If then you have law courts dealing with matters of this life, do you appoint them as judges who are of no account in the church? I say this to your shame. Is it so, that there is not among you one wise man who will be able to decide between his brethren, but brother goes to law with brother, and that before unbelievers? (6:1-6)

A case against translates three Greek words (a noun, verb, and preposition) that were commonly used to indicate a lawsuit. **His neighbor** is literally "another" and is probably best rendered that way. **Unrighteous** does not refer to the moral character but to the spiritual standing of those before whom the Christians were taking their cases. The public arbitrators and jurors were unsaved and therefore unjustified, or unrighteous. Christians were bringing lawsuits against one another before unbelievers, and Paul was shocked and grieved. Because he already knew the answer, his question was rhetorical. He was saying, "How can it be? Is it really true that some of you are actually suing each other, and that you are even doing it in public, pagan courts?" The verb *tolmaō* (**dare**) is in the present tense, indicating a continuing reality.

Paul's concern was not that believers would get an unfair hearing in the public courts. They may have been given as fair judgments there as they would have received from fellow Christians. Paul was concerned because they had so little respect for the church's authority and ability to settle its own disputes. Christians are members of Christ's own Body and are indwelt by His own Spirit. Christians are **saints,** the holy ones of God, who are "enriched in Him" and "not lacking in any gift" (1:2-7). "How," Paul asks, "can you think of taking your problems outside of the family to be settled?" All the resources of truth, wisdom, equity, justice, love, kindness, generosity, and understanding reside in the people of God.

Christians are not to take other Christians to worldly courts. When we put ourselves under the authority of the world in this way, we confess that we do not have right actions and right attitudes. Believers who go to court with believers are more concerned with revenge or gain than with the unity of the Body and the glory of Jesus

Christ. Disputes between Christians should be settled by and among Christians. If we as Christians, with our wonderful gifts and resources in Christ, cannot settle a dispute, how can we expect unbelievers to do it? Paul insists that Christians *are* able to solve disputes, always. **Do you not know that the saints will judge the world? And if the world is judged by you, are you not competent to constitute the smallest law courts?** "If you are one day going to sit in God's supreme court over the world, aren't you qualified to judge in the small, everyday matters that come up among you now?" It should be noted that the term **law courts** can also be translated "law suits."

When Jesus Christ returns to set up His millennial kingdom, believers from throughout all of history will be His coregents, sitting with Him on His throne (Rev. 3:21; cf. Dan. 7:22). Part of our responsibility as rulers with Christ will be to judge the world. The apostles will have special authority, ruling from "twelve thrones, judging the twelve tribes of Israel" (Matt. 19:28). But every believer will participate in some way. He "who overcomes, and he who keeps My deeds until the end, to Him I will give authority over the nations; and he shall rule them with a rod of iron, as the vessels of the potter are broken to pieces, as I also have received authority from My Father" (Rev. 2:26-27).

If the saints will one day help rule the entire earth, they surely are able to rule themselves within the church now. That future rule will be based on perfect adherence to the Word of God and proper godly attitudes, which are available now. There will not then be any different principles of wisdom and justice than we have revealed to us in Scripture now.

The Corinthian Christians, however, not only were not ruling themselves but were making a spectacle of themselves before unbelievers, airing their pride, carnality, greed, and bitterness before the whole world—the world that one day they would be called on by the Lord to help judge and rule in righteousness.

Believers will one day even **judge angels.** Scripture is not clear as to which angels we will judge. The fallen angels will be judged by the Lord (2 Pet. 2:4; Jude 6), but we are not told if believers will participate in that judgment. The Greek (*krinō*) for **judge** can also mean "to rule or govern." That certainly would be the meaning if we are to have authority over the holy angels, for they will have no sin for which to be condemned. One cannot be dogmatic, but I am inclined to think that glorified believers will help judge the fallen angels and exercise some rule over the holy angels. If Christ was exalted above all the angels (Eph. 1:20-23), if we are in Him and are like Him, and if we are to reign with Him, it must be that somehow we will share in His authority. Whatever the sphere and extent of that heavenly judgment or ruling, Paul's point here is the same: If we are to judge and rule over the world and over angels in the age to come, we are surely able, under the guidance of Scripture and the Holy Spirit, to settle any matters of disagreement among ourselves today.

If then you have law courts dealing with matters of this life, do you appoint them as judges who are of no account in the church? As the different renderings of English versions suggest, verse 4 is difficult to translate, and we should not be dogmatic about the specific wording. But the basic meaning is clear: When Christians have earthly quarrels and disputes among themselves, it is inconceivable that those who will rule eternally should try to settle them through tribunals run by unbelievers, by

judges who are of no account in the church. If two Christian parties cannot agree between themselves, they should ask fellow Christians to settle the matter for them, and be willing to abide by that decision. The poorest equipped believer, who seeks the counsel of God's Word and Spirit, is much more competent to settle disagreements between fellow believers than is the most highly trained and experienced unbelieving judge who is devoid of divine truth. Because we are in Christ, Christians rank above the world and even above angels. And by settling our own disputes, we give a testimony of our resources and of our unity, harmony, and humility before the world. When we go to public court, our testimony is the opposite.

Paul was ashamed of the behavior of those whom he had taught and among whom he had ministered. They knew better. **I say this to your shame.** He continues with a note of sarcasm, **Is it so, that there is not among you one wise man who will be able to decide between his brethren, but brother goes to law with brother, and that before unbelievers?** The mark that should most characterize Christian brothers is love. John makes it absolutely clear that "anyone who does not practice righteousness is not of God, nor the one who does not love his brother. For this is the message which you have heard from the beginning, that we should love one another" (1 John 3:10-11). Love, however, did not characterize the Corinthian brothers and sisters. They were acting like the unredeemed, and, as Paul would remind them a few chapters later, a Christian without love is "a noisy gong or a clanging cymbal"; he is, in fact, "nothing" (13:1-2).

Sometimes in our society a quarrel between Christians over rights and property cannot help coming before a secular court. When, for instance, a Christian is being divorced by his or her spouse, the law requires a secular court to be involved. Or, in the case of child abuse or neglect, a Christian parent may be forced to seek court protection from a backslidden former spouse. But even in those kinds of exceptions, when for some reason a Christian finds himself unavoidably in court with a fellow believer, his purpose should be to glorify God, and never to gain selfish advantage. The general rule is: Do not go to court with fellow Christians, but settle matters among yourselves.

The True Attitude of Christians

Actually, then, it is already a defeat for you, that you have lawsuits with one another. Why not rather be wronged? Why not rather be defrauded? On the contrary, you yourselves wrong and defraud, and that your brethren. (6:7-8)

Christians who take fellow Christians to court lose spiritually before the case is heard. The fact that they have **lawsuits** at all is a sign of moral and spiritual **defeat** (*hēttēma*, a word used of defeat in court). A believer who takes a fellow believer to court for any reason always loses the case in God's sight. He has already suffered a spiritual **defeat.** He is selfish, and he discredits the power, wisdom, and work of God, when he tries to get what he wants through the judgment of unbelievers.

The right attitude of a Christian is to **rather be wronged,** to **rather be**

defrauded, than to sue a fellow Christian. It is far better to lose financially than to lose spiritually. Even when we are clearly in the legal right, we do not have the moral and spiritual right to insist on our legal right in a public court. If the brother has wronged us in any way, our response should be to forgive him and to leave the outcome of the matter in God's hands. The Lord may give or take away. He is sovereign and has His will and purpose both in what we gain and in what we lose. We should gratefully accept that.

When Peter asked Jesus how often he should should forgive a brother who sinned against him, the Lord replied, "seventy times seven" (Matt. 18:21-22), a figure that represented an unlimited amount. To illustrate the principle, Jesus told the parable of the unforgiving slave. After being forgiven a huge, unpayable sum by the king, the man refused to forgive a fellow slave for a pittance, and was handed "over to the torturers" by the irate king. "So shall My heavenly Father also do to you," Jesus said, "if each of you does not forgive his brother from your heart" (vv. 23-35). Because God in Christ has forgiven each us of such great sin against Himself, no Christian has the right to be unforgiving, especially of fellow Christians. If he is unforgiving, the Lord will deliver him to chastening until he repents or is removed.

If we are **wronged** or **defrauded** we should be forgiving, not bitter. If we cannot convince the brother to make things right, and if he will not listen to fellow believers, we are better off to suffer the loss or the injustice than to bring a lawsuit against him. "Do not resist him who is evil," Jesus commanded, "but whoever slaps you on your right cheek, turn to him the other also. And if anyone wants to sue you, and take your shirt, let him have your coat also" (Matt. 5:39-40). Contrary to the world's standard, it is better to be sued and lose than to sue and win. Spiritually, it is impossible for a Christian to sue and win. When we are deprived wrongfully we are to cast ourselves on the care of God, who is able to work that for our good and His glory.

An attorney friend of mine says that over the years he has counseled dozens of Christians to drop lawsuits against each other. In some ninety percent of the cases he has been successful, and he reports that, without exception, those believers have been blessed. Also without exception, those who insisted on resolving their disputes in court became bitter and resentful—whether they won or lost their cases. If they went to court they always lost spiritually.

The Lord knows the needs of His children and will see that we have what we need. We are to "seek first His kingdom and His righteousness; and all these things shall be added" (Matt. 6:33). A Christian's primary concern should not be to protect his possessions or his rights but to protect his relationship with His Lord and with his fellow believers.

The True Character of Christians

Or do you not know that the unrighteous shall not inherit the kingdom of God? Do not be deceived; neither fornicators, nor idolaters, nor adulterers, nor effeminate, nor homosexuals, nor thieves, nor the covetous, nor drunkards, nor revilers, nor swindlers, shall inherit the kingdom of God.

And such were some of you; but you were washed, but you were sanctified, but you were justified in the name of the Lord Jesus Christ, and in the Spirit of our God. (6:9-11)

Paul's purpose here is not to give a list of sins that will indicate one has lost his salvation. There are no such sins. He is rather giving a catalog of sinners who are typical of the unsaved. Persons whose lives are totally characterized by such sins are not saved and therefore **unrighteous,** unjustified. They **shall not inherit the kingdom of God,** because they are not right with God. They are outside the kingdom, the sphere of salvation.

The application to believers is clear. "Why, then," Paul asks the Corinthians, "do you keep living like the unsaved, the unrighteous? Why do you keep falling into the ways of your old life, the life from which Christ has saved you? Why are you following the old standards, and having the old selfish, ungodly motives? You are to be separated from the world's ways, not following them. And specifically, why are you taking your problems to the world's courts?"

A believer is a new creation (2 Cor. 5:17), with a new inner personhood made after God's own person (2 Pet. 1:4), and there is no longer unbroken unrighteousness. But the flesh can become dominant in the disobedient Christian, so that he may take on the appearance of an unbeliever.

The catalog of sins in verses 9-10 is not exhaustive, but those sins represent all the major types of moral sin, the types of sin that have always characterized ungodly societies and that ought never to characterize the godly society of the redeemed.

Fornicators has to do with sexual immorality in general and to that by unmarried persons in particular. Scripture continually condemns it. The sin is characteristic of our own western society today. It is portrayed and exalted in books, magazines, movies, and television as the norm of human living. But fornication in any form is an abomination to God and should be an abomination to His people. Those who habitually practice and defend it cannot possibly belong to God, for the heirs of His **kingdom** do not habitually practice and defend sexual immorality. True believers may do it, but no matter how involved and weak they are, deep within them they recognize its evil. (See Rom. 7:15-25 for Paul's discussion of this conflict.)

Idolaters refers to those who worship any false gods and false religious systems, not simply to those who bow down to images. Our society has never been so engulfed by and enamored of false religions and cults as in our day. No belief, claim, or practice seems to be too bizarre to get a following.

Adulterers refers specifically to married persons who indulge in sexual acts outside the marriage partnership. Because marriage is sacred, that is an especially heinous sin in God's sight. The Old Testament required the death penalty for it. In addition to corrupting the participants themselves it also corrupts the family. It defiles the unique, God-established relationship between husband and wife and it inevitably brings harm to their children. And those may be only the initial effects.

Effeminate and **homosexuals** both refer to those who exchange and corrupt normal male-female sexual roles and relations. Transvestism, sex change, homosexuality, and other gender perversions are included. God's unique creation, those created in His own image, were created "male and female" (Gen. 1:27), and the Lord strictly forbids the two roles to be blurred, much less exchanged. "A woman shall not wear man's clothing, nor shall a man put on a woman's clothing; for whoever does these things is an abomination to the Lord your God" (Deut. 22:5). The Hebrew terms in that verse indicate more than clothing, and include any tool, implement, or apparatus.

Homosexuality is condemned throughout Scripture. It was so characteristic of Sodom that the term *sodomy* is a synonym for that sin. The Sodomite men were inflamed with perverted sexual desire, and on one occasion they surrounded Lot's house and demanded that the two angels (who had come in the form of men) be sent outside so that they could "have relations with them" (Gen. 19:4-5). God completely destroyed Sodom and Gomorrah because "their sin [was] exceedingly grave" (18:20). Since that time *sodomy* has stood for sexual perversion and the phrase *Sodom and Gomorrah* has stood for moral corruption. For believers the terms also have come to stand for God's hatred and judgment of moral corruption.

By Paul's day homosexuality had been rampant in Greece and Rome for centuries. In his commentary on this passage, William Barclay reports that Socrates was a homosexual and Plato probably was. Plato's *Symposium on Love* is a treatise glorifying homosexuality. It is likely that fourteen of the first fifteen Roman emperors were homosexuals. Nero, who reigned close to the time Paul wrote 1 Corinthians, had a boy named Sporis castrated in order for the boy to become the emperor's "wife," in addition to his natural wife. After Nero died, the boy was passed on to one of Nero's successors, Otho, to use in the same way.

Confusion of sex roles, like adultery, is particularly evil because it attacks the family. It corrupts the biblical plan for the family, including the standards for authority and submission within the family, and thus retards the passing of righteousness from one generation to the next. The most ungodly societies of history have been plagued by sex role perversions, no doubt because Satan is so intent on destroying the family. Churches who, in the name of love, defend homosexuality and condone homosexual ministers, "marriages," and congregations not only pervert God's standards of morality but encourage their members in sin. Encouragement in sin has no part in love. True love of others is not doing for them what they want but doing for them what God wants. "By this we know that we love the children of God, when we love God and observe His commandments. For this is the love of God, that we keep His commandments" (1 John 5:2-3). Condoning sin is never an act of love, either for God or for those whose sins we condone.

Thieves and **covetous** relate to the same basic sin of greed. The covetous person desires that which belongs to others; the thief actually takes it. Greed is a manifestation of selfishness and, like all selfishness, is never satisfied. The greedy demand more and more. In our day it is difficult to find a person, even a Christian, who is satisfied with his income and possessions. But greed is not to characterize the heirs of God's kingdom. It has no place in the Christian life.

Drunkards is self-explanatory. Like the other sins listed here, it is almost inevitably found to be a serious problem where God's name and Word are disregarded or despised. Today alcoholism is spreading even to the elementary ages. Preteen and young teen alcoholics are becoming more and more common, as are alcoholics among their elders. The harm that alcohol does to individuals and to families is beyond measure.

Revilers are those who destroy with their tongues; they wound with words. God does not consider their sin to be mild, because it comes from hearts full of hate and causes misery, pain, and despair in the lives of those it attacks.

Swindlers are thieves who steal indirectly. They take unfair advantage of others to promote their own financial gain. Extortioners, embezzlers, confidence men, promoters of defective merchandise and services, false advertisers, and many other types of swindlers are as common to our day as to Paul's.

And such were some of you, Paul continues. The Corinthian church, as churches today, had ex-fornicators, ex-adulterers, ex-thieves, and so on. Though many Christians have never been guilty of the particular sins just discussed, every Christian was sinful before he was saved. Every Christian is an ex-sinner. Christ came for the purpose of saving sinners (Matt. 9:13). That is the great truth of Christianity: no person has sinned too deeply or too long to be saved. "Where sin increased, grace abounded all the more" (Rom. 5:20). But **some** had ceased to be like that for a while, and were reverting to their old behavior.

Paul uses **but** (*alla,* the strongest Greek adversative particle) three times to indicate the contrast of the Christian life with the worldly life he has just been describing. **But you were washed, but you were sanctified, but you were justified.** It made no difference what they were before they were saved. God can save a sinner from any sin and all sin. But it makes a great deal of difference what a believer is like after salvation. He is to live a life that corresponds to his cleansing, his sanctification, and his justification. His Christian life is to be pure, holy, and righteous. The new life produces and requires a new kind of living.

Washed speaks of new life, of regeneration. Jesus "saved us, not on the basis of deeds which we have done in righteousness, but according to His mercy, by the washing of regeneration and renewing by the Holy Spirit" (Titus 3:5). Regeneration is God's work of re-creation. "Therefore if any man is in Christ, he is a new creature; the old things passed away; behold, new things have come" (2 Cor. 5:17). "We are His workmanship, created in Christ Jesus" (Eph. 2:10). When a person is washed by Christ he is born again (John 3:3-8).

Sanctified speaks of new behavior. To be sanctified is to be made holy inwardly and to be able, in the Spirit's power, to live a righteous life outwardly. Before a person is saved he has no holy nature and no capacity for holy living. But in Christ we are given a new nature and can live out the new kind of life. Sin's total domination is broken and is replaced by a life of holiness. By their fleshly sinfulness the Corinthians were interrupting that divine work.

Justified speaks of new standing before God. In Christ we are clothed in His righteousness and God now sees in us His Son's righteousness instead of our sin.

Christ's righteousness is credited to our account (Rom. 4:22-25). We are declared and made in the new nature righteous, holy, innocent, and guiltless because God is "the justifier of the one who has faith in Jesus" (Rom. 3:26).

The Corinthian believers had experienced transformation **in the name of the Lord Jesus Christ, and in the Spirit of our God.** God's name represents His will, His power, and His work. Because of Jesus' willing submission to the Father's will, His death on the cross in our behalf, and His resurrection from the dead, He has provided our washing, our sanctification, and our justification.

A transformed life should produce transformed living. Paul is saying very strongly that it was unacceptable that some believers were behaving like those outside the kingdom. They were acting like their former selves. They were not saved for that, but from that.

Christian Liberty and Sexual Freedom

15

(6:12-20)

All things are lawful for me, but not all things are profitable. All things are lawful for me, but I will not be mastered by anything. Food is for the stomach, and the stomach is for food; but God will do away with both of them. Yet the body is not for immorality, but for the Lord; and the Lord is for the body. Now God has not only raised the Lord, but will also raise us up through His power. Do you not know that your bodies are members of Christ? Shall I then take away the members of Christ and make them members of a harlot? May it never be! Or do you not know that the one who joins himself to a harlot is one body with her? For He says, "The two will become one flesh." But the one who joins himself to the Lord is one spirit with Him. Flee immorality. Every other sin that a man commits is outside the body, but the immoral man sins against his own body. Or do you not know that your body is a temple of the Holy Spirit who is in you, whom you have from God, and that you are not your own? For you have been bought with a price: therefore glorify God in your body. (6:12-20)

Freedom in Christ was a truth Paul never tired of emphasizing. "It was for freedom that Christ set us free; therefore keep standing firm and do not be subject again to a yoke of slavery. . . . For you were called to freedom, brethren" (Gal. 5:1, 13).

He continually rejoiced in "the freedom of the glory of the children of God" (Rom. 8:21). Believers "are not under law, but under grace" (Rom. 6:14). We are not saved by works or kept saved by works. "For by grace you have been saved through faith; and that not of yourselves, it is the gift of God; not as a result of works, that no one should boast" (Eph. 2:8-9; cf. Rom. 3:20). "Now we have been released from the Law, having died to that by which we were bound, so that we serve in newness of the Spirit and not in oldness of the letter" (Rom. 7:6).

God's grace alone saves and God's grace alone keeps salvation. Christians are justified, counted righteous and holy in God's sight (Rom. 4:22-25). "Who," therefore, "will bring a charge against God's elect? God is the one who justifies" (Rom. 8:33). A Christian can commit no sin that is not already covered by God's grace. No sin can forfeit his salvation. No accusation can succeed against the believer. God is the highest court, and He has declared that believers are righteous. There is no higher appeal. That settles the issue.

The Corinthian church had been taught this truth many times while Paul was among them, but they were using it as a theological excuse for sin. They ignored the truth, "only do not turn your freedom into an opportunity for the flesh" (Gal. 5:13), which he surely had also taught them. When Paul spoke of Christian freedom it was always in relation to freedom from works righteousness—that is, earning salvation by good deeds—whether by the Mosaic law, Pharisaic tradition, or any other means. The Corinthians had perverted this truth to justify their sinning. They possibly used the same argument that Paul anticipated when he was explaining grace to the Roman church: "What shall we say then? Are we to continue in sin that grace might increase?" (Rom. 6:1). They pretended to have theological justification for living as they wanted.

They may have had a philosophical argument for their sin as well, perhaps implied in 6:13, "Food is for the stomach, and the stomach is for food." Much Greek philosophy considered everything physical, including the body, to be basically evil and therefore of no value. What was done with or to the body did not matter. Food was food, the stomach was the stomach, and sex was sex. Sex was just a biological function like eating, to be used just as food was used, to satisfy their appetites. The argument sounds remarkably modern.

Like many people today, the Corinthian Christians rationalized their sinful thinking and habits. They were clever at coming up with seemingly good reasons for doing wrong things. They also lived in a society that was notoriously immoral, a society that, in the temple prostitution and other ways, actually glorified promiscuous sex. To have sexual relations with a prostitute was so common in Corinth that the practice came to be called "Corinthianizing." Many believers had formerly been involved in such immorality, and it was hard for them to break with the old ways and easy to fall back into them. Just as it was hard for them to give up their love of human wisdom, their worldliness, their pride, their divisive spirit, and their love for suing, it was also hard for them to give up their sexual immorality.

In 6:12-20 Paul shows three of the evils of sexual sin: it is harmful to everyone involved; it gains control over those who indulge in it; and it perverts God's purpose for the body.

SEXUAL SIN HARMS

All things are lawful for me, but not all things are profitable. (6:12*a*)

The statement, **All things are lawful** may have been a common Corinthian saying in that liberated society. Paul borrows it and, playing off it, says, "It is so **for me**, too. Every sin I as a Christian commit is forgiven in Jesus Christ." But no sin is ever right or good, and no sin ever produces anything right or good. Sin can never be worthwhile or profitable. **Profitable** (*sumpherō*) means "to be to advantage." In the sense that believers are free and no longer under the penalty of the law in any way, **all things are lawful** for them. But the price for doing some things is terribly high, terribly unprofitable. Sin never brings profit; it always brings loss.

The particular type of sin Paul has in mind here (vv. 13-20) is sexual sin. No sin that a person commits has more built-in pitfalls, problems, and destructiveness than sexual sin. It has broken more marriages, shattered more homes, caused more heartache and disease, and destroyed more lives than alcohol and drugs combined. It causes lying, stealing, cheating, and killing, as well as bitterness, hatred, slander, gossip, and unforgivingness.

The dangers and harm of sexual sin are nowhere presented more vividly and forcefully than in Proverbs. "The lips of an adulteress drip honey, and smoother than oil is her speech" (Prov. 5:3). The basic truth applies to a prostitute or to any other woman who tries to seduce a man. It also applies to a man who tries to seduce a woman. The point is that sexual allurement is extremely enticing and powerful. It seems nice, enjoyable, and good. It promises nothing but pleasure and satisfaction. But what it ends up giving "is bitter as wormwood, sharp as a two-edged sword. Her feet go down to death, her steps lay hold of Sheol. She does not ponder the path of life; her ways are unstable, she does not know it" (vv. 4-6). The first characteristic of sexual sin is deceit. It never delivers what it promises. It offers great satisfaction but gives great disappointment. It claims to be real living but is really the way to death. Illicit sexual relationships are always "unstable." Nothing binds those involved except the temporary and impersonal gratification of physical impulses. That is poor cement. Another tragedy of sexual sin is that often those involved do "not know it" is unstable, do not realize perhaps for a long time that their relationship cannot be lasting. Thus they fall deeper and deeper into the pit of their doomed relationship, which makes the dissolution all the more devastating and painful.

Those who consider all sex to be basically evil, however, are as far from the truth as those who consider all sex to be basically good and permissible. God is not against sex. He created and blessed it. When used exclusively within marriage, as the Lord intends, sex is beautiful, satisfying, and stabilizing. "Let your fountain be blessed," Scripture says, "and rejoice in the wife of your youth. . . . Be exhilarated always with her love" (Prov. 5:18-19).

The Bible's advice for avoiding sexual involvement outside marriage is simple: stay as far away as possible from the persons and places likely to get you in trouble.

"Keep your way far from her, and do not go near the door of her house" (Prov. 5:8). When repeatedly enticed by Potiphar's wife, Joseph refused not only "to lie beside her" but even to "be with her" (Gen. 39:10). When she tried to force him into adultery and grabbed his coat, "he left his garment in her hand and fled, and went outside" (v. 12). It was not the time for argument or explanation but for flight. When we unavoidably get caught in such a situation, the only sensible thing to do is to get away from it as quickly as we can. Passion is not rational or sensible, and sexually dangerous situations should be avoided or fled, not debated.

Involvement in illicit sex leads to loss of health, loss of possessions, and loss of honor and respect. Every person who continues in such sins does not necessarily suffer all of those losses, but those are the types of loss that persistent sexual sin produces. The sex indulger will come to discover that he has lost his "years to the cruel one," that his "hard-earned goods" have gone "to the house of an alien," and that he will "groan" in his latter years and find his "flesh and [his] body are consumed" (Prov. 5:9-11). The "stolen water" of sexual relations outside of marriage "is sweet; and bread eaten in secret is pleasant"; but "the dead are there" (Prov. 9:17-18). Sexual sin is a "no win" situation. It is never profitable and always harmful.

God looks on sexual immorality with extreme seriousness. Because of this sin in Israel, "twenty-three thousand fell in one day" (1 Cor. 10:8). David was a man after God's own heart and was greatly used of the Lord in leading Israel and even in writing Scripture. But David was not exempted from the consequences of his sin. He committed adultery with Bathsheba and she became pregnant. He then arranged for her husband to be killed in battle and took her as his own wife. "But the thing that David had done was evil in the sight of the Lord" (2 Sam. 11:27). Through His prophet Nathan, God told David that because of his sin, "the sword shall never depart from your house, . . . I will raise up evil against you from your own household," and "the child also that is born to you shall surely die" (12:10-11, 14). David paid for those sins almost every day of his life. Several of his sons were rebellious, jealous, and vengeful, and his family life was for the most part a tragic shambles.

David repented and was forgiven. "The Lord also has taken away your sin" (12:13), but the Lord did not take away the consequences of the sin. After that experience the king wrote Psalm 51, in gratitude but also in deep remorse and agony. He had experienced God's marvelous and gracious forgiveness, but he had also come to see the awfulness of his sin. "Against Thee, Thee only, I have sinned, and done what is evil in Thy sight" (v. 4). God's grace is free, but the cost of sin is high.

Sexual Sin Controls

All things are lawful for me, but I will not be mastered by anything. (6:12b)

Paul was free in the grace of Christ to do as he pleased, but he refused to allow himself to be **mastered** by anything or anyone but Christ. He would not become enslaved to any habit or custom and certainly not to any sin. "For sin shall not be master over you, for you are not under law, but under grace" (Rom. 6:14).

No sin is more enslaving than sexual sin. The more it is indulged, the more it controls the indulger. Often it begins with small indiscretions, which lead to greater ones and finally to flagrant vice. The progression of sin is reflected in Psalm 1: "Blessed is the man who does not walk in the counsel of the wicked, nor stand in the path of sinners, nor sit in the seat of scoffers" (v. 1). When we willingly associate with sin, we will soon come to tolerate it and then to practice it. Like all other sins that are not resisted, sins of sex will grow, and eventually they will corrupt and destroy not only the persons directly involved but many innocent persons besides.

The Corinthians were no strangers to sins of sex, and unfortunately many believers there had gone back to them. In the name of Christian freedom they had become controlled by their own fleshly desires.

Paul wrote the Thessalonians, "For this is the will of God, your sanctification; that is, that you abstain from sexual immorality; that each of you know how to possess his own vessel in sanctification and honor, not in lustful passion, like the Gentiles who do not know God" (1 Thess. 4:3–5). The context argues that "vessel" is here a synonym for body rather than for wife, as many interpreters hold. Every believer is to rightly possess, rightly control, his own body. If we are living in the Spirit, we "are putting to death the deeds of the body" (Rom. 8:13).

It is not as easy to be in control of ourselves as we sometimes think. Many people are deceived in thinking they are perfectly in control of their thoughts and actions, simply because they always do what they want. The fact, however, is that their desires and passions are telling them what to do, and they are going along. They are not masters of their desires, but are willing slaves. Their flesh is controlling their minds.

Paul himself testifies that he had to "buffet [his] body and make it [his] slave, lest possibly, after [he had] preached to others, [he himself] should be disqualified" (1 Cor. 9:27). Buffet (*hupōpiazō*) means literally, "to give a black eye, or to beat the face black and blue." To keep his body from enslaving him, he had to enslave his body. Otherwise he could become disqualified, not for salvation but for holy living and useful service to God.

Sexual Sin Perverts

Sexual sin not only harms and controls but also perverts. It especially perverts God's plan and purpose for the bodies of His people. A Christian's body is for the Lord; it is a member of Christ; and it is the temple of the Holy Spirit.

THE BODY IS FOR THE LORD

Food is for the stomach, and the stomach is for food; but God will do away with both of them. Yet the body is not for immorality, but for the Lord; and the Lord is for the body. Now God has not only raised the Lord, but will also raise us up through His power. (6:13-14)

Food and the **stomach** were created by God for each other. Their relationship is purely biological. It is likely the Corinthians were using this truth as an analogy to justify sexual immorality. The Greek text says literally, "The foods the belly, the belly the foods." Perhaps this was popular proverb meant to celebrate the idea that "Sex is no different from eating: the stomach was made for food, and the body was made for sex." But Paul stops them short. "It is true that food and the stomach were made for each other," he is saying, "but it is also true that that relationship is purely temporal." One day, when their purpose has been fulfilled, **God will do away with both of them.** That biological process has no place in the eternal state.

Not so with the body itself. The bodies of believers are designed by God for much more than biological functions. **The body is not for immorality, but for the Lord; and the Lord is for the body.** Paul had a better proverb in mind with that statement. The body is to be the instrument of the Lord, for His use and glory.

Now God has not only raised the Lord, but will also raise us up through His power. Our bodies are designed not only to serve in this life but in the life to come. They will be changed bodies, resurrected bodies, glorified bodies, heavenly bodies—but they will still be our own bodies.

The stomach and food have only a horizontal, temporal relationship. At death the relationship ceases. But our bodies are far more than biological. For believers they also have a spiritual, vertical relationship. They belong to God and they will forever endure with God. That is why Paul says, "For our citizenship is in heaven, from which also we eagerly wait for a Savior, the Lord Jesus Christ; who will transform the body of our humble state into conformity with the body of His glory" (Phil. 3:20-21). We need to take serious care of this body because it will rise in glory to be the instrument that carries our eternally glorious and pure spirit throughout eternity.

THE BODY IS A MEMBER OF CHRIST

Do you not know that your bodies are members of Christ? Shall I then take away the members of Christ and make them members of a harlot? May it never be! Or do you not know that the one who joins himself to a harlot is one body with her? For He says, "The two will become one flesh." But the one who joins himself to the Lord is one spirit with Him. Flee immorality. Every other sin that a man commits is outside the body, but the immoral man sins against his own body. (6:15-18)

The believers' bodies not only are *for* the Lord now and in the future, but they are *of* the Lord, a part of the Lord's own body, **members of Christ.** Christ is "head over all things to the church, which is His body, the fulness of Him who fills all in all" (Eph. 1:22-23). "We, who are many, are one body in Christ" (Rom. 12:5). We are, in this age, the living spiritual temple in which Christ lives. We are His body, the incarnation of His person in the church.

Paul's next point follows logically. For a Christian to commit sexual immorality is to make **the members of Christ . . . members of a harlot.** It is to use a part of Christ's own body in an act of fornication or adultery. The idea is incomprehensible to Paul, as it should be to every believer. **May it never be!**

Sexual relations involve a union; the man and woman **become one flesh.** This indicates that the most essential meaning of the phrase **one flesh** (see Gen. 2:24; etc.) is sexual union. In his *Screwtape Letters* C. S. Lewis writes, "Every time a man and a woman enter into a sexual relationship a spiritual bond is established between them which must be eternally enjoyed or eternally endured." God takes sexual sin seriously because it corrupts and shatters spiritual relationships, both human and divine.

Christ's people are **one spirit with Him.** That statement is filled with profound meaning and wondrous implications. But for his purpose here, Paul uses it to show that a Christian who commits sexual immorality involves his Lord. All sex outside of marriage is sin, but when it is committed by believers it is especially reprehensible, because it profanes Jesus Christ, with whom the believer is one (cf. John 14:18-23; 15:4, 7; 17:20-23). Since we are one with Christ, and the sex sinner is one with his partner, Christ is placed in an unthinkable position in Paul's reasoning. Christ is not personally tainted with the sin, any more than the sunbeam that shines on a garbage dump is polluted. But His reputation is dirtied because of the association.

Paul's counsel regarding sexual sin is the same as Solomon's in the book of Proverbs: **Flee immorality.** The present imperative of the Greek indicates the idea is to flee continually and to keep fleeing until the danger is past. When we are in danger of such immorality, we should not argue or debate or explain, and we certainly should not try to rationalize. We are not to consider it a spiritual challenge to be met but a spiritual trap to be escaped. We should get away as fast as we can.

Paul does not elucidate on what he means by **Every other sin that a man commits is outside the body, but the immoral man sins against his own body.** I believe he is saying that, although sexual sin is not necessarily the worst sin, it is the most unique in its character. It rises from within the body bent on personal gratification. It drives like no other impulse and when fulfilled affects the body like no other sin. It has a way of internally destroying a person that no other sin has. Because sexual intimacy is the deepest uniting of two persons, its misuse corrupts on the deepest human level. That is not a psychological analysis but a divinely revealed fact. Sexual immorality is far more destructive than alcohol, far more destructive than drugs, far more destructive than crime.

Some years ago a sixteen-year-old girl came to my office in complete despair. She had committed so many sex sins that she felt utterly worthless. She had not looked in a mirror for months, because she could not stand to look at herself; and to me she looked nearer 40 than 16. She was on the verge of suicide, not wanting to live another day. I had a special joy in leading her to Jesus Christ and seeing the transformation He made in her life. She said, "For the first time in years I feel clean."

Many of the Corinthians needed that cleaning again.

THE BODY IS A TEMPLE OF THE HOLY SPIRIT

Or do you not know that your body is a temple of the Holy Spirit who is in you, whom you have from God, and that you are not your own? For you have been bought with a price: therefore glorify God in your body. (6:19-20)

As Christians our bodies are not our own. Paul puts sting into this verse by framing it as a sarcastic question. They are the Lord's, members of Christ, and temples of the Holy Spirit, who has been given by God to indwell us. So Paul calls for sexual purity not only because of the way sexual sin affects the body, but because the body it affects is not even the believer's own. Understanding the reality of the phrase **the Holy Spirit who is in you, whom you have from God** should give us as much commitment to purity as any knowledge of divine truth could.

To commit sexual sin in a church auditorium, disgusting as that would be, would be no worse than committing the sin anywhere else. Offense is made within God's sanctuary wherever and whenever sexual immorality is committed by believers. Every act of fornication, every act of adultery by Christians, is committed in God's sanctuary: their own bodies. "For we are the temple of the living God" (2 Cor. 6:16). The fact that Christians are the dwelling place of the Holy Spirit is indicated in passages such as John 7:38-39; 20:22; Acts 1:8; Romans 8:9; and 1 Corinthians 12:3. The fact that God sent the Holy Spirit is clear from John 14:16-17; 15:26; and Acts 2:17, 33, 38.

We no longer belong to ourselves because we **have been bought with a price.** We were not "redeemed with perishable things like silver or gold from [our] futile way of life inherited from [our] forefathers, but with precious blood, as of a lamb unblemished and spotless, the blood of Christ" (1 Pet. 1:18-19).

Christians' bodies are God's temple, and a temple is for worship. Our bodies, therefore, have one supreme purpose: to **glorify God.** This is a call to live so as to bring honor to the person of God, who alone is worthy of our obedience and adoration.

A friend once took a visitor to a large Catholic cathedral in the east. The visitor wanted to pray at the station of his favorite saint. But upon arriving at that station, he was startled to find no candles lit, and a sign saying, "Do not worship here; closed for cleaning." The Corinthians provided no divine focus, either, no place for seeking souls to worship, since they were unclean. That, Paul said, had to change.

To Marry or Not to Marry (7:1-7)

16

Now concerning the things about which you wrote, it is good for a man not to touch a woman. But because of immoralities, let each man have his own wife, and let each woman have her own husband. Let the husband fulfill his duty to his wife, and likewise also the wife to her husband. The wife does not have authority over her own body, but the husband does; and likewise also the husband does not have authority over his own body, but the wife does. Stop depriving one another, except by agreement for a time that you may devote yourselves to prayer, and come together again lest Satan tempt you because of your lack of self-control. But this I say by way of concession, not of command. Yet I wish that all men were even as I myself am. However, each man has his own gift from God, one in this manner, and another in that. (7:1-7)

Chapters 7-11 of 1 Corinthians comprise Paul's answers to practical questions about which the believers in Corinth had written him (7:1), in a letter probably delivered by Stephanas, Fortunatus, and Achaicus (16:17).

The first of those questions had to do with marriage, an area in which the Corinthians had serious problems. As with their many other problems, much of their marital trouble reflected the pagan and morally corrupt society in which they lived and from which they had not fully separated. Their society tolerated fornication, adultery, homosexuality, polygamy, and concubinage. Juvenal (60-140 A.D.), the Roman poet, wrote about women who rejected their own sex: they wore helmets, delighted in feats of strength, and with exposed breasts hunted pigs with spears. He also said they wore out their bridal veils with so many marriages.

Under Roman law and customs of that day, four types of marriage were practiced. Slaves generally were considered to be subhuman chattel. If a man and woman slave wanted to be married, they might be allowed to live together in what was called a *contubernium,* which means "tent companionship." The arrangement lasted only as long as the owner permitted. He was perfectly free to separate them, to arrange for other partners, or to sell one or the other. Many of the early Christians were slaves, and some of them had lived—perhaps were still living—in this sort of marital relationship.

A second type of marriage was called *usus,* a form of common law marriage that recognized a couple to be husband and wife after they had lived together for a year. A third type was the *coemptio in manum,* in which a father would sell his daughter to a prospective husband.

The fourth type of marriage was much more elevated. The Patrician class, the nobility, were married in a service called the *confarreatio,* on which the modern Christian marriage ceremony is based. It was adopted by the Roman Catholic church and used with certain Christian modifications—coming, with little change, into Protestantism through the Reformation. The original ceremony involved participation by both families in the arrangements for the wedding, a matron to accompany the bride and a man to accompany the groom, exchanging of vows, the wearing of a veil by the bride, the giving of a ring (placed on the third finger of the left hand), a bridal bouquet, and a wedding cake.

In the Roman empire of Paul's day divorce was common, even among those married under the *confarreatio.* It was not impossible for men and women to have been married 20 times or more. An active and vocal feminist movement had also developed. Some wives competed with their husbands in business and even in feats of physical strength. Many were not interested in being housewives and mothers, and by the end of the first century childless marriages were common. Both men and women were determined to live their own lives, regardless of marriage vows or commitments.

The early church had members that had lived together, and were still living together, under all four marriage arrangements. It also had those who had had multiple marriages and divorces. Not only that, but some believers had gotten the notion that being single and celibate was more spiritual than being married, and they disparaged marriage entirely. Perhaps someone was teaching that sex was "unspiritual" and should be altogether forsaken.

The situation was difficult and perplexing even for mature Christians. For the immature Corinthians it was especially confusing. The great question was: "What do we do now that we are believers? Should we stay together as husband and wife if we are both Christians? Should we get divorced if our spouse is an unbeliever? Should we become, or remain, single?" The chaos of marital possibilities posed myriad perplexities, which Paul approaches in this section of the letter.

In the first seven verses of chapter 7 Paul starts with the question of singleness. He teaches that celibacy is good, that it can be tempting, that it is wrong for married people, and that it is a gift from God.

CELIBACY IS GOOD

Now concerning the things about which you wrote, it is good for a man not to touch a woman. (7:1)

To touch a woman was a common Jewish euphemism for sexual intercourse. The phrase is used in that sense in passages such as Gen. 20:6; Ruth 2:9; and Prov. 6:29. Paul uses it to state that it is a good thing for Christians not to have sexual intercourse, that is, to be single, unmarried. He does not say, however, that singleness is the only good condition or that marriage is in any way wrong or inferior to singleness. He says only that singleness, as long as it is celibate, can be good.

God Himself declared at creation that "it is not good for the man to be alone; I will make him a helper suitable for him" (Gen. 2:18). All people need companionship and God ordained marriage to be, among other things, the most fulfilling and common means of companionship. God allowed for singleness and did not require marriage for everyone under the Old Covenant, but Jewish tradition not only looked on marriage as the ideal state but looked on singleness as disobedience of God's command to "be fruitful and multiply, and fill the earth" (Gen. 1:28).

It is possible that, as a result of this, some of the Jewish Christians in Corinth were pressuring single Gentile believers to become married. Some of the Gentiles, on the other hand, perhaps because of past experiences they had had, were inclined to remain single. As the Jews had done with marriage, those Gentiles, reacting to the sexual sin of their past, came to look on celibacy not only as the ideal state but the only truly godly state. Paul acknowledges that singleness is **good**, honorable, and excellent, but he does not support the claim that it is a more spiritual state or that it is more acceptable to God than marriage.

CELIBACY IS TEMPTING

But because of immoralities, let each man have his own wife, and let each woman have her own husband. (7:2)

But because of immoralities does not imply that every Corinthian church member was immoral, although many of them were. Paul is speaking of the *danger* of fornication for those who are single. Because sexual desire is unfulfilled and can be very strong, there is great temptation to sexual immorality for those who are not married, especially in societies—such as that of ancient Rome and our own—where sexual license is freely practiced and glorified.

Marriage cannot be reduced simply to being God's escape valve for the sex drive. Paul does not suggest that Christians go out and find another Christian to marry only to keep from getting into moral sin. He had a much higher view of marriage than that (see Eph. 5:22-23). His purpose here is to stress the reality of the sexual temptations of singleness and to acknowledge that they have a legitimate outlet in marriage. Therefore, **let each man have his own wife, and let each woman have her own husband.**

Scripture gives numerous reasons for marriage. First, marriage is for *procreation*. God commanded Adam and Eve to "be fruitful and multiply" (Gen. 1:28). God intends for mankind to reproduce itself. Marriage is also for *pleasure*. Proverbs speaks of a man's being "exhilarated always" with the wife of his youth (5:18-19), and the Song of Solomon centers around the physical attractions and pleasures of marital love. Marriage is a *partnership*. Woman was created for man to be "a helper suitable for him" (Gen. 2:18). Friendship between husband and wife is one of the key ingredients of a good marriage. Marriage is a *picture* of the church. Husbands are to have authority over and to love their wives as Christ has authority over and loves the church (Eph. 5:23-32). And marriage is for *purity*. It protects from sexual **immorality** by meeting the need for physical fulfillment.

Although celibacy is good, it is not superior to marriage, and it has dangers and temptations that marriage does not have.

CELIBACY IS WRONG FOR MARRIED PERSONS

Let the husband fulfill his duty to his wife, and likewise also the wife to her husband. The wife does not have authority over her own body, but the husband does; and likewise also the husband does not have authority over his own body, but the wife does. Stop depriving one another, except by agreement for a time that you may devote yourselves to prayer, and come together again lest Satan tempt you because of your lack of self-control. (7:3-5)

That celibacy is wrong for those who are married should be an obvious truth, but it was not obvious to some of the Corinthian believers. Because of their erroneous belief in the spiritual superiority of total sexual abstinence, some members in the church practiced it even within marriage. Some overzealous husbands apparently had decided to set themselves apart wholly for God. In doing so, however, they neglected or even denied their responsibilities to their wives, especially in the area of sexual relations. Some wives had done the same thing. The practice of deprivation probably was most common when the spouse was not a believer. But Paul applies his command to all marriages, as is clear from vv. 10-17. Married believers are not to sexually deprive their spouses, whether or not the spouse is a Christian.

The apostle made no exception to the instruction that **the husband fulfill**

his duty to his wife, and likewise also the wife to her husband. God holds all marriage to be sacred and He holds sexual relations between husband and wife not only to be sacred but proper and even obligatory. Paul makes it clear that physical relations within marriage are not simply a privilege and a pleasure but a responsibility. Husbands and wives have a **duty** to give sexual satisfaction to each other. There is no distinction between men and women. The husband has no more rights in this regard than the wife.

In verse 4 Paul reinforces the mutuality of obligation. **The wife does not have authority over her own body, but the husband does; and likewise also the husband does not have authority over his own body, but the wife does.** God honors sexual desire and expression within marriage. In fact, failure for Christian husbands and wives to submit sexually to the **authority** of their spouses brings dishonor to God because it dishonors marriage.

The present tense of *exousiazei* (**have authority over**) indicates a general statement that is always true. Spouses' mutual authority over each other's bodies is continuous; it lasts throughout marriage. In the normal realms of life, a Christian's body is his own, to take care of and to use as a gift from God. And in the deepest spiritual sense, of course, it belongs entirely to God (Rom. 12:1). But in the marital realm, it also belongs to the marriage partner.

Sexual expression within marriage is not an option or an extra. It is certainly not, as it has sometimes been considered, a necessary evil in which spiritual Christians engage only to procreate children. It is far more than a physical act. God created it to be the expression and experience of love on the deepest human level and to be a beautiful and powerful bond between husband and wife.

God intends for marriage to be permanent and for the sexual relationship within it to be permanent. His original plan for marriage did not allow for divorce or for celibacy. Christians are not to forsake unbelieving spouses (vv. 12-17), and they are not to sexually deprive spouses, whether believing or unbelieving. The prohibition is inclusive: **Stop depriving one another.** It is an emphatic command. Sexual relations between a husband and his wife are God-ordained and commanded.

The only exception is both mutual and temporary: **by agreement for a time that you may devote yourselves to prayer.** As in the case of fasting, if both partners agree to abstain from sexual activity for a brief period to allow one or both of them to spend time in intensive prayer, they may do so. Both the ideas of a specific period of **time** and of a specific purpose for **prayer** are implied. The length of time for physical separation and the specific need and purpose of the prayer should be agreed on in advance.

God may give us a strong burden about a person or a ministry, a burden that requires our undivided attention and concentrated prayer. Grief or serious illness, for example, may lead to this. Or we may fall into a particularly harmful sin and need to withdraw for awhile to get straightened out with the Lord.

After the covenant at Sinai had been given, the Lord planned to come down and manifest Himself before Israel "in a thick cloud, in order that the people may hear when I speak with [Moses]." In preparation for His coming, the people were to consecrate themselves by washing their clothes and by abstaining from sexual intercourse for three days (Ex. 19:9-15).

Hundreds of years later, in response to Judah's extreme wickedness, the Lord commanded:

> Return to Me with all your heart, and with fasting, weeping, and mourning; and rend your heart and not your garments. Now return to the Lord your God, . . . Who knows whether He will not turn and relent, . . . Gather the people, sanctify the congregation, assemble the elders. Gather the children and the nursing infants. Let the bridegroom come out of his room and the bride out of her bridal chamber. (Joel 2:12-14, 16)

The need of forgiveness was so great that even brides and grooms were to leave their nuptial chambers to join in national mourning and penitence.

When Jesus Christ returns He will "pour out on the house of David and on the inhabitants of Jerusalem, the Spirit of grace and of supplication, so that they will look on Me whom they have pierced; and they will mourn for Him, . . . the land will mourn, every family by itself; the family of the house of David by itself, and their wives by themselves" (Zech. 12:10, 12). Marriage relations will be forsaken during that time of mourning.

But when such urgent spiritual needs are past, normal marital relationships are to resume. Husbands and wives then are to **come together again.**

The reason for coming back together is explicit: **lest Satan tempt you because of your lack of self-control.** When the time of concentrated prayer is over, normal desires and temptations will return, often with greater intensity. Satan knows that Christians can be especially vulnerable after a mountaintop experience. Our defenses are apt to be down and our pride may be up. Or, because of the experience, we may simply not have the desire for sex for a while afterward. Our spouse, on the other hand, especially if he or she has not shared in the prayer, may have developed a particularly strong desire during the separation. As a guard against falling into temptation ourselves, or of causing our marriage partner to fall into temptation, sexual relations are to resume immediately.

Unless it is by mutual consent, for a specific prayer need and for a brief period of time, sexual abstinence can become a tool of Satan. It is never to be used as pretense for spiritual superiority or as a means of intimidating or manipulating one's spouse. Physical love is to be a normal and regular experience shared by both marriage partners alike, as a gift from God.

Celibacy Is a Gift

But this I say by way of concession, not of command. Yet I wish that all men were even as I myself am. However, each man has his own gift from God, one in this manner, and another in that. (7:6-7)

I do not believe **concession** is the best translation. The Greek (*sungnōmē*) means "to think the same thing as someone, to have a joint opinion, a common mind or understanding." It can also mean "awareness." **But this I say** refers back to what has just been said about marriage. I think Paul was saying that he was *aware* of the goodness of being single and celibate, yet aware also of the privileges and responsibilities of marriage. His comments were **not** meant as a **command** for every believer to be married. Marriage was instituted by God and is the norm for man-woman relationships, and it is a great blessing to mankind. But it is not required for believers or for anyone else. His point was: If you are single that is good, and if you are married or get married, stay married and retain normal marital relations, for that is of God. Spirituality is not determined by marital status.

In one sense, Paul wished that all believers could be unmarried, **even as I myself am.** He said that in light of the great freedom and independence he had as a single person to serve Christ. But he did not expect all believers to be unmarried. He did not expect all who were then single to stay single. And for those who were already married it would be wrong to live as if they were single, to become celibate while married.

Although celibacy is good for Christians who are not married, it is a **gift from God** that He does not give to every believer. Just as it is wrong to misuse a gift that we have, it is also wrong to try to use a gift we do not have. For a person who does not have the gift of celibacy, trying to practice it brings moral and spiritual frustration. But for those who have it as God's gift, singleness, like all His gifts, is a great blessing.

The attitude among Christians today about singleness, however, is often like that of Jewish tradition in Paul's day. It is looked on as a second-class condition. "Not so," says the apostle. If singleness is God's gift to a person, it is God's will for that person to accept and exercise the gift. If that person is submissive to God, he can live in singleness all his life in perfect contentment and happiness.

Obviously, singleness has many practical advantages. It allows much greater freedom in where and how a person serves the Lord. He is freer to move around and to set his own hours and schedule. As Paul points out later in the chapter, married persons have many cares and concerns that the unmarried do not have (vv. 32-34).

Rachel Saint served as a single missionary among the Auca Indians of Ecuador for many years without companionship. She poured out her life and her love to the Indians and found great blessing and fulfillment.

Jesus told the disciples on one occasion, "Not all men can accept this statement, but only those to whom it has been given. For there are eunuchs who were born that way from their mother's womb; and there are eunuchs who were made eunuchs by men; and there are also eunuchs who made themselves eunuchs for the sake of the kingdom of heaven. He who is able to accept this, let him accept it" (Matt. 19:12).

Both Jesus and Paul make it clear that the celibate life is not required by God for all believers and that it can be lived satisfactorily only by those to whom God has given it.

Each man has his own gift from God, one in this manner, and another in that. Our purpose should be to discover the gifts he has given us and to use those gifts faithfully and joyfully in His service, without either envying or disparaging the gifts we do not have.

Divine Guidelines for Marriage (7:8-16)

But I say to the unmarried and to widows that it is good for them if they remain even as I. But if they do not have self-control, let them marry; for it is better to marry than to burn. But to the married I give instructions, not I, but the Lord, that the wife should not leave her husband (but if she does leave, let her remain unmarried, or else be reconciled to her husband), and that the husband should not send his wife away. But to the rest I say, not the Lord, that if any brother has a wife who is an unbeliever, and she consents to live with him, let him not send her away. And a woman who has an unbelieving husband, and he consents to live with her, let her not send her husband away. For the unbelieving husband is sanctified through his wife, and the unbelieving wife is sanctified through her believing husband; for otherwise your children are unclean, but now they are holy. Yet if the unbelieving one leaves, let him leave; the brother or the sister is not under bondage in such cases, but God has called us to peace. For how do you know, O wife, whether you will save your husband? Or how do you know, O husband, whether you will save your wife? (7:8-16)

In the United States today about every other marriage ends in divorce. There are nearly as many divorces as marriages each year. Love today is loudly acclaimed and sought after but it is not much evident—even within marriages.

Marriage problems are not unique to modern times. They have occurred throughout history, and were rampant in New Testament times in the Roman empire. As would have been expected, the church in Corinth was severely afflicted. As has been noted, it is to marriage and some of the problems related to it that the seventh chapter of 1 Corinthians is devoted. Here Paul deals with the serious misconceptions and misbehavior of the Corinthian believers in regard to singleness, celibacy, and marriage. In verses 1-7 he establishes the general principle that marriage is the norm for Christians but that singleness as a special gift of God is good.

In verses 8-16 Paul applies that basic truth to four groups of believers: (1) those who are formerly married; (2) those who are married to believers; (3) those who are married to unbelievers and who want to remain married; and (4) those who are married to unbelievers and who want to leave the marriage. In the first situation God offers an option; in the other three He does not.

GUIDELINES FOR SINGLE CHRISTIANS

But I say to the unmarried and to widows that it is good for them if they remain even as I. But if they do not have self-control, let them marry; for it is better to marry than to burn. (7:8-9)

These verses answer the question, "Should those who were married and divorced before becoming Christians remarry?" No doubt that was a key question in the Corinthian church. Formerly married people came to salvation in Christ and asked if they now had the right to marry someone else. Paul's response here is uniquely fitted to those who want to know their options.

The **unmarried** and **widows** are the two categories of single people mentioned here, but there is a third category of single people ("virgins") indicated in verse 25. Understanding the distinctions in regard to these three groups is essential. "Virgins" (*parthenoi*) clearly refers to single people who have never been married. **Widows** (*chērais*) are single people who formerly were married but were severed from that relationship by the death of the spouse. That leaves the matter of the **unmarried**. Who are they?

The term **unmarried** (*agamos*, from "wedding, or marriage," with the negative prefix *a*) is used only four times in the New Testament, and all four are in this chapter. We need go nowhere else for understanding of this key term. Verse 32 uses it in a way that gives little hint as to its specific meaning; it simply refers to a person who is not married. Verse 34 uses it more definitively: "the woman who is unmarried, and the virgin." We assume Paul has two distinct groups in mind: whoever the unmarried are, they are not virgins. Verse 8 speaks to "the unmarried and to widows," so we can conclude that the **unmarried** are not **widows**. The clearest insight comes in the use of the term in verses 10 and 11: "the wife should not leave [divorce] her husband (but if she does leave, let her remain unmarried. . . .)." The term **unmarried** indicates those who were previously married, but are not widows; people who are now single, but are not virgins. The **unmarried** woman, therefore, is a divorced woman.

Paul is speaking to people who were divorced before coming to Christ. They wanted to know if they had the right to marry. His word to them is that **it is good for them** who are now free of marriage to **remain even as I.** By that statement Paul affirms that he was formerly married. Because marriage seems to have been required for membership in the Sanhedrin, to which Paul may once have belonged, because he had been so devoutly committed to Pharisaic tradition (Gal. 1:14), and because he refers to one who could have been his wife's mother (Rom. 16:13), we may assume that he was once married. His statement here to the previously married confirms that— **even as I.** Likely he was a widower. He does not identify with the virgins but with the unmarried and widows, that is, with the formerly married.

The point is that those who are single when converted to Christ should know that it is good for them to stay that way. There is no need to rush into marriage. Many well-meaning Christians are not content to let people remain single. The urge to play cupid and matchmaker can be strong, but mature believers must resist it. Marriage is not necessary or superior to singleness, and it limits some potential for service to Christ (vv. 32-34).

One of the most beautiful stories associated with Jesus' birth and infancy is that of Anna. When Mary and Joseph brought the baby Jesus to the Temple to present Him to the Lord and to offer a sacrifice, the prophetess Anna recognized Jesus as the Messiah. Much as Simeon had done a short while before, "she came up and began giving thanks to God, and continued to speak of Him to all those who were looking for the redemption of Jerusalem." Her husband had lived only seven years after their marriage, and she had since remained a widow. At the age of 84 she was still faithfully serving the Lord in His Temple, "serving night and day with fastings and prayers" (Luke 2:21-38). She did not look on her lot as inferior and certainly not as meaningless. She had the gift of singleness and used it joyfully in the Lord's work.

Later in the chapter Paul advised believers to remain as they were. Staying single was not wrong, and becoming married or staying married were not wrong. But "in view of the present distress" the Corinthian believers were experiencing, it seemed much better to stay as they were (7:25-28).

If, however, a single believer did **not have self-control,** that person should seek to **marry.** If a Christian is single but does not have the gift of singleness and is being strongly tempted sexually, he or she should pursue marriage. **Let them marry** in the Greek is in the aorist imperative, indicating a strong command. "Get married," Paul says, **for it is better to marry than to burn.** The term means "to be inflamed," and is best understood as referring to strong passion (cf. Rom. 1:27). A person cannot live a happy life, much less serve the Lord, if he is continually burning with sexual desire—even if the desire never results in actual immorality. And in a society such as Corinth's, or ours, in which immorality is so prevalent and accepted, it is especially difficult not to succumb to temptation.

I believe that once a Christian couple decides to get married they should do it fairly soon. In a day of lowered standards, free expression, and constant suggestiveness, it is extremely difficult to stay sexually pure. The practical problems of an early marriage are not nearly as serious as the danger of immorality.

Deciding about marriage obviously is more difficult for the person who has strong sexual desires but who has no immediate prospect for a husband or wife. It is never God's will for Christians to marry unbelievers (2 Cor. 6:14), but neither is it right just to marry the first believer who will say yes. Though we may want very much to be married, we should be careful. Strong feelings of any sort tend to dull judgment and make one vulnerable and careless.

There are several things that Christians in this dilemma ought to do. First, they should not simply seek to be married, but should seek a person they can love, trust, and respect, letting marriage come as a response to that commitment of love. People who simply want to get married for the sake of getting married run a great risk of marrying the wrong person. Second, it is fine to be on the lookout for the "right person," but the best way to *find* the right person is to *be* the right person. If believers are right with God and it is His will for them to be married, He will send the right person—and never too late.

Third, until the right person is found, our energy should be redirected in ways that will be the most helpful in keeping our minds off the temptation. Two of the best ways are spiritual service and physical activity. We should avoid listening to, looking at, or being around anything that strengthens the temptation. We should program our minds to focus only on that which is good and helpful. We should take special care to follow Paul's instruction in Philippians: "Whatever is true, whatever is honorable, whatever is right, whatever is pure, whatever is lovely, whatever is of good repute, if there is any excellence and if anything worthy of praise, let your mind dwell on these things" (4:8).

Fourth, we should realize that, until God gives us the right person, He will provide strength to resist temptation. "God is faithful, who will not allow you to be tempted beyond what you are able, but with the temptation will provide the way of escape also, that you may be able to endure it" (1 Cor. 10:13).

Finally, we should give thanks to the Lord for our situation and be content in it. Salvation brings the dawning of a new day, in which marriage "in the Lord" (v. 39) is an option.

GUIDELINES FOR CHRISTIANS MARRIED TO OTHER CHRISTIANS

But to the married I give instructions, not I, but the Lord, that the wife should not leave her husband (but if she does leave, let her remain unmarried, or else be reconciled to her husband), and that the husband should not send his wife away. (7:10-11)

No distinction is made as to the type of marriage involved. As seen in the last chapter, at least four marital arrangements were practiced in that day—ranging from the common-law *usus* to the noble *confarreatio*. **To the married** covers every type.

That both partners of the marriage in view here were Christians is clear from Paul's giving them **instructions** (which he never gave to unbelievers) and from the fact that in verses 12-16 he deals specifically with marriages in which only one partner is a believer.

Lest there be any doubt as to the source of the teaching here, the apostle adds, **not I, but the Lord.** Jesus had taught the truth during His earthly ministry. Quoting Genesis 2:24, Jesus said, "For this cause a man shall leave his father and mother, and shall cleave to his wife; and the two shall become one flesh," and then added, "What therefore God has joined together, let no man separate" (Matt. 19:5-6). In answer to the disciples' question, Jesus explained that God allowed Moses to permit divorce only because of His peoples' "hardness of heart" (vv. 7-8), and that it was permissible only in the case of adultery (Matt. 5:31-32). "I hate divorce," God declared through Malachi (Mal. 2:16). Divorce is contrary to God's plan for mankind, and when allowed in cases of adultery is only a gracious concession to the innocent party in an irreconcilable case of unfaithfulness. Where there is repentance, there can be restoration.

We do not know why some of the Corinthians wanted to divorce their partners. In light of verses 1-7 it is likely some church members thought they could live holier and more dedicated lives as celibates and wanted to divorce for that reason. Some probably wanted to leave their mates because they saw someone more desirable, or simply because they felt unfulfilled with them. Whatever the reasons, however, they were not to divorce. **The wife should not leave her husband** and **the husband should not send his wife away.** The terms **leave** (*chōrizō*) and **send away** (*aphiēmi*) in this context of man-woman relationships mean divorce, and such action is forbidden.

Paul was not discussing divorce based on adultery, for which Jesus specifically affirmed provision (Matt. 5:32; 19:8-9). He was talking about divorce for other reasons, even supposedly spiritual ones.

Some of the believers in Corinth had already divorced each other or were in motion to that end. To those persons the apostle says, **but if she does leave, let her remain unmarried, or else be reconciled to her husband.** If a Christian does divorce another Christian, except for adultery, neither partner is free to marry another. They must stay single or rejoin their former mate. In God's eyes that union has never been broken. These are not a counselor's suggestions, but the Lord's commands.

GUIDELINES FOR CHRISTIANS MARRIED TO UNBELIEVERS WHO WANT TO STAY MARRIED

But to the rest I say, not the Lord, that if any brother has a wife who is an unbeliever, and she consents to live with him, let him not send her away. And a woman who has an unbelieving husband, and he consents to live with her, let her not send her husband away. For the unbelieving husband is sanctified through his wife, and the unbelieving wife is sanctified through her believing husband; for otherwise your children are unclean, but now they are holy. (7:12-14)

What were Christians to do who were already married to unbelievers, possibly even to immoral and idolatrous pagans? Were they free to divorce the one to whom they were unequally yoked and then free either to live singly or marry a believer? Those were honest questions. In light of Paul's teaching that their bodies were members of Christ and were temples of the Holy Spirit (6:15-20), the Corinthian Christians were justifiably concerned about whether or not to maintain marital union with an unbeliever. Some may have thought that such a union joined Christ to Satan, defiling the believer and the children and dishonoring the Lord. The desire for a Christian partner would be very strong.

Jesus had not taught directly about that problem, and so Paul says, **to the rest say I, not the Lord.** That is not a denial of inspiration or an indication that Paul is only giving his own human opinion. It is only to say that God had not given any previous revelation on the subject, but Paul was now setting it forth. **If any brother has a wife who is an unbeliever, and she consents to live with him, let him not send her away.**

Christians married to unbelievers were not to worry that they themselves, their marriage, or their children would be defiled by the unbelieving spouse. On the contrary, the very opposite was the case. Both the children and the unbelieving spouse would be **sanctified through** the believing **wife** or **husband.**

Being unequally yoked, one flesh with an unbeliever, can be frustrating, discouraging, and even costly. But it need not be defiling because one believer can sanctify a home. In this sense **sanctify** does not refer to salvation; otherwise the spouse would not be spoken of as **unbelieving.** It refers to being set apart, the basic meaning of **sanctify** and **holy,** terms that are from the same Greek root. The sanctification is matrimonial and familial, not personal or spiritual. In God's eyes a home is set apart for Himself when the husband, wife, or, by implication, any other family member, is a Christian. Such a home is not Christian in the full sense, but it is immeasurably superior to one that is totally unbelieving. Even if the Christian is ridiculed and persecuted, unbelievers in the family are blessed because of that believer. One Christian in a home graces the entire home. God's indwelling that believer and all the blessings and graces that flow into the believer's life from heaven will spill over to enrich all who are near.

In addition, although the believer's faith cannot suffice for the salvation of anyone but himself, he is often the means of other family members coming to the Lord by the power of his testimony.

A young woman came up to me after the service one Sunday morning and told me that when she was growing up her grandmother was the only Christian in the family. The grandmother used to speak of her love for Christ and witnessed to the family in what she said and by what she did. Eventually, three of the four grandchildren came to know the Lord, and each one declared that their grandmother had the greatest influence on their decision for Christ.

When God was about to destroy Sodom, Abraham pleaded with Him to spare the city if fifty righteous people lived there. "So the Lord said, 'If I find in Sodom fifty righteous within the city, then I will spare the whole place on their account'" (Gen.

18:26). When that many could not be found, the patriarch reduced the number to forty-five, then to forty, thirty, twenty, and finally ten. In each case the Lord agreed to spare the city, but not even ten righteous could be found. But God was willing to bless many wicked people for the sake even of a few of His own people in their midst.

Furthermore, God looks on the family as a unit. Even if it is divided spiritually, and most of its members are unbelieving and immoral, the entire family is graced by a believer among them. Therefore, if an unbelieving spouse is willing to stay, the believer is not to seek a divorce.

The Christian need not fear that the **children** will be **unclean**, defiled by the unbelieving father or mother. God promises that the opposite is true. They would **otherwise** be **unclean** if both parents were unbelievers. But the Lord guarantees that the presence of just one Christian parent will protect the children. It is not that their salvation is assured but that they are protected from undue spiritual harm and that they will receive spiritual blessing. Because they share in the spiritual benefits of their believing parent, **they are holy.** Often the testimony of the believing parent in this situation is especially effective, because the children see a clear contrast to the unbelieving parent's life, and that leads them to salvation.

GUIDELINES FOR CHRISTIANS MARRIED TO UNBELIEVERS WHO WANT TO LEAVE

Yet if the unbelieving one leaves, let him leave; the brother or the sister is not under bondage in such cases, but God has called us to peace. For how do you know, O wife, whether you will save your husband? Or how do you know, O husband, whether you will save your wife? (7:15-16)

Tertullian (160-230 A.D.), the theologian of Carthage, wrote about heathen husbands being angry with their Christian wives because they wanted to kiss martyrs' bonds, embrace Christians, and visit the cottages of the poor. Often when an unbelieving spouse wants to leave the marriage the believer has no control over the outcome. But Paul says that Christians should not even try to insist on the spouse's staying if he or she is determined to go. **If the unbelieving one leaves, let him leave.** If the unbeliever begins divorce proceedings, the Christian partner is not to contest. Again the word **leave** (*chōrizō*) refers to divorce.

The brother or the sister is not under bondage in such cases. In God's sight the bond between a husband and wife is dissolved only by death (Rom. 7:2), adultery (Matt. 19:9), and an unbeliever's leaving. When the bond, or **bondage,** is broken in any of those ways, a Christian is free to remarry. Throughout Scripture, whenever legitimate divorce occurs, remarriage is assumed. Where divorce is permitted, remarriage is permitted. It is clearly forbidden in the case in verse 11, but here and in other texts dealing with divorce because of adultery it is not. By implication, the permission given for a widow or widower to remarry (Rom. 7:3; because the person is no longer "joined," or bound, to the dead partner) can extend to the present case, where a believer is also no longer bound, **not under bondage.**

God allows divorce in such a case of desertion because He **has called us to peace**. If the unbelieving husband or wife cannot tolerate the spouse's faith and desires to be free from the union, it is better that the marriage be dissolved in order to preserve the peace of His child. Fighting, turmoil, bickering, criticism, and frustration disrupt the harmony and peace that God wants His children to have. Again, it is a concession.

"If possible," Paul says in Romans, "so far as it depends on you, be at peace with all men" (12:18). But when an unbeliever wants out of a marriage, the peace no longer depends on the Christian. Many Christians have tried to keep a marriage together even when the spouse was unbelieving and wanted a divorce. But that course is against God's will. **Let him leave** is not permission but a command.

A **wife** has no assurance that she **will save** her **husband**, and a **husband** has no assurance that he **will save** his **wife**. Regardless of a Christian's motives and hopes, the likelihood of leading the partner to Christ is minimal. If the partner stays in the marriage unwillingly or reluctantly, the likelihood is even less, and the disruption of family **peace** is assured. The Lord therefore allows no option.

Evangelism is not cause enough to maintain a marriage, especially if the unbelieving partner wants to leave. The believer should let God follow that spouse's soul with the message of salvation, and use whomever He will to take up the call to faith.

Christians and Social Revolution

18

(7:17-24)

Only, as the Lord has assigned to each one, as God has called each, in this manner let him walk. And thus I direct in all the churches. Was any man called already circumcised? Let him not become uncircumcised. Has anyone been called in uncircumcision? Let him not be circumcised. Circumcision is nothing, and uncircumcision is nothing, but what matters is the keeping of the commandments of God. Let each man remain in that condition in which he was called. Were you called while a slave? Do not worry about it; but if you are able also to become free, rather do that. For he who was called in the Lord while a slave, is the Lord's freedman; likewise he who was called while free, is Christ's slave. You were bought with a price; do not become slaves of men. Brethren, let each man remain with God in that condition in which he was called. (7:17-24)

Much has been said and written about the social role and responsibility of the church. Periodically throughout church history, and strongly in our own day, people have claimed that Christianity should be an agent of external social reform, even of revolution if necessary.

Most sensitive believers have wondered how and to what extent they should be involved, if at all, in promoting social, economic, and political change. All human institutions and forms of government are imperfect; some are obviously corrupt, cruel, and unjust. But what are Christians, individually or collectively, to do about wrongs and abuses in civil systems and social practices?

First Corinthians 7:17-24 is not a full treatise on that subject, but it plainly teaches the basic principle by which Christians should look at and respond to the civil and social conditions in which they live. The principle is this: Christians should willingly accept the situation into which God has placed them and be content to serve Him there. It is a principle against which human nature rebels, and Paul states it three times in these 8 verses, so that his readers could not miss his point. We should not be preoccupied with changing our outward circumstances.

THE PRINCIPLE STATED

Only, as the Lord has assigned to each one, as God has called each, in this manner let him walk. And thus I direct in all the churches. Was any man called already circumcised? Let him not become uncircumcised. Has anyone been called in uncircumcision? Let him not be circumcised. Circumcision is nothing, and uncircumcision is nothing, but what matters is the keeping of the commandments of God. (7:17-19)

Christians individually and corporately are to minister in many ways, including the practical, material ways of feeding the hungry, healing the sick and injured, and other such services. Christianity has far and away been the leader in building hospitals and orphanages, in visiting prisoners, in helping the poor, and in ministering in countless other ways that are considered social services. But those are ministries Christians do as Christians, not services that they persuade society to perform.

Christ made it clear that He did not come to instigate an external social revolution, as many Jews of His days thought the Messiah would do. Jesus told Pilate, "My kingdom is not of this world. If My kingdom were of this world, then My servants would be fighting, that I might not be delivered up to the Jews; but as it is, My kingdom is not of this realm" (John 18:36). Christ's mission was "to seek and to save that which was lost" (Luke 19:10), and that is the mission of His church. When Christianity becomes closely identified with a social movement, the message of the gospel is in danger of being lost.

When it is faithfully followed, however, biblical Christianity cannot help having radical effects on every person, institution, and practice around it. But the primary purpose of the gospel is to change people, not change society. Its focus is on inward change, not outward. We should be satisfied to be where God has put us, to accept what **the Lord has assigned** us, and to be faithful in whatever condition **God has called** us.

Obviously the apostle is not telling believers to stay in occupations, professions, or habits that are inherently immoral or illegal. A thief was not to keep stealing, a temple priestess was not to continue in prostitution, or a drunkard was not to keep getting drunk. Everything sinful is to be forsaken. The issue has to do with believers being content in the social conditions and situations they are in when saved.

Several areas of discontent were prevalent in the Corinthian church. Some believers wanted to change their marital status—from single to married, from married to single, or from an unbelieving partner to a believing one. Some were slaves and wanted to be free. They had misinterpreted, and often abused, the truth of Christian freedom—taking it to mean freedom to do as they pleased, instead of freedom to do as God pleased.

The unity of the church at Corinth was seriously fractured. Not only were there numerous parties and factions, but some groups were encouraging those with the gift of celibacy to get married, while other groups were encouraging those who were married to become celibate. Slaves were chafing under their bondage and were trying to find spiritual justification for demanding freedom. Although the gospel is the antithesis of the standards and values of the world, it does not disdain or seek to destroy governments, societies, or families. Rather where the gospel is believed and obeyed, some of the most obvious by-products are better government, better societies, and better families.

But Christians can be Christians in a dictatorship, a democracy, or even under anarchy. We can be Christians whether we are man, woman, child, married, single, divorced, Jew, Gentile, slave, or free. We can be Christians in Russia or the United States, in Cuba or China, in France or Japan. Whatever we are and wherever we are, we can be Christians.

God does not justify corrupt governments or immoral societies, and they will be judged in His time and in His way. But the purpose of the gospel of His Son Jesus Christ is not to revolutionize social institutions but to revolutionize hearts. The gospel is directed at the human heart, not at human society. Because faithful Christians are better husbands or wives, better friends, better slaves or masters, better sons or daughters, and better citizens, they cannot help contributing to better societies. But using natural means to try to effect a better society is not their ministry.

The gospel can be planted and take root wherever there is a person to hear and accept it, even in countries or in families that are pagan, atheistic, humanistic, and avowedly anti-Christian. As the saying goes, we should bloom where we are planted. Where **the Lord has assigned** and where **God has called** is where we should **walk.**

The principle is universal. It was not given only to the divided, contentious, and immature Corinthians, but to **all the churches.** God's primary purpose for His church in every nation is for them to evangelize, to change the world through spiritual regeneration, not social revolution.

The first illustration Paul gives of that general principle has to do with identity as Jew or Gentile. **Was any man called already circumcised? Let him not become uncircumcised.** In the epistles, being **called** by God (cf. v. 17) always refers to an effectual call to salvation. When a Jew is saved, he should not try to become like a Gentile.

This had a very specific application. Circumcision was an embarrassment in the Roman world. According to the Maccabees, some Jewish men "made themselves uncircumcised." Josephus tells us that during the Greek rule of the eastern Mediterranean several centuries before Christ, some Jewish men who wanted to be accepted into Greek society had surgery performed to make themselves appear uncircumcised when they bathed or exercised at the gymnasiums. They literally became **uncircumcised** surgically. The Roman encyclopedist Celsus, in the first century A.D., wrote a detailed description of the surgical procedure for decircumcision.

The practice was so common that considerable rabbinic literature addressed the problem (e.g., Aboth 3:11; Jerushalmi Peah 1 and 16b; Lamentations Rabbah 1:20). Jews who had such surgery were referred to as epispatics, a name taken from the euphemistic term *epispaomai,* meaning "to draw over," or "to pull towards." That is the very term Paul uses here for **uncircumcised.** Perhaps some Jewish Christians thought that was a way to demonstrate their break with Judaism.

The apostle's meaning here can also be figurative. **Circumcised** and **uncircumcised** were commonly used to represent Jew and Gentile, respectively. By extension, the terms may even have related to women, for whom literal circumcision obviously does not apply. And the idea could also be that, when they become Christians, Jews are not to give up their Jewishness and try to appear like Gentiles. Many religious beliefs must be changed, but not racial or cultural identity as Jews.

The same principle applies to Gentiles. **Has anyone been called in uncircumcision? Let Him not be circumcised.** Gentiles who become Christians are not to become like Jews.

The problem concerning circumcision was not as serious in Corinth as it was in Galatia, where Judaizers taught that circumcision was necessary for salvation (Gal. 5:2-3). In Corinth the practice may have been viewed as a mark of special dedication and a means of special blessing. But circumcision is not necessary either for salvation or for blessing. It has no spiritual significance or value for Christians at all. **Circumcision is nothing, and uncircumcision is nothing.**

For Jews to want to appear as Gentiles or for Gentiles to subscribe to things unique to Jews was both spiritually and practically wrong. It was spiritually wrong because it added an outward form to the gospel that the Lord does not require and that has no spiritual merit or meaning. It was practically wrong because it unnecessarily separated believers from their families and friends and made witnessing to them much more difficult.

What matters is the keeping of the commandments of God. Obedience is the only mark of faithfulness the Lord recognizes. Obedience is sometimes costly, but it is always possible. We can be obedient anywhere and in any circumstance. The issue is internal.

THE PRINCIPLE REPEATED

Let each man remain in that condition in which he was called. Were you called while a slave? Do not worry about it; but if you are able also to become

free, rather do that. For he who was called in the Lord while a slave, is the Lord's freedman; likewise he who was called while free, is Christ's slave. You were bought with a price; do not become slaves of men. Brethren, let each man remain with God in that condition in which he was called. (7:20-24)

For the second time Paul states the principle of being content to stay in the condition we were in when saved, whether it is racial or social. The focus of a Christian's concern should be on divinely supernatural things.

Another illustration is given, this time concerning slaves. Paul's point is not to approve of slavery or to suggest that it is as good a condition to live under as freedom. His point is that, if a person is a slave, he is still able to live a Christian life. He is every bit as able to obey and serve Christ in slavery as in freedom. No circumstance, no matter how terrible, painful, or unjust, can keep us from being in every sense a Christian.

A slave can, in fact, serve Christ through his slavery. Paul wrote the Ephesians,

> Slaves, be obedient to those who are your masters according to the flesh, with fear and trembling, in the sincerity of your heart, as to Christ; not by way of eyeservice, as men-pleasers, but as slaves of Christ, doing the will of God from the heart. With good will render service, as to the Lord, and not to men, knowing that whatever good thing each one does, this he will receive back from the Lord, whether slave or free. (Eph. 6:5-8)

Paul consistently taught that principle. Slaves were to serve their masters honestly and sincerely, "as for the Lord rather than for men" (Col. 3:23). Slaves had a unique opportunity to testify for the Lord. They were to show their human masters that they worked hard and honestly not because they were forced to but because they wanted to, out of love for and obedience to their true Lord and Master. They could demonstrate true contentment and peace in the midst of slavery, thus showing the inner provision of salvation.

The book of Philemon centers around the runaway slave Onesimus, whom Paul had led to Christ while in prison (v. 10). As it happens, Onesimus's owner, Philemon, was a Christian. He was Paul's "beloved brother and fellow worker," and the church in Colossae met in his house (vv. 1-2). The apostle makes a strong personal and spiritual appeal for Philemon to forgive Onesimus and to accept him back, not just as a slave but as a Christian brother (v. 16). Yet, as embarrassing as it has been to some Christian activists, Paul did not condemn slavery or question Philemon's legal rights over his slave. He did not ask for social equality for Onesimus. In fact, he even used slavery as an analogy for the believer's walk with God.

In the Roman empire of Paul's time, perhaps fifty percent of the population were slaves. But unlike most slaves throughout history, the slave of that day often was better educated, more skilled, and more literate and cultured than the average free person. A large percentage of the doctors, teachers, accountants, and other professionals were slaves. Many of them lived in relative ease and were treated with respect. Others, of course, lived in constant poverty and humiliation under cruel and merciless owners.

Paul made no distinction. Any slave, in any circumstance, was to be willing to remain as he was. Only sin can keep us from obeying and serving the Lord; circumstance cannot. Therefore if we are in a difficult, uncomfortable, and restricting situation, we should **not worry about it,** but should determine to be faithful as long as the Lord leaves us there.

Even having affirmed that principle, Paul makes it clear that he did not consider slavery to be the most desirable state. **But if you are able also to become free, rather do that.** Freedom is immeasurably better than slavery, and a Christian is not more spiritual for staying in slavery. If he has opportunity to become free, as did many slaves in New Testament times, a believer should take advantage of it. Paul was content to be in jail and to serve the Lord as long as he was jailed. He carried on much of his ministry from a jail cell. But when he was freed he left jail. If a Christian slave has the opportunity to become free, he should **rather do that.**

Although the gospel does not approve of removing slavery by social revolution, the gospel throughout history has brought the freedom of more slaves than any human philosophy, movement, or political system. In past times, some Christians, unfortunately, have supported and tried to justify slavery. But the Bible does not; and where Christians are faithful to Scripture, slavery cannot flourish.

Even while he is a slave, a Christian is **the Lord's freedman.** No bondage is as terrible or enslaving as that from which Christ redeems us. In Him we are freed from sin, from Satan, from judgment and condemnation, from hell, and from the curse of the Law. From the slavery that really matters, every Christian has already been delivered. In Christ we have the greatest, most complete, and most glorious freedom possible. A person who is **the Lord's freedman,** and who will remain so throughout all eternity, should not be overly concerned about remaining in human bondage for a few years.

Lest Christians who were physically free should gloat, thinking they were more favored by God than slaves or that their freedom meant license to do as they pleased, Paul reminds them, **likewise he who was called while free, is Christ's slave.** Our freedom in Christ is not *to* sin but *from* sin, not freedom to do our own will but freedom to do His will. In Christ we are "freed from sin and enslaved to God" (Rom. 6:22).

When we focus on our spiritual freedom and our slavery in God, our freedom or slavery among men is not all-important, and we can look at it in the right perspective and live in it in the right attitude. It does not matter whether we are physically bound or free, only that we are both spiritually bound and free—in the wonderful paradox of the gospel.

Because we have been **bought with a price,** our great concern, whether we are free or in bondage, should be that we do not allow ourselves to **become slaves of men.** Here Paul does not mean physical slavery but spiritual slavery. He is speaking of becoming slaves of the ways of men, the ways of the world, the ways of the flesh. That is the slavery into which many of the Corinthian believers had fallen, the slavery that caused their divisions and strife and their immaturity and immorality.

We have been bought with the inestimable **price** of the "precious blood, as of a lamb unblemished and spotless, the blood of Christ" (1 Pet. 1:19). We have been bought by God and we belong to God. We must never become the moral and spiritual **slaves of men,** living by their standards and seeking to please them.

For a third time Paul gives the principle: **Brethren, let each man remain with God in that condition in which he was called.** However it is that we have been saved (**called**), and in whatever **condition** we now are in, we should be willing to **remain.** God allows us to be where we are and to stay where we are for a purpose. Conversion is not the signal for a person to leave his social condition, his marriage or his singleness, his human master, or his other circumstances. We are to leave sin and anything that encourages sin; but otherwise we are to stay where we are until God moves us.

Reasons for
Remaining Single
(7:25-40)

19

Now concerning virgins I have no command of the Lord, but I give an opinion as one who by the mercy of the Lord is trustworthy. I think then that this is good in view of the present distress, that it is good for a man to remain as he is. Are you bound to a wife? Do not seek to be released. Are you released from a wife? Do not seek a wife. But if you should marry, you have not sinned; and if a virgin should marry, she has not sinned. Yet such will have trouble in this life, and I am trying to spare you. But this I say, brethren, the time has been shortened, so that from now on those who have wives should be as though they had none; and those who weep, as though they did not weep; and those who rejoice, as though they did not rejoice; and those who buy, as though they did not possess; and those who use the world, as though they did not make full use of it; for the form of this world is passing away. But I want you to be free from concern. One who is unmarried is concerned about the things of the Lord, how he may please the Lord; but one who is married is concerned about the things of the world, how he may please his wife, and his interests are divided. And the woman who is unmarried, and the virgin, is concerned about the things of the Lord, that she may be holy both in body and spirit; but one who is married is concerned about the things of the world, how she may please her husband. And this I say for your own benefit; not to put a restraint upon you, but to promote what is seemly, and to secure undistracted devotion to the Lord.

But if any man thinks that he is acting unbecomingly toward his virgin daughter, if she should be of full age, and if it must be so, let him do what he wishes, he does not sin; let her marry. But he who stands firm in his heart, being under no constraint, but has authority over his own will, and has decided this in his own heart, to keep his own virgin daughter, he will do well. So then both he who gives his own virgin daughter in marriage does well, and he who does not give her in marriage will do better.

A wife is bound as long as her husband lives; but if her husband is dead, she is free to be married to whom she wishes, only in the Lord. But in my opinion she is happier if she remains as she is; and I think that I also have the Spirit of God. (7:25-40)

In his discussion of marriage and singleness, Paul has made it clear that neither state is spiritually better than the other. The Roman Catholic idea that celibate priests and nuns are necessarily more devoted to God is contrary to this teaching. Being married or single has nothing in itself to do with spirituality. A married person for whom it is the Lord's will to be married is no more or less spiritual than a single person for whom it is the Lord's will to be single. Spirituality is based on obedience to God. Just as in relation to circumcision, "what matters is the keeping of the commandments of God" (7:19).

Many books, magazine articles, conferences, and programs today focus on the biblical standards for marriage and the family. Many of those are excellent and helpful. Much less attention, however, is given to what the Bible says about singleness. A great deal of the literature and programs for singles is directed toward helping them "cope," and seems to reflect an underlying assumption that being single is not quite normal and is certainly not desirable.

Admittedly, many who are single have difficulty because sin has brought on the singleness, and they have to lie in the empty bed they made for themselves. But for the person to whom God has given the gift of singleness (7:7) that state has many practical advantages. Continuing to answer the questions about which the Corinthians had written him (7:1), Paul gives six reasons for remaining single: (1) the pressure of the system (vv. 25-27); (2) the problems of the flesh (v. 28); (3) the passing of the world (vv. 29-31); (4) the preoccupations of marriage (32-35); (5) the promises of fathers (vv. 36-38); and (6) the permanency of marriage (vv. 39-40).

THE PRESSURE OF THE SYSTEM

Now concerning virgins I have no command of the Lord, but I give an opinion as one who by the mercy of the Lord is trustworthy. I think then that this is good in view of the present distress, that it is good for a man to remain as he

is. Are you bound to a wife? Do not seek to be released. Are you released from a wife? Do not seek a wife. (7:25-27)

The principle here is **that it is good . . . to remain as** [one] **is,** and those in view are **virgins,** including both women and men (**a man**).

Again (cf. v. 12) Paul points out that Jesus gave no direct teaching on the goodness of singleness (**I have no command of the Lord**), although He alludes to it in Matt. 19:12. Yet the apostle's teaching is no less divine and authoritative. **Opinion** (*gnōmē*) can carry the ideas of "judgment, consideration, and conviction." As an apostle **who by the mercy of the Lord is trustworthy,** Paul's conviction was that it is better for single Christians to remain single, if they have the gift from God.

But although this perspective is authoritative, it is not given as an absolute or as a command. It is an authoritative guideline, thoroughly dependable advice, and is twice stated in verse 26 to be **good.** Paul and the Lord are saying that singleness makes good sense.

The first reason Paul gives for remaining single is the pressure of the system, the world situation of that day, that he called **the present distress.** *Anankē* (**distress**) means "a stress, calamity," or sometimes "the means of calamity" (such as torture or violence). Some suggest that the reference is to the violent conflict between the new creation in Christ and the old cosmos, the world system. When a person becomes a Christian he immediately gets into some degree of conflict with the ungodly system around him.

Mention of **the present** distress, however, may also indicate that Paul had a more specific and severe type of conflict in mind. Countless Christians had been arrested, beaten, imprisoned, and even killed because of the gospel. Jesus had warned the disciples that they would be made "outcasts from the synagogue," and that "an hour is coming for everyone who kills you to think that he is offering service to God" (John 16:2).

Paul seemed to sense the coming terrible Roman persecutions, the first of which would begin under Nero some ten years after Paul wrote 1 Corinthians. That emperor refined torture to a diabolical art, and his name became synonymous with sadistic cruelty. He had Christians sewn up in animal skins and thrown before wild dogs to be torn apart and eaten. Other believers were dressed in clothes soaked in wax, tied to trees, and set on fire—to become human candles for his garden.

Corinth itself would furnish one of the early Christian martyrs. According to Foxe's *Christian Martyrs,* Erastus, the treasurer of that city (Rom. 16:23) and probably a convert of Paul's, was tortured to death in Philippi.

Persecution is difficult enough for a single person, but the problems and pain are multiplied for one who is married. If Paul had been married, his suffering would have been magnified by his worry about his family and knowledge of their worry about him. They would have suffered every time he was beaten or stoned or imprisoned and would have been constantly fearful for his life. Who would have taken care of them in his absence? Who would have taught his children and comforted his wife? His suffering and his practical problems would have increased and the effectiveness of his ministry decreased. Married believers who go through social turmoil and persecution cannot escape carrying a much heavier load than those who are single.

Those who are already married, however, must **not seek to be released.** Marriage is a lifelong bond that can be broken only by death, adultery, or divorce by an unbelieving spouse. Other problems, no matter how severe, are never grounds for divorce.

For those who have the gift of singleness, therefore, it is much wiser to remain single. **Are you released from a wife? Do not seek a wife.** "Cherish your singleness as a blessing from God," Paul is saying. "Take advantage of its many advantages."

God still gives the gift of singleness to some of His children. And many signs point to times of increasing conflict and even persecution for Christians in our world. In Matthew 24 Jesus vividly pictured the turmoil and terror of the end times. It would be characterized by wars, apostasy, persecution, false prophets, and universal tribulation. We can already see overpopulation, pollution, rampant crime and immorality, false prophets and cults, apostasy, and increased threat of global war. The turn of the century could produce widespread warfare, civil strife, revolution, famine, disease, persecution, despotism, natural disasters, and economic stagnation and depression.

THE PROBLEMS OF THE FLESH

But if you should marry, you have not sinned; and if a virgin should marry, she has not sinned. Yet such will have trouble in this life, and I am trying to spare you. (7:28)

Paul again makes it clear that it is not a sin for single believers to get married, as long as it is to another believer (v. 39; cf. 2 Cor. 6:14). Even those with the gift of singleness do not sin if they get married. So **if you should marry,** for whatever reason, **you have not sinned.** The point is that marriage is a legitimate option, but it is good to consider first the option of singleness.

Yet such will have trouble in this life, and I am trying to spare you. The apostle is giving practical advice, not a moral or spiritual command. Believers are still sinful and subject to limitations and weaknesses of the flesh. It is hard enough for a sinner to live with himself, let alone with another sinner. When two people are bound together in marriage the problems of human nature are multiplied. Close living allows us to see our partner's faults more clearly, and vice versa. Children of Christian parents are born sinful just as is every child, and they do not become sinless when they are saved. They will have some measure of conflict with each other and with their parents.

It is not that marriage is not rewarding, or that family life is uninterrupted trouble. A loving, devoted, spiritual family not only is a great joy and strength to its members but also strengthens and blesses those around it. Paul is simply pointing out that marriage may cause some problems while it solves others. It is not intended by God to resolve all personal, emotional, or spiritual difficulties. It definitely intensifies some of them.

Trouble (*thlipsis*) literally means "pressed together, or under pressure." Marriage presses two people together in the closest possible ways. The two become one, but they are still two personalities, two distinct people with their own likes and dislikes, their own characteristics, emotions, temperaments, and wills. Each partner has some degree of anger, selfishness, dishonesty, pride, forgetfulness, and thoughtlessness. That is true even of the best marriages. When one partner is an unbeliever, or is immature, self-centered, temperamental, or domineering, every conflict is magnified.

Marriage involves conflicts, demands, hardships, sacrifices, and adjustments that singleness does not. Marriage is ordained of God, good, holy, and fulfilling; but it does not solve all problems. It brings more. Marriage never should be used as a way of escape, even from loneliness. Many people carry their loneliness right into marriage, and end up making another person lonely. And although it is God's means for normal sexual fulfillment, marriage does not end temptation to lust and immorality. Paul tells those who do not have sexual self-control to "marry; for it is better to marry than to burn" (7:9). But even though there is the satisfaction of physical desire, the mind may be drawn to illicit fulfillment. Sexual sins will not be corrected by marriage. They may only be worsened by adding another person to their list of afflicted people. Through repentance and forgiveness they can, of course, be removed after a person is married—but they will not be removed *by* the marriage. Nor is marriage a guarantee that sexual sin will not return. There are troubles unique to singleness, but they may be exceeded by those in marriage.

THE PASSING OF THE WORLD

But this I say, brethren, the time has been shortened, so that from now on those who have wives should be as though they had none; and those who weep, as though they did not weep; and those who rejoice, as though they did not rejoice; and those who buy, as though they did not possess; and those who use the world, as though they did not make full use of it; for the form of this world is passing away. (7:29-31)

The focus of this passage is at the end of verse 31: **for the form of this world is passing away. Form** (*schēma*) means "fashion, manner of life, way of doing things, or mode of existence." The mode of the **world** is impermanence; it **is passing away.**

Although God-ordained and blessed, marriage is not an eternal relationship. Speaking of the angels in heaven, Jesus said that "they neither marry, nor are given in marriage" (Matt. 22:30). Godly marriages are "made in heaven," but they will not carry over into heaven. Marriage will disappear with this world, because it is designed only for this world, not the next. Cults that teach of marriage in heaven contradict one of the Lord's clearest and most specific teachings. Marriage **is passing away.**

The time (*kairos*) refers to a definite period, a fixed, appointed time; and that period **has been shortened**, or drawn together so that it is a small amount. Human life at its longest is brief, "a vapor that appears for a little while and then vanishes away" (James 4:14). "All flesh is like grass, and all its glory like the flower of grass. The grass withers, and the flower falls off" (1 Pet. 1:24; cf. Isa. 40:6-8). In times of persecution life is often made even more brief.

For husbands and wives to live **as though they had none,** does not teach that marriage is no longer binding on believers or that their marital responsibilities are reduced. Marriage lasts only for life, and is therefore as brief as life. Yet a brief life and hard circumstances do not lessen the obligations of husbands and wives. Among other things wives are to be subject to their husbands, husbands are to love their wives (Eph. 5:22-25, 28, 33; Col. 3:18-19), and neither is to deprive the other of marital rights (1 Cor. 7:3-5). Paul is teaching that marriage should not reduce a Christian's obligation and devotion to the Lord and His work. The responsibilities of marriage are no excuse for slacking the Lord's work. That is to invert the priorities.

Today it has become increasingly difficult, because of close attachment to families, to get Christians—including missionaries—to be strongly dedicated to serving the Lord. In many cases they do not want to be separated from the companionship of their wives for more than a week or two at most, even though an important ministry may need more time than that. There must be a balance, a scriptural balance, between fulfilling marriage needs and serving the Lord.

The primary affections of all Christians, whether married or single, should be set "on the things above, not on the things that are on the earth" (Col. 3:2). "Do not love the world, nor the things in the world. If anyone loves the world, the love of the Father is not in him. . . . And the world is passing away, and also its lusts; but the one who does the will of God abides forever" (1 John 2:15, 17). We must understand the priority of the eternal over the temporal.

In addition to marriage, Paul gives four other areas in which priorities and perspectives must be kept right. The second and third areas have to do with the emotions of sorrow and joy. **Those who weep** should live **as though they did not weep; and those who rejoice, as though they did not rejoice.** Emotions are more controllable than we sometimes think, especially for Christians. We are not to be emotionless, and certainly not hard-hearted or indifferent. Love does not allow such attitudes. But Christian love is much more than emotion; it is an act of will, not simply a reaction to circumstances. True love will, in fact, help keep our emotions in proportion and perspective. When a husband, wife, child, or dear friend dies or becomes crippled or diseased, we do not laugh or celebrate. On the other hand, the mature Christian does not fall apart and lose all hope and purpose and motivation.

With our emphasis on celebration and happiness it is also easy for believers to get carried away with rejoicing over those things that pass away. A personal success, an inheritance, or a business promotion sometimes excites us more than a spiritual victory. Even when we give the Lord credit for the blessing, we can lose our perspective and be controlled more by our emotions than by our good judgment and spiritual priorities.

The fourth area of concern is that of finances and possessions: **and those who buy, as though they did not possess.** Corinthian Christians were in no more danger in this area than many believers today. The accumulation of money and of the things it can **buy** is a preoccupation of many Christians, who in this regard cannot be distinguished from the unbelieving world around them. Many of us are more concerned about our bank accounts, houses, and cars than about our spirituality— more concerned about the outward than the inward. We are strongly attached to the **form of this world,** even though we know it **is passing away.**

The fifth area of concern is that of pleasure: **and those who use the world, as though they did not make full use of it.** In times of affluence, ease, permissiveness, and inordinate self-acceptance it is easy to live for pleasure. Pleasures that are not immoral or extravagant may still be worldly. More leisure, more vacation time, earlier retirement, more comfortable homes, and such things can so occupy our interest and time that the things of the Spirit are neglected.

None of the five areas about which Paul warns is inherently bad. Marriage, sorrow, rejoicing, possessions, and pleasure all have a proper place in the Christian life. In fact, each is a part of God's provision for life here. Asceticism not only is not taught in Scripture, it is forbidden (Col. 2:18, 23; 1 Tim. 4:3). But human relationships, emotions, possessions, and pleasures become sinful when they dominate thought and behavior, and especially when they detract us from the Lord's work. We are to hold marriage in the highest honor (Heb. 13:4), to "rejoice with those who rejoice, and weep with those who weep" (Rom. 12:15), and not despise earthly possessions. Our "heavenly Father knows that [we] need all these things" (Matt. 6:32). But we should not overvalue those things, knowing that they are **passing away.**

THE PREOCCUPATIONS OF MARRIAGE

But I want you to be free from concern. One who is unmarried is concerned about the things of the Lord, how he may please the Lord; but one who is married is concerned about the things of the world, how he may please his wife, and his interests are divided. And the woman who is unmarried, and the virgin, is concerned about the things of the Lord, that she may be holy both in body and spirit; but one who is married is concerned about the things of the world, how she may please her husband. And this I say for your own benefit; not to put a restraint upon you, but to promote what is seemly, and to secure undistracted devotion to the Lord. (7:32-35)

The fourth reason for staying single is the preoccupations that marriage brings. Both husbands and wives are **concerned about the things of the world.** They are concerned about the earthly needs of each other, as they should be. The husband is concerned about **how he may please his wife,** and the wife about **how** she may please her husband. The one who is unmarried (here *agamos* is used in a general way) is concerned about the things of the Lord, how he may please the Lord and how she may be holy both in body and spirit. But the married person's interests are divided between the earthly and the heavenly. And so it should be.

The woman who is unmarried, (here *agamos* is used in the sense of divorced) and the virgin (in contrast to those single by divorce) are able to be holy in body and spirit. Holy is used here in its basic sense of separation, being set apart. Single Christians, whether formerly married or never married, are not intrinsically more righteous or faithful than married ones. But they are able, because of fewer family demands and obligations, to be more devoted to the Lord's work. Being holy, or separated, is contrasted with being divided. It is not that the married believer has divided spiritual loyalties or that the unmarried is more spiritually faithful. Many married believers are holy in the sense of being highly devoted to the Lord, and many single believers are divided in their spiritual interests. But *practically,* the unmarried person, both in body and spirit, is potentially able to set himself or herself apart from the things of this life more exclusively for the Lord's work than is the married.

Married Christians should not feel guilty about being married and unmarried Christians should not feel guilty about getting married. The apostle is not trying to add to the burdens and cares that married persons already have, and he is not trying to force single believers into the permanent mold of singleness. This I say for your own benefit; not to put a restraint upon you, but to promote what is seemly, and to secure undistracted devotion to the Lord.

Marriage does not prevent great devotion to the Lord, and singleness does not guarantee it. But singleness has fewer hindrances and more advantages. It is easier for a single person to be singleminded in the things of the Lord. The married Christian has no choice. His interests *must* be divided. He cannot be faithful to the Lord if he is unfaithful to his family. "If anyone does not provide for his own, and especially for those of his household, he has denied the faith, and is worse than an unbeliever" (1 Tim. 5:8). The single person, however, has a choice. He is free to marry or not. He is not under restraint to remain single. His choice is not between right and wrong but between good and better.

Paul was not putting a legalistic noose (the literal meaning of restraint) around the necks of single Christians. They are not under compulsion either to marry or to remain single. In advising them to remain as they were, he had two motives, both of them for their own benefit. He wanted to spare them trouble (v. 28; cf. v. 32), and he wanted them to have undistracted devotion to the Lord. The word devotion has the idea of waiting alongside the Lord as those who serve (cf. 9:13).

THE PROMISES OF FATHERS

But if any man thinks that he is acting unbecomingly toward his virgin daughter, if she should be of full age, and if it must be so, let him do what he wishes, he does not sin; let her marry. But he who stands firm in his heart, being under no constraint, but has authority over his own will, and has decided this in his own heart, to keep his own virgin daughter, he will do well. So then both he who gives his own virgin daughter in marriage does well, and he who does not give her in marriage will do better. (7:36-38)

In Jewish culture, parents, and particularly fathers, had long had a dominant role in deciding whom their children would marry. The same general custom prevailed in many ancient societies, including that of Rome. Some historians credit Rome's decline in part to the weakening of the family caused by loss of parental control in arranging marriages. In New Testament times the arranged marriage, especially for young people, was the norm.

In light of the extant teaching about the advantages of singleness, some of the fathers in Corinth apparently had dedicated their young daughters to the Lord as permanent virgins. But when the daughters became of marriageable age, many of them no doubt wanted to be married, and their fathers were in a quandary. Should they break the vow they made for the girl? It is likely that many of the girls did not have the gift of singleness and were struggling with their desire to get married and their desire to please their fathers and the Lord. The problem was among those mentioned in the church's letter to Paul (7:1).

Again the emphasis is on the option believers have in regard to marriage. If the intended partner is a Christian, marriage is always permissible. A father who had vowed his daughter's remaining single in order to serve the Lord more devotedly was free to change his mind and allow her to marry if she were insistent. After all, it was a vow made for someone else, and was therefore subject to that person's spiritual needs. **If she should be of full age, and if it must be so, let him do what he wishes, he does not sin; let her marry.** Just as unmarried people themselves are under no restraint (v. 35) and do not commit sin by marrying (v. 28), neither does a father who has made a vow do wrong by changing his mind. His making the vow is good; but if his daughter is not able or inclined to follow it, both she and her father are free to do as they wish. **If it must be so** indicates that she really is designed for marriage, and the father should allow it.

But if the father **stands firm in his heart,** that is, does not change his mind about the promise; and is **under no constraint** by the daughter to change his mind; and has a good and pure motive (**has authority over his own will**) and is deeply committed (**decided this in his own heart**); he may **keep his own virgin daughter. Constraint** is better translated "necessity," referring to the daughter's necessity to get married (cf. "if it must be so," v. 36). Only the daughter's unwillingness to keep the vow should cause the father to change his mind. His steadfastness in his vow will encourage his daughter to be steadfast in hers. In doing that **he will do well.**

Paul repeats the option: **So then both he who gives his own virgin daughter in marriage does well, and he who does not give her in marriage will**

do better. As with the single themselves (v. 28), the choice is not between right and wrong but between good (**well**) and **better.**

THE PERMANENCY OF MARRIAGE

A wife is bound as long as her husband lives; but if her husband is dead, she is free to be married to whom she wishes, only in the Lord. But in my opinion she is happier if she remains as she is; and I think that I also have the Spirit of God. (7:39-40)

This additional word about singleness is not tacked on to Paul's discussion, as some interpreters suggest. It focuses on the permanency of the marriage relationship. The relationship is not permanent in the sense of being eternal but in the sense of being lifelong. It is binding as long as both partners are alive. The disciples responded to this teaching of our Lord by saying, "If the relationship of the man with his wife is like this, it is better not to marry" (Matt. 19:10). Although Christians with the gift of singleness are free to get married, they should keep in mind that they are bound for the rest of their lives if they should die before their partners. In any case the believer will be **bound as long as her husband** [or wife] **lives,** which is often well into old age and past the time for the most productive service to the Lord.

If the partner **is dead,** the believer is **free to be married,** as long as the new partner is **in the Lord** (cf. 9:5). The particular advice here is to widows, but it applies also to widowers. The two main points are that widowed believers are not bound to stay single but that, if they do remarry, it must be to another believer.

But remarriage is not the ideal; it is not God's best for everyone. **In my opinion she is happier if she remains as she is.** Again (cf. vv. 28, 32, 35) Paul makes it clear that he is not giving a command, but is giving counsel for the benefit and blessing of those who take it. A widowed person who has God's grace for singleness will be **happier** to remain single.

Paul's statement **I think that I also have the Spirit of God** does not lessen but strengthen his point. With a touch of sarcasm he was saying that he, too, had access to the leading of the Holy Spirit—a claim apparently made both by the group that advocated celibacy only and by the group that advocated marriage only. He was still speaking as "an apostle of Jesus Christ by the will of God" (1:1). His command was God's command and his advice was God's advice.

The Limits of
Christian Liberty
(8:1-13)

20

Now concerning things sacrificed to idols, we know that we all have knowledge. Knowledge makes arrogant, but love edifies. If anyone supposes that he knows anything, he has not yet known as he ought to know; but if anyone loves God, he is known by Him. Therefore concerning the eating of things sacrificed to idols, we know that there is no such thing as an idol in the world, and that there is no God but one. For even if there are so-called gods whether in heaven or on earth, as indeed there are many gods and many lords, yet for us there is but one God, the Father, from whom are all things, and we exist for Him; and one Lord, Jesus Christ, by whom are all things, and we exist through Him.

However not all men have this knowledge; but some, being accustomed to the idol until now, eat food as if it were sacrificed to an idol; and their conscience being weak is defiled. But food will not commend us to God; we are neither the worse if we do not eat, nor the better if we do eat. But take care lest this liberty of yours somehow become a stumbling block to the weak. For if someone sees you, who have knowledge, dining in an idol's temple, will not his conscience, if he is weak, be strengthened to eat things sacrificed to idols? For through your knowledge he who is weak is ruined, the

brother for whose sake Christ died. And thus, by sinning against the brethren and wounding their conscience when it is weak, you sin against Christ. Therefore, if food causes my brother to stumble, I will never eat meat again, that I might not cause my brother to stumble. (8:1-13)

Chapters 8-10 of 1 Corinthians continue Paul's answers to questions asked in the letter to him mentioned in 7:1. All three chapters deal with the problem of questionable practices, which in Corinth centered around eating food that had been offered to idols.

That specific problem still exists in parts of the world for Christians saved out of idolatrous religions. Even for the rest of us, however, the basic problem that confronted the Corinthians faces all of us. The issue is: How far does Christian freedom go in regard to behavior not specifically forbidden in Scripture?

During the past several generations some of the strongest debate among fundamentalists and evangelicals has centered around questionable practices—practices that many believers feel to be wrong but that are not specifically forbidden in Scripture. Some of the key issues have been drinking alcoholic beverages, smoking, card playing, wearing makeup, dancing, Sunday sports, styles of music, and going to the theater or movies. One reason Christians have spent so much time arguing those issues is that the Bible does not specifically forbid them.

It is not that those and many similar issues may not be important. But we cannot speak as authoritatively about them as we can such things as stealing, murder, slander, adultery, or covetousness—which Scripture plainly forbids as sinful. Both the Old and New Testaments mention many things that believers are prohibited from doing. Likewise both testaments teach many things that are always good to do—loving and worshiping God, loving our neighbor, helping the poor, and so on. Those specific things are black or white, wrong or right.

Many behaviors, however, are not commanded, commended, or forbidden in Scripture. They are neither black nor white, but gray. Such issues in one age or area may not be the same as those in other times or places; but every age and every place has had to deal with the gray areas of Christian living. The first major council of the Christian church, reported in Acts 15, was called primarily to deal with such issues. Some Jewish believers were insisting that all male Gentile converts be circumcised (v. 1) and others were afraid to socialize with believing Gentiles, especially over a meal, for fear they would break Jewish dietary laws. The council decided that Gentiles need not be circumcised (v. 19) but that believers "abstain from things contaminated by idols and from fornication and from what is strangled and from blood" (v. 20). By following those policies they would "do well" (v. 29).

Because there could have been no question about the sinfulness of fornication, the mention of it in this list must be figurative, probably referring to the nonincestuous marriage of a near relative. The Jews had very clear teaching as to the fact that consanguine marriage in extended degrees was forbidden to them as a part of their unique identity. The practices mentioned were not in themselves sinful, but the council advised the churches to abstain from them in order not to needlessly offend Jewish brothers who had strong convictions about them.

Christian liberty is a central truth of the New Testament. "If you abide in My word," Jesus said, "then you are truly disciples of Mine; and you shall know the truth, and the truth shall make you free" (John 8:31-32). "Where the Spirit of the Lord is, there is liberty" (2 Cor. 3:17). "It was for freedom that Christ set us free" (Gal. 5:1).

But Christian liberty is not unbridled license. It is never freedom to sin, and often it should exclude things that in themselves are not sin but that may become sinful or lead others to sin. Peter says, "Act as free men, and do not use your freedom as a covering for evil, but use it as bond-slaves of God" (1 Pet. 2:16).

Two common extremes are often followed in regard to doubtful things. One is legalism; the other is license. Legalism believes that every act, every habit, every type of behavior is either black or white. Legalists live by rules rather than by the Spirit. They classify everything as either good or bad, whether the Bible mentions it or not. They develop exhaustive lists of do's and don'ts. Doing the things on the good list and avoiding the things on the bad list is their idea of spirituality, no matter what the inner person is like. Their lives are law controlled, not Spirit controlled. But refraining from doing things is not spirituality; walking in the Spirit is spirituality. Legalism stifles liberty, stifles conscience, stifles the Word, and stifles the Holy Spirit.

License is the opposite extreme. It is like legalism in that it too has no gray areas—but neither does it have much black. Almost everything is white; everything is acceptable as long as it is not strictly forbidden in Scripture. Such advocates believe that Christian freedom is virtually absolute and unqualified. As long as your own conscience is free you can do as you please. That seems to have been the philosophy of the group Paul addresses in 1 Corinthians 8. They probably agreed with him that believers should "maintain always a blameless conscience both before God and before men" (Acts 24:16). Beyond that, however, they wanted no restrictions.

But Paul teaches that it can also be wrong to offend the consciences of fellow believers when they are less mature ("weak") and when what we are doing is not necessary in our service to the Lord.

In answer to the specific question about eating food offered to idols, Paul gives a general and universal principle that can be applied to all doubtful behavior. He states and explains the principle in chapter 8; he illustrates it in 9:1–10:13; and he applies it in 10:14–11:1. The principle is: "Take care lest this liberty of yours somehow become a stumbling block to the weak" (8:9). Before we exercise our Christian liberty in a given area not forbidden by Scripture, we should consider how it will affect others, especially our fellow believers.

In preparation for giving the principle, Paul responds to three reasons some of the Corinthians gave for feeling completely free to act as they pleased in regard to practices not specifically forbidden by God. The reasons were: (1) We know we all have knowledge; (2) We know that an idol is nothing; and (3) We know that food is not an issue with God. The apostle agrees that each reason is basically valid, but then goes on to show how none of those reasons should be applied to practices that might cause someone else to stumble spiritually.

We Know That We All Have Knowledge

Now concerning things sacrificed to idols, we know that we all have knowledge. Knowledge makes arrogant, but love edifies. If anyone supposes that he knows anything, he has not yet known as he ought to know; but if anyone loves God, he is known by Him. (8:1-3)

Things sacrificed to idols is one word in Greek and can be translated simply as "idol sacrifices." The sacrifices were food offerings, symbolically presented in worship to the god in whose temple they were given. The particular issue was that of eating food that had been offered in those sacrifices.

The Greeks and Romans were polytheistic, worshiping many gods. They had a god, or a group of gods, for every circumstance, every need, and every activity of any consequence. They had a god of war, a goddess of love, a god of travel, a goddess of justice, and on and on. They were also polydemonistic, believing in many evil spirits. They believed the air was filled with evil spirits of all sorts.

Giving food sacrifices, which were usually meat, was of great importance in regard to both of those beliefs. It was believed that the evil spirits were constantly trying to invade human beings and that the easiest way to do that was to attach themselves to food before it was eaten. The only way the spirits could be removed from food was through its being sacrificed to a god. The sacrifice therefore served two purposes; it gained the favor of the god and cleansed the meat from demonic contamination.

Idol offerings were divided into three parts. One part was burned on an altar as the sacrifice proper. The second part was given as payment to the priests who served at the temple, and the remaining part was kept by the offerer. Because of the large number of offerings, the priests were not able to eat all of their portion, and they sold in the marketplace what they did not need. That meat was highly valued because it was cleansed of evil spirits, and was thus the meat served at feasts and to guests.

The eating of meat offered to idols therefore had the same two associations for Christians, especially for those who had grown up in that religious atmosphere. The meat was associated with pagan gods and goddesses, having been part of an offering to them, and it was associated with the superstition that it had once been contaminated by evil spirits.

It was almost impossible for a believer who had any personal contact with Gentiles to avoid facing the question of eating idol sacrifices. Most social occasions, including weddings, involved pagan worship of some sort, and a great many of the festivities were held in temples. Idol food was always served. If a relative was getting married, or a long-time friend was giving a banquet, a Christian either had to make excuses for not attending—which he could not do indefinitely—or he had to eat food that he knew had been part of an idol offering.

Some sensitive Gentile believers refused to buy such meat because it brought back memories of their previous pagan lives or because those who saw them buy it might think they had reverted to paganism. Also many believers, both Gentile and Jewish, were reluctant to eat at the homes of pagan Gentiles—and even of some Christian Gentiles—because they were afraid of being served that meat. Such food could only be doubly unclean according to Jewish dietary law—from which many Jewish Christians found it hard to separate themselves.

On the other hand, some Christians were not bothered. To them, meat was meat. They knew pagan deities did not really exist and that evil spirits did not contaminate food. They were mature, well-grounded in God's truth, and their consciences were clear in the matter. That group gave Paul the three reasons for freely exercising their liberty.

Paul's responses to the reasons were *directed to* that group of more mature believers. But his responses *centered on* the other group. He told the mature believers not to focus on their liberty but on the spiritual welfare of those who were less mature. He was saying, "Don't look at your freedom; look at their need. Your own freedom should be limited by your love for fellow believers. If you love them as God calls you to love, you will not use your liberty in any way that will offend, confuse, or weaken their faith."

The first reason that had been given for exercising freedom is summarized by Paul: **we know that we all have knowledge.** The statement was true but egotistical. It reflected a feeling of superiority. The believers who made the claim were not suggesting they were omniscient, but that they had more than enough knowledge and understanding of God's Word to know that pagan gods and idols were not real and that food sacrificed to them was still just food. They knew that eating the food could not contaminate them spiritually, that it had no affect on their Christian lives. They felt totally free to eat whatever they wanted, no matter what others thought.

But they are reminded that **knowledge makes arrogant.** Those believers were mature in knowledge, but were not mature in love. **Love edifies,** or builds up others; and that edification they did not have. They were solid in doctrine but weak in love. They were strong in self-love but weak in brotherly love.

Of all the apostles, Paul is least likely to be charged with belittling doctrine, the knowledge of God's Word. He was the theologian's theologian. "For whatever was written in earlier times was written for our instruction," he tells the Romans (15:4). He prayed that the Colossian believers might "be filled with the knowledge of His will in all spiritual wisdom and understanding" (Col. 1:9) and encouraged them to be "renewed to a true knowledge according to the image of the One who created [them]" (3:10). In the long list of ways in which his ministry was commended, Paul includes "knowledge" and "the word of truth" (2 Cor. 6:4-10). In that same letter he commends the Corinthians themselves for their "faith and utterance and knowledge" (8:7). Numerous times the apostle tells those to whom he is writing that he did not want them to be ignorant about certain truths (Rom. 1:13; 11:25; 1 Cor. 10:1; 12:1; 2 Cor. 1:8; 1 Thess. 4:13).

Knowledge of God's Word is extremely important. It is impossible to believe or obey what is not known. The Lord told Israel, "My people are destroyed for lack of knowledge. Because you have rejected knowledge, I also will reject you from being My priest" (Hos. 4:6). Among other things, God is "He who teaches man knowledge" (Ps. 94:10). The Bible places no premium on ignorance.

But knowledge, even of God's Word, is not enough. It is essential but not sufficient. By itself **knowledge makes arrogant.** To have love but no knowledge is unfortunate; but to have knowledge and no love is equally tragic.

Among the many spiritual problems of the Corinthian Christians was arrogance, a word Paul uses six times in relation to them. They were proud and self-satisfied. They had knowledge without love. As they are reminded several chapters later, a person who has all sorts of abilities and virtues but has no love is "nothing," and "love does not brag and is not arrogant" (1 Cor. 13:1-4).

Knowledge that idols were not real and that idol food was not spiritually corrupted was right knowledge and helpful knowledge. But by itself it turned inward those who had it. They saw the truth as it applied to them and nothing else. They were insensitive as to how it might apply to those who did not "have this knowledge" (1 Cor. 8:7). Flaunting the liberty of this knowledge could seriously offend other believers. And as Jesus said, it would be better to be drowned than to offend another child of God (Matt. 18:6-14).

The truly well-rounded Christian thinks and acts in two ways: conceptually and relationally. He has the ability to understand biblical truths and the ability to relate them to people, to himself, and to others. He has knowledge plus love, because love is the medium through which truth is to be communicated. "Speaking the truth in love, we are to grow up in all aspects into Him, who is the head, even Christ" (Eph. 4:15). Knowledge by itself brings arrogance, not maturity.

Division in the church may be caused by problems of behavior as well as problems of doctrine. When some believers insist on exercising their liberty without regard for the feelings and standards of fellow believers, the church is weakened and frequently divided.

Love edifies, and the knowledgeable believer without the edification of love is not as mature as he is inclined to think. **If anyone supposes that he knows anything, he has not yet known as he ought to know.** The unloving orthodox are arrogant but not edified. They have right knowledge but not right understanding.

The truly edified person has some idea of what he has yet to learn. Someone has defined knowledge as "the process of passing from the unconscious state of ignorance to the conscious state of ignorance." Ignorance does not know that it does not know. True knowledge does not know and knows it.

But if anyone loves God, he is known by Him. It is impossible to know God and not love Him. Loving God is the most important evidence of a right relationship to Him. Without love for God, made possible by His love for us (1 John 4:19), we can have no right knowledge of Him, because we will not have a right relation to Him. The only ones who know God and are **known by Him** are those who have a love relationship with Him (John 14:21). Knowledge is important, immensely important. But, as everything else, without love it is nothing. Loving and being loved by God is everything. Paul here implies that if one is loved by God and loves God, he will also love other believers, whom God loves (1 John 5:1).

Love is the key to behavior. Knowing what is not forbidden is not enough. When we "do not merely look out for [our] own personal interests, but also for the interests of others" (Phil. 2:4), we are on the road to mature, loving Christian behavior. Love sets the limits of Christian liberty.

WE KNOW THAT AN IDOL IS NOTHING

Therefore concerning the eating of things sacrificed to idols, we know that there is no such thing as an idol in the world, and that there is no God but one. For even if there are so-called gods whether in heaven or on earth, as indeed there are many gods and many lords, yet for us there is but one God, the Father, from whom are all things, and we exist for Him; and one Lord, Jesus Christ, by whom are all things, and we exist through Him.

However not all men have this knowledge; but some, being accustomed to the idol until now, eat food as if it were sacrificed to an idol; and their conscience being weak is defiled. (8:4-7)

In verses 4-6 Paul states his agreement with the Corinthians who were theologically well taught. First he agrees **that there is no such thing as an idol in the world.** The stone, precious metal, or wood is real, but there is no god behind it. The image is not of anything that really exists. It only reflects the imagination of the one who designed it, or the impersonation of the demon who deceives through it (10:20).

When I was in Hawaii some years ago I visited a Buddhist temple. An old lady was bowing down to a large brass statue of Buddha and throwing small stones toward it. The stones were rolled somewhat like dice, and the way they landed indicated good or bad fortune. Other people came in and brought food offerings, which they left in front of the idol. I had a strong desire to tell them, "Nobody's there. Nobody's home. There is nothing there but brass." **There is no God but one.**

It is not that there are no imaginary gods, **so-called gods whether in heaven or on earth, as indeed there are many gods and many lords.** Some are outright fakes and some are manifestations of demons, but none are truly gods. The **so-called gods** have a certain type of reality, but not as deity.

Paul taught that truth throughout his ministry and was often persecuted for it. Demetrius, a pagan silversmith in Ephesus, stirred up his fellow tradesmen by charging, "You see and hear that not only in Ephesus, but in almost all of Asia, this Paul has persuaded and turned away a considerable number of people, saying that gods made with hands are no gods at all" (Acts 19:26). The apostle agreed with the psalmist:

> Their idols are silver and gold,
> The work of man's hands.
> They have mouths, but they cannot speak;
> They have eyes, but they cannot see;

> They have ears, but they cannot hear;
> They have noses, but they cannot smell;
> They have hands, but they cannot feel;
> They have feet, but they cannot walk;
> They cannot make a sound with their throat.
> Those who make them will become like them,
> Everyone who trusts in them. (Ps. 115:4-7)

Paul repeats the truth that **there is but one God.** He is the one **from whom are all things, and we exist for Him; and one Lord, Jesus Christ, by whom are all things, and we exist through Him.** There is only one true God. He has come to us in the person of the Son, **Jesus Christ,** and we are brought to the **Father** through the divine Son. Everything comes **from** the Father, and all believers **exist for** the Father. Everything is **by** the Son, and everyone who comes to the Father comes **through** the Son. This is a powerful and clear affirmation of the equality of essence of God the Father and the Lord Jesus Christ.

It is absolutely true that idols are not real, that so-called gods are not real, and that the only real God is the God of Scripture revealed in Jesus Christ. In those doctrines the freedom-loving Corinthian Christians were completely orthodox. But they were not right in how they applied the truths to their daily living. They had the right concepts, but did not carry them over to make the right relationships.

Paul reminds them of an additional truth, one they must have known but that they did not take into consideration when exercising their Christian liberty. **However not all men have this knowledge.** Not all believers were mature in their knowledge and understanding of spiritual truths. Some were new Christians, freshly out of paganism and its many temptations and corruptions. They still imagined that idols, though evil, were real and that the gods the idols represented were real. They knew that there is only one *right* God but perhaps they had not yet fully grasped the truth that there is only one *real* God.

Even if they did understand that there was only one real God, the experiences of their past paganism were so fresh that they rejected all that was related to it. To participate in any way was to be tempted to fall back into former practices.

Some, being accustomed to the idol until now, eat food as if it were sacrificed to an idol; and their conscience being weak is defiled. Some new converts wanted to take no chance of being contaminated again by the evil influences that for so long had governed everything they thought and did. The pagan gods were not real, but the wicked practices associated with them were real and fresh on their minds. They recoiled from having contact with anything associated with their past paganism. Their consciences were not yet strong enough to allow them to eat idol food without having it pull them back to their former idolatrous activity.

If such persons, following the example of more knowledgeable believers, go ahead and eat what their consciences tell them not to eat, **their conscience being weak is defiled.** Even though the act in itself is not morally or spiritually wrong, it becomes wrong when it is committed against conscience. A **defiled** conscience is one that has been ignored and violated. Such a conscience brings confusion, resentment, and feelings of guilt. A person who violates his conscience willingly does what he thinks to be wrong. In his own mind he has committed sin; and until he fully understands that the act is not sin in God's eyes, he should have no part in it. "He who doubts is condemned if he eats, because his eating is not from faith; and whatever is not from faith is sin" (Rom. 14:23). Defiled conscience is defiled faith. Such behavior brings guilt feelings, despair, and loss of joy and peace. It may also lead to sinful thoughts connected with former pagan practices and even lead a person back into some of them.

Paul's primary point in the present passage is that anyone who causes such a weaker brother to defile his conscience and his faith helps lead that brother into sin. Knowledge may tell us that something is perfectly acceptable, but love will tell us that, because it is not acceptable to a fellow believer's conscience, we should not take advantage of our freedom.

WE KNOW THAT FOOD IS NOT AN ISSUE WITH GOD

But food will not commend us to God; we are neither the worse if we do not eat, nor the better if we do eat. But take care lest this liberty of yours somehow become a stumbling block to the weak. For if someone sees you, who have knowledge, dining in an idol's temple, will not his conscience, if he is weak, be strengthened to eat things sacrificed to idols? For through your knowledge he who is weak is ruined, the brother for whose sake Christ died. And thus, by sinning against the brethren and wounding their conscience when it is weak, you sin against Christ. (8:8-12)

The third truth with which Paul agreed was that eating or not eating food has no spiritual significance in itself. Neither act will **commend us to God. Commend** (*paristēmi*) means "to place near, bring beside, present to." Neither eating or not eating **food** will bring us closer to God or make us approved by Him. The general point is that doing things not forbidden by God has no significance in our relationship to Him. They are spiritually neutral. Food is an excellent illustration of that fact.

Common sense and concern for the bodies God has given us should make us careful about what and how much we eat. Gluttony is harmful and eating foods to which we are allergic is harmful. No sensible, mature person will do those things. But, in itself, eating or not eating certain foods has absolutely no spiritual significance. Jesus made it plain that "there is nothing outside the man which going into him can defile him; but the things which proceed out of the man are what defile the man" (Mark 7:15). The Lord's command to Peter to "kill and eat" was both figurative, referring to accepting Gentiles, and literal, referring to eating food previously considered ceremonially unclean (Acts 10:10-16; cf. v. 28). And Paul told Timothy to receive all food with thankfulness (1 Tim. 4:4).

Food makes no difference for food's sake, for ceremony's sake, or for God's sake. But it can make a great difference for the sake of the conscience of some of His children. What would not otherwise be wrong for us becomes wrong if it is **a stumbling block to the weak**. Obviously, some Corinthian believers could not handle such liberty; it would pull them down into the pit from which they had been delivered. If an immature brother sees us doing something that bothers his conscience, his spiritual life is harmed. We should never influence a fellow Christian to do anything that the Holy Spirit, through that person's conscience, is protecting him from.

A mature believer rightly sees no harm for himself in **dining in an idol's temple** in some family or community event. He does not accept the pagan beliefs or participate in the pagan practices, but he can associate with pagan people because he is spiritually strong; he has spiritual **knowledge**.

But if a Christian who has a **conscience** that is **weak** sees a mature believer eating in the temple, the weak brother is likely to be tempted to go against his own conscience and to eat in the temple himself. That could be dangerous to him, causing him to go against his own conscience. Consequently, **through your knowledge he who is weak is ruined, the brother for whose sake Christ died. Ruined** has the idea of "to come to sin." We cause that person to sin by leading him into a situation he cannot handle.

It is never right to cause another believer to violate his conscience. To do so runs the risk of ruining a **brother for whose sake Christ died** (cf. Acts 20:28; 1 Pet. 1:18-19). Our Christian liberty must never be used at the expense of a Christian brother or sister who has been redeemed at such a price.

The voice of a Christian's conscience is the instrument of the Holy Spirit. If a believer's conscience is weak it is because he is spiritually weak and immature, not because the leading of his conscience is weak. Conscience is God's doorkeeper to keep us out of places where we could be harmed. As we mature, conscience allows us to go more places and to do more things because we will have more spiritual strength and better spiritual judgment.

A small child is not allowed to play with sharp tools, to go into the street, or to go where there are dangerous machines or electrical appliances. The restrictions are gradually removed as he grows older and learns for himself what is dangerous and what is not.

God confines His spiritual children by conscience. As they grow in knowledge and maturity the limits of conscience are expanded. We should never expand our actions and habits before our conscience permits it. And we should never encourage, either directly or indirectly, anyone else to do that. **By sinning against the brethren and wounding their conscience when it is weak, you sin against Christ.** Causing a brother to stumble is more than an offense against him; it is an offense against our Lord. That is a strong warning. Surely no believer would desire to **sin against Christ**.

We should be eager to limit our liberty at any time and to any degree in order to help a fellow believer—a brother whom we should love, and a precious soul for whom Christ died.

Therefore, if food causes my brother to stumble, I will never eat meat again, that I might not cause my brother to stumble. (8:13)

Paul restates the principle he has been explaining. In regard to doubtful things a Christian's first concern should not be to exercise his liberty to the limit but to care about the welfare of his brother in Christ. Paul set the example. He would **never eat meat again,** or do anything else his own conscience allowed him to do, if that would cause his **brother to stumble.**

In deciding about whether or not to participate in any behavior that is doubtful, the following principles make a good checklist to follow.

Excess. Is the activity or habit necessary, or is it merely an extra that is not really important? Is it perhaps only an encumbrance that we should willingly give up (Heb. 12:1)?

Expediency. "All things are lawful for me," Paul says, "but not all things are profitable," or expedient (1 Cor. 6:12). Is what I want to do helpful and useful, or only desirable?

Emulation. "The one who says he abides in Him ought himself to walk in the same manner as He walked" (1 John 2:6). If we are doing what Christ would do, our action not only is permissible but good and right.

Example. Are we setting the right example for others, especially for weaker brothers and sisters? If we emulate Christ, others will be able to emulate us, to follow our example (1 Tim. 4:12).

Evangelism. Is my testimony going to be helped or hindered? Will unbelievers be drawn to Christ or turned away from Him by what I am doing? Will it help me conduct myself "with wisdom toward outsiders, making the most of the opportunity" (Col. 4:5)?

Edification. Will I be built up and matured in Christ; will I become spiritually stronger? "All things are lawful, but not all things edify" (1 Cor. 10:23).

Exaltation. Will the Lord be lifted up and glorified in what I do? God's glory and exaltation should be the supreme purpose behind everything we do. "Whether, then, you eat or drink or whatever you do, do all to the glory of God" (1 Cor. 10:31).

Supporting the Man of God (9:1-14)

21

Am I not free? Am I not an apostle? Have I not seen Jesus our Lord? Are you not my work in the Lord? If to others I am not an apostle, at least I am to you; for you are the seal of my apostleship in the Lord.

My defense to those who examine me is this: Do we not have a right to eat and drink? Do we not have a right to take along a believing wife, even as the rest of the apostles, and the brothers of the Lord, and Cephas? Or do only Barnabas and I not have a right to refrain from working? Who at any time serves as a soldier at his own expense? Who plants a vineyard, and does not eat the fruit of it? Or who tends a flock and does not use the milk of the flock? I am not speaking these things according to human judgment, am I? Or does not the Law also say these things? For it is written in the Law of Moses, "You shall not muzzle the ox while he is threshing." God is not concerned about oxen, is He? Or is He speaking altogether for our sake? Yes, for our sake it was written, because the plowman ought to plow in hope, and the thresher to thresh in hope of sharing the crops. If we sowed spiritual things in you, is it too much if we should reap material things from you? If others share the right over you, do we not more? Nevertheless, we did not use this right, but we endure all things, that we may cause no hindrance to the gospel of Christ. Do you not know that those who perform sacred services eat the food of the temple, and those who attend regularly to the altar have their share with the

altar? So also the Lord directed those who proclaim the gospel to get their living from the gospel. (9:1-14)

In chapter 8 Paul set out the limits of Christian liberty, limits that are to be determined by brotherly love, by concern for the welfare of fellow Christians. He summarizes the principle as, "Take care lest this liberty of yours somehow become a stumbling block to the weak" (8:9). Our rights end when another person is offended.

In chapter 9 the apostle illustrates how he followed the principle in his own life. In verses 1-18 he discusses his right to be financially supported by those to whom he ministers. Verses 1-14 set forth his right, and verses 15-18 give the reason why he would not take advantage of it. In verses 19-27 he explains that he would give up any and every right for the sake of winning men to Jesus Christ.

In the first section of the chapter Paul gives six reasons why he had the right to be supported by the churches to whom he ministered: (1) he was an apostle; (2) it is customary to pay workers; (3) it is according to God's law; (4) other leaders exercise the right; (5) it is the universal pattern; (6) and Jesus ordained it. The first reason related only to apostles, and therefore does not apply today. The other five reasons, however, apply to every minister and Christian worker in every time of church history.

Paul Was an Apostle

Am I not free? Am I not an apostle? Have I not seen Jesus our Lord? Are you not my work in the Lord? If to others I am not an apostle, at least I am to you; for you are the seal of my apostleship in the Lord.

My defense to those who examine me is this: Do we not have a right to eat and drink? Do we not have a right to take along a believing wife, even as the rest of the apostles, and the brothers of the Lord, and Cephas? Or do only Barnabas and I not have a right to refrain from working? (9:1-6)

Verse one is composed of four questions. All of them are rhetorical, the answer to each being assumed.

The first question is **Am I not free?** In their letter to Paul (see 7:1) the Corinthians must have made much of their liberty in Christ—a liberty they had been taught largely by Paul himself. Now he states his own freedom and his own rights. "I have no less freedom than you do," he implies. "And I cherish my freedom no less than you do. But I cherish some other things even more."

The second question, **Am I not an apostle?** is closely related to the first. As an apostle he would, if anything, have greater freedom than the average Christian. Paul was always conscious of his apostleship. He did not preach and teach his own philosophy or minister and serve in his own name and power. He was the Lord's apostle, commissioned to take the gospel to the Gentiles (Acts 9:15).

At this point he gives two verifications of his apostleship. First, he had seen the Lord: **Have I not seen Jesus our Lord?** An apostle had to be an eyewitness of Christ and of His resurrection (Acts 1:21-22). Paul was not among the original disciples who were with Jesus during His earthly ministry, but he had seen the resurrected Christ on at least three occasions. The Lord appeared to Paul at his conversion (Acts 9:4-5) and in two visions that we know of (Acts 18:9-10; 22:17-18). Paul could witness to having personally met the risen Christ.

The second proof of his apostleship was the Corinthian believers themselves. **Are you not my work in the Lord? If to others I am not an apostle, at least I am to you.** The church at Corinth was one of the fruits of Paul's apostolic labors. Their saving faith and their knowledge of God's Word came from Paul's faithful evangelism and discipling (Acts 18:1-11).

The Corinthian church was **the seal of**[his] **apostleship in the Lord.** In ancient times seals were used on containers of merchandise, on letters, and on other things to indicate the authenticity of what was inside and to prevent the contents from being substituted or altered. The seal was the official representation of the authority of the one who sent the merchandise or letter. What was under the seal was guaranteed to be genuine. The Corinthian church was a living **seal** of Paul's apostleship, the proof of his genuineness.

Paul next gives a **defense to those who examine me in this. Examine** (*anakrinō*) was a legal term for the investigation or inquiry made before a decision was reached in a case. He desires to clearly defend his rights.

The first right defended was that of being supported financially by those to whom he ministered. **Do we not have a right to eat and drink?** That is, "As a minister of God, not to mention as an apostle, don't I have the right to expect that at least food and drink will be provided to me?" (cf. 1 Tim. 5:17-18; Gal. 6:6).

Or, he continues, **Do we not have a right to take along a believing wife, even as the rest of the apostles, and the brothers of the Lord, and Cephas?** "Don't I have the right to marry a Christian woman and have her minister with me wherever I go?" The other apostles, including **Cephas** (Peter), were married, as were Jesus' brothers—the sons born naturally to Joseph and Mary after Jesus. Paul probably was a widower. In any case he had a right to marry a believer. Though he chose the status of singleness, he had every right in the Lord to be married. He also had the right, as did the other apostles, to take his wife with him as he ministered and to have her supported along with him.

I believe that verse supports the principle of paying pastors, evangelists, missionaries, and other such Christian workers enough so that their wives do not have to work; so they can have more time to be with their husbands in the ministry.

The verse can be applied to the principle of paying for the wife's expenses when she travels with her husband in his ministry, **even as the rest of the apostles, and the brothers of the Lord, and Cephas.** The term **to take along** (*periagō*) means "to carry about in one's company." A wife's support and companionship is especially helpful when the husband is ministering away from home. No doubt one of the contributing causes of divorce among ministers today is that many of them are not able to spend enough time with their wives and families. Obviously a wife with small children at home or with other such commitments is limited in the trips she can take.

The point is that, when it is possible for her to go along, every effort should be made by the sponsoring group to pay her way. It is a question of the right attitude, the attitude of generosity in supporting the Lord's full-time workers.

With a touch of sarcasm Paul asks, **Or do only Barnabas and I not have a right to refrain from working?** Paul and Barnabas had as much right as the others to get their livelihood from the ministry, without having to work on the side. They did not pay their own ways because they were obligated to do so. They did it voluntarily.

IT IS CUSTOMARY

Who at any time serves as a soldier at his own expense? Who plants a vineyard, and does not eat the fruit of it? Or who tends a flock and does not use the milk of the flock? (9:7)

Paul gives three illustrations to show that paying workers is customary. As he does in much of this chapter, Paul makes his point through rhetorical questions, the answers to which are obvious. The answer expected to each question is none.

Soldiers do not fight during the day and then work at a civilian job at night in order to eat, buy clothes, and have a place to stay. Soldiers do not serve at their **own expense.** They are provided food, clothing, arms, lodging, and whatever else is needed to live and fight effectively.

Farmers do not plant **a vineyard** or cultivate a crop for someone without being paid. They do not farm for free and then do other work to make a living. They **eat the fruit of** their farming, being paid either in money or with a share of the crop (cf. 2 Tim. 2:6). Shepherds do not work for free, either. They expect at least some of **the milk of the flock** in payment.

All three types of workers are paid for their work. It is the customary, rightful, and expected thing. Why should it not be true for God's workers as well?

IT IS GOD'S LAW

I am not speaking these things according to human judgment, am I? Or does not the Law also say these things? For it is written in the Law of Moses, "You shall not muzzle the ox while he is threshing." God is not concerned about oxen, is He? Or is He speaking altogether for our sake? Yes, for our sake it was written, because the plowman ought to plow in hope, and the thresher to thresh in hope of sharing the crops. If we sowed spiritual things in you, is it too much if we should reap material things from you? (9:8-11)

The principle of workers being paid for their work is not merely **according to human judgment,** as in the previous illustrations. God's Law teaches the same thing. **You shall not muzzle the ox while he is threshing.** That quotation from

Deuteronomy 25:4 refers to the general practice **written in the Law of Moses** that oxen were to be allowed to eat as they worked. That was their "payment."

The comment that **God is not concerned about oxen** does not mean that He has no interest in the welfare of animals. The Lord "prepares for the raven its nourishment" (Job 38:41) and "He gives the beast its food" (Ps. 147:9). Jesus spoke of the heavenly Father feeding "the birds of the air" (Matt. 6:26). In spite of that, ultimately God's concern is not for animals but for people. If He wants to be certain that oxen are "paid" for their work, how much more is He concerned that men be compensated for theirs.

So the primary purpose even of the quoted Old Testament command had to do with human beings. Deuteronomy 25 pertains to social and economic relationships among men, and in verse 4 the well-established practice of not muzzling working oxen is used to teach that human workers should be paid for their work. As Paul explains, God was **speaking altogether for our sake.** Men should earn their living from their labor. **The plowman** and **the thresher** should be able to work **in hope of sharing the crops.**

Paul had every right to apply the principle to himself. If men working for men should be paid for their labor, surely men working for God should be paid for theirs. **If we sowed spiritual things in you, is it too much if we should reap material things from you?** The only difference in the principle as applied to the Lord's service is that material payment is given for spiritual work. The Lord provides His own spiritual rewards, but His people are to provide material reward, and provide it generously as unto Him. Paul calls for "double honor" (1 Tim. 5:17).

The Lord's servants deserve to be supported well. There should not be a double standard, applying to preachers, missionaries, and other Christian ministers a standard that is considerably lower than that set for those laboring in the system of man. We should pay them as generously as is feasible and leave the stewardship of that money to them, just as we expect the stewardship of our own money to be left to us.

Obviously we should give our money only to ministries that are biblically sound and responsible. Every appeal made in the Lord's name does not deserve the support of the Lord's people. Being wise in our giving is part of our stewardship. But when we give to a servant who is worthy, we should give happily, generously, and trustingly. The **if** (*ei* with the indicative) in Paul's statement **if we sowed spiritual things,** presents a condition assumed to be true. That is, if that genuine spiritual ministry has occurred, and it has, it should not be **too much** to ask **material things from you.**

The churches of Macedonia—those at Philippi, Thessalonica, Berea, and perhaps others (see Acts 16:11–17:13)—consistently supported Paul financially, as a pastor while he worked among them and as a missionary after he left. In addition they gave to help other churches. They had little wealth and were undergoing considerable persecution, but,

> in a great ordeal of affliction their abundance of joy and their deep poverty overflowed in the wealth of their liberality. For I testify that according to their ability, and beyond their ability they gave of their own accord, begging us with much entreaty for

> the favor of participation in the support of the saints, and this, not as we had expected, but they first gave themselves to the Lord and to us by the will of God. (2 Cor. 8:1-5)

Their attitude and their pattern of giving is a model for all Christians.

Giving to the Lord's workers is giving to the Lord. God gives to His children beyond measure, so that, as Paul had already reminded the Corinthians, we "are not lacking in any gift" (1 Cor. 1:7). Peter tells us that "His divine power has granted to us everything pertaining to life and godliness" (2 Pet. 1:3). God supplies all our "needs according to His riches in glory in Christ Jesus" (Phil. 4:19). God's children are to reflect their heavenly Father's generosity. "He who sows sparingly shall also reap sparingly; and he who sows bountifully shall also reap bountifully" (2 Cor. 9:6). As individuals and as churches, Christians who give generously to the Lord's work and to the support of His servants will be blessed.

It is our Lord's will that we be generous to our pastors, our educational workers, our missionaries, and to those leaders of any kind who come and minister to us—just as He has been so immeasurably generous to us.

It Is Done for Others

If others share the right over you, do we not more? Nevertheless, we did not use this right, but we endure all things, that we may cause no hindrance to the gospel of Christ. (9:12)

Paul's fourth reason for having a right to be supported in his ministry was that the Corinthians apparently had always supported their pastors. Those they now supported, or had supported, doubtlessly included Apollos and Peter (cf. 1:12; 3:22). As the church's founding pastor and as an apostle, Paul had **more** claim on their support than the **others**. But he **did not use this right**.

In spite of the many reasons he had to justify his right to be supported, he waived the right. **But we endure all things, that we may cause no hindrance to the gospel of Christ.** The basic meaning of **endure** (*stegō*) is "to bear or to pass over in silence." Paul used the present tense, indicating that throughout his ministry he continued to bear uncomplainingly whatever was necessary to fulfill his work. His customary way of life was self-denial.

He worked as a tentmaker (Acts 18:3) to pay his way while he preached and taught. Paul could tell the Corinthians the same thing he told the Ephesians: "You yourselves know that these hands ministered to my own needs and to the men who were with me" (Acts 20:34). He not only supported himself but many of those who worked closely with him (2 Thess. 3:8).

Paying his own way was one means of causing no **hindrance to the gospel of Christ.** Paul did not want new converts or potential converts to have reason to think he was preaching the gospel for selfish motives. He wanted no one thinking he was in the ministry for the sake of money or an easy living. That policy was no doubt especially significant for Paul's work, because he, more than any other apostle of which we know, worked in virgin territory among the Gentiles. Not only the gospel itself but its Old Testament background was completely new to those he reached, and he did not want that message clouded in any way. The other apostles and New Testament prophets worked largely among Jews, who were accustomed to the Lord's ministers being supported by His people.

In new ministries today it is wise for those working in them to be able to support themselves, or to be supported by fellow Christians, until a group of believers is well established. Particularly in light of some preachers who make merchandise of the gospel, Christian workers should be careful not to give grounds for any such charge against them. Calling people at the same time to come to Christ and to give their money is offensive.

IT IS THE UNIVERSAL PATTERN

Do you not know that those who perform sacred services eat the food of the temple, and those who attend regularly to the altar have their share with the altar? (9:13)

The fifth reason for Paul's having a right to be supported by the churches he served was that it had been the universal pattern since the founding of the priesthood in Israel. The priests, **those who perform sacred services**, were supported by the tithes of crops and animals as well as sacrifices from the people to whom they ministered in **the temple**, and before that in the tabernacle (Num. 18:8-24). Hundreds of years before the Aaronic priesthood, in fact, Abraham gave tithes to Melchizedek, "a priest of God Most High" (Gen. 14:18-20). Since they **attend regularly** to the service of God as a way of life, they need to be provided for.

JESUS ORDAINED IT

So also the Lord directed those who proclaim the gospel to get their living from the gospel. (9:14)

Paul had the right to ask for support because the Lord had ordained the principle. **Those who proclaim the gospel** are **to get their living from the gospel.** Both God's Law and God's Son teach that His prophets, teachers, and ministers are to be paid for their work in the Lord. The New Testament teaching reiterates that of the Old. Paul may have been referring to Jesus' instruction to the seventy (Luke 10:7), to an otherwise unrecorded teaching of the Lord, or to a special revelation given to the apostle. In any case Jesus personally taught that truth.

The Lord commands His people to offer support to those who minister to them, but He does not command those who minister to accept the support. Paul did not. He had the right, as much as any and more than most. But for the gospel's sake, for the brethren's sake, and for love's sake, he gladly limited his liberty. He willingly waived his right.

Refusing to Use Your Liberty (9:15-27)

22

But I have used none of these things. And I am not writing these things that it may be done so in my case; for it would be better for me to die than have any man make my boast an empty one. For if I preach the gospel, I have nothing to boast of, for I am under compulsion; for woe is me if I do not preach the gospel. For if I do this voluntarily, I have a reward; but if against my will, I have a stewardship entrusted to me. What then is my reward? That, when I preach the gospel, I may offer the gospel without charge, so as not to make full use of my right in the gospel.

For though I am free from all men, I have made myself a slave to all, that I might win the more. And to the Jews I became as a Jew, that I might win Jews; to those who are under the Law, as under the Law, though not being myself under the Law, that I might win those who are under the Law; to those who are without law, as without law, though not being without the law of God but under the law of Christ, that I might win those who are without law. To the weak I became weak, that I might win the weak; I have become all things to all men, that I may by all means save some. And I do all things for the sake of the gospel, that I may become a fellow partaker of it.

Do you not know that those who run in a race all run, but only one receives the prize? Run in such a way that you may win. And everyone who competes in the games exercises self-control in all things. They then do it to

receive a perishable wreath, but we an imperishable. Therefore I run in such a way, as not without aim; I box in such a way, as not beating the air; but I buffet my body and make it my slave, lest possibly, after I have preached to others, I myself should be disqualified. (9:15-27)

In 9:15-27 Paul restates (v. 15) and then continues to illustrate the principle that love limits Christian liberty as well as his own policy of not using his right to be supported financially by those to whom he ministered. He gives two reasons why he refused to accept such support. First, he did not want to lose his reward for preaching the gospel without charge (vv. 16-18). Second, and more importantly, he wanted absolutely nothing to hinder his reaching the lost with that gospel (vv. 19-27).

He has just given six reasons (9:1-14) why he had the right to be supported. **But I have used none of these things,** he continues. He would not take advantage of the right for any reason.

Lest the Corinthians think he had changed his mind and had given those six reasons to convince them to begin supporting him, he adds, **And I am not writing these things that it may be done so in my case.** His thinking had not changed. He was not using subterfuge, hoping that, despite his protest, they would begin to pay him. He had never taken pay from those he served and he never intended to. Nor was he now asking for that in a disguised way.

That was Paul's policy wherever he went. He reminded the Thessalonian church, "you recall, brethren, our labor and hardship, how working night and day so as not to be a burden to any of you, we proclaimed to you the gospel of God" (1 Thess. 2:9). In his next letter to that church he repeats the reminder: "Nor did we eat anyone's bread without paying for it, but with labor and hardship we kept working night and day so that we might not be a burden to any of you" (2 Thess. 3:8). He would not accept so much as a free meal from them.

Paul received support from the Thessalonians after he left them, but not while he worked among them. Without doubt that church was among the Macedonian churches that helped support the apostle while he was in Corinth. "I robbed [a word used for plundering a temple] other churches, taking wages from them to serve you; and when I was present with you and was in need, I was not a burden to anyone; for when the brethren came from Macedonia, they fully supplied my need, and in everything I kept myself from being a burden to you, and will continue to do so" (2 Cor. 11:8-9).

Paul's refusal to accept wages from those he was serving was the result of a deep conviction. **It would be better for me to die than have any man make my boast an empty one.** He would rather have been dead than have anyone think he preached and taught for money. He was not a prophet for hire, as was Balaam (Num. 22), or in the ministry "for sordid gain" (1 Pet. 5:2). It is this commitment that he declares to the Ephesian elders: "I have coveted no one's silver or gold or clothes. You yourselves know that these hands ministered to my own needs and to the men who were with me. In everything I showed you that by working hard in this manner you must help the weak and remember the words of the Lord Jesus, that He Himself said, 'It is more blessed to give than to receive'" (Acts 18:33-35).

Boast (*kauchēma*) refers to that in which one glories or to the basis for glorying. It also carries the idea of rejoicing or reveling. Because it is frequently done in pride, boasting is usually a sin; but it need not be proud and sinful. Paul's **boast** was not intended to convey arrogance but joy. He was so glad for that spiritual privilege and commitment in which he rejoiced that he would rather die than contradict it. He had his priorities right, receiving his joy from exercising his privilege to restrict his freedoms rather than from using them. His boasting was far different from boasting of his accomplishments, as he immediately makes clear.

To Keep from Losing His Reward

For if I preach the gospel, I have nothing to boast of, for I am under compulsion; for woe is me if I do not preach the gospel. For if I do this voluntarily, I have a reward; but if against my will, I have a stewardship entrusted to me. (9:16-18)

THE REWARD WAS NOT FOR THE MESSAGE OR THE MINISTRY OF THE GOSPEL

Paul spoke of boasting in the Lord (1 Cor. 1:31), "boasting in things pertaining to God" (Rom. 15:17), and such. Even more often he spoke of rejoicing in the gospel, of glorying in the cross, and supremely of glorying in Jesus Christ. But he says, **if I preach the gospel, I have nothing to boast of.**

He gloried *in* the gospel but not *for* it. He had absolutely nothing to do with the giving or the content of the gospel. He simply received the revelation. Nor was he boasting of his commitment to or ability in preaching the gospel. He did **preach the gospel,** more diligently than anyone of whom we know, but for this he was **under compulsion.** The Lord stopped him short one day on the road to Damascus, as he was on his way there to persecute Christians. At that time he was set apart as the apostle to the Gentiles (Acts 9:3-6, 15; 26:13-18; cf. Rom. 11:13). Paul chose God's call in the sense that he was not "disobedient to the heavenly vision" (Acts 26:19), but he really had no choice. He was **under compulsion.**

As Paul realized later, God had set him apart even from his "mother's womb" (Gal. 1:15). Like Jeremiah (Jer. 1:5) and John the Baptist (Luke 1:13-17), Paul was called and ordained by God before he was born. And like Jeremiah, Paul could refrain from preaching. When frustrated and despondent because of rejection and ridicule, Jeremiah tried to stop preaching but could not. "But if I say, 'I will not remember Him or speak anymore in His name,' then in my heart it becomes like a burning fire shut up in my bones; and I am weary of holding it in, and I cannot endure it" (Jer. 20:9). To the Colossians Paul said, "I was made a minister according to the stewardship from God bestowed on me" (Col. 1:25).

At some time or another, every preacher whom the Lord has called will realize that he is under God's compulsion. It is not that God's calling cannot be ignored, neglected, or slighted, but that it cannot be changed. The man who resists God's call or tries to give it up will, like Jeremiah, experience a "burning fire shut up in [his] bones" until he obeys. He has no choice.

Ramond Lull, the Spanish mystic, lived a careless and luxurious life for many years. He wrote that in a vision one night Christ came to him carrying a cross and said, "Carry this cross for me, Ramond." He pushed Christ away and refused. In a later vision the same thing happened: Christ offered the cross and Ramond refused it. In a third vision Christ laid the cross in the man's arms and walked away. "What else could I do," Ramond explained, "but take it up?"

Added to that sense of constraint is a serious and compelling responsibility, which Paul articulates in the words, **woe is me if I do not preach the gospel**. In effect, he says that failure to obey that call would result in his suffering serious chastisement. The severest judgments are promised on unfaithful ministers (James 3:1).

Paul gladly preached the gospel, but he did not do it **voluntarily**. **Against my will** does not indicate he was unwilling to obey but that his will had no part in the call itself. It was not his choice to serve Christ, so consequently, he did not receive a **reward** but **a stewardship**. He was under obligation to preach, for which he neither deserved nor expected reward.

Stewardship indicates that someone gives us something or some responsibility that is valued to them, which we are to care for properly. That is the case in every call to minister. God gives the minister what He highly values for safe care, and promises stern discipline to the one who falls short. Paul uses the interjection **woe** (*ouai*) to indicate the impending pain.

THE REWARD WAS FOR PREACHING WITHOUT CHARGE

Having mentioned what his reward could not be for, Paul now mentions what it would be for.

What then is my reward? That, when I preach the gospel, I may offer the gospel without charge, so as not to make full use of my right in the gospel. (9:18)

The gospel was thrust on Paul; he was under compulsion to preach it, and would have been in serious trouble with Lord if he had not. But he was not under compulsion in regard to payment for it. In that he was entirely free to expect support from those he served. He chose not to be paid because he wanted it that way, not because it was necessary. In that choice he found great satisfaction and joy, and for that choice he knew he would receive a reward.

He was determined **not to make full use of** [his] **right in the gospel**. He would work after hours, day and night, to earn his own living rather than be a burden to those he served or cause them to think he was in the ministry for the money.

With great happiness and satisfaction Paul forsook a liberty, he refused to take advantage of a right, in order to make a contribution of his very own to the work of Christ.

To Win the Lost to Christ

Paul's second, and more important, reason for forsaking his right to financial support was to be able to win the lost to Christ without hindrance.

In verses 19-27 he explains two ways in which he sought to enhance his preaching of Christ: through self-denial and self-control.

THROUGH SELF-DENIAL

For though I am free from all men, I have made myself a slave to all, that I might win the more. And to the Jews I became as a Jew, that I might win Jews; to those who are under the Law, as under the Law, though not being myself under the Law, that I might win those who are under the Law; to those who are without law, as without law, though not being without the law of God but under the law of Christ, that I might win those who are without law. To the weak I became weak, that I might win the weak; I have become all things to all men, that I may by all means save some. And I do all things for the sake of the gospel, that I may become a fellow partaker of it. (9:19-23)

The primary purpose of Paul's not taking full advantage of his Christian liberty was **that** [he] **might win the more.** He deeply believed that "he who is wise wins souls" (Prov. 11:30) and was willing to do anything and to sacrifice anything to win people to Jesus Christ. As far as his rights were concerned he **was free from all men,** but because of his love for all men he would gladly limit those rights for their sakes. He had, figuratively, become **a slave to all.** He would modify his habits, his preferences, his entire life-style if any of those things caused someone to stumble, to be offended, or to be hindered from faith in the Lord.

Again we are reminded that in the gray areas of living, those that involve practices about which the Bible does not speak, Paul, as all believers, was free to do as his conscience allowed. But love would not let him do anything that the consciences of weaker believers would not allow. Love would not even allow him to do things that would be offensive to unbelievers to whom he witnessed. He would put every questionable thing in his life under the control of love.

Under the Mosaic law every Hebrew who was enslaved by another Hebrew had to be offered his freedom after six years. But if he loved his master and preferred to remain in that household, he could become a permanent slave, and his ear was pierced as a sign of his voluntary enslavement (Ex. 21:2-6).

In a figurative way Paul made himself such a slave to other men. **I have made**

myself a slave is only two words in Greek (*edoulōsa,* "I enslave," and *emauton,* "myself"). That word for enslavement is very strong. It is used to describe Israel's 400-year experience in Egypt (Acts 7:6), the marriage bond (1 Cor. 7:15), addiction to wine (Titus 2:3), and the Christian's new relationship to righteousness (Rom. 6:18). It was not a small or easy thing that Paul enslaved himself **to all.** But his Lord had taught that "whoever wishes to be first . . . shall be slave of all" (Mark 10:44).

Paul's willing adjustment of his living in order to identify with those to whom he witnessed was part of what today we call preevangelism. What he did in this regard was not a part of the gospel; it had nothing to do with the gospel. But it helped many unbelievers to listen to the gospel and be more open to receive it.

To illustrate his voluntary slavery Paul mentions three ways in which he had adapted, and would continue to adapt, his living in order to help others be more receptive to Christ. Each of these illustrations, like the statement of the principle itself (v. 19), ends with a purpose clause ("that I might/may . . . ") indicating his great desire to win people to Christ.

To the Jews I became as a Jew. First, within scriptural limits he would be as Jewish as necessary when working with Jews. In Christ he was no longer bound to the ceremonies, rituals, and traditions of Judaism. Following or not following any of those things had no affect on his spiritual life. But if following them would open a door for his witnessing to Jews, he would gladly accommodate. What had once been legal restraints now had become love restraints. His motive was clearly to win **Jews** to salvation in Jesus Christ.

Speaking of his fellow Jews, Paul said, "My heart's desire and my prayer to God for them is for their salvation" (Rom. 10:1). Even if preaching to the Gentiles caused some Jews to accept Christ out of jealousy, that would be good (11:14). Earlier in that same letter he said, "For I could wish that I myself were accursed, separated from Christ for the sake of my brethren, my kinsmen according to the flesh" (9:3).

If he was willing to do that for the sake of his fellow Jews, he could surely abide by their ceremonial regulations, observe a special day, or refrain from eating certain foods—if doing those things would help **win those who are under the Law.** When Paul wanted to take Timothy with him in his ministry he had him circumcised, "because of the Jews who were in those parts" where he intended to go (Acts 16:3). Timothy's circumcision was of no benefit to him and certainly not to Paul. But it could be of great benefit to their ministry among Jews and was a small price for the prospect of winning some of them to the Lord.

At the advice of James and other leaders of the Jerusalem church, Paul willingly paid for and participated in a Jewish purification ceremony with four other Jewish Christians. He took part in the ritual in order to prove to the Jewish critics of Christianity that he was not teaching Jews to completely abandon Moses and the Old Testament law (Acts 21:20-26). The special Jewish vow Paul took in Cenchrea (Acts 18:18) may have been for the sake of some Jews.

Because Jews were still **under the Law,** Paul would himself act **as under the Law** when he worked among them. He did not believe, teach, or give the least suggestion that following the law was of any spiritual benefit. It could not gain or keep salvation, but it was a way of opening doors to work among the Jews.

To those who are without law, as without law. Second, Paul was willing to live like a Gentile when he worked among Gentiles.

To keep from being misunderstood, he makes it clear that he is not talking about ignoring or violating God's moral law. The Ten Commandments and all of God's other moral laws have, if anything, been strengthened under the New Covenant. For example, not only is it sin to commit murder but also to be inordinately angry with your brother or to call him a fool. Not only is adultery sinful, but so is lust (Matt. 5:21-30). Love does not abrogate God's moral law but fulfills it (Rom. 13:8, 10; cf. Matt. 5:17). None of us in Christ is **without** [outside] **the law of God,** but rather are **under the law of Christ.** Every believer is under complete legal obligation to Jesus Christ—even though love, rather than the externalities of the law, is to be the guiding force.

In other than moral matters, however, Paul identified as closely as possible with Gentile customs. He ate what they ate, went where they went, and dressed as they dressed. The purpose again was to **win** the Gentiles to Christ.

To the weak I became weak. Third, Paul was willing to identify with those, whether Jew or Gentile, who did not have the power of understanding to grasp the gospel. When among those who were **weak** he acted **weak.** He stooped to the level of their weakness of comprehension. To those who needed simple or repeated presentations, that is what he gave them. No doubt he demonstrated that kind of consideration in the case of the Corinthians themselves (cf. 2:1-5). His purpose was to **win** them to salvation.

In summary, Paul became **all things to all men, that** he might **by all means save some.** He did not compromise the gospel. He would not change the least truth in the least way in order to satisfy anyone. But he would condescend in any way for anyone if that would in any way help bring him to Christ. He would never set aside a truth of the gospel, but he would gladly restrict his liberty in the gospel. He would not offend Jew, Gentile, or those weak in understanding.

If a person is offended by God's Word, that is his problem. If he is offended by biblical doctrine, standards, or church discipline, that is his problem. That person is offended by God. But if he is offended by our unnecessary behavior or practices—no matter how good and acceptable those may be in themselves—his problem becomes our problem. It is not a problem of law but a problem of love, and love always demands more than the law. "Whoever slaps you on your right cheek, turn to him the other also. And if anyone wants to sue you, and take your shirt, let him have your coat also. And whoever shall force you to go one mile, go with him two" (Matt. 5:39-41).

Paul's life centered in living out the gospel and in preaching and teaching the gospel. Nothing else was of any concern to him. **I do all things for the sake of the gospel.** His life was the gospel. He therefore set aside anything that would hinder its power and effectiveness.

Fellow partaker (*sunkoinōnos*) refers to joint participation, joint sharing. The idea here is that Paul wanted everyone else to be a **fellow partaker** with him in the benefits and blessing of the gospel. He wanted them to be with him in the family of God.

THROUGH SELF-CONTROL

Do you not know that those who run in a race all run, but only one receives the prize? Run in such a way that you may win. And everyone who competes in the games exercises self-control in all things. They then do it to receive a perishable wreath, but we an imperishable. Therefore I run in such a way, as not without aim; I box in such a way, as not beating the air; but I buffet my body and make it my slave, lest possibly, after I have preached to others, I myself should be disqualified. (9:24-27)

Liberty cannot be limited without self-control. Our sinfulness resents and resists restrictions, sometimes even in the name of spiritual freedom. It is one thing to acknowledge the principle of living by love; it is another to follow it. Paul followed it because he wanted to be a winner.

The Greeks had two great athletic festivals, the Olympic games and the Isthmian games. The Isthmian games were held at Corinth and were therefore intimately familiar to those to whom Paul was writing. Contestants in the games had to prove rigorous training for ten months. The last month was spent at Corinth, with supervised daily workouts in the gymnasium and athletic fields.

The race was always a major attraction at the games, and that is the figure Paul uses to illustrate the faithful Christian life. **Those who run in a race all run, but only one receives the prize.** No one would train so hard for so long without intending to win. Yet out of the large number of runners, only one wins.

A great difference between those races and the Christian "race" is that every Christian who will pay the price of careful training can win. We do not compete against each other but against the obstacles—practical, physical, and spiritual—that would hinder us. In a sense, every Christian runs his own race, enabling each one of us to be a winner in winning souls to Christ. Paul therefore counsels all believers to **run in such a way that you may win,** by setting aside anything that might hinder the reception of the gospel.

Holding tightly to liberties and rights is a sure way to lose the race of soul-winning. Many of the Corinthian Christians seriously limited their testimony because they would not limit their liberty. They refused to give up their rights, and in so doing they won few and offended many.

If the Olympic and Isthmian athletes exercised such great discipline and **self-control in all things,** why cannot Christians, Paul asks. **They then do it to receive a perishable wreath, but we an imperishable.**

In the Isthmian games the prize was a pine **wreath.** The contestants competed for more than that, of course. The wreath represented fame, acclaim, and the life of a hero. Winners were immortalized, much as they are today. But that "immortality" was just as mortal as the wreath itself, and lasted little longer. Both were **perishable.**

Christians do not run for a short-lived pine wreath or for short-lived fame. They already have true immortality. They run in order to receive a "crown of righteousness, which the Lord, the righteous judge, will award . . . on that day" (2 Tim. 4:8), "an inheritance which is imperishable and undefiled and will not fade away, reserved in heaven" (1 Pet. 1:4). That prize is **imperishable**.

But the imperishable requires self-control just as the perishable. No Christian will be successful in witnessing, or in anything else worthwhile, without discipline. Every good thing we accomplish—whether in learning, business, artistic skill, marriage, spiritual living, witnessing, or whatever—is accomplished through discipline and self-control.

If an athlete expects to excel, he voluntarily, and often severely, restricts his liberty. His sleep, his diet, and his exercise, are not determined by his rights or by his feelings but by the requirements of his training. Professional athletes today often are highly paid. But the Isthmian games were amateur, as the Olympics are today. Amateur athletes train rigorously for years, often at considerable expense, for the sake of an inexpensive prize and the brief acclaim that goes with it.

The athlete's disciplined self-control is a rebuke of half-hearted, out-of-shape Christians who do almost nothing to prepare themselves to witness to the lost—and consequently seldom do.

Paul had a purpose in running. He was **not without aim**. His goal, which he states four times in verses 19-22, was to win as many people to Jesus Christ as possible by as many means as possible.

Changing metaphors, he says that he boxed **in such a way, as not beating the air**. He did not shadow box; he was always fighting the real fight, "the good fight" (1 Tim. 1:18). He was not just working up a sweat, but engaging in a real battle.

A considerable part of that fight was against Paul's own body. **I buffet my body and make it my slave. Buffet** (*hupōpiazō*) literally means to hit under the eye. He figuratively would give his body a black eye, knock it out if necessary. **Make it my slave** (*doulagōgeō*) is from the same root as "made . . . a slave" in verse 19. Paul put his body into subjection, into slavery to his mission of winning souls for Christ.

Most people, including many Christians, are instead slaves to their bodies. Their bodies tell their minds what to do. Their bodies decide when to eat, what to eat, how much to eat, when to sleep and get up, and so on. An athlete cannot allow that. He follows the training rules, not his body. He runs when he would rather be resting, he eats a balanced meal when he would rather have a chocolate sundae, he goes to bed when he would rather stay up, and he gets up early to train when he would rather stay in bed. An athlete leads his body; he does not follow it. It is his slave, not the other way around.

Paul trained rigorously **lest possibly, after I have preached to others, I myself should be disqualified**. Here is another metaphor from the Isthmian games. A contestant who failed to meet the training requirements was disqualified. He could not even run, much less win. Paul did not want to spend his life preaching the requirements to others and then be disqualified for not meeting the requirements himself.

Many believers start the Christian life with enthusiasm and devotion. They train carefully for a while but soon tire of the effort and begin to "break training."

Before long they are disqualified from being effective witnesses. They do not have what it takes, because they are unwilling to pay the price. The flesh, the world, everyday affairs, personal interests, and often simple laziness hinder spiritual growth and preparation for service.

Even good things can interfere with the best. Fulfillment of freedoms can interfere with fulfillment of love. Following our own ways can keep others from knowing the Way. Souls are won by those who are prepared to be used when the Spirit chooses to use them.

The Danger of Overconfidence
(10:1-13)

For I do not want you to be unaware, brethren, that our fathers were all under the cloud, and all passed through the sea; and all were baptized into Moses in the cloud and in the sea; and all ate the same spiritual food; and all drank the same spiritual drink, for they were drinking from a spiritual rock which followed them; and the rock was Christ. Nevertheless, with most of them God was not well-pleased; for they were laid low in the wilderness. Now these things happened as examples for us, that we should not crave evil things, as they also craved. And do not be idolaters, as some of them were; as it is written, "The people sat down to eat and drink, and stood up to play." Nor let us act immorally, as some of them did, and twenty-three thousand fell in one day. Nor let us try the Lord, as some of them did, and were destroyed by the serpents. Nor grumble, as some of them did, and were destroyed by the destroyer. Now these things happened to them as an example, and they were written for our instruction, upon whom the ends of the ages have come. Therefore let him who thinks he stands take heed lest he fall. No temptation has overtaken you but such as is common to man; and God is faithful, who will not allow you to be tempted beyond what you are able, but with the temptation will provide the way of escape also, that you may be able to endure it. (10:1-13)

In chapter 8 Paul sets forth the principle that, although Christians are free to do whatever Scripture does not forbid as being morally wrong, if we love as God calls us to love, we will limit our liberty for the sake of weaker believers. In chapter 9 he illustrates this limitation from his own life and ministry. To keep from giving them reason to think he was preaching for the money, he accepted no wages from those to whom he was ministering. He also modified and adapted his life-style in whatever ways were scripturally permissible in order to witness more effectively.

The second half of chapter 8 and all of chapter 9 illustrate how using our freedom affects others. Chapter 10 illustrates how our use of freedom affects our own lives. In verses 1-13 Paul shows how misuse of liberty can disqualify us from effective service to Christ.

One of the surest ways to fall into temptation and sin is to become overconfident. Many of the Corinthian believers thought, and perhaps had said in the letter to Paul (7:1), that they felt perfectly secure in their Christian lives, that they had arrived. Paul surely had that attitude in mind in the sarcastic rebuke of 4:8-14. They were saved, baptized, well taught, lacking in no gift, and presumably mature. They thought they were strong enough to freely associate with pagans in their ceremonies and social activities and not be affected morally or spiritually, as long as they did not participate in outright idolatry or immorality.

Paul tells them they were self-deceived. Abusing their liberty not only harmed weaker believers whose consciences were offended but also endangered their own spiritual lives. They could not live long on the far edge of freedom without falling into temptation and then into sin. The mature, loving Christian does not try to stretch his liberty to the extreme, to see how close to evil he can come without being harmed.

When a Christian becomes so confident of his strength that he thinks he can handle any situation, he is overconfident and in great danger of falling. The warning is summarized in verse 12: "Therefore let him who thinks he stands take heed lest he fall." The danger is not of falling from salvation but of falling from holiness and from usefulness in service. It is a serious danger and one the Lord does not take lightly.

Ancient Israel provided Paul with sobering illustrations of the pitfalls of overconfident living. Using incidents from their forty-year wandering between Egypt and Canaan, Paul discusses the assets of liberty (vv. 1-4), the abuse of liberty (vv. 5-10), and the application of liberty (vv. 11-13).

The Assets of Liberty

For I do not want you to be unaware, brethren, that our fathers were all under the cloud, and all passed through the sea; and all were baptized into Moses in the cloud and in the sea; and all ate the same spiritual food; and all drank the same spiritual drink, for they were drinking from a spiritual rock which followed them; and the rock was Christ. (10:1-4)

For refers back to the disqualification for service of which Paul had just spoken (9:27) and introduces the examples that follow. **I do not want you to be unaware, brethren,** prepares his readers for new insights into old and familiar stories. It is an urgent statement, pleading with his readers to remember what happened to Israel in the wilderness. He is partly reminding and partly giving new teaching.

All Hebrews were the physical descendants of Abraham. But to truly be God's children they also had to be his spiritual descendants. "For they are not all Israel who are descended from Israel . . . That is, it is not the children of the flesh who are children of God, but the children of the promise are regarded as descendants" (Rom. 9:6, 8). Abraham was father of all the faithful (Rom. 4:11; Gal. 3:29), and in this sense Paul's reference to **our fathers** could be addressed to Gentile as well as Jewish Christians, for they were spiritual descendants of all who believed.

In verses 1-4 Paul emphasizes the oneness of Israel as a corporate community and the commonness of their experiences under Moses' leadership. **All** is used five times in those four verses to indicate that oneness in experience and blessing.

Three basic areas of blessing are mentioned: liberation from Egypt, baptism into Moses, and spiritual sustenance.

LIBERATION FROM EGYPT

After a few years of favored treatment because of Joseph, Israel spent 400 years as slaves in Egypt. They were under total subjection to a foreign and pagan people, who abused, maligned, and severely overworked them. After the ten plagues He sent against the Egyptians, God miraculously delivered Israel. He opened the Red Sea for them to pass **through the sea** on dry land and then closed the waters on their pursuers. He guided them by "a pillar of cloud by day" and "a pillar of fire by night" (Ex. 13:21). As the Lord's supreme deliverance of His chosen people from bondage to freedom, the Exodus became the touchstone of Jewish religion and remains that today.

The Exodus did not represent the spiritual salvation of God's people. Men have always been spiritually saved only by personal faith in God. Many Israelites believed wholly in God while they were in Egypt and no doubt many came to personal faith during the wilderness wanderings. Israel was never saved *spiritually* as a nation, yet their national deliverance is a symbol of New Covenant salvation given to individuals. The Exodus was God's calling His chosen people, believing and unbelieving, out of their bondage in Egypt and His deliverance of them into His own land that He had promised to them through Abraham (Gen. 12:7). They were to be His witnessing community to the world. That was the "race" that Israel as a nation was called by God to run (1 Cor. 9:24). It was in that race that the nation misused its freedom and became disqualified, by falling into idolatry, immorality, and rebelliousness. Paul was saying to the self-confident Corinthians, "Don't let what happened to the nation of Israel happen to you."

BAPTISM INTO MOSES

Ordinarily baptism refers to the ceremony in which water is used to symbolize cleansing from sin. Many Christians, therefore, interpret **and all were**

baptized into Moses in the cloud and in the sea as a reference to this ceremony. They take it to mean that the people were sprinkled by rain from the cloud or immersed when passing through the **sea**. But the pillar of cloud that guided the Israelites by day was the Shekinah cloud, the cloud of God's presence, which at night turned into a pillar of fire, not a cloud of water. And the sea was parted so that the people could walk through on dry land (Ex. 14:16).

The basic Christian significance for baptism is identification with Christ. As Paul explains later in Romans 6:1-10, water baptism is an outward sign of spiritual union with Christ in His death and resurrection. Water baptism symbolizes the baptism believers have already experienced. When we trust in Jesus Christ we are baptized into Him, identified with Him, made one with Him. "For all of you who were baptized into Christ have clothed yourselves with Christ" (Gal. 3:27). It is that idea of spiritual identification, rather than the physical ceremony, that I believe Paul has in mind in the present passage. The Israelites **were baptized into Moses** in the sense that they identified with him as the Lord's appointed leader over them. There was solidarity between the people and Moses.

SPIRITUAL SUSTENANCE

The fact that **all** the Israelites **ate the same spiritual food** indicates that Paul is not speaking of God's working in the spirits of individual Israelites. He could not do that because many of them did not believe in Him. Paul is speaking of the source, not the type, of sustenance. It is true that God spiritually strengthened the Israelites who believed in Him. But He provided physical **food** and **drink**, through **spiritual** means, for **all** of Israel, believers and unbelievers alike. The Lord miraculously provided manna for food (Ex. 16:15) and water for drink (17:6). In this sense they were all spiritually sustained, that is, given provisions from a divine source rather than a natural one.

The source of their **spiritual drink** was **a spiritual rock which followed them; and the rock was Christ.** Even at the time of the Exodus, the Messiah was with Israel providing for them!

The Jews had a popular legend, still known and believed by many in Paul's day, that the actual rock that Moses struck followed Israel throughout her wilderness travels, providing water wherever they went. I believe the apostle may have been alluding to this legend, saying, "Yes, a rock did follow Israel in the wilderness. But it was not a physical rock that provided merely physical water. It was a spiritual rock, the Messiah (the Hebrew term for Christ) whom you have long awaited, who was with our fathers even then."

The term Paul uses here for **rock** is not *petros,* a large stone or boulder, but *petra,* a massive rock cliff. God used a boulder to provide water for Israel on one occasion. But the **spiritual rock which followed them** throughout their journeys was not that small boulder but the great rock of **Christ.** That supernatural rock protected and sustained His people and would not allow them to perish. Old Testament believers did not have the indwelling of the Holy Spirit, but even during the

Exodus they had the sustaining presence of the preexistent Messiah, the preincarnate **Christ,** caring for and fulfilling the needs of His people.

The point of all these affirmations is to recount the privileges of Israel, the assets of her deliverance.

THE ABUSES OF LIBERTY

Nevertheless, with most of them God was not well-pleased; for they were laid low in the wilderness. Now these things happened as examples for us, that we should not crave evil things, as they also craved. And do not be idolaters, as some of them were; as it is written, "The people sat down to eat and drink, and stood up to play." Nor let us act immorally, as some of them did, and twenty-three thousand fell in one day. Nor let us try the Lord, as some of them did, and were destroyed by the serpents. Nor grumble, as some of them did, and were destroyed by the destroyer. (10:5-10)

All Israel shared in the common blessings of liberty, baptism, and sustenance in the wilderness. **Nevertheless, with most of them God was not well-pleased. Most of them** is an understatement. Of the entire great number of Israelites who left Egypt only two, Joshua and Caleb, were allowed to enter the Promised Land. Even Moses and Aaron were disqualified from entering because the rock at Meribah was struck with Moses' rod rather than spoken to as God had commanded (Num. 20:8-12, 24).

Because of disobedience all but two Israelites **were laid low in the wilderness. Laid low** (*katastrōnnumi*) means literally "to strew or spread over." The corpses of those with whom God was not pleased were strewn all over the wilderness. All Israel had been graciously blessed, liberated, baptized, and sustained by the Lord in the wilderness, but in that "race," that test of obedience and service, most of them were "disqualified" (cf. 9:24, 27). They misused and abused their freedom and their blessings. In self-centeredness and self-will they tried to live on the edge of their liberty, and they fell into temptation and then into sin. Overconfidence was their undoing.

Many of the disqualified Israelites were believers who became unfit for God's service. They became what Paul elsewhere refers to as vessels of dishonor. They had not cleansed themselves "from youthful lusts" and had not pursued "righteousness, faith, love and peace." Consequently they did not become vessels that were "sanctified, useful to the Master, prepared for every good work" (2 Tim. 2:21-22). They were scattered about the wilderness as potsherds, pieces of broken vessels that were no longer useful.

The judgments experienced by the disobedient Israelites in the wilderness were **examples for us, that we should not crave evil things, as they also craved.** Those who "were laid low in the wilderness" had not brought their bodies under control as Paul had done with his (9:27) but had indulged their every desire, lust, and craving. A controlled body is useful to the Lord; an indulged one is not. The Christian who controls his body and his life-style is qualified to serve the Lord; the one who indulges his body and is careless in his life-style is disqualified.

The Israelites had become disqualified because of four major sins: idolatry (v. 7), sexual immorality (v. 8), trying God (v. 9), and complaining (v. 10).

IDOLATRY

Idols were more than familiar to Corinthians, because their entire society was built around them. No religious, social, political, or business function was conducted without some involvement with idol worship or recognition.

Many of the Corinthian Christians, overconfident in their own moral and spiritual strength, had become careless about their participation in activities where false gods were worshiped, consulted, or appealed to. They believed they could be associated with such pagan activities without being spiritually harmed. Some of the believers, or professed believers, in Corinth had slipped back into actual idolatry (5:11). Others were in danger of doing the same thing.

Still using Israel as an example, Paul warned, **And do not be idolaters, as some of them were.** The Israelites were hardly out of Egypt before they fell into idolatry. There were no pagan priests, temples, or idols to lure them, but they managed to make their own idols and improvise their own ceremonies.

Exodus 32 records the sordid story. After Moses went up on Mt. Sinai to receive the tablets of God's commandments, the people became impatient at his delay in returning. With little difficulty they persuaded Aaron to make a golden calf. Although the calf was a representation of a popular Egyptian god, the Israelites planned to use it to worship Jehovah. They referred to the calf as the god who had brought them out of Egypt (32:4), and when Aaron built an altar to the idol he declared "a feast to the LORD," that is to Jehovah, or Yahweh, the covenant name of Israel's God (3:14-15). Aaron even offered the same sacrifices, the burnt and peace offerings, customarily offered to God. Yet somehow they thought they could use a pagan idol to worship the true God. They had for so long been around the pagan ceremonies of Egypt that it seemed almost natural to add a pagan practice to true worship. Even Aaron, the first high priest of Israel and next in command under Moses, did not resist when approached by the people with their wicked idea. It was he who suggested that they make the calf from jewelry received from the Egyptians.

Quoting Exodus 32:6 Paul continues, **The people sat down to eat and drink, and stood up to play.** The eating and drinking refer to the excessive feasting that followed the sacrifices. **Play** is a euphemism for sexual relations. It means sexual play and is the same word translated "caressing" in Gen. 26:8. Some three thousand of the Israelites who had instigated that idolatrous and immoral orgy at Sinai were put to death (Ex. 32:28).

Some of the believers in Corinth had also reverted to their old ways of worship. Idols represent false gods, gods who are really demons, and Paul warns later in chapter 10 that "You cannot drink the cup of the Lord and the cup of demons"

(1 Cor. 10:20-21). The right God can only be worshiped in the right way. Those who try to honor God with immoral and pagan practices bring dishonor on Him and judgment on themselves.

When Christians worship anyone or anything besides God, that is idolatry. Worshiping the virgin Mary, saints, icons, or angels is idolatry. No matter how sincerely they are meant to honor to God, such practices are false worship and are strictly forbidden in Scripture. The first commandment God gave Moses was "You shall have no other gods before Me" (Ex. 20:3). There is only one God, and only God is to be worshiped. The injunction of Revelation 22:9, "worship God," is still the exclusive command. And "My little children, guard yourselves from idols" (1 John 5:21) is still the comprehensive prohibition.

All idols, of course, are not physical. They do not have to be made of wood, stone, or metal. Any concept of God that is not biblical is false, and if believed and followed it becomes an idol. Those who follow a man-made god may claim they worship the God of Scripture, just as the Israelites claimed their calf worship was to the Lord. But no false god has anything in common with the God of the Bible.

Churches and philosophies have developed that virtually make gods of success, love, social service, self-image, or simply mankind. Anything that takes our first loyalty and allegiance is an idol. Many people who would not take a second glance at a carved idol will sacrifice health, time, family, moral standards, and anything else required in order to achieve the idol of success or recognition they want. The sin of idolatry, like every other sin, is of the heart. As God told Ezekiel about the elders of Israel, "These men have set up their idols in their hearts, and have put right before their faces the stumbling block of their iniquity" (Ezek. 14:3).

Christians in churches that practice any form of idolatry—ceremonial, theological, or practical—cannot stay there long without being contaminated. They should not want to stay. They should not want to support and encourage, even indirectly, those who hold to doctrines or practices that are unscriptural and ungodly. In doing so they dishonor God, confirm others in wrongdoing, and endanger their own spiritual well-being.

SEXUAL IMMORALITY

The second major sin was alluded to in the previous verse (**play**) but is treated explicitly in verse 8. **Nor let us act immorally, as some of them did, and twenty-three thousand fell in one day.** The incident to which Paul refers is recorded in Numbers. While in the wilderness, "the people began to play the harlot with the daughters of Moab. For they invited the people to the sacrifices of their gods, and the people ate and bowed down to their gods" (25:1-2). Twenty-four thousand Israelites were slain because of that orgy (v. 9). The difference in numbers between the two accounts is probably best explained by taking 23,000 to mean those killed during one day and 24,000 to include others who died later due to the plague.

Idolatry and sexual immorality were closely associated in virtually all ancient religions. They were especially associated in Corinth, whose temple to Aphrodite had a thousand ritual prostitutes. Just as most social occasions involved some form of idolatry, they also usually involved some form of sexual immorality. It is clear from Paul's warning that the self-confident Corinthian believers were no more immune to immorality than idolatry. Thinking they could live carelessly around corruption without being corrupted, they first were tempted and then gave in to temptation. As the apostle had already told them in this letter (6:18), and probably had told them many times when he was with them in person, immorality is to be fled, not flirted with. Christ gives us freedom so that we may serve him more effectively in righteousness, not so we can see how close we can come to unrighteousness.

Many Christians fall into moral problems simply because they are overconfident in themselves. They enter into and continue relationships that may not be wrong in themselves but which offer strong temptations. And when temptations come they think they can handle it, often finding out too late that they could not. Or they go places and do things that are closely associated with immorality, stopping short of doing anything immoral themselves. But even if a person never commits an immoral act in such situations, his mind is filled with vulgar ideas and images, and his spiritual life and testimony are seriously weakened.

TRYING GOD

The third major sin of which the Corinthians were in danger was that of trying, or tempting, God. **Nor let us try the Lord, as some of them did, and were destroyed by the serpents.** Numbers 21 gives the story behind this reference. "And the people spoke against God and Moses, 'Why have you brought us up out of Egypt to die in the wilderness? For there is no food and no water, and we loathe this miserable food'" (Num. 21:5). God had provided manna to eat and water to drink, but the people were not satisfied. They wanted more variety and more spice. They complained and complained, questioning God's goodness and trying His patience. They had no concern for pleasing God, only for His pleasing themselves. They did not use their new freedom to serve Him better but to demand that He serve them better.

Christians sometimes use their freedom to push God to the limit, trying to see how much they can get out of Him and how much they can get by with before Him. Ananias and Sapphira sold some property to raise money for the church in Jerusalem. Keeping part of the proceeds for themselves was within their freedom and was not sinful. But they decided to appear more generous by claiming they gave the entire amount, and their lying hypocrisy pushed the Lord too far. They not only lied to God's people but to God Himself. In rebuking them Peter asked Ananias, "Why has Satan filled your heart to lie to the Holy Spirit? . . . You have not lied to men, but to God," and later asked Sapphira, "Why is it that you have agreed together to put the Spirit of the Lord to the test?" (Acts 5:3-4, 9). Lying to God cost them their lives (vv. 5, 10).

Many of the Corinthians were pushing their liberty to the limits, to see how much of the flesh they could indulge and how much of the world they could enjoy. They were trying God and risking severe discipline. As some Christians today, they probably said, "This is the age of grace. We are free and God is forgiving. We can't lose our salvation so why not get everything out of life that we can?"

The Israelites found the answer to that question. "And the Lord sent fiery serpents among the people and they bit the people, so that many people of Israel died" (Num. 21:6). God's people have always lived under His grace. Every blessing Israel had, including her being called as God's special people, was by His grace. She had been delivered from Egypt by God's grace and she was being sustained and protected by His grace. When she put the Lord to the test, however, she discovered that He had limits which He would not let them cross over without punishment. Some of the Corinthians had gone past that limit and become sick or even died (1 Cor. 11:30).

COMPLAINING

The fourth major sin about which Paul warns is complaining. **Nor grumble, as some of them did, and were destroyed by the destroyer.** After Korah, Dathan, Abiram, and their fellow rebels were destroyed by the Lord (Num. 16:32-35), "all the congregation of the sons of Israel grumbled against Moses and Aaron, saying, 'You are the ones who have caused the death of the Lord's people'" (v. 41). God was so incensed at their complaints about divine justice that He immediately sent a plague that killed 14,700 people. The **destroyer** was the same angel who had slain the firstborn of the Egyptians before Israel left Egypt (Ex. 12:23), who would kill 70,000 men because of David's census (2 Sam. 24:15-16), and who, in response to the prayer of Isaiah and Hezekiah, would destroy the entire Assyrian army that was besieging Jerusalem (2 Chron. 32:21).

Murmuring is dissatisfaction with God's sovereign will for our lives and the lives of others, and is a sin that He does not take lightly, even in view of His grace. When God's people question or complain, they are challenging His wisdom, His grace, His goodness, His love, and His righteousness. Our need for contentment is not merely for our own well-being, which it is, but for God's honor and glory. Complaining dishonors our heavenly Father; contentment glorifies Him.

Paul had "learned to be content in whatever circumstances" he was in (Phil. 4:11) and advises the Corinthians to have this same contentment, lest they suffer God's discipline.

THE APPLICATION OF LIBERTY

Now these things happened to them as an example, and they were written for our instruction, upon whom the ends of the ages have come. Therefore let him who thinks he stands take heed lest he fall. No temptation has overtaken you but such as is common to man; and God is faithful, who will not allow you to be tempted beyond what you are able, but with the temptation will provide the way of escape also, that you may be able to endure it. (10:11-13)

The punishments that came upon the disobedient Israelites not only were **an**

225

example to their fellow Hebrews but also to believers in every age since. More than that they were given for **our instruction,** for the benefit of Christians, those **upon whom the ends of the ages have come.** Instruction (*nouthesia*) is more than ordinary teaching. It means admonition and carries the connotation of warning. It is counsel given to persuade a person to change behavior in light of judgment. **The ends of the ages** refers to the time of Messiah, the time of redemption, the last days of world history before the messianic kingdom comes.

We are living in a greatly different age from that of the Hebrews in the wilderness under Moses, but we can learn a valuable lesson from their experience. Like them we can forfeit our blessing, reward, and effectiveness in the Lord's service if, in overconfidence and presumption, we take our liberties too far and fall into disobedience and sin. We will not lose our salvation, but we can easily lose our virtue and usefulness, and become disqualified in the race of the Christian life.

Every believer, especially when he becomes self-confident in his Christian liberty and spiritual maturity, should **take heed lest he fall.** Paul expresses a timeless principle, articulated in Proverbs as "Pride goes before destruction, and a haughty spirit before stumbling" (16:18). It is easy to substitute confidence in ourselves for confidence in the Lord—accepting His guidance and blessing and then taking credit for the work He does through us. It is also easy to become so enamored of our freedom in Christ that we forget we are His, bought with a price and called to obedience to His Word and to His service.

When I visited Israel several years ago I was shown the place at the Golan Heights where, in 1967, the Israelis penetrated the Syrian defenses and secured that strategic area for themselves. From those heights Syrian guns overlooked most of the Galilee region of northern Israel and were a constant threat. The entire Golan area was closely guarded by the Syrians, except for one spot where the cliffs were so high and sheer that they seemed perfectly safe from attack. One night, however, Israeli bulldozers cut out the cliffs enough to push tanks up to the top. By morning a large contingent of tanks, followed by infantry and supported by fighter planes, completely overran the Syrian positions and secured an area that extended ten miles inland. The spot the Syrians thought to be the safest turned out to be the most vulnerable.

The Bible is filled with examples of the dangers of overconfidence. The book of Esther centers around the plan of a proud and overconfident man who saw his plan backfire. King Ahasuerus of Persia promoted Haman to be his second in command, with instructions for the people to bow before Haman as they would the king. Mordecai, however, would not bow to him, and when the proud and arrogant Haman was told that Mordecai was a Jew, he persuaded Ahasuerus to declare an edict that would give him revenge on all Jews in the land by having them destroyed. Through the intercession of Queen Esther, also a Jew and the niece of Mordecai, the king issued a far different edict, which allowed and even encouraged the Jews to defend themselves—which they did with great success. Haman was hanged on the gallows he had prepared for Mordecai, who was given all of Haman's possessions and the royal honor Haman had expected for himself.

Sennacherib, king of Assyria, taunted Israel with the boast that her God could no more save her than the gods of other lands had saved them. A short time later, "the angel of the Lord went out, and struck 185,000 in the camp of the Assyrians; and when men arose early in the morning, behold, all of these were dead." A few days after the defeated king returned to Assyria, he was assassinated by two of his own sons and succeeded on the throne by a third (Isa. 37:36-38).

Peter discovered that where he thought he was strongest and most dependable he actually was the weakest. He assured Jesus, "Lord, with You I am ready to go both to prison and to death!" But, as Jesus then predicted, before dawn Peter three times denied even knowing Jesus (Luke 22:33-34, 54-62).

The church at Sardis was proud of her reputation for being spiritually alive, but the Lord warned her that she was really dead and needed to repent (Rev. 3:1-2). If she did not He would come upon her like a thief (v. 3)—just as one night enemy soldiers under Cyrus had sneaked into the seemingly impregnable acropolis at Sardis by way of an unguarded footpath. A handful of soldiers crept up the path and opened the gates to the rest of the army. Overconfidence led to carelessness, and carelessness led to defeat.

The self-confident believers at Thyatira thought they were "wealthy" and in "need of nothing," but were told by the Lord that they were really "wretched and miserable and poor and blind and naked" (3:17).

Christians who become self-confident become less dependent on God's Word and God's Spirit and become careless in their living. As carelessness increases, openness to temptation increases and resistance to sin decreases. When we feel most secure in ourselves—when we think our spiritual life is the strongest, our doctrine the soundest, and our morals the purest—we should be most on our guard and most dependent on the Lord.

After the strong warning about self-confidence and pride, Paul gives a strong word of encouragement about God's help when we are tempted (v. 13). First he assures us that none of us has temptations that are unique. Then he assures us that we can also resist and overcome every temptation if we rely on God.

By this time the Corinthians were no doubt wondering how they could possibly avoid all the pitfalls Paul had just described and illustrated. "How do we keep from craving evil things as Israel did (cf. v. 6)? How do we keep from falling into idolatry in our hearts? How can we live righteous lives when the society around us is so wicked? How can we avoid trying the Lord and how can we keep from grumbling?"

Paul's answer is that a Christian should recognize that victory is always available, because a believer can never get into temptation that he cannot get out of. For one thing, Paul explains, **No temptation has overtaken you but such as is common to man.**

The basic meaning of **temptation** (*peirasmos*) is simply to test or prove, and has no negative connotation. Whether it becomes a proof of righteousness or an inducement to evil depends on our response. If we resist it in God's power, it is a test that proves our faithfulness. If we do not resist, it becomes a solicitation to sin. The Bible uses the term in both ways, and I believe that Paul has both meanings in mind here.

When "Jesus was led up by the Spirit into the wilderness to be tempted by the devil" (Matt. 4:1) it is clear that both God and Satan participated in the testing. God intended the test to prove His Son's righteousness, but Satan intended it to induce Jesus to misuse His divine powers and to give His allegiance to Satan. Job was tested in much the same way. God allowed Job to be afflicted in order to prove His servant was an "upright man, fearing God and turning away from evil" (Job 1:8). Satan's purpose was the opposite: to prove that Job was faithful only because of the blessings and prosperity the Lord had given him and that, if those things were taken away, Job would would "surely curse Thee to Thy face" (v. 11).

God's tests are never a solicitation to evil, and James strongly corrects those who suggest such a thing. "Let no one say when he is tempted, 'I am being tempted by God'; for God cannot be tempted by evil, and He Himself does not tempt anyone" (James 1:13). "By evil" is the key to the difference between the two types of temptation. In the wilderness God tested Jesus by righteousness, whereas Satan tested Him by evil. A temptation becomes an inducement to evil only when a person "is carried away and enticed by his own lust. Then when lust has conceived, it gives birth to sin" (James 1:14-15).

Earlier in his letter James wrote, "Consider it all joy, my brethren, when you encounter various trials" (1:2). The nouns *trials* (see also verse 12) and *testing* (v. 3) are from the same Greek root as the verb *tempted* in verses 13-14. The context indicates which sense is meant.

God often brings circumstances into our lives to test us. Like Job we usually do not at the time recognize them as tests, certainly not from God. But our response to them proves our faithfulness or unfaithfulness. How we react to financial difficulty, school problems, health trouble, or business setbacks will always test our faith, our reliance on our heavenly Father. If we do not turn to Him, however, the same circumstances can make us bitter, resentful, and angry. Rather than thanking God for the test, as James advises, we may even accuse Him. An opportunity to cheat on our income tax or take unfair advantage in a business deal will either prove our righteousness or prove our weakness. The circumstance or the opportunity is only a test, neither good nor evil in itself. Whether it results in good or evil, spiritual growth or spiritual decline, depends entirely on our response.

In the Lord's Prayer Jesus says that we should ask God not to "lead us into temptation, but deliver us from evil" (Matt. 6:13). "Evil" is better translated "the evil one," referring to Satan. In other words we should pray that God will not allow tests to become temptations, in the sense of inducement to evil. The idea is, "Lord, stop us before Satan can turn your test into his temptation."

Common to man is one word (*anthrōpinos*) in Greek and simply means "that which is human, characteristic of or belonging to mankind." In other words, Paul says there is no such thing as a superhuman or supernatural temptation. Temptations are human experiences. The term also carries the idea of usual or typical, as indicated by **common**. Temptations are never unique experiences to us. We can never have a temptation that has not been experienced by millions of other people. Circumstances differ but basic temptations do not. Even the Son of God was "tempted in all things as we are" (Heb. 4:15), and because of that "He is able to come to the aid of those who are tempted" (2:18). And because temptations are common to us all we are able to "confess [our] sins to one another" (James 5:16) and to "bear one another's burdens" (Gal. 6:2). We are all in the same boat.

Not only are temptations common to men but **God is faithful, who will not allow you to be tempted beyond what you are able.** No believer can claim that he was overwhelmed by temptation or that "the devil made me do it." No one, not even Satan, can make us sin. He cannot even make an unbeliever sin. No temptation is inherently stronger than our spiritual resources. People sin because they willingly sin.

The Christian, however, has his heavenly Father's help in resisting temptation. **God is faithful.** He remains true to His own. "From six troubles He will deliver you, even in seven evil will not touch you" (Job 5:19). When our faithfulness is tested we have God's own faithfulness as our resource. We can be absolutely certain that He **will not allow** [us] **to be tempted beyond what** [we] **are able.** That is God's response when we pray, "do not lead us into temptation, but deliver us from evil" (Matt. 6:13). He will not let us experience any test we are not able to meet.

When the soldiers came to arrest Jesus in the Garden of Gethsemane, He asked them twice whom they had come for, who was designated on their arrest order. After they answered for the second time, "Jesus the Nazarene," He said, "If therefore you seek Me, let these go their way" (John 18:4-9). John explains that Jesus prevented the disciples from being arrested with Him in order "that the word might be fulfilled which He spoke, 'Of those whom Thou hast given Me I lost not one'" (v. 9). The disciples were not yet ready for such a test. Had they been arrested, they would have been devastated, and Jesus would not permit it. As best we know from church history, most of those eleven disciples died a martyr's death. The other, John, was exiled for life on the island of Patmos. All of them went through persecution, imprisonment, and countless hardships for the sake of the gospel. But they did not go though those things until they were ready to handle them.

But with the temptation will provide the way of escape also, that you may be able to endure it. The phrase **the way** is formed by the definite article and a singular noun. In other words, there is only one way. The **way of escape** from every temptation, no matter what it is, is the same: it is *through*. Whether we have a test by God to prove our righteousness or a test by Satan to induce to sin, there is only one way we can pass the test. We **escape** temptation not by getting out of it but by passing through it. God does not take us out; He sees us through by making us **able to endure it.**

God's own Spirit led Jesus into the wilderness to be tempted. It was the Father's will that the Son be there, and Jesus did not leave until all three temptations were over. He met the temptations head-on. He "escaped" the temptations by enduring them in His Father's power.

God provides three ways for us to endure temptation: prayer, trust, and focusing on Jesus Christ.

"Keep watching and praying, that you may not come into temptation," Jesus told His disciples (Mark 14:38). If we do not pray, we can be sure a test will turn into temptation. Our first defense in a test or a trial is to pray, to turn to our heavenly Father and put the matter in His hands.

Second, we must trust. When we pray we must pray believing that the Lord will answer and help us. We also trust that, whatever the origin of the trial, God has allowed it to come for our good, to prove our faithfulness. God has a purpose for everything that comes to His children, and when we are tested or tempted we should gladly endure it in His power—for the sake of His glory and of our spiritual growth.

Third, we should focus on our Lord Jesus Christ. "For consider Him who has endured such hostility by sinners against Himself, so that you may not grow weary and lose heart. You have not yet resisted to the point of shedding blood in your striving against sin" (Heb. 12:3-4). Christ endured more than we could ever be called on to endure. He understands our trials and He is able to take us through them.

In John Bunyan's *Pilgrim's Progress* Christian and Hopeful fall asleep in a field belonging to giant Despair. The giant finds them and takes them into Doubting Castle, where he puts them in a dark and stinking dungeon, without food or water. On his wife's advice, the giant first beats them mercilessly and then suggests they commit suicide. After the giant leaves, the two companions discuss what they should do. Finally Christian remembers the key in his pocket. "I have a key in my bosom called Promise, that will, I am persuaded, open any lock in Doubting Castle." Sure enough, it opened all the doors in the castle and even the gate. "Then they went on, and came to the King's highway again."

The Truth About Idolatry (10:14-22)

Therefore, my beloved, flee from idolatry. I speak as to wise men; you judge what I say. Is not the cup of blessing which we bless a sharing in the blood of Christ? Is not the bread which we break a sharing in the body of Christ? Since there is one bread, we who are many are one body; for we all partake of the one bread. Look at the nation Israel; are not those who eat the sacrifices sharers in the altar? What do I mean then? That a thing sacrificed to idols is anything, or that an idol is anything? No, but I say that the things which the Gentiles sacrifice, they sacrifice to demons, and not to God; and I do not want you to become sharers in demons. You cannot drink the cup of the Lord and the cup of demons; you cannot partake of the table of the Lord and the table of demons. Or do we provoke the Lord to jealousy? We are not stronger than He, are we? (10:14-22)

As Paul has made clear in 10:1-13, idolatry, immorality, and complaining against God are not questionable things; they are outright sins. Christians have no liberty in regard to such things. In the next nine verses (14-22) the apostle explains why the sin of idolatry is especially abominable to God. It is not a moral issue to eat something offered to an idol, but it is a serious sin to engage in any form of idol worship. Some of the Corinthians were taking their liberty in questionable things too far, and were becoming involved in the evil of idolatry. They were free to attend pagan functions but were not free to participate in the false worship. With strong words Paul here rebukes those who would do that.

Therefore, my beloved, flee from idolatry. I speak as to wise men; you judge what I say. (10:14-15)

Paul first assures his fellow believers, his brothers and sisters in Christ, that he is speaking to them as one who loves and cares for them. The Corinthian Christians were deeply loved by their former pastor, who was the spiritual father of many of them. They were his **beloved**, in spite of their many problems.

Many of the believers in Corinth were still spiritually immature (3:1-3). But because of their salvation, all of them had divine guidance in understanding, and so are addressed here as **wise men**. Paul gives them the benefit of any doubt and assumes that, if they listen carefully, they will by the Spirit be able to **judge** correctly what he says. His exhortation is simple, scriptural, and logical.

Before he goes into defining the specific evils of idolatry, he tells them to **flee from idolatry.** Even before they understand its full danger they should get away from it (cf. 1 John 5:21). If they had slipped back into idolatry or were strongly tempted to do so, they first should get far away from it, and then study Paul's argument. "First, get out of immediate danger. You won't be able to pay attention to or appreciate what I am saying as long as you are associated with the practice in any way."

Because idolatry is worshiping something other than the true God in the true way, it is the most serious and contaminating of sins. It strikes at the very character of God. Those who worship an idol declare that the Lord is not the only true God and that other "so-called gods" (8:5) are worthy to share His glory and honor. They testify that the Lord is deficient, that He is not all-wise, all-powerful, and all-sufficient. A Pandora's box is opened to other loyalties and other moral and spiritual standards. It is not accidental or incidental that the first two of the Ten Commandments are prohibitions that have to do with idolatry. If we do not have the right view of God, nothing else can be in the right perspective.

Since the Fall men have wanted to make God over into their own images and to their own liking. "For even though they knew God, they did not honor Him as God, or give thanks; but they became futile in their speculations, and their foolish heart was darkened. Professing to be wise, they became fools, and exchanged the glory of the incorruptible God for an image in the form of corruptible man and of birds and four-footed animals and crawling creatures" (Rom. 1:21-23). As A. W. Tozer observed, "A god begotten in the shadows of a fallen heart will, quite naturally, be no true likeness of the true God."

Idolatry includes much more than bowing down or burning incense to a physical image. Idolatry is having any false god—any object, idea, philosophy, habit, occupation, sport, or whatever that has one's primary concern and loyalty or that to any degree decreases one's trust in and loyalty to the Lord.

There is no other God but the God of the Bible, and He is a jealous God who will not tolerate the worship of another. In Isaiah 48:11, God says: "My glory will I not give to another." Exodus 34:14 says, "You shall not worship any other god, for the Lord, whose name is Jealous, is a jealous God."

Yet the world worships false gods. Romans 1:21 indicts all of mankind: "Even though they knew God," Paul wrote, speaking of the human race, "they did not honor Him as God, or give thanks." In fact, when they refused to worship God, they began to make images. They "exchanged the glory of the incorruptible God for an image in the form of corruptible man and of birds and fourfooted animals and crawling creatures" (v. 23).

They refused to worship God, turning instead to false gods, and that is unacceptable. Verse 24 tells the consequences of worshiping a false god: "God gave them over in the lusts of their hearts to impurity." Verse 28 adds, "God gave them over to a depraved mind."

The result of their improper worship was that God simply gave them over to their sin and its consequences. Can you think of anything worse? Their sin increasingly became the dominating factor in their lives, and ultimately they faced judgment without any excuses (Rom. 1:32–2:1).

Everyone worships—even an atheist. He worships himself. When men reject God they worship false gods. That, of course, is what God forbids in the first commandment.

False gods may be either material objects or mythical, supernatural beings. Material gods may be worshiped even without the conscious thought that they are deities. Job wrote,

> If I have put my confidence in gold,
> And called fine gold my trust,
> If I have gloated because my wealth was great,
> And because my hand had secured so much;
> If I have looked at the sun when it shone,
> Or the moon going in splendor,
> And my heart became secretly enticed,
> And my hand threw a kiss from my mouth,
> That too would have been an iniquity calling for
>   judgment,
> For I would have denied God above. (Job 31:24-28)

That describes a man who refuses the inclination to worship his material wealth. If you worship what you possess, if you center your life on yourself, your possessions, or even your needs, you have denied God.

Habakkuk 1:16 describes the false worship of the Chaldeans: "The Chaldeans bring all of them [the righteous] up with a hook, drag them away with their net, and gather them together in their fishing net. Therefore, they rejoice and are glad. Therefore, they offer a sacrifice to their net, and burn incense to their fishing net." Their "net" was their military might, and the god they worshiped was armed power—a false god.

Some formulate supernatural gods, supposed deities. That, too, is unacceptable. Things sacrificed to idols are really sacrificed to demons (1 Cor. 10:20). Therefore, if men worship false beings, they are actually worshiping the demons that impersonate those false gods.

Acts 17:29 contains a marvelous observation by Paul: "Being then the offspring of God, we ought not to think that the Divine Nature is like gold or silver or stone, an image formed by the art and thought of man." We are made in God's image, and we are not silver, stone, or wood. How could any man think that his Creator would be such?

Idolatry has many forms. *Libeling the character of God* is idolatry. This form includes believing the true God to be something other than He is. We are guilty of idolatry, for example, when we think of the Son of God only as Jesus and use that name almost to the exclusion of His other names. He is first of all the Lord Jesus Christ, the second person of the Trinity. He is our friend and brother, but infinitely more important than that He is our Lord and Savior, our God.

We are also guilty of libeling God when we do not trust Him, when we doubt that He is able or willing to meet every need we have. When we doubt God we say in our hearts, "I question whether your Word is reliable, your promises are true, your power is sufficient, or your love unlimited."

Worshiping the true God in the wrong way is idolatry. Whenever men establish unbiblical forms and rituals and neglect worship from the heart, they set up idols that come between worshipers and God, even though the forms and rituals are intended to be in His name and for His honor and glory. Any time they adopt worldly practices in church services they set up idols that detract from true worship.

Worshiping God in the wrong form is unacceptable worship. For example, the Israelites were idolatrous when they worshiped the golden calf in the wilderness despite the fact that they intended the image to represent the true God (Ex. 32:1-4). Making idols of any sort was strictly forbidden in the second commandment (Ex. 20:4), and was a practice they knew was pagan even before the law was given.

Exodus 32:7-9 records God's response when the Israelites made the golden calf to worship:

> Then the Lord spoke to Moses, "Go down at once, for your people, whom you brought up from the land of Egypt, have corrupted themselves. They have quickly turned aside from the way which I commanded them. They have made for themselves a molten calf, and have worshiped it, and have sacrificed unto it, and said, 'This is your god, O Israel, who brought you up from the land of Egypt!'"

When the Israelites constructed the molten calf, they worshiped it in the name of the true God, but they had reduced Him to an image.

Years later, as recorded in Deuteronomy 4:14-19, Moses said to the assembled Israelites:

> And the Lord commanded me at that time to teach you statutes and judgments, that you might perform them in the land where you are going over to possess it. So watch yourselves carefully, since you did not see any form on the day the Lord spoke to you at Horeb from the midst of the fire. Lest you act corruptly and make a graven image for yourselves in the form of any figure, the likeness of male or female, the likeness of any animal that is on the earth, the likeness of any winged bird that flies in the sky, the likeness of anything that creeps on the ground, the likeness of any fish that is in the water below the earth. And beware, lest you lift up your eyes to heaven and see the sun and the moon and the stars, all the host of heaven, and be drawn away and worship them and serve them, those which the Lord your God has allotted to all the peoples under the whole heaven.

In other words, when God revealed Himself to the Israelites, He was not represented in any visible form. There was no physical representation of God—and that is true of God throughout the Scriptures. Why? Because God does not want to be reduced to any image.

The idea that God is an old man with a beard sitting in a chair is completely contrary to Scripture and is unacceptable. Idolatry does not begin with a sculptor's hammer; it begins in the mind. When we think of God we should visualize absolutely nothing. No visual conception of Him could properly represent His eternal nature and glory.

Worshiping any image is idolatry. That is the most literal and obvious kind of idolatry, the kind so frequently denounced in the Old Testament. It is the kind in which a person makes an image with his own hands and then "falls down before it and worships; he also prays to it and says, 'Deliver me, for thou art my god'" (Isa. 44:17).

Even statues or other images of Christ are not to be revered or worshiped. Only Christ is to be worshiped, not likenesses of Him. They do not represent Jesus Christ, no matter what our claims and intentions are. "God is spirit, and those who worship Him must worship in spirit and truth" (John 4:24). Even nonliturgical Christians should be on guard, whether in public worship or private devotions, about associating any place, picture, or pattern of worship too closely with God. It is easy for such a thing to come between us and Him, though we may think it helps draw us closer.

Worshiping angels is idolatry. Paul warns, "Let no one keep defrauding you of your prize by delighting in self-abasement and the worship of the angels" (Col. 2:18). When, overcome with awe, John fell at the feet of the angel who was speaking to him, the angel said, "Do not do that; I am a fellow servant of yours and your brethren who hold the testimony of Jesus; worship God" (Rev. 19:10). Angels are created beings and, whether holy or fallen, are not to be venerated or worshiped.

Worshiping demons is idolatry, and is closely associated with worshiping images, behind which are often demons. In Satan cults demons are worshiped directly. Speaking of the Tribulation, John foretells that "The rest of mankind, who were not killed by these plagues, did not repent of the works of their hands, so as not to worship demons, and the idols of gold and of silver and of brass and of stone and of wood" (Rev. 9:20).

Worshiping dead men is idolatry. Referring to idolatry that Israel learned from Moab, the psalmist wrote, "They joined themselves also to Baal-peor, and ate sacrifices offered to the dead. Thus they provoked Him to anger with their deeds; and the plague broke out among them" (Ps. 106: 28-29). We do not worship human beings, whether they are alive or dead, saintly or otherwise. Even the great heroes of Scripture—such as Abraham, Moses, David, the prophets, Mary, or the apostles—are never to be worshiped. That is idolatry.

Supreme loyalty in our heart to anything other than God is idolatry. Every person is tempted with ambitions, desires, possessions, recognition, and a host of other such things that easily can become idols. "Where your treasure is, there will your heart be also," Jesus said (Matt. 6:21). The greatest heart treasure, or heart idol, is self.

Covetousness is idolatry. Those who covet or are greedy worship at the shrine of materialism, one of the most popular and powerful idols of our day. But Paul says, "For this you know with certainty, that no immoral or impure person or covetous man, who is an idolator, has an inheritance in the kingdom of Christ and God" (Eph. 5:5; cf. Col. 3:5).

Inordinate desire, or lust, is idolatry. Paul speaks of "enemies of the cross of Christ, whose end is destruction, whose god is their appetite, and whose glory is in their shame, who set their minds on earthly things" (Phil. 3:18-19). The person whose mind, desires, longings, and appetites are set on fleshly things is an idolater.

Idolatry brings guilt on everyone who is involved in it, as well as bringing God's vengeance on unbelievers and His chastening on believers. "The Levites who went far from Me, when Israel went astray, who went astray from Me after their idols, shall bear the punishment for their iniquity" (Ezek. 44:10). To those whose idolatry is less obvious the Lord says, "I have spread out My hands all day long to a rebellious people, who walk in the way which is not good, following their own thoughts" (Isa. 65:2).

Idolatry is listed among the vilest sins of the flesh (Gal. 5:19-21), and the Lord makes it clear that no idolater will inherit His kingdom (Rev. 21:8; 22:15).

Idolatry not only is an offense against God but is harmful to men. It defiles those who practice it and is harmful to everyone around them. Idolatry defiles a person by rendering him spiritually impure. Whether he worships a carved god of stone or a sophisticated god of his mind and heart, that worship has a corrupting effect on his moral and spiritual life. It has that effect both on believers and unbelievers. An unbeliever is pushed further from God and His way, and a believer violates the purity of his relationship with his heavenly Father. God graciously keeps forgiving and cleansing the believer, but his idolatry is no less defiling and sinful. Idolatry harms those around the idolater by giving them a false testimony and example. It is a degrading influence on all of the society in which it is practiced.

Not only that, but no idol can help men. A carved image cannot forgive, save, give peace of mind, or solve problems; nor can money, fame, education, social prestige, or any other such thing that men come to trust in. Every idol is man-made, and every idol is helpless to help. Idols only defile. They never glorify God but always dishonor Him. Since no good can come of idolatry, the only response to it should be to **flee.**

In verses 16-22 Paul gives three reasons for fleeing from idolatry: it is inconsistent; it is demonic; and it is offensive to God.

Idolatry Is Inconsistent

Is not the cup of blessing which we bless a sharing in the blood of Christ? Is not the bread which we break a sharing in the body of Christ? Since there is one bread, we who are many are one body; for we all partake of the one bread. Look at the nation Israel; are not those who eat the sacrifices sharers in the altar? (10:16-18)

The cup of blessing could be the last cup of wine drunk at the end of a meal, as a final testimony of thanksgiving for all that God had provided. It also was the proper name given to the third cup passed during the Passover feast. In the upper room, on the night before His crucifixion, Jesus may have used the third cup as the symbol of His blood shed for sin. That cup then became the instrument to institute the Lord's Supper. In any case He set apart the cup as a token of special thanksgiving before He passed it to the disciples (Matt. 26:26), and whenever believers partake of Communion they partake of this blessed sacred cup. For Christians it is the supreme **cup of blessing,** which in turn **we bless** and are thankful for His death each time we use it in remembrance of our Lord.

Paul's words are so framed as to assume that participating in the Lord's Supper is a regular practice of faithful Christians. It is commanded by our Lord (Luke 22:19; 1 Cor. 11:24-25) to remind us of His sacrifice for us and of our oneness with Him and with fellow believers. When believers participate they are **sharing in the blood of Christ** and **sharing in the body of Christ.** It is communing with the Lord and with His people. Celebrating our common salvation and eternal life is the ultimate fellowship of believers while we are on earth, and reflects the perfect fellowship we will have in heaven.

Sharing (*koinōnia*) means to have in common, to participate with, to have partnership. The same Greek word is used of our being "called into *fellowship* with His Son, Jesus Christ our Lord" (1 Cor. 1:9), of the "*fellowship* of the Spirit" (Phil. 2:1), of the "*fellowship* of His sufferings" (Phil. 3:10), and of "*participation* in the support of the saints" (2 Cor. 8:4). When we properly share in Communion we spiritually participate in fellowship with Jesus Christ and with other believers. It is much more than a symbol; it is a profound celebration of common spiritual experience.

The picture of someone we love is not the same as that person; it only represents the person. But the feelings of love, care, desire to be with them, and of remembering experiences we have had with them are totally real. We have an experience of real fellowship and kinship with that person whenever we see the picture. Our minds are flooded with reality.

While we are thinking of them, our earthly loved ones are seldom aware of it; but our Lord is intensely aware of it when we think of Him. When we remember His death for us, His becoming sin for us, His taking our penalty upon Himself, His redeeming us—all of which are represented by His shed **blood**—we participate in the most intimate and real communion with Him and with all others in Him.

In this passage, and in many places in the New Testament, Jesus' **blood** and **body** are used as metonyms. A metonym is a figure of speech in which the name of one thing is used to represent another thing of which it is a part or with which it is associated. When we say, "I was reading Shakespeare last night," we mean that we were reading a play written by him. The name of the author is used to represent the works he has written. In the Old Testament, blood is frequently used to represent life, "For the life of the flesh is in the blood" (Lev. 17:11). Similarly, shedding of blood is often used to represent death, which is the loss of life. In the New Testament, therefore, blood is often used to represent Christ's sacrificial death, the death in which His physical blood was shed on behalf of those who trust in Him. There was nothing in the physical blood of Christ that could remove sin. It was His death, represented by His shed blood, that paid the penalty for our sin and redeemed us.

The bread which we break [is] **a sharing in the body of Christ**. The bread symbolizes Christ's body just as the cup symbolizes His blood. And as the blood represents His death, so the body represents His life.

In the Old Testament the human body was associated with the totality of life, with man's earthliness, his humanness. Adam's body was formed "of the dust from the ground" (Gen. 2:7), and his very name is from the same Hebrew root as earth, or land (*'adāmâ*). When we share **in the body of Christ** we remember and celebrate His earthliness, His humanness, His incarnation, and also His death as a human sacrifice for the salvation of humankind.

The New Testament makes a special point of the fact that Jesus' body was not broken on the cross. "For these things came to pass, that the Scripture might be fulfilled, 'Not a bone of Him shall be broken'" (John 19:36). The bread represents Christ's body, but the breaking of the bread does not represent the breaking of His body, because that never took place.

Jesus broke the bread in order to distribute it among the disciples, representing His sharing His life with them. When we eat the bread we remember Christ's emptying Himself in order to live among us as a man (Phil. 2:7), His suffering as we suffer, and His being tempted as we are tempted, in order that "He might become a merciful and faithful high priest" (Heb. 2:17).

The Lord's Supper is a spiritual experience. The bread and wine are not transubstantiated—turned into the actual body and blood of Christ—as Roman Catholics believe, or consubstantiated—having the actual body and blood existing alongside them—as many Lutherans believe. Christ cannot be sacrificed again, because He was offered only "once to bear the sins of many" (Heb. 9:28). Nor can His body and blood actually be consumed by us, either in place of the bread and wine or along with them (cf. John 6:52). Not only that, but at the first Lord's Supper, in which Christ Himself passed the cup and the bread, He had not yet been crucified; His physical blood had not yet been shed. When believers partake of Communion in faith, the Holy Spirit uses those symbols as sensitizers to kindle our spirits in awareness and appreciation of our Lord's great ministry and sacrifice for us.

Christ's body also symbolizes our unity in Jesus Christ. **Since there is one bread, we who are many are one body; for we all partake of the one bread.** Because we are one with Christ we are one with each other. As we come into fellowship with Christ through Communion, we come into fellowship with each other in a unique and deep way (cf. 1 Cor. 6:17). All believers stand on the same ground at the foot of the cross, as forgiven sinners who possess the eternal life principle within them.

Again Paul uses Israel to illustrate his point. **Are not those who eat the sacrifices sharers in the altar?** When the Israelites sacrificed to the Lord, some of the offering was burnt as the sacrifice proper, some of it was eaten by the priests, and some was eaten by those who offered it. Everyone was involved with the offering, with God and with each other.

Likewise, to sacrifice to an idol is to identify with it, to participate with the idol and with all others who sacrifice to it. Religious ceremonies, whether Christian or pagan, involve participation of the worshipers with the object of their worship and with each other. Thus it is completely inconsistent for believers to participate in any expression of worship that is apart from and contrary to their Lord.

Idolatry Is Demonic

What do I mean then? That a thing sacrificed to idols is anything, or that an idol is anything? No, but I say that the things which the Gentiles sacrifice, they sacrifice to demons, and not to God; and I do not want you to become sharers in demons. You cannot drink the cup of the Lord and the cup of demons; you cannot partake of the table of the Lord and the table of demons. (10:19-21)

Much worse than being inconsistent, idolatry is also demonic. The **thing sacrificed** has no spiritual power or nature (cf. 8:8); nor does the physical **idol** to which it is sacrificed (cf. 8:4). Those things are nothing in themselves. But more importantly than their not being **anything**, idols represent that which is demonic.

Demons are the spiritual force behind all idolatry. Those who sacrifice to idols **sacrifice to demons.** When worshipers believe an idol represents an actual god, Satan sends one of his demon emissaries to act out the part of that imaginary god. There is never a god behind an idol, but there is always a spiritual force; and that force is always evil, always demonic.

Demons can exhibit considerable power. Many cultic and pagan religious claims are faked and exaggerated; but many are true. They are evil but true. Much that goes under the name of astrology, for instance, is simply exploitation of the gullible. But many predictions come true through the work of demonic forces. Demons are not unlimited in power, but they have power to perform enough wonders and to make enough predictions come true to keep superstitious worshipers deceived and loyal (cf. 2 Thess 2:9-11).

Satan is the prince of this world system and he rules this world with the aid of his demons. To participate in the corrupt things of this world, especially in idolatrous acts of worship, is to participate with Satan and his demons. It is **to become sharers in demons.** Moses wrote of Jeshurun, an affectionate name for Israel, as having "sacrificed to demons who were not God" (Deut. 32:17). The ones they worshiped were not divine but they were real. The psalmist, also speaking of Israel, tells of her following pagan practices to the extent even of sacrificing "their sons and their daughters to the demons" (Ps. 106:37).

A Christian **cannot drink the cup of the Lord and the cup of demons.** He **cannot partake of the table of the Lord and the table of demons.** Paul is not giving advice but stating a fact. Jesus made it clear that we cannot "serve two masters" (Matt. 6:24). It is not simply that we should not but that we cannot. It is impossible to do both at the same time. It must be one or the other. We will "hate the one and love the other," or we will "hold to the one and despise the other." When we fellowship with **the Lord** we cannot also fellowship with **demons,** and vice versa. Some attempted it in Corinth, but they were not truly fellowshipping with the Lord. Their worship was hypocrisy.

Christians are not immune from the influence of demons. When we willingly ignore the Lord's way and flirt with the things of Satan by setting up idols of any kind, we open ourselves up to demonic influence. In rebuking Ananias, Peter said, "Why has Satan filled your heart to lie to the Holy Spirit?" (Acts 5:3). Through the idol of their greed, he and his wife, Sapphira, left themselves open to being corrupted by the chief of demons. It is clear from our wrestling with demons (Eph. 6:12) that there is some intimate contact between believers and those vile fallen angels.

John warns, "If anyone comes to you and does not bring this teaching, do not receive him into your house, and do not give him a greeting; for the one who gives him a greeting participates in his evil deeds" (2 John 10-11). Even showing hospitality to those who promote false teaching causes us to participate with the demonic influence behind those teachings. To do that in any way and then come to the Lord's table in true communion with the Savior and His people is impossible.

Idolatry Is Offensive to the Lord

Or do we provoke the Lord to jealousy? We are not stronger than He, are we? (10:22)

Idolatry is inconsistent, demonic, and offensive to the Lord. It will **provoke**

the Lord to jealousy. God has holy jealousy because He will have no competition. That is why God said Israel "made Me jealous with what is not God; they have provoked Me to anger with their idols" (Deut. 32:21). The Lord deals strongly with idolatry because nothing is more offensive to Him than idolatry, which is the most detestable sign of unbelief. Because Judah had gone "after other gods to serve them and to worship them, . . . 'behold, I will send and take all the families of the north,' declares the Lord, 'and I will send to Nebuchadnezzar king of Babylon, My servant, and will bring them against this land, and against its inhabitants, and against all these nations round about; and I will utterly destroy them, and make them a horror, and a hissing, and an everlasting desolation'" (Jer. 25:6, 9). John pictures an even more terrible judgment. "But for the cowardly and unbelieving and abominable and murderers and immoral persons and sorcerers and idolaters and all liars, their part will be in the lake that burns with fire and brimstone, which is the second death" (Rev. 21:8).

Paul's question, **We are not stronger than He, are we?** obviously is rhetorical. Does the idolater foolishly think he is more powerful than God? God will not allow idolatry to go unpunished, and no one can escape. Even His own children will not escape His severe chastisement if they persist in worshiping any sort of idol. Some of the Corinthians had done that and had paid with their health, or even their lives (1 Cor. 11:30).

Using Freedom for God's Glory (10:23–11:1)

25

All things are lawful, but not all things are profitable. All things are lawful, but not all things edify. Let no one seek his own good, but that of his neighbor. Eat anything that is sold in the meat market, without asking questions for conscience' sake; for the earth is the Lord's, and all it contains. If one of the unbelievers invites you, and you wish to go, eat anything that is set before you, without asking questions for conscience' sake. But if anyone should say to you, "This is meat sacrificed to idols," do not eat it, for the sake of the one who informed you, and for conscience' sake; I mean not your own conscience, but the other man's; for why is my freedom judged by another's conscience? If I partake with thankfulness, why am I slandered concerning that for which I give thanks? Whether, then, you eat or drink or whatever you do, do all to the glory of God. Give no offense either to Jews or to Greeks or to the church of God; just as I also please all men in all things, not seeking my own profit, but the profit of the many, that they may be saved. Be imitators of me, just as I also am of Christ. (10:23–11:1)

Paul's central message in this passage, and the Bible's central message for believers in all ages, is summarized in verse 31: **whatever you do, do all to the glory of God**. God created man to glorify Himself, and that is man's purpose in life. Fallen man cannot purpose to glorify God, because he does not know God or have a godly nature through Jesus Christ.

God is glorified in His wrath against the unredeemed. Pharaoh did not seek to glorify God, nor could he; but God said, "I will be honored through Pharaoh and all his army, through his chariots and his horsemen" (Ex. 14:17). And He was glorified through all those means. God's message to Pharaoh was, "Indeed, for this cause I have allowed you to remain, in order to show you My power, and in order to proclaim My name through all the earth (Ex. 9:16). Although Pharaoh could not glorify God with his life, God was glorified in his destruction (cf. Jer. 13:15-16; Rom. 1:22-26).

Redeemed man, however, is able to glorify the Lord, and he will glorify Him if he is faithful.

The first question and answer in The Shorter Catechism are: "What is the chief end of man? Man's chief end is to glorify God, and to enjoy Him forever." The catechism is right in declaring that the pinnacle of man's being is glorifying and enjoying God. The highest purpose any individual can have is to be totally absorbed in the person of God, and to view all of life through eyes filled with His wonder and glory. That is the perspective of the true worshiper, the one who truly glorifies God.

The word *glory* means "something that is worthy of praise or exaltation; brilliance; beauty; renown." God's glory has two aspects. First is His inherent, or intrinsic, glory. God is the only being in all of existence who can be said to possess inherent glory. No one can give it to Him; it already completely belongs to Him by virtue of who He is. If no one ever gave God praise, He would still be the glorious God that He is, because He was fully glorious before He created any other beings to worship Him.

The second aspect of God's glory is ascribed glory. "Ascribe to the Lord, O sons of the mighty," the psalmist says, "ascribe to the Lord glory and strength. Ascribe to the Lord the glory due to His name; worship the Lord in holy array" (Ps. 29:1-2). Obviously, we cannot give God glory in the sense of adding to His glory, any more than we can add to His strength. The psalmist is simply urging us to recognize and acclaim the glory God already has.

Practical ways of glorifying God frequently are given in Scripture. A list would include confession of sin (Josh. 7:19), trusting God (Rom. 4:20), bearing fruit for Him (John 15:8), thanking Him (Ps. 50:23), suffering for Christ (1 Pet. 4:14-16), being content (Phil. 4:10-20), praying (John 14:13), and spreading the Word (2 Thess. 3:1). Anything and everything a Christian says and does should be to God's glory.

In 10:23–11:1 Paul explains three things believers must understand about their Christian freedom if they are to glorify God in everything they do: (1) the basic principles for using Christian freedom, (2) the purpose of Christian freedom, and (3) the pattern for using Christian freedom.

THE PRINCIPLES FOR USING CHRISTIAN FREEDOM

In verses 23-30 four basic principles are given to guide us in using our Christian liberty for God's glory.

EDIFICATION OVER GRATIFICATION

All things are lawful, but not all things are profitable. All things are lawful, but not all things edify. (10:23)

Here Paul summarizes what he has been saying about Christian freedom. Because the apostle refers to it several times, he had probably used the phrase **all things are lawful** when he preached in Corinth, and some of the believers there apparently had taken it as a slogan to justify anything they wanted to do. The apostle explains earlier in this letter, however, that his use of that phrase in relation to Christian liberty means all things not specifically identified in Scripture as sinful. Before he first mentions that "all things are lawful" (6:12), he specifically says that "the unrighteous shall not inherit the kingdom of God," and proceeds to give an extensive list of sins that characterize the unrighteous (6:9-10). His use of **all things are lawful** always refers to questionable practices, the gray areas of Christian living that are not specifically forbidden in the Bible.

The basic meaning of **edify** (*oikodomeō*) is "to build a house," and, by extension, the term refers to the literal or figurative building of anything. It is often used in the New Testament to describe the spiritual growth, or upbuilding, of believers. Whatever contributes to spiritual growth constitutes what is **profitable**, or beneficial, helpful, advantageous, or useful. Only things that are **profitable** are able to **edify**. Those two present active indicative verbs basically convey the same truth.

There are many ways in which we are built up, in which we "grow in the grace and knowledge of our Lord and Savior Jesus Christ" (2 Pet. 3:18), but there are four basic tools to help us grow in Him. First is His Word. In his counsel to the Ephesian elders who had come to Miletus to see him for the last time, Paul said, "And now I commend you to God and to the word of His grace, which is able to build you up and to give you the inheritance among all those who are sanctified" (Acts 20:32). God's Word is His supreme means of building us up (cf. 2 Tim. 3:16-17). Second is preaching and teaching. Later in this letter to the Corinthians Paul tells them that, rather than being so concerned about speaking in tongues, they should focus on prophesying, or preaching, which "speaks to men for edification and exhortation and consolation." The "one who prophesies edifies the church" (1 Cor. 14:3-4). Third is love. Knowledge tends to make us proud and arrogant, whereas "love edifies" (1 Cor. 8:1). Fourth is obedient service. The purpose of the Christian ministry is to equip "the saints for the work of service, to the building up of the body of Christ" (Eph. 4:12).

Desiring the spiritual benefit and edification of ourselves and of others is a hallmark of Christian maturity. Paul told the Ephesian elders that he had not withheld from them "anything that was profitable" (Acts 20:20). He called Timothy to be faithful to the Scriptures, which are profitable (2 Tim. 3:16). And to the Corinthians he said, "Let all things be done for edification" (1 Cor. 14:26). Paul's supreme purpose in ministering to believers was to promote their upbuilding, or edification (2 Cor. 12:19). His advice to all Christians is that everything we say be "for edification according to the need of the moment, that it may give grace to those who hear" (Eph. 4:29; cf. 1 Thess. 5:11). When we are faced with a decision about a practice, we should first ask if we have a right to do it. If it is not forbidden in Scripture the answer is yes. But our next question should be, Is it profitable, edifying, and upbuilding for ourselves and for others? If the answer to both questions is yes, then we can do it to God's glory. If the answer to either question is no, we cannot do it to His glory.

OTHERS OVER SELF

Let no one seek his own good, but that of his neighbor. (10:24)

The second principle for using Christian freedom for the glory of God is even more demanding. Even if something will build us up we should not do it if it is not also for the good of others. Our primary concern should be for the **good** of our **neighbor,** a principle contrary to basic human nature.

A pastor friend of mine, after preaching on this passage, had a time of testimony. He asked the congregation to share experiences of giving up something for the sake of someone else. Except for one man who said he did not drink or smoke around other Christians, no one responded. After the service a number of people told the pastor, "For the first time in my life I realized that I don't really give up anything for the sake of others." Apparently some of the believers at Philippi had the same problem, and Paul wrote them, "Do nothing from selfishness or empty conceit, but with humility of mind let each of you regard one another as more important than himself; do not merely look out for your own personal interests, but also for the interests of others" (Phil. 2:3-4).

LIBERTY OVER LEGALISM

Eat anything that is sold in the meat market, without asking questions for conscience' sake; for the earth is the Lord's, and all it contains. If one of the unbelievers invites you, and you wish to go, eat anything that is set before you, without asking questions for conscience' sake. (10:25-27)

The third principle for using Christian liberty to the Lord's glory is that of following liberty over legalism. To some degree this principle counterbalances the previous one. The true welfare of others should be our first concern, but their standards should not rule everything we do. As much as possible we should keep from offending the weak consciences of fellow believers, but we should not go to the legalistic extreme of making great issues out of everything we do.

Again Paul uses the illustration of food offered to idols. "When you go to the **meat market** don't ask whether or not the meat you buy has been offered to an idol. Just go ahead and buy it **without asking questions for conscience' sake.** If it doesn't bother your own conscience, then buy it and eat it."

Quoting Psalm 24:1, Paul says, **for the earth is the Lord's, and all it contains.** Christians have no business participating in an idolatrous ceremony, because to do so is "to become sharers in demons" (1 Cor. 10:20). But after idol meat is sent to the market it is just meat like all other meat. It is food that the Lord provides from **the earth,** and can be eaten with a clear conscience and with thanksgiving. "For everything created by God is good, and nothing is to be rejected, if it is received with gratitude; for it is sanctified by means of the word of God and prayer" (1 Tim. 4:4-5).

If an unbeliever invites you to eat with him, you should act in the same way, **without asking questions for conscience' sake.** If you want to accept his invitation, do so without asking embarrassing questions. If the possibility of eating idol food does not bother you, go and enjoy the meal. **Eat anything that is set before you.** Freedom in Christ is a privilege to be forfeited only when it clearly may offend another person.

"It was for freedom that Christ set us free; therefore keep standing firm and do not be subject again to a yoke of slavery" (Gal. 5:1). We should not give up our liberty unless it is clearly for the upbuilding of someone else. If we refrain from doing certain questionable things, we do not do so from a sense of legalistic compulsion but from the voluntary restriction of our liberty in order to help build up someone else.

When we restrict our liberty for the sake of a weaker brother, we should also try to help him grow in the understanding of his own Christian freedom. In other words, we should help his conscience grow stronger, in order that he can come to enjoy his full liberty in Christ and not be restricted in the enjoyment of his privileges.

CONDESCENSION OVER CONDEMNATION

But if anyone should say to you, "This is meat sacrificed to idols," do not eat it, for the sake of the one who informed you, and for conscience' sake; I mean not your own conscience, but the other man's; for why is my freedom judged by another's conscience? If I partake with thankfulness, why am I slandered concerning that for which I give thanks? (10:28-30)

The fourth principle is also illustrated by the hypothetical meal at a pagan's house. **If anyone,** in this case another believer, happens to be there and tells you, **"This is meat sacrificed to idols,"** then **do not eat it, for the sake of the one who informed you.** Do not argue or condemn or insist on your own freedom. Give up your liberty so that his conscience will not be offended.

Paul makes it clear that **for conscience' sake** refers to **the other man's** conscience, not our own. We are to modify our actions for the sake of others, but we are not to modify our consciences. The legalism of a weaker brother should not make us legalistic, only gracious.

But our brother's **conscience' sake** is important, more important than the feelings of an unbelieving host. It is better to offend the host by not eating the idol meat than to offend a weaker believer by eating it. If we have to choose between offending a Christian and offending a non-Christian, we should offend the non-Christian. The profit and edification of our brother or sister in Christ is of greater importance. Not only that, but our testimony will be harmed more by arguing with and condemning fellow believers than by standing by them in love. Unbelievers will be inclined to respect us for showing loving concern for the convictions of a fellow Christian.

Our own **freedom** should not be **judged by another's conscience.** That is, we should not cause our freedom to be slandered by expressing it in ways that offend a weaker brother. We should **give thanks** for the food and for our liberty and then express our liberty by choosing not to eat the food that offends the brother. How can we be thankful to the Lord for something a Christian brother or sister is going to stumble over?

The Purpose of Christian Freedom

Whether, then, you eat or drink or whatever you do, do all to the glory of God. Give no offense either to Jews or to Greeks or to the church of God. (10:31-32)

The purpose of using our liberty carefully and selflessly is to glorify God. The idea of eating and drinking is in the context of things offered to idols, but is not limited to that. Paul is saying that even in the most mundane, routine, nonspiritual things of life, like ordinary eating and drinking, God is to be glorified. His glory is to be our life commitment. It is the purpose of our whole life, which now belongs to the Lord because we have been "bought with a price" (1 Cor. 7:23). Not only when we **eat or drink** but in **whatever** [we] **do** we should **do all to the glory of God.** (For further material on glorifying God, see the opening section of this chapter.)

A person either lives a life that honors God or that dishonors Him. God's own people had become such a reproach to Him that He allowed Israel to be conquered and exiled by Assyria in 722 B.C. and Judah to be conquered and exiled by Babylonia in 586. Those conquests, however, at first caused His name to suffer even more reproach, because the heathen nations around Israel and Judah were saying that Jehovah God was not strong enough even to save His own people. Through His prophet Ezekiel, who himself had been taken captive to Babylon, God promised that He would deliver and regather His people. But the purpose would be primarily to "vindicate the holiness of My great name which has been profaned among the nations, which you have profaned in their midst. Then the nations will know that I am the Lord" (Ezek. 36:23). God's glory is His supreme concern and should also be our supreme concern.

God is dishonored when anyone sins, but He is especially dishonored when His own people sin. Because he has specially honored us by His forgiving grace, we specially dishonor Him by our sin. When in justice He is forced to chastise us, He is further dishonored by unbelievers, who charge, as did the nations around Israel and

Judah, that He does not even take care of His own people. Sin of any sort takes glory from God.

In the same way God is specially honored and glorified when His people are faithful and obedient. Just as our sin reflects against His honor, so our loving obedience reflects to His honor. When we resist and forsake sin we glorify our heavenly Father. And when we willingly use our Christian liberty for His sake and for the sake of His other children, we glorify Him still more.

Our living should be so righteous, loving, and selfless that we **give no offense either to Jews or to Greeks or to the church of God.** Those three groups cover all of humanity. No action of ours should prevent an unbeliever, whether Jew or Gentile, from coming to Christ (cf. Acts 15:20-29), or should cause a weak brother in Christ to stumble (1 Pet. 2:11-19). That many people are offended by the gospel is their problem, but when they are needlessly offended by our way of living, that is our problem; and it dishonors the Lord. The term *aproskopos,* here translated **give no offense,** is rendered as "be . . . blameless" in Philippians 1:10.

The Pattern of Christian Freedom

just as I also please all men in all things, not seeking my own profit, but the profit of the many, that they may be saved. Be imitators of me, just as I also am of Christ. (10:33–11:1)

Paul closes this section, which in thought extends into chapter 11, with a practical suggestion for following the principles of Christian liberty.

Because the apostle lived in such a way as to **please all men in all things, not seeking** [his] **own profit, but the profit of the many, that they may be saved,** he could safely tell the Corinthians to follow his example. He had lived and ministered in Corinth for eighteen months, and the believers there knew him well. "You remember how I lived when I was with you," he is saying. "Live like that yourselves." Paul's goal was to bring people to salvation. He was willing to set aside anything for that (cf. 9:19-23).

The reason Paul was so confident and successful in his Christian living in general, and in the responsible use of his Christian liberty in particular, was that he was an imitator **of Christ,** the supreme example of One who set aside His rights for the sake of others, the One who "emptied Himself, taking the form of a bond-servant" and "humbled Himself by becoming obedient to the point of death" (Phil. 2:7-8). Paul called the Corinthians to imitate him as he imitated the God-glorifying condescension of Christ (cf. 4:16; Phil. 3:17).

The Subordination and Equality of Women (11:2-16)

26

Now I praise you because you remember me in everything, and hold firmly to the traditions, just as I delivered them to you. But I want you to understand that Christ is the head of every man, and the man is the head of a woman, and God is the head of Christ. Every man who has something on his head while praying or prophesying, disgraces his head. But every woman who has her head uncovered while praying or prophesying, disgraces her head; for she is one and the same with her whose head is shaved. For if a woman does not cover her head, let her also have her hair cut off; but if it is disgraceful for a woman to have her hair cut off or her head shaved, let her cover her head. For a man ought not to have his head covered, since he is the image and glory of God; but the woman is the glory of man. For man does not originate from woman, but woman from man; for indeed man was not created for the woman's sake, but woman for the man's sake. Therefore the woman ought to have a symbol of authority on her head, because of the angels. However, in the Lord, neither is woman independent of man, nor is man independent of woman. For as the woman originates from the man, so also the man has his birth through the woman; and all things originate from God. Judge for yourselves: is it proper for a woman to pray to God with head uncovered? Does not even nature itself teach you that if a man has long hair, it is a dishonor to him, but if a woman has long hair, it is a glory to her? For her hair

is given to her for a covering. But if one is inclined to be contentious, we have no other practice, nor have the churches of God. (11:2-16)

The role of women has become a battleground in society during the last several decades. The struggle for women's rights has escalated to a place of imbalance in society that threatens the future. In our day, the efforts of the enemy began with secular society and worked back into the church, which so often catches the world's diseases and adopts the spirit of the age. Some leaders and writers, in the name of Christianity, have gone so far as to teach principles that attempt to redefine, or even alter, biblical truths to accommodate the standards of contemporary thinking in the world. To do that, of course, they have to believe that Paul, Peter, and other scriptural writers added some of their own opinions to God's revealed truth or that the apostles sometimes taught culturally determined customs rather than divinely revealed standards. When that approach is taken, man must decide for himself what part of Scripture is revealed and what is not—making him the judge over God's Word. Satan feverishly tries to upset the divine order in any way he can, and one foundational way is by perverting male-female roles and relationships.

The Corinthian church faced a situation similar to the one we face today, and the believers who wrote Paul (7:1) apparently had asked for his word on the submission of women. The apostle was pleased that they sought God's revelation in this and the other matters, that they loved and respected him, and that basically they held to sound doctrine. **Now I praise you because you remember me in everything, and hold firmly to the traditions, just as I delivered them to you.** The term **remember** means to be continually remembering, as indicated by the perfect tense. Despite their immaturity and their many problems, they respected Paul's apostolic authority and divine wisdom, and in some areas of doctrine were seeking to know and follow the Lord's will.

Traditions (*paradosis*) means "that which is passed along by teaching" and is used in a negative way in the New Testament when it refers to man-made ideas or practices (as is Matt. 15:2-6; Gal. 1:14; Col. 2:8). But the term is also applied to divinely revealed teaching, as here and in 2 Thess. 2:15. To Paul's inspired apostolic teaching the Corinthian believers had held **firmly.**

The basic problem in the Corinthian church did not concern doctrine but morals, not theology but life-style. They were orthodox but not pure. They remembered and believed the cardinal truths about God's nature and work, but they did not live godly lives. And so Paul praises them for their strengths before he again begins to correct their weaknesses—in this case their misunderstanding of male-female roles and relationships.

The Principle Stated

But I want you to understand that Christ is the head of every man, and the man is the head of a woman, and God is the head of Christ. (11:3)

Paul begins his corrective by stating succinctly the basic divine principle he is going to discuss, and he uses the phrase **I want you to understand** to introduce something he was greatly concerned about but had not taught before (cf. Col. 2:1). Women in that Greek culture lived in the background and were often only to be used for prostitution. The gospel of the Lord Jesus Christ gave them dignity and honor, which was apparently abused in some cases. Paul responded to the situation by showing that men and women were not on the same level of function in God's design.

The principle of subordination and authority pervades the entire universe. Paul shows that woman's subordination to man is but a reflection of that greater general truth. **Christ is the head of every man, and the man is the head of a woman, and God is the head of Christ.** If Christ had not submitted to the will of **God,** redemption for mankind would have been impossible, and we would forever be doomed and lost. If individual human beings do not submit to Christ as Savior and Lord, they are still doomed and lost, because they reject God's gracious provision. And if women do not submit to men, then the family and society as a whole are disrupted and destroyed. Whether on a divine or human scale, subordination and authority are indispensable elements in God's order and plan.

Head refers to the ruling and sovereign part of the body. In stating the general principle, Paul gives three ways in which headship is manifested. First, **Christ is the head of every man.** He is uniquely the head of the church as its Savior and Lord (Eph. 1:22-23; 4:15; Col. 1:18; etc.). He has redeemed and bought it with His own blood (1 Cor. 6:20; 1 Pet.1:18-19; Rev. 5:9). But in His divine authority Christ is head of *every* human being, believer and nonbeliever. "All authority has been given to Me in heaven and on earth," Jesus declared (Matt. 28:18). Most of mankind has never acknowledged Christ's authority, but all things have been put "in subjection under His feet" (Heb. 2:8), and one day "every knee [will] bow, of those who are in heaven, and on earth, and under the earth, and . . . every tongue [will] confess that Jesus Christ is Lord, to the glory of God the Father" (Phil. 2:10-11). Those who willingly submit to His authority constitute the church, and those who rebel against His authority constitute the world. In His patience and forbearance God has allowed rebellious unbelievers to ignore Christ's lordship, but one day even they will acknowledge their subjection to Him. He is in ultimate control of all men, now and forever.

Second, **the man is the head of a woman.** The principle of subordination and authority applies to all men and all women, not just to husbands and wives. It extends beyond the family to all aspects of society. That is the basic order of creation, as Paul explains later (vv. 8-9). That is the way God planned and created mankind; it is the way He has made us.

It seems that most of the fads and misconceptions of the world eventually find their way into the church. Worldly Christians continually try to find ways to justify their worldliness, if possible on the basis of Scripture. Christian feminists appeal to such passages as Galatians 3:28 ("there is neither male nor female") and 1 Peter 3:7 ("and grant her honor as a fellow heir of the grace of life") to disprove the idea that husbands are to have authority over their wives and that wives should be submissive to their husbands—not to mention the idea that women in general are to be submissive to men in general. But it is impossible honestly to interpret what Paul says as being supportive of contemporary feminism. He is therefore often charged as being a male chauvinist, who frequently taught his own prejudices instead of God's Word.

But he makes no distinction between men and women as far as personal worth, abilities, intellect, or spirituality are concerned. Both as human beings and as Christians, women in general are completely equal to men spiritually. Some women obviously are even superior to some men in abilities, intellect, maturity, and spirituality. God established the principle of male authority and female subordination for the purpose of order and complementation, not on the basis of any innate superiority of males. An employee may be more intelligent and more skilled than his boss, but a company cannot be run without submission to proper authority, even if some of those in authority are not as capable as they ought to be. Elders and deacons are to be chosen from among the most spiritual men of the congregation, but there may be other men in the church who are even more spiritual. Yet, for the very reason that they *are* spiritual, those who are not in positions of leadership will submit to those who are.

A church may have some women who are better Bible students, better theologians, and better speakers than any of the men, including the pastor. But if those women are obedient to God's order they will submit to male leadership and will not try to usurp it—simply because that is God's design. A wife may be better educated, better taught in Scripture, and more spiritually mature than her husband. But because she *is* spiritual, she will willingly submit to him as head of the family. That proper relationship is specifically described in Ephesians 5:22-33. Isaiah spoke judgment on his generation because they had allowed women to rule over them (Isa. 3:12).

Third, **God is the head of Christ**. Jesus made nothing clearer than the fact that He submitted Himself to His Father's will (John 4:34; 5:30; 6:38; cf. 1 Cor. 3:23; 15:24-28; etc.). Christ has never been—before, during, or after His incarnation—in any way inferior in essence to the Father. But in His incarnation He willingly subordinated Himself to the Father in His role as Savior and Redeemer. He lovingly subjected Himself completely to His Father's will as an act of humble obedience in fulfilling the divine purpose.

Paul inseparably ties the three aspects of the principle together. As Christ is submissive to the Father and Christians are to be submissive to Christ, women are to be submissive to men. You cannot reject one part without rejecting the others. You cannot, for example, reject the principle of woman's submission to man without also rejecting Christ's submission to the Father and believers' submission to Christ. It is clear that the man's being head of the woman means the same thing as Christ's being head of man—that is, sovereign leadership requiring submission that recognizes the benefit of such leadership of love.

The authority and submission in each of these cases is based on love, not tyranny. The Father sent Christ out of love, not under compulsion, to redeem the world; and the Son submitted to the Father out of love, not compulsion. Christ loves the church, so much that He died for it; and He rules the church in love, not in tyranny. In response, the church submits to Him in love. Likewise, men in general and husbands in particular should exercise their authority in love, not in tyranny. They do not have authority because of greater worth or greater ability, but simply because of God's wise design and loving will. Women respond in loving submission as they were designed to do (cf. 1 Tim. 2:11-15). This is not a matter of relative dignity or worth but of task and responsibility.

THE PRINCIPLE APPLIED

Every man who has something on his head while praying or prophesying, disgraces his head. But every woman who has her head uncovered while praying or prophesying, disgraces her head; for she is one and the same with her whose head is shaved. For if a woman does not cover her head, let her also have her hair cut off; but if it is disgraceful for a woman to have her hair cut off or her head shaved, let her cover her head. (11:4-6)

It is best to understand that Paul is here referring to activities of believers in ministry before the Lord and the public, where a clear testimony is essential.

In the most general senses **praying** is talking to God about people, including ourselves, and **prophesying** is talking to people about God. One is vertical (man to God) and the other is horizontal (man to man), and they represent the two primary dimensions of believers' ministry. Admittedly, the detail of this passage related to head coverings is difficult because of the scarcity of historical data. But the content helps to clarify the principle Paul has in mind, whatever the special covering may have been. He wants the church to live according to divine standards.

When Paul said a man **disgraces his head** if he **has something on his head while praying or prophesying,** he had to be referring to local Corinthian custom. The phrase **has something on his head** literally means "having down from head," and is usually taken to refer to a veil. The context here implies that in Corinth such a head covering would have been completely ridiculous for a man and completely proper for a woman. For Jews, who came to wear head coverings, the practice seems to have come in the fourth century A.D., though some may have tried it in the time of the apostles. But generally it was regarded as a disgrace for a man to worship with his head covered.

It seems, therefore, that Paul is not stating a divine universal requirement but simply acknowledging a local custom. The local Christian custom, however, reflected the divine principle. In Corinthian society a man's praying or prophesying without a head covering was a sign of his authority over women, who were expected to have their heads covered in these ministries. Consequently, for a man to cover his head would be a disgrace, because it suggested a reversal of the proper relationships. **Disgraces her head** could refer to her own head literally and to her husband's metaphorically.

In Paul's day numerous symbols were used to signify the woman's subordinate relationship to men, particularly of wives to husbands. Usually the symbol was in the form of a head covering, and in the Greek-Roman world of Corinth the symbol apparently was a veil of some kind. In many Near East countries today a married woman's veil still signifies that she will not expose herself to other men, that her beauty and charms are reserved entirely for her husband, that she does not care even to be noticed by other men. Similarly, in the culture of first-century Corinth wearing a head covering while ministering or worshiping was a woman's way of stating her devotion and submission to her husband and of demonstrating her commitment to God.

It seems, however, that some women in the Corinthian church were not covering their heads **while praying or prophesying.** We know from secular history that various movements of women's liberation and feminism appeared in the Roman empire during New Testament times. Women would often take off their veils or other head coverings and cut their hair in order to look like men. Much as in our own day, some women were demanding to be treated exactly like men and they attacked marriage and the raising of children as unjust restrictions of their rights. They asserted their independence by leaving their husbands and homes, refusing to care for their children, living with other men, demanding jobs traditionally held by men, wearing men's clothing and hairdos, and by discarding all signs of femininity. It is likely that some of the believers at Corinth were influenced by those movements and, as a sign of protest and independence, refused to cover their heads at appropriate times.

As with meat that had been offered to idols, there was nothing in the wearing or not wearing of the head covering itself that was right or wrong. It is the rebellion against God-ordained roles that is wrong, and in Corinth that rebellion was demonstrated by women praying and prophesying with their heads uncovered.

Dress is largely cultural and, unless what a person wears is immodest or sexually suggestive, it has no moral or spiritual significance. Throughout biblical times, as in many parts of the world today, both men and women wore some type of robe. But there always were some clear distinctions of dress between men and women, most often indicated by hair length and head coverings.

It is the principle of women's subordination to men, not the particular mark or symbol of that subordination, that Paul is teaching in this passage. The apostle is not laying down a universal principle that Christian women should always worship with their heads covered.

The mention here of women's **praying or prophesying** is sometimes used to prove that Paul acknowledged the right of their teaching, preaching, and leading in church worship. But he makes no mention here of the church at worship or in the time of formal teaching. Perhaps he has in view praying or prophesying in public places, rather than in the worship of the congregation. This would certainly fit with the very clear directives in 1 Corinthians (14:34) and in his first letter to Timothy (2:12). The New Testament has no restrictions on a woman's witnessing in public to others, even to a man. Nor does it prohibit women from taking nonleadership roles of praying with believers or for unbelievers; and there is no restriction from teaching children and other women (cf. Titus 2:3-4; 1 Tim. 5:16). Women may have the gift of prophecy, as did Philip's four daughters (Acts 21:9), but they are normally not to prophesy in the meetings of the church where men are present.

In other words, it is only necessary to combine the relevant passages to get the composite truth. Women may pray and prophesy within the boundaries of God's revelation, and with a proper sense of submission. And it is critical that their deportment in so doing reflects God's order. Certainly they must not appear rebellious against God's will.

Paul's point in verses 4-5 is that, whenever and wherever it is appropriate for men and women to pray or prophesy, they should do so with proper distinction between male and female. **Every man** should speak to or for the Lord clearly as a man, and **every woman** should speak to or for the Lord clearly as a woman. God does not want the distinction to be blurred.

For a Corinthian woman to pray or prophesy with her head uncovered disgraced or shamed her and made her the **same with her whose head is shaved.** If a woman took off her head covering she might as well make the symbol of her role rejection complete by taking off all of her hair, the God-given identifier of her special role as a woman. **For if a woman does not cover her head, let her also have her hair cut off.** In that day only a prostitute or an extreme feminist would shave her head.

The Talmud indicates that a Jew considered a woman with a shaved head extremely ugly, and Chrysostom records that women guilty of adultery had their hair shaved off and were marked as prostitutes. Aristophanes even taught that the mother of unworthy children should have her hair shorn.

Paul therefore is saying, "If you are not willing to look like a prostitute or a rebellious feminist by cutting off your hair, don't pray or prophesy with your head uncovered either."

It is remarkable that any Christian woman would seek such an identification, until we think of how some appear today so worldly as to make the same comparison possible.

THE PRINCIPLE DEFENDED

For a man ought not to have his head covered, since he is the image and glory of God; but the woman is the glory of man. For man does not originate from woman, but woman from man; for indeed man was not created for the woman's sake, but woman for the man's sake. Therefore the woman ought to have a symbol of authority on her head, because of the angels. (11:7-10)

As has been mentioned, covering the head appears to have been a customary symbol of subordination in Corinthian society, as in much of the ancient world. But the principle of male headship is not a matter of custom but a matter of God's order and creation and should never be compromised. Because a covered head was a sign of subordination, **a man ought not to have his head covered, since he is the image and glory of God.** Man was created in the moral, mental, and spiritual **image** of

God. He was created with intellect, will, emotion, knowledge, and holiness, to which he is restored in Jesus Christ (Eph. 4:24).

Man is also uniquely created to bear the image of God as a ruler, who is given a sphere of sovereignty. In that sense, he was also created to be the **glory of God.** God gave man dominion over all the created world, to care for according to His divine plan. Man was given rulership of the world. Both men and women are created in God's image, but as Paul points out in verse 8, the original creation from the "dust from the ground" was of Adam only (Gen. 2:7). Eve was created later from part of Adam himself (2:21-22). The male was given the dominion and authority over God's created world, and is by that fact the **glory of God.**

The fall confirmed these roles in an even more dramatic way, as Genesis 3:16-17 indicates by saying, "Your desire shall be for your husband, and he shall rule over you." So the man is to represent God in authority and rulership, thus being the **glory of God.** After the fall man's rule was strengthened. Consequently he is not to wear any symbol of subordination.

Because some ancient rabbis had misinterpreted Exodus 34:33-35, they taught that Jewish men should cover their heads when they prayed because Moses veiled his face in the presence of God's glory. But it was in the people's presence, not God's presence, that Moses wore the veil. As Paul explains in his next letter to Corinth, Moses "used to put a veil over his face that the sons of Israel might not look intently at the end of what was fading away" (2 Cor. 3:13). He did not want them to see the glory of God, which he had received in God's presence, fading from his face. The Jewish tradition of men covering their heads to pray is therefore a human tradition, not a divine one.

On the other hand, **woman is the glory of man.** Woman was made to manifest man's authority and will as man was made to manifest God's authority and will. The woman is viceregent, who rules in the stead of man or who carries out man's will, just as man is God's viceregent who rules in His stead or carries out His will. The woman shines not so much with the direct light of God as with the derived light from man. Man is both the **image and glory** of God, while woman is only the image of God (Gen. 1:27) and not the image of man, and the **glory of man,** not the glory of God. The point is that man shows how magnificent a creature God can create from Himself, while woman shows how magnificent a creature God can make from a man (Gen. 2:21-22).

Yet as far as saving and sanctifying grace is concerned a woman comes as deeply into communion with God as a man. She was made equally in the image of God, and that image is equally restored through faith in Jesus Christ. She will be as much like Jesus as any man when we see our Lord face to face (1 Cor. 13:12). But though woman is fully in the image of God she is not directly the glory of God. She is directly the glory of man, the indirect outshining of man's glory of God. Her role in the world is to submit to the direction of man, to whom is given the divine dominion.

To further defend that truth Paul points out that **man does not originate from woman, but woman from man.** Adam was created first and was given dominion over the earth before the woman was created; and when she was created she was created from him. She was given the very name "Woman, because she was taken out of Man" (Gen. 2:9-23; cf. 1 Tim. 2:11-13).

Woman not only was created from man but for man. **For indeed man was not created for the woman's sake, but woman for the man's sake.** She is not intellectually, morally, spiritually, or functionally inferior to man. She is unique from him. Her role is to come under the leadership, protection, and care of man, and she is to be "a helper suitable for him" (Gen. 2:20).

In verse 10 Paul returns to the application of the principle. **Therefore the woman ought to have a symbol of authority on her head, because of the angels.** The cultural use of a head covering represents the divine and universal principle of a woman's subordination to man's authority. **Symbol of authority** is one word (*exousia*) in the Greek and means "rightful power," or "authority." The covered head was the woman's authority or right to pray and worship, since it demonstrated her submissiveness. **Symbol** is implied because of the obvious reference here to the head covering mentioned in verses 4-7. In that culture, a woman was to wear such a symbol as an indication of her subordinate role to man.

The basic meaning of **angels** is "messenger." Paul here is speaking of the holy angels, God's ministering angels, whose supreme characteristic is total and immediate obedience to God. Throughout Scripture God's holy angels are shown as creatures of great power, but it is always derived power and submissive power. Satan and the other angels who followed him were thrown out of heaven for the very reason that they sought to use their power to their own selfish purposes and glory rather than to God's. The holy angels, on the other hand, are the supreme example of proper creaturely subordination. Hebrews 1:4–2:18 focuses on Christ's superiority to the angels and their willing subservience to Him.

These messengers are God's protectors of His church, over which they stand perpetual guard. It is proper for a woman to cover her head as a sign of subordination **because of the angels,** in order that these most submissive of all creatures will not be offended by nonsubmissiveness. Furthermore, the angels were present at creation (Job 38:7) to be witnesses of God's unique design for man and woman, and would be offended at any violation of that order. The idea of caring about the response and attitude of angels is also seen in Ephesians 3:9-10 and Matthew 18:10. The Midrash taught that angels are the guardians of the created order.

THE PRINCIPLE HARMONIZED

However, in the Lord, neither is woman independent of man, nor is man independent of woman. For as the woman originates from the man, so also the man has his birth through the woman; and all things originate from God. (11:11-12)

If Satan cannot get men to deny or disregard God's Word he will try to get them to misinterpret it and carry it to extremes the Lord did not intend. Lest men abuse their authority over women, Paul reminds them of their equality and mutual dependence. Man's authority over woman is a delegated authority and a derived authority, given by God to be used for His purposes and in His way. Man as a fellow creature has no innate superiority to woman and has no right to use his authority tyrannically or selfishly. Male chauvinism is no more biblical than feminism. Both are perversions of God's plan.

Far from oppressing women, the church has been their greatest liberator. In Greek and Roman societies most women were little more than slaves, the possessions of their husbands, who often virtually bought and traded their wives at will. It was largely because of this inhumane treatment of women that feminism became so popular in the Roman empire. In many Jewish communities the woman's situation was not much better. Divorce had become easy and commonplace, but it was almost entirely the prerogative of the man. Some Jewish men held women in such low esteem that they developed a popular prayer in which they thanked God that they were not born a slave, a Gentile, or a woman.

But in Christ all believers, male and female, are **in the Lord,** and are alike under the Lord. In His work women are as important as men. Their roles are different in function and relationships, but not in spirituality or importance. **Neither is woman independent of man, nor is man independent of woman.** Men and women are complementary in every way in life, but particularly in the Lord's work do they function together as a divinely ordained team. They serve each other and they serve with each other. In this regard "there is neither male nor female, for you are all one in Christ Jesus" (Gal. 3:28). This equality is supported in many biblical passages. Our Lord, for example, commended Mary's act of listening to theological discourse over Martha's work in the kitchen (Luke 10:38-42), and women are given spiritual gifts (1 Cor. 12:7-11).

From the earliest history of God's people women have had a vital role in His work and ministry. The psalmist declared that "The women who proclaim the good tidings are a great host" (Ps. 68:11), indicating that many of God's greatest workers have been women. Immediately after our Lord's ascension, some 120 believers, including the apostles and a number of women, gathered in the upper room for prayer (Acts 1:12-15). The entire last chapter of Romans is devoted to Paul's commendation of and greetings to various friends in the church at Rome, among whom are eight honored women. He begins with a beautiful commendation of "our sister Phoebe, who is a servant of the church which is at Cenchrea" and the request "that you receive her in the Lord in a manner worthy of the saints, and that you help her in whatever matter she may have need of you; for she herself has also been a helper of many, and of myself as well" (Rom. 16:1-2). Among her many other works, Phoebe ministered even to an apostle. Mary, the mother of John Mark, opened her home as a meeting place for the Jerusalem believers (Acts 12:12) and Lydia opened her home in the same way to believers in Philippi (Acts 16:40). When Apollos, "an eloquent man . . . mighty in the Scriptures," began preaching in Ephesus, both Aquilla and his wife, Priscilla, "took him aside and explained to him the way of God more accurately" (Acts 18:24-26).

In many times and places, faithful women have kept the church alive with little or no support from men. Many mission fields would not exist if it were not for God's elect women. A church without godly women cannot be a strong and effective church. The man's proper authority does not make him independent of woman, nor does her proper subordination make her alone dependent. Neither is independent of the other; they are mutually dependent.

God created both men and women. The first woman was created from the man, but since that time every man has been created through a woman. **For as the woman originates from the man, so also the man has his birth through the woman.** Most importantly, **all things originate from God.** Men and women have different roles but not different importance. Women are equal to men in the world, in the church, and before God. That is God's wise and gracious harmony and balance— difference in roles but equality in nature, personhood, work, and spirit. He created both for His glorious purposes.

Women are not to be teachers of men, but they are usually the most influential shapers of men. Bearing and nurturing children give women salvation from any thought of lower status than men (1 Tim. 2:15). As mothers they have a unique and indispensable role in training and developing boys, who are men in the making. From conception to adulthood a man is dependent upon and shaped by his mother in a unique and marvelous way. And throughout adulthood, whether married or single, he is dependent on women in more ways than he is often willing to acknowledge. In marriage men cannot be faithful to the Lord unless they are willingly and lovingly dependent on the wife He has given them. In the Lord's work men cannot be faithful to Him unless they are dependent on the women to whom He has given responsibility in His church. They are perfect complements—one the head, leader, provider, and the other the helper, supporter, and companion.

THE PRINCIPLE RESPONDED TO

Judge for yourselves: is it proper for a woman to pray to God with head uncovered? Does not even nature itself teach you that if a man has long hair, it is a dishonor to him, but if a woman has long hair, it is a glory to her? For her hair is given to her for a covering. But if one is inclined to be contentious, we have no other practice, nor have the churches of God. (11:13-16)

Paul asks the Corinthians to disregard his apostolic authority for a moment. **Judge for yourselves,** he tells them. The principle of authority and subordination is not only given by God in His divine revelation but is self-evident from His creation itself. The cultural practice of a woman's covering her head as a symbol of subordination to man is a reflection of the natural order. **Does not even nature itself teach you that if a man has long hair, it is a dishonor to him, but if a woman has long hair, it is a glory to her.**

Men and women have distinctive physiologies in many ways. One of them is in the process of hair growth on the head. Hair develops in three stages—formation and growth, resting, and fallout. The male hormone testosterone speeds up the cycle so that men reach the third stage earlier than women. The female hormone estrogen causes the cycle to remain in stage one for a longer time, causing women's hair to grow longer than men's. Women are rarely bald because few even reach stage three. This physiology is reflected in most cultures of the world in the custom of women wearing longer hair than men.

Nature (*phusis*) also carries the idea of instinct, an innate sense of what is normal and right. This is an appeal to human consciousness. Paul is saying that as man looks around himself he recognizes that, but for rare exceptions, both nature and human instinct testify that it is normal and proper for a woman's hair to be longer than a man's. Beautifully dressed hair is **a glory** to a woman, God's special gift to show the softness and tenderness of a woman. The Greek word (*komē*) for **long hair** can mean both long hair and a neat hairdo.

A woman's hair is itself **given to her for a covering.** Her hair is her natural covering or veil, and headwear is a cultural symbolic covering, both representing her subordinate role. Both nature and general custom reflect God's universal principle of man's role of authority and woman's role of subordination. The unique beauty of a woman is gloriously manifest in the distinctive femininity portrayed by her hair and her attendance to feminine customs.

In modern cultures where the wearing of a hat or veil does not symbolize subordination, that practice should not be required of Christians. But women's hair and women's dress is to be distinctively feminine and demonstrate her womanly loveliness and submissiveness. There should be no confusion about male and female identities, because God has made the sexes distinct—physiologically and in roles and relationships. He wants men to be masculine, to be responsibly and lovingly authoritative. He wants women to be feminine, to be responsibly and lovingly submissive.

As in almost every age and every church, some of the believers in Corinth were not satisfied with God's way and wanted to disregard it or modify it to suit themselves. Paul anticipated their objection to what he had just taught. He knew that some would be **inclined to be contentious,** but he could say nothing additional to them that would be more convincing than what he had already said.

In summing up his argument, we note that Paul has established that women are to be submissive to men because of the relationship in the Godhead (v. 3), the divine design of male and female (v. 7), the order of creation (v. 8), the role of woman (v. 9), the interest of the angels (v. 10), and the characteristics of natural physiology (vv. 13-15).

That is why he declares that neither God, represented by His apostles, nor the faithful congregations of His church will recognize any other principle or follow any other pattern of behavior. The argument is utterly convincing. "If you want to find a sympathetic ear to your dissent," he says, "you won't find it among the apostles or in the churches." **We have no other practice, nor have the churches of God.** The apostles and the other churches were firmly committed to the practice that women should wear longer hair than men and should have distinctively female hairdos. And where custom dictated it, they should wear proper head coverings to distinguish themselves as submissive.

Celebrating the Lord's Supper (11:17-34) 27

But in giving this instruction, I do not praise you, because you come together not for the better but for the worse. For, in the first place, when you come together as a church, I hear that divisions exist among you; and in part, I believe it. For there must also be factions among you, in order that those who are approved may have become evident among you. Therefore when you meet together, it is not to eat the Lord's Supper, for in your eating each one takes his own supper first; and one is hungry and another is drunk. What! Do you not have houses in which to eat and drink? Or do you despise the church of God, and shame those who have nothing? What shall I say to you? Shall I praise you? In this I will not praise you. For I received from the Lord that which I also delivered to you, that the Lord Jesus in the night in which He was betrayed took bread; and when He had given thanks, He broke it, and said, "This is My body, which is for you; do this in remembrance of Me." In the same way He took the cup also, after supper, saying, "This cup is the new covenant in My blood; do this, as often as you drink it, in remembrance of Me." For as often as you eat this bread and drink the cup, you proclaim the Lord's death until He comes. Therefore whoever eats the bread or drinks the cup of the Lord in an unworthy manner, shall be guilty of the body and the blood of the Lord. But let a man examine himself, and so let him eat of the bread and drink of the cup. For he who eats and drinks, eats and drinks

judgment to himself, if he does not judge the body rightly. For this reason
many among you are weak and sick, and a number sleep. But if we judged
ourselves rightly, we should not be judged. But when we are judged, we are
disciplined by the Lord in order that we may not be condemned along with
the world. So then, my brethren, when you come together to eat, wait for one
another. If anyone is hungry, let him eat at home, so that you may not come
together for judgment. And the remaining matters I shall arrange when I
come. (11:17-34)

By instruction and by example Christ instituted two ordinances, baptism and
Communion, ordinances that those who believe in Him are to follow faithfully. Jesus
commanded His disciples to "Go therefore and make disciples of all the nations,
baptizing them in the name of the Father and the Son and the Holy Spirit" (Matt.
28:19), following His own example of being baptized by John the Baptist (Matt.
3:13-17). During His last Passover meal in the upper room Jesus initiated the
Communion (or Lord's Supper, as it has come to be known), telling the disciples to
continue the ordinance as a remembrance of Him (Luke 22:19-20).

Paul had been faithful in establishing these ordinances in Corinth. Although
he did not personally baptize many of the believers there (1 Cor. 1:14-16), he affirmed
baptism as a non-optional act of obedience to the Lord. The present passage makes it
clear that the Corinthians regularly celebrated the Lord's Supper, in which the apostle
had shared with them many times.

It was not incidental that Christ initiated Communion rites during the
Passover meal. God instituted the Passover when He delivered His people from their
400 years of bondage in Egypt. The meal celebrated the death angel's passing over the
houses of those whose doorposts and lintels were smeared with lamb's blood. The
lamb itself was roasted and eaten, along with unleavened bread and bitter herbs. "Now
this day will be a memorial to you, and you shall celebrate it as a feast to the Lord;
throughout your generations you are to celebrate it as a permanent ordinance" (Ex.
12:1-14). Throughout her history Israel celebrated this meal in remembrance of the
Lord's supreme deliverance of them, from Egypt to the Promised Land. It is still the
holiest of Jewish feasts.

Jesus transformed the Passover meal into the celebration of the infinitely
greater deliverance He came to bring, of which the Passover was only a foreshadow.
When we eat His body and drink His blood, we remember the spiritual and eternal
redemption that He bought with the sacrifice of that body and the offering of that
blood. The Passover celebrated the temporary, physical deliverance of the Old
Covenant. The Lord's Supper celebrates the permanent and spiritual deliverance of the
New. "This cup which is poured out for you is the new covenant in My blood" (Luke
22:20). The Lord's table reminds us of the cross of Jesus Christ.

Luke tells us that the four marks of the daily life of early Christians were
obedience to apostolic teaching, fellowship, breaking of bread, and prayer (Acts 2:42).
We may be sure that the breaking of bread included frequent celebration of the Lord's

death with the bread and the cup. Some scholars and historians of the early church believe that in some households Communion was celebrated at every meal.

The early church developed special fellowship meals that came to be called love feasts (Jude 12) and that usually were closed with the observance of Communion. Those were congregational meals stressing fellowship, affection, and mutual caring among the believers. The emphasis on oneness led very readily into a celebration of the unifying accomplishment of the Savior on the cross. The church at Corinth followed this custom but, like those whom Peter condemns (2 Pet. 2:13), they had turned the meals into gluttonous, drunken revelry. And when the meal was connected to the bread and cup remembrance, it was a flagrant desecration of the holy ordinance.

When he introduced the discussion of women's head coverings, Paul praised the Corinthians for holding firmly to the doctrines he had taught them (11:2). Now he has no praise. **But in giving this instruction, I do not praise you, because you come together not for the better but for the worse.**

Giving . . . instruction (*parangellō*) means "to command," specifically to give a charge or order. The basic idea of the word is "to pass along from one to another." It was used especially for the order given by a military commander and passed along the line by his subordinates. Paul made it clear that what he was about to say was not merely personal advice. It was apostolic **instruction** that his readers were commanded to accept and follow.

It would have been much better for those Corinthians never to have had a love feast, and even never to have observed the Lord's Communion, than to have so abused them. They came together **not for the better but for the worse.** The term for **worse** is a comparative of *kakos,* which represents moral evil. Instead of the celebrations being times of loving fellowship and spiritual enrichment they involved selfish indulgence, shaming the poorer brethren, mocking the Lord's sacrificial death, and scandalizing the church before the unbelieving world around them.

In calling the Corinthians to sanctity in their observance of the Lord's Supper, Paul discusses their perversion of it, the Lord's purpose for it, and the right preparation for it.

THE PERVERSION OF THE LORD'S SUPPER

For, in the first place, when you come together as a church, I hear that divisions exist among you; and in part, I believe it. For there must also be factions among you, in order that those who are approved may have become evident among you. Therefore when you meet together, it is not to eat the Lord's Supper, for in your eating each one takes his own supper first; and one is hungry and another is drunk. What! Do you not have houses in which to eat and drink? Or do you despise the church of God, and shame those who have nothing? What shall I say to you? Shall I praise you? In this I will not praise you. (11:18-22)

Church (*ekklēsia*) means "assembly," or "congregation," and in the New

Testament is never used of a building or meeting place but always of believers. Apparently wherever and whenever the Corinthian Christians got together they bickered and quarreled. **When you come together as a church, I hear that divisions exist among you.** Divisions (*schismata,* from which we get schism) literally refers to tearing or cutting, and metaphorically to division or dissension. The Corinthians apparently could not agree on anything, nor did they seek to serve each other. Instead of sharing together in fellowship and worship they spent their time in selfish indulgence, arguing, and disputing. Perhaps because he suspected that some of the reports had been exaggerated, the apostle wanted to give them the benefit of any doubt. So he added, **and in part, I believe it.**

Yet the reports would not have been hard to believe. Paul began this letter by strongly rebuking them for their divisions based on party loyalties (1:10-17; 3:1-3). Those divisions inevitably ended in "quarrels" (v. 11). The believers were also divided socially, as this passage indicates. Those who were well off brought their food and selfishly ate it before the poorer members arrived. Far from having "all things in common" and "sharing . . . with all, as anyone might have need," as did the first Christians in Jerusalem (Acts 2:44), the Corinthian upper class disdained even sharing in a "pot luck supper" with their less fortunate brothers and sisters. It was every person for himself.

Paul's first appeal to them had been, "Now I exhort you, brethren, by the name of our Lord Jesus Christ, that you all agree, and there be no divisions among you, but you be made complete in the same mind and in the same judgment" (1 Cor. 1:10). "As fellow followers of Christ you ought to have the same understanding, the same opinions, the same attitude, the same outlook," he was saying. The reasons for their division were carnality, selfishness, and worldliness. "I, brethren, could not speak to you as to spiritual men, but as to men of flesh, as to babes in Christ" (3:1). They were walking in the flesh rather than in the Spirit and following their own wills rather than the Lord's.

One of the most fearful things in the church is division, because it is one of the first and surest signs of spiritual sickness. One of the first symptoms of worldliness and backsliding, often before it shows up in compromised doctrine or life-style, is dissension within a congregation.

Paul was well aware that division cannot be entirely avoided. Until the Lord returns, there will always be tares among the wheat, and disobedient believers as well. **For there must also be factions among you. There . . . must be** translates the single word *dei,* which means "it is necessary" or "it must be," and denotes necessity or compulsion of any kind. When Peter and the other apostles were told by the Sanhedrin to stop preaching the gospel, they replied, "We must [*dei*] obey God rather than men" (Acts 5:29). The word is often used in the New Testament to represent divine necessity. Jesus used the term on numerous occasions in relation to certain scripturally predicted and divinely appointed events, including His crucifixion and resurrection (Matt. 24:6; 26:54; John 3:14; etc.). He even said, "For it is inevitable that stumbling blocks come; but woe to that man through whom the stumbling block comes!" (Matt. 18:7). That is the sense in which Paul uses the term here.

The paradox is that it was necessary for there to be factions in the Corinthian church **in order that those who are approved may have become evident among you.** The worldliness and fleshly disobedience of those who caused the divisions would expose and highlight the love, harmony, and spirituality of **those who are approved. Approved** (*dokimos*) refers to that which has passed a test. The term was used of precious metals tried in fire and proved to be pure. Church division, ungodly and sinful as it is, nevertheless is used by the Lord to prove the worth of His faithful saints. In the midst of bickering and divisiveness they are separated out as pure gold is from the dross. Evil helps manifest good. Trouble in the church creates a situation in which true spiritual strength, wisdom, and leadership can be manifested.

Paul spoke to the Thessalonians of the *dokimos,* those who "have been approved by God to be entrusted with the gospel" (1 Thess. 2:4). In every congregation of believers God has His approved people in whom He entrusts the work of His church. Those approved ones are especially made manifest in adversity and hardship, and it is only to such tried and tested saints that a church should entrust its leadership. A major cause of pastors, missionaries, and other Christian leaders leaving the ministry or being unproductive in it is that they are not approved, they are not fully qualified spiritually in the first place to do the Lord's work. "Blessed is a man who perseveres under trial," James says, "for once he has been approved, he will receive the crown of life, which the Lord has promised to those who love Him" (James 1:12).

Factions are not merely disruptive; they are destructive. Initially they help reveal the strong, spiritual leaders, but when left unchallenged they will undermine any Christian group and are not to be tolerated. "Reject a factious man after a first and second warning," Paul wrote Titus, "knowing that such a man is perverted and is sinning, being self-condemned" (Titus 3:10-11). By the very fact that he is factious and divisive a person proves his carnality and his unfitness to be a part of the Christian fellowship. It is necessary that factions appear, but it is not necessary that they be tolerated or allowed to lead to division in the church.

The focal point of this evil was **the Lord's Supper.** The term *deipnon* (**Supper**) was the normal word used for the evening meal. The addition of **the Lord's** gives it special and much greater significance. This was a genuine meal, where the church congregated to eat the "love feast," a meal followed by the Communion. The Communion was connected to this supper in the Corinthian church, but abuses were obscuring its divine purpose and destroying its sanctity. In the early church the love feast and Communion customarily were held together, but abuses such as those in Corinth eventually forced the two to be separated in order to protect the Communion. The love feast soon disappeared altogether.

The factious members of the Corinthian church had so perverted the congregation that the celebration of Communion was a mockery; in fact it was not Communion at all. **Therefore when you meet together, it is not to eat the Lord's Supper.** They could not properly say it was devoted to the Lord. Neither the meal nor the Communion was honoring to Him. They had the ceremony but not the reality, the form but not the substance. "You may be breaking some bread, passing the cup, and repeating some of Jesus' words," Paul said in effect, "but what you are doing has nothing to do with the ordinance the Lord instituted. Christ has no part in it." **For in your eating each one takes his own supper first; and one is hungry and another is drunk.** The poorer believers came to the supper expecting to share in the food brought by the wealthy, but they went away hungry—physically as well as spiritually. Those who brought food and drink gorged themselves and became drunk. They mocked the very purpose of the occasion, which was to bring harmony and unity among those who belonged to Christ, as they remembered His sacrifice to make them one in Him. "Is not the cup of blessing which we bless a sharing in the blood of Christ? Is not the bread which we break a sharing in the body of Christ? Since there is one bread, we who are many are one body; for we all partake of the one bread" (1 Cor. 10:16-17).

In seeming frustration, as if trying to find a rational explanation, Paul asks, **What! Do you not have houses in which to eat and drink? Or do you despise the church of God, and shame those who have nothing?** If they intended to selfishly indulge themselves, could they not do that at home? Or were they actually trying to destroy the fellowship by flagrantly despising God's church? Or were they so contemptuous of their poor brothers and sisters in Christ that they purposely embarrassed and shamed them? Whatever the reasons may have been, they could not justify the harm being brought to the church. If they could not show love, why have a love feast?

Again Paul tells them that he can say nothing in their defense. **What shall I say to you? Shall I praise you? In this I will not praise you.** "You will get no approval from me," he said. "And you will certainly get no praise."

A Christian's attitudes and motives should be pure at all times. But when believers come to the table of the Lord, sharing the bread of His body and the cup of His blood, it is absolutely necessary that they leave behind all sin, all bitterness, all racial and sexual prejudice, all class pride, and all feelings of superiority. Of all places and occasions, those attitudes are most out place at the Lord's Supper. They grievously profane that holy, beautiful, and unifying ordinance of God.

THE PURPOSE OF THE LORD'S TABLE

For I received from the Lord that which I also delivered to you, that the Lord Jesus in the night in which He was betrayed took bread; and when He had given thanks, He broke it, and said, "This is My body, which is for you; do this in remembrance of Me." In the same way He took the cup also, after supper, saying, "This cup is the new covenant in My blood; do this, as often as you drink it, in remembrance of Me." For as often as you eat this bread and drink the cup, you proclaim the Lord's death until He comes. (11:23-26)

These verses are like a diamond dropped in a muddy road. One of the most beautiful passages in all of Scripture is given in the middle of a strong rebuke of worldly, carnal, selfish, and insensitive attitudes and behavior. The rebuke, in fact, is of

Christians who have perverted the very ceremony that these verses so movingly describe.

As he often did when about to present an especially important or controversial truth, Paul makes it clear that what he is teaching is not his own opinion but God's revealed Word. From the tenses in verse 23 we know that what he is about to tell the Corinthian believers is not new to them. He is reminding them of what he had already taught them. **For I received from the Lord that which I also delivered to you.**

Most conservative scholars agree that 1 Corinthians probably was written before any of the gospels. If that is true, Paul's account here is the first biblical record of the institution of the Lord's Supper, and includes direct quotations from Jesus. It is perfectly consistent with the gospel accounts, but Paul's revelation most likely was **received from the Lord** directly, not through the other apostles (cf. Gal. 1:10-12), even though the terms here speak of a chain of tradition that had come from the Lord to Paul and then to the Corinthians.

In the night in which He was betrayed gives the historical setting, which many of the believers may not have known, because, as just noted, probably none of the gospels was yet written. Again we see a jewel against a filthy backdrop. This most beautiful and meaningful of Christian celebrations was instituted on the very night the Lord was betrayed and arrested. In the midst of the world's evil, God establishes His good; in the midst of Satan's wickedness, God plants His holiness. Just as, by contrast, the fleshly factions cause the Lord's approved saints to "become evident" (11:19), so Jesus' betrayal and arrest cause His gracious sacrifice to become more evident. In the midst of Satan's absolute worst, the condemnation of the Son of God on the cross, God accomplished His absolute best, the sacrifice for the redemption of the world through that cross.

Although Jesus was celebrating the Passover meal with His disciples in the upper room, neither the gospels nor Paul's account here give all the details of the meal. They concentrate on Jesus' institution of the new meal, the new supper, which now supersedes the old.

The Passover meal began with the host's pronouncing a blessing over the first cup of red wine and passing it to the others present. Four cups of wine were passed around during the meal. After the first cup was drunk bitter herbs dipped in a fruit sauce were eaten and a message was given on the meaning of Passover. Then the first part of a hymn, the Hallel (which means "praise" and is related to hallelujah, "praise ye the Lord"), was sung. The Hallel is comprised of Psalms 113-118, and the first part sung was usually 113 or 113 and 114. After the second cup was passed, the host would break and pass around the unleavened bread. Then the meal proper, which consisted of the roasted sacrificial lamb, was eaten. The third cup, after prayer, was then passed and the rest of the Hallel was sung. The fourth cup, which celebrated the coming kingdom, was drunk immediately before leaving.

It was the third cup that Jesus blessed and that became the cup of Communion. "And in the same way He took the cup after they had eaten, saying, 'This cup which is poured out for you is the new covenant in My blood'" (Luke 22:20). After

Jesus gave some brief words of warning, rebuke, and instruction (vv. 21-38), the meal was concluded with the singing of a hymn (Matt. 26:30).

When He, that is, Jesus, **had given thanks, He broke it** (cf. John 6:11). In the Greek **had given thanks** is a participle of *eucharisteō,* from which we get Eucharist, the name by which some Christians refer to the Lord's Supper.

The **bread** that had represented the Exodus now came to represent the **body** of Jesus Christ, the Messiah. To the Jewish mind the body represented the whole person, not just his physical body. Jesus' body represents the great mystery of His whole incarnate life, His whole teaching, ministry, and work—all He was and all He did.

The word *broken* (as in the KJV of verse 24) does not appear in the best manuscripts or in most modern translations. Though the Romans frequently broke the legs of crucified victims in order to hasten death as an act of mercy, John specifically tells us that Jesus' legs were not broken. In order "that the Scripture might be fulfilled, 'Not a bone of Him shall be broken'" (John 19:33, 36). The best reading therefore is simply **This is My body, which is for you.**

For you are two of the most beautiful words in all of Scripture. Jesus gave His body, His entire incarnate life, for us who believe in Him. "I became a man for you; I gave the gospel to you; I suffered for you; and I died for you." Our gracious, loving, magnanimous, merciful God became incarnate not for Himself but for us. Whether a person wants and receives the benefit of that sacrifice is his choice; but Jesus made it and offers it for every person. He paid the ransom for everyone who will be freed.

The **cup** that had represented the lamb's blood smeared on the doorposts and lintels now came to represent the **blood** of the Lamb of God, shed for the salvation of the world. The Old Covenant was ratified repeatedly by the blood of animals offered by men; but the New Covenant has been ratified once and for all by the blood of Jesus Christ (Heb. 9:28), which God Himself has offered. The old deliverance was merely from Egypt to Canaan. So Jesus took the cup and said it **is the new covenant in My blood.** It is important to realize that this was not new in the sense that it was a covenant of grace replacing one of works. It is new in that it is the saving covenant to which all the Old Testament shadows pointed. The new deliverance is from sin to salvation, from death to life, from Satan's realm to God's heaven. Passover was transformed into the Lord's Supper. We now eat the bread and drink the cup not to remember the Red Sea and the Exodus but to remember the cross and the Savior.

Do this in remembrance of Me is a command from the lips of our Lord Himself. Sharing in the Lord's Supper is therefore not an option for believers. We must have Communion on a regular basis if we are to be faithful to the Lord who bought us through the act we are called to remember. Not to partake of the Lord's Supper is disobedience and a sin.

For the Hebrew to remember meant much more than simply to bring something to mind, merely to recall that it happened. To truly remember is to go back in one's mind and recapture as much of the reality and significance of an event or experience as one possibly can. To remember Jesus Christ and His sacrifice on the cross is to relive with Him His life, agony, suffering, and death as much as is humanly possible. When we partake of the Lord's Supper we do not offer a sacrifice again; we remember His once-for-all sacrifice for us and rededicate ourselves to His obedient service.

For as often as you eat this bread and drink the cup, you proclaim the Lord's death until He comes. As often as we are willing to remember and to proclaim the death of Christ, we will celebrate Communion. No frequency is given, but it is a permanent feast. It is more than a remembrance for our own sakes; it is also a proclamation for the world's sake. It is a testimony to the world that we are not ashamed of our Lord or of His blood, that we belong to Him and are obedient to Him.

Communion is also a reminder of the Lord's coming again, for He tells us to proclaim His death by this means **until He comes.** It helps keep us looking forward to the day when we will be with Him. It is a celebration of His present life and of His future return in glory.

There is much involved in that remembrance. When a believer comes to the Lord's table, he remembers Christ's work on the cross (11:25), he partakes of Christ's spiritual presence in the fellowship, not the elements themselves (10:16), he communes with the saints (10:17), he worships in holiness (10:20-22), he proclaims salvation in Christ (11:24-25), and he anticipates the return of the Lord (11:26) and the coming Kingdom (Matt. 26:29).

The Preparation for the Lord's Supper

Therefore whoever eats the bread or drinks the cup of the Lord in an unworthy manner, shall be guilty of the body and the blood of the Lord. But let a man examine himself, and so let him eat of the bread and drink of the cup. For he who eats and drinks, eats and drinks judgment to himself, if he does not judge the body rightly. For this reason many among you are weak and sick, and a number sleep. But if we judged ourselves rightly, we should not be judged. But when we are judged, we are disciplined by the Lord in order that we may not be condemned along with the world. So then, my brethren, when you come together to eat, wait for one another. If anyone is hungry, let him eat at home, so that you may not come together for judgment. And the remaining matters I shall arrange when I come. (11:27-34)

Again Paul returns to warning. Because of all that is involved in the ordinance, **whoever** participates in the Lord's Supper **in an unworthy manner, shall be guilty of the body and blood of the Lord.** One can come to His table unworthily in many ways. It is common for people to participate in it ritualistically, without participating with their minds and hearts. They can go through the motions without going through any emotions, and treat it lightly rather than seriously. They can believe it imparts grace or merit, that the ceremony itself, rather than the sacrifice it represents, can save or keep one saved. Many come with a spirit of bitterness or hatred toward another believer, or come with a sin of which they will not repent. If a believer comes with anything less than the loftiest thoughts of the Father, Son, and Holy Spirit, and anything less than total love for his brothers and sisters in Christ, he comes unworthily.

To come unworthily to the Lord's table is to become **guilty of the body and blood of the Lord**. To trample our country's flag is not to dishonor a piece of cloth but to dishonor the country it represents. To come unworthily to Communion does not simply dishonor the ceremony; it dishonors the One in whose honor it is celebrated. We become **guilty** of dishonoring His body and blood, which represent His total gracious life and work for us, His suffering and death on our behalf. We become guilty of mocking and treating with indifference the very person of Jesus Christ (cf. Acts 7:52; Heb. 6:6; 10:29).

Every time he comes to the Lord's Supper, therefore, a person should **examine himself, and so let him eat of the bread and drink of the cup**. Before we partake we are to give ourselves a thorough self-examination, looking honestly at our hearts for anything that should not be there and sifting out all evil. Our motives, our attitudes toward the Lord and His Word, toward His people, and toward the Communion service itself should all come under private scrutiny before the Lord. The table thus becomes a special place for the purifying of the church. That is a vital use of Communion, and Paul's warning reinforces that ideal.

A person who partakes without coming in the right spirit **eats and drinks judgment to himself, if he does not judge the body rightly. Judgment** (*krima*) here has the idea of chastisement. Because "there is therefore now no condemnation for those who are in Christ Jesus" (Rom. 8:1), the KJV rendering of *damnation* is especially unfortunate. The great difference in Paul's use here of *krima* (**judgment**) and *katakrima* (**condemned**) is seen in verse 32, where it is clear that *krima* refers to discipline of the saved and *katakrima* refers to condemnation of the lost. That chastening comes **if he does not judge the body rightly**, that is, the blood and body used in Communion. To avoid God's judgment, one must properly discern and respond to the holiness of the occasion.

The types of chastening the Lord may use are illustrated in verse 30. **For this reason many among you are weak and sick, and a number sleep.** God does not eternally condemn those who abuse the Lord's table, but His punishment may be severe illness. **Sleep** is here, as in several other places in the New Testament, used metaphorically to speak of the death of believers (as of Lazarus, John 11:11; and Stephen, Acts 7:60). God actually put to death **a number** (*hikanos*, lit., "sufficient") of believers in Corinth because they continually despised and corrupted the Supper of His Son, just as He had put to death Ananias and Sapphira for lying to the Holy Spirit (Acts 5:1-11). As in the Old Testament, such divine executions were to serve as examples of what all sinners deserve, and might receive (cf. Luke 13:1-5).

There is a remedy for unworthiness. **If we judged ourselves rightly, we should not be judged.** This involves discerning what we are and what we ought to be. If we confess our sins, our wrong attitudes and motives, God "is faithful and righteous to forgive us our sins and to cleanse us from all unrighteousness" (1 John 1:9).

As has already been mentioned, if we come unworthily and are judged by God, it is not for condemnation. It is for the very opposite. **But when we are judged, we are disciplined by the Lord in order that we may not be condemned along with the world.** God sends individual chastening to push offenders back toward righteous behavior, and sends death to some in the church to encourage those who remain to choose holiness rather than sin. Even if the Lord were to strike us dead for profaning His table, it would be to discipline us, to keep us from being condemned. The thought is powerful. We are kept from condemnation not only by decree, but also by divine intervention. God chastens us to keep us from falling from salvation, and will even take our life, if need be, before that could happen.

Paul closes by admonishing the Corinthians to get their lives and their attitudes straightened out, to completely discard their prejudices, their selfishness, and their indifference to God's holy ordinance. The fact that he says **when you come together to eat** assumes that he supported the idea of their fellowship meal, but they should **wait for one another** before they partake of it. If any were only attending in order to satisfy their physical hunger they should **eat at home.** Otherwise they pervert the love feast. When they come to the love feast, and especially to the Lord's table, they should come to satisfy their spiritual hunger. There is no point in gathering to sin, because that is simply coming **together for judgment.**

Because they are mentioned here, rather than at the close of the letter, Paul's closing remarks in this section, **the remaining matters I shall arrange when I come,** must refer to other issues related to worship, the Lord's Supper, or both. He would take care of those matters when he arrived in Corinth personally.

The Background and Testing of Counterfeit Spiritual Gifts (12:1-3)

28

Now concerning spiritual gifts, brethren, I do not want you to be unaware. You know that when you were pagans, you were led astray to the dumb idols, however you were led. Therefore I make known to you, that no one speaking by the Spirit of God says, "Jesus is accursed"; and no one can say, "Jesus is Lord," except by the Holy Spirit. (12:1-3)

This passage introduces the section (chaps. 12–14) that focuses on spiritual gifts, a controversial subject today within many parts of professing Christianity. Perhaps no area of biblical doctrine has been more misunderstood and abused, even within evangelicalism, than that of spiritual gifts. Yet no area of doctrine is more important to the spiritual health and effectiveness of the church. Apart from the direct energizing of God's Spirit, nothing is more vital to believers than the ministry of their spiritual gifts, their God-given endowments for Christian service.

Contrary to the thinking of many people, the true church of Jesus Christ is not a visible human organization run by a hierarchy of officials. It is not a social agency to meet the needs and demands of the community or simply a convenient place in which to be married, buried, or baptized. It is certainly not a religious social club in which people of like-minded beliefs and standards get together for fellowship and occasional service activities.

The church, as established by Jesus Christ and described and defined in the New Testament, is a living organism. It is the spiritual body of Christ, who is its Head, its Lord. The members of that body are entirely and exclusively those who have become new creatures through faith in Him as their Savior and Lord. Though composed of human members, it is not a human organization. It is a supernatural organism, created, established, empowered, and led by the Lord Himself. Because its Head is eternal and indestructible, the church is eternal and indestructible. Jesus assures us that even "the gates of Hades shall not overpower it" (Matt. 16:18).

Every member of Christ's church has been given supernatural endowments, gifts of God's Holy Spirit, which through the Spirit are God's divine means of ministering His Word and power among His people and to the world. They are God's supernatural provision for the edification of the church and the evangelization of the world. They are the means through which believers are to grow, worship, witness, and serve.

True spiritual gifts are given by God to strengthen and manifest oneness, harmony, and power. Satan's counterfeit gifts are meant to divide, disrupt, and weaken. God's gifts build up; Satan's counterfeits tear down.

The Corinthian church, like much of the church today, was seriously affected by counterfeiting as well as by misunderstanding and misuse of spiritual gifts. Some of the Corinthian believers recognized the problem, and 1 Corinthians 12–14 continues to answer questions about which they had written Paul (7:1). In addition to the problems raised and reflected in that letter, Paul had learned of other problems from "Chloe's people" (1:11) and from "Stephanas and Fortunatus and Achaicus" (16:17). Judging by the apostle's teaching in this section, the questions included those such as: What are spiritual gifts? How many are there? Does every believer have them? How can a person know which one or ones he has? How important are they to individual Christian living and to the life of the church? What is the baptism of the Holy Spirit and how does it relate to spiritual gifts? Are all of the gifts given for every age of the church, or were some given only for a special purpose and a limited time? Can the gifts be counterfeited and, if so, how can believers tell the true ones from the false? Those and many other questions Paul carefully answers.

Just as the Corinthians had perverted almost everything else, they also had perverted the nature, purpose, and use of spiritual gifts. This perversion, as the others, largely was due to ideas and practices they had dragged from their pagan society into the church. The old life continually contaminated the new. They had not separated themselves from their former ways and were still handling, in fact strongly holding on to, that which was "unclean" (2 Cor. 6:14-17). Although they were rich and complete in spiritual gifts (1 Cor. 1:7), they were poor in understanding them and irresponsible in using them.

PAGAN BACKGROUNDS

The pagan cults of Greece and Rome were part of what are commonly called the mystery religions. By Paul's time they had dominated the near eastern world for thousands of years and indirectly would dominate much of western culture through the Middle Ages and, to some extent, even until today.

The mystery religions had many forms and variations, but a common source. In his vision on the island of Patmos John was shown "the judgment of the great harlot who sits on many waters," on whose "forehead a name was written, a mystery, 'Babylon the great, the mother of harlots and of the abominations of the earth'" (Rev. 17:1, 5). Here the Lord pictures His judgment of world religion. At the end of the Tribulation the true church will have been raptured (1 Thess. 4:13-18; Rev. 3:10) and the world will begin to establish a religion of its own that will be truly universal. It will be the composite of all the world's false religions, which will "give their power and authority to the beast," the Antichrist (Rev. 17:13). The final form of that all-powerful, universal religion will represent the completion of the mystery religions that historically originated in ancient Babylon.

In its organized form false religion began with the tower of Babel, from which Babylon derives its name. Cain was the first false worshiper, and many individuals after him followed his example. But organized pagan religion began with the descendants of Ham, one of Noah's three sons, who decided to erect a great monument that would "reach into heaven" and make themselves a great name (Gen. 10:9-10; 11:4). Under the leadership of the proud and apostate Nimrod they planned to storm heaven and unify their power and prestige in a great worldwide system of worship. That was man's first counterfeit religion, from which every other false religion in one way or another has sprung.

God's judgment frustrated their primary purpose of making a grand demonstration of humanistic unity. By confusing "their language, that they may not understand one another's speech," and scattering "them abroad from there over the face of the whole earth" (Gen. 11:7-8) the Lord halted the building of the tower and fractured their solidarity. But those people took with them the seeds of that false, idolatrous religion, seeds that they and their descendants have been planting throughout the world ever since. The ideas and forms were altered, adapted, and sometimes made more sophisticated, but the basic system remained, and remains, unchanged. That is why Babel, or Babylon, is called "the mother of harlots and of the abominations of the earth" (Rev. 17:5). She was the progenitor of all false religions.

From various ancient sources, it seems that Nimrod's wife, Semiramis (the First), apparently was high priestess of the Babel religion and the founder of all mystery religions. After the tower was destroyed and the multiplicity of languages developed, she was worshiped as a goddess under many different names. She became Ishtar of Syria, Astarte of Phoenicia, Isis of Egypt, Aphrodite of Greece, and Venus of Rome—in each case the deity of sexual love and fertility. Her son, Tammuz, also came to be deified under various names and was the consort of Ishtar and god of the underworld.

According to the cult of Ishtar, Tammuz was conceived by a sunbeam, a counterfeit version of Jesus' virgin birth. Tammuz corresponded to Baal in Phoenicia, Osiris in Egypt, Eros in Greece, and Cupid in Rome. In every case, the worship of those gods and goddesses was associated with sexual immorality. The celebration of Lent has no basis in Scripture, but rather developed from the pagan celebration of Semiramis's mourning for forty days over the death of Tammuz (cf. Ezek. 8:14) before his alleged resurrection—another of Satan's mythical counterfeits.

The mystery religions originated the idea of baptismal regeneration, being born again merely through the rite of water baptism, and the practice of mutilation and flagellation to atone for sins or gain spiritual favor. They also began the custom of pilgrimages, which many religions follow today, and the paying of penance for forgiveness of sins for oneself and for others.

Several pagan practices were especially influential in the church at Corinth. Perhaps the most important, and certainly the most obvious, was that of ecstasy, considered to be the highest expression of religious experience. Because it seemed supernatural and because it was dramatic and often bizarre, the practice strongly appealed to the natural man. And because the Holy Spirit had performed many miraculous works in that apostolic age, some Corinthian Christians confused those true wonders with the false wonders counterfeited in the ecstasies of paganism.

Ecstasy (Greek, *ekstasia,* a term not used in Scripture) was held to be a supernatural, sensuous communion with a deity. Through frenzied hypnotic chants and ceremonies worshipers experienced semiconscious euphoric feelings of oneness with the god or goddess. Often the ceremony would be preceded by vigils and fastings, and would even include drunkenness (see Eph. 5:18). Contemplation of sacred objects, whirling dances, fragrant incense, chants, and other such physical and psychological stimuli customarily were used to induce the ecstasy, which would be in the form of an out-of-body trance or an unrestrained sexual orgy. The trance is reflected in some forms of Hindu yoga, in which a person becomes insensitive to pain, and in the Buddhist goal of escaping into Nirvana, the divine nothingness. Sexual ecstasies were common in many ancient religions and were so much associated with Corinth that the term *Corinthianize* meant to indulge in extreme sexual immorality. A temple to Bacchus still stands in the ruins of Baalbek (in modern Lebanon) as a witness to the debauchery of the mystery religions.

A similar form of mystical experience was called enthusiasm (Greek, *enthusiasmos),* which often accompanied but was distinct from ecstasy. Enthusiasm involved mantic formulas, divination, and revelatory dreams and visions, all of which are found in many pagan religions and philosophies today.

THE SITUATION IN CORINTH

New Testament Corinth was filled with priests, priestesses, religious prostitutes, soothsayers, and diviners of the mystery religions who claimed to represent a god or gods and to have supernatural powers that proved their claims. Unbelievably, some of their dramatic and bizarre practices were mimicked in the church.

The Corinthian believers knew of the prophet Joel's prediction:

> And it will come about after this
> That I will pour out My Spirit on all mankind;
> And your sons and daughters will prophesy,
> Your old men will dream dreams,
> Your young men will see visions.
> And even on the male and female servants
> I will pour out My Spirit in those days. (2:28-29)

They also knew that Jesus had said that the coming of the Holy Spirit would be accompanied by amazing signs and events (Mark 16:17-18). They had heard, perhaps firsthand from Peter, of the miraculous events of Pentecost, with the tongues of fire and speaking with other languages (Acts 2:3-4). Perhaps they were so determined to experience those wonders that they tried to manufacture them.

First Corinthians was one of the earliest written epistles of the New Testament. Yet even in a short period of time Satan had begun to confuse believers about many doctrines, practices, and signs. The pure water of God's truth was being muddied, and nowhere more than in Corinth. Satan began to counterfeit the gospel and its wonders in earnest, and the gullible, worldly, self-centered, thrill-seeking Corinthians with their pagan backgrounds were prime targets for his assaults.

People do not counterfeit what is not valuable. Satan counterfeits the Spirit's gifts because he knows they are so valuable in God's plan. If Satan can get God's people to become confused about or abusive of those gifts, he can undermine and corrupt the worship and work of the church. Counterfeit gifts, whether through false manifestations or through misguided and selfish use, poison God's spiritual organism and make it weak and ineffective.

One of the chief evidences of the spiritual immaturity of the Corinthian Christians was lack of discernment. If an occult practice seemed to have supernatural effect, they assumed it was of God. If a priest or soothsayer performed a miracle, they assumed it was by God's power. Like many Christians today, they believed that if something "works" it must be right and good. Some of the believers, however, realized that the confusion, division, and immoral practices that characterized many of the church members could not be of God. They asked Paul to tell them how to determine what was of the Holy Spirit and what was of some other spirit (cf. 1 John 4:1).

THE IMPORTANCE OF SPIRITUAL GIFTS

Now concerning spiritual gifts, brethren, I do not want you to be unaware. (12:1)

Paul's use here of **Now concerning** was much like saying, "Now in the second place," the first being mentioned in 11:18. Just as the Corinthians had been abusing the Lord's Supper, they also had been abusing their spiritual gifts.

As indicated by italics in many translations, **gifts** is supplied by the translators to indicate a word only implied in the original. The Greek (*pneumatikos*) literally means "spirituals," or "spiritualities," referring to that which has spiritual qualities or characteristics or is under spiritual control. Because the masculine and neuter forms of the word are the same, it can indicate either spiritual persons or spiritual things. Some interpreters have taken it to refer to spiritual persons, in contrast to the unspiritual and carnal ones about whom Paul has been saying so much. But the context makes it clear that the reference is to spiritual *things*, specifically to "gifts" of the Spirit (12:4, 9, 28, 30-31). The same word is used in 14:1 (cf. v. 12), where it could not possibly refer to persons. Except in Ephesians 6:12, the word *spiritual* is always used in the New Testament of that which is in some way related to the Holy Spirit.

Paul wants to make sure that the Corinthians have a clear and complete understanding of their **spiritual gifts,** the special equipment for ministry that the Holy Spirit gives in some measure to all believers and that are to be wholly under His control and used for Christ's glory.

After the harsh words he has just given about abusing the Lord's table (11:17-34), Paul again assures the Corinthian believers that he considers them to be **brethren,** his spiritual brothers and sisters in Jesus Christ. They were not acting spiritual or acting like Christian brothers, but they still belonged to Christ.

Paul was deeply concerned that those brethren have a proper understanding of the work of the Holy Spirit, especially in relation to His gifts to them. He uses the same phrase here (**I do not want you to be unaware**) that he used in 10:1 concerning the experiences of Israel in the wilderness under Moses. It was an idiomatic phrase often used to introduce an exceptionally important subject. Paul used it to encourage his readers to pay close attention to a critical truth (see Rom. 1:13; 11:25; 1 Thess. 4:13). The Greek *agnoeō* literally means "not to know," or "to be ignorant of." It is the term from which we get agnostic. Paul wanted the Corinthians to have no ignorance and no doubts, no uncertainty or agnosticism, about the identification and use of their spiritual gifts. The church cannot function, and it certainly cannot mature, without properly and faithfully using the gifts God gives His people for ministry. Satan will try to counterfeit the Spirit's gifts, and he will try to induce believers to ignore, neglect, misunderstand, abuse, and pervert them. Consequently, Paul's teaching here is critical.

The apostle assured the Corinthians that it was possible for them to know the truth about spiritual gifts and that he was determined to teach them. He therefore proceeds to tell them how to determine which gifts were true and godly and which were counterfeit and satanic. Because they misused the true gifts, he also tells them how to use those gifts properly.

All the gifts are given to the church to build up God's people into the image of Christ its Lord. In Ephesians Paul speaks of the specially gifted men who are given to the church "for the equipping of the saints for the work of service, to the building up of the body of Christ; until we all attain to the unity of the faith, and of the knowledge of the Son of God, to a mature man, to the measure of the stature which belongs to the fulness of Christ" (4:11-13). Christ indwells each believer (Rom.8:9; 1 Cor. 3:16) and

He indwells the church (Eph. 2:22). Individually and corporately the church represents Christ. Spiritual gifts are the Lord's primary channel of making Christians become Christ in the world, His visible and manifest body.

Spiritual gifts are divine enablements for ministry, characteristics of Jesus Christ that are to be manifested through the body corporate just as they were manifested through the body incarnate. Each gift the Holy Spirit now gives to believers had its perfect expression in Jesus' own life and ministry. His church continues to live out His life on earth through the power of His Spirit working through His gifted people.

THE SOURCE OF COUNTERFEIT GIFTS

You know that when you were pagans, you were led astray to the dumb idols, however you were led. (12:2)

Pagans translates *ethnē,* which commonly was used to represent all non-Jews, that is, Gentiles in general. But in the New Testament the term also is sometimes used, as here, to refer specifically to non-Christians (cf. 1 Thess. 4:5; 1 Pet. 2:12).

One of the chief characteristics of most pagan religions was idolatry. As former pagans, the Corinthian Christians had once been **led astray to the dumb idols. Led astray** (*apagō*) was often used of prisoners being taken under armed guard to prison or execution (Mark 14:44; 15:16; Acts 12:19; cf. 2 Tim. 3:6). Before a person is saved he is a captive of Satan and of his own depraved nature. He is spiritually blind and spiritually weak, and cannot help being led into idolatry.

One of the most common misconceptions about the ungodly life—a misconception shared by many immature believers—is that it is free, in contrast to the Christian life, which is hemmed in by rigid restrictions. As Paul teaches in this passage, just the opposite is true. The unbeliever is a captive of sin and of Satan. He has some choice as to the type of sin, but he has no choice as to whether or not to sin. **However you were led,** the apostle says, you were led. You had no choice. Whether you went into idolatry willingly or not, you could not help it.

I often think of a man to whom I have witnessed for many years. Each time I ask him to believe in Christ and confess Him as Lord he says, in one way or another, "I would become a Christian, but I don't want to give up my freedom. I don't want to be restricted. I want to do what I want." I have shared with him 1 Corinthians 12:2 and other texts that teach the same truth. I remind him that all unbelievers are "slaves of sin" (Rom. 6:17), that they are not free at all. But he is convinced that he is doing entirely what he wants and refuses to give up his delusion.

Unbelievers not only are bound but blinded. They cannot see their chains. They live "in the futility of their mind, being darkened in their understanding, excluded from the life of God, because of the ignorance that is in them, because of the hardness of their heart" (Eph. 4:17-18). Unbelievers think they are free because they are "deceived," unknowingly "enslaved to various lusts and pleasures" (Titus 3:3). It is true, of course, that most people are quite content to be in sin; they like it and want to stay there (John 3:19). But the point is that, even if they wanted to do so, they could not escape.

Part of the unbeliever's bondage is to the worship of false gods, which even the atheist and agnostic have. They can no more keep from worshiping their sophisticated idols of various sorts than a primitive tribesman can keep from worshiping his carved fetish. Each is a slave of sin, **led astray to the dumb idols, however** [he is] **led**.

Dumb (*aphōnos*) does not mean unintelligent but speechless, literally "without voice." No idol can respond to man's needs. By definition an idol is man-made and impersonal. No idol, primitive or sophisticated, can answer a person's questions, give him revelation, assure him of truth, forgive him of sin, or endow him with dignity, meaning, and peace. Just as no unregenerate person can help being led into some form of idolatry, no idol can help being **dumb**. Whether or not a demon is behind it (1 Cor. 10:20), an idol is totally helpless to benefit the one who worships it.

Tragically, many of the Corinthian Christians had fallen back into some of their old idolatrous beliefs and practices. They could no longer distinguish the work of God's Spirit from that of demonic spirits, God's true spiritual gifts from Satan's counterfeits, or true worship of God from the perverted worship of idols. They forfeited God's blessing and received none from their dumb gods.

THE TEST OF SPIRITUAL GIFTS

Therefore I make known to you, that no one speaking by the Spirit of God says, "Jesus is accursed"; and no one can say, "Jesus is Lord," except by the Holy Spirit. (12:3)

Satan spends a lot of time in church. Nowhere is he more anxious to pervert God's people than where they are worshiping. Some members of the church at Corinth apparently became so fleshly and confused, and their worship so paganized and frenzied, that they even allowed the Lord to be cursed within their own congregation. Paul rebukes the entire church for allowing such ungodliness and for being so undiscerning about what is spiritual and what is demonic. He gives two principles, one negative and one positive, for testing the validity of gifts and their use. It is the first of several tests the apostle mentions in chapters 12-14.

THE NEGATIVE TEST

The clear implication, as recognized by most evangelical interpreters, is that those who were saying **Jesus is accursed** claimed to be **speaking by the Spirit of God**. They actually claimed to be "speaking in the Spirit," manifesting some gift of prophecy or teaching, while cursing the name of the Savior and Lord they were supposed to be worshiping! **Accursed** (*anathema*) refers to severe condemnation. To say that Jesus is accursed is to condemn His nature, His character, and His work—not to mention His holiness and glory.

Paul tells the Corinthians that no such blasphemous utterance could possibly be **by the Spirit of God.** Nothing should have been more logical and obvious, but the Corinthians had come to judge the nature and use of gifts on the basis of experience rather than content. The more impressive, showy, unusual, and bizarre, the more a practice was accepted and respected. They had fallen back so deeply into ecstasy and enthusiasm that their judgment was completely warped. As long as it took place in the church and was presented by someone who claimed to be a Christian, any teaching or practice was accepted without question. Content was ignored, even to the extent of disregarding that which was obviously immoral and blasphemous.

It is possible that the person who called Jesus accursed was Jewish. Because the law taught that a person who is hanged on a tree "is accursed of God" (Deut. 21:23), many Jews considered Jesus to have been cursed by being crucified. It may have been that the apostle himself, as Saul the persecutor, had once urged Christians to blaspheme the Lord by saying, "Jesus is accursed" (see Acts 26:11).

But whether a person is Jewish or Gentile, his claiming to be a Christian and claiming that what he says or does is spiritual does not make it so. Paul hits them over the head with the obvious. Incredulously he asks, "How can you possibly be so confused? When you were pagans you could not help being blind and deceived. You could not help being led astray. But how can you who are truly Christians fail to recognize those who so obviously are not? How can you who have been so blessed with spiritual gifts be so utterly incapable of recognizing Satan's counterfeit gifts? How can you even believe that cursing the Lord and Savior could be of the Holy Spirit?"

Only one thing seems to explain why such a wicked condition could have come to exist, especially in a church established and pastored by Paul himself. During the first century the philosophy of early-developing gnosticism was a great threat to the church. It taught that everything physical and natural is evil and that everything supernatural and spiritual is good. When adapted to Christianity it taught that the supernatural Christ only *appeared* to be the natural Jesus. The human Jesus was an imperfect, evil, and poor representation of the spiritual Son of God, who, because of His divine nature, could not possibly have taken on a physical form. Christ's Spirit descended upon Jesus at His baptism but returned to heaven before the crucifixion. Therefore Jesus died an accursed death as no more than a mere man. So while glorifying the divine Christ the Corinthians may have felt perfectly justified in cursing the human Jesus.

Because they considered everything physical to be evil, Gnostics vehemently denied the idea of resurrection. The human body was the last thing with which they would want to be reunited after death. It is this part of the heresy that Paul so strongly challenges in 1 Corinthian 15. In the following chapter Paul states that it is the person who does not love the Lord Jesus Christ who is accursed (16:22-24). Some manuscripts do not have "Jesus Christ" in verse 22, but the two following verses show that the three names are inseparable. There is no Lord apart from Jesus and there is no Christ apart from Jesus. The resurrected, historical Jesus is the divine, heavenly Christ.

A person who will not claim the resurrected Jesus as Lord cannot claim the divine Christ as Lord. The incarnated Lord is the only Lord.

The heresy obviously continued to plague the Corinthian church for many years. "I am afraid," Paul writes in his next letter to them, "lest as the serpent deceived Eve by his craftiness, your minds should be led astray from the simplicity and purity of devotion to Christ. For if one comes and preaches another Jesus whom we have not preached, or you receive a different spirit which you have not received, or a different gospel which you have not accepted, you bear this beautifully" (2 Cor. 11:3-4). The basic meaning of "simplicity" (*haplotēs*) is singleness, oneness. The Corinthians were still being led astray concerning the unity of Jesus and Christ. Some of the church members were still holding to false teachings about the nature of Jesus, the Holy Spirit, and the gospel. They had heard "another Jesus" preached and had received "a different spirit" and "a different gospel."

The first test of a spiritual gift is doctrinal. If a person holds a derogatory view of Jesus Christ, then what he says and does is not of God. We should always compare a teaching or a practice with God's Word. That is the test of its being of the Holy Spirit. A Christian today cannot receive new revelation. The only way to be sure if something is spiritual is to be sure it is scriptural. If it agrees with Scripture, a new revelation from the Spirit is unnecessary; if it does not agree with Scripture, a new revelation cannot be from the Spirit and is false.

THE POSITIVE TEST

The second part of the test is also doctrinal and is simply the reverse side of the negative. **No one can say, "Jesus is Lord," except by the Holy Spirit.** Paul is of course speaking of sincere confession. An unbeliever can easily utter those words. Jesus warned, "Not everyone who says to Me, 'Lord, Lord,' will enter the kingdom of heaven; but he who does the will of My Father who is in heaven" (Matt. 7:21). True confession is based on true faith, of which obedience to God's Word is the true mark. Confessing Jesus as **Lord** means nothing unless it involves affirming who He really is and obeying what He commands. One whom we do not really know and obey cannot truly be our Lord (Luke 6:46).

The title **Lord** (*kurios*) implies deity. *Kurios* and its Old Testament Hebrew counterpart (*adonay*) are often used in the Bible as terms of respect shown to people of high rank or distinction, much as we use "your honor" when addressing a judge. But they are also used in a unique way of God. Because Jews considered God's covenant name (Yahweh, or Jehovah) to be too sacred to say aloud, it was instead spoken as "Lord." The custom is reflected in many translations by the use of capital and small capital letters (LORD) to render the Hebrew YHWH (Yahweh).

The early church soon came to reserve *kurios* entirely for use in referring to God. Confessing **Jesus is Lord**, therefore, was always understood as confessing Jesus as God. A Gnostic may have confessed Christ as Lord, but he would not have confessed Jesus as Lord.

Lord implies sovereign authority. There is overwhelming biblical evidence that the word means rulership. If the **Lord** is creator, sustainer, and controller, He obviously is sovereign. Thomas's words, "My Lord and my God" (John 20:28) must mean more than deity, or "my God" would have been sufficient. In Romans 10:9-10, confessing Jesus as Lord indicates His sovereign rule, because the context (v. 13) includes a quote from Joel 2:32 (Greek Septuagint version), where the Greek *kurios* translates the Hebrew *yhwh,* which means sovereign authority, and is most often rendered in English as Lord. In the use of "Lord" in Acts 2:36, the context again gives us insight; verses 34-35 are from Psalm 110:1, where the Hebrew *adon* means sovereign rulership.

The term **Lord** is used about 700 times in the New Testament ("Savior," under 10 times). The lordship, deity, and sovereignty of Jesus Christ was and is central to the true faith, and such affirmation is the work of the Spirit.

What a person truly believes about Jesus Christ is the test of whether or not what he teaches and does is **by the Holy Spirit.** The Holy Spirit always leads men to ascribe lordship to Jesus Christ as one indivisible and divine Person, to be obeyed completely. That is the testimony of the Father (Matt. 3:17; 17:5; John 5:26-27, 36-38; Acts 2:36; Eph. 1:20-21; Phil. 2:9-11), of the Holy Spirit (John 15:26; 1 Cor. 2:8-14; 1 John 5:6-8), and of Jesus Himself (Matt. 16:27; 26:64; 28:18).

The Source and Purpose of Spiritual Gifts (12:4-7)

29

Now there are varieties of gifts, but the same Spirit. And there are varieties of ministries, and the same Lord. And there are varieties of effects, but the same God who works all things in all persons. But to each one is given the manifestation of the Spirit for the common good. (12:4-7)

After reminding the Corinthians of the pagan and idolatrous lives most of them had once lived, Paul gave two tests, one negative and one positive, for determining if a professing Christian is truly saved out of that paganism and if what he says is genuinely of the Holy Spirit (12:1-3). It is God Himself who gives right understanding of Jesus as Lord to individual believers and who gives oneness and power to the church.

Because the Corinthian Christians were behaving in response to the flesh rather than the Spirit, they quarreled, became factious, took each other to court, fell back into immoral and idolatrous practices, corrupted marriage relationships, abused their Christian liberty, and became self-centered, overconfident, and worldly. Their misunderstanding and misuse of spiritual gifts was a major result of their carnal divisiveness.

The Spirit gives gifts (capacities for spiritual ministry) to believers to express and strengthen the unity they have in their Lord Jesus Christ. But misuse of those gifts shatters unity, divides believers, ruins their testimony before the world, and short-circuits their growth and effectiveness in the Lord's service.

Paul no doubt had taught the Corinthians carefully about spiritual gifts when he ministered among them for a year and a half. But they had forgotten or perverted much of what he had taught. He now reiterates and reinforces what they already should have known.

In this passage the apostle explains that the Spirit gives a variety of gifts, to be used in a variety of ministries that have a variety of effects, but a common source and a common purpose.

Varieties of Gifts

Now there are varieties of gifts, but the same Spirit. (12:4)

Charisma (plural, **gifts**) means essentially "gift of grace" or "free gift," and in sixteen of its seventeen New Testament uses is connected to God as the Giver. In Romans, Paul uses it in reference to the gift of salvation (5:15-16; 6:23), the blessings of God (1:1; 11:29), and divine enablements for ministry (12:6). Every other use of the word by Paul, and the one by Peter (1 Pet. 4:10), relates it to the divine enablements for believers to minister in the power of the Holy Spirit.

Spiritual gifts are not talents. Natural talents, skills, and abilities are granted by God just as everything good and worthwhile is a gift from Him. But those things are natural abilities shared by believer and unbeliever alike. An unbeliever can be a highly skilled artist or musician. An atheist or agnostic can be a great scientist, carpenter, athlete, or cook. If a Christian excels in any such abilities it has nothing to do with his salvation. Though he may use his natural talents quite differently after he is saved, he possessed them before he became a Christian. Spiritual gifts come only as a result of salvation.

Spiritual gifts, however, are not natural, but rather are supernaturally given by the Holy Spirit only and always to believers in Jesus Christ, without exception (v. 7). Spiritual gifts are special capacities bestowed on believers to equip them to minister supernaturally to others, especially to each other. Consequently, if those gifts are not being used, or not being used rightly, the body of Christ cannot be the corporate manifestation of its Head, the Lord Jesus Christ, and the work of God is hindered.

Essential to unity is diversity. Unity of spirit and purpose can be maintained only through diversity of ministry. But unity is not uniformity. A football team whose players all wanted to play quarterback would have uniformity but not unity. It could not function as a team if everyone played the same position. That is Paul's point here. God gives His people **varieties of gifts** just as players on a team have varieties of positions.

Varieties (*diaireseis*) basically means "apportionments," "allotments," or "distributions," with the derived idea of varieties. God distributes His gifts in many forms, in many varieties, to His children. He has a multiplicity of gifts, which are given to every believer. They fall into two general types, speaking gifts and serving gifts (see 1 Pet. 4:11).

The New Testament contains several lists of the categories of spiritual gifts, one of which is here in 1 Corinthians 12:8-10, 28 (see also Rom. 12:6-8; cf. 1 Pet. 4:11). Bible scholars do not agree on the exact number and distinction of kinds of gifts. Because the scriptural lists are not identical, it seems clear that God did not intend to give His church either a rigid or a precise and exhaustive compilation, but rather general categories. One should be careful not to overdefine the gifts. Because they may resist overclassification, there is not much value in taking tests, formal or informal, to determine what spiritual gifts we have. A believer's gifts can be an overlapping combination, taken in different proportions from the categories of gifts. One person may be obviously strong in a single gift, such as teaching. Another may not be strong in any one gift but have some measure of three or four categories. It is best to see each person's gift as a unique blend of the categories of giftedness, granted to that individual in connection with his or her traits and experiences and the needs of the church. Each believer becomes as unique spiritually as his fingerprints are physically.

VARIETIES OF MINISTRIES

And there are varieties of ministries, and the same Lord. (12:5)

God gives His gifts to be used in **varieties of ministries.** Even Christians with the same basic gift may be led to manifest that gift in many different ways. One teacher may be especially gifted in teaching young children; another may have special ability with the original biblical languages and be highly qualified to teach seminarians. One evangelist may be able to powerfully address large crowds, while another's strength is in one-on-one witnessing. One person's service of teaching may emphasize exhortation and doctrine, while another's may focus on comfort and mercy. The emphasis here is on variety.

Ministries is from the same basic Greek term as *serve, servant,* and *deacon* (one who serves). Speaking of Himself, Jesus said, "For even the Son of Man did not come to be served, but to serve" (Mark 10:45). Jesus came to minister to others for God, and His Spirit gives gifts to His people so they can do the same. Spiritual gifts are not given as badges of privilege or prestige but as tools for ministry. The Lord gives them to His servants so they can serve, and He gives them for a limitless variety of services. All gifts are for service, but the types of service are immeasurable.

It is critical to understand that spiritual gifts are not given for self-edification. A teacher who studies the Word and then writes lessons that only he reads, or records messages that only he hears prostitutes his gift. A person with the gift of discernment who keeps his Spirit-given insights to himself is an unfaithful steward. Nor are God's gifts given for self-service. A Christian with the gift of helps must, by definition, be involved in serving others, just as service, by definition, involves helping others. In the broad sense, therefore, *every* gift is a helps gift because every gift is a service gift. A gift exercised in private is a perverted gift. God gives His gifts *to* us but *for* others. We are personally blessed when we use our gifts in the Spirit's power to serve others in His name, but that blessing is the by-product not the purpose.

"As each one has received a special gift, employ it in serving one another, as good stewards of the manifold grace of God" (1 Pet. 4:10). We are stewards of God's gifts. They are loaned to us; they belong to Him. They are for us to use, but by its power in His service and to His glory. Peter uses "gift" in the singular, emphasizing that each of us has a gift, which is the unique single enablement for us by God's design and grace, so that we are unique in our service for Christ.

Varieties of Effects

And there are varieties of effects, but the same God who works all things in all persons. (12:6)

Effects (*energēma*) means literally "what is worked out or energized." The One who provides the spiritual gifts also provides the energy and power, as well as the faith (Rom. 12:3*b*), to make them effective. Just as spiritual gifts are given supernaturally, so they are energized supernaturally. Christians, no matter how well trained and experienced or how unselfishly motivated, cannot exercise their gifts in their own power. We may exercise our talents, skills, intelligence, and other natural abilities in our own power, but only the Giver of spiritual gifts can empower them and make them effective. Just as God gives no commands for which He does not also give the ability to obey, He does not give spiritual gifts for which He does not also give the power to use. We must be pure from sin and be willing to be used, in order that the Holy Spirit can make our gifts productive. Both the bestowing and the empowering are the Lord's exclusive domain. A "self-made" Christian is a self-contradiction. He cannot be in the right place and cannot be doing the right thing. He harms himself, he harms those to whom he tries to minister, and he harms the Lord's work. Obviously, the Word of God carries enough power on its own to accomplish divine results through the gifts He gives; but used by a carnal believer, a gift is not able to bring personal fruitfulness and blessing to that believer.

Like the gifts themselves, the energizing of spiritual gifts is sovereignly varied (cf. Matt. 13:23). The same gift may be used by the Lord in countless ways, in many **varieties**. Even the same person exercising the same gift will not always see the same kind or extent of result. We should not all expect to have the same gifts, nor should we expect them to operate in the same ways or produce the same quantity of fruit. God's people and God's gifts are like snowflakes; no two are exactly alike.

The natural man, however, is always more concerned with uniformity than with unity. In their immaturity and carnality, the Corinthian believers tended to be superficial copiers. They were more interested in appearance than in substance, and they tried to copy the gifts and practices of those who seemed to be the most successful, popular, and powerful. Like many Christians today, they liked formulas for solving problems, formulas for success, and even formulas for doing the Lord's work. They were more interested in being "successful" than in being submissive, and in being noticed and praised than in being obedient and faithful. That is why they so highly valued the more dramatic gifts, especially speaking in tongues. They were not concerned with using the Lord's gifts in His power to serve Him and His church but in using them in their own power and for their own selfish and proud purposes.

The emphasis here on **varieties** seems to imply that the Corinthians thought that the more dramatic gifts were the only gifts, or at least the only gifts worth having. But Paul tells them that the Holy Spirit gives gifts to *all* Christians, that He gives a variety of gifts, and that every gift is as spiritual and important as any other. We should not envy those who seem to be greatly gifted. Our concern should be to discover, to faithfully use, and to be grateful for the gift the Lord has given us. God makes no mistakes. His gifts to us are the best possible ones He could give us for doing what he wants us to do. Not only is every believer gifted, but every believer is perfectly gifted.

No child in the the world could substitute for one of our own children. No matter how many children we might have, none could ever be replaceable. Neither are God's children replaceable or the ministries He has given them replaceable. No other believer can take our place in God's heart, and no other believer can take our place in God's work. He has given no one the exact gift He has given us and He has given no one the exact ministry He has given us. If we do not use our gift no one else will; if we do not fulfill our ministry it will not be fulfilled.

One Source and One Purpose

But to each one is given the manifestation of the Spirit for the common good. (12:7)

The manifestation of the Spirit restates what Paul has emphasized in each of the three previous verses: God is the source of all spiritual gifts. They are all given by and are manifestations of the divine Trinity. The gifts are given by "the same Spirit" (v. 4); the ministries are assigned by "the same Lord" (v. 5); and the effects are energized by "the same God" (v. 6).

Manifestation (*phanerōsis*) has the basic idea of making known, clear, or evident. That is what spiritual gifts do: they make the Holy Spirit known, clear, and evident in the church and in the world. They manifest the Spirit. The meaning is the opposite of hidden or private. Spiritual gifts are never given to be hidden or to be used privately. They are given to manifest the Holy Spirit, to put Him on display.

They are also given **for the common good** (*sumpheron*, from a verb meaning literally "to bring together"). The term also came to mean "to help, confer a benefit, or be advantageous," and in the context of this verse means "mutually beneficial or advantageous." Spiritual gifts are to be edifying and helpful to the church, to God's people whom He brings together in His name.

Not only does the exercise of our spiritual gifts minister to others but it also helps them to better use their own gifts. A pastor, for example, who faithfully preaches and teaches his congregation not only builds them up spiritually but prepares them to be better stewards of their own gifts. God uses him "for the equipping of the saints for the work of service, to the building up of the body of Christ" (Eph. 4:12). The Christian who ministers his gift of helps not only serves other believers but encourages them to be more helpful. The believer who exercises his gift of mercy helps his fellow believers to be more merciful. As we each minister our own gifts we help others to better minister theirs.

On the other hand, as we fail to minister our own gifts we hinder others in ministering theirs. A Christian who does not exercise his spiritual gifts cripples his own ministry and the ministry of others—to say nothing of forfeiting the blessing and reward that would have come to his own life.

Some years ago I attended an olympic decathlon, the grueling contest in which each athlete competes in ten different track and field events. I marveled at how a human body can function with such amazing coordination, endurance, and efficiency. Every muscle, every organ, every blood vessel, every nerve, every cell is harnessed in a completely unified effort to win. How wonderful it would be if we who comprise Christ's body, the church, would function with such efficiency and harmony! How wonderful if every part of His body would work together in total unity and interdependence. What an impact the church would have on the world if every believer would be as wholly responsive to the mind of Jesus Christ as the bodies of dedicated athletes are responsive to the minds of their owners.

When the church ministers its gifts as it should, at least four important blessings result. First, Christians themselves receive great blessing—both from exercising their own gifts and from the exercising of other's gifts for their benefit. God never intended for the ministry of His church to be carried on by a few professional or specially talented men, while everyone else sits back and watches.

Second, when everyone does his part in ministry the church forms a dynamic witness, with power and effectiveness it cannot otherwise have. Not only are those with the gift of evangelism empowered to witness more effectively but every believer is used directly or indirectly in strengthening the testimony of the gospel before unbelievers. So all share in the results. When Peter preached at Pentecost three thousand people were saved (Acts 2:41). And when the Jerusalem church, including many of those new converts, began to faithfully and sacrificially exercise their various gifts, "the Lord was adding to their number day by day those who were being saved" (v. 47).

Third, when the church ministers its gifts, God's leaders become apparent. In a faithfully functioning church, spiritual leadership inevitably emerges. Capable leadership is essential for the church to operate as it should, but a faithful church is also necessary to provide the environment in which leaders can develop and lead as they should. God's leaders are not made by attending leadership seminars built on worldly techniques for creating success. God equips His leaders when they are saved, and when they come to have the spiritual and moral qualifications that come from obedience to His Word, their leadership blossoms and becomes evident. Spirit-filled leadership appears rapidly when God is freely at work in His body.

Fourth, a church that faithfully uses its gifts in the Spirit's power experiences the joy of great unity, love, and fellowship—in ways that no amount of human ability, planning, or effort can produce.

Varieties of Spiritual Gifts (12:8-11)

30

For to one is given the word of wisdom through the Spirit, and to another the word of knowledge according to the same Spirit; to another faith by the same Spirit, and to another gifts of healing by the one Spirit, and to another the effecting of miracles, and to another prophecy, and to another the distinguishing of spirits, to another various kinds of tongues, and to another the interpretation of tongues. But one and the same Spirit works all these things, distributing to each one individually just as He wills. (12:8-11)

A thorough examination will yield the truth that spiritual gifts fill two major purposes: the permanent gifts edify the church and the temporary gifts are signs to confirm the Word of God. God will continue to give the permanent gifts to believers for the duration of the church age, and those gifts are to be ministered by His people at all times in the life of the church. Those gifts include first the speaking or verbal gifts—prophecy, knowledge, wisdom, teaching, and exhortation, and, second, the serving or nonverbal gifts—leadership, helps, giving, mercy, faith, and discernment. The temporary sign gifts were limited to the apostolic age and therefore ceased after that time. Those gifts included miracles, healing, languages, and the interpretation of languages. The purpose of temporary sign gifts was to authenticate the apostolic message as the Word of God, until the time when the Scriptures, His written Word,

297

were completed and became self-authenticating.

In the present passage Paul mentions some of those gifts that illustrate the "varieties" he spoke of in verse 4. This list includes both permanent and temporary gifts, and is only representative of the varieties, as seen from the fact that additional gifts are mentioned elsewhere in the New Testament, including in verse 28 of this chapter (see also Rom. 12:6-8; cf. 1 Pet. 4:11). The apostle does not here explain the functions of the particular gifts. His point is to illustrate the variety in kinds of gifts and to emphasize the common source of the gifts, each of which is given for "the manifestation of the Spirit for the common good" (v.7). As we have mentioned, because of their uniqueness in the lives and ministries of the millions of Christians, the gifts are not narrowly defined. We can define them only generally by the terms used in Scripture.

REPRESENTATIVE SPIRITUAL GIFTS

THE GIFT OF WISDOM

The word of wisdom is a broad term. The use of *logos* (**word**) indicates this is a speaking ability. In the apostolic age it may have been revelation at times. In the New Testament, **wisdom** (*sophia*) is used most often to refer to the ability to understand God's will and apply it obediently (see, e.g., Matt. 11:19; 13:54; Mark 6:2; Luke 7:35; Acts 6:10; James 1:5; 3:13, 17; 2 Pet. 3:15). **Wisdom**, then, refers basically to applying truths discovered, to the ability to make skillful and practical application of the truth to life situations. Communicating wisdom is the function of the expositor, who draws not only from his own study of Scripture but from the many insights and interpretations of commentators and other Bible scholars. It is also the ability a counselor must have in order to apply God's truth to the questions and problems brought to him. It is a feature in the gift of the pastor, who must know, understand, and be able to apply God's Word in order to lead his people as he should.

THE GIFT OF KNOWLEDGE

I believe that this second gift mentioned in verse 8 logically precedes the first, because ordinarily knowledge comes before wisdom. **The word of knowledge** is also a broad term, which basically refers to perceiving and understanding the truths of God's Word. It, too, may have been revelatory in the first century, but it is especially the gift of communicating insight into the mysteries of His revelation, those truths that could not be known apart from God's revelation (Rom. 16:25; Eph. 3:3; Col. 1:26; 2:2; 4:3; cf. 1 Cor. 13:2). God gives certain of His saints a special ability to study His Word and discover the full meaning of the text and context, of individual words and phrases, and of related passages and truths, and thereby help provide understanding for others. Perhaps the best insight on this text is found in 13:2 in the phrase, "know all mysteries and all knowledge." The gift of **knowledge** is the capability of grasping the meaning of God's revelation, which is mystery to the natural mind.

That gift is foundational for all Christian teaching and preaching, as well as for the proper exercise of counseling, leadership, wisdom and all other ministries and gifts. If a person does not have that ability himself, he must rely heavily on those who do in order to exercise his own gifts rightly. The teacher or preacher is especially dependent on **knowledge**, because he is commissioned to teach and interpret God's truths to others.

A Christian with the gift of knowledge may be highly trained in biblical languages, history, archaeology, and theology. God can use that training in the working of his gift. But another person with the same gift may have limited formal education. In either case, the ability to comprehend spiritual truth is God-given. The gifted person is supernaturally enabled not only to discover truths from the facts of Scripture but to explain and interpret those truths in order to help others understand them. As all the other gifts, it comes in many forms and degrees. One believer may have great ability in this one area alone, while another may have moderate ability here, mixed with several other spiritual capabilities.

The human writers of Scripture had the gift of knowledge in a unique way. God gave them truths directly, which they recorded as part of His written Word. Since the closing of the canon of Scripture, however, that gift has not involved the receiving of new truth but only understanding of truth previously revealed. Anyone today who claims to have a divine revelation is a deceiver and contradicts God's own Word, which expressly warns that if anyone adds to it or takes away from it he will suffer God's judgment (Rev. 22:18). Any word of divine knowledge or wisdom must be based on the Word of God, "once for all delivered" (Jude 3).

THE GIFT OF FAITH

This sovereign, Spirit-given **faith** obviously is distinct from saving faith or the daily faith by which every believer lives. This category of giftedness is limited to certain Christians and has to do with an intensive ability to trust God in difficult and demanding ways. It is the ability to trust Him in the face of overwhelming obstacles and human impossibilities.

The gift of faith is primarily expressed toward God through prayer, appealing to and trusting God to do that which is beyond His normal provision. Jesus said, "For truly I say to you, if you have faith as a mustard seed, you shall say to this mountain, 'Move from here to there,' and it shall move; and nothing shall be impossible to you" (Matt. 17:20). Paul alludes to that type of faith later in this letter: "If I have all faith, so as to remove mountains, but do not have love, I am nothing" (13:2). Paul was not disparaging faith but simply pointing out its emptiness without love. His phrase "all faith" seems to indicate that it is possessed in degrees.

Those with the gift of faith have a special ability to lay claim on the promises of God. According to His own plan and will, faith activates God (cf. James 5:16b-18). When Paul was sailing to Rome as a captive, the ship encountered a terrible storm. After throwing all cargo and tackle overboard, they went for many days without food and without letup of the storm. At the height of danger Paul told his fellow travelers, "I urge you to keep up your courage, for there shall be no loss of life among you, but only of the ship. For this very night an angel of the God to whom I belong and whom I serve stood before me, saying 'Do not be afraid, Paul; you must stand before Caesar; and behold, God has granted you all those who are sailing with you'" (Acts 27:22-24). Paul's confidence took special faith. His great faith exercised in the midst of disaster laid hold of God's promise and brought hope and safety to everyone with him. Abraham was also "strong in faith, giving glory to God" (Rom. 4:20).

On the basis of one person's strong faith others are always helped and served. Through the history of the church thousands of saints with gifts of faith have believed God in the face of great danger and often death, and in exercising their faith have strengthened the faith of their brothers and sisters in the Lord. Hudson Taylor believed God would win many Chinese converts through him, and without any money or support, refusing to ask for a penny of help, he began what became the great and fruitful China Inland Mission. George Mueller, solely through trusting God in prayer, continually saw Him provide for his orphanage in miraculous ways. Countless missionaries have claimed tribes or nations for the Lord, and evangelists have claimed cities for the Lord, and seen Him faithfully respond to their faith. Their prayers are answered and their faith itself is strengthened and multiplied.

THE GIFTS OF HEALINGS

Again it is interesting to note that **gifts** here is plural, supporting what has been said in chapter 29: namely, that Paul is speaking of categories of giftedness in which there may be great variety. The **gifts of healing** were the first temporary sign gifts Paul mentions in this passage. And since all these gifts were in operation then, the sign gifts are not placed in a separate category. The word **healing** also is plural in the Greek (*iamatōn*), emphasizing the many kinds of afflictions that need healing. These gifts were for Christ (Matt. 8:16-17), the apostles (Matt.10:1), the seventy (Luke 10:1), and some associates of the apostles such as Philip (Acts 8:5-7).

God may still heal directly and miraculously today, in response to the faithful prayers of His children. But no Christian today has the gifts of healings. This is apparent because no one today can heal as did Jesus and the apostles—who with a word or touch instantaneously and totally healed all who came to them, and who raised the dead. The Corinthian church may have seen God perform healings through Paul or others who had those abilities, and in that case Paul mentions them here simply to remind the Corinthians of the variety of ways in which God equips His people to do His work.

The gifts of healings, like the other sign gifts, were temporary, given to the church for authenticating the apostolic message as the Word of God. The Great Commission does not include a call to heal bodies but only the call to heal souls through the preaching of the gospel. It is not that God became no longer interested in men's physical health and well-being or that the church should have no such concern. Medical work has long been a God-blessed part of Christian service and is one of the cutting edges of modern missions. But God's healing work, whether through medicine or miracle, is no longer an authenticating sign, and He no longer endows His church with such gifts.

As did all the others with the gifts of healings, Paul used it sparingly and only for its intended purpose. It was never used solely for the purpose of bringing physical health. Paul himself was sick, yet he never healed himself nor asked a fellow gifted believer to heal him. Paul's dear friend and fellow worker Epaphroditus had been terribly ill and would have died but for God's intervention. "God had mercy on him, and not on him only but also on me, lest I should have sorrow upon sorrow" (Phil. 2:27). God miraculously healed Epaphroditus, but if the apostle had freely exercised the gift of healing, he would not have had to make a special plea to God. When Timothy, another co-worker, had stomach trouble and other ailments Paul did not heal him but rather advised him to drink some wine (1 Tim. 5:23). Trophimus, still another associate, Paul "left sick at Miletus" (2 Tim. 4:20). He did not exercise the gift of healing except as necessary to confirm the power of the gospel, not to make Christians healthy.

A Christian today has the right to ask God for the healing of any illness. God may choose to heal in order to accomplish some purpose of His and to show His glory. But He is under no obligation to heal, because He has made no blanket promise to heal during any age (cf. Num. 12:9-10; Deut. 28:21-22; 2 Kings 5:15-27; 2 Chron. 26:5, 21; Ps. 119:67; 1 Cor.11:30), and He no longer is authenticating His Word, because the completed Word is its own verification.

THE GIFT OF MIRACLES

The effecting of miracles also was a temporary sign gift. A miracle is a supernatural intrusion into the natural world and its natural laws, explainable only by divine intervention. God often leads us, helps us, or warns us by working through other Christians, through ordinary circumstances, or through natural laws. Those are supernatural workings of providence by God, but they are not miracles. A miracle is an act of God that is contrary to the ordinary working and laws of nature, an act that only He could accomplish by overruling nature and that could not otherwise occur through any circumstances.

John tells us that Jesus' turning the water into wine at the wedding feast was the beginning of the "signs Jesus did in Cana of Galilee, and manifested His glory, and His disciples believed in Him" (John 2:11). That was the purpose. The miracle was not to improve the party or to show off great power to the curious. Even with Jesus, the working of miracles, just as the work of healing, was confirmation of His coming as Messiah, the carrier of God's power and message. Near the end of his gospel John says, "Many other signs therefore Jesus also performed in the presence of the disciples, which are not written in this book; but these have been written that you may believe that Jesus is the Christ, the Son of God; and that believing you may have life in His name" (20:30-31). Jesus performed miracles to prove that God was being revealed in Him, that is, in Jesus. At Pentecost Peter told the crowd to whom he was preaching, "Men of Israel, listen to these words: Jesus the Nazarene, [was] a man attested to you by God with miracles and wonders and signs which God performed through Him in your midst, just as you yourselves know" (Acts 2:22).

Jesus performed miracles and healed the sick only for the three years of His ministry. Contrary to certain myths and legends that have cropped up through the centuries, Scripture indicates that Jesus lived a quiet, normal life as a child and as a young man, exercising absolutely no supernatural powers until the wedding at Cana. As is clear from the quotation from John 2 above, Jesus' miracles began when His ministry began.

The apostles and a few other early church leaders also performed miracles as confirming signs of the gospel message. In Iconium Paul and Barnabas "spent a long time there speaking boldly with reliance upon the Lord, who was bearing witness to the word of His grace, granting that signs and wonders be done by their hands" (Acts 14:3). Paul later wrote the Corinthians, "The signs of a true apostle were performed among you with all perseverance, by signs and wonders and miracles" (2 Cor. 12:12). Miraculous signs were a mark of apostleship, authenticating the apostles' message and work as being of the Lord. In Hebrews we read, "After it [the gospel] was the first spoken through the Lord, it was confirmed to us by those who heard [the apostles], God also bearing witness with them, both by signs and wonders and by various miracles and by gifts of the Holy Spirit according to His own will" (2:3-4).

Just what were the miracles the apostles did? Jesus made wine, made food, walked on water with Peter, took a coin from the mouth of a fish, disappeared from a hostile crowd, and ascended in a cloud to heaven. All those miracles were related to nature and were done only by Him. No disciple is ever reported to have done a miracle of nature. What miracles did they do? The answer is in the word for miracle, *dunamis,* which means "power." In fact, the term is translated "power" in the gospels, and is frequently connected with the casting out of demons (Luke 4:36; 6:18; 9:42). It is precisely that power, to cast out demons, that the Lord gave to the twelve and to the seventy (Luke 9:1; 10:17-19). We have no such power today by which certain of us can successfully go about commanding demons to come out of unsaved people, as the disciples did. Philip and Stephen demonstrated the gift of miracles (Acts 6:8; 8:7). Paul used it to confirm "the teaching of the Lord" and bring a man to faith (Acts 13:6-12). Some Jews who tried to cast out demons without the true gift were beaten up and chased out by the demons they were trying to exorcise (Acts 19:14-16).

Those signs accompanied God's Word only so long as He was revealing the Word. When revelation stopped, the sign gifts stopped. B. B. Warfield wrote, "These miraculous gifts were part of the credentials of the apostles, as authoritative agents of God in founding the church. Their function confined them distinctly to the apostolic church, and they necessarily passed away with it."

THE GIFT OF PROPHECY

To some Christians God has given the gift of **prophecy.** There has long been a difference of interpretation among evangelicals as to whether or not prophecy is a continuing, permanent gift or, like healings and miracles, passed away with the apostolic age. The primary argument for those who maintain it was a temporary sign gift—that it was a revelatory gift only, and therefore ceased when revelation ceased—is based on 1 Corinthians 13:8, where the gifts of prophecy, tongues, and knowledge all are referred to together as ceasing. As will be discussed when treating that passage, though they all appear in that verse, prophecy and knowledge are not in the same category as tongues, and the mention of them together in 13:8 does not prove they are of the same type—any more than the mention of the various gifts in 12:8-10 proves they are all of the same type. We will assume here that prophecy is a permanent edifying gift.

Like its Hebrew equivalent (*nābā'*), the Greek verb (*prophēteuō*) behind **prophecy** simply means "to speak forth, to proclaim." It assumes the speaker is before an audience, and could mean "to speak publicly." The connotation of prediction was added sometime in the Middle Ages. Although many of the prophets made predictions, that was not their basic ministry and the idea is not involved in the original terms used to describe them and their work. The original terms, in fact, did not necessarily carry the idea of revelation. God revealed a great deal of His Word through the prophets, but much of their ministry was simply proclaiming, expounding, and exhorting with revelation already given. The biblical prophets sometimes revealed (see 1 Tim. 4:14; 2 Pet. 1:21) and sometimes only reiterated what had already been revealed. A prophet of God, therefore, is simply one who speaks forth God's Word, and **prophecy** is the proclaiming of that Word. The gift of prophecy is the Spirit-given and Spirit-empowered ability to proclaim the Word effectively. Since the completion of Scripture, prophecy has no longer been the means of new revelation, but has only proclaimed what has already been revealed in Scripture.

The simplest and clearest definition of this function is given by Paul in 1 Corinthians 14:3, "But one who prophesies speaks to men for edification and exhortation and consolation."

I do not believe there has been a time in the history of God's dealing with men that He has not endowed some of His people with gifts of this kind. During the Old and New Testament periods and throughout history between and since, the Lord always has equipped some of His saints to speak for Him with special power and effectiveness. In 1 Corinthians 14:1 Paul urges believers in general to "pursue love, yet desire earnestly spiritual gifts, but especially that you may prophesy." He makes the same plea again in verse 39. The apostle is not suggesting that every Christian should seek *personally* to have a gift of proclamation, but that all Christians *collectively* should want that gift to be ministered among them. Throughout chapter 14 Paul contrasts the gift of tongues, a sign gift needing interpretation before either believers or unbelievers ever can understand it, with the gift of prophecy, which has the specific purpose of edifying all those who hear.

In speaking of spiritual gifts in Romans 12, Paul says, "let each exercise them accordingly: if prophecy, according to the proportion of his faith" (v. 6). The term *analogia* ("proportion") refers to a right relationship to or agreement with, and the Greek of this verse reads literally, "of the faith." A better rendering therefore would be, "according to the measured-out faith." "The faith" is used several times in the New Testament as a synonym of the gospel, the God-given body of Christian belief (Acts 6:7; Jude 3, 20). Believers today with the gift of prophecy are empowered to speak forth not according to their personal subjective faith but according to God's already-revealed objective faith, His Word. That primary purpose of prophecy is given in the book of Revelation: "The testimony of Jesus is the spirit of prophecy" (19:10). And the Bible is the testimony of Jesus (cf. John 5:39). Prophecy can never deviate from the Word of God written, as Paul makes plain when he says, "If anyone thinks he is a prophet or spiritual, let him recognize that the things which I write to you are the Lord's commandment" (1 Cor. 14:37). The gift of prophecy is the Spirit's special enablement of a Christian to testify of Jesus. No one is to "despise prophetic utterances" (1 Thess. 5:20), but the Corinthians apparently did look down on it, and even replaced it with ecstatic utterances, as chapter 14 reveals.

THE GIFT OF DISCERNMENT

An important gift for the protection of the church is that of discernment, **the distinguishing of spirits.** The basic meaning of **distinguishing** has to do with separating out for examination and judging in order to determine what is genuine and what is spurious. Satan is the great deceiver, "the father of lies" (John 8:44), and ever since the Fall he and his demons have counterfeited God's message and God's work. All Christians should judge carefully what they hear and read and "not believe every spirit, but test the spirits to see whether they are from God" (1 John 4:1). That is what the God-fearing and "noble-minded" Jews of Berea did when they first heard the gospel from Paul (Acts 17:11). They tested Paul's word against what they knew of God's Word, and because the two words matched they believed that what he preached was from God and not from demons. That is what every believer should do with every message that claims to be from God. No preacher or teacher of the gospel should resent having what he says judged against Scripture.

Those to whom God has given the gift of discernment have a special ability to recognize lying spirits, and this gift is the Spirit's watchdog. Some ideas that are given as scriptural and that on the surface *seem* scriptural actually are clever counterfeits that would deceive most believers. Those with the gift of discernment are the Holy Sprit's inspectors, His counterfeit experts to whom He gives special insight and understanding. The gift was especially valuable in the early church because the New Testament had not been completed. Because of the difficulty and expense of copying, for many years after its completion the Bible was not widely available. The Holy Spirit's discerners were the church's protectors.

The gift of discernment is also especially valuable when the church and the gospel are considered acceptable in society. When Christianity is persecuted, counterfeit teachers usually are scarce, because the price for being identified with the gospel is too high. They are much more likely to appear in times and in places where Christianity is considered respectable or at least is tolerated. In parts of the world today, evangelicalism is popular and often profitable. All sorts of teachers, preachers, writers, and counselors claim to be evangelical and biblical. Although any thinking person realizes that all the ideas cannot be biblical, simply because many of them are so contradictory of each other, it is not always easy to know which are true and which are not. Most often they are a mixture. Counterfeit teachers used by Satan usually have some truth in what they say. Unfortunately, many basically sound teachers sometimes undiscerningly pick up ideas from psychology, philosophy, or popular thinking that seem biblical but are not. It is the ministry of those with the gift of discernment to help separate the wheat from the chaff.

The Corinthian believers who had that gift either were not using it or were being ignored. Otherwise the perverted ideas and practices that Paul deals with in this letter could not have flourished as they did. Discernment is the gift, along with prophecy, that the apostle urges the Corinthians to use in relation to judging the use and interpretation of tongues. Those with discernment are to judge even those who prophesy (1 Cor. 14:29).

Obviously, the gift of discernment is valuable to the church in assisting Christians to settle disputes among themselves rather than going to court. That seems to be the gift needed by the person Paul speaks of in 1 Corinthians 6, the "wise man who will be able to decide between his brethren" (v.5).

Even praise of the gospel can be deceitful and misleading. When Paul and Silas began to minister in Philippi, Luke reports that "a certain slave-girl having a spirit of divination met us, who was bringing her masters much profit by fortunetelling. Following after Paul and us, she kept crying out, saying, 'These men are bond-servants of the Most High God, who are proclaiming to you the way of salvation'" (Acts 16:16-17). What the girl said not only was true but seemed to be favorable to the gospel and to those who were proclaiming it. But the purpose and motivation of what she said was exactly the opposite. The demons who controlled her meant to attract the people and, gaining their trust, then ridicule and undercut God's Word and the work of His ministers. In that case Paul could not judge by what was said, because the girl's words were true. He knew she was a demonic instrument only because the Holy Spirit revealed the false spirit that controlled her.

False teaching can be judged by comparing it with Scripture, but false spirits can be judged only by the true Spirit's gift of discernment. That gift may be called the Spirit's gift on gifts, because God uses it to reveal to His church whether or not a manifestation of the other gifts is of Him. All imitation of the gifts is not demonic. Much of it is simply the work of the flesh, carnal Christians trying to serve the Lord in their own power and for their own benefit and glory. Summarizing, it can be said that the gift of discernment is given to tell if the other gifts are of the Holy Spirit, if they are merely natural imitations, or if they are demonic counterfeits. I believe God still empowers some of His people to unmask false prophets and carnal hypocrites. He gives them insight to expose imitations and deceptions that most Christians would take as genuine.

The gift of discernment, however, can easily deteriorate into a critical, proud, and self-righteous spirit. It can be judgmental instead of corrective when it is imitated in the flesh. But rightly used it is a great protection to God's people.

THE GIFTS OF TONGUES AND OF INTERPRETATION OF TONGUES

The most controversial spiritual gift in our day is that of speaking in **various kinds of tongues.** Because this gift, and that of **interpretation of tongues,** will be discussed in detail in the exposition of 1 Corinthians 14, it is necessary only to mention here that these are temporary sign gifts that are not genuinely active in the church today. Their ministry in the New Testament church was, like the other sign gifts, to validate the message and power of the gospel. They were disproportionately exalted and seriously abused in Corinth. But that is not yet Paul's point. Now he is simply naming them to show the great diversity in the gifts sovereignly given by the Spirit of God.

GOD'S SOVEREIGN CONTROL OF SPIRITUAL GIFTS

But one and the same Spirit works all these things, distributing to each one individually just as He wills. (12:11)

This verse summarizes verses 4-10. Just as he did when illustrating the varieties in the nature, ministries, and effects of spiritual gifts (vv. 4-6), Paul continues to stress that each gift, though different in many ways from the others, is supernaturally and sovereignly given by **one and the same Spirit** (cf. vv. 8-9). In fact, this is the fifth reference in this paragraph to the Holy Spirit as the giver. He also emphasizes again that every believer (**distributing to each one individually**) is spiritually gifted (cf. vv. 6-7). Those with gifts are not a spiritual elite but comprise the whole church, the entire Body of Christ. All of us are gifted, and all of us are called by the Lord to minister the gifts He has supplied.

There is no indication here that gifts should be sought. That would violate both the idea of a gift of grace and the intent of the text, which is to instruct the Corinthians to recognize that all believers have gifts that are different. In God's sovereignty He has given gifts to be the fulfillment of His divine purpose. They are not a smorgasbord from which believers may choose.

The point is further emphasized in seeing that the Holy Spirit not only gives the gifts, but that it is the **Spirit who works all these things. Works** is the same term as in verse 6, and means "energizings." In the deepest sense a believer does not even use his gift, but allows God to work through it by the power of the Holy Spirit. God energizes and makes effective the gifts He sovereignly gives **just as He wills** to His people—to all of His people. The Spirit is the messenger of the Head of the church, giving and energizing the spiritual gifts as deity has designed.

When the Spirit of God rules and energizes a church at least eight evidences will be manifested:

The Spirit-controlled church is *unified*. The Holy Spirit is the source and preserver of unity, a unity that does not crush individuality.

The Spirit-controlled church is characterized by *fellowship*. Its fellowship is deep and wide, honest and intimate, inclusive of every believer who cares and participates.

The Spirit-controlled church is *worshipful*. Its worship is meaningful, genuine, God-centered, and shared by all, as it honors God the Father, the Son, and the Holy Spirit. It sings praise, talks praise, and lives praise.

The Spirit-controlled church is *evangelistic*. The Holy Spirit is the true instrument of every conversion, every new spiritual birth, and a church that is responsive to Him wins souls spontaneously and joyfully. Bringing unbelievers to new life in Christ is the top priority and natural outflow of its own life.

The Spirit-controlled church is *loving*. It is an assembly of people who care and help, a body of believers where selflessness and sacrifice are normal.

The Spirit-controlled church is *obedient*. It walks in the path that God prescribes, and only in that path. What the Bible teaches it believes, and what the Bible commands it does.

The Spirit-controlled church is *submissive*. Submissiveness is willing obedience, obedience that comes gladly from the heart. It submits to its Lord because it loves its Lord and seeks to please only Him.

The Spirit-controlled church *ministers*. Like its Lord Jesus Christ, its call and its goal is not to be served but to serve. It is a community of believers in which each one ministers by the gifting and empowering of the Holy Spirit.

When the church today does not understand the pattern and intent of God's spiritual gifts, but rather attempts to grade them according to human standards, exalts certain gifts above others, and seeks gifts other than those that have been given, the Corinthian confusion returns.

Unified and Diversified (12:12-19)

For even as the body is one and yet has many members, and all the members of the body, though they are many, are one body, so also is Christ. For by one Spirit we were all baptized into one body, whether Jews or Greeks, whether slaves or free, and we were all made to drink of one Spirit. For the body is not one member, but many. If the foot should say, "Because I am not a hand, I am not a part of the body," it is not for this reason any the less a part of the body. And if the ear should say, "Because I am not an eye, I am not a part of the body," it is not for this reason any the less a part of the body. If the whole body were an eye, where would the hearing be? If the whole were hearing, where would the sense of smell be? But now God has placed the members, each one of them, in the body, just as He desired. And if they were all one member, where would the body be? (12:12-19)

The Corinthians' misuse of spiritual gifts was one of many reflections of their fleshly worldliness, and was closely related to their divisiveness, which Paul now continues to reprove.

While illustrating the diversity of spiritual gifts (12:4-11) the apostle repeatedly stresses their one source in God (vv. 4, 5, 6, 8, 9, 11). He also stresses their one purpose, to reveal the Holy Spirit's work and power for the common good of the church (v. 7). These unifying realities lead the apostle's thought to a general discussion of the oneness of the redeemed community.

In the present passage he explains and illustrates the nature and importance of the unity of the church itself, and then again the importance of diversity as a key factor in that unity. The diversity of the church is a God-ordained means of bringing the fellowship to oneness, but unless each diverse member recognizes and accepts his part in the whole body, diversity will divide rather than unite, destroy rather than build up, bring discord rather than harmony, and result in self-serving rather than self-giving.

In verse 12 Paul gives an illustration of unity and in verse 13 he explains its origin.

UNIFIED IN ONE BODY

For even as the body is one and yet has many members, and all the members of the body, though they are many, are one body, so also is Christ. (12:12)

Paul again (cf. 10:17) uses the human body to illustrate the unity and interrelationship of the members of Christ's Body, the church. Through verse 27 of chapter 12 Paul uses the term *body* some 16 times, and he uses the metaphor many other places in his writings (Rom. 12:5; Eph. 1:23; 2:16; 4:4, 12, 16; Col. 1:18; etc.).

The human body is by far the most amazing organic creation of God. It is marvelously complex yet unified, with unparalleled harmony and interrelatedness. It is a unit; it cannot be subdivided into several bodies. If it is divided, the part that is cut off ceases to function and dies, and the rest of the body loses some of its functions and effectiveness. The body is immeasurably more than the sum of its parts.

Christ's Body is also one. There are many Christian organizations, denominations, agencies, clubs, and groups of every sort. But there is only one church, of which every true believer in Christ is a member. Paul is so intent on driving home the point of oneness in the church that he refers to Christ *as* the church: **so also is Christ**. We can no more separate Christ from His church than we can separate a body from its head. When Christ is referred to as the head of the church it is always in the sense of mind, spirit, and control. When a body loses its mind and spirit it ceases to be a body and becomes a corpse. It still has structure but it does not have life. It is still organized but it is no longer a living organism.

Through another figure for the church Jesus tells us the same truth. "I am the vine, you are the branches," He said. "He who abides in Me, and I in him, he bears much fruit; for apart from Me you can do nothing" (John 15:5). A severed branch not only is an unproductive branch but a lifeless branch.

It is for that reason that the New Testament speaks of our being in Christ and of Christ's being in us. He is more than simply *with* His church; He is in His church and His church is in Him. They are totally identified. The church is an organic whole, the living manifestation of Jesus Christ that pulses with the eternal life of God. The common denominator of all believers is that they possess the very life of God. Jesus said, "Because I live, you shall live also" (John 14:19). "He who has the Son has the life" (1 John 5:12), because "the one who joins himself to the Lord is one spirit with Him" (1 Cor. 6:17).

While He was on earth Christ was incarnate in a single body. Now He is incarnate in another body, the great, diverse, and precious Body that is His church. Christ is now incarnate in the world through His church. There is no true church life without Christ life. Paul did not say, "For to me, to live is being a Christian," but "For to me, to live is Christ" (Phil. 1:21). He could say, in fact, "It is no longer I who live, but Christ lives in me" (Gal. 2:20). This same Christ life is possessed by every believer, and every believer therefore is a part of Christ, a part of His Body, the church. The church is **one body** because **so also is Christ.** For illustrations of the implications of this solidarity, see Matthew 18:5 and 25:31-46, where our Lord teaches that what one does to a child of God he does to Christ Himself.

BAPTIZED BY ONE SPIRIT

For by one Spirit we were all baptized into one body, whether Jews or Greeks, whether slaves or free, and we were all made to drink of one Spirit. (12:13)

In this verse Paul presents two important truths about Christ's Body: its formation and its filling.

THE FORMING OF THE BODY

The church is formed as believers are baptized by Christ with the Holy Spirit. **For by one Spirit we were all baptized into one body.** The Holy Spirit is the agent of baptism but Christ is the baptizer. At Jesus' own baptism John the Baptist tells us that it is Jesus Christ, "He who is coming after me [and] is mightier than I," who would baptize "with the Holy Spirit and fire" (Matt. 3:11; cf. Mark 1:8; Luke 3:16; John 1:33). As explained in the following verse, the baptism of fire is the judgment of hell, the burning of "the chaff with unquenchable fire." As Savior, Christ baptizes with the Holy Spirit; as Judge, He baptizes with fire. All believers receive baptism with the Holy Spirit; all unbelievers will receive baptism with fire. Therefore every living soul will be baptized by Christ.

Parenthetically, it should be noted that Paul is not speaking here of water baptism. Water baptism is an outward, physical ordinance believers submit to themselves and which is performed by other believers, in obedience to Christ's command (Matt. 28:19; cf. Acts 2:38). Water baptism plays no part in conversion, but is a testimony to the church and to the world of conversion that has already taken place inwardly. Spirit baptism, on the other hand, is entirely the work of God and is virtually synonymous with salvation. The term *baptizō* ("to baptize") is used in the New Testament to refer to figurative immersion in trouble (Matt. 20:22-23, KJV) or to spiritual immersion (Rom. 6:3-5) in Christ's death and resurrection. As one can be immersed in water, so a believer is immersed spiritually into the Body of Christ.

It should also be noted that the phrase "baptism *of* the Holy Spirit" is not a correct translation of any passage in the New Testament, including this one. *En heni pneumati* (**by one Spirit**) can mean "by or with one Spirit." Because believers are baptized by Christ, it is therefore best to translate this phrase as "with one Spirit." It is not the Holy Spirit's baptism but Christ's baptism *with* the Holy Spirit that gives us new life and places us into the Body when we trust in Christ.

It is not possible to be a Christian and not be baptized by Christ with the Holy Spirit. Nor is it possible to have more than one baptism with the Spirit. There is only one Spirit baptism, the baptism *of* Christ *with* the Spirit that all believers receive when they are born again. By this the Son places all believers into the sphere of the Spirit's power and Person, into a new environment, a new atmosphere, a new relationship with others, and a new union with Jesus Christ (cf. 1 Cor. 10:2, where Paul shows how the nation of Israel left Pharaoh and Egypt to become immersed and identified with a new leader, Moses, and a new land, Canaan).

The pouring forth of the Holy Spirit at Pentecost also reveals that this baptism was *by* Jesus Christ (Acts 2:32-33), in fulfillment of John the Baptist's prediction (Matt. 3:11; etc.) and of Jesus' own promise (John 7:37-39; 15:7-15; Acts 1:5). We are not told exactly how this is done, any more than we are told exactly how God can give a person a new heart and new life. Those are mysteries beyond our comprehension. But there is no mystery as to the divine roles in salvation. The Father sent the Son and the Son sends the Spirit. The Son is the divine Savior, and the Holy Spirit is the divine Comforter, Helper, and Advocate. The Son is the baptizer and the Holy Spirit is the agent of baptism.

Paul's central point in 1 Corinthians 12:13 is that baptism with the one Spirit makes the church one Body. If there were more than one Spirit baptism, there would be more than one church, and Paul's whole point here would be destroyed. He is using the doctrine of baptism with the Spirit to show the unity of all believers in the Body. Many erring teachers today have used a wrong interpretation of the baptism with the Spirit to divide off from the Body an imagined spiritual elite who have what the rest do not. That idea violates the whole teaching here.

For by one Spirit we were baptized into one body, whether Jews or Greeks, whether slaves or free. The apostle could not have stated the truth more clearly. One Spirit baptism establishes one church. There are no partial Christians, no partial members of Christ's Body. The Lord has no halfway houses for His children, no limbo or purgatory. All of His children are born into His household and will forever remain in His household. "For you are all sons of God through faith in Christ Jesus. For all of you who were baptized into Christ have clothed yourselves with Christ" (Gal. 3:26-27). All believers in Jesus Christ become full members of His Body, the church, when they are saved. "There is one body and one Spirit, just as also you were called in one hope of your calling; one Lord, one faith, one baptism, one God and Father of all who is over all and through all and in all" (Eph. 4:4-6).

It is interesting that those who advocate Christians' seeking the baptism *by* the

Spirit in order to belong to the spiritual elite cannot seem to agree on how that is to be done. They have many ideas and many theories but no scriptural method. The reason is simple: Scripture contains no command, suggestion, or method for believers to seek or receive the baptism of the Spirit. You do not seek or ask for that which you already possess. The believers in Samaria who were converted under the ministry of Philip had to wait a short while to receive baptism with the Holy Spirit, until Peter and John came up to Samaria and laid hands on the converts (Acts 8:17). In that unique transitional situation as the church was beginning, those particular believers had to wait for the Holy Spirit, but they were not told to seek Him. The purpose for that exception was to demonstrate to the apostles, and to bring word back to the Jewish believers in general, that the same Holy Spirit baptized and filled Samaritan believers as baptized and filled Jewish believers—just as a short while later Peter and a few other Jewish Christians were sent to witness to Cornelius and his household in order to be convinced that the gospel was for all men and to see that "the Holy Spirit had been poured out upon the Gentiles also" (Acts 10:44-45). Those special transitional events did not represent the norm, as our present text makes clear, but were given to indicate to all that the Body was one (Acts 11:15-17).

THE FILLING OF THE BODY

When we were born again the Lord not only placed us into His Body, but placed the Holy Spirit in us. At salvation we are **all made to drink of one Spirit.** We are in the Spirit, who is in us. Just as there are no partially saved Christians there are no partially indwelt Christians. The Spirit is not parceled out to us in installments. God "gives the Spirit without measure" (John 3:34).

Like being baptized with the Spirit, being indwelt by the Spirit is virtually synonymous with conversion. It is a separate facet of the same glorious, transforming act. "However, you are not in the flesh but in the Spirit, if indeed the Spirit of God dwells in you. But if anyone does not have the Spirit of Christ, he does not belong to Him" (Rom. 8:9). A person who does not have the Holy Spirit does not have eternal life, because eternal life is the life of the Spirit. Thus Peter can affirm "that His divine power has granted to us everything pertaining to life and godliness, through the true knowledge of Him who called us by His own glory and excellence. For by these He has granted to us His precious and magnificent promises, in order that by them you might become partakers of the divine nature" (2 Pet. 1:3-4; cf. Col. 2:10; 1 Cor. 6:19).

Well-meaning and otherwise sound Christian leaders have caused great confusion, frustration, and disappointment in the lives of many believers by holding out the prospect of a second working of grace—which is called by many names. Time and energy that could be used in simply obeying the Lord and relying on what He has already given is spent striving for that which is possessed completely and in abundance. A person cannot enjoy what he has if he is forever seeking a nonexistent second blessing. An inadequate doctrine of salvation will always lead to an erroneous doctrine of sanctification. It is an ironic tragedy that those who seek a second blessing of grace cannot enjoy either. They do not enjoy the first blessing, although it is complete, because they are continually seeking the second, which does not exist.

The idea of the second blessing probably originated in the Middle Ages with the teaching that a person is saved when baptized, even though as an infant, and later receives the Holy Spirit at confirmation after coming of age. Sincere and otherwise biblical evangelicals modified the idea as a means for trying to enliven lifeless Christians. Because the church was lethargic, carnal, worldly, and fruitless, they sought to infuse vitality by encouraging believers to seek an additional work of God. But the problem has never been the insufficiency or incompleteness of God's work. Christ gives no salvation but perfect salvation. And it is tragic that so many are seeking some "triumphalistic experience" of "deeper life," some formulized key to instant spirituality, when the Lord calls for obedience and trust in what has been given in His perfect work of salvation (Heb. 10:14).

The being "filled up to all the fulness of God" of which Paul speaks in Ephesians 3:19 has to do with living out fully that which we already possess fully, just as does the working out of our salvation (Phil. 2:12). When we trust in Christ we are completely immersed into the Spirit and completely indwelt by Him. God has nothing more to put into us. He has put His very self into us, and that cannot be exceeded. What is lacking is our full obedience, our full trust, our full submission, not His full salvation, indwelling, or blessing.

DIVERSIFIED IN ONE BODY

For the body is not one member, but many. If the foot should say, "Because I am not a hand, I am not a part of the body," it is not for this reason any the less a part of the body. And if the ear should say, "Because I am not an eye, I am not a part of the body," it is not for this reason any the less a part of the body. If the whole body were an eye, where would the hearing be? If the whole were hearing, where would the sense of smell be? (12:14-17)

The most important characteristic of the Body is unity; but diversity is essential to that unity. The church is one Body, but **the body is not one member, but many.**

The Corinthian church, as many churches today, was divided where it should have been unified and tried to be uniform where it should have been diverse. On the one hand it was divided, for example, over leadership—whether to follow Paul, Apollos, or Peter (1:12)—when it should have been unified under the perfect leadership of Jesus Christ, their Lord. On the other hand, the members tried to be alike in all having certain spiritual gifts, especially the showy ones such as speaking in tongues, instead of being glad for and faithfully using the many diverse gifts the Lord had given them (12:27-31).

Many of the Corinthian believers were unhappy with their gifts. Envy is a sure sign of carnality, and it seems that everyone wanted a gift that someone else had. Paul's analogy is graphic as he extends the illustration of the human body. The person with a

foot thought he could not really be a part of the church body because he was not a **hand**. One with an **ear** thought he was left out because he was not an **eye**. It is almost certain that, had the gifts been changed to suit the complainers, their reactions would have been the same. Selfishness is never satisfied and envy is never content.

Envy is also frequently petulant and pouting. If it cannot have its own way it takes its marbles and goes home, and will not play with the others. That is what some of the immature believers at Corinth were doing. In seeming humility, they said, "I don't have a spiritual gift, so I am not really a part of the church," or "My gift is second-rate and unimportant. I have nothing to offer, so why participate?" But that attitude does not reflect humility. It is self-centered, selfish, and an affront to God's wisdom and love.

Disclaiming responsibility does not remove it. Refusing to function as part of the body does not make us **any the less a part of the body** or any less responsible for ministering within it. We have no right to remove ourselves from our God-given responsibilities just because we are dissatisfied with what we are and what we have. Many Christians have never known the joy of ministry and of pleasing the Lord simply because they do not recognize or refuse to use the gifts and opportunities God has given them. That is disobedience.

Continuing his analogy, Paul reminds us that a body could not possibly function if it were all the same part. **If the whole body were an eye, where would the hearing be? If the whole were hearing, where would the sense of smell be?** Common sense should have told the Corinthians that, as a fellowship of believers, they could operate more effectively with members performing different ministries. With everyone doing the same thing, at best their life and service would be lopsided.

Gifted by One Lord

But now God has placed the members, each one of them, in the body, just as He desired. And if they were all one member, where would the body be? (12:18-19)

Discontentment with their spiritual gifts, however, was much worse than lack of common sense. By wanting gifts they did not have, the Corinthian believers questioned God's wisdom and goodness by implying He had made a mistake. They also opened themselves up to fleshly and demonic counterfeits. Their primary problem was not intellectual but spiritual. They did not see their gifts rightly because they did not see the sovereign God rightly. They had not received their gifts by accident or whim. **But now God has placed the members, each one of them, in the body, just as He desired.** Questioning our spiritual gifts is questioning God, and not using our spiritual gifts is disobeying God. "Who are you, O man," Paul writes in the book of Romans, "who answers back to God? The thing molded will not say to the molder, 'Why did you make me like this,' will it? Or does not the potter have a right over the clay?" (Rom. 9:20-21).

A Christian who does not have a ministry is a contradiction. He is disobedient and denies God the right to use him in the way He intends and for which He has gifted him. When we refuse to follow God's will and God's plan we deny His authority and Lordship as well as His wisdom and goodness. As members of Christ's Body we are not to do our own will but the Lord's. The arm does not have one will, the foot another, and the eye still another. Each is controlled by the head—the mind, will, and spirit. It is possible for the body to be so remarkably coordinated only because it is directed by one will. One will tells each part of the body to do what it is best designed and equipped to do, and consequently they work in marvelous harmony together. How much more should the Lord Jesus Christ control His own Body, the church, of which He not only is Head but Creator.

As Creator and Lord **God has placed the members, each one of them, in the body.** God has created us, re-created us, placed each of us in His Body exactly where He wants us to be, and equipped us to do exactly what He wants us to do.

Because they were discontent and disobedient the Corinthian believers were also unproductive. They did not use the gifts they had, and, in light of Paul's repeated emphasis in 12:4-11 that every Christian is gifted, it seems apparent that some thought they did not have a gift at all. In any case their gifts either were not being used or were being misused.

Churches often fall back on organization because the organism is not functioning right. Because a hand is not doing its job, a foot is called on to do that work, and so on. If most of the congregation is inactive, the active members must do work for which they are not equipped. The answer to an inactive organism, however, is not an active organization. Carnality cannot be overcome by compensation. No human substitutions can satisfactorily replace God's plan and God's power. The only way the church can function properly is by using the Spirit's gifts in the Spirit's power as it should, **just as He** [God] **desired.** We all have what God desires for us (cf. Rom. 12:3b) and are to receive the privileged gift with joyful thanks.

It is terribly tragic when believers are discontent with their spiritual gifts, their circumstances, or with anything the Lord has given them. In God's Body, which is also His family, there is no place for discontent, envy, selfishness, or conceit. No Christian would be better off, or happier, with a showier or more prominent gift. We cannot be happy except with what God has given us, because He gives each and every one of His children the very best possible. What He has given another believer would not be His best for us.

If they were all one member, where would the body be? Paul expands on his point in verse 17. A body that had only one part would not be a body. A church whose members all had the same gift and the same ministry would not really be a church. It is foolish and immature not to be content with or use what the Lord has given us. We are not perfect, but His gifts to us are perfect and the ministry in which he has called us to use them is perfect. His design for the church is perfect and His gifting of the church is equally perfect.

Interdependence, Not Independence

(12:20-31)

32

But now there are many members, but one body. And the eye cannot say to the hand, "I have no need of you"; or again the head to the feet, "I have no need of you." On the contrary, it is much truer that the members of the body which seem to be weaker are necessary; and those members of the body, which we deem less honorable, on these we bestow more abundant honor, and our unseemly members come to have more abundant seemliness, whereas our seemly members have no need of it. But God has so composed the body, giving more abundant honor to that member which lacked, that there should be no division in the body, but that the members should have the same care for one another. And if one member suffers, all the members suffer with it; if one member is honored, all the members rejoice with it. Now you are Christ's body, and individually members of it. And God has appointed in the church, first apostles, second prophets, third teachers, then miracles, then gifts of healings, helps, administrations, various kinds of tongues. All are not apostles, are they? All are not prophets, are they? All are not teachers, are they? All are not workers of miracles, are they? All do not have gifts of healings, do they? All do not speak with tongues, do they? All do not interpret, do they? But earnestly desire the greater gifts. And I show you a still more excellent way. (12:20-31)

Paul continues the theme of oneness, stressing Christians' mutual dependence on each other and on each other's callings and gifts.

Rugged individualism has long been considered a hallmark of Americanism. The explorer who supposedly relied on no one for anything, the pioneers who grew their own food, made their own clothes, soap, and many of their own tools and implements—these have been our heroes. We still see ads that glorify the nonconformist who goes off into the woods and lives off nature, the man who crosses the ocean alone in a small boat or raft, or who singlehandedly accomplishes some other demanding feat of skill and perseverance.

Individualism is appealing because the natural man is inclined not only to do his own thing but to do it alone, or at least do it without depending on or obeying others. Since Cain first renounced his responsibility for his brother's welfare (Gen. 4:9), man has disdained the thought of responsibility for others.

The philosophy that we are basically self-sufficient and do not need anyone else is Satan's philosophy and the opposite of God's plan and will for men. The well-known lines from *Invictus*—"I am the captain of my fate; I am the master of my soul"—express the heart of fallen man, his great desire to be his own god.

Even as Christians we sometimes fall prey to the notion that, because we are complete in Christ and because He is our sufficiency, we therefore do not really need anyone else to live a faithful Christian life. Yet the idea completely contradicts Scripture. God has made us and redeemed us not only for Himself but for each other. We would never have heard of God or of the gospel had it not been for someone leading us to Christ or providing material for us to read. We could not have grown in faith and obedience had it not been for Christian teachers and friends who helped us and guided us. We cannot possibly fulfill our own ministry, whatever it is, without being mutually dependent on others.

Some years ago I gave a series of messages at a seminary I had never visited before. I knew none of the faculty members personally and only a few of the students. But I had been indebted to that school and its ministry for many years because of the outstanding books and articles written by the faculty. My own life was richer and my own ministry was strengthened by a seminary I never attended and by people I had never met.

Our Lord Jesus Christ might have been a truly independent person, because He was the incarnate Son of God and had no need of other men in the ways that the rest of us need each other. Yet before His public ministry began when He was thirty years old, He lived with and helped support His family. The next three years of His life were spent in almost constant companionship with the twelve men that were His disciples. The apostle Paul, who stands out so visibly among the early church leaders, sometimes is characterized as having been independent and individualistic. Yet that image is far from the truth. He always traveled and worked in the company of other believers with whom he shared companionship and ministry. He traveled thousands of miles with Barnabas, Silas, Mark, Luke, and others.

It is true that Paul would not compromise the gospel for the sake of any person, not even another apostle. When Peter yielded to the Judaizers and started requiring Gentile converts to be circumcised, Paul publicly rebuked him (Gal. 2:14). In that sense he would stand alone if necessary. But he continually learned from and was encouraged by other believers. He was anxious to go to Rome not only to preach there but to be benefited there. "For I long to see you," he wrote, "in order that I may impart some spiritual gift to you, that you may be established; that is, that I may be encouraged together with you while among you, each of us by the other's faith, both yours and mine'" (Rom. 1:11-12). Those are not the words of an independent individualist but of a person who clearly and humbly understood his need not only for God but for fellow Christians. With John Wesley he would have said, "There is no such thing as solitary Christianity."

In this chapter Paul deals with the two primary reasons some Christians never become involved in ministry. Some feel they have no gifts or abilities that are worthwhile, and so sit back and let others do the work. Those are the believers described in 1 Corinthians 12:15-17. Others feel they are so highly qualified that they do not really need the help of others to perform their ministry. Those are the believers described in verse 21 and counseled in the following verses. But neither the individualism of supposed inferiority nor the individualism of proud independence is biblical or pleasing to God.

BELIEVERS' PROPER RELATIONSHIPS

And the eye cannot say to the hand, "I have no need of you"; or again the head to the feet, "I have no need of you." On the contrary, it is much truer that the members of the body which seem to be weaker are necessary; and those members of the body, which we deem less honorable, on these we bestow more abundant honor, and our unseemly members come to have more abundant seemliness, whereas our seemly members have no need of it. But God has so composed the body, giving more abundant honor to that member which lacked, that there should be no division in the body, but that the members should have the same care for one another. And if one member suffers, all the members suffer with it; if one member is honored, all the members rejoice with it. Now you are Christ's body, and individually members of it. (12:21-27)

Whereas the first kind of individualist says, "They don't need me," the second says, "I don't need them." That attitude is wrong enough in the world, because God has made all of His creation interrelated, especially mankind, whom He has made in His own image. The attitude is much worse in the church, whose members have a common Savior and Lord and a common spiritual body. No **eye** in the church has a right to say to a **hand, "I have no need of you," or again the head to the feet, "I have no need of you."** That attitude was common in the Corinthian assembly. A few prominent and gifted members acted as if they were self-sufficient, as if they could carry on their ministries and daily Christian living completely by themselves or with only a few select friends. They overestimated their own importance and underestimated that of other believers. Disobeying the principles of Matthew 18:10 and Romans 14:1–15:7, these people were disdaining those they saw as weak and less significant.

On the contrary, Paul continues, **it is much truer that the members of the body which seem to be weaker are necessary.** As important as some of the prominent members of the human body are it is possible to live without them. They are important but not absolutely **necessary.** You can lose an eye or ear, a hand or leg, and still live. But you cannot lose your heart or liver or brain and live. Those organs are more hidden than the others but also are more vital. You can notice the breathing of your lungs and the pulse of your heartbeat, but their work is not nearly as obvious as what we do with our hands or feet. Those less noticed parts (internal organs) **seem to be weaker** than much of the rest of the body (external limbs), but they also are more **necessary.** Consequently they are more guarded by the skeleton and the rest of the body. They are more vital and more vulnerable, and are therefore given more protection. You can live without legs, but not without lungs.

The most vital ministries in a church always include some that are not obvious. The faithful prayers and services of a few dedicated saints who hold no office frequently are the most reliable and productive channels of spiritual power in a congregation. The Corinthian church had failed to be considerate and appreciative of those who did not have the "out front" gifts such as prophecy, languages, or healing. Those with less noticeable ministries are sometimes vulnerable to misunderstanding, and often to neglect and lack of appreciation. They should be protected by fellow believers just as the body protects its vital organs.

Continuing the analogy, Paul reminds us that **those members of the body, which we deem less honorable, on these we bestow more abundant honor, and our unseemly members come to have more abundant seemliness.**

Less honorable probably refers to the parts of our body that are not particularly attractive. It seems best to see this as referring to the torso in general—the part on which we hang clothes. It might include flabby thighs or a paunch, but is usually covered and considered less attractive. The use of the verb *peritithēmi* (**bestow,** literally "to put around") suggests the idea of clothing the body in general. We spend more time and money clothing those parts of our body than the ones that are more presentable (such as face and hands), and by doing so, **on these we bestow more abundant honor.**

Unseemly (*aschēmōn*) means shameful, indecent, or unpresentable, and here refers to those parts of the body that are considered private and to be covered. In virtually all societies of history, with the exceptions of a few primitive tribes, those parts of the body have been treated with modesty. The fact that many people today are discarding this natural modesty and are exploiting the display of traditionally private parts indicates the extent of modern depravity.

When people treat these **unseemly members** with care and modesty they **come to have more abundant seemliness.** It is not those parts of the body themselves, but the display of them, that is unseemly and shameful. When they are properly treated they become more decent, just as the less honorable parts, when properly treated, become more attractive.

It is from a warped sense of values that a Christian, well known because of a prominent gift, looks down on other Christians who possess no obvious gift and seeks great honor for his own. That attitude is a direct contradiction of the principle of concern that characterizes a body. It is far more consistent with self-preservation that members of the body that have greater outward beauty and more functional abilities devote themselves to the well-being of those parts that are not so well equipped but are essential to life. Every sensible person is more concerned with his heart than his hair.

Those in positions of leadership and prominence not only should not look down on those whose gifts are less noticeable but should take special care to show them appreciation and to protect them when necessary. Specially gifted Christians are specially obligated to "encourage the fainthearted, help the weak, [and] be patient with all men" (1 Thess. 5:14).

Those who have the more noticeable and attractive gifts are the more **seemly members** [who] **have no need of** encouragement and protection. Honor comes to them almost as a matter of course, and that honor they should share with members whose gifts and temperaments are less attractive and more likely to be ignored. They should give **more abundant honor to that member which lacked.**

I believe that the most surprising experience Christians will have is that of seeing the Lord present His rewards at the *bēma,* the judgment seat of Christ, where every believer will "be recompensed for his deeds in the body, according to what he has done, whether good or bad" (2 Cor. 5:10). If there is such a thing as shock in heaven, I believe that is what most of us will feel when the secrets are revealed (cf. 1 Cor. 4:3-5). Jesus said that those who seek to be first in this life will be last in the next (Matt. 19:30), and that spiritual greatness is determined by the spirit of servanthood not by high position or impressive achievements (Matt. 20:27). Jesus' response to the request of the mother of James and John reveals that suffering is more related to reward than is success (Matt. 20:20-23).

It is clear from what Paul says in the present text that heavenly reward will be based not only on what we do with our own gifts and ministries but on our attitudes toward and support of the gifts and ministries of other believers.

Mutual support and encouragement is necessary to avoid both underconfidence and overconfidence. It is also necessary to avoid **division in the body.** In our eyes, as in God's eyes, every believer should be of the highest importance and every ministry of the highest importance (cf. Phil. 2:1-4). In a mature and spiritual congregation, church members will **have the same care for one another.** We should care as much for the nursery teacher as for the pastor, as much for the janitor as for the Sunday school superintendent.

In the obedient and loving church that God has planned for His children, **if one member suffers, all the members suffer with it; if one member is honored, all the members rejoice with it.** Only that sort of mutual love and concern can prevent or heal division and preserve unity. The one who is hurt is consoled and the one who is blessed is rejoiced with. There is no disdain for one another, no rivalry or competition, no envy or malice, no inferiority or superiority, but only love—love that is patient, kind, and not jealous, boastful, or arrogant; love that does not act unbecomingly or seek its own and is not easily provoked; love that never rejoices in unrighteousness but always rejoices in the truth (1 Cor. 13:4-6).

The only people that can love in that way and be unified in that way are Christians, who **are Christ's body, and individually members of it**. And only Christ's love can produce such love.

Paul reminded the Corinthian believers that, individually and collectively, they were Christ's very body, the church for whom He died. They *were* one in Him and so should be one in each other. They were "not lacking in any gift" (1:7) and were perfectly equipped to represent and serve the Lord. As a local congregation they were Christ's body in miniature, a representation of Jesus Christ to all of Corinth. Every local church is fully equipped to serve the Lord, just as every believer is fully equipped to serve Him. Any lacking, any deficiency, is always in our recognition and use of what He has provided.

God's Perfect Provision

And God has appointed in the church, first apostles, second prophets, third teachers, then miracles, then gifts of healings, helps, administrations, various kinds of tongues. All are not apostles, are they? All are not prophets, are they? All are not teachers, are they? All are not workers of miracles, are they? All do not have gifts of healings, do they? All do not speak with tongues, do they? All do not interpret, do they? (12:28-30)

Paul again reminds the Corinthians of God's sovereign and perfect provision in equipping His church. It is unified and diversified. "One and the same Spirit works all these things, distributing to each one individually just as He wills" (12:11). As in 12:8-10, the apostle does not here give an exhaustive list of gifts but simply illustrates them—repeating some, deleting some, and adding others—to show the variety of ways in which the Lord calls and equips His people to do His work harmoniously. He continues to stress the same three key points: sovereignty, unity, and diversity.

In verse 28 Paul first mentions certain gifted men and then certain spiritual gifts. The gifted men are **appointed,** just as members are placed, or appointed, in the church as God plans (v. 18, where the same Greek verb, *tithēmi,* is used). The term basically means to set or place, but is often used, as in these two verses, to indicate official appointment to an office (cf. John 15:16; Acts 20:28, "made"; 2 Tim. 1:11). God has sovereignly appointed **first apostles, second prophets, third teachers.** The other divinely appointed offices are those of evangelist and pastor, or pastor-teacher (Eph. 4:11).

The first two offices mentioned in verse 28, those of apostle and of prophet, had three basic responsibilities: (1) to lay the foundation of the church (Eph. 2:20); (2) to receive and declare the revelation of God's Word (Acts 11:28; 21:10-11; Eph. 3:5);

and (3) to give confirmation of that Word through "signs and wonders and miracles" (2 Cor. 12:12; cf. Acts 8:6-7; Heb. 2:3-4).

The **first** of the gifted men in the New Testament church were the apostles, of whom Jesus Christ Himself is foremost (Heb. 3:1). The basic meaning of **apostle** (*apostolos*) is simply that of one sent on a mission. In its primary and most technical sense *apostle* is used in the New Testament only of the twelve, including Matthias, who replaced Judas (Acts 1:26), and of Paul, who was uniquely set apart as apostle to the Gentiles (Gal. 1:15-17; cf. 1 Cor. 15:7-9; 2 Cor. 11:5). The qualifications for that apostleship were having been chosen directly by Christ and having witnessed the resurrected Christ (Mark 3:13; Acts 1:22-24). Paul was the last to meet those qualifications (Rom. 1:1; etc.). It is not possible therefore, as some claim, for there to be apostles in the church today. Some have observed that the apostles were like delegates to a constitutional convention. When the convention is over, the position ceases. When the New Testament was completed, the office of apostle ceased.

The term *apostle* is used in a more general sense of other men in the early church, such as Barnabas (Acts 14:4), Silas and Timothy (1 Thess. 2:6), and a few other outstanding leaders (Rom. 16:7; 2 Cor. 8:23; Phil. 2:25). The false apostles spoken of in 2 Cor. 11:13 no doubt counterfeited this class of apostleship, since the others were limited to thirteen and were well known. The true apostles in the second group were called "messengers (*apostoloi*) of the churches" (2 Cor. 8:23), whereas the thirteen were apostles of Jesus Christ (Gal. 1:1; 1 Pet. 1:1; etc).

Apostles in both groups were authenticated "by signs and wonders and miracles" (2 Cor. 12:12), but neither group was self-perpetuating. In neither sense is the term *apostle* used in the book of Acts after 16:4. Nor is there any New Testament record of an apostle in either group being replaced when he died.

The text here affirms that **prophets** were also appointed by God as specially gifted men, and differ from those believers who have the gift of prophecy (12:10). Not all such believers could be called prophets. It seems that the office of prophet was exclusively for work within a local congregation, whereas that of apostleship was a much broader ministry, not confined to any area, as implied in the word *apostolos* ("one who is sent on a mission"). Paul, for example, is referred to as a prophet when he ministered locally in the Antioch church (Acts 13:1), but elsewhere is always called an apostle.

The prophets sometime spoke revelation from God (Acts 11:21-28) and sometimes simply expounded revelation already given (as implied in Acts 13:1, where they are connected with teachers). They always spoke for God but did not always give a newly revealed message from God. The prophets were **second** to the apostles, and their message was to be judged by that of the apostles (1 Cor. 14:37). Another distinction between the two offices may have been that the apostolic message was more general and doctrinal, whereas that of the prophets was more personal and practical.

Like the apostles, however, their office ceased with the completion of the New Testament, just as the Old Testament prophets disappeared when that testament was completed, some 400 years before Christ. The church was established "upon the foundation of the apostles and prophets, Christ Jesus Himself being the corner stone"

(Eph. 2:20). Once the foundation was laid, the work of the apostles and prophets was finished. The work of interpreting and proclaiming the now-written Word was taken over by evangelists, pastor-teachers, and teachers. The purpose of apostles and prophets was to equip the church with right doctrine; the purpose of evangelists, pastor-teachers, and teachers is to equip the church for effective ministry. The offices are listed here in 1 Corinthians without chronological distinctiveness or reference to duration, because at that time they were all operative.

The third office is that of **teacher**, which may be the same as that of pastor-teacher (see Eph. 4:11; Acts 13:1). I am inclined, however, to consider them as being separate. The teacher not only has the gift of teaching but God's calling to teach. He is called and gifted for the ministry of studying and interpreting the Word of God to the church. All who have the office of teaching also have the gift of teaching, but not everyone with the gift has the office.

The second half of verse 28 lists several representative spiritual gifts, both temporary and permanent. The temporary sign gifts of **miracles** and **healings** are discussed under 12:9-10. Various kinds of tongues will be discussed in following chapters. The other two are permanent serving gifts.

The gift of **helps** is a gift for service in the broadest sense of helping and supporting others in day-by-day, often unnoticed, ways. It is the same gift as that of serving (Rom. 12:7), though another Greek word is used in that text. **Helps** (*antilēmpsis*) is an especially beautiful word, meaning to take the burden off someone else and place it on oneself. That gift doubtlessly is one of the most widely distributed of any, and is a gift that is immeasurably important in supporting those who minister other gifts. Paul used the same term in his final words to the Ephesian elders, as he met with them at Miletus on his way to certain arrest in Jerusalem: "In everything I showed you that by working hard in this manner you must *help* the weak and remember the words of the Lord Jesus, that He Himself said, 'It is more blessed to give than to receive'" (Acts 20:35).

To the Philippians Paul speaks of Epaphroditus as my "fellow worker and fellow soldier, who is also your messenger and minister to my need, . . . risking his life to complete what was deficient in your service to me" (Phil. 2:25, 30). Whatever other gifts he may have had, Epaphroditus clearly had the gift of helps and ministered it faithfully.

The gift of helps is not glamorous or showy and, as in the Corinthian church, often is not highly prized or appreciated. But it is God's gift, and its faithful ministry is highly prized by Him and by any leader who knows the value of supporting people behind the scenes.

The gift of **administrations** is the gift of leadership. The term comes from *kubernēsis*, literally meaning "to steer or pilot" a ship, and is so used in Acts 27:11. It refers to one who keeps a ship, or a church, on course toward its proper destination. In the Septuagint (Greek version of the Old Testament) the term is used several times, in each case in relation to wisdom. In Proverbs 12:5 it is translated "counsels," and in Ezekiel, wise men are compared to "pilots" (27:8).

The gift of the "word of wisdom" (1 Cor. 12:8) has to do with understanding and practically applying the truths of God's Word. The wisdom of those with the gift of administrations lies in the ability to make wise decisions and to mobilize, motivate, and direct others toward an objective. A pastor most often has the gift of administrations, a necessary ability if he is to lead the church well (cf. 1 Tim. 5:17; Heb. 13:7, 17, 24). Like the pilot of a ship, he is not owner but steward. The church belongs to the Lord Jesus Christ; the one gifted with administrations is His steward. There is nothing to indicate that the gift is limited to pastors. It is found in many others to whom the Lord has given the ministry of leading in various ways.

Because it was "not lacking in any gift," we know that the Corinthian church had gifted leaders. And because the leaders apparently were not doing their work "properly and in an orderly manner" (14:40; cf. v. 33), we also know that they were not exercising their gifts, or else the people refused to follow their leadership.

Paul's primary point in listing the offices and gifts of 12:28 was to emphasize again the "varieties of ministries" (v. 5) God gives to His church. Mentioning the offices and most of the gifts again, he asks rhetorically about each: **all are not** that type of minister **are they?** or **all do not have** that gift **do they?** God does not intend for everyone to have the same gift, and He does not intend for everyone to have gifts that are out front and noticed. He distributes the offices and the gifts according to His sovereign purpose, "just as He wills" (12:11). The responsibility of believers is to accept the ministries they are given with gratitude and to use them with faithfulness.

It is interesting that the two gifts mentioned in verse 28 that are not mentioned in verses 29-30 are helps and administrations, probably the ones least prized by the Corinthians, but clearly the ones for which they had the greatest need.

Believers' Proper Response

But earnestly desire the greater gifts. And I show you a still more excellent way. (12:31)

In light of the entire chapter up to this point, in which Paul stresses God's sovereignty in distributing the gifts and believers' responsibility to be content with them, it seems impossible to interpret verse 31, as some do, as an appeal to seek the showier gifts such as tongues. Paul's repeated point has been that we do not choose or seek the gifts. He has also made plain that the value and importance of gifts does not lie in their prominence or in their appeal to human nature.

Because *zēloō* (**earnestly desire**) usually has the negative connotation of coveting jealously or enviously (but contrast 2 Cor. 11:2), and because the Greek indicative and imperative forms are identical, the first half of the verse could be translated, "But you earnestly desire the greater gifts." That rendering seems much more appropriate to the context, both of what precedes and of what follows. It certainly is consistent with the tone of the letter and the sin of the Corinthians. Because they clearly prized the showier gifts, the seemingly **greater gifts,** it would seem foolish of Paul to command them to do what they already were eagerly doing.

The Corinthians were to stop seeking gifts, because to do so is both presumptuous and purposeless. Every believer already is perfectly gifted in the way that God planned and which best suits their ministry for Him. What they needed to seek was **a still more excellent way,** the way of contentment and harmony that he has been exhorting in chapter 12 and the way of love that he is about to **show** them in chapter 13. These things they did not have but desperately needed.

(Note: Further insight into the subjects contained in these chapters can be obtained by reading the author's book *The Charismatics* [Grand Rapids: Zondervan, 1978] and noting the sources in the bibliography.)

The Prominence of Love (13:1-3)

If I speak with the tongues of men and of angels, but do not have love, I have become a noisy gong or a clanging cymbal. And if I have the gift of prophecy, and know all mysteries and all knowledge; and if I have all faith, so as to remove mountains, but do not have love, I am nothing. And if I give all my possessions to feed the poor, and if I deliver my body to be burned, but do not have love, it profits me nothing. (13:1-3)

The Bible's simplest description of God—and therefore God's own description of Himself—is "God is love" (1 John 4:16). Love is the most blessed manifestation of the character of God. John continues, "and the one who abides in love abides in God, and God abides in him" (v. 16b). Therefore the simplest and most profound description of Christian character also is love.

It is tragic that in many churches, as in the one in ancient Corinth, the love that is basic to Christian character does not characterize the membership or the ministry. Love was missing in Corinth. Spiritual gifts were present (1:7); right doctrine for the most part was present (11:2); but love was absent. Throughout history it seems that the church has found it difficult to be loving. It is easier to be orthodox than to be loving, and easier to be active in church work than to be loving. Yet the supreme characteristic that God demands of His people is love. In opposing that love the enemy of the church makes some of his supreme efforts.

The thirteenth chapter of 1 Corinthians may be, from a literary viewpoint, the greatest passage Paul ever penned. Among many other things, it has been called the hymn of love, a lyrical interpretation of the Sermon on the Mount and the Beatitudes set to music. Studying it is somewhat like taking apart a flower; part of the beauty is lost when the components are separated. But the Spirit's primary purpose in this passage, as in all Scripture, is to edify. When each part is understood more clearly, the whole can become even more beautiful.

This chapter is a breath of fresh air, an oasis in a desert of problems. It is a positive note in the midst of almost continual reproof and correction of wrong understandings, wrong attitudes, wrong behavior, and wrong use of God's ordinances and gifts. Paul's scribe must have breathed a sigh of relief and amazement when the apostle began dictating these beautiful, Holy Spirit-inspired words.

This gem cannot properly be understood, however, apart from its setting. Its message is integral to what Paul says before and after it. The full impact and depth of its truths cannot be discovered in isolation. Much of the power, and even much of the purpose and beauty, is missed when the passage is studied and applied out of context.

Chapter 13 is the central chapter in Paul's lengthy discussion of spiritual gifts (chaps. 12-14). Chapter 12 discusses the endowment, receipt, and interrelatedness of the gifts. Chapter 14 presents the proper exercise of the gifts, especially that of languages. In this middle chapter we see the proper attitude and atmosphere, the proper motive and power, the "more excellent way" (12:31), in which God has planned for all of the gifts to operate. Love is certainly more excellent than feeling resentful and inferior because you do not have the showier and seemingly more important gifts. It is also more excellent than feeling superior and independent because you do have those gifts. And it is more excellent than trying to operate spiritual gifts in your own power, in the flesh rather than in the Spirit, and for selfish purposes rather than for God's.

The truly spiritual life is the only life in which the gifts of the Spirit can operate. The health of spiritual living is not reflected in spiritual gifts but in spiritual fruit, the first and chief of which is love (Gal. 5:22). Without the fruit of the Spirit the gifts of the Spirit cannot operate except in the flesh, in which they become counterfeit and counterproductive. Through the fruit of the Spirit God gives the motivation and power to minister the gifts of the Spirit. The fruit of the Spirit, like all of spiritual living, comes only from walking in the Spirit (Gal.5:16, 25). Having a spiritual gift does not make one spiritual. Even having the fruit of the Spirit does not make one spiritual but is simply evidence that one is spiritual. Only walking in the Spirit makes the believer spiritual. Walking by the Spirit is Paul's way of defining day-to-day obedience to the Word of God and submission to the Lord (Col. 3:16).

The Corinthian Christians were not walking in the Spirit. They were selfish, self-designing, self-willed, self-motivated, and doing everything possible to promote their own interests and welfare. Everyone was doing his own thing for his own good, with little or no regard for others. The Corinthians did not lack in any gift, but they were terribly deficient in spiritual fruit, because they were not walking in the source and power both of the gifts and of the fruit. Among the many things those believers lacked, the most significant was love. Like the church at Ephesus, they had left their first love for the Lord (Rev. 2:4). When we stray from the Source of love, it is impossible to be loving.

Agapē (**love**) is one of the rarest words in ancient Greek literature, but one of the most common in the New Testament. Unlike our English *love,* it never refers to romantic or sexual love, for which *erōs* was used, and which does not appear in the New Testament. Nor does it refer to mere sentiment, a pleasant feeling about something or someone. It does not mean close friendship or brotherly love, for which *philia* is used. Nor does *agapē* mean charity, a term the King James translators carried over from the Latin and which in English has long been associated only with giving to the needy. This chapter is itself the best definition of *agapē*.

Dr. Karl Menninger, the famous psychiatrist and founder of the Menninger Clinic, has written that "Love is the medicine for our sick old world. If people can learn to give and receive love, they will usually recover from their physical or mental illness."

The problem, however, is that few people have any idea of what true love is. Most people, including many Christians, seem to think of it only in terms of nice feelings, warm affection, romance, and desire. When we say, "I love you," we often mean, "I love me and I want you." That, of course, is the worst sort of selfishness, the very opposite of *agapē* love.

Alan Redpath tells the story of a young woman who came to her pastor desperate and despondent. She said, "There is a man who says he loves me so much he will kill himself if I don't marry him. What should I do?" "Do nothing," he replied. "That man doesn't love you; he loves himself. Such a threat isn't love; it is pure selfishness."

Self-giving love, love that demands something of us, love that is more concerned with giving than receiving, is as rare in much of the church today as it was in Corinth. The reason, of course, is that *agapē* love is so unnatural to human nature. Our world has defined love as "romantic feeling" or "attraction," which has nothing to do with true love in God's terms.

The supreme measure and example of *agapē* love is God's love. "God so loved the world, that He gave His only begotten Son" (John 3:16). Love is above all sacrificial. It is sacrifice of self for the sake of others, even for others who may care nothing at all for us and who may even hate us. It is not a feeling but a determined act of will, which always results in determined acts of self-giving. Love is the willing, joyful desire to put the welfare of others above our own. It leaves no place for pride, vanity, arrogance, self-seeking, or self-glory. It is an act of choice we are commanded to exercise even in behalf of our enemies: "I say to you, love your enemies, and pray for those who persecute you in order that you may be sons of your Father who is in heaven" (Matt. 5:44-45). If God so loved us that, even "while we were enemies, we were reconciled to God through the death of His Son" (Rom. 5:10; Eph. 2:4-7), how much more should we love those who are *our* enemies.

With the same love by which the Father sent Jesus into the world, Jesus "loved His own who were in the world" and "He loved them to the end" (John 13:1). A more literal translation would be, "He loved them to perfection," or "to completion." Jesus loved to the fullest degree and measure. He loved to the limits of love.

At the Last Supper Jesus took off His outer garments and began to wash the disciples' feet as a practical demonstration of love to those who, contrary their Master, were then thinking only of themselves. While Jesus was facing the agony of the cross, His unloving disciples argued about which of them was the greatest (Luke 22:24). They were humanly unattractive, undeserving, selfish, and insensitive. But the Savior chose to love them supremely, and taught them to love not in word but in deed. In His kind act, He showed them that love is not an emotional attraction, but selfless, humble service to meet another's need, no matter lowly the service or how undeserving the person served.

Love is so much an absolute of the Christian life that Jesus said to those disciples, "A new commandment I give to you, that you love one another, even as I have loved you, that you also love one another. By this all men will know that you are My disciples, if you have love for one another" (John 13:34-35). Again He said, "Just as the Father has loved Me, I have also loved you; abide in My love" (John 15:9). Jesus left no doubt that love—*agapē* love, self-sacrificing love—is the supreme mark of discipleship to Him. He both taught it and demonstrated it in the footwashing.

"He who loves his neighbor," Paul tells us, "has fulfilled the law. For this, 'You shall not commit adultery, You shall not murder, You shall not steal, You shall not covet,' and if there is any other commandment, it is summed up in this saying, 'You shall love your neighbor as yourself'" (Rom. 13:8-9). Lovelessness is behind all disobedience to the Lord, and love is behind all true obedience.

Everything a Christian does should be done in love (1 Cor. 16:14). Right theology is no substitute for love. Religious works are no substitute for love. Nothing substitutes for love. Christians have no excuse for not loving, "because the love of God has been poured out within our hearts through the Holy Spirit who was given to us" (Rom. 5:5). We do not have to manufacture love; we only have to share the love we have been given. We do not have to be humanly taught to love, because we ourselves "are taught by God to love one another" (1 Thess. 4:9). We are therefore told to "pursue love" (1 Cor. 14:1), to "put on love" (Col. 3:14), to "increase and abound in love" (1 Thess. 3:12; Phil. 1:9), to be sincere in love (2 Cor. 8:8), to be unified in love (Phil. 2:2), to be "fervent" in love (1 Pet. 4:8), and to "stimulate one another to love" (Heb. 10:24).

Those teachings can be summarized in five keys to loving: (1) love is commanded; (2) love is already possessed by Christians; (3) love is the norm of Christian living; (4) love is the work of the Spirit; and (5) love must be practiced to be genuine.

ELOQUENCE WITHOUT LOVE IS NOTHING

If I speak with the tongues of men and of angels, but do not have love, I have become a noisy gong or a clanging cymbal. (13:1)

In verses 1-2 Paul uses considerable hyperbole. To make his point he exaggerates to the limits of imagination. Using various examples, he says, "If somehow I were able to do or to be . . . to the absolute extreme, but did not have love, I would be absolutely nothing."

In the spirit of the love about which he is talking, Paul changes to the first person. He wanted to make it clear that what he said applied as fully to himself as to anyone in Corinth.

First Paul imagines himself able to speak with the greatest possible eloquence, **with the tongues of men and of angels.** Although *glōssa* can mean the physical organ of speech, it can also mean language—just as it does when we speak of a person's "mother tongue." **Tongues,** therefore is a legitimate translation, but I believe that *languages* is a more helpful and less confusing rendering.

In the context there is no doubt that Paul here includes the gift of speaking in languages (see 12:10, 28; 14:4-6, 13-14; etc.). That is the gift the Corinthians prized so highly and abused so greatly, and it will be discussed in detail in the exposition of chapter 14.

Paul's basic point in 13:1, however, is to convey the idea of being able to speak all sorts of languages with great fluency and eloquence, far above the greatest linguist or orator. That the apostle is speaking in general and hypothetical terms is clear from the expression **tongues . . . of angels.** There is no biblical teaching of a unique or special angelic language or dialect. In the countless records of their speaking to men in Scripture, they always speak in the language of the person being addressed. There is no indication that they have a heavenly language of their own that men could learn. Paul simply is saying that, were he to have the ability to speak with the skill and eloquence of the greatest men, even with angelic eloquence, he would only **become a noisy gong or a clanging cymbal** if he did **not have love.** The greatest truths spoken in the greatest way fall short if they are not spoken in love. Apart from love, even one who speaks the truth with supernatural eloquence becomes so much noise.

The gift of language is especially meaningless without love. Paul chooses this as his illustration of lovelessness because it was a sought-after experience that made the people proud. One of the results of the Corinthians' trying to use that gift in their own power and for their own selfish and proud ends was that it could not be ministered in love. Because they did not walk in the Spirit, they did not have the fruit of the Spirit and could not properly minister the gifts of the Spirit. Because the most important fruit was missing from what they thought was the most important gift, their exercising the gift became nothing more than babble.

In New Testament times, rites honoring the pagan deities Cybele, Bacchus, and Dionysus included speaking in ecstatic noises that were accompanied by smashing gongs, clanging cymbals, and blaring trumpets. Paul's hearers clearly got his point: unless it is done in love, ministering the gift of languages, or speaking in any other human or angelic way, amounts to no more than those pagan rituals. It is only meaningless jibberish in a Christian guise.

PROPHECY, KNOWLEDGE, AND FAITH WITHOUT LOVE ARE NOTHING

And if I have the gift of prophecy, and know all mysteries and all knowledge; and if I have all faith, so as to remove mountains, but do not have love, I am nothing. (13:2)

PROPHECY WITHOUT LOVE

In the beginning of the next chapter Paul speaks of prophecy as the greatest of the spiritual gifts because the prophet proclaims God's truth to people so they can know and understand it (14:1-5). The apostle was himself a prophet (Acts 13:1) and had the highest regard both for the office of prophet and the gift of prophecy.

Continuing his hyperbole, however, Paul says that even the great **gift of prophecy** must be ministered in love. The most gifted man of God is not exempt from ministering in love. If anything, he is the *most* obligated to minister in love. "From everyone who has been given much shall much be required" (Luke 12:48). Of all persons, the prophet should speak the truth in love (Eph. 4:15).

Balaam was a prophet of God. He knew the true God and he knew God's truth, but he had no love for God's people. With little hesitation he agreed to curse the Israelites in return for a generous payment by Balak, king of Moab. Because God could not convince his prophet not to do that terrible thing, He sent an angel to stop the prophet's donkey (Num. 22:16-34). Several other times Balaam would have cursed Israel had he not been prevented by God. But what the prophet failed to do through cursing Israel he accomplished by misleading them. Because he led Israel into idolatry and immorality, Balaam was put to death (Num. 31:8, 16). The prophet knew God's Word, spoke God's Word, and feared God in a self-protecting way, but he had no love for God and no love for God's people.

Some years ago a young Sunday school teacher came to me and said, "I thought I really loved the girls in my class. I prepared my lesson carefully and tried to make everyone feel a part of the class. But I have never made any personal sacrifice for those girls." She sensed that, with all her study of the Bible, her careful preparation of lessons, and her nice feelings about the class members, she still lacked the key ingredient of *agapē* love, love that is self-giving and self-sacrificing.

The power behind what we say and what we do is our motive. If our motive is self-interest, praise, promotion, or advantage of any sort, our influence for the Lord will be undercut to that extent—no matter how orthodox, persuasive, and relevant our words are or how helpful our service seems superficially to be. Without the motivation of love, in God's sight we are only causing a lot of commotion.

Jeremiah's ministry was in stark contrast to Balaam's. He was the weeping prophet, not because of his own problems, which were great, but because of the wickedness of his people, because of their refusal to turn to the Lord, and because of the punishment he had to prophesy against them. He wept over them much as Jesus later wept over Jerusalem (Luke 19:41-44). Early in his ministry Jeremiah was so moved by the spiritual plight of his people that he cried out, "My sorrow is beyond healing, my heart is faint within me! . . . For the brokenness of the daughter of my people I am broken; I mourn, dismay has taken hold of me. . . . Oh, that my head were waters, and my eyes a fountain of tears, that I might weep day and night for the slain of the daughter of my people!" (Jer. 8:18, 21; 9:1). Jeremiah was a prophet with a broken heart, a loving heart, a spiritual heart.

Paul also often ministered with tears, frequently for fellow Jews who would not accept Jesus Christ. It was they who caused him most of his trials, but it was their turning against the gospel, not their turning against him, that caused him to minister "with tears" (Acts 20:19). In Romans he gives the touching testimony, "I am telling the truth in Christ, I am not lying, my conscience bearing me witness in the Holy Spirit, that I have great sorrow and unceasing grief in my heart. For I could wish that I myself were accursed, separated from Christ for the sake of my brethren, my kinsmen according to the flesh" (9:1-3). Paul ministered with great power in large measure because he ministered with great love. To proclaim the truth of God without love is not simply to be less than you should be, it is to be *nothing*.

KNOWLEDGE WITHOUT LOVE

Just as prophecy without love is nothing, so is the understanding of **all mysteries and all knowledge.** Paul uses that comprehensive phrase to picture ultimate human understanding. **Mysteries** may represent divine spiritual understanding and **knowledge** may represent factual human understanding. In Scripture the term *mystery* always signifies divine truth that God has hidden from men at some time. Most often it refers to truths hidden to Old Testament saints that have been revealed in the New Testament (cf. Eph. 3:3-5). If he could perfectly understand all unrevealed divine mysteries, along with all the mysteries that are revealed, Paul insists that he could still be **nothing.** That spiritual understanding would count for nothing without the supreme spiritual fruit of love. This indicates the great importance of love; without it, we can know as God knows and still be nothing.

Adding **all knowledge** would not help. One could fathom all the observable, knowable facts of the created universe, be virtually omniscient, and he would still be **nothing** without love. In other words, if somehow he could comprehend all of the Creator and all of the creation, he would be zero without love.

If all of that would amount to nothing without love, how much less do our very limited intellectual accomplishments, including biblical and theological knowledge and insights, amount to without love? They are *less* than nothing. That sort of knowledge without love is worse than mere ignorance. It produces spiritual snobbery, pride, and arrogance. It is Pharisaic and ugly. Spiritual knowledge is good, beautiful, and fruitful in the Lord's work when it is held in humility and ministered in love. But it is ugly and unproductive when love is missing. Mere knowledge, even of God's truths, "makes arrogant"; love is the absolutely essential ingredient for edification (1 Cor. 8:1).

Paul did not depreciate knowledge, especially knowledge of God's Word. To the Philippians he wrote, "And this I pray, that your love may abound still more and more in real knowledge and all discernment" (1:9). We cannot be edified by or obey what we do not know. But we can know and not obey and not be strengthened. Only love brings "real knowledge and all discernment." We can know and not be edified. Love is the divine edifier.

FAITH WITHOUT LOVE

If Paul did not depreciate knowledge, even less did he depreciate faith. No one preached the necessity for faith, especially saving faith, more strongly than he. But he is not speaking here of saving faith but of the **faith** of confidence and expectancy in the Lord. He is addressing believers, who already have saving faith. **All faith, so as to remove mountains** refers to trusting God to do mighty things in behalf of His children. It especially refers to believers who have the gift of faith. Even with this wonderful gift from God—of making the impossible possible—Paul says a Christian is **nothing** if he does not have love.

It is not by coincidence that the apostle uses the same figure used on one occasion by Jesus. After His disciples failed to heal the demon-possessed boy, Jesus told them, "Truly I say to you, if you have faith as a mustard seed, you shall say to this mountain, 'Move from here to there,' and it shall move" (Matt. 17:20). Jesus was speaking in hyperbole just as Paul is in 1 Corinthians 13:1-3. The Lord's point to His disciples was that, by trusting Him completely, nothing in their ministry would "be impossible." Paul's point is that, even if a person had that great degree of prayerful trust in the Lord, but was unloving, he would be **nothing**.

Jonah had great faith. It was because of his great belief in the effectiveness of God's Word that he resisted preaching to Nineveh. He was not afraid of failure but of success. He had great faith in the power of God's Word. His problem was that he did not want the wicked Ninevites to be saved. He had no love for them, not even after they repented. He did not want them saved and was resentful of the Lord's saving them. As the direct result of the prophet's preaching, everyone in the city from the king down repented. Even the animals were covered with sackcloth as a symbol of repentance. God miraculously spared Nineveh, just as Jonah knew he would. Then we read of one of the strangest and most hardhearted prayers in all Scripture: "But it greatly displeased Jonah, and he became angry. And he prayed to the Lord and said, 'Please Lord, was not this what I said while I was still in my own country? Therefore, in order to forestall this I fled to Tarshish, for I knew that Thou art a gracious and compassionate God, slow to anger and abundant in lovingkindness, and one who relents concerning calamity. Therefore now, O Lord, please take my life from me, for death is better to me than life'" (Jonah 4:1-3). Everything Jonah acknowledged the Lord to be, the prophet himself was not and did not want to be. A more loveless man of God is hard to imagine. His faith told him that a great success would come in Nineveh, but the prophet was a great failure. The preaching wrought a great miracle, as he believed it would, but the preacher was a **nothing**.

Benevolence and Martyrdom Without Love Are Nothing

And if I give all my possessions to feed the poor, and if I deliver my body to be burned, but do not have love, it profits me nothing. (13:3)

Agapē love is always self-sacrificing, but self-sacrifice does not necessarily come from love. Throughout the history of the church certain groups and movements have believed that self-denial, self-humiliation, and even self-affliction in themselves bring spiritual merit. Many cults and pagan religions place great emphasis on the giving up of possessions, on sacrifice of various sorts, and on religious acts of supposed self-effacement, self-deprivation, self-affliction, and monasticism. Even for Christians, however, such things are worse than worthless without love. Without love, in fact, they are anything but selfless. The real focus of such practices is not God nor others, but self—either in the form of legalistic fear of not doing those things or for the praise and imagined blessing for doing them. The motive is self, and is neither spiritual nor loving.

BENEVOLENCE WITHOUT LOVE

The term for **give** means to dole out in small quantities, and signifies a long-term, systematic program of giving away everything one possesses. Such an ultimate act of benevolence, giving **all** one's **possessions to feed the poor,** would not be a spiritual deed if not done out of genuine love, no matter how great the sacrifice or how many people were fed. The rabbis taught that people did not ever need to give more than twenty percent, so Paul's illustration suggested unheard of generosity. Even so, the people who received such generosity would be benefited by full stomachs, but the giver would be benefited by **nothing.** Both his bank account and his spiritual account would be left empty. Giving from legalistic obligation, from desire for recognition and praise, or as a way to salve a guilty conscience is worthless. Only love qualifies giving to be spiritual.

Jesus' command to give secretly (Matt. 6:3) helps protect us from being tempted by some of those false, unspiritual, and unloving motives. Benevolence with love is of great worth; benevolence without love is nothing.

MARTYRDOM WITHOUT LOVE

Finally, Paul says, **if I deliver my body to be burned, but do not have love, it profits me nothing.** Some interpreters believe that the apostle was referring to becoming a slave, the mark of which was a brand made with a hot iron. But in keeping with the extremes he has been using in these verses, it is best to assume he was referring to being burned alive. Execution by burning at the stake, a fate suffered by many Christian martyrs, was not begun in the Roman empire until some years later. Yet that seems to be the form of suffering to which Paul refers. Whether or not such execution was common at that time, it represented a horrible, agonizing death.

When persecution of the early church became intense, some believers actually sought martyrdom as a way of becoming famous or of gaining special heavenly credit. But when sacrifice is motivated by self-interest and pride it loses its spiritual value. Even accepting agonizing death for the faith **profits . . . nothing** if it is done without true divine love. No matter how much a person may suffer because of his Christian service and testimony, he has no spiritual gain if his witness and work are not ministered in love.

The loveless person produces nothing, is nothing, and gains nothing.

The Qualities of Love—part 1 (13:4-5)

34

Love is patient, love is kind, and is not jealous; love does not brag and is not arrogant, does not act unbecomingly; it does not seek its own, is not provoked, does not take into account a wrong suffered. (13:4-5)

The previous passage (vv. 1-3) focuses on the emptiness produced when love is absent. In verses 4-5 we find the most comprehensive biblical description of the fullness of love. Paul shines love through a prism and we see 15 of its colors and hues, the spectrum of love. Each ray gives a facet, a property, of *agapē* love. Unlike most English translations, which include several adjectives, the Greek forms of all those properties are verbs. They do not focus on what love is so much as on what love does and does not do. *Agapē* love is active, not abstract or passive. It does not simply feel patient, it practices patience. It does not simply have kind feelings, it does kind things. It does not simply recognize the truth, it rejoices in the truth. Love is fully love only when it acts (cf. 1 John 3:18).

The purpose of Paul's prism is not to give a technical analysis of love, but to break it down into smaller parts so that we may more easily understand and apply its full, rich meaning. As with all of God's Word, we cannot truly begin to understand love until we begin to apply it in our lives. Paul's primary purpose here is not simply to instruct the Corinthians but to change their living habits. He wanted them carefully and honestly to measure their lives against those characteristics of love.

To change the metaphor, Paul is painting a portrait of love, and Jesus Christ is sitting for the portrait. He lived out in perfection all of these virtues of love. This beautiful picture of love is a portrait of Him.

LOVE IS PATIENT

Love practices being **patient** or long-suffering, literally, "long-tempered" (*makrothumeō*). The word is common in the New Testament and is used almost exclusively of being patient with people, rather than with circumstances or events. Love's patience is the ability to be inconvenienced or taken advantage of by a person over and over again and yet not be upset or angry. Chrysostom, the early church Father, said, "It is a word which is used of the man who is wronged and who has it easily in his power to avenge himself but will never do it." Patience never retaliates.

Like *agapē* love itself, the patience spoken of in the New Testament was a virtue only among Christians. In the Greek world self-sacrificing love and nonavenging patience were considered weaknesses, unworthy of the noble man or woman. Aristotle, for example, taught that the great Greek virtue was refusal to tolerate insult or injury and to strike back in retaliation for the slightest offense. Vengeance was a virtue. The world has always tended to make heroes of those who fight back, who stand up for their welfare and rights above all else.

But love, God's love, is the very opposite. Its primary concern is for the welfare of others, not itself, and it is much more willing to be taken advantage of than to take advantage, much less to avenge. Love does not retaliate. The Christian who acts like Christ never takes revenge for being hurt or insulted or abused. He refuses to "pay back evil for evil" (Rom. 12:17), but if he is slapped on the right cheek, he will turn the left (Matt. 5:39).

Paul said that patience was a characteristic of his own heart (2 Cor. 6:6) and should characterize every Christian (Eph. 4:2). Stephen's last words were ones of patient forgiveness: "Lord, do not hold this sin against them!" (Acts 7:60). As he lay dying under the painful, crushing blows of the stones, his concern was for his murderers rather than for himself. He was long-tempered, patient to the absolute extreme.

The supreme example of patience, of course, is God Himself. It is God's patient love that prevents the world from being destroyed. It is His patience and long-suffering that allows time for men to be saved (2 Pet. 3:9). As He was dying on the cross, rejected by those He had come to save, Jesus prayed, "Father, forgive them; for they do not know what they are doing" (Luke 23:34).

Robert Ingersoll, the well-known atheist of the last century, often would stop in the middle of his lectures against God and say, "I'll give God five minutes to strike me dead for the things I've said." He then used the fact that he was not struck dead as proof that God did not exist. Theodore Parker said of Ingersoll's claim, "And did the gentleman think he could exhaust the patience of the eternal God in five minutes?"

Since Adam and Eve first disobeyed Him, God has been continually wronged and rejected by those He made in His own image. He was rejected and scorned by His chosen people, through whom he gave the revelation of His Word, "the oracles of God" (Rom. 3:2). Yet through the thousands of years, the eternal God has been eternally long-suffering. If the holy Creator is so infinitely patient with His rebellious creatures, how much more should His unholy creatures be patient with each other?

One of Abraham Lincoln's earliest political enemies was Edwin M. Stanton. He called Lincoln a "low cunning clown" and "the original gorilla." "It was ridiculous for people to go to Africa to see a gorilla," he would say, "when they could find one easily in Springfield, Illinois." Lincoln never responded to the slander, but when, as president, he needed a secretary of war, he chose Stanton. When his incredulous friends asked why, Lincoln replied, "Because he is the best man." Years later, as the slain president's body lay in state, Stanton looked into the coffin and said through his tears, "There lies the greatest ruler of men the world has ever seen." His animosity was finally broken by Lincoln's long-suffering, nonretaliatory spirit. Patient love won out.

Love Is Kind

Just as patience will take anything from others, kindness will give anything to others, even to its enemies. Being **kind** is the counterpart of being **patient**. To be kind (*chrēsteuomai*) means to be useful, serving, and gracious. It is active goodwill. It not only feels generous, it is generous. It not only desires others' welfare, but works for it. When Jesus commanded His disciples, including us, to love their enemies, He did not simply mean to feel kindly about them but to be kind to them. "If anyone wants to sue you, and take your shirt, let him have your coat also. And whoever shall force you to go one mile, go with him two" (Matt. 5:40-41). The hard environment of an evil world gives love almost unlimited opportunity to exercise that sort of kindness.

Again God is the supreme model. "Do you think lightly of the riches of His kindness and forbearance and patience, not knowing that the kindness of God leads you to repentance?" (Rom. 2:4), Paul reminds us. To Titus he wrote, "But when the kindness of God our Savior and His love for mankind appeared, He saved us, not on the basis of deeds which we have done in righteousness, but according to His mercy, by the washing of regeneration and renewing by the Holy Spirit, whom He poured out upon us richly through Jesus Christ our Savior" (Titus 3:4-6). Peter tells us that we should "long for the pure milk of the word" and thereby "grow in respect to salvation," because we "have tasted the kindness of the Lord" (1 Pet. 2:2-3). To His disciples Jesus says, "For My yoke is easy, and My load is light" (Matt. 11:30). The word He used for "easy" is the one translated **kind** in 1 Cor. 13:4. In His love for those who belong to Him, Jesus makes His yoke "kind," or mild. He makes sure that what His people are called to bear for Him is bearable (see 1 Cor. 10:13).

The first test of Christian kindness, and the test of every aspect of love, is the home. The Christian husband who acts like a Christian is kind to his wife and children. Christian brothers and sisters are kind to each other and to their parents. They have more than kind feelings toward each other; they do kind, helpful things for each other—to the point of loving self-sacrifice, when necessary.

For the Corinthians, kindness meant giving up their selfish, jealous, spiteful, and proud attitudes and adopting the spirit of loving-kindness. Among other things, it would allow their spiritual gifts to be truly and effectively ministered in the Spirit, rather than superficially and unproductively counterfeited in the flesh.

Love Is Not Jealous

Here is the first of eight negative descriptions of love. Love **is not jealous.** Love and jealousy are mutually exclusive. Where one is, the other cannot be. Shakespeare called jealousy the "green sickness." It also has been called "the enemy of honor" and "the sorrow of fools." Jesus referred to it as "an evil eye" (Matt. 20:15, KJV).

Jealousy, or envy, has two forms. One form says, "I want what someone else has." If they have a better car than we do, we want it. If they are praised for something they do, we want the same or more for ourselves. That sort of jealousy is bad enough. A worse kind says, "I wish they didn't have what they have" (see Matt. 20:1-16). The second sort of jealousy is more than selfish; it is desiring evil for someone else. It is jealousy on the deepest, most corrupt, and destructive level. That is the jealousy Solomon uncovered in the woman who pretended to be a child's mother. When her own infant son died, she secretly exchanged him for the baby of a friend who was staying with her. The true mother discovered what had happened and, when their dispute was taken before the king, he ordered the baby to be cut in half, a half to be given to each woman. The true mother pleaded for the baby to be spared, even if it meant losing possession of him. The false mother, however, would rather have had the baby killed than for the true mother to have him (1 Kings 3:16-27).

One of the hardest battles a Christian must fight is against jealousy. There is always someone who is a little better or who is potentially a little better than you are. We all face the temptation to jealousy when someone else does something better than we do. The first reaction of the flesh is to wish that person ill.

The root meaning of *zēloō* ("to be **jealous**") is "to have a strong desire," and is the term from which we get *zeal*. It is used both favorably and unfavorably in Scripture. In 1 Corinthians 13:4 the meaning is clearly unfavorable, which is why 12:31, part of the immediate context, should be taken as a *statement of fact* ("you are now earnestly desiring the greater, or showier, gifts") and not a *command to seek* "the greater gifts." The Greek word there translated "earnestly desire" is the same as that translated here **is . . . jealous.** One of the basic principles of hermeneutics is that identical terms appearing in the same context should be translated identically.

When love sees someone who is popular, successful, beautiful, or talented, it is glad for them and never jealous or envious. While Paul was imprisoned, probably in Rome, some of the younger preachers who then served where he had ministered were trying to outdo the apostle out of envy. They were so jealous of Paul's reputation and accomplishments that, with their criticism, they intended to cause him additional "distress" while he suffered in prison. But Paul did not resent their freedom, their success, or even their jealousy. Though he did not condone their sin, he would not return envy for envy, but was simply glad that the gospel was being preached, whatever the motives (Phil. 1:15-17). He knew the message was more powerful than the messenger, and that it could transcend weak and jealous preachers in order to accomplish God's purpose.

Jealousy is not a moderate or harmless sin. It was Eve's jealousy of God, sparked by her pride, to which Satan successfully appealed. She wanted to be like God, to have what He has and to know what He knows. Jealousy was an integral part of that first great sin, from which all other sin has descended. The next sin mentioned in Genesis is murder, caused by Cain's jealousy of Abel. Joseph's brothers sold him into slavery because of jealousy. Daniel was thrown into the lion's den because of the jealousy of his fellow officials in Babylon. Jealousy caused the elder brother to resent the father's attention to the prodigal son. And there are many more biblical illustrations of the same kind.

"Wrath is fierce and anger is a flood, but who can stand before jealousy?" (Prov. 27:4). In its extreme, jealousy has a viciousness shared by no other sin. "If you have bitter jealousy and selfish ambition in your heart," says James, "do not be arrogant and so lie against the truth. This wisdom is not that which comes down from above, but is earthly, natural, demonic. For where jealousy and selfish ambition exist, there is disorder and every evil thing" (James 3:14-16). Selfish ambition, which is fueled by jealousy, is often clever and successful. But its "wisdom" is demonic and its success is destructive.

In stark contrast to the many accounts of jealousy in Scripture is the story of Jonathan's love for David. David not only was a greater and more popular warrior than Jonathan but was a threat to the throne that Jonathan normally would have inherited. Yet we are told of nothing but Jonathan's great respect and love for his friend David, for whom he would willingly have sacrificed not only the throne but his life. "He loved him [David] as he loved his own life" (1 Sam. 20:17). Jonathan's father, Saul, lost his throne and his blessing because of his jealousy, primarily of David. Jonathan willingly forsook the throne and received a greater blessing, because he would have nothing of jealousy.

Eliezer of Damascus was the heir to Abram's estate, because Abram had no son (Gen. 15:2). When Isaac was born, however, and Eliezer lost the privileged inheritance, his love for Abram and Isaac never wavered (see Gen. 24). A loving person is never jealous. He is glad for the success of others, even if their success works against his own.

Love Does Not Brag

When the loving person is himself successful he does not boast of it. He **does not brag**. *Perpereuomai* ("to brag") is used nowhere else in the New Testament and means to talk conceitedly. Love does not parade its accomplishments. Bragging is the other side of jealousy. Jealousy is wanting what someone else has. Bragging is trying to make others jealous of what we have. Jealousy puts others down; bragging builds us up. It is ironic that, as much as most of us dislike bragging in others, we are so inclined to brag ourselves.

The Corinthian believers were spiritual show-offs, constantly vying for public attention. They clamored for the most prestigious offices and the most glamorous gifts. They all wanted to talk at once, especially when speaking esctatically. Most of their tongues-speaing was counterfeit, but their bragging about it was genuine. They cared nothing for harmony, order, fellowship, edification, or anything else worthwhile. They cared only for flaunting themselves. "What is the outcome then, brethren? When you assemble, each one has a psalm, has a teaching, has a revelation, has a tongue, has an interpretation" (1 Cor. 14:26). Each did his own thing as prominently as possible, in total disregard for what others were doing.

Charles Trumbull once vowed: "God, if you will give me the strength, every time I have the opportunity to introduce the topic of conversation it will always be Jesus Christ." He had only one subject that was truly worth talking about. If Christ is first in our thoughts, we cannot possibly brag.

C. S. Lewis called bragging "the utmost evil." It is the epitome of pride, which is the root sin of all sins. Bragging puts ourselves first. Everyone else, including God, must therefore be of less importance to us. It is impossible to build ourselves up without putting others down. When we brag, we can be "up" only if others are "down."

Jesus was God incarnate, yet never exalted Himself in any way. "Although He existed in the form of God, [He] did not regard equality with God a thing to be grasped, but emptied Himself, taking the form of a bond-servant, and . . . being found in appearance as a man, He humbled Himself" (Phil. 2:6-8). Jesus, who had everything to boast of, never boasted. In total contrast, we who have nothing to boast of are prone to boast. Only the love that comes from Jesus Christ can save us from flaunting our knowledge, our abilities, our gifts, or our accomplishments, real or imagined.

Love Is Not Arrogant

The Corinthian believers thought they had arrived at perfection. Paul already had warned them "not to exceed what is written, in order that no one of you might become arrogant in behalf of one against the other. For who regards you as superior? And what do you have that you did not receive? But if you did receive it, why do you boast as if you had not received it? You are already filled," he continues sarcastically, "you have already become rich, you have become kings without us; and I would indeed that you had become kings so that we also might reign with you" (1 Cor. 4:6-8). Becoming still more sarcastic, he says, "We [the apostles] are fools for Christ's sake, but you are prudent in Christ; we are weak, but you are strong; you are distinguished, but we are without honor" (v. 10). A few verses later the apostle is more direct: "Now some of you have become arrogant, as though I were not coming to you" (v. 18).

Everything good that the Corinthians had came from the Lord, and they therefore had no reason to boast and be arrogant. Yet they were puffed up and conceited about their knowledge of doctrine, their spiritual gifts, and the famous teachers they had had. They were so jaded in their pride that they even boasted about their carnality, worldliness, idolatry, and immorality, including incest, which was not even practiced by pagans (5:1). They were arrogant rather than repentant; they bragged rather than mourned (v. 2). Love, by contrast, **is not arrogant.**

William Carey, often referred to as the father of modern missions, was a brilliant linguist, responsible for translating parts of the Bible into no fewer than 34 different languages and dialects. He had been raised in a simple home in England and in his early manhood worked as a cobbler. In India he often was ridiculed for his "low" birth and former occupation. At a dinner party one evening a snob said, "I understand, Mister Carey, that you once worked as a shoemaker." "Oh no, your lordship," Carey replied, "I was not a shoemaker, only a shoe repairman."

When Jesus began to preach He soon overshadowed the ministry of John the Baptist. Yet John spoke of Him as "He who comes after me, the thong of whose sandal I am not worthy to untie" (John 1:27). When John's disciples later became jealous of Jesus' popularity, John rebuked them, saying, "He must increase, but I must decrease" (3:30).

Like wisdom, love says, "Pride and arrogance and the evil way, and the perverted mouth, I hate" (Prov. 8:13). Other proverbs remind us that "when pride comes, then comes dishonor" (11:2), that "through presumption comes nothing but strife" (13:10), and that "pride goes before destruction, and a haughty spirit before stumbling" (16:18; cf. 29:23).

Pride and arrogance breed contention, with which the Corinthian church was filled. In such things love has no part. Arrogance is big-headed; love is big-hearted.

LOVE DOES NOT ACT UNBECOMINGLY

Love **does not act unbecomingly.** The principle here has to do with poor manners, with acting rudely. It is not as serious a fault as bragging or arrogance, but it stems from the same lovelessness. It does not care enough for those it is around to act becomingly or politely. It cares nothing for their feelings or sensitivities. The loveless person is careless, overbearing, and often crude.

The Corinthian Christians were models of unbecoming behavior. Acting unseemly was almost their trademark. Nearly everything they did was rude and unloving. Even when they came together to celebrate the Lord's Supper they were self-centered and offensive. "Each one takes his own supper first; and one is hungry and another is drunk" (1 Cor. 11:21). During worship services each one tried to outdo the other in speaking in tongues. Everyone talked at once and tried to be the most dramatic and prominent. The church did everything improperly and in disorder, the opposite of what Paul had taught them and now advised them against (14:40).

On one occasion Jesus was dining in the home of a Pharisee named Simon. During the meal a prostitute came and washed Jesus' feet with her tears, dried them with her hair, and then anointed them with expensive perfume. Simon, embarrassed and offended, thought to himself, "If this man were a prophet He would know who and what sort of person this woman is who is touching Him, that she is a sinner." Jesus then told the parable of the moneylender who forgave two debtors, one for 500 denarii and the other for 50. He asked Simon which debtor would be more grateful, to which the Pharisee answered,

"I suppose the one whom he forgave more." . . . Turning toward the woman, He said to Simon, "Do you see this woman? I entered your house; you gave Me no water for My feet, but she has wet My feet with her tears, and wiped them with her hair. You gave Me no kiss; but she, since the time I came in, has not ceased to kiss My feet. You did not anoint My head with oil, but she anointed My feet with perfume. For this reason I say to you, her sins, which are many, have been forgiven, for she loved much; but he who is forgiven little, loves little." (Luke 7:36-47)

The primary example of love in that story is not the woman's, sincere and beautiful as it was. It is Jesus' love that is the most remarkable, and that is in such contrast to Simon's lovelessness. By His loving acceptance of the woman's loving act, as well as by the parable, Jesus showed Simon that it was not her actions or His response that was improper, but Simon's attitude. What the woman did and what Jesus did had everything to do with love. What Simon did had nothing to do with love.

William Barclay translates our text as, "Love does not behave gracelessly." Love is gracious. Graciousness should begin with fellow believers, but it should not end there. Many Christians have forfeited the opportunity for witnessing by rudeness to an unbeliever who offends them by a habit the Christian considers improper. As with Simon, sometimes our attitude and behavior in the name of righteousness are more improper, and less righteous, than some of the things we criticize.

Love is much more than being gracious and considerate, but it is never less. To the extent that our living is ungracious and inconsiderate it is also unloving and un-Christian. Self-righteous rudeness by Christians can turn people away from Christ before they have a chance to hear the gospel. The messenger can become a barrier to the message. If people do not see the "gentleness of Christ" (2 Cor. 10:1) clearly in us, they are less likely to see Him clearly in the gospel we preach.

Love Does Not Seek Its Own

I understand that the inscription on a tombstone in a small English village reads,

> Here lies a miser who lived for himself,
>   and cared for nothing but gathering wealth.
> Now where he is or how he fares,
>   nobody knows and nobody cares.

In contrast, a plain tombstone in the courtyard at St. Paul's Cathedral in London reads, "Sacred to the memory of General Charles George Gordon, who at all times and everywhere gave his strength to the weak, his substance to the poor, his sympathy to the suffering, his heart to God."

Love **does not seek its own.** Here is probably the key to everything. The root evil of fallen human nature is in wanting to have its own way. R. C. H. Lenski, the well-known Bible commentator, has said, "Cure selfishness and you have just replanted the garden of Eden." Adam and Eve rejected God's way so that they could have their own. Self replaced God. That is the opposite of righteousness and the opposite of love. Love is not preoccupied with its own things but with the interests of others (Phil.2:4).

Again, the Corinthian believers were models of what loving Christians should *not* be. They were selfish in the extreme. They did not share their food at love feasts, they protected their rights to the point of suing fellow believers in pagan law courts, and they wanted what they thought were the "best" spiritual gifts for themselves. Instead of using spiritual gifts for the benefit of others, they tried to use them to their own advantage. Paul therefore tells them, "Since you are zealous of spiritual gifts, seek to abound for the edification of the church" (14:12). They did not use their gifts to build up the church but to try to build up themselves.

The story is told of a chauffeur who drove up to a cemetery and asked the minister who served as caretaker to come to the car, because his employer was too ill to walk. Waiting in the car was a frail old lady with sunken eyes that showed years of hurt and anguish. She introduced herself and said she had been sending five dollars to the cemetery for the past several years to be used for flowers for her husband's grave. "I have come in person today," she said, "because the doctors have given me only a few weeks to live and I wanted to see the grave for one last time." The minister replied, "You know, I am sorry you have been sending money for those flowers." Taken aback, she said, "What do you mean?" "Well, I happen to be a part of a visiting society that visits patients in hospitals and mental institutions. They dearly love flowers. They can see them and smell them. Flowers are therapy for them, because they are living people." Saying nothing, she motioned the chauffeur to leave. Some months later the minister was surprised to see the same car drive up, but with the woman herself at the wheel. She said, "At first I resented what you said to me that day when I came here for a last visit. But as I thought about it, I decided you were right. Now I personally take flowers to the hospitals. It *does* make the patients happy and it makes me happy, too. The doctors can't figure out what made me well, but I know. I now have someone else to live for."

As always, Jesus is our perfect model. He "did not come to be served, but to serve" (Matt. 20:28). The Son of God lived His life for others. God incarnate was love incarnate. He was the perfect incarnation of self-giving love. He never sought His own welfare, but always the welfare of others.

LOVE IS NOT PROVOKED

The Greek *paroxunō*, here translated **provoked,** means to arouse to anger and is the origin of the English *paroxysm*, a convulsion or sudden outburst of emotion or action. Love guards against being irritated, upset, or angered by things said or done against it. It **is not provoked.**

The apostle does not rule out righteous indignation. Love cannot "rejoice in unrighteousness" (1 Cor. 13:6). To be angered by the mistreatment of the unfortunate or by the maligning and contradiction of God's Word is righteous indignation. But when it is truly righteous, indignation will never be provoked by something done against us personally. When Jesus cleansed the Temple, He was angered at the profaning of His Father's house of worship (Matt. 21:11-12). But on the many occasions when He was personally vilified or abused, He did not once become angry or defensive.

Like his Lord, Paul was only angered by the things that anger God. He responded strongly against such things as heresy, immorality, and misuse of spiritual gifts. But he did not become angry at those who beat him, jailed him, or lied about him (see Acts 23:1-5).

The being provoked that Paul is talking about here has to do with things done against us or that are personally offensive. Love does not get angry at others when they say or do something that displeases us or when they prevent us from having our own way (cf. 1 Pet. 2:21-24). Love never reacts in self-defense or retaliation. Being **provoked** is the other side of seeking one's own way. The person who is intent on having his own way is easily provoked, easily angered.

The great colonial preacher and theologian Jonathan Edwards had a daughter with an uncontrollable temper. When a young man fell in love with her and asked her father for her hand in marriage, Dr. Edwards replied, "You can't have her." "But I love her and she loves me," he protested. "It doesn't matter," the father insisted. Asked why, he said, "Because she is not worthy of you." "But she is a Christian isn't she?" "Yes," said Edwards, "but the grace of God can live with some people with whom no one else could ever live."

Surely the number one reason both for mental and physical illness in our society today is the overwhelming preoccupation with our rights and the consequent lovelessness. When everyone is fighting for his own rights, no one can really succeed or be happy. Everyone grabs, no one gives, and everyone loses—even when one gets what he wants. Lovelessness can never win in any meaningful or lasting way. It always costs more than it gains.

We get angry when another person gains a privilege or recognition we want for ourselves, because it is our "right." But to put our rights before our duty and before loving concern for others comes from self-centeredness and lovelessness. The loving person is more concerned about doing what he should and helping where he can than in having what he thinks are his rights and his due. Love considers nothing its right and everything its obligation.

Telling our wives or husbands that we love them is not convincing if we continually get upset and angry at what they say and do. Telling our children that we love them is not convincing if we often yell at them for doing things that irritate us and interfere with our own plans. It does no good to protest, "I lose my temper a lot, but it's all over in a few minutes." So is a nuclear bomb. A great deal of damage can be done in a very short time. Temper is always destructive, and even small temper "bombs" can leave much hurt and damage, especially when they explode on a regular basis. Lovelessness is the cause of temper, and love is the only cure.

Love that takes a person outside of himself and centers his attention on the well-being of others is the only cure for self-centeredness.

LOVE DOES NOT TAKE INTO ACCOUNT A WRONG SUFFERED

Logizomai (**take into account**) is a bookkeeping term that means to calculate or reckon, as when figuring an entry in a ledger. The purpose of the entry is to make a permanent record that can be consulted whenever needed. In business that practice is necessary, but in personal matters it is not only unnecessary but harmful. Keeping track of things done against us is a sure way to unhappiness—our own and that of those on whom we keep records.

The same Greek word is used often in the New Testament to represent the pardoning act of God for those who trust in Jesus Christ. "Blessed is the man whose sin the Lord will not *take into account*" (Rom. 4:8). "God was in Christ reconciling the world to Himself, not *counting* their trespasses against them" (2 Cor. 5:19). Once sin is placed under the blood of Christ there is no more record of it. It is blotted out, "wiped away" (Acts 3:19). In God's heavenly record the only entry after the names of His redeemed is "righteous," because we are counted righteous in Christ. Christ's righteousness is placed to our credit. No other record exists.

That is the sort of record love keeps of wrongs done against it. No wrong is ever recorded for later reference. Love forgives. Someone once suggested that love does not forgive and forget, but rather remembers and still forgives. Resentment is careful to keep books, which it reads and rereads, hoping for a chance to get even. Love keeps no books, because it has no place for resentment or grudges. Chrysostom observed that a wrong done against love is like a spark that falls into the sea and is quenched. Love quenches wrongs rather than records them. It does not cultivate memories out of evils. If God so completely and permanently erases the record of our many sins against Him, how much more should we forgive and forget the much lesser wrongs done against us (cf. Matt. 18:21-35; Eph. 4:32)?

The Qualities of Love —part 2 (13:6-7)

[Love] does not rejoice in unrighteousness, but rejoices with the truth; bears all things, believes all things, hopes all things, endures all things. (13:6-7)

Love Does Not Rejoice in Unrighteousness

Love never takes satisfaction from sin, whether our own sin or that of others. Doing wrong things is bad enough in itself; bragging about them makes the sins even worse. To **rejoice in unrighteousness** is to justify it. It is making wrong appear to be right. "Woe to those who call evil good, and good evil," Isaiah warns, "who substitute darkness for light and light for darkness" (Isa. 5:20). That is turning God's truth upside down.

Among the most popular magazines, books, and TV programs are those that glorify sin, that literally rejoice in unrighteousness. More and more explicitly they declare that anything goes and that every person sets his own standards of right and wrong. What is right is doing what you want. Even much news amounts to rejoicing in unrighteousness, because violence, crime, immorality, slander, and the like are attractive to the natural mind and heart. Christians are not immune from enjoying such things, either because we find them entertaining or because we feel self-righteous about not doing them ourselves.

Sometimes rejoicing in unrighteousness takes the form of hoping someone will make a mistake or fall into sin. I have known Christians who wanted to be rid of their marriage partners or were already divorced. But because they did not believe in remarriage unless the other party was unfaithful, they actually hoped their spouses would commit adultery so that they themselves could be scripturally free to remarry!

Rejoicing in sin is wrong first of all because sin is an affront to God. We cannot imagine taking delight in a tragedy that befalls a friend or loved one; yet when we delight in sin, we are delighting in that which offends and grieves our heavenly Father and which is tragedy to Him. If we love God, what offends Him will offend us and what grieves Him will grieve us. "The reproaches of those who reproach Thee have fallen on me," David said (Ps. 69:9). When God was dishonored David was grieved, because the One whom he loved above all others was maligned. When we enjoy sin, either directly or vicariously in seeing others sin, we prove our lack of love for God.

One of the most common forms of rejoicing in sin is gossip. Gossips would do little harm if they did not have so many eager listeners. This sin, which many Christians treat lightly, is wicked not only because it uncaringly reveals the weaknesses and sins of others, and therefore hurts rather than helps them, but because the heart of gossip is rejoicing in evil. Gossip that is true is still gossip. It is the *way* unfavorable truth is passed on, and often simply the fact that it *is* passed on, that makes gossip gossip. It has been defined as vice enjoyed vicariously. The essence of gossip is gloating over the shortcomings and sins of others, which makes gossip a great sin itself. A person is never helped by spreading the news of his sin. Granville Walker said,

> There are times when silence is yellow, times when we ought to stand on our feet and regardless of the consequences challenge the gross evils of the time, times when not to do so is the most blatant form of cowardice. But there are other times when silence is golden, when to tell the truth is to make many hearts bleed needlessly and when nothing is accomplished and everything is hurt by a loose tongue.

Second, rejoicing in sin is wrong because of the consequences it has on the one who sins. Sin can produce nothing but harm. In the unsaved person sin is evidence of his lostness. In a believer sin is evidence of disobedience and broken fellowship with God. To love a person is to hate his sin. Discipline in the church is necessary not only to protect the purity of the body but to help the sinning believer confront his wrong and to repent (cf. Matt. 18:15-20). Paul had reminded the Corinthians of his command "not to associate with any so-called brother if he should be an immoral person, or covetous, or an idolater, or a reviler, or a drunkard, or a swindler—not even to eat with such a one" (1 Cor. 5:11). In his second letter to Thessalonica he said, "Now we command you, brethren, in the name of our Lord Jesus Christ, that you keep aloof from every brother who leads an unruly life and not according to the tradition which you received from us" (2 Thess. 3:6). That the apostle considered this principle entirely consistent with love, in fact a necessary part of love, is seen in the previous verse: "And may the Lord direct your hearts into the love of God and into the steadfastness of Christ" (v. 5). Love cannot tolerate evil or rejoice in it in any way.

LOVE REJOICES WITH THE TRUTH

After mentioning eight negatives, things that love is not or does not do, Paul lists five more positives (see v. 4a). The first is a contrast with the last negative: love **rejoices with the truth.**

At first glance it may seem strange to contrast not rejoicing in unrighteousness with rejoicing in the truth. But the truth Paul is speaking about here is not simply factual truth. He is speaking of God's truth, God's revealed Word. Righteousness is predicated on God's truth and cannot exist apart from it. Love always rejoices in God's truth and never with falsehood or false teaching. Love cannot tolerate wrong doctrine. It makes no sense to say, "It doesn't make a great difference if people don't agree with us about doctrine. What matters is that we love them." That is the basic view of what is commonly called the ecumenical movement. But if we love others it will matter a great deal to us whether or not what they believe is right or wrong. What they believe affects their souls, their eternal destinies, and their representation of God's will, and therefore should be of the highest concern to us. It also affects the souls and destinies of those whom they influence.

Love is consistent with kindness but it is not consistent with compromise of the truth. Compromising the truth is not kind to those whom we mislead by our failure to stand firmly in the truth. "This is love," John tells us, "that we walk according to His commandments" (2 John 6). To compromise, for example, with those who cast doubt on the incarnation is not loving, and it risks losing reward (vv. 7-8). Love, truth, and righteousness are inseparable. When one is weakened the others are weakened. A person who teaches falsehood about God's truth should not even be received into our home or given a greeting (v. 10). We are not to rejoice in a wrong doctrine that he teaches or in a wrong way in which he lives. Love rejoices in the truth and never in falsehood or unrighteousness.

On the other hand, love does not focus on the wrongs of others. It does not parade their faults for all the world to see. Love does not disregard falsehood and unrighteousness, but as much as possible it focuses on the true and the right. It looks for the good, hopes for the good, and emphasizes the good. It rejoices in those who teach the truth and live the truth.

A Scottish minister was known for his love and encouragement of the people of his church and village. When he died someone commented, "There is no one left to appreciate the triumphs of ordinary folk." Love appreciates the triumphs of ordinary folk. Our children are built up and strengthened when we encourage them in their accomplishments and in their obedience. Love does not rejoice in falsehood or wrong, but its primary business is to build up, not tear down, to strengthen, not weaken.

William Gladstone, a prime minister of England in the nineteenth century, one night was working late on an important speech he was to give to the House of

Commons the next day. At about two o'clock in the morning a woman knocked on his door, asking the servant if Mr. Gladstone would come and comfort her young crippled son who lay dying in a tenement not far away. Without hesitation the busy man set his speech aside and went. He spent the rest of the night with the boy, comforting him and leading him to accept Jesus Christ as Savior. The boy died about dawn, and Gladstone returned home. He told a friend later that morning, "I am the happiest man in the world today." The true greatness of Gladstone was not in his political position or attainments but in his great love, a love that would risk his political future to show the love of Christ to a young boy in great need. As it turned out, that morning he also made what some historians claim was the greatest speech of his life. He gained that victory, too, but he had been willing to lose it for the sake of a greater one. Love's victory was more important.

LOVE BEARS ALL THINGS

The four qualities mentioned in verse 7 are hyperbole, exaggerations to make a point. Paul has made it clear that love rejects jealousy, bragging, arrogance, unseemliness, selfishness, anger, resentment, and unrighteousness. It does not bear, believe, hope, or endure lies, false teaching, or anything else that is not of God. By **all things** Paul is speaking of all things acceptable in God's righteousness and will, of everything within the Lord's divine tolerance. The four qualities listed here are closely related and are given in ascending order.

Stegō (to **bear**) basically means to cover or to support and therefore to protect. Love **bears all things** by protecting others from exposure, ridicule, or harm. Genuine love does not gossip or listen to gossip. Even when a sin is certain, love tries to correct it with the least possible hurt and harm to the guilty person. Love never protects sin but is anxious to protect the sinner.

Fallen human nature has the opposite inclination. There is perverse pleasure in exposing someone's faults and failures. As already mentioned, that is what makes gossip appealing. The Corinthians cared little for the feelings or welfare of fellow believers. It was every person for himself. Like the Pharisees, they paid little attention to others, except when those others were failing or sinning. Man's depravity causes him to rejoice in the depravity of others. It is that depraved pleasure that sells magazines and newspapers that cater to exposés, "true confessions," and the like. It is the same sort of pleasure that makes children tattle on brothers and sisters. Whether to feel self-righteous by exposing another's sin or to enjoy that sin vicariously, we all are tempted to take a certain kind of pleasure in the sins of others. Love has no part in that. It does not expose or exploit, gloat or condemn. It **bears**; it does not bare.

"Hatred stirs up strife, but love covers all transgressions" (Prov. 10:12). We can measure our love for a person by how quick we are to cover his faults. When one of our children does something wrong we are inclined to put the best face on it. "He didn't understand what he was doing," we explain, or "She didn't really mean what she said." With a person we do not like, however, our reaction is likely to be the opposite: "That is typical of John," or, "What would you expect from someone like her?"

Love does not justify sin or compromise with falsehood. Love warns, corrects, exhorts, rebukes, and disciplines. But love does not expose or broadcast failures and wrongs. It covers and protects. Henry Ward Beecher said, "God pardons like a mother who kisses the offense into everlasting forgetfulness."

The mercy seat, where the blood of atonement was sprinkled (Lev. 16:14), was a covering, not only for the ark itself but for the sins of the people. The mercy seat was a place of covering. That covering prefigured the perfect and final covering of sin accomplished by Jesus on the cross in His great propitiatory sacrifice (Rom. 3:25-26; Heb. 2:17; 1 John 2:2). In the cross God threw the great mantle of His love over sin, forever covering it for those who trust in His Son. By nature, love is redemptive. It wants to buy back, not condemn, to save, not judge.

Love feels the pain of those it loves and helps carry the burden of the hurt. True love is even willing to take the consequences of the sin of those it loves. Isaiah wrote of Jesus Christ, "Surely our griefs He Himself bore, and our sorrows He carried; . . . He was pierced through for our transgressions, He was crushed for our iniquities; the chastening for our well-being fell upon Him" (Isa. 53:4-5). As Peter knew firsthand from Jesus' great patience and kindness, "love covers a multitude of sins" (1 Pet. 4:8).

During Oliver Cromwell's reign as lord protector of England a young soldier was sentenced to die. The girl to whom he was engaged pleaded with Cromwell to spare the life of her beloved, but to no avail. The young man was to be executed when the curfew bell sounded, but when the sexton repeatedly pulled the rope the bell made no sound. The girl had climbed into the belfry and wrapped herself around the clapper so that it could not strike the bell. Her body was smashed and bruised, but she did not let go until the clapper stopped swinging. She managed to climb down, bruised and bleeding, to meet those awaiting the execution. When she explained what she had done, Cromwell commuted the sentence. A poet beautifully recorded the story as follows:

> At his feet she told her story,
> > showed her hands all bruised and torn,
> And her sweet young face still haggard
> > with the anguish it had worn,
> Touched his heart with sudden pity,
> > lit his eyes with misty light.
> "Go, your lover lives," said Cromwell;
> > "Curfew will not ring tonight."

LOVE BELIEVES ALL THINGS

In addition to bearing all things, love also **believes all things.** Love is not suspicious or cynical. When it throws its mantle over a wrong it also believes in the best outcome for the one who has done the wrong—that the wrong will be confessed and forgiven and the loved one restored to righteousness.

Love also believes all things in another way. If there is doubt about a person's guilt or motivation, love will always opt for the most favorable possibility. If a loved one is accused of something wrong, love will consider him innocent until proven guilty. If he turns out to be guilty, love will give credit for the best motive. Love trusts; love has confidence; love **believes.**

In our church we continually try to develop a spirit of mutual trust, within the the staff and within the congregation as a whole. We believe that each person is dedicated to the Lord and is responsible for serving Him. We believe each person is living in fellowship with the Lord. When someone fails, as we all do, then our desire is to help cover that wrong and help it be made right. Whenever there is doubt, we would rather err on the favorable side.

Job's friends showed few signs of love. They were ready to believe the worst about him, being thoroughly convinced that his problems could only have been caused by his sins. Job did not himself understand why he was suffering so terribly, but he knew it was not because of his sins. "Behold, I know your thoughts," he responded to his friends, "and the plans by which you would wrong me" (Job 21:27). They gave Job no benefit of doubt because they had no true love for him. Knowing the uprightness of Job's life, loving friends would have realized that his sufferings were out of proportion to whatever shortcomings he had.

The lovelessness of the scribes and Pharisees is seen in their predisposition to see the worst in others, including Jesus. When Jesus forgave the paralytic of his sins, the Pharisees immediately concluded He was blaspheming (Luke 5:21). To further evidence His divine power Jesus then healed the man of his affliction. Most of the crowd marveled at the miracle and glorified God (v. 26), but we know from their later words and actions that the scribes and Pharisees remained convinced that Jesus was evil. Hatred believes the worst; love believes the best.

Love is a harbor of trust. When that trust is broken, love's first reaction is to heal and restore. "Brethren, even if a man is caught in any trespass, you who are spiritual, restore such a one in a spirit of gentleness; each one looking to yourself, lest you too be tempted" (Gal. 6:1).

Love Hopes All Things

Even when belief in a loved one's goodness or repentance is shattered, love still **hopes.** When it runs out of faith it holds on to hope. As long as God's grace is operative human failure is never final. God would not take Israel's failure as final. Jesus would not take Peter's failure as final. Paul would not take the Corinthians' failure as final. There are more than enough promises in the Bible to make love hopeful.

The parents of backslidden children, the spouse of an unbelieving marriage partner, the church that has disciplined members who do not repent—all hope in love that the child, the spouse, or the erring brother or sister will be saved or restored. Love refuses to take failure as final. The rope of love's hope has no end. As long as there is life, love does not lose hope. When our hope becomes weak, we know our love has become weak.

I heard the story of a dog who stayed at the airport of a large city for over five years waiting for his master to return. Employees and others fed the dog and took care of him, but he would not leave the spot where he last saw his master. He would not give up hope that someday they would be reunited. If a dog's love for his master can produce that kind of hope, how much longer should our love make hope last?

Love Endures All Things

Hupomenō ("to endure") was a military term used of an army's holding a vital position at all costs. Every hardship and every suffering was to be endured in order to hold fast.

Love holds fast to those it loves. It **endures all things** at all costs. It stands against overwhelming opposition and refuses to stop bearing or stop believing or stop hoping. Love will not stop loving.

Stephen lovingly bore the ridicule and rejection of those to whom he witnessed. Their taunts would not make him stop believing they would believe, and their stones would not make him stop hoping they would be saved. He died praying, "Lord, do not hold this sin against them!" (Acts 7:60). Like his Lord, he loved to the end even the unloving enemies who put him to death. His love endured.

Love bears what otherwise is unbearable; it believes what otherwise is unbelievable; it hopes in what otherwise is hopeless; and it endures when anything less than love would give up. After love bears it believes. After it believes it hopes. After it hopes it endures. There is no "after" for endurance, for endurance is the unending climax of love.

The Permanence of Love (13:8-13)

Love never fails; but if there are gifts of prophecy, they will be done away; if there are tongues, they will cease; if there is knowledge, it will be done away. For we know in part, and we prophesy in part; but when the perfect comes, the partial will be done away. When I was a child, I used to speak as a child, think as a child, reason as a child; when I became a man, I did away with childish things. For now we see in a mirror dimly, but then face to face; now I know in part, but then I shall know fully just as I also have been fully known. But now abide faith, hope, love, these three; but the greatest of these is love. (13:8-13)

The theme of the final section of 1 Corinthians 13 is **love never fails.** Throughout all eternity love will never end. Love lasts.

Many of the Corinthians continually had their eyes on the wrong things. They were overly concerned about the temporary and little concerned about the permanent. Instead of being God's salt in Corinth, they were being flavored by the culture around them. Instead of penetrating Corinth with a spirit of godliness, Corinth's spirit of ungodliness had penetrated the church. Instead of being obedient to God's Spirit and controlled by the fruit He gives, they were infected by materialism, pride, antagonism, selfishness, compromise, indulgence, hatred, sexual immorality, jealousy, and virtually every other sin imaginable. They were called to be light, but they did deeds of darkness. They were called to be righteous, but lived in sin. Instead of Corinth being Christianized, the church was being paganized.

Of all their many failings the Corinthian believers' greatest failure was in love. Just as the presence of "love covers a multitude of sins" (1 Pet. 4:8), the lack of love *causes* a multitude of sins. The Corinthians had great lovelessness and great sin. What they needed above all else was great love and great righteousness. That which most completely characterizes God Himself should characterize His children.

In 1 Corinthians 13:8-13 Paul proves that, because of its enduring quality, love is God's greatest gift, His gift above all gifts. In contrast to love's permanence, spiritual gifts are temporary, partial, and elementary.

GIFTS ARE TEMPORARY

Love never fails; but if there are gifts of prophecy, they will be done away; if there are tongues, they will cease; if there is knowledge, it will be done away. (13:8)

Fails (from *piptō*) has the basic meaning of falling, especially the idea of final falling, and was used of a flower or leaf that falls to the ground, withers, and decays. **Never** refers to time, not to frequency, and the idea is that at no time will divine **love** ever fall, wither, and decay. By nature it is permanent. It is never abolished.

Love cannot fail because it shares God's nature and God's eternity. In heaven we not only will have no more need for faith and hope, but no more need for the gifts of teaching, preaching, helps, prophecy, discernment, knowledge, wisdom, tongues, miracles, healings, faith, mercy, or leadership. None of those gifts will have a purpose or place in heaven. Yet love is, and forever will be, the very air of heaven.

It is important to note that **never fails** does not refer to success. Love is not a magic key that Christians use to unlock every opportunity and guarantee every endeavor. Love is not a spiritual formula that, faithfully applied, automatically fulfills our desires and produces human success. Love does not always win, at least not in the usual sense. Jesus Christ was love incarnate, yet He did not by His perfect love succeed in winning every person to Himself. He was ridiculed, maligned, denied, rejected, and crucified. Paul could be called the apostle of love, yet he did not leave a trail of perfect successes wherever he ministered. He was persecuted, arrested, beaten, imprisoned, and, like his Lord, put to death because of what he said and did in love.

On the other hand, whenever and wherever Christians *are* successful in their living and ministering, it will always be through love. Because love does not overpower human will, we cannot always accomplish our purposes, no matter how loving, spiritual, and selfless we may be. But no godly work can be accomplished without love. Success will not always be a part of love, but love will always be a part of true spiritual success.

Paul, however, is not speaking of love's successes or failures, but of its lastingness, its permanence as a divine quality. **Love never fails** in the sense that it outlasts any failures. For the Christian, love is life, and both are eternal. Love is the supreme characteristic of the life God gives, because love is the supreme characteristic of God Himself. "God is love, and the one who abides in love abides in God, and God abides in him" (1 John 4:16). That is Paul's point, the truth he hoped the Corinthians somehow could understand, accept, and follow. He wanted them to be successful in love, successful in being like God.

Paul strengthens his emphasis on the supreme nature of love by comparing love's permanence to the impermanence of three spiritual gifts: **prophecy, tongues,** and **knowledge**. Each of those gifts eventually will fall and disappear, but love will continue.

Though we are told here that all three gifts would someday cease to exist, two different verbs are used to indicate their cessation. **Prophecy** and **knowledge** will be **done away,** whereas **tongues** will **cease.**

Done away is from *katargeō*, which means "to reduce to inactivity," or "to abolish." The gifts of prophecy and knowledge one day will be made inoperative. Both forms of this verb in verse 8, as well as its form in verse 10, are passive; that is, something or someone will cause them to stop. As will be discussed below, that something is the coming of "the perfect" (v. 10).

Cease is from *pauō*, which means "to stop, to come to an end." Unlike *katargeō*, this verb is here used in the Greek middle voice, which, when used of persons, indicates intentional, voluntary action upon oneself. Used of inanimate objects it indicates reflexive, self-causing action. The cause comes from within; it is built in. God gave the gift of **tongues** a built-in stopping place. "That gift will stop by itself," Paul says. Like a battery, it had a limited energy supply and a limited lifespan. When its limits were reached, its activity automatically ended. Prophecy and knowledge will be stopped by something outside themselves, but the gift of tongues will stop by itself. This distinction in terms is unarguable.

The question remains as to *when* and *how* these gifts will end. Prophecy and knowledge are said to end "when the perfect comes" (vv. 9-10), and we will discuss the what and the when of "perfect" when we come to those verses.

The cessation of **tongues,** however, is not mentioned in relation to the coming of the perfect. They will have ceased at an earlier time. That is why they are not stopped by the same thing that stops the other two gifts. As was discussed in some detail under 12:8-10, I believe that gift ended with the apostolic age.

In the first place, tongues was a sign gift and, as with the gifts of healing and miracles, it ceased to operate when the New Testament was completed. God has never ceased to perform miracles, and He continues today to heal miraculously and to work in other supernatural ways according to His sovereign will. But the Bible records only three periods of history in which human beings were given the gift of performing miracles. The first period was during the ministries of Moses and Joshua, the second during the ministries of Elijah and Elisha, and the third during the ministries of Jesus and the apostles. Each period lasted only about 70 years and then abruptly ended. The only other age of miracles will be in the millennial kingdom, and the sources of those miracles are described as "the powers of the age to come" (Heb. 6:5). The last miracle recorded in the New Testament in which God worked directly through a human instrument occurred about the year 58 (Acts 28:8). From that time until about 96, when John completed the writing of Revelation, not a single miracle of that sort is mentioned.

The New Testament miracle age was for the purpose of confirming the Word as given by Jesus and the apostles, of offering the kingdom to Israel, and of giving a taste, a sample, of the kingdom. When Israel turned its back on Christ and His kingdom, it was "impossible to renew them again to repentance" (Heb. 6:6), and the gospel was then offered to the Gentiles. The teaching of Christ and the apostles had been confirmed to Israel "both by signs and wonders and by various miracles and by gifts of the Holy Spirit" (Heb. 2:3-4). It is interesting that, though Hebrews was written as early as 67 or 68, the writer there speaks of this confirmation (*ebebaiōthē*, aor. pass. ind.) in the past tense, as if the signs, wonders, and miracles had ceased. Those gifts were uniquely tied to the apostles (2 Cor. 12:12).

The second evidence that the gift of tongues ended with the apostles is that its purpose as a judicial sign of Israel's judgment ceased to apply at that time. Paul reminds the Corinthians that "In the Law it is written, 'By men of strange tongues and by the lips of strangers I will speak to this people, and even so they will not listen to Me,' says the Lord" (1 Cor. 14:21; cf. Isa. 28:11-12). In other words, because Israel refused to listen and believe when God spoke to them in clear language, the prophet said the day would come when He would speak to them in a language they could not understand, as a testimony against their rejection of Him.

Tongues were not given as a sign to believers "but to unbelievers" (1 Cor. 14:22), specifically unbelieving Jews. With the destruction of the Temple by the Roman general Titus in A.D. 70, Judaism ended except as a shadow religion. When the Temple was destroyed, the sacrificial system was destroyed, and the need for a Jewish priesthood was destroyed. From that day it has been impossible for the requirements of the Old Covenant to be fulfilled. When that destruction occurred, some 15 years after Paul wrote this epistle, the need for tongues as a judicial sign to Israel had no further value. There is no need today for a sign that God is moving from Israel to the world.

Third, tongues ceased because they were an inferior means of edification. When properly interpreted, tongues had the ability to edify in a limited way (1 Cor. 14:5; 12-13; 27-28). But the primary purpose of 1 Corinthians 14 is to show that tongues were an inferior means of communication (vv.1-12), an inferior means of praise (vv. 13-19), and an inferior means of evangelism (vv. 20-25). Tongues provided limited and inferior edification, whereas prophecy is far superior in every way (vv. 1, 3-6, 24, 29, 31, 39). Five words spoken intelligently and intelligibly in ordinary language are of more value "than ten thousand words in a tongue" (v. 19).

Fourth, the gift of tongues has ceased because its purpose as a confirming sign of apostolic authority and doctrine ended when the New Testament was completed. Genuine tongues-speaking involved direct revelation of God to the speaker, though it was veiled revelation that always needed translation or interpretation, often even to the speaker himself (1 Cor. 14:27-28). Revelation of God's Word was completed, however, when the New Testament was completed, and to that nothing is to be added or subtracted (Rev. 22:18-19). The confirming purpose of tongues was completed.

Fifth, it is reasonable to believe that tongues have ceased because their use is mentioned only in the earlier New Testament books. Most of the books, in fact, do not mention it. Paul mentions it only in this one letter, and James, Peter, John, and Jude make no mention of it at all. Nor does reference to it appear in the book of Acts after 19:6. It seems clear from the New Testament record itself that tongues not only ceased to be an issue but ceased to be practiced well before the end of the apostolic age. Nowhere in the epistles is it commanded or enjoined on believers as a responsibility or spiritual exercise.

Finally, the gift of tongues has evidently ceased because, since the apostolic age, it has reappeared only spasmodically and questionably throughout nineteen centuries of church history. The gift of tongues is nowhere alluded to or found in any writings of the church Fathers. Clement of Rome wrote a letter to the Corinthian church in the year 95, only about four decades after Paul wrote 1 Corinthians. In discussing problems in the church, Clement made no mention of tongues. Apparently both the use and misuse of that gift had ceased. Justin Martyr, the great church Father of the second century, visited many of the churches of his day, yet in his voluminous writings he mentions nothing of tongues. It is not mentioned even among his several lists of spiritual gifts. Origen, a brilliant church scholar who lived during the third century, makes no mention of tongues. In his polemic against Celsus he explicitly argues that the sign gifts of the apostolic age were temporary and were not exercised by Christians of his day. Chrysostom, perhaps the greatest of the post-New Testament writers, lived from 347 until 407. Writing on 1 Corinthians 12 he states that tongues and the other miraculous gifts not only had ceased but could not even be accurately defined. Augustine, in his comments on Acts 2:4, wrote, "In the earliest times the Holy Spirit fell on them that believed and they spoke with tongues. These were signs adapted to that time, for there behooved to be that betokening of the Holy Spirit. That thing was done for betokening and it passed away."

The historians and theologians of the early church unanimously maintained that tongues ceased to exist after the time of the apostles. The only exception of which we know was within the movement led by Montanus, a second century heretic who believed that divine revelation continued through him beyond the New Testament.

Apparently no other tongues-speaking was practiced in Christianity until the seventeenth and eighteenth centuries, when it appeared in several Roman Catholic groups in Europe (Cevenols and Jansenists) and among the Shakers in New England. The nineteenth century Irvingites of London were marked by unbiblical claims of revelations and by "tongues-speak." For over 1800 years the gift of tongues, along with the other miracle gifts, was unknown in the life and doctrine of orthodox Christianity. Then, around the turn of the twentieth century, tongues became a major emphasis within the holiness movement, a large section of which developed into modern Pentecostalism. The charismatic movement, which began in 1960, carried the practice of tongues beyond traditional Pentecostalism into many other denominations, churches, and groups, both Catholic and Protestant, filling the void in true spiritual living with false experience.

Many charismatics defend as biblical the modern tongues-speaking as part of the latter-day signs spoken of by Joel (2:28-32) and quoted by Peter in his Pentecost sermon (Acts 2:17-21). But it is clear from a careful examination of those passages that the prophecy does not apply either to Pentecost or to modern times. From earlier in Joel 2 we see that the time referred to is the second coming of Christ (of which Pentecost was only a sample), when the Lord "will remove the northern army far from [Israel]" (v. 20), just before the millennial kingdom is established and God's chosen people turn to Him (vv. 21-27; cf. Ezek. 36:23-38). It is only "after this" (v. 28) that the miraculous signs in the heavens and on the earth will appear.

There were no blood, columns of smoke, darkening of the sun, or changing of the moon to blood associated with Pentecost. Nor have any such things happened in modern times. Peter was not saying that Pentecost completely fulfilled Joel's prophecy, because obviously it did not. He was saying that the limited miraculous signs that had occurred shortly before he began his sermon were a glimpse of much greater and far-reaching signs and wonders that would come in "the last days" (Acts 2:17). There simply is no biblical explanation here for the modern reappearance of tongues or of any of the other miracle gifts.

Some charismatics also maintain that "the early and latter rain" of Joel 2:23 refer to the outpouring of the Holy Spirit at Pentecost and in modern times, respectively. But the early rain was the literal rainfall that came in the autumn and the latter rain was that which came in the spring. Joel's point is simply that God will make crops grow profusely in the kingdom, as the following verses (24-27) make abundantly clear.

George N. H. Peters, a Bible scholar of the last century, said, "The Baptism of Pentecost is a pledge of fulfillment in the future, evidencing what the Holy Ghost will yet perform in the coming age." A contemporary theologian, Helmut Thielicke, describes the miracles of the first century, including tongues, as "the lightning on the horizon of the Kingdom of God."

GIFTS ARE PARTIAL

For we know in part, and we prophesy in part; but when the perfect comes, the partial will be done away. (13:9-10)

The cessation of tongues took place a short while after Paul wrote this letter, but the gifts of prophecy and knowledge have not yet been **done away**, because **the perfect** has not yet come. Like tongues and all other gifts, those two gifts are temporary, but they are less temporary than tongues. The unique and isolated purpose of the gift of tongues is seen in the fact that, unlike knowledge and prophecy, it did not exist either before or after the apostolic era. As far as his discussion of love is concerned, Paul considers tongues already to have stopped, because that gift is not mentioned after verse 8.

Paul's first emphasis in verses 9-10 is the partiality of knowledge and prophecy: **we know in part, and we prophesy in part.** Those gifts are representative of all the gifts, which will be **done away** when **the perfect comes,** because at that time no gift will have further reason for existence.

God's gifts are complete, but those to whom He gives them are limited. Paul included himself in the **we.** Even the apostles knew **in part** and prophesied **in part.** Paul had cautioned the Corinthians that "If anyone supposes that he knows anything, he has not yet known as he ought to know" (1 Cor. 8:2). "Knowing Christ Jesus" better was Paul's supreme purpose and joy in life, yet even near the end of his life he insisted, "Not that I have already obtained it, or have already become perfect, but I press on in order that I may lay hold of that for which also I was laid hold of by Christ Jesus" (Phil. 3:8, 12).

Zophar asked Job, "Can you discover the depths of God? Can you discover the limits of the Almighty? They are high as the heavens, what can you do? Deeper than Sheol, what can you know? Its measure is longer than the earth, and broader than the sea" (Job 11:7-9). Sometime later Job himself declares, "Behold, these are the fringes of His ways; and how faint a word we hear of Him! But His mighty thunder, who can understand?" (26:14). David sang in awe, "Many, O Lord my God, are the wonders which Thou hast done, and Thy thoughts toward us; there is none to compare with Thee; if I would declare and speak of them, they would be too numerous to count" (Ps. 40:5). God knows us perfectly, but we can know Him now only imperfectly.

> O Lord, Thou hast searched me and known me.
> Thou dost know when I sit down and when I rise up;
> Thou dost understand my thought from afar.
> Thou dost scrutinize my path and my lying down,
> And art intimately acquainted with all my ways.
> Even before there is a word on my tongue,
> Behold, O Lord, Thou dost know it all.
> Thou hast enclosed me behind and before,
> And laid Thy hand upon me.
> Such knowledge is too wonderful for me;
> It is too high, I cannot attain to it. (Ps. 139:1-6)

To the Romans Paul wrote, "Oh, the depth of the riches both of the wisdom and knowledge of God! How unsearchable are His judgments and unfathomable His ways! For who has known the mind of the Lord, or who became His counselor?" (Rom. 11:33-34).

Through God's Word and the enlightenment of the Holy Spirit, we can have "a true knowledge of God's mystery, that is, Christ Himself," but even our true knowledge is still imperfect knowledge, because only in Him "are hidden all the treasures of wisdom and knowledge" (Col. 2:2-3). God has provided all the truth we *need* to know. "And we know that the Son of God has come, and has given us understanding, in order that we might know Him who is true, and we are in Him who is true, in His Son Jesus Christ" (1 John 5:20). God's "divine power has granted to us everything pertaining to life and godliness, through the true knowledge of Him who called us by His own glory and excellence" (2 Pet. 1:3). The Lord has provided all the knowledge we need in order to know and serve Him—more, in fact, than any man could ever comprehend. Yet God's written Word does not exhaust truth about Him.

For several reasons infinite revelation about the infinite God would be ridiculous and useless. In the first place, finite minds could not encompass or comprehend infinite truth. In the second place, man's mind not only is finite but depraved. Not until our minds are perfected will we be able "to know fully just as [we] also have been fully known" (1 Cor. 13:12). So we wait for the time and experience of perfection.

When **the perfect comes** we will have no more need of knowledge or wisdom, preaching or teaching, prophecy or interpretation. We will not even have need of the Bible. We will no longer need the written Word because we will be eternally in the presence and full comprehension of the living Word.

THE PERFECT IS NOT THE COMPLETION OF SCRIPTURE

What, precisely, is **the perfect** thing that is to come? Some Christians believe the perfect has already come in the completion of Scripture. But that idea would have been meaningless to the Corinthians. Nowhere in this letter does he mention or allude to such a scriptural completion. The Corinthian believers would have taken Paul's meaning in the plainest and simplest way: as a reference to spiritual and moral perfection, the perfection to which the Lord calls all of His people: "Therefore you are to be perfect, as your heavenly Father is perfect" (Matt. 5:48). Paul was speaking of completed holiness, of our one day actually becoming what God now counts, or reckons, us to be.

If **the perfect** refers to the completion of Scripture, then prophecy and knowledge have already been stopped, and all believers since that time would have been without benefit of two of the most important gifts for proclaiming, interpreting, and understanding Scripture. The gift of prophecy was only partly used for revelation. In most cases it was used for proclaiming and interpreting what already had been revealed. The church would be in dire straits if the gifts of knowledge and prophecy had ceased with the completion of the New Testament.

We know, furthermore, that prophecy will be active in the Kingdom age. At that time the Lord says, "I will pour out My Spirit on all mankind; and your sons and daughters will prophesy, your old men will dream dreams, your young men will see visions" (Joel 2:28; Acts 2:17). Prior to the kingdom, during the Tribulation, God will raise up two great prophetic witnesses who "will prophesy for twelve hundred and sixty days, clothed in sackcloth" (Rev. 11:3).

Still another reason **the perfect** cannot refer to the completion of Scripture is found in Paul's statement that we will see "face to face" (1 Cor. 13:12). Scripture gives a wonderful and reliable picture of God, but it does not allow us to see Him "face to face." Peter speaks of the many believers even of his own day who "have not seen Him" (1 Pet. 1:8). The Bible does not give a "face to face" vision of God. No Christian, before or after the completion of the New Testament, has known the Lord as he has "been fully known" (1 Cor. 13:12). We love One whom we have not seen.

Nor is it possible that prophecy stopped after completion of the New Testament and will resume during the Tribulation and the Kingdom. In the first place the verb *katargeō* means to be abolished completely and finally, not temporarily. In the second place, an interruption of prophecy would not fit Paul's point here, which is to show the permanency of love over the temporariness of gifts.

THE PERFECT IS NOT THE RAPTURE

Many interpreters hold the coming of **the perfect** to be the rapture of the church. But if knowledge and prophecy have been permanently **done away**, they could no more be resumed after the rapture and during the Tribulation or the Kingdom. Paul makes it clear that once those gifts end, they will end permanently. But they appear to be inoperative in both the Tribulation and the millennial Kingdom.

THE PERFECT IS NOT THE MATURING CHURCH

A relatively new interpretation is that **the perfect** refers to the maturing, or completion, of the church. It is true that *perfect* often has the meaning of maturity or completion. But such a completion would amount to the rapture, which this view eliminates. When the Lord's work with His church is completed, He will rapture it; and we are still left with the question of prophecy during the Tribulation and Kingdom.

THE PERFECT IS NOT THE SECOND COMING

Some believe **the perfect** refers to Christ's second coming. But **perfect** is neuter in the Greek (*teleion*), eliminating the possibility that it relates to a person. In addition, that view also has the problem of the reappearance of prophecy, and the widespread preaching and teaching of the Word, during the Kingdom period. "For the earth will be full of the knowledge of the Lord as the waters cover the sea" (Isa. 11:9) and "on that day the deaf shall hear words of a book, and out of their gloom and darkness the eyes of the blind shall see" (29:18; cf. 32:3-4). Jeremiah tells us of the shepherds whom the Lord will raise up to tend His people in that day. "'They will not be afraid any longer, nor be terrified, nor will any be missing,' declares the Lord" (Jer. 23:4). The Kingdom will have an abundance of preachers and teachers.

THE PERFECT IS THE ETERNAL STATE

By process of elimination, the only possibility for **the perfect** is the eternal, heavenly state of believers. Paul is saying that spiritual gifts are only for time, but that love will last for all eternity. The point is simple, not obscure.

The eternal state allows for the neuter form of **the perfect** and allows for the continuation of knowledge and prophecy during the church age, the Tribulation, and the Kingdom. It fits the context of Paul's emphasis on the permanence of love. It also fits his mention of our then seeing "face to face," which will come about only with our glorification, when we will be illumined by the very glory of God Himself (Rev. 21:23). Finally, only in heaven will we "know fully just as [we] also have been fully known" (1 Cor. 13:12).

The eternal state begins for Old Testament believers at the first resurrection, when they will be raised to be with Him forever (Dan. 12:2). For Christians the eternal state begins either at death, when they go to be with the Lord, or at the rapture, when the Lord takes His own to be with Himself. For Tribulation and Kingdom saints it will occur at death or glorification.

GIFTS ARE ELEMENTARY

When I was a child, I used to speak as a child, think as a child, reason as a child; when I became a man, I did away with childish things. For now we see in a mirror dimly, but then face to face; now I know in part, but then I shall know fully just as I also have been fully known. (13:11-12)

Paul is here illustrating what happens when "the perfect comes." In their earthly lives all Christians are children compared to what they will be when they are perfected in heaven.

Perhaps Paul was comparing His present spiritual state to his boyhood, **as a child.** A Jewish male was considered a boy until his bar mitzvah ("son of the law"), after which he was considered **a man.** One moment he was a boy; the next he was a man. Our perfection in Christ will be a type of spiritual bar mitzvah, a coming into immediate, complete, and eternal spiritual adulthood and maturity. At that moment everything **childish** will be done away with. All immaturity, all childishness, all imperfection, and all limitations of knowledge and understanding will be forever gone.

In this present life, even with God's Word completed and the illumination of His Spirit, **we see in a mirror dimly.** In our present state we are not capable of seeing more. But when we enter into the Lord's presence, we then will see Him **face to face.** Now we can only **know in part, but then** [we] **shall know fully just as** [we] **also have been fully known.**

LOVE IS ETERNAL

But now abide faith, hope, love, these three; but the greatest of these is love. (13:13)

Returning to the temporal, to the Christian's earthly life, Paul mentions the three greatest spiritual virtues: **faith, hope,** and **love.** Actually **faith** and **hope** are encompassed by **love,** which "believes all things," and "hopes all things" (v. 7). Because faith and hope will have no purpose in heaven, where everything true will be known and everything good will be possessed, they are not equal to love.

Love is **the greatest of these** not only because it is eternal, but because, even in this temporal life, where we now live, love is supreme. Love already is the greatest, not only because it will outlast the other virtues, beautiful and necessary as they are, but because it is inherently greater by being the most God-like. God does not have faith or hope, but "God *is* love" (1 John 4:8).

Gifts, ministries, faith, hope, patience, all one day will cease to exist because they will cease to have purpose or meaning. But in that perfect day, when we see our Lord "face to face," love will for us be just beginning. But our showing love, practicing love, living love *now* are of utmost importance, more important than having any of the other virtues or gifts, because love is the link God gives us with His eternal Self.

The Position of the Gift of Tongues

(14:1-19)

Pursue love, yet desire earnestly spiritual gifts, but especially that you may prophesy. For one who speaks in a tongue does not speak to men, but to God; for no one understands, but in his spirit he speaks mysteries. But one who prophesies speaks to men for edification and exhortation and consolation. One who speaks in a tongue edifies himself; but one who prophesies edifies the church. Now I wish that you all spoke in tongues, but even more that you would prophesy; and greater is one who prophesies than one who speaks in tongues, unless he interprets, so that the church may receive edifying. But now, brethren, if I come to you speaking in tongues, what shall I profit you, unless I speak to you either by way of revelation or of knowledge or of prophecy or of teaching? Yet even lifeless things, either flute or harp, in producing a sound, if they do not produce a distinction in the tones, how will it be known what is played on the flute or on the harp? For if the bugle produces an indistinct sound, who will prepare himself for battle? So also you, unless you utter by the tongue speech that is clear, how will it be known what is spoken? For you will be speaking into the air. There are, perhaps, a great many kinds of languages in the world, and no kind is without meaning. If then I do not know the meaning of the language, I shall be to the one who speaks a barbarian, and the one who speaks will be a barbarian to me. So also you, since you are zealous of spiritual gifts, seek to abound for the edification of the church. Therefore let one who speaks in a tongue pray that he may interpret. For if I pray in a tongue, my spirit prays, but my mind is unfruitful. What is the outcome then? I shall pray with the spirit and I shall pray with the mind also; I shall sing with the spirit and I shall sing with the mind also. Otherwise if you bless in the spirit only, how will the one who fills the place of the ungifted say the "Amen" at your giving of thanks, since he does not know what you are saying? For you are giving thanks well enough, but the other man is not edified. I thank God, I speak in tongues more than you all; however, in the church I desire to speak five words with my mind, that I may instruct others also, rather than ten thousand words in a tongue. (14:1-19)

After presenting love as the "more excellent way" above all ministries and gifts, Paul directly and forcefully confronts the Corinthians in regard to their sin against love in misunderstanding and misusing the gift of tongues. Believers there had so abused the gift that they rivaled Babel in confusion of speaking, and the apostle devotes an entire chapter to the problem, which was so representative of their sinfulness.

As commented on under 12:10, the practice of ecstatic utterances was common in many of the pagan Graeco-Roman religions of Paul's day, including those active in Corinth. Devotees of a god would drink and dance themselves into frenzies until they went into semiconsciousness or even unconsciousness—an experience they considered to be the highest form of communion with the divine. They believed that in such drunkenness their spirits left their bodies and communed directly with the god or gods, a practice to which Paul alludes in Ephesians 5:18. The ecstatic speaking that often accompanied such experiences was thought to be the language of the gods.

The terms *lalein glōssēi/glōssais* (to speak in a tongue/in tongues) that Paul uses so frequently in chapter 14 were commonly used in his day to describe pagan ecstatic speech. The Greeks also used *erōs* to describe the experience. Though commonly used of sexual love, *erōs* also was used for any strongly sensual feeling or activity, and pagan ecstatic frenzies often were accompanied by sexual orgies and perversions of all sorts.

In the church at Corinth much of the tongues-speaking had taken on the form and flavor of those pagan ecstasies. Emotionalism all but neutralized their rational senses, and selfish exhibitionism was common, with everyone wanting to do and say his own thing at the same time (v.26). Services were bedlam and chaos, with little worship and little edification taking place.

Because of the extreme carnality in the church at Corinth, we can be sure that much of the tongues-speaking there was counterfeit. Believers were in no spiritual condition to properly use true spiritual gifts or properly manifest true spiritual fruit. How could a congregation so worldly, opinionated, selfish, cliquish, envious, jealous, divisive, argumentative, arrogant, disorderly, defrauding, inconsiderate, gluttonous, immoral, and desecrative of the Lord's Supper exercise the gifts of the Spirit? For them to have done so would have defied every biblical principle of spirituality. You cannot walk in the Spirit while exercising the flesh.

Against the backdrop of such false experiences Paul teaches three basic truths about the gift of tongues: its position is secondary to prophecy (vv. 1-19); its purpose was as a sign to unbelievers (vv. 20-25); and its proper procedure, or use, was systematic and orderly (vv. 26-40).

Within the first section, the apostle gives three reasons why the position of tongues is secondary to that of prophecy: prophecy edifies the whole congregation; tongues are unintelligible; and the effects of tongues are emotional rather than rational.

PROPHECY EDIFIES THE WHOLE CONGREGATION

Pursue love, yet desire earnestly spiritual gifts, but especially that you may prophesy. For one who speaks in a tongue does not speak to men, but to God; for no one understands, but in his spirit he speaks mysteries. But one who prophesies speaks to men for edification and exhortation and consolation. One who speaks in a tongue edifies himself; but one who prophesies edifies the church. Now I wish that you all spoke in tongues, but even more that you would prophesy; and greater is one who prophesies than one who speaks in tongues, unless he interprets, so that the church may receive edifying. (14:1-5)

Diōkō (to **pursue**) means to follow, hunt, or chase after with intensity, and is sometimes translated "persecute," as in 2 Corinthians 4:9. Above all else, as Paul emphasized in the previous chapter, the Corinthians should **pursue love**. Lovelessness was by far their greatest problem, to which all of their other problems were related in one way or another. The only strong affection many of them had was for themselves. Paul here commands them to pursue love.

The fact that love is primary, however, does not mean that everything else is to be disregarded. **Yet desire earnestly spiritual gifts**, Paul continues. Love is no substitute for other virtues, or even for good works; in fact, love is the great motivator, the only true motivator, of good works. It is also the great motivator of every spiritual ministry and of the proper use of every spiritual gift.

The strong desire the Corinthians had for gifts was not wrong in itself but wrong in that it was selfishly directed only toward "the greater gifts" (12:31), the showy and attention-getting gifts. They were right to have desired spiritual gifts, but their concern should have been for using the gifts they had, not for enviously wanting gifts that others had. Their desire should have been to see their gifts minister to others, not to show off.

And particularly they should have followed after prophecy. **Especially that you may prophesy** is a plural form, indicating not that individuals should desire to prophesy, but that the whole church should desire that gift to be used in their assembly. It was the more significant gift because it was able to accomplish what tongues could not.

The type of tongues the Corinthians practiced had no edifying value at all. It could **not speak to men**; it could give them no instruction or exhortation. It could only speak **to God**. I believe a better translation, however, is "to a god." The Greek has no definite article, and such anarthrous constructions usually are translated with an indefinite article (see Acts 17:23, where the same form of *theō* [god] is used in reference to "*an* unknown god").

The translation here of "a god" is supported by the fact that the Bible records no instance of believers speaking to God in anything but normal, intelligible language. Even in Jesus' great high priestly prayer (John 17), in which the Son poured out His heart to the Father, when deity communed with deity, the language is remarkably simple and clear. Jesus in fact warned against using "meaningless repetition, as the Gentiles do, for they suppose that they will be heard for their many words" (Matt. 6:7). His reference included the repetitious and unintelligible gibberish of pagan tongues-speaking, in which certain meaningless sounds were repeated over and over again. The instructional prayer Jesus then gave, commonly called the Lord's Prayer, is a model of simplicity and clarity.

The carnal Corinthians, however, were much more interested in the sophisticated than the simple, in the mysterious rather than the edifying. They did not care that **no one understands,** or literally, "no one hears." Their concern was for the excitement and self-gratification of speaking **mysteries** in the **spirit.** They did not care that the mysteries had no meaning to themselves or to anyone else.

The **mysteries** Paul has in mind here are of the type associated with the pagan mystery religions, out of which many of the Corinthian Christians had come. Unlike the mysteries of the gospel, which are revelations of things previously hidden (Matt. 13:11; Eph. 3:9; etc.), the pagan mysteries intentionally remained mysterious, as unknown truths and principles that supposedly only the initiated elite were privileged to know.

The **spirit** to which Paul refers is not the Holy Spirit, as some interpreters claim, but the person's own spirit, as implied in the Greek (locative case) and indicated in the NASB by **his** (cf. vv. 14-16). Paul is not advocating tongues, but simply characterizing the uselessness of efforts to counterfeit them.

A believer who properly ministers a true spiritual gift ministers not to a false god, but to others. **One who prophesies,** for example, **speaks to men for edification and exhortation and consolation.** The purpose of prophecy is to build up by **edification,** to encourage through exhortation, and to comfort through **consolation.** Spiritual gifts are meant to accomplish something spiritually and practically worthwhile, and are always meant to be of benefit to others, believer or unbeliever.

On the other hand, **one who speaks in a tongue edifies himself.** I believe Paul's point here is sarcastic. (His sarcasm can also be seen in 4:8-10, and reaches its height in 14:16, "was it from you that the word of God first went forth?") Because even true tongues must be interpreted in order to be understood, they cannot possibly edify anyone, including the person speaking, without such interpretation. They cannot, therefore, be intended by God for private devotional use, as many Pentecostals and charismatics claim. Paul here is referring to the *supposed* value the Corinthians placed on their self-styled tongues-speaking. The satisfaction many of the believers experienced in their abuse of tongues was *self*-satisfaction, which came from pride-induced emotion, not from spiritual edification. It is an illegitimate self-building, often building up nothing more than spiritual pride.

The believer, however, who **prophesies edifies the church.** That person uses his gift to minister, as all the gifts are meant to do. The purpose of gifts, Paul was saying, is to minister *for* God but not *to* God. Their purpose certainly is not to selfishly minister to ourselves, as some of the Corinthian believers thought they were doing by speaking in tongues. Our gifts are to minister to others for God's glory. "To each one is given the manifestation of the Spirit for the common good" (12:7).

Why, many people wonder, did Paul say, **I wish that you all spoke in tongues?** He has been warning them about their abuse of tongues, and is beginning a chapter devoted to showing the inferiority of tongues. Why would he have wanted the problem to be compounded by getting everyone involved?

But Paul was wishing the impossible for the sake of emphasis. He knew that all Christians do not have the same gifts. "All do not have gifts of healings, do they? All do not speak with tongues, do they? All do not interpret, do they?" (12:30). The apostle certainly was not suggesting that his wisdom was greater than that of the Holy Spirit, who "works all these things, distributing to each one individually just as He wills" (12:11). To have wished literally that all the Corinthian believers had the gift of tongues would have presumed to improve on the Spirit's wisdom. Paul simply was making it clear that he did not despise the genuine gift of tongues, the true manifestation of which is of God. "If the Holy Spirit chose to endow every one of you with the gift of tongues," he was saying, "that would be fine with me."

Even more, however, Paul wished that all of the Corinthian believers **would prophesy.** He knew that that also was impossible, for the same reason that their all having the gift of tongues was impossible. His point was that, if they insisted on clamoring after the same gift, it would be much better if they clamored after prophecy. Not only was prophecy superior to tongues in edifying the church, but it was a longer-lasting gift, one Paul knew would continue to be used by the Lord long after tongues had ceased.

It is an interpretive key to this chapter to note that in verses 2 and 4 **tongue** is singular (cf. vv. 13, 14, 19, 27), whereas in verse 5 Paul uses the plural **tongues** (cf. vv. 6, 18, 22, 23, 39). Apparently the apostle used the singular form to indicate the counterfeited gift and the plural to indicate the true. Recognizing that distinction may be the reason the King James translators supplied *unknown* before the singular. The singular is used of the false because gibberish is singular; it cannot be gibberishes. There are no kinds of pagan ecstatic speech; there are, however, kinds of languages in the true gift, for which the plural **tongues** is used. The only exception is in v. 27, where the singular is used to refer to a single man speaking a single genuine language.

In any case, even a believer with the genuine gift of **tongues** was never to exercise it **unless he interprets.** Either the tongues-speaker himself or another person (v. 28) was always to interpret, **so that the church may receive edifying** (a Greek purpose clause). Any private, self-building expression could not be the genuine gift, because the purposer of tongues is only realized when it is exercised and interpreted publicly so that the whole assembly may be built up.

Tongues Are Unintelligible

But now, brethren, if I come to you speaking in tongues, what shall I profit you, unless I speak to you either by way of revelation or of knowledge or of prophecy or of teaching? Yet even lifeless things, either flute or harp, in producing a sound, if they do not produce a distinction in the tones, how will it be known what is played on the flute or on the harp? For if the bugle produces an indistinct sound, who will prepare himself for battle? So also you, unless you utter by the tongue speech that is clear, how will it be known what is spoken? For you will be speaking into the air. There are, perhaps, a great many kinds of languages in the world, and no kind is without meaning. If then I do not know the meaning of the language, I shall be to the one who speaks a barbarian, and the one who speaks will be a barbarian to me. So also you, since you are zealous of spiritual gifts, seek to abound for the edification of the church. (14:6-12)

Paul's second major truth regarding the secondary position of tongues is that, in themselves, they are unintelligible. To strengthen his point he uses himself as an illustration, saying **if I come to you.** Even by an apostle, **speaking in tongues** gives no **profit** apart from interpretation, through which the **revelation** or **knowledge** (internal) or the **prophecy** or **teaching** (external) is made understandable to those who hear. Any message is useless if it cannot be comprehended. Again the private use of this gift is excluded. It is useless if it is not edifying to the church.

It is incredible that some Christians put a premium on private or en masse unintelligible utterances that no one, including the speaker, can even attempt to understand. In some instances, what is claimed to be an interpretation has been proved to have no relationship with what was spoken. Persons who have tested an interpreter by speaking in Hebrew, or another language known to them but unknown by the interpreter, have had their words "translated" into messages that had absolutely no correspondence to what was spoken. Like some of the Corinthians, such abusers not only put self-glorification above the edification of the church but add deception to the abuse.

Even lifeless things, such as a **flute or harp,** are expected to make sensible sounds. Rhythm, structure, harmony, and other such orderly qualities make a group of notes music instead of mere noise. For music to be music it must be intelligible in its own way; it must make musical sense. Each note, chord, and phrase has a musical purpose—to communicate joy, sadness, militancy, peace, strife, or whatever the composer intends. **If they do not produce a distinction in the tones, how will it be known what is played on the flute or on the harp?** Without variation, order, and **distinction** of notes, a musical instrument makes only noise. The Corinthians could especially appreciate the musical illustration because their city contained one of the great ancient music halls, seating about 20,000 people.

Changing the figure somewhat, Paul points out that if a **bugle produces an indistinct sound, who will prepare himself for battle?** Hearing a bugle means nothing to a soldier if a definite military call is not being played. Mere bugle notes are meaningless, even if played by the official bugler on the best instrument available. A soldier gets no message from a bunch of random notes. He only gets ready for battle when "Call to Arms," "Charge," or other such calls are played.

In the same way, we cannot communicate Christian truth through meaningless sounds. **Unless you utter by the tongue speech that is clear, how will it be known what is spoken? For you will be speaking into the air.**

The Corinthians were so carnally self-centered that they could not have cared less about communication. They were interested in impressing others, not communicating with them, much less edifying them. Paul compares those Christians to musical instruments blown into by one who is not a musician or a bugle played so poorly that what comes out is unrecognizable. From such incompetence, produced by pride and lovelessness, the Corinthian assembly could not have been other than it was: confused, disorderly, and unproductive (11:21; 14:23; etc.).

Paul continues to hammer away at the same point. **There are, perhaps, a great many kinds of languages in the world, and no kind is without meaning.** He simply mentions the obvious. A language without meaning is pointless. A language without meaning is not really a language. It is meaning that makes language language. The **great many kinds of languages in the world** all sound differently. But each has a single common purpose: to communicate, to transmit **meaning** among those who speak it.

Not only must a legitimate language be used in order to communicate, but both the speaker and hearer must understand it. By definition communication must be two-sided. Otherwise, **I shall be to the one who speaks a barbarian, and the one who speaks will be a barbarian to me. Barbarian** was an onomatopoeic word derived from the twin syllables "bar-bar." To a person who does not know a language it often sounds as if the words are all alike and all meaningless. To most Greeks of Paul's day, anyone who did not speak Greek was a barbarian. His language was unintelligible.

If, therefore, even true tongues are meaningless without interpretation, Paul says, how much more meaningless is pagan-like gibberish that is a counterfeit of the true thing? **Since you are zealous of spiritual gifts, seek to abound for the edification of the church.** In other words, "If you are so eager to minister spiritual gifts, minister them in the way God intended: for the benefit of the church, in particular for the church's edification." Again the clear word is that this gift is for public, not private, use and benefit. The present tense of *zēteō* (**seek**) indicates continuous, habitual action.

The purpose of the gift of tongues, just as the purpose of all languages, was to communicate. Although it was a miraculous sign gift, it also was a communicative gift. From its first occurrence at Pentecost the Lord intended it to be a means of communication. The very miracle of tongues at Pentecost was in the fact that everyone present, though from many different countries, heard the apostles "speak in his own language" (Acts 2:6; cf.vv. 8, 11).

That was always a characteristic of genuine tongues. The Pentecost tongues, and every true manifestation of tongues after that time until their cessation, were understandable—either directly (Acts 2:6) or through an interpreter (1 Cor. 14:27). God did not give two kinds of tongues, one intelligible and the other unintelligible. The Bible speaks of only one gift, whose characteristics and purpose did not change.

THE EFFECTS OF TONGUES ARE EMOTIONAL RATHER THAN RATIONAL

Therefore let one who speaks in a tongue pray that he may interpret. For if I pray in a tongue, my spirit prays, but my mind is unfruitful. What is the outcome then? I shall pray with the spirit and I shall pray with the mind also; I shall sing with the spirit and I shall sing with the mind also. Otherwise if you bless in the spirit only, how will the one who fills the place of the ungifted say the "Amen" at your giving of thanks, since he does not know what you are saying? For you are giving thanks well enough, but the other man is not edified. I thank God, I speak in tongues more than you all; however, in the church I desire to speak five words with my mind, that I may instruct others also, rather than ten thousand words in a tongue. (14:13-19)

In this section Paul continues to teach about counterfeit tongues, and therefore continues to speak sarcastically (cf. 4:8-10). This is indicated in the first place by the fact that he uses the singular **tongue** (see discussion above under vv. 1-5), which refers to the false gift, except in verse 27, where the reference is to one man speaking on one occasion. In the second place, what he says here does not, for the most part, apply to the true gift of tongues. If Paul were not speaking sarcastically of counterfeited tongues he would be asking the Corinthians to seek the true gift of interpretation. But he has already made it clear that the Holy Spirit sovereignly distributes gifts "individually just as He wills" (12:11). Gifts are not to be sought by individuals, but only accepted and properly used.

Paul sarcastically reproaches carnal believers for their immaturity (cf. v. 20), saying in effect, "While you are jabbering away in your unintelligible pseudo-tongues, you could at least ask God to give you some means of making them beneficial to the church. As you now exercise them they are both pagan and pointless."

In the pagan rites with which the Corinthians were so familiar, speaking in ecstatic utterances was considered to be communing with the gods spirit-to-spirit. The experience was intended to bypass the mind and normal understanding. As noted above, its mysteries were meant to remain mysterious. Paul here may have used *pneuma* (which can be translated "spirit," "wind," or "breath") in the sense of breath. If so, He was saying, **If I pray in a** [self-manufactured] **tongue, my** [breath] **prays, but my mind is unfruitful.**

It certainly seems impossible that **spirit** here refers to the Holy Spirit, as some charismatics believe—His Spirit being manifested through our spirits. All Christians are indwelt by the Holy Spirit, but if Paul was speaking of the Holy Spirit in relation to **my spirit**, then grammatically and theologically he also was speaking of the Holy Spirit in relation to **my mind.** The Holy Spirit could not be praying through a person while bypassing his mind. And he certainly was not saying that the mind of the Holy Spirit sometimes can be unfruitful. The apostle has to be speaking entirely of himself, and that hypothetically. "If I, though an apostle, were to speak the gibberish that many of you speak, my mind would have no part in it. I would only be making wind, blowing air (cf. v. 9). What I would say would be as empty and mindless as the ecstasies you used to witness in your pagan temples."

What is the outcome then? The answer is that there is no place for mindless ecstatic prayer. Praying and singing **with the spirit** must be accompanied by praying and singing **with the mind also.** It is obvious that edification cannot exist apart from the mind. Spirituality involves more than the mind, but it never excludes the mind (cf. Rom. 12:1-2; Eph. 4:23; Col. 3:10). In Scripture, and certainly in the writings of Paul, no premium is placed on ignorance. Quoting Deuteronomy 6:5, Jesus reinforced the Old Testament command that we should "love the Lord [our] God with all [our] hearts, and with all [our] soul, and with all [our] mind" (Matt. 22:37).

Praying or singing in tongues could serve no purpose, and Paul would not do it. **Otherwise if you bless in the spirit only, how will the one who fills the place of the ungifted say the "Amen" at your giving of thanks, since he does not know what you are saying?** Ungifted (*idiōtēs*) is, I believe, better translated in its usual sense of ignorant, unlearned, or unskilled. A person who is ignorant of a language being spoken cannot possibly understand what he hears. In a worship service, for example, he could not know when to **say the "Amen" at your giving of thanks.** Prayers or songs of thanks could not include anyone else if they were given in unintelligible sounds.

Amen is a Hebrew word of agreement and encouragement, meaning "So let it be," and was commonly used by worshipers in the synagogue. The practice carried over into some early Christian churches and, in fact, is common in many churches today. A person cannot know when to "Amen," however, if he does not know what is being said. The person speaking in a tongue may feel he is **giving thanks well enough,** but no one else will know what is being said. **The other man is not edified,** as he should be when the gift is ministered properly (14:5, 12).

Lest the Corinthians, after reading this, think he no longer recognized the true gift of tongues, Paul says, **I thank God, I speak in tongues more than you all.** He made it clear that he was not condemning true tongues or enviously criticizing a gift he did not himself possess.

Here he uses the plural **tongues.** He is no longer speaking hypothetically (cf. vv. 6, 11, 14-15), and he is no longer speaking of a counterfeited gift. Paul had had more experience than any of the Corinthians (**you all**) in speaking in tongues, though we have no record of a specific instance. He knew what the proper use of the true gift involved and did not inolve. We can be sure that he did not use the gift in any perverted way for personal gratification. He may have used it as it was used at Pentecost, to bring a supernatural message to those God wanted to reach, and as a miraculous sign verifying the gospel and his apostolic authority. Yet he considered that gift so low in value as compared to his other gifts and ministries that in none of his writings does he mention a specific use of it by him or any other believer.

The gift of languages had a proper place for a prescribed time as a miraculous confirming sign to unbelievers, with an accompanying purpose of edification through interpretation. **However, in the church,** Paul continues, **I desire to speak five words with my mind, that I may instruct others also, rather than ten thousand words in a tongue.** Using the singular (**tongue**) again to refer to pagan gibberish, he emphasizes that an uncountable number of sounds in unintelligible tones has no place in the church and is useless. Five understandable words are far more desirable.

The apostle was not speaking of an exact mathematical ratio. Although *murioi* can mean **ten thousand** (cf. Matt. 18:24), the largest number for which Greek had a specific word, it was commonly used to indicate an inestimable number. It is the term from which we get *myriad,* as it is sometimes translated. In the book of Revelation, for example, the term is repeated ("myriads of myriads") and then added to "thousands of thousands" (5:11) to indicate a completely immeasurable figure.

It is in that general sense that the term is used in our text. To speak a very short sentence of **five words with** [his] **mind,** giving a message that would instruct or encourage his hearers, was more valuable to Paul than a limitless number of **words in a tongue** that was incomprehensible to them.

Because Paul knew that the gift of tongues would cease in a few years, he was not giving instructions for governing tongues in the church today. He was not even giving such instruction to the Corinthians, because he was speaking of counterfeit tongues, which were based in self-centered emotionalism and did not originate with the Holy Spirit. He was giving them, as well as Christians of all ages, warning against using self-serving, worldly, carnal, ineffective, and God-dishonoring substitutes for the true spiritual gifts God has ordained to be ministered in the power and in the fruit of the Spirit and for the blessing and edification of His church.

The Purpose and Procedure for the Gift of Tongues

38

(14:20-28)

Brethren, do not be children in your thinking; yet in evil be babes, but in your thinking be mature. In the Law it is written, 'By men of strange tongues and by the lips of strangers I will speak to this people, and even so they will not listen to Me,' says the Lord. So then tongues are for a sign, not to those who believe, but to unbelievers; but prophecy is for a sign, not to unbelievers, but to those who believe. If therefore the whole church should assemble together and all speak in tongues, and ungifted men or unbelievers enter, will they not say that you are mad? But if all prophesy, and an unbeliever or an ungifted man enters, he is convicted by all, he is called to account by all; the secrets of his heart are disclosed; and so he will fall on his face and worship God, declaring that God is certainly among you.

What is the outcome then, brethren? When you assemble, each one has a psalm, has a teaching, has a revelation, has a tongue, has an interpretation. Let all things be done for edification. If anyone speaks in a tongue, it should be by two or at the most three, and each in turn, and let one interpret; but if there is no interpreter, let him keep silent in the church; and let him speak to himself and to God. (14:20-28)

In this passage Paul first reviews the primary purpose of the gift of languages and then gives the procedure, or guidelines, for its proper use. This is an unusually important section, because it gives a clear picture of what the gift of languages was designed to do and therefore gives another basic criterion for judging whether or not that gift is valid today.

The apostle has just pointed out that even the true gift was inferior to prophecy and teaching, because it was not primarily intended for edification of the church, though edification came when what was spoken was translated or interpreted (14:5). It was therefore true, technically, that the gift of translation, a distinct gift from speaking in tongues (12:10, 30), was the edifying gift.

Earlier in the letter Paul makes it clear that tongues-speaking was not an evidence or proof of the baptism of the Holy Spirit: "For by one Spirit we were all baptized into one body" (12:13). Every Christian is baptized by the Holy Spirit, but not every Christian is given the gift of tongues (12:30). At no time has every believer received or been promised the gift of tongues, not even during apostolic times, when that gift was active. Immediately after the first and most dramatic occurrence of the language miracle, when three thousand people believed in Christ and received the gift of the Holy Spirit, there is no record of a single one of them speaking in tongues! We are told that the new converts listened to the apostles' teaching, fellowshipped with each other, ate and prayed together, shared their possessions, worshiped in the Temple together, and praised God (Acts 2:37-47). But no mention is made of their speaking in tongues.

A short while later, as Peter and John met with some of the disciples, the group was "all filled with the Holy Spirit." The result of that filling was speaking "the word of God with boldness," not speaking in tongues (4:31).

The Purpose of Tongues: a Sign

Brethren, do not be children in your thinking; yet in evil be babes, but in your thinking be mature. In the Law it is written, 'By men of strange tongues and by the lips of strangers I will speak to this people, and even so they will not listen to Me,' says the Lord. So then tongues are for a sign, not to those who believe, but to unbelievers; but prophecy is for a sign, not to unbelievers, but to those who believe. If therefore the whole church should assemble together and all speak in tongues, and ungifted men or unbelievers enter, will they not say that you are mad? But if all prophesy, and an unbeliever or an ungifted man enters, he is convicted by all, he is called to account by all; the secrets of his heart are disclosed; and so he will fall on his face and worship God, declaring that God is certainly among you. (14:20-25)

As Paul begins to explain the true purpose of tongues, he appeals to the Corinthians to be **mature** in their **thinking**. It was their loveless immaturity and carnality that caused their theological, spiritual, and moral problems, including their misuse and counterfeiting of the gifts. Before they could comprehend what the apostle was trying to say, they would have to stop being **children** in their **thinking.**

In evil the Corinthians were anything but **babes.** They were highly advanced in every sort of sin. They had virtually all the manifestations of the flesh and almost none of the fruit of the Spirit (Gal. 5:19-23). They were "children, tossed here and there by waves, and carried about by every wind of doctrine, by the trickery of men, by craftiness in deceitful scheming" (Eph. 4:14). By their selfish, ego-building abuse of the gift of tongues they were, among other things, ignoring the rest of the family of God.

They could not be taught because they were not interested in learning. They were interested only in using spiritual means and fellow believers in whatever ways would serve their own ends. They were not interested in truth but in experience, not in right doctrine or right living but only in good feelings. They were not interested in pleasing the Lord or their fellow Christians but only themselves. Experience always won out over truth, emotions always won out over reason, and self-will always won out over God's will. Unlike the Bereans (Acts 17:11), the Corinthians did not bother to check what they heard against Scripture. They did not bother to "test the spirits to see whether they [were] from God" (1 John 4:1). If something sounded good, they believed it; if it felt good, they did it. Like the Israelites in the time of the judges, everyone "did what was right in his own eyes" (Judg. 17:6; 21:25).

Hopefully having shamed the Corinthians into attention by confronting their abuse of the gifts, Paul explains to them the true purpose of tongues. He begins with a freely rendered passage from Isaiah 28:11-12. Hundreds of years before Christ, the Lord told Israel that one day He would **speak to this people by strange tongues** from **the lips of strangers.** Despite this miraculous sign, however, she would **not listen to Me.**

Those **strange tongues,** Paul says, are what you now know and experience as the gift of languages. God has given that gift as **a sign, not to those who believe, but to unbelievers.** Here is the heart of chapter 14 and the most important truth about this phenomenon: it was given as **a sign,** and as a sign to **unbelievers,** specifically unbelieving Jews, the unbelievers among **this people.** *The gift of tongues was given solely as a sign to unbelieving Israel.*

The sign was threefold: a sign of cursing, a sign of blessing, and a sign of authority.

A SIGN OF CURSING

Some 15 years or so before Isaiah prophesied about the strange tongues from the lips of strangers, the northern kingdom of Israel had been conquered and taken captive by the Assyrians (in 722 B.C.) because of unbelief and apostasy. The prophet then warned the southern kingdom, Judah, that the same judgment awaited her at the hands of the Babylonians. The proud religious leaders of Judah would not listen to Isaiah. His teaching was too simple. He talked to them, they claimed, as if they were babies, "Those just weaned from milk" and "just taken from the breast." He taught them as if they were kindergartners: "Order on order, order on order, line on line, line on line, a little here, a little there" (Isa. 28:9-10). God had indeed spoken to them simply, in order that the least mature among them could understand and so that no Israelite would have an excuse for not knowing the Lord's will and promise. The essence of His promise was, "Here is rest, give rest to the weary," and "Here is repose"; yet Israel "would not listen" (v. 12).

About 800 years before Isaiah, God had warned Israel that "The Lord will bring a nation against you from afar, from the end of the earth, as the eagle swoops down, a nation whose language you shall not understand" (Deut. 28:49). The strange language of their conquerors would be a sign of God's judgment. About 100 years after Isaiah, the Lord warned through Jeremiah, "Behold, I am bringing a nation against you from afar, O house of Israel, . . . a nation whose language you do not know, nor can you understand what they say" (Jer. 5:15). The sign of judgment would be a language they could not understand.

When the apostles spoke at Pentecost and were heard in their own language by Jews from many countries (Acts 2:7-11), those Jews should have known that God's judgment was imminent. His judgment had fallen on rebellious Israel and then on rebellious Judah. How much more would it fall on those of His people who now had crucified the Son of God? In A.D. 70 that great judgment fell, when Jerusalem was utterly destroyed by the Roman general Titus (later emperor). Over one million Jews were slaughtered; thousands more were taken captive; the Temple was plundered, desecrated, and then utterly destroyed; and the rest of the city was burned to the ground. One historian comments that Jerusalem had no history for 60 years. Just as Jesus had predicted when He wept over the city, "Your enemies will throw up a bank before you, and surround you, and hem you in on every side, and will level you to the ground and your children within you, and they will not leave in you one stone upon another, because you did not recognize the time of your visitation" (Luke 19:44; cf. 21:20-24).

After the destruction of Jerusalem, and especially of the Temple, the reason for tongues ceased to exist. The judgment of which it was a sign had come. After the Pentecost manifestation of tongues, Peter, by implication, reminded his hearers of that judgment: "Therefore let all the house of Israel know for certain that God has made Him both Lord and Christ—this Jesus whom you crucified" (Acts 2:36; cf. vv. 22-23).

A SIGN OF BLESSING

The second sign was a residual benefit of the first. The gift of tongues was a sign that God would no longer work through one nation, and favor one people. The church of Jesus Christ was for all peoples of all nations, a church in which there are many languages but no barriers. "There is neither Jew nor Greek, there is neither slave nor free man, there is neither male nor female; for you are all one in Christ Jesus" (Gal. 3:28).

With great compassion and sorrow for his fellow Jews, Paul wrote in Romans, "But by their transgression salvation has come to the Gentiles, to make them jealous." But with a note of great hope he continued, "Now if their transgression be riches for the world and their failure be riches for the Gentiles, how much more will their fulfillment be!" (11:11-12). A few verses later he explains more fully: "For I do not want you, brethren, to be uninformed of this mystery, lest you be wise in your own estimation, that a partial hardening has happened to Israel until the fullness of the Gentiles has come in; and thus all Israel will be saved; just as it is written" (vv. 25-26). The way would always be open for individual Jews to come into the kingdom, for the hardening was only partial, and one day the entire nation of Israel would be brought back to her Lord. The sign of tongues was repeated when the Gentiles were included in the church, as recorded in Acts 10:44-46.

A SIGN OF AUTHORITY

Those who preached the judgment and promised the blessing were the apostles and prophets, whose authority was validated by "signs and wonders and miracles" (2 Cor. 12:12; cf. Rom. 15:19). Among the authenticating signs was the gift of tongues, in which Paul spoke "more than you all" (1 Cor. 14:18).

As a sign, the purpose of tongues ended when that to which it pointed ended. A person driving to Los Angeles may see the first mileage sign about 300 miles away. Later he sees one that reads "200 miles to Los Angeles," and then "50 miles," and then "10 miles." After he passes through the city, however, the mileage signs to Los Angeles cease. They have no further purpose, because that to which they pointed has been reached and passed. The gift of tongues was attached irretrievably to one point in history, and that point has long been passed.

It is interesting, and I believe highly significant, that no record is given of a single word spoken in tongues or even interpreted. Every reference to tongues is general. They are always mentioned in relation to their purpose and significance, never in relation to their specific content. The messages given in tongues were not new revelations or new insights, but, as at Pentecost, simply unique expressions of old truths, "the mighty deeds of God" (Acts 2:11). Though tongues could edify when interpreted, their purpose was not to teach, but to point, not to reveal God's truth but to validate the truth of His appointed spokesmen.

Since the destruction of Jerusalem in A.D. 70 there has been no purpose for the sign gift of tongues, because that to which it pointed has been reached and passed. Israel has been set aside, the Gentiles have been brought in, and the apostles have given the faith once-for-all delivered to the saints.

But prophecy, Paul goes on to say, is for a sign, not to unbelievers, but to those who believe. As indicated by italics in the NASB text, is for a sign is not in the Greek text and was supplied by the translators. According to Greek grammar such a meaning is possible, but it is not required. Because prophesying is nowhere else spoken of as a sign, I do not believe that is Paul's meaning here. He was not saying that prophecy is a sign to believers as tongues was a sign to unbelievers. Prophecy is given to those who believe, and is not given as a sign pointing to something else but for edification in itself (vv. 4, 31).

The limited function of the genuine gift of tongues can be seen in the fact that, even during its proper time in history, it could be misused and become a hindrance to worship and to evangelism. If everyone with the gift spoke at once, **and ungifted men or unbelievers enter, will they not say that you are mad?** As in v. 16, I believe that *idiōtēs* (**ungifted**) is better rendered in its more common meaning of unlearned or ignorant.

An unbelieving Gentile would have been turned off **if . . . the whole church should assemble together and all speak in tongues,** because he would have seen no meaning in the sign. An unbelieving Jew would have been turned off because of the bedlam and confusion. *Mainomai* (**mad**) means to be in a frenzied rage, to be beside oneself in anger. An unbeliever, Gentile or Jew, would go away from such a service thinking it was just another wild and meaningless ritual, much like those of paganism.

Though they were not given for edification, tongues were nevertheless to be understood, not to cause bewilderment. The amazement of the Jewish visitors in Jerusalem at Pentecost was in the fact that they understood what was spoken in tongues in their "own tongues" (Acts 2:11).

On the other hand, **if all prophesy, and an unbeliever or an ungifted man enters, he is convicted by all, he is called to account by all.** These judicial verbs indicate that preaching the Word brings men to the conviction that the argument is true, and that they will be judged on the basis of their response. Paul continues to contrast tongues with prophecy, again showing prophecy's superiority. **Prophecy** is used here in its most general sense of speaking forth God's Word. When the Word is proclaimed it speaks to men's hearts and brings conviction of sin, the first step in coming to faith. The convicted person comes to see himself as he really is, because **the secrets of his heart are disclosed.** His sinful intentions and acts are revealed to him. Consequently, he will **fall on his face and worship God, declaring that God is certainly among you.** The church's most powerful testimony is not in its ecstasies, but in its clear proclamation of the powerful Word of God (Heb. 4:12).

When tongues were misused, there was only confusion, frustration, and bewilderment. Unbelievers were repelled and believers were unedified. But prophecy edifies believers and evangelizes unbelievers. God is honored and men are blessed when His Word is clearly declared. Our desire should be that every service, every activity, everything that we say or do in the Lord's name will cause people to say **God is certainly among you.**

THE PROCEDURE FOR TONGUES: SYSTEMATIC

What is the outcome then, brethren? When you assemble, each one has a psalm, has a teaching, has a revelation, has a tongue, has an interpretation. Let all things be done for edification. If anyone speaks in a tongue, it should be by two or at the most three, and each in turn, and let one interpret; but if there is no interpreter, let him keep silent in the church; and let him speak to himself and to God. (14:26-28)

The New Testament always gives a doctrinal basis for Christian behavior. There is always a theological reason to do what we are called to do. Just as Paul uses the first eleven chapters of Romans to lay the doctrinal foundation for the exhortations of chapters 12-16, so here he uses the first twenty-five verses of 1 Corinthians 14 to lay the doctrinal foundation for the exhortations of verses 26-40.

The primary emphasis of verses 26-40 is that the biblical procedure for the use of languages is to be systematic and orderly, according to divine pattern—contrary to the confused way in which the Corinthian believers seemed to do everything. Whether they had **a psalm, a teaching, a revelation, a tongue,** or **an interpretation,** they all wanted to participate at the same time. They were not interested in serving, or learning, or edifying, but only in self-expression and self-glory. Everyone vied for attention and preeminence.

A psalm referred to reading, or perhaps singing, one of the Old Testament psalms. **A teaching** probably indicates a favorite doctrine or pet subject that was presented and expounded. Other members had what they claimed was a new **revelation** from God. Others spoke in **a tongue,** true or counterfeited, while still others gave **an interpretation.**

Except for the possibility of counterfeited tongues, all of those things were good and legitimate parts of worship. The problem was that they were all done at the same time. No one was left to listen, except for the few bewildered visitors, who no doubt thought the whole group was crazy (see v. 23). No one could benefit from such bedlam.

In light of such confusion and disorder, Paul gives a clear command: **Let all things be done for edification.**

Oikodomē (**edification**) literally means "housebuilding," the construction of a house. Figuratively, it refers to growing, improving, or maturing. The spiritual lives of Christians need to be built up and improved, expanded to fulness and completeness. The primary responsibility of Christians to each other is to build each other up. Edification is a major responsibility of church leaders (Eph. 4:11-12), but it is also the responsibility of all other Christians. *Every* believer is called to be an edifier. "Therefore encourage one another, and build up one another, just as you also are doing" (1 Thess. 5:11). "Let each of us please his neighbor for his good, to his edification. For even Christ did not please Himself" (Rom 15:2-3). Jesus "did not come to be served, but to serve, and to give His life a ransom for many" (Matt. 20:28). Our Lord did not seek what was beneficial to Himself but what was beneficial to those He came to save.

As Paul repeatedly points out in this fourteenth chapter, a major evidence of the Corinthians' loveless immaturity was their selfish concern for themselves, the other side of which was lack of concern for the edification, the building up, of their brothers and sisters in Christ (vv. 3-5, 12, 17, 26, 31). They did not, as Paul commanded, "pursue the things which make for peace and the building up of one another" (Rom.14:19). That which builds others up is also that which brings harmony, just as that which is selfish is also that which brings disharmony.

Christians are built up by only one thing, the Word of God. That is the tool with which all spiritual building is done. "All Scripture is inspired by God and profitable for teaching, for reproof, for correction, for training in righteousness; that the man of God may be adequate, equipped for every good work" (2 Tim. 3:16-17). That is the tool with which every believer should be skilled.

REGULATIONS FOR SPEAKING IN TONGUES

In verses 27-28 Paul gives four regulations for the use of tongues: (1) only two or three persons should speak; (2) they should speak in turn; (3) what they say should be interpreted; and (4) if no one is present to interpret, they should not speak.

Contrary to the pagan ecstasies that many of the Corinthian Christians were mimicking, the Holy Spirit does not work through persons who are out of self-control or "slain in the spirit." He ministers all of His gifts through the conscious, aware minds of the saints.

First, **If anyone speaks in a tongue, it should be by two or at the most three.** In any one service no more than three persons, and preferably no more than two, were permitted to speak in tongues. Although Paul has regularly used the singular **tongue** to refer to the counterfeited gift, it seems clear that here he is speaking of the genuine thing. He hardly would have given regulations for using a counterfeit. Here he uses the singular **tongue** to correspond to the singular subject, **anyone**, since a given person at a given time would speak only in one language.

Second, those two or three persons should not speak simultaneously as they were accustomed to doing, but **each in turn**. Orderliness, understandability, and courtesy all demand such a procedure. Several persons speaking in the same language at the same time would be confusing enough, but doing so in different languages would be bedlam.

One of the strongest indictments of the modern charismatic movement is the common practice of many persons speaking, praying, and singing at the same time, with no one paying attention to what others are doing or saying. It is everyone for himself, just as it was in the Corinth, and is in clear violation of Paul's command that **each** speak **in turn.**

Third, **let one interpret.** Everything spoken in a tongue must be interpreted, and apparently by only one interpreter. In the Greek construction, one is in the emphatic position, indicating that a single person is involved. The interpreters in Corinth were as self-serving as those who spoke in tongues, and each tried to outdo the other. Verse 26 implies that everyone, whatever they were doing, tried to shout everyone else down. Paul tells them that, whereas two or three were allowed to speak in turn, only **one** was to **interpret.**

Fourth, **if there is no interpreter, let him keep silent in the church.** Although speaking in languages and translating those languages were distinct gifts, they were not to be used apart from one another. An interpreter *could not* exercise his gift unless there were speaking, and a speaker *should not* exercise his gift unless there were interpretation. Paul's instruction presupposed that the congregation knew which believers had the gift of interpretation. If one of those persons was not present, there was to be no speaking in tongues. The rule was clear and simple: no interpreter, no speaking out loud. A person who still felt compelled to speak was to meditate and pray, to speak silently **to himself and to God.**

The Procedure for Prophecy (14:29-40)

And let two or three prophets speak, and let the others pass judgment. But if a revelation is made to another who is seated, let the first keep silent. For you can all prophesy one by one, so that all may learn and all may be exhorted; and the spirits of prophets are subject to prophets; for God is not a God of confusion but of peace, as in all the churches of the saints.

Let the women keep silent in the churches; for they are not permitted to speak, but let them subject themselves, just as the Law also says. And if they desire to learn anything, let them ask their own husbands at home; for it is improper for a woman to speak in church. Was it from you that the word of God first went forth? Or has it come to you only?

If anyone thinks he is a prophet or spiritual, let him recognize that the things which I write to you are the Lord's commandment. But if anyone does not recognize this, he is not recognized.

Therefore, my brethren, desire earnestly to prophesy, and do not forbid to speak in tongues. But let all things be done properly and in an orderly manner. (14:29-40)

In this section the apostle concludes his critical discussion of matters related to spiritual gifts. He pulls together a few remaining exhortations to summarize what had been left unsaid in the previous correctives. Admittedly, as has been obvious, some things in this whole passage are difficult to understand, because we cannot fully reconstruct the scene in Corinth. The last few exhortations, however, leave little confusion about their meaning.

And let two or three prophets speak, and let the others pass judgment. But if a revelation is made to another who is seated, let the first keep silent. For you can all prophesy one by one, so that all may learn and all may be exhorted; and the spirits of prophets are subject to prophets; for God is not a God of confusion but of peace. (14:29-33a)

Like that of the apostles, and unlike that of pastors and teachers, however, the unique office of prophet ceased to exist while the church was still very young. Judging from Paul's pastoral epistles (1 & 2 Timothy and Titus), prophets ceased to function in the church even before the end of the apostolic age. In those letters he makes considerable mention of church leadership—elders, deacons, deaconesses, and bishops—but makes no mention of prophets. Along with the apostles, prophets were a part of the foundation of the church (Eph. 2:20), and are the first office to have disappeared from the New Testament church.

But when Paul wrote this letter to Corinth, prophets were still very central to the work of that church. In fact, nowhere in this letter is there mention of a pastor, elder, or overseer. The prophets seem to have been the key leaders in the early days of the church (cf. Acts 13:1). Because this was obviously the case in Corinth, Paul was compelled to give some principles for the prophets to follow.

In verses 29-33a Paul gives four regulations for prophesying: (1) only two or three prophets were to speak; (2) the other prophets were to judge what was said; (3) if someone else had a revelation, the first speaker was to yield to him; and (4) each prophet was to speak in turn.

First, only **two or three prophets** were to **speak** at any given service. Those New Testament **prophets** spoke for the Lord in two ways. In some instances they gave new revelation from God to the church. And, by reiterating what the apostles taught, they also proclaimed what had previously been revealed, much as preachers and teachers of the Word do today.

Second, when prophets spoke in a meeting, the other prophets present were to **pass judgment** (from *diakrinō*). The judging prophets may have had the gift of discernment (cf. 12:10; *diakrisis*, "distinguishing") or they may simply have measured what was said against their own knowledge of the Word and will of God. In any case they were collectively to evaluate the validity of all prophetic messages. The Holy Spirit enabled those evaluating prophets to "test the spirits to see whether they [were] from God" (1 John 4:1). Since the prophets sometimes were entrusted with new revelation, it was especially vital that everything they preached and taught was absolutely true and consistent. Because they were helping build the foundation of the church, the validity of their teaching was of the utmost importance. No prophet acted unilaterally in teaching. There was accountability among all of them.

Third, **if a revelation is made to another who is seated, let the first keep silent.** A new revelation took precedence over the reiteration of something that had already been taught. It was not that the truths in the new revelation were necessarily more important than those then being proclaimed, but that, at the moment, the new should be heard while it was fresh from the Lord. That is not an issue in the church today, because the revelation aspect of the prophetic ministry ceased with the completion of the New Testament. But apparently in the early church such conflicts sometimes occurred. When they did, the prophet with the new revelation was to be given the floor. In other words, when God spoke directly, everyone was to listen.

Fourth, whether to give new revelation or to reinforce previous revelation, the prophets were to **prophesy one by one.** Just as with speaking in tongues, it was imperative that only one person speak at a time, **so that all may learn and all may be exhorted.** The conjunction *hina* (**so that**) is used to express the twofold purpose for all such prophesying: learning and exhortation (cf. v. 3).

Paul reinforces the principle of prophets judging one another's messages (cf. 29). **The spirits of prophets are subject to prophets** (cf. v. 29). Not only are prophets to judge the authenticity of what other prophets say, but each prophet is to have control of his own spirit. The Bible knows nothing of out-of-spirit or out-of-mind revelations. Those to whom God revealed His Word did not always fully comprehend the message they were given, but they were always fully aware of what the message was and aware that it was given to them by God. God does not bypass men's minds either to reveal or to teach His Word. There were no ecstatic, bizarre, trancelike experiences related to divine action or the prophet, such as occurred and occurs with demonic revelations. That was one clear test to distinguish the work of the Holy Spirit from the work of demons, and assumes the Corinthians were having difficulty so distinguishing (cf. 12:3).

For God is not a God of confusion but of peace. Here is the key to the whole chapter. Our worship of God should reflect the character and nature of God. He is the God of **peace** and harmony, not of strife and **confusion** (cf. Rom. 15:33; 2 Thess. 3:16; Heb. 13:20). God cannot be honored where there is disharmony and confusion, competition and frenzy, self-serving and self-glorying. Chaos and dischord in a church meeting is certain proof that the Spirit of God is not in control. Where His Spirit rules there is always **peace** (cf. James 3:14-18).

OTHER GENERAL REGULATIONS

As in all the churches of the saints. Let the women keep silent in the churches; for they are not permitted to speak, but let them subject themselves, just as the Law also says. And if they desire to learn anything, let them ask their own husbands at home; for it is improper for a woman to speak in church. Was it from you that the word of God first went forth? Or has it come to you only?

If anyone thinks he is a prophet or spiritual, let him recognize that the things which I write to you are the Lord's commandment. But if anyone does not recognize this, he is not recognized. (14:33b-38)

The second half of verse 33 seems to fit best with verse 34. The phrase **as in all the churches of the saints** is not logically related to God's not being a God of confusion. The phrase does, however, make a logical introduction to **Let the women keep silent in the churches; for they are not permitted to speak.** Paul was emphasizing the fact that the principle of women's not speaking in church services was not local, geographical, or cultural, but universal, **in all the churches of the saints.** Though it embraces tongues, the context here refers to prophecy. Women are not to exercise any such ministries.

The women who joined in the chaotic self-expression which Paul has been condemning not only added to the confusion but should not have been speaking in the first place. In God's order for the church, women should **subject themselves, just as the Law also says.** The principle was first taught in the Old Testament and is reaffirmed in the New. In reflection of that principle, no women were permitted to speak at the Jewish synagogues.

One of the designs of creation, as well as one of the primary consequences of the Fall, was the submission of women (Gen. 3:16). Paul reflected that principle explicitly when he said, "Let a woman quietly receive instruction with entire submissiveness. But I do not allow a woman to teach or exercise authority over a man, but to remain quiet" (1 Tim. 2:11-12). Paul's argument was not based on cultural standards but on two historic and foundational facts: (1) "Adam . . . was first created, and then Eve" and (2) "it was not Adam who was deceived, but the woman" (vv. 13-14). Men are to lead in love; women are to submit in love. That is God's design.

It is not coincidental that, like Corinth, many of the churches today that practice speaking in tongues and claim gifts of healing also permit women to engage in speaking ministry. Many charismatic groups, in fact, were begun by women, just as many of the cults that have sprung from Christianity were founded by women. When women usurp man's God-ordained role, they inevitably fall into other unbiblical practices and delusions.

Women may be highly gifted teachers and leaders, but those gifts are not to be exercised over men in the services of the church. God has ordained order in His creation, an order that reflects His own nature and that therefore should be reflected in His church. When any part of His order is ignored or rejected, His church is weakened and He is dishonored. Just as God's Spirit cannot be in control where there is confusion and chaos in the church, He cannot be in control where women take upon themselves roles that He has restricted to men. **It is improper** [*aischros,* "shameful, disgraceful"] **for a woman to speak in church.** That statement leaves no question as to its meaning.

If they desire to learn anything, let them ask their own husbands at home. The implication is present in this statement that certain women were out of order in asking questions in the church service. If they desired to learn, the church was no place for them to express their questions in a disruptive way. Paul also implies, of course, that Christian husbands should be well taught in the Word. Many women are tempted to go beyond their biblical roles because of frustration with Christian men, often including their own husbands, who do not responsibly fulfill the leadership assignments God has given them. But God has established the proper order and relationship of male-female roles in the church, and they are not to be transgressed for any reason. For a woman to take on a man's role because he has neglected it merely compounds the problem. It is not possible for a woman to substitute for a man in such things. God often has led women to do work that men have refused to do, but He does not lead them to accomplish that work through roles He has restricted to men.

There are times in informal meetings and Bible studies where it is entirely proper for men and women to share equally in exchanging questions and insights. But when the church comes together as a body to worship God, His standards are clear: the role of leadership is reserved for men.

Obviously many of the Corinthian believers, men as well as women, had contended with Paul about this matter. They were determined to follow their own principles and standards regardless of what the apostle or other mature leaders said. In its pride and arrogance the church wanted to be a law unto itself, deciding on its own what was right and proper. They acted as if they had a corner on truth and dared others to question them.

The Corinthians put themselves above Scripture, either ignoring it or interpreting it in ways that fit their predisposed notions. So Paul challenges them in his most biting and sarcastic words yet: **Was it from you that the word of God first went forth? Or has it come to you only?** He said, in effect, "If you didn't write Scripture, then obey it. If you are not the sole receivers of God's Word, then subject yourselves to it as faithful children of God, as Christians everywhere else are obliged to do." No believer has a right to overrule, ignore, alter, or disobey the Word of God. To do so is to put himself above God's Word.

He continues the challenge: **If anyone thinks he is a prophet or spiritual, let him recognize that the things which I write to you are the Lord's commandment.** In the context of what Paul has been focusing on in reference to prophets and tongues, it seems that **spiritual** must refer primarily to those who spoke in tongues, the special spiritual language the Corinthians prized so highly. His point is this: "If a person claims to be a prophet or to have the gift of tongues or any other spiritual gift, the mark of his true calling and faithful ministry will be his acknowledging that what I teach as an apostle are the truths of God. If a person is truly called or gifted of God and is sincerely trying to follow God, he will submit the exercise of his calling and gift to the principles God has revealed to me as His commandments." What the apostle taught was not optional.

On the other side, **But if anyone does not recognize this, he is not recognized.** This play on words carries the idea that anyone who disregards the Word should himself be disregarded. The mark of a false prophet or a counterfeiter of tongues, or of a person who misuses a true calling or gift, was his rejection of what Paul taught. Because such persons rejected the apostle's teaching, they were rejected as legitimate servants of God. Because it was the revelation of God as Scripture, Paul's teaching was absolutely authoritative (cf. 2 Pet. 3:15-16).

This emphasis on authority comes at an appropriate place, because so many Corinthian believers had wanted to disregard Paul's words about tongues and women. Paul says the church should ignore such ignorant, self-styled rejectors.

In verses 37-38 Paul gives perhaps his strongest claim to authority as God's apostle. Paul had personal limitations and blind spots, which he freely recognized (see, e.g., Phil. 3:12-14). But when He spoke for God, his views were not tainted by cultural or personal bias. He did not, for instance, teach the submission of women in the church because of his Jewish background or in order to conform to any personal male chauvinism. He taught that truth because he himself had been so taught by the Lord. Paul did not claim omniscience, but he claimed unequivocally that everything he taught about God, about His gospel, and about His church was God's own teaching, **the Lord's commandment.**

No matter what their position, training, experience, expertise, or talents, Christians who reject Paul's teaching reject God's teaching, and are themselves to be rejected as teachers or leaders in His church.

SUMMARY EXHORTATION

Therefore, my brethren, desire earnestly to prophesy, and do not forbid to speak in tongues. But let all things be done properly and in an orderly manner. (14:39-40)

Paul concludes the chapter with a summary exhortation for the Corinthians to hold prophecy in the superior position in their services, but not to despise or reject legitimate speaking in tongues. And whatever they did in the Lord's name should be done in the right way.

In their assemblies they were collectively to **desire earnestly** [second person plural] **to prophesy,** because prophecy is the great edifier, the great instructor and teacher. Prophecy is so important because edification is so important. Again, as the verb form proves, Paul is not suggesting that individuals seek the gift of prophecy (see comments in chap. 37 on 14:1).

But, although secondary to prophecy, legitimate **tongues** that are legitimately exercised should also be recognized as of the Lord, and not ridiculed or forbidden. **Do not forbid** is also in the plural and does not advocate individual seeking of tongues, but refers to the church as a group allowing the proper gifts to be exercised. Tongues was a limited gift, both in purpose and in duration, but it was the Lord's gift, and, as long as it was active, was not to be despised or hindered.

Right revelation should be obeyed in the right way, and right gifts should be exercised in the right way. The basic meaning of *euschēmonōs* (**properly**) is gracefully, becomingly, harmoniously, beautifully. **Orderly** has the meaning of "in turn" or "one at a time" (cf. v. 27). God is a God of beauty and harmony, of propriety and order, and **all things** that His children do should reflect those divine characteristics.

The Evidence for Christ's Resurrection (15:1-11)

40

Now I make known to you, brethren, the gospel which I preached to you, which also you received, in which also you stand, by which also you are saved, if you hold fast the word which I preached to you, unless you believed in vain. For I delivered to you as of first importance what I also received, that Christ died for our sins according to the Scriptures, and that He was buried, and that He was raised on the third day according to the Scriptures, and that He appeared to Cephas, then to the twelve. After that He appeared to more than five hundred brethren at one time, most of whom remain until now, but some have fallen asleep; then He appeared to James, then to all the apostles; and last of all, as it were to one untimely born, He appeared to me also. For I am the least of the apostles, who am not fit to be called an apostle, because I persecuted the church of God. But by the grace of God I am what I am, and His grace toward me did not prove vain; but I labored even more than all of them, yet not I, but the grace of God with me. Whether then it was I or they, so we preach and so you believed. (15:1-11)

Unlike most of 1 Corinthians, chapter 15 is devoted entirely to doctrine, and to a single doctrine at that. In these 58 verses Paul gives the most extensive treatment of the resurrection in all of Scripture.

Just as the heart pumps life-giving blood to every part of the body, so the truth of the resurrection gives life to every other area of gospel truth. The resurrection is the pivot on which all of Christianity turns and without which none of the other truths would much matter. Without the resurrection, Christianity would be so much wishful thinking, taking its place alongside all other human philosophy and religious speculation.

The resurrection was the focal point of every other truth Christ taught. He taught His disciples that "the Son of Man must suffer many things and be rejected by the elders and the chief priests and the scribes, and be killed, and after three days rise again" (Mark 8:31; cf. 9:9, 31). He said, "I am the resurrection and the life; he who believes in Me shall live even if he dies" (John 11:25). The first two sermons preached after Pentecost both focused on the resurrection of Christ (Acts 2:14-36; 3:12-26). Because of that truth the heart-broken followers of the crucified Rabbi were turned into the courageous witnesses and martyrs who, in a few years, spread the gospel across the Roman empire and beyond. Belief in the resurrection, the truth that this life is only a prelude to the life to come for those who trust in Jesus Christ, could not be obliterated by ridicule, prison, torture, or even death. No fear or dread in this life can quench the hope and joy of an assured life to come.

True New Testament Christianity is a religion of the resurrection. John Locke, the 18th-century British philosopher, said, "Our Saviour's resurrection is truly of great importance in Christianity, so great that His being or not being the Messiah stands or falls with it."

Because it is the cornerstone of the gospel, the resurrection has been the target of Satan's greatest attacks against the church. If the resurrection is eliminated, the life-giving power of the gospel is eliminated, the deity of Christ is eliminated, salvation from sin is eliminated, and eternal life is eliminated. "If we have hoped in Christ in this life only, we are of all men most to be pitied" (1 Cor. 15:19). If Christ did not live past the grave, those who trust in Him surely cannot hope to do so.

Without the resurrection salvation could not have been provided, and without belief in the resurrection salvation cannot be received. "If you confess with your mouth Jesus as Lord, and believe in your heart that God raised Him from the dead, you shall be saved" (Rom. 10:9). It is not possible, therefore, to be a Christian and not believe in the resurrection of Jesus Christ.

The doctrinal problem on which this chapter focuses was not the Corinthians' disbelief in Christ's resurrection but confusion about their own. Paul was not trying to convince them that Christ rose from the dead but that one day they, too, would be raised with Him to eternal life. Nevertheless, to lay the foundation, in the first eleven verses he reviews the evidences for Jesus' resurrection, a truth he acknowledges they already believed (vv. 1, 11). The five evidences, or testimonies, he presents are: the church; the Scriptures; the eyewitnesses; a special witness, the apostle himself; and the common message.

THE TESTIMONY OF THE CHURCH

Now I make known to you, brethren, the gospel which I preached to you,

which also you received, in which also you stand, by which also you are saved, if you hold fast the word which I preached to you, unless you believed in vain. (15:1-2)

The first testimony is not stated explicitly but is implied. The very fact that the Corinthian Christians themselves, and all other Christians everywhere, had received the gospel and believed in Jesus Christ and had been miraculously changed, was in itself a strong evidence of the power of the gospel, which power is in the resurrection of Christ.

By addressing them again as **brethren** (cf. 1:10; 2:1; 3:1; 10:1; etc.) Paul assures those to whom he writes that he recognizes them to be fellow Christians. The term not only expresses his spiritual identity with them but also his love (cf. 15:58).

The apostle tells them that what he is about to say is nothing new to them, but is simply **the gospel which I preached to you, which also you received.** Not until verses 3-4 does he specify what the heart of the gospel is: "that Christ died for our sins, . . . and that He was buried, and that He was raised on the third day." The point of the first two verses is that the Corinthian believers were themselves living evidence that this doctrine was true. The fact that they came out of the spiritual blindness and deadness of Judaism or paganism and into the light and life of Christ testified to the power of the gospel, and therefore to the power of the resurrection. It also testified that they already believed in the truth of Christ's resurrection. It was the gospel of the resurrection of Jesus Christ that Paul had **preached** to them, that they had **received**, and in which he assures them they now **stand** and by which they **are saved**, delivered from sin's power and condemnation. Because of the reality of Christ's resurrection and of their trust in it, they were now a part of His church and thereby were evidence of the power of that resurrection.

Paul's qualifying phrase—**if you hold fast the word which I preached to you, unless you believed in vain**—does not teach that true believers are in danger of losing their salvation, but it is a warning against non-saving faith. So a clearer rendering would be, " . . . if you hold fast what I preached to you, unless your faith is worthless or unless you believed without effect." The Corinthians' holding fast to what Paul had preached (see 11:2) was the result of and an evidence of their genuine salvation, just as their salvation and new life were an evidence of the power of Christ's resurrection. It must be recognized, however, that some lacked the true saving faith, and thus did not continue to obey the Word of God.

Paul's teaching about the security of believers was unambiguous. "For whom He foreknew, He also predestined to become conformed to the image of His Son, that He might be the firstborn among many brethren; and whom He predestined, these He also called; and whom He called, these He also justified; and whom He justified, these He also glorified" (Rom. 8:29-30; cf. vv. 35-39; 5:9-10; 9:23; 1 Cor. 2:7; etc.). It is only by God's power that we are saved and only by His power that we are kept saved. Our salvation is kept by Christ's holding us fast, not primarily by our holding Him fast. Our holding onto Him is evidence that He is holding onto us.

A professing Christian who holds to orthodox doctrine and living and then fully rejects it proves that his salvation was never real. He is able to let go of the things of God because he is doing the holding. He does not belong to God and therefore God's power cannot keep him. Such a person does not **hold fast the word** because his faith is **in vain**. It was never real. He cannot hold fast because he is not held fast.

Our Lord repeatedly spoke of sham believers who had useless, non-saving faith. The parable of the sower (Matt. 13:1-23) tells us that some of the seeds of the gospel fall on shallow or weedy soil, and that tares often look like wheat, but are not (13:24-30, 34-43). Jesus spoke of many kinds of fish being caught in the same net, with the good being kept and the bad being thrown away (13:47-50). He spoke of houses without foundations (7:24-27), virgins without oil for their lamps, and servants who wasted their talents and so were "cast out" (25:1-30). He warned of gates and paths that seem right, but that lead to destruction (7:13-14).

Some of the Corinthians apparently had intellectually and/or outwardly acknowledged Jesus' lordship, saviorhood, and resurrection, but had not trusted in Him or committed themselves to Him. They believed only as the demons believe (James 2:19). They acknowledged Christ, but they had not **received** Him, did not **stand** in Him, were not **saved** by Him, and did not **hold fast** to His **word**, which Paul had **preached** to them. As Jesus made clear in the illustrations just cited above, many people make positive responses of one sort or another to the gospel, but only genuine faith in Jesus Christ results in salvation.

Many people have useless faith. "Many" will say, "Lord, Lord," in the day of judgment, but be excluded because of their empty, sham faith (Matt. 7:22-23; 25:11-12). Those who forsake Christ and His church prove that they never really belonged to Him or to His true Body (cf. 1 John 2:19). It is those who "abide in My word," Jesus said, those who **hold fast the word**, who "are truly disciples of Mine" (John 8:31; cf. 2 Cor. 13:5; 2 John 9). The truly justified and righteous not only are saved by faith but continue to "live by faith" (Heb. 10:38). Obedience and continuous faithfulness mark the redeemed.

The fact that, despite their great immaturity and many weaknesses, the Corinthian church even continued to exist was a strong testimony to the power of the gospel. Who but the risen, living Christ could have taken extortioners, thieves, adulterers, fornicators, homosexuals, liars, idolaters, and such thoroughly worldly pagans and transformed them into a community of the redeemed? Despite their shortcomings and failures, and despite the presence of false followers in their assembly, Christ lived in and through the true saints. Paul was ashamed of much of what they did and did not do, but he was not ashamed to call them **brethren**.

Though it is largely a subjective proof, the endurance of the church of Jesus Christ through 2,000 years is evidence of His resurrection reality. His church and His Word have survived skepticism, persecution, heresy, unfaithfulness, and disobedience. Critics have denounced the resurrection as a hoax and fabrication, but have never explained the power of such a fabrication to produce men and women who gave up everything, including their freedom and lives when necessary, to love and to follow a dead Lord! His living church is evidence that Christ Himself is alive; and He could be alive only if He had been raised from the dead.

H. D. A. Major, former principal of Ripon Hall, Oxford, has written,

> Had the crucifixion of Jesus ended his disciples' experience of him, it is hard to see how the Christian Church could have come into existence. That church was founded on faith in the Messiahship of Jesus. A crucified Messiah was no Messiah at all. He was one rejected by Judaism and a curse of God. It was the resurrection of Jesus, as St. Paul declares in Romans 1:4, which proclaimed Him to be "the Son of God with power."

Church historian Kenneth Scott Latourette wrote in *History of the Expansion of Christianity,*

> It was the conviction of the resurrection of Jesus which lifted his followers out of the despair into which his death had cast them and which led to the perpetuation of a movement begun by him. But for their profound belief that the crucified had risen from the dead and they had seen him and talked with him, the death of Jesus and even Jesus himself, would probably have been all but forgotten.

A follower of Buddha writes of that religious leader, "When Buddha died it was with that utter passing away in which nothing whatever remains." Mohammed died at Medina on June 8, 632, at the the age of 61, and his tomb there is visited yearly by tens of thousands of Muslims. But they come to mourn his death, not to celebrate his resurrection. Yet the church of Jesus Christ, not just on Easter Sunday but at every service of immersion baptism, celebrates the victory of her Lord over death and the grave.

THE TESTIMONY OF SCRIPTURE

For I delivered to you as of first importance what I also received, that Christ died for our sins according to the Scriptures, and that He was buried, and that He was raised on the third day according to the Scriptures. (15:3-4)

The second evidence for Christ's resurrection was the Old Testament, **the Scriptures** of Judaism and of the early church. The Old Testament clearly predicted Christ's death, burial, and resurrection. When Paul says **I delivered to you,** he means he *brought* authoritative teaching, not something of his own origination. He did not design it, he only **delivered** what God had authored.

To the two disciples on the road to Emmaus, Jesus said, "'O foolish men and slow of heart to believe in all that the prophets have spoken! Was it not necessary for the Christ to suffer these things and to enter into His glory?' And beginning with Moses and with all the prophets, He explained to them the things concerning Himself in all the Scriptures" (Luke 24:25-27). When the unbelieving Jews asked for a sign of

Jesus' messiahship, He responded, "An evil and adulterous generation craves for a sign; and yet no sign shall be given to it but the sign of Jonah the prophet; for just as Jonah was three days and three nights in the belly of the sea monster, so shall the Son of Man be three days and three nights in the heart of the earth" (Matt. 12:39-40).

At Pentecost Peter quoted from Psalm 16 and then commented that David, the author of the psalm, "looked ahead and spoke of the resurrection of the Christ, that He was neither abandoned to Hades, nor did His flesh suffer decay" (Acts 2:25-31). Paul proclaimed before King Agrippa, "And so, having obtained help from God, I stand to this day testifying both to small and great, stating nothing but what the Prophets and Moses said was going to take place; that the Christ was to suffer, and that by reason of His resurrection from the dead He should be the first to proclaim light both to the Jewish people and to the Gentiles" (Acts 26:22-23).

Jesus, Peter, and Paul quoted or referred to such Old Testament passages as Genesis 22:8, 14; Psalm 16:8-11; Psalm 22; Isaiah 53; and Hosea 6:2. Over and over again, either directly or indirectly, literally or in figures of speech, the Old Testament foretold Jesus' death, burial, and resurrection. No Jew who believed and understood **the Scriptures,** referring to what we now call the Old Testament, should have been surprised that the Messiah was ordained to die, be buried, and then resurrected. Twice Paul repeats the phrase **according to the Scriptures,** to emphasize that this is no new thing, and no contradiction of true Jewish belief.

The Testimony of Eyewitnesses

And that He appeared to Cephas, then to the twelve. After that He appeared to more than five hundred brethren at one time, most of whom remain until now, but some have fallen asleep; then He appeared to James, then to all the apostles. (15:5-7)

Throughout history the testimony of responsible and honest eyewitnesses has been considered one of the most reliable forms of evidence in a court of law. Paul's third evidence for Christ's resurrection is in that form.

Lawyer Sir Edward Clarke said,

> As a lawyer I have made a prolonged study of the evidences for the events of the first Easter day. For me, the evidence is conclusive, and over and over again in the high court I have secured the verdict on evidence not nearly so compelling. Inference follows on evidence, and a truthful witness is always artless and disdains effect; the gospel evidence for the resurrection is of this class, and as a lawyer I accept it unreservedly as the testimony of truthful men to facts they were able to substantiate.

The historian Thomas Arnold of Oxford has written,

The evidence for our Lord's life and death and resurrection may be and often has been shown to be satisfactory. It is good according to the common rules for distinguishing good evidence from bad. Thousands and tens of thousands of persons have gone through it piece by piece as carefully as every judge summing up on an important case. I have myself done it many times over, not to persuade others but to satisfy myself. I have been used for many years to study the history of other times, and to examine and weigh the evidence of those who have written about them, and I know of no one fact in the history of mankind which is better proved by fuller evidence than the great sign that God has given us that Christ died and rose again from the dead.

JESUS' APPEARANCE TO PETER

It is significant that Paul says that Jesus **appeared** to those who saw Him after the resurrection. Until He revealed His identity to them, not even Mary Magdelene (John 20:14-16), the two disciples on the Emmaus road (Luke 24:15, 31), or the disciples gathered together on Easter evening (John 20:19-20) recognized Him. The gospel accounts consistently speak of Jesus' appearing or manifesting Himself after His resurrection (Matt. 28:9; Mark 16:9, 12, 14; Luke 24:31-39; John 21:1; etc.). He was recognized only by those to whom He chose to reveal Himself, and there is no record that He revealed Himself to any other than His followers.

One of the requirements for apostleship was having seen the resurrected Christ (Acts 1:22), and the first apostle to whom **He appeared** was **Cephas**, that is, Peter. We are not told the exact time or occasion for that appearance. We only know that it was sometime after His appearance to Mary and before His appearance to the two disciples on the road to Emmaus (Luke 24:34). We are not told why the Lord appeared to Peter first or separately, but it possibly was because of Peter's great remorse over having denied his Lord, and because his role as a leader among the apostles and in the primitive church until the Council of Jerusalem (Acts 15). In going to Peter first, Jesus emphasized His grace. Peter had forsaken the Lord, but the Lord had not forsaken him. Christ did not appear to Peter because Peter deserved to see Him most, but perhaps because Peter needed to see Him most. Peter was the Lord's spokesman at Pentecost and was crucially used in the expansion of the church for several years. As such he was the prime witness to the resurrected Christ.

JESUS' APPEARANCE TO THE TWELVE

Jesus next appeared **to the twelve**. As mentioned above, He appeared to the eleven disciples (though still often referred to as "the twelve" even before Judas was replaced) as they were fearfully assembled on Easter evening (John 20:19; Luke 24:36).

The apostles laid the foundation of the church (Eph. 2:20), which from the beginning based its beliefs and practices on their teaching (Acts 2:42). Those men whom the Lord used to establish His church on earth all saw Him in His resurrected body (Acts 1:22). They were capable, honest, and reliable witnesses to the most important event of history.

JESUS' APPEARANCE TO THE FIVE HUNDRED

After that He appeared to more than five hundred brethren at one time. The quality of specific witnesses is represented by the apostles, all of whom were known by name and could easily be questioned. The quantity of witnesses is seen in the **five hundred brethren** who all saw the risen Christ **at one time.** Scripture gives no indication of who those people were, or where Jesus appeared to them, but they were surely well known in the early church, and, like the twelve, would often have been questioned about seeing the risen Savior. Even at the time of Paul's writing, more than two decades later, most of the witnesses were still alive. They **remain until now,** he adds, **but some have fallen asleep,** that is, died.

At the same time and same place five hundred witnesses saw Jesus alive after His resurrection!

JESUS' APPEARANCE TO JAMES

We are not told to which **James** Christ **then . . . appeared.** Two of the apostles, one the son of Zebedee and the other the son of Alphaeus, were named James (Mark 3:17-18). I am inclined to believe, however, that this James was the half-brother of the Lord, the author of the letter of James and a key leader in the Jerusalem church (Acts 15:13-21).

James originally was a skeptic. Like his brothers he did not at first believe that Jesus was the Messiah (John 7:5). But now this member of Jesus' own household, this one who for several years did not recognize Jesus as the Christ, was a witness, a powerful and convincing witness, to His resurrection. Perhaps, as with Paul, it was the experience of seeing the resurrected Christ that finally brought **James** to saving faith. In any case, the convincing testimony of a family member and former unbeliever was added to that of the apostles and the five hundred.

"Over a period of forty days" (Acts 1:3), between His resurrection and ascension, Jesus appeared **to all the apostles** on other occasions that are not specified (see John 21:1-14).

THE TESTIMONY OF A SPECIAL WITNESS

And last of all, as it were to one untimely born, He appeared to me also. For I am the least of the apostles, who am not fit to be called an apostle, because I persecuted the church of God. But by the grace of God I am what I am, and His grace toward me did not prove vain; but I labored even more than all of them, yet not I, but the grace of God with me. (15:8-10)

The fourth major testimony of Christ's resurrection was that of the apostle Paul himself, a special and unique witness of the risen Lord. Paul was not among the original apostles, all of whom had been disciples of Jesus during His earthly ministry.

He was not among the five hundred other believers who had seen the resurrected Christ. Rather, he had for many years been an unbeliever and a chief persecutor of the church.

He was, however, **last of all** allowed to see the risen Christ. The Lord's appearance to Paul not only was postresurrection but postascension, making Paul's testimony more unique still. It was not during the forty days in which He appeared to all the others but several years later. All the others to whom Christ appeared, except perhaps James, were believers, whereas Paul (then known as Saul) was a violent, hateful unbeliever when the Lord manifested Himself on the Damascus road (Acts 9:1-8). There were also other appearances (Acts 18:9-10; 23:11; cf. 2 Cor. 12:1-7).

Jesus appeared to Paul **as it were to one untimely born.** *Ektrōma* (**untimely born**) ordinarily referred to an abortion, miscarriage, or premature birth—a life unable to sustain itself. In Paul's figure, the term could indicate hopelessness for life without divine intervention, and convey the idea that he was born without hope of meeting Christ. But the use of the term in the sense of an ill-timed birth, too early or too late, seems to fit Paul's thought best. He came too late to have been one of the twelve. In carrying the idea of unformed, dead, and useless, the term was also used as a term of derision. Before his conversion, which coincided with his vision of the resurrected Lord, Paul was spiritually unformed, dead, and useless, a person to be scorned by God. Even when he was born it was wrong timing. Christ was gone. How could he be an apostle? Yet, by special divine provision, **He appeared to me also,** Paul testifies.

Though Paul never doubted his apostleship or hesitated to use the authority that office brought, he also never ceased to be amazed that, of all persons, Christ would have called him to that high position. He not only considered himself to be **the least of the apostles,** but not even **fit to be called an apostle, because** [he] **persecuted the church of God.**

Paul knew all of his sins were forgiven, and he was not plagued by feelings of guilt over what he had once done against God's people. But he could not forget that for which he had been forgiven, and it continually reminded him that **by the grace of God I am what I am.** That he deserved God's forgiveness so little was a constant reminder of how graciously His grace is given.

It is possible that Paul's memory of having **persecuted the church of God** was a powerful motivation for his being determined that **His grace would not prove vain.** (Compare his testimony in 1 Tim. 1:12-17.) As is clearly substantiated in the New Testament, Paul was able to truthfully say, **I labored even more than all of them.** (Compare his commitment as chronicled in 2 Cor. 11:23–12:12.) Yet he was not boasting in his own spirituality or power but in God's, because, as he hastened to add, **yet not I, but the grace of God with me.** The same grace responsible for his calling was responsible for his faithfulness. God sovereignly appointed Paul an apostle and sovereignly blessed his apostolic ministry. Paul believed, responded, obeyed, and was continually sensitive to the Lord's leading and will. But apart from God's prevenient grace the apostle knew that everything he did would have been in vain and worthless (cf. Eph. 4:15-16; Col. 1:28-29; etc.).

The truth and power of the resurrected Christ had brought three great changes in Paul. First was deep recognition of sin. For the first time he realized how far his external religious life was from being internally godly. He saw himself as he really was, an enemy of God and a persecutor of His church. Second, he experienced a revolution of character. From a persecutor of the church he became her greatest defender. His life was transformed from one characterized by self-righteous hatred to one characterized by self-giving love. He changed from oppressor to servant, from imprisoner to deliverer, from judge to friend, from a taker of life to a giver of life. Third, he experienced a dramatic redirection of energy. As zealously as he had once opposed God's redeemed he now served them.

The Testimony of the Common Message

Whether then it was I or they, so we preach and so you believed. (15:11)

The last testimony to Christ's resurrection was that of the common message that every true apostle, prophet, and pastor preached. **Whether then it was I or they**—Peter, the twelve, the five hundred, James, or anyone else—**so we preach and so you believed.** Without exception, the preaching and teaching in the early church centered on the death, burial, and resurrection of Christ. Wherever Christ was preached and by whomever He was preached, His resurrection was the pivotal message that was proclaimed. There was no dispute about the truth or the importance of the doctrine, which hardly would have been the case had it been a fabrication.

Except for a few isolated heresies, the doctrine of Christ's resurrection has not been questioned within the church until our modern age of skepticism and humanism. New Testament Christianity, whether ancient or modern, knows nothing of a gospel whose heart is not the risen Lord and Savior, Jesus Christ.

The Importance of
Bodily Resurrection
(15:12-19)

41

Now if Christ is preached, that He has been raised from the dead, how do some among you say that there is no resurrection of the dead? But if there is no resurrection of the dead, not even Christ has been raised; and if Christ has not been raised, then our preaching is vain, your faith also is vain. Moreover we are even found to be false witnesses of God, because we witnessed against God that He raised Christ, whom He did not raise, if in fact the dead are not raised. For if the dead are not raised, not even Christ has been raised; and if Christ has not been raised, your faith is worthless; you are still in your sins. Then those also who have fallen asleep in Christ have perished. If we have hoped in Christ in this life only, we are of all men most to be pitied. (15:12-19)

As Paul reminded them in verses 1-11, the Corinthian Christians already believed in Christ's resurrection, else they would not have been Christians. That affirmation of the reality of the resurrection formed the basis for his double-edged argument in chapter 15: Because Christ was raised, resurrection from the dead obviously is possible; and, on the other hand, unless men in general can be resurrected, Christ could not have been raised. The two resurrections stand or fall together; there could not be one without the other. Furthermore, if there is no resurrection, the gospel is meaningless and worthless.

It seems strange that some of those believers could have accepted one part of the truth without the other. The cause of this confusion, as of many of their other problems, lay in the continuing influence of the pagan philosophies and religions out of which many of them had come. The philosophical and spiritualistic thought of Paul's day, just as in our own, had many erroneous ideas of what happens to human beings after death.

Some religions have taught soul sleep, in which the body dies and disintegrates, while the soul or spirit rests. Materialists believe in utter extinction, total annihilation. Nothing human, physical or otherwise, survives after death. Death ends it all. Some religions teach reincarnation, wherein the soul or spirit is continually recycled from one form to another—even from human to animal or animal to human. Others believe in what is generally described as absorption, in which the spirit, or at least a certain part of the spirit, returns back to its source and is absorbed back into the ultimate divine mind or being. That belief is reflected in a statement of the contemporary philosopher Leslie Weatherhead: "Would it really matter if I were lost like a drop of water in the ocean, if I could be one shining particle in some glorious wave that broke in utter splendour in perfect beauty on the shores of some eternal sea?"

In all those views, human personhood and individuality are forever lost at death. Whatever, if anything, survives is no longer a person, no longer an individual, no longer a unique being.

A basic tenet of much ancient Greek philosophy was dualism, a concept generally attributed to Plato. Dualism considered everything spiritual to be intrinsically good and everything physical to be intrinsically evil. To anyone holding that view the idea of a resurrected body was repugnant. For them, the very reason for going to an afterlife was to escape all things physical. They considered the body a tomb or a corpse, to which, in this life, their souls were shackled. For those Greeks, their bodies were the last things they would want to take along to the next life. They believed in the immortality of the soul but strongly opposed the idea of a resurrection of the body—as Paul had experienced when he preached on the Areopagus: "Now when they [the Athenian philosophers] heard of the resurrection of the dead, some began to sneer" (Acts 17:32). The typical view of dualism was expressed by Seneca: "When the day shall come which shall part this mixture of divine and human here where I found it, I will leave my body, and myself I will give back to the gods."

It is possible that even some of the Jewish members of the Corinthian church doubted the resurrection. Despite the fact that resurrection is taught in the Old Testament, some Jews, such the Sadducees, did not believe in it.

In the ancient book of Job we read, "Even after my skin is destroyed, yet from my flesh I shall see God" (Job 19:26; cf. Ps. 17:15). Ezekiel's vision of the dry bones (37:1-14) pictures the restored nation of Israel but also suggests the bodily resurrection of God's people. Daniel's prediction of resurrection is clear, speaking of the resurrection of the lost as well as of the saved. "And many of those who sleep in the dust of the ground will awake, these to everlasting life, but the others to disgrace and everlasting contempt" (Dan. 12:2).

But whereas the Old Testament teaching about the resurrection was limited and incomplete, the New Testament teaching is extensive. Though the gospels were not yet written, Jesus' life was well known and the Corinthians doubtless had learned of His teaching from Peter and others. "No one can come to Me unless the Father who sent Me draws him; and I will raise him up on the last day" (John 6:44), He proclaimed to some of His Jewish critics near the Sea of Galilee. To Martha He said, "I am the resurrection and the life; he who believes in Me shall live even if he dies" (John 11:25).

The foundation of apostolic teaching was that Christ rose from the dead and that all who believed in Him would also be raised. As Peter and John were preaching in Jerusalem soon after Pentecost, "the priests and the captain of the temple guard, and the Sadducees, came upon them, being greatly disturbed because they were teaching the people and proclaiming in Jesus the resurrection from the dead" (Acts 4:1-2). Paul had written the Thessalonians several years before he wrote 1 Corinthians, "For the Lord Himself will descend from heaven with a shout, with the voice of the archangel, and with the trumpet of God; and the dead in Christ shall rise first" (1 Thess. 4:16). He doubtlessly had taught the Corinthians the same truth, and in his next letter to them he says, "He who raised the Lord Jesus will raise us also with Jesus and will present us with you" (2 Cor. 4:14).

In spite of the fact that the resurrection of believers is taught in the Old Testament, in the teaching of Jesus during His earthly ministry, and in the teaching of the apostles, serious doubts about it had infected many of the Corinthian Christians. It is those doubts that Paul forcefully counters in 1 Corinthians 15.

His first argument is simple and logical: **Now if Christ is preached, that He has been raised from the dead, how do some among you say that there is no resurrection of the dead?** The construction here (*ei* with the indicative) implies a condition that is true. The Corinthians believed in Christ's resurrection (1 Cor. 15:1, 11) and that He was presently alive (emphasized by the perfect tense of *egeirō,* **has been raised**). How then could they logically deny the general truth of resurrection? If Christ has been raised, resurrection obviously is possible.

In verses 13-19 the apostle demonstrates that the resurrection is not only possible but essential to the faith, by giving seven disastrous consequences, four theological and three personal, that would result if there were no resurrection: (1) Christ would not be risen; (2) preaching of the gospel would be meaningless; (3) faith in Christ would be worthless; (4) all witnesses to and all preachers of the resurrection would be liars; (5) all men would still be in their sins; (6) all former believers would have eternally perished; and (7) Christians would be the most pitiable people on earth.

THE THEOLOGICAL CONSEQUENCES OF NO RESURRECTION

But if there is no resurrection of the dead, not even Christ has been raised; and if Christ has not been raised, then our preaching is vain, your faith also is vain. Moreover we are even found to be false witnesses of God, because we witnessed against God that He raised Christ, whom He did not raise, if in fact the dead are not raised. (15:13-15)

CHRIST WOULD NOT BE RISEN

The first and most obvious consequence of there being no resurrection would be that **not even Christ has been raised**. "As anyone should easily deduce," Paul argues, "if the dead cannot rise, Christ did not rise."

It is likely that the disbelieving Corinthians got around that problem by claiming that Christ was not really a man, or was not fully a man. Because of their dualistic orientation, as discussed above, they assumed that because Christ was divine He could not possibly have been human, and therefore only appeared to be human. Consequently He did not really die but only appeared to die. According to this view, His appearances between the crucifixion (an illusion) and the ascension were simply continuing manifestations that only *seemed* to be bodily.

That view, of course, cannot square with what the gospel writers, Jesus Himself, and the apostles taught. The gospel accounts of Jesus' earthly life and ministry are of a person who was entirely human. He was born to a human mother, and He ate, drank, slept, became tired, was crucified, was stabbed, bled, and died. At His first appearance to the twelve after the crucifixion, Jesus made a point of having the disciples touch Him in order to prove that He was not simply a spirit, which "does not have flesh and bones as you see that I have." He next asked for something to eat and then "took it and ate it before them" (Luke 24:39-43).

At Pentecost Peter proclaimed that "Jesus the Nazarene [was] a man attested to you by God" and that "this Man delivered up by the predetermined plan and foreknowledge of God, you nailed to a cross" (Acts 2:22-23). Later in the same message he proclaimed that Jesus was still alive, not merely in spirit but in body. He told of David's speaking "of the resurrection of the Christ, that He was neither abandoned to Hades, nor did His flesh suffer decay. This Jesus God raised up again" (Acts 2:31-32). In his opening words to the Romans, Paul makes it clear that "the gospel of God" for which he was set apart was "concerning His Son, who was born of a descendant of David according to the flesh, who was declared the Son of God with power by the resurrection from the dead" (Rom. 1:1-4). Jesus' resurrection evidenced both His humanity and His deity.

In His vision to John on Patmos Christ declared, "I am the first and the last, and the living One; and I was dead, and behold, I am alive forevermore, and I have the keys of death and of Hades" (Rev. 1:17-18). In his second letter John points up the crucial importance of believing that Jesus was born, lived, died, and was raised up a human being: "For many deceivers have gone out into the world, those who do not acknowledge Jesus Christ as coming in the flesh. This is the deceiver and the antichrist" (2 John 7).

The Corinthians could not fall back on the pagan notion that Christ only appeared to be human. He was fully human; He physically lived and died and lived again. Therefore, if there is no such thing as physical resurrection, **not even Christ has been raised**.

PREACHING OF THE GOSPEL WOULD BE MEANINGLESS

The second consequence of there being no resurrection would be that

preaching of the gospel would be **vain,** completely meaningless. As Paul had just said, the heart of the gospel is Christ's death and resurrection on our behalf. "For I delivered to you as of first importance what I also received, that Christ died for our sins according to the Scriptures, and that He was buried, and that He was raised on the third day according to the Scriptures" (15:3-4). Apart from the resurrection Jesus could not have conquered sin or death or hell, and those three great evils would forever be man's conquerors.

Without the resurrection the good news would be bad news, and there would be nothing worth preaching. Without the resurrection the gospel would be an empty, hopeless message of meaningless nonsense. Unless our Lord conquered sin and death, making a way for men to follow in that victory, there is no gospel to proclaim.

FAITH IN CHRIST WOULD BE WORTHLESS

Just as no resurrection would make preaching Christ meaningless, it would also make faith in Him worthless. Faith in such a gospel would be **vain** (*kenos,* empty, fruitless, void of effect, to no purpose). A dead savior could not give life. If the dead do not rise, Christ did not rise and we will not rise. We then could only say with the psalmist, "Surely in vain I have kept my heart pure" (Ps. 73:13), or with the Servant in Isaiah, "I have toiled in vain, I have spent My strength for nothing and vanity" (Isa. 49:4).

If there were no resurrection, the hall of the faithful in Hebrews 11 would instead be the hall of the foolish. Abel, Enoch, Noah, Abraham, Sarah, Moses, Rahab, David, the prophets, and all the others would have been faithful for nothing. They would have been mocked, scourged, imprisoned, stoned, afflicted, ill-treated, and put to death completely in **vain.** All believers of all ages would have believed for nothing, lived for nothing, and died for nothing.

ALL WITNESSES TO AND PREACHERS OF THE RESURRECTION WOULD BE LIARS

Moreover we are even found to be false witnesses of God, because we witnessed against God that He raised Christ, whom He did not raise, if in fact the dead are not raised. If there is no such thing as resurrection of the dead, then every person who claimed to have witnessed the risen Christ and every person who preached the risen Christ was a liar, including Paul and the other apostles (**we**). They would be pseudo-witnesses, claiming falsely to be from God and witnessing falsely **against** [concerning] **God that He raised Christ.**

To deny the resurrection is to call the apostles and every other leader of the New Testament church not simply mistaken but willfully mistaken, that is, liars. There is no possibility, as many liberals claim, that such a mistake could have been innocent or naive. Those witnesses could not have been honest men who unwittingly gave bad advice. If Christ was not raised from the dead, they not only were not sent by God with a message from Him, but were liars who would have had to conspire together in order for their lies to have been so consistent and harmonized.

If the apostles, the prophets, and the New Testament writers lied about the heart of the gospel why should they be believed about anything else? Why should their moral teachings be considered inspired and lofty if they so blatantly falsified their teaching about Jesus' resurrection? All New Testament truth stands or falls together based on the resurrection.

Not only that, but those witnesses would have testified, preached, and taught a lie for which they were maligned, beaten, imprisoned, and often martyred. Such self-sacrifice, however, is not the stuff of which charlatans are made. People do not die to preserve a lie.

Although Paul does not mention it specifically, it clearly follows that if the resurrection were not true, Christ Himself lied, or at best was tragically mistaken. In either case, He hardly would have qualified as the divine Son of God or the world's Savior and Lord. Jesus would not have been Victor but victim. Or, if the New Testament writers completely misrepresented what both Christ and the apostles taught, then the New Testament would be a worthless document that no reasonable person would trust.

The Personal Consequences of No Resurrection

For if the dead are not raised, not even Christ has been raised; and if Christ has not been raised, your faith is worthless; you are still in your sins. Then those also who have fallen asleep in Christ have perished. If we have hoped in Christ in this life only, we are of all men most to be pitied. (15:16-19)

Next Paul gives what may be described as three personal consequences that would result if there were no such thing as resurrection from the dead. Like the other four, these consequences have serious theological significance, but they also state much more directly how believers would be affected.

ALL MEN WOULD STILL BE IN THEIR SINS

In verse 16 Paul restates his major argument: **If the dead are not raised, not even Christ has been raised.** A dead Christ would be the chief disastrous consequence from which all the other consequences would result.

The next consequence Paul mentions is both personal and serious: **if Christ has not been raised, your faith is worthless; you are still in your sins.** After repeating the consequence that believers' faith would be **worthless,** or vain (v. 14), the apostle points to the obvious additional result that believers would be no better off spiritually than unbelievers. Christians would **still** be in their **sins** just as much as the most wicked and unbelieving pagan. We would all be in the same boat as the unbelievers to whom Jesus said, "You . . . shall die in your sin" (John 8:21).

If Jesus did not rise from the dead, then sin won the victory over Christ and therefore continues to be victorious over all men. If Jesus remained dead, then, when we die, we too will remain dead and damned. "The wages of sin is death" (Rom. 6:23), and if we remain dead, then death and eternal punishment are the only prospects of believer and unbeliever alike. The purpose of trusting in Christ is for forgiveness of sins, because it is from sin that we need to be saved. "Christ died for our sins" and "was buried, and . . . raised on the third day" (1 Cor. 15:3-4). If Christ was not raised, His death was in vain, our faith in Him is in vain, and our sins are still counted against us. We are still dead in trespasses and sins and will forever remain spiritually dead and sinful. If Christ was not raised, then He did not bring forgiveness of sins or salvation or reconciliation or spiritual life, either for now or for eternity.

But God *did* raise "Jesus our Lord from the dead, He who was delivered up because of our transgressions, and was raised because of our justification" (Rom. 4:24-25). Because Christ *does* live, we too shall live (John 14:19). "The God of our fathers raised up Jesus, whom you had put to death by hanging Him on a cross. He is the one whom God exalted to His right hand as a Prince and a Savior, to grant repentance to Israel, and forgiveness of sins" (Acts 5:30-31).

ALL FORMER BELIEVERS WOULD HAVE ETERNALLY PERISHED

If there is no resurrection, **then those also who have fallen asleep in Christ have perished. Fallen asleep** does not refer to what is often called soul sleep but was a common euphemism for death (cf. vv. 6, 20; Matt. 27:52; Acts 7:60; 2 Pet. 3:4). Every saint, Old Testament or Christian, who had died would have forever **perished.** Obviously the same consequence would apply to every saint who has died since Paul wrote. Paul himself, the other apostles, Augustine, Calvin, Luther, Wesley, D. L. Moody, and every other believer of every other age would spend eternity in torment, without God and without hope. Their faith would have been in vain, their sins would have been unforgiven, and their destiny would be damnation.

CHRISTIANS WOULD BE THE MOST PITIABLE PEOPLE ON EARTH

In light of the other consequences, the last is rather obvious. **If we have hoped in Christ in this life only** [and we have; *ei* with the indicative] **we are of all men most to be pitied.** Without the resurrection, and the salvation and blessings it brings, Christianity would be pointless and pitiable. Without the resurrection we would have no Savior, no forgiveness, no gospel, no meaningful faith, no life, and no hope of any of those things.

To have **hoped in Christ in this life only** would be to teach, preach, suffer, sacrifice, and work entirely for nothing. If Christ is still dead, then He not only cannot help us in regard to the life to come but He cannot help us now. If He cannot grant us eternal life, He cannot improve our earthly life. If He is not alive, where would be our source of peace, joy, or satisfaction *now.* The Christian life would be a mockery, a charade, a tragic joke.

A Christian has no Savior but Christ, no Redeemer but Christ, no Lord but Christ. Therefore if Christ was not raised, He is not alive, and our Christian life is lifeless. We would have nothing to justify our faith, our Bible study, our preaching or witnessing, our service for Him or our worship of Him, and nothing to justify our hope either for this life or the next. We would deserve nothing but the compassion reserved for fools.

But we are *not* to be pitied, for Paul immediately continues, "But now Christ has been raised from the dead, the first fruits of those who are asleep" (15:20).

The Resurrection
Plan (15:20-28)

42

But now Christ has been raised from the dead, the first fruits of those who are asleep. For since by a man came death, by a man also came the resurrection of the dead. For as in Adam all die, so also in Christ all shall be made alive. But each in his own order: Christ the first fruits, after that those who are Christ's at His coming, then comes the end, when He delivers up the kingdom to the God and Father, when He has abolished all rule and all authority and power. For He must reign until He has put all His enemies under His feet. The last enemy that will be abolished is death. For He has put all things in subjection under His feet. But when He says, "All things are put in subjection," it is evident that He is excepted who put all things in subjection to Him. And when all things are subjected to Him, then the Son Himself also will be subjected to the One who subjected all things to Him, that God may be all in all. (15:20-28)

Theologian Erich Sauer has written, "The present age is Easter time. It begins with the resurrection of the Redeemer and ends with the resurrection of the redeemed. Between lies the spiritual resurrection of those called into life through Christ. So we live between two Easters, and in the power of the first Easter we go to meet the last Easter."

The last Easter to which Sauer refers is, of course, the bodily resurrection of the saved. Scripture speaks of that resurrection of the righteous (Rev. 20:6; 1 Thess. 4:13-18; 2 Cor. 5:1-5; Luke 14:14; John 5:29), calling it the first resurrection. The second is the resurrection of the unrighteous (John 5:29). It is of the first resurrection that Paul speaks in 1 Corinthians 15.

The apostle has reminded the Corinthians that they already believed in Christ's resurrection (15:1-11) and that logically they must also believe in their own resurrection and that of all saints, mentioning seven disastrous and absurd consequences that would result if they were not raised (vv. 12-19). Moving into verses 20-28 Paul discusses three aspects of the resurrection of the righteous: (1) The Redeemer; (2) the redeemed; and (3) the restoration. The first and third focus on Christ; the second focuses on believers.

THE REDEEMER

But now Christ has been raised from the dead, the first fruits of those who are asleep. For since by a man came death, by a man also came the resurrection of the dead. For as in Adam all die, so also in Christ all shall be made alive. (15:20-22)

First Paul reaffirms Christ's resurrection: **But now Christ has been raised from the dead,** a truth his readers already acknowledged and believed (vv. 1-2). The words "and become," found in some translations (e.g., the KJV), do not come first in the original text and are misleading. Christ did not become the **first fruits** at some time after His resurrection, but at the moment of His resurrection, by the very fact of His resurrection. His being raised made Him the first fruits of all who would be raised.

Before Israelites harvested their crops they were to bring a representative sample, called the first fruits, to the priests as an offering to the Lord (Lev. 23:10). The full harvest could not be made until the first fruits were offered. That is the point of Paul's figure here. Christ's own resurrection was **the first fruits** of the resurrection "harvest" of the believing dead. In His death and resurrection Christ made an offering of Himself to the Father on our behalf.

The significance of the first fruits, however, not only was that they preceded the harvest but that they were a first installment of the harvest. The fact that Christ was **the first fruits** therefore indicates that something else, namely the harvest of the rest of the crop, is to follow. In other words, Christ's resurrection could not have been in isolation from ours. His resurrection *requires* our resurrection, because His resurrection was part of the larger resurrection of God's redeemed.

The resurrection of which Paul speaks here is permanent resurrection. Both the Old and New Testaments tell of persons who died and were miraculously brought back to life (1 Kings 17:22; 2 Kings 4:34-36; 13:21; Luke 7:15; John 11:44). But all of those persons died again. Even those whom Jesus raised—the son of the widow of Nain, Jairus's daughter, and Lazarus—eventually died again. Christ Himself, however, was the first to be raised never to die again.

As in 15:6, 18 (cf. Matt. 27:52; Acts 7:60; 2 Pet. 3:4), **those who are asleep** refers to the dead, in this instance to the righteous dead, whose spirits have gone to be with the Lord (2 Cor. 5:8; cf. Phil. 1:23) but whose remains are in the grave, awaiting recomposition and resurrection.

Through Christ, as a **man, came the resurrection of the dead,** just as through Adam, the first **man, came death.** Paul's point here is that Jesus' humanness was inextricably involved both in His resurrection and in ours. It was because Jesus died, was buried, and was raised as a **man** that He could become the **first fruits** of all other men who would be raised to glory. As already noted, the first fruits and the harvest were from the same crop.

In verse 22 Paul continues to explain how the great truth of the one resurrection of Christ affects believers. The convincing analogy comes from the first man: **For as in Adam all die, so also in Christ all shall be made alive.** Just as Adam was the progenitor of everyone who dies, so Christ is the progenitor of everyone who will be raised to life. In each case, one man doing one act caused the consequences of that act to be applied to every other person identified with him. Those who are identified with Adam—every person who has been born—is subject to death because of Adam's sinful act. Likewise, those who are identified with Christ— every person who has been born again in Him—is subject to resurrection to eternal life because of Christ's righteous act. **In Adam all** have inherited a sin nature and therefore will **die. In Christ all** who believe in Him have inherited eternal life, and **shall be made alive,** in body as well as in spirit. "For as through the one man's disobedience the many were made sinners, even so through the obedience of the One the many will be made righteous" (Rom. 5:19).

From countless other passages of Scripture we know that the two **alls** in verse 22, though alike in some respects, cannot be equal. Those who attempt to read universalism into this passage must contradict those other passages that teach reprobation (Matt. 5:29; 10:28; 25:41, 46; Luke 16:23; 2 Thess. 1:9; Rev. 20:15; etc.). The **alls** are alike in that they both apply to descendants. Every human being is a descendant of Adam, and therefore the first **all** is universal. With only the exceptions of Enoch and Elijah, whom the Lord took directly to be with Himself, and of those saints who will be raptured, every person born will die.

Only those who trust in Jesus Christ, however, are *His* descendants (as illustrated in John 8:44), and the second **all** therefore applies only to the saved. It is only **all** the fellow sons of God and joint heirs with Jesus Christ (Gal. 3:26, 29; 4:7; Eph. 3:6; cf. Acts 20:32; Titus 3:7) who **shall be made alive. In Adam** is simply to be human, to have been born once. **In Christ** is to have eternal life, to be born again. By natural descent from Adam, having inherited his sin, **all die.** By supernatural descent from Christ, having inherited His righteousness, **all shall be made alive.**

Though the inheritance in both cases is bodily as well as spiritual, Paul's major emphasis here is on the bodily. Through Adam's sin, man died spiritually and became subject to death bodily. Likewise, through Christ believers are given life spiritually and will be raised bodily. But our spirits, because they go to be with the Lord at death, will not wait to be resurrected. Only our bodies will be resurrected, and that is the truth stressed here.

THE REDEEMED

But each in his own order: Christ the first fruits, after that those who are Christ's at His coming. (15:23)

In the scheme of resurrection, **Christ** is **the first fruits** and **those who are Christ's at His coming** are the full harvest. Unlike the grain harvest, however, that of the resurrection is far removed in time from the **first fruits.** We do not know—in fact, are told we cannot know (Matt. 24:36, 42, 44, 50; 25:13)—when the Lord will come to raise and rapture His people and set up His kingdom. We do not know the time, the specific generation or moment, but we know the **order.**

Most obvious is that Christ was **first** and that our resurrection will follow at **His coming.** From other parts of Scripture we learn that even the "harvest" will not be all at once, but will have its own **order,** its own sequence. The first resurrection has two major parts—Christ's resurrection and believers' resurrection. The resurrection of believers, **those who are Christ's,** will be in three stages, according to different groups of believers.

Initially will be the resurrection of the church, those believers who will have come to saving faith from Pentecost to the rapture. "For the Lord Himself will descend from heaven with a shout, with the voice of the archangel, and with the trumpet of God; and the dead in Christ shall rise first" (1 Thess. 4:16). They will be joined by living saints to meet the Lord in the air and ascend to heaven.

Next will be the resurrection of the Tribulation saints. Many will come to trust in Christ during the Tribulation, that unimaginably horrible seven-year ordeal during which many godly people will be put to death for their faith. At the end of that period, however, all those who will have come to faith in Christ will be raised up to reign with Him during the Millennium (Rev. 20:4).

Following that will be the resurrection of Old Testament saints, promised by the prophet Daniel: "And many of those who sleep in the dust of the ground will awake, these to everlasting life, but the others to disgrace and everlasting contempt" (Dan. 12:2; cf. Isa. 26:19-20). That resurrection, I believe, will occur simultaneously with that of the Tribulation saints.

Then during the millennial Kingdom there will, of necessity, be the resurrection of those who die during that time. It is interesting to think that they may well be raised as soon as they die, no burial being necessary. It would make death for a believer during the Kingdom nothing more than an instant transformation into his eternal body and spirit.

The only resurrection remaining will be that of the unrighteous, who will be raised to damnation and eternal punishment at the end of Christ's thousand-year reign (John 5:29). The saved will have been raised to eternal life, but the unsaved will be raised to eternal death, the second death (Rev. 21:8; cf. 2:11).

THE RESTORATION

Then comes the end, when He delivers up the kingdom to the God and Father, when He has abolished all rule and all authority and power. For He must reign until He has put all His enemies under His feet. The last enemy that will be abolished is death. For He has put all things in subjection under His feet. But when He says, "All things are put in subjection," it is evident that He is excepted who put all things in subjection to Him. And when all things are subjected to Him, then the Son Himself also will be subjected to the One who subjected all things to Him, that God may be all in all. (15:24-28)

The third aspect of the resurrection plan that Paul discusses here is what may be called the restoration. The apostle summarizes some of the things that will happen in the last times.

Then (*eita*, "after this") may imply an interval of time between the resurrection at His coming and the establishment of His kingdom. That would coincide with the teaching of our Lord in Matthew 24 and 25, where He tells of all the signs that will precede His kingdom, even the sign of the Son of Man in heaven and the gathering together of the elect (24:30-31).

Telos (**end**) not only can refer to that which is final but also to that which is completed, consummated, or fulfilled. In the final culmination of the ages, **when He delivers up the kingdom to the God and Father**, all things will be restored as they were originally designed and created by God to be. In the end it will be as it was in the beginning. Sin will be no more, and God will reign supremely, without enemy and without challenge. That gives us great insight into the divine redemptive plan. Here is the culmination: Christ turns over the restored world to God His Father, who sent Him to recover it.

Christ's final act will be to conquer permanently every **enemy** of God, every contending **rule** and **authority** and **power**. They will forever be abolished, never to exist again, never again to oppose God or to deceive, mislead, or threaten His people or corrupt any of His creation.

This final act of Christ, the turning over the world to His Father, will be worked out over the period of a thousand years, during the millennial rule of Christ on earth. As vividly and dramatically portrayed in the symbols and statements of Revelation 5-20, Christ will take back to Himself the earth that He created and that is rightfully His. The scene of Revelation 5 depicts the Son taking rightful possession of the title deed to the earth, His going out to take it back from the usurper to present it to the Father. In doing that He will quell all rebellions and subdue all enemies. **He must reign until He has put all His enemies under His feet.** It is necessary for Him to rule.

The figure of putting **His enemies under His feet** comes from the common practice in ancient times of kings and emperors always sitting enthroned above their subjects, so that when the subjects bowed they were literally under, or lower, than the sovereign's feet. With enemies, a king often would literally put his foot on the neck of the conquered king or general, symbolizing the enemy's total subjection. In His millennial reign, all of Christ's **enemies** will be put in subjection to Him, **under His feet,** so that God's sovereign plan may be fulfilled.

During the Millennium no open rebellion will be tolerated, but there will still be rebelliousness in the hearts of Christ's enemies. Because His enemies will not submit to Him willingly, He will have to "rule them with a rod or iron" (Rev. 19:15). But they *will be ruled.* At the end of the thousand years Satan will be unleashed for a brief period to lead a final insurrection against God and His kingdom (20:7-9), after which he, with all who belong to him, will be banished to hell, to suffer eternally in the lake of fire (Rev. 20:10-15).

The last enemy, both of God and of man, **is death,** which, with all the other enemies, **will be abolished.** Christ broke the power of Satan, "him who had the power of death" (Heb. 2:14), at the cross, but Satan and death will not be permanently **abolished** until the end of the Millennium. The victory was won at Calvary, but the eternal peace and righteousness that that victory guarantees will not be consummated and completed until the enemies who were conquered are also banished and **abolished.** Then, His final work having been accomplished, Christ **delivers up the kingdom to the God and Father.**

When He took the assignment of salvation from His Father, Christ came to earth as a baby, and lived and grew up as a man among men. He taught, preached, healed, and did miraculous works. He died, was buried, was raised and ascended to His Father, where He now intercedes for those who are His. When He returns He will fight, conquer, rule, judge, and then, as His last work on the Father's behalf, forever subdue and finally judge all the enemies of God (Rev. 20:11-15), re-create the earth and heavens (Rev. 21:1-2), and finally deliver **the kingdom to the God and Father.**

The **kingdom** that Christ **delivers up** will be a redeemed environment indwelt by His redeemed people, those who have become eternal subjects of the everlasting kingdom through faith in Him. In light of Paul's major argument in this chapter, it is obvious that his point here is that, if there were no resurrection, there would be no subjects for God's eternal kingdom; and there would be no Lord to rule. Unless He and they were raised, all of God's people eventually would die, and that would be the end—the end of them and the end of the kingdom. But Scripture assures us that "His kingdom will have no end" (Luke 1:33), and He and His subjects will have no end.

Lest any of his readers misunderstand, Paul goes on to explain the obvious: **But when He says, "All things are put in subjection," it is evident that He is excepted who put all things in subjection to Him.** God the Father is the exception who will not be subject to Christ, for it is the Father who gave the rule and authority to the Son (Matt. 28:18; John 5:27), and whom the Son faithfully and perfectly served.

From the time of His incarnation until the time when He presents the kingdom to the Father, Christ is in the role of a Servant, fulfilling His divine task as assigned by His Father. But when that final work is accomplished, He will assume His former, full, glorious place in the perfect harmony of the Trinity. **And when all things are subjected to Him, then the Son Himself also will be subjected to the One who subjected all things to Him, that God may be all in all.** Christ will continue to reign, because His reign is eternal (Rev. 11:15), but He will reign with the Father in trinitarian glory, subject to the Trinity in that way eternally designed for Him.

When God created man He made him perfect, righteous, good, and subservient. At the Fall, this supreme creature of God, along with all the rest of His creation, was corrupted and ruined. But the new men He creates through His Son will never be corrupted or ruined. They will be raised up to live and reign eternally in His eternal kingdom with His eternal Son.

Resurrection Incentives (15:29-34)

43

Otherwise, what will those do who are baptized for the dead? If the dead are not raised at all, why then are they baptized for them? Why are we also in danger every hour? I protest, brethren, by the boasting in you, which I have in Christ Jesus our Lord, I die daily. If from human motives I fought with wild beasts at Ephesus, what does it profit me? If the dead are not raised, Let us eat and drink, for tomorrow we die. Do not be deceived: "Bad company corrupts good morals." Become sober-minded as you ought, and stop sinning; for some have no knowledge of God. I speak this to your shame. (15:29-34)

When the Sadducees, who did not believe in resurrection, asked Jesus the mocking and insincere question about whose wife a certain woman would be in the resurrection, He first told them that they understood neither the Scriptures nor the power of God. After declaring that there is no marriage in heaven, He continued, "But regarding the resurrection of the dead, have you not read that which was spoken to you by God, saying, 'I am the God of Abraham, and the God of Isaac, and the God of Jacob'? He is not the God of the dead but of the living" (Matt. 22:23-32; Ex. 3:6). The emphasis in His statement was on the verb tense ("I am"). Abraham, Isaac, and Jacob were spiritually alive at the time Jesus spoke, and one day would be reunited with their glorified bodies in the resurrection. He was saying, in effect, "Presently, right now, I am the God Abraham, Isaac, and Jacob." That was true because there is life after death.

Scripture is not theoretical, impractical, or irrelevant. Because the Sadducees denied resurrection, they could not think or live right, as is obvious in their response to the life and work of Christ. Right doctrine is inseparably connected to right moral behavior; right principles are given to lead to right conduct. God's truth not only is to be believed but properly responded to. We should live the words we love to sing, "Trust and obey, for there's no other way, to be happy in Jesus than to trust and obey." Scriptural truth is not something God gave just to be discussed by theologians and written into creeds. He gave it to be lived out. When its truth is denied there are devastating moral and spiritual consequences.

The first eleven chapters of Romans are almost pure doctrine, pure theology. Chapter 12 begins, "I urge you therefore, brethren, by the mercies of God, to present your bodies a living and holy sacrifice, acceptable to God, which is your spiritual service of worship" (v. 1). From this point on in the letter the apostle's teaching is primarily practical, a series of exhortations based on the preceding truths. The "therefore" means "because." "Because of what I have just said, this is the way you should live." Paul echoes the psalmist who wrote, "What shall I render to the Lord for all His benefits toward me?" (Ps. 116:12). In Paul's writings, as in Scripture in general, believers' behavior and morality are built on the foundation of God's redemptive work. What *God* has done is the greatest possible motive for *our* doing what He wants *us* to do. To deny the resurrection is, in effect, to deny the need for righteous conduct.

Paul's major thrust in 15:29-34 is: if you remove the resurrection, if you deny this crucial and wonderful truth of God's redemptive work, you have removed one of the greatest motivations the Lord gives for coming to Christ and for living for Christ. He therefore points out three powerful incentives the resurrection gives: (1) an incentive for salvation; (2) an incentive for service; and (3) an incentive for sanctification. The first is for unbelievers, the other two are for believers.

An Incentive for Salvation

Otherwise, what will those do who are baptized for the dead? If the dead are not raised at all, why then are they baptized for them? (15:29)

This verse is one of the most difficult in all of Scripture, and has many legitimate possible interpretations; it has also, however, been used to support many strange and heretical ideas. The careful and honest interpreter may survey the several dozen interpretations offered and still not be dogmatic about what it means. But we can be dogmatic, from the clear teaching of other parts of Scripture, about some of the things it does *not* mean. As to what this verse does mean, we can only guess, since history has locked it into obscurity.

We can be sure, for example, that it does not teach vicarious, or proxy, baptism for the dead, as claimed by ancient gnostic heretics such as Marcion and by the Mormon church today. Paul did not teach that a person who has died can be saved, or helped in any way, by another person's being baptized in his behalf. Baptismal regeneration, the idea that one is saved by being baptized, or that baptism is in some way necessary for salvation, is unscriptural. The idea of vicarious baptismal regeneration is still further removed from biblical truth. If a person cannot save himself by being baptized, he certainly cannot save anyone else through that act. Salvation is by personal faith in Jesus Christ alone. "For by grace you have been saved through faith; and that not of yourselves, it is the gift of God" (Eph. 2:8; cf. Rom. 3:28; etc.). That is the repeated and consistent teaching of both the Old and New Testaments. Quoting from Genesis 15:6, Paul says, "For what does the Scripture say? 'And Abraham believed God, and it was reckoned to him as righteousness'" (Rom. 4:3). The only way any person has ever come to God is by personal faith.

If one person's faith cannot save another, then certainly one person's baptism cannot save another. Baptism is simply an act of obedient faith that proclaims identity with Christ (Rom. 6:3-4). No one is saved by baptism—not even living persons, much less dead ones. "It is appointed for men to die once and after this comes judgment" (Heb. 9:27). Death ends all opportunity for salvation and for spiritual help of any sort.

In the New Testament baptism is closely associated with salvation, of which it is an outward testimony. Although a person does not have to be baptized to be a Christian, he has to be baptized to be an obedient Christian—with the obvious exception of a believer who has no opportunity to be baptized before death. Baptism is an integral part of Christ's Great Commission (Matt. 28:19). In the early church a person who was saved was assumed to have been baptized; and a person was not baptized unless the church was satisfied he was saved. To ask, then, if a person was baptized, was equivalent to asking if he was saved.

If we assume that Paul was using the term *baptized* in that sense, then **those . . . who are baptized** could refer to those who were giving testimony that they were Christians. In other words, he was simply referring to believers under the title of **those who are baptized,** not to some special act of baptism. **The dead** could also refer to Christians, to deceased believers whose lives were a persuasive testimony leading to the salvation of the **baptized.** This seems to be a reasonable view that does no injustice to the text or context.

The Greek *huper,* translated **for** in verse 29, has a dozen or more meanings, and shades of meaning—including "for," "above," "about," "across," "beyond," "on behalf of," "instead of," "because of," and "in reference to"—depending on grammatical structure and context. Although **for** is a perfectly legitimate translation here, in light of the context and of Paul's clear teaching elsewhere, "because of" could also be a proper rendering.

In light of that reasoning and interpretation, we could guess that Paul may have simply been saying that people were being saved (baptism being the sign) because of the exemplary lives and witness of faithful believers who had died. Whether this is the right interpretation of this verse we cannot be certain, but we can be certain that people often come to salvation because of the testimony of those whom they desire to emulate.

Some years ago a young man in our church was told by his doctors that he had only a short time to live. His response was not one of regret or bitterness but of joy at the prospect of soon being with his Savior. Because of his confident faith and contentment in face of death, one person I know of, and perhaps more, came to a saving knowledge of Christ.

During the Finnish-Russian war seven captured Russian soldiers were sentenced to death by the Finnish army. The evening before they were to be shot, one of the soldiers began singing "Safe in the Arms of Jesus." Asked why he was singing such a song, he answered tearfully that he had heard it sung by a group of Salvation Army "soldiers" just three weeks earlier. As a boy he had heard his mother talk and sing of Jesus many times, but would not accept her Savior. The previous night, as he lay contemplating his execution, he had a vision of his mother's face, which reminded him of the hymn he had recently heard. The words of the song and verses from the Bible that he had heard long ago came to his mind. He testified before his fellow prisoners and his captors that he had prayed for Christ to forgive his sins and cleanse his soul and make him ready to stand before God. All the men, prisoners and guards alike, were deeply moved, and most spent the night praying, weeping, talking about spiritual things, and singing hymns. In the morning, just before the seven were shot, they asked to be able to sing once more "Safe in the Arms of Jesus," which they were allowed to do.

At least one other of the Russian soldiers had confessed Christ during the night. In addition, the Finnish officer in charge said, "What happened in the hearts of the others I don't know, but . . . I was a new man from that hour. I had met Christ in one of His loveliest and youngest disciples, and I had seen enough to realize that I too could be His."

It may be that the first seeds of faith were planted in Paul's own heart by the testimony of Stephen, whose death the young Paul (then Saul) witnessed and whose confident and loving dying testimony he heard (Acts 7:59–8:1).

In 1 Corinthians 15:29 Paul may be affirming the truth that Christians who face death with joy and hope are a powerful testimony. The prospect of eternal life, of resurrection life, of reunion with loved ones, is a strong motive for people to listen to and accept the gospel. Resurrection is one of the greatest assurances that God gives to those who trust in His Son. For those who believe in Jesus Christ, the grave is not the end. At death our spirits are not absorbed back into some cosmic divine mind. When we die we will go immediately to be with the Lord—as an individual, personal being. Not only that, but one day our glorified bodies will rejoin our spirits, and we will live as whole, completed human beings throughout all of eternity with all who have loved and worshiped God.

Another way in which the believing **dead** are used as a means of salvation is through the hope of reunion. Many believers have been drawn to the Savior because of a strong desire to be united with a loved one who has gone to be with the Lord. I have never led a funeral service in which I did not make such an appeal. I have seen a husband who would not come to Christ until his wife died. Because he could not bear the thought of not seeing her again, committing his own life and eternity into the hands of the One he knew was her Lord was made more attractive. I have seen children come to Christ after their mother's death, motivated in part by the desire one day to be united with her. What her pleading and praying could not do, her death accomplished.

It is also true, of course, that the resurrection holds out great reunion hope for those who already are believers. The hope that sustained David after the death of his infant son was that, though "he will not return to me," "I shall go to him" (2 Sam. 12:23). David knew that one day he and his son would be reunited.

Perhaps confused by some of the same pagan philosophy that plagued the Corinthian church, the Thessalonian believers were concerned because they thought their believing loved ones and friends who had died somehow had no prospect of a future life. "But we do not want you to be uninformed, brethren, about those who are asleep," Paul wrote them, "that you may not grieve, as do the rest who have no hope. For if we believe that Jesus died and rose again, even so God will bring with Him those who have fallen asleep in Jesus" (1 Thess. 4:13-14). "Like you," He was assuring them, "they will be resurrected, and you will all be reunited by the Lord when He returns."

If there is no resurrection, no hope of a future life, Paul asked, why are people coming to Christ because of the testimony of believers who have died? **If the dead are not raised at all, why then are they** [many present Christians] **baptized for** [become believers because of the testimony of] **them** [deceased faithful believers]?

An Incentive for Service

Why are we also in danger every hour? I protest, brethren, by the boasting in you, which I have in Christ Jesus our Lord, I die daily. If from human motives I fought with wild beasts at Ephesus, what does it profit me? If the dead are not raised, Let us eat and drink, for tomorrow we die. (15:30-32)

The second incentive that hope of the resurrection gives is that for service. Why, otherwise, would believers endure and sacrifice so much? If this life were the end, what would be the reason for Paul's and the other apostles' being **in danger every hour?**

If there were no resurrection of the believing dead, then suffering and dying for the sake of the gospel would be masochistic, suffering for suffering's sake. As Paul had already pointed out, "If we have hoped in Christ in this life only, we are of all men most to be pitied" (15:19).

The only thing that makes Christians willing to work hard, willing to suffer, willing to be abused and ridiculed, willing to endure in the work of Christ is that Christ's own supreme finished work, the redemption of sinners, will last past this present life (cf. Rom. 8:18). What would be the purpose of suffering for Christ if we would never see Him face to face? What would be the purpose of winning others to Christ if they would never see Him face to face? Where would be the good news in such a gospel? Where would be the incentive for preaching or believing such a gospel?

Why make this life miserable if this life is all there is? Why be **in danger every hour,** if we have no security to look forward to? Why **die daily,** that is, risk your life in self-denying ministry, if death ends it all? **I protest,** Paul says vehemently, "You who deny the resurrection make a shambles of Christian service. Nothing makes sense if there is no resurrection." If Christ's resurrection on Easter morning was the only resurrection, as some of the Corinthians believed, then His being raised was no victory for us. He would not have conquered death but only made death a greater mockery for those who put their trust in Him.

If from human motives I fought with wild beasts at Ephesus, what does it profit me? What **human motives** could Paul have had for continually risking his safety and his life? We cannot be certain that Paul **fought** literal **wild beasts at Ephesus,** but it seems entirely possible that such was the case, and this interpretation is supported by tradition. It may be that Paul was speaking metaphorically of the wild crowd of Ephesians that was incited against him by the silversmith Demetrius (Acts 19:23-34). In any case, he was speaking of one of his many dangerous, life-threatening experiences.

Why would he have endured that, he was saying, and have continued to endure such things, if his only purpose and only hope was merely human and temporary? If we live only to die and remain dead, it makes more sense to say, **Let us eat and drink, for tomorrow we die**—a direct quotation from Isaiah 22:13 that reflected the hopeless and hedonistic view of the backslidden Israelites. It also reflects the dismal futility repeatedly expressed in Ecclesiastes: "'Vanity of vanities! All is vanity.' What advantage does man have in all his work which he does under the sun?" (Eccles. 1:2-3).

The Greek historian Herodotus tells of an interesting custom of the Egyptians. "In social meetings among the rich, when the banquet was ended, a servant would often carry around among the guests a coffin, in which was a wooden image of a corpse carved and painted to resemble a dead person as nearly as possible. The servant would show it to each of the guests and would say, 'Gaze here and drink and be merry, for when you die such you shall be.'"

If this life is all there is, why should the sensual not rule? Why not grab all we can, do all we can, live it up all we can? If we die only to remain dead, hedonism makes perfect sense.

What would *not* make sense is the godly self-sacrifice of those "who by faith conquered kingdoms, performed acts of righteousness, obtained promises, shut the mouths of lions, quenched the power of fire, escaped the edge of the sword, . . . wandering in deserts and mountains and caves and holes in the ground" (Heb. 11:33-34, 38). Their hope that "they might obtain a better resurrection" (v. 35) would have been futile and empty.

"Jesus, the author and perfecter of faith, . . . for the joy set before Him endured the cross, despising the shame, and has sat down at the right hand of the throne of

God" (Heb. 12:2). It was anticipation of the resurrection, of being raised to be again with His Father, that gave our Lord the motive for dying on our behalf. He was willing to die for us because He knew He would be raised for us.

AN INCENTIVE FOR SANCTIFICATION

Do not be deceived: "Bad company corrupts good morals." Become sober-minded as you ought, and stop sinning; for some have no knowledge of God. I speak this to your shame. (15:33-34)

The third incentive the hope of resurrection gives is for sanctification. Looking forward to resurrection should lead to more godly living and spiritual maturity. Verses 32 and 33 are closely related. Denying the resurrection destroys the incentives both for service and for sanctification. Why then bother serving the Lord or serving others in His name, and why bother to be holy and pure?

Paul warned the Corinthians that they should **not be deceived** about the danger of **bad company.** *Homilia* (**company**) basically means an association of people, but also can have the connotation of a lecture or sermon. It seems possible, therefore, that the Corinthians were both listening to some wrong teaching and associating with some evil people. Whether the teaching was in formal messages or not, it was **bad** and corrupting.

People who think wrongly invariably behave wrongly. Wrong behavior comes from wrong thinking, from wrong beliefs and wrong standards. It is impossible to associate regularly with wicked people without being contaminated both by their ideas and by their habits. The context implies that the **bad company** was teaching the heretical theology that there is no resurrection of the dead, and that bad theology had corrupted **good morals.**

Just as hoping in the resurrection is an incentive to obedience and holiness, so disbelief of it is an incentive to disobedience and immorality. As Paul has just pointed out, if there is no resurrection, we might as well **eat and drink, for tomorrow we die.** If death is the end, what great difference does it make what we do?

Some in the Corinthian congregation had **no knowledge of God,** and therefore no knowledge of His truth. Their bad theology was leading to bad behavior, especially because they denied the resurrection.

The Greek historian Thucydides reported that when a deadly plague came to Athens, "People committed every shameful crime and eagerly snatched at every lustful pleasure." They believed life was short and there was no resurrection, so they would have to pay no price for their vice. The Roman poet Horace wrote, "Tell them to bring wine and perfume and the too short-lived blossoms of the lovely rose while circumstance and age and the black threads of the three sisters fate still allow us to do so." Another Roman poet, Catullus, penned the lines: "Let's live my Lesbia and let's love, and let's value the tales of austere old men at a single half penny. Suns can set and then return again, but for us when once our brief light sets there is but one perpetual night through which we must sleep."

Without the prospect of a resurrection, and of the accountability it brings, there is no incentive for doing anything but what we feel like doing here and now. If behavior has no reward or condemnation, it is uncontrollable.

Become sober-minded as you ought, and stop sinning, Paul pleads in the imperative. "Those of you who believe in the resurrection know better, and you should be leading those who do not believe in the resurrection into a true **knowledge of God,** rather than allowing their heresy and their immorality to mislead and corrupt you." The apostle spoke **this to** [their] **shame.** They had the truth, but they did not fully believe it and therefore did not fully follow it. He commands them to cease the sin they were involved in.

What tremendous power the resurrection has, and what wonderful hope it gives! Jesus rose from the dead; He is alive; and we also shall live because one day He will raise us up to be with Him eternally. What greater incentive, what greater motive, could we have for coming to Him, for serving Him, and for living for Him?

Our Resurrection Bodies (15:35-49)

44

But someone will say, "How are the dead raised? And with what kind of body do they come?" You fool! That which you sow does not come to life unless it dies; and that which you sow, you do not sow the body which is to be, but a bare grain, perhaps of wheat or of something else. But God gives it a body just as He wished, and to each of the seeds a body of its own. All flesh is not the same flesh, but there is one flesh of men, and another flesh of beasts, and another flesh of birds, and another of fish. There are also heavenly bodies and earthly bodies, but the glory of the heavenly is one, and the glory of the earthly is another. There is one glory of the sun, and another glory of the moon, and another glory of the stars; for star differs from star in glory. So also is the resurrection of the dead. It is sown a perishable body, it is raised an imperishable body; it is sown in dishonor, it is raised in glory; it is sown in weakness, it is raised in power; it is sown a natural body, it is raised a spiritual body. If there is a natural body, there is also a spiritual body. So also it is written, "The first man, Adam, became a living soul." The last Adam became a life-giving spirit. However, the spiritual is not first, but the natural; then the spiritual. The first man is from the earth, earthy; the second man is from heaven. As is the earthy, so also are those who are earthy; and as is the heavenly, so also are those who are heavenly. And just as we have borne the image of the earthy, we shall also bear the image of the heavenly. (15:35-49)

The first major problem Paul deals with in chapter 15 is denial of general resurrection. Some of the Corinthians, though they had accepted the truth of Christ's resurrection, refused to believe that other men would or could be resurrected. Verses 12-34 show the error and dangers of such denial. Now the apostle deals with another troublesome issue, one that is really a part of the first, namely, the question of how a general resurrection could be possible. The idea of resurrecting all the human race seems inconceivable because of its complexity and the power demanded to accomplish it.

But someone will say, "How are the dead raised? And with what kind of body do they come?" (15:35)

Those in Corinth who denied the resurrection did so primarily because of the influence of gnostic philosophy, which considered the body to be inherently evil and only the spirit to be good. They therefore believed that resurrection of the body is *undesirable*. Paul now challenges the idea that resurrection also is *impossible*. "Supposing," they argued, "that resurrection were a good thing, how could it happen?"

Part of the problem some Greeks had may have been traceable to a false view of resurrection taught by many rabbis of that time. By misinterpreting such passages as Job 19:26 ("Yet from my flesh I shall see God"), they concluded that resurrection bodies will be identical to earthly bodies in every way. The writer of the Jewish apocryphal book of Baruch wrote, for example, that "the earth shall then [at the resurrection] assuredly restore the dead; it shall make no change in form, but as it has received so shall it restore." To Gnostics, that view made resurrection seem even *less* desirable and possible.

But why would anyone who acknowledges a creator God think His restoring bodies, in whatever way, would be any more difficult for Him than making them in the first place? As Paul asked before King Agrippa, "Why is it considered incredible among you people if God does raise the dead?" (Acts 26:8). Why do people still today, including some Christians, become perplexed and bothered about how God could restore the bodies of those who have been lost at sea, blown up in an explosion, or cremated? Why is His restoring those bodies more miraculous and unbelievable than His creating the universe? And besides, every dead body, no matter how well embalmed, eventually disintegrates.

Yet one objection to the idea of resurrection was, and still is, its seeming impossibility. **But someone will say,** Paul's experience led him to anticipate, **"How are the dead raised?"** How could God possibly reassemble the bodies of everyone who has died throughout the ages of history? A closely related question was, **And with what kind of body do they come?**

In verses 36-49 Paul answers the questions of verse 35 in four ways: (1) he gives an illustration from nature, (2) he tells what kind of body resurrection bodies will be, (3) he contrasts earthly and resurrection bodies, and (4) he reminds them of the prototype resurrection, in which they already believed.

AN ILLUSTRATION OF RESURRECTION

You fool! That which you sow does not come to life unless it dies; and that which you sow, you do not sow the body which is to be, but a bare grain, perhaps of wheat or of something else. But God gives it a body just as He wished, and to each of the seeds a body of its own. (15:36-38)

Like denial of resurrection because it seems undesirable, denial of resurrection because it seems impossible came from the skepticism of pagan philosophy. It did not come from honest doubt or ignorance, and Paul responds accordingly: **You fool.** The word was used derisively of one who does not use or does not have understanding.

The questions mentioned in verse 35 were not those of someone who wanted to know but were the mocking taunts of someone who thought he already knew. As with most of the questions put to Jesus by the scribes, Pharisees, and Sadducees, the purpose was to entrap and embarrass, not discover truth.

To point up the foolishness of the objection, Paul gives a common illustration from nature. In three significant ways resurrection is similar to the planting and growth of crops: the original form is dissolved, the original and final forms are different in kind, and yet the two forms have a continuity. Resurrection is not impossible, because it occurs on a small scale continuously in the plant world.

DISSOLUTION

First is the similarity of dissolution, or dying. **That which you sow does not come to life unless it dies.** When a seed is planted in the ground it dies, actually decomposing as a seed: it must cease to exist in its original form as a seed before it can **come to life** in its final form as a plant.

Applying the same figure, Jesus said, "Truly, truly, I say to you, unless a grain of wheat falls into the earth and dies, it remains by itself alone; but if it dies, it bears much fruit" (John 12:24). Before Christ could bear the fruit of salvation for us, He had to die. Likewise, before we can participate in the fruit of His resurrection, or bear fruit in His service, we too must die. "He who loves his life loses it; and he who hates his life in this world shall keep it to life eternal" (v. 25).

When Jesus was crucified His earthly body died; it ceased to exist as an earthly body. Just as with growing crops, there had to be an end to the old before there could be a beginning of the new. In the case of men, one body will die to give life to another.

DIFFERENCE

Second, both in the growing of crops and in the resurrection of bodies there is a difference between the original and final forms. The seed loses its identity as a seed and becomes more and more like the mature plant. But the seed itself, **that which you sow**—whether it is **wheat or . . . something else**—looks nothing like the

433

mature plant, **the body which is to be**. Only after ceasing to be a seed does it become the mature plant the farmer harvests.

When Jesus was raised from the dead His glorified body was radically different from the one which died. What came out of the grave was different from what was placed in the grave. It was no longer limited by time, space, and material substance. During His appearances, Jesus went from one place to another without traveling in any physical way. He appeared and disappeared at will, and entered rooms without opening the door (Luke 24:15, 31, 36; John 20:19; etc.). In His earthly body He had done none of those things. Resurrection changed Jesus' body in marvelous and radical ways, and at His return *all* resurrection bodies will be changed marvelously and radically.

CONTINUITY

Third, in spite of the differences, there is nevertheless a continuity between the old and the new. **But God gives it a body just as He wished, and to each of the seeds a body of its own.** The seed changes radically, but it continues as the same life form. A wheat seed does not become barley, and a flax seed does not become corn. **God** has given each type of seed **a body of its own,** whose identity continues into the grown plant.

After Jesus was raised, no one recognized Him unless He revealed Himself to them. But once revealed, He was recognizable. The disciples knew His face, and they recognized His wounded side and His pierced hands. In a similar way, our resurrected bodies as believers will have a continuity with the bodies we have now. Our bodies will die and they will change form, but they will still be *our* bodies. Surely it is not too hard to believe that the God who has worked this process daily through the centuries in His creation of plants, can do it with men.

The Form of Resurrection Bodies

All flesh is not the same flesh, but there is one flesh of men, and another flesh of beasts, and another flesh of birds, and another of fish. There are also heavenly bodies and earthly bodies, but the glory of the heavenly is one, and the glory of the earthly is another. There is one glory of the sun, and another glory of the moon, and another glory of the stars; for star differs from star in glory. So also is the resurrection of the dead. (15:39-42a)

These verses expand on Paul's previous point that our resurrection bodies will be different from our earthly bodies. Seeing the vast differences in God's creation, we should not question His ability to create bodies that are different and yet continuous.

All flesh is not the same flesh indicates the amazing variety of earthly bodies God has made. We need only look around us to see the virtually infinite assortment of created beings and things. In the biological world the flesh of men is absolutely distinct from the **flesh of beasts,** the **flesh of birds,** and the **flesh of fish.** All flesh is not of the same kind.

I have read that there are some six hundred octodecillion different combinations of amino acids. An octodecillion is 10 to the 108th power, or 1 followed by 108 zeros. Amino acids are the building blocks of all life. Not only does each type of plant and animal life have a distinct pattern of amino acids, but each individual plant, animal, and human being has its own unique grouping of them. No two flowers, snowflakes, seeds, blades of grass, or human beings—even identical twins—are exactly alike. Yet each is completely identified with its own species or kind.

Those two facts make one of the strongest scientific evidences against evolution. No matter what we may eat, no matter how specialized or unbalanced our diet may be, and no matter what our environment may be, we will never change into another form of life. We may become healthier or more sickly, heavier or lighter, but we will never be anything but a human being and never any human being but the one we are. The biological codes are binding and unique. There is no repeatable or demonstrable scientific proof that one form of life has changed or could change into another.

There are also heavenly bodies, which obviously differ greatly from **earthly bodies** in **glory,** that is, in nature, manifestation, and form. Not only are the heavenly bodies vastly different from the earthly; they are greatly different from each other. The **sun** is greatly different from the **moon,** and both are different from the **stars.** From astronomy we know that many of what normally are called stars actually are planets, and therefore similar to the earth and moon, and that true stars are themselves suns. But Paul was speaking from the perspective of normal human observation, not from the perspective of science. From either perspective, however, his basic point is true. The stars generate their own light, while the planets and moons only reflect light produced by the stars. In that way the two types of heavenly bodies are greatly different in **glory,** that is, in character and manifestation.

Even **star differs from star in glory.** Donald Peattie has written,

> Like flowers, the stars have their own colors. At your first upward glance all gleam white as frost crystals, but single out this one and that for observation and you will find a subtle spectrum in the stars. The quality of their lights is determined by their temperatures. In the December sky you will see Aldebaran as pale rose, Rigel as bluish white and Betelgeuse orange to topaz yellow.

Every star is different, just as every plant is different, every animal is different, and every human being is different. God has infinite creative capacity, including the capacity to make infinite variety. Why would anyone think it hard for Him to re-create and resurrect human bodies, no matter what the form might be?

So also is the resurrection of the dead. Resurrection bodies will differ from earthly bodies just as radically as heavenly bodies differ from earthly. And resurrection bodies will be as individual and unique as are all the other forms of God's creation.

When Moses and Elijah appeared on the Mount of Transfiguration they were as distinctly individual as they had been while living on earth. They did not then have resurrected bodies, but they were distinct beings of heaven, who one day will have distinct heavenly bodies. God *is*, not was, the God of Abraham, Isaac, and Jacob—the God of the living, not of the dead (Matt. 22:32). Those patriarchs are not merely alive in heaven, but are alive as the same persons they were on earth. Jesus knows *all* His sheep by name (John 10:3), whether they are in heaven or still on earth. Our resurrection bodies will be as uniquely ours as our spirits and our names.

THE CONTRASTS OF RESURRECTION

It is sown a perishable body, it is raised an imperishable body; it is sown in dishonor, it is raised in glory; it is sown in weakness, it is raised in power; it is sown a natural body, it is raised a spiritual body. If there is a natural body, there is also a spiritual body. (15:42b-44)

Focusing more directly on the resurrection body, Paul here mentions specific ways, given as four sets of contrasts, in which our glorified bodies will be different from our earthly bodies.

PERISHABLE/IMPERISHABLE

The first contrast pertains to durability. One of the most obvious characteristics of all natural life, including human life, is that it is **perishable,** subject to deterioration and eventual death. Even in the healthy infant the process of aging and deterioration has begun. "All go to the same place. All came from the dust and all return to the dust" (Eccles. 3:20). "For He Himself knows our frame; He is mindful that we are but dust. As for man, his days are like grass; as a flower of the field, so he flourishes. When the wind has passed over it, it is no more; and its place acknowledges it no longer" (Ps. 103:14-16).

Even the healthiest of people, as they get older, become weaker and more subject to disease and various physical problems. Death, of course, rapidly accelerates decay. Martha objected to Lazarus's tomb being opened, because "by this time there will be a stench, for he has been dead four days" (John 11:39). The purpose of embalming is to retard deterioration of the body as long as possible. But even the remarkable Egyptian mummification could not prevent deterioration, much less restore life.

One of the tragic consequences of the Fall was that men's bodies from that time on were irreversibly mortal, subject to death. Without exception, every human being is **sown,** that is, born with, **a perishable body.**

But the resurrection body of the believer will be **raised an imperishable body.** "Blessed be the God and Father of our Lord Jesus Christ, who according to His great mercy has caused us to be born again to a living hope through the resurrection of

Jesus Christ from the dead, to obtain an inheritance which is imperishable and undefiled and will not fade away, reserved in heaven for you" (1 Pet. 1:3-4). Our new bodies will know no sickness, decay, deterioration, or death. "When this perishable will have put on the imperishable, and this mortal will have put on immortality, then will come about the saying that is written, 'Death is swallowed up in victory'" (1 Cor. 15:54).

DISHONOR/GLORY

The second contrast has to do with value and potential. At the Fall man's potential for pleasing and serving God was radically reduced. Not only his mind and spirit but also his body became of immeasurably less value in doing what God had designed it to do. The creature that was made perfect, and in the very image of his Creator, was made to manifest his Creator in all that he did. But through sin, that which was created to honor God became characterized instead by **dishonor.**

We dishonor God by our inability to take advantage fully of what He has given us in His creation. We dishonor God by misusing and abusing the bodies through which He desires us to honor and serve Him. Even the most faithful believer dies with his body in a state of dishonor, a state of imperfection and incompleteness.

But that imperfect and dishonored body one day will be **raised in glory.** Throughout eternity our new immortal bodies will also be honorable bodies, perfected for pleasing, praising, and enjoying the Creator who made them and the Redeemer who restored them.

WEAKNESS/POWER

The third contrast has to do with ability. Our present bodies are characterized by **weakness.** We are weak not only in physical strength and endurance but also in resistance to disease and harm. Despite the marvelous natural protective mechanisms of the human body, no one is immune from breaking a bone, cutting a leg, catching various infections, and eventually from dying. We can and should minimize unnecessary dangers and risks to our bodies, which for believers are temples of the Holy Spirit (1 Cor. 6:19-20). But we cannot completely protect them from harm, much less from death. Our earthly "temples" are inescapably temporary and fragile.

But not so our new bodies, which will be **raised in power.** We are not told what that power will entail, but it will be immeasurable compared to what we now possess. We will no longer have to say that "the spirit is willing, but the flesh is weak" (Matt. 26:41). Anything our heavenly spirits determine to do our heavenly bodies will be able to accomplish.

Martin Luther said, "As weak as it [the human body of believers] is now without all power and ability when it lies in the grave, just so strong will it eventually become when the time arrives, so that not a thing will be impossible for it if it has a mind for it, and it will be so light and agile that in an instant it can float here below on earth or above in heaven."

NATURAL/SPIRITUAL

The fourth area of contrasts has to do with the sphere, or realm, of existence. Our earthly body is strictly **natural**. That is the only realm in which it can live and function. The physical body is suited for and limited to the physical world. Even with the imperfections and limitations caused by the Fall, our present bodies are wonderfully made for life on earth, marvelously suited for earthly living. But that is the only realm and the only living for which they are suited.

The new body of the believer, however, will be **raised a spiritual body**. Our spirits now reside in earthly bodies, but one day they will reside in spiritual bodies. In every way we then will be spiritual beings. In both spirit and body we will be perfectly suited for heavenly living.

"The sons of this age marry and are given in marriage," Jesus said, "but those who are considered worthy to attain to that age and the resurrection from the dead, neither marry, nor are given in marriage; for neither can they die anymore, for they are like angels, and are sons of God, being sons of the resurrection" (Luke 20:34-36).

In the resurrection everything about us will be perfected for all eternity. We will not be the same as angels, but will be "like" them in that we too will be perfectly equipped and suited for heavenly, spiritual, supernatural, living.

THE PROTOTYPE OF RESURRECTION

So also it is written, "The first man, Adam, became a living soul." The last Adam became a life-giving spirit. However, the spiritual is not first, but the natural; then the spiritual. The first man is from the earth, earthy; the second man is from heaven. As is the earthy, so also are those who are earthy; and as is the heavenly, so also are those who are heavenly. And just as we have borne the image of the earthy, we shall also bear the image of the heavenly. (15:45-49)

The fourth way in which Paul answers the questions "How are the dead raised? And with what kind of body do they come?" (v. 35) is by showing the prototype of resurrection and by further explaining the differences between natural and spiritual bodies.

He begins with a quotation from Genesis 2:7, with the addition of the two words **first** and **Adam. So also it is written, "The first man, Adam, became a living soul."** Adam was created with a natural body. It was not glorified, but it was perfect and "good" in every way (Gen. 1:31).

Adam and Eve originally were in a probationary period. Had they proved faithful rather than disobedient, their bodies would have been glorified and immortalized by eating the fruit of the tree of life, which they then could have eaten (see Gen. 2:9). Because they sinned, however, they were put out of the garden lest they eat of the tree of life and live forever in a state of sin (3:22).

The last Adam, however, **became a life-giving spirit. The last Adam** is Jesus Christ. "As through the one man's disobedience the many were made sinners, even so through the obedience of the One the many will be made righteous. And . . . as sin reigned in death, even so grace might reign through righteousness to eternal life through Jesus Christ our Lord" (Rom. 5:19, 21; cf. vv. 12, 15). Through Adam we have inherited our natural bodies; through Christ we will inherit spiritual bodies in the resurrection.

Adam's was the prototype of our natural bodies, whereas Christ's was the prototype of our spiritual bodies. All the descendants of Adam have natural bodies, and all the descendants of Christ will have spiritual bodies. Christ's resurrection, therefore, was the prototype of all subsequent resurrection.

In verse 46 Paul points out the obvious: **However, the spiritual is not first, but the natural; then the spiritual.** Every human being, starting with Adam and including Christ, has begun human life in a natural, physical body. The body that was raised from the dead on Easter morning had been a natural body, the incarnate body in which Christ was born and in which He lived and died. In the resurrection it was a spiritual, eternal body.

Adam, **the first man,** from whom came the natural race, originated on the earth, in fact was created directly **from the earth** (Gen. 2:7). In every way he was **earthy.** But Christ, called **the second man** because He has produced a spiritual race, existed eternally before He became a man. He lived on earth in a natural body, but He came **from heaven.** Adam was tied to earth; Christ was tied to heaven.

Because of our natural descent from Adam we are a part of **those who are earthy.** But because of our inheritance in Jesus Christ, we also have become a part of **those who are heavenly.** In Adam we are **earthy;** in Christ we have become **heavenly.** One day our natural bodies from Adam will be changed into our heavenly bodies from Christ.

And just as we have borne the image of the earthy, we shall also bear the image of the heavenly. Just as we will exchange Adam's natural body for Christ's spiritual body, we will also exchange Adam's **image** for Christ's.

From Jesus' postresurrection appearances we get some idea of the greatness, power, and wonder of what our own resurrection bodies will be like. Jesus appeared and disappeared at will, reappearing again at another place far distant. He could go through walls or closed doors, and yet also could eat, drink, sit, talk, and be seen by those who He wanted to see Him. He was remarkably the same, yet even more remarkably different. After His ascension, the angel told the amazed disciples, "This Jesus, who has been taken up from you into heaven, will come in just the same way as you have watched Him go into heaven" (Acts 1:11). The body the disciples saw after Jesus' resurrection is the same body that will be seen when He returns again.

Just as with our Lord, our bodies, which are now perishable, dishonored, weak, and natural, will be raised into bodies that are imperishable, glorious, powerful, and spiritual. That which hindered our service and manifestation of God will now be the marvelous channel of fulfillment. We will have His own power in which to serve and praise Him, and His own glory by which to manifest and magnify Him. "Then the righteous will shine forth as the sun in the kingdom of their Father" (Matt. 13:43). In heaven we will radiate like the sun, in the blazing and magnificent glory which the Lord will graciously share with those who are His. Christ will "transform the body of our humble state into conformity with the body of His glory, by the exertion of the power that He has even to subject all things to Himself" (Phil. 3:21).

We cannot imagine exactly what that will be like. Even our present spiritual eyes cannot envision our future spiritual bodies. "Beloved, now we are children of God, and it has not appeared as yet what we shall be. We know that, when He appears, we shall be like Him, because we shall see Him just as He is" (1 John 3:2). We will not see our own resurrected bodies, or even have our own resurrected bodies, until we first see Christ's.

"So the graveyards of man become the seed plots of resurrection," Erich Sauer beautifully observes, "and the cemeteries of the people of God become through the heavenly dew the resurrection fields of the promised perfection."

The coming resurrection is the hope and motivation of the church and of all believers. Whatever happens to our present bodies—whether they are healthy or unhealthy, beautiful or plain, short-lived or long-lived, or whether they are indulged or tortured—they are not our permanent bodies, and we should not hold them too dearly. Our blessed hope and assurance is that these created natural bodies one day will be recreated as spiritual bodies. Although we have only a glimpse of what those new bodies will be like, it should be enough to know that "we shall be like Him."

Victory over Death
(15:50-58)

Now I say this, brethren, that flesh and blood cannot inherit the kingdom of God; nor does the perishable inherit the imperishable. Behold, I tell you a mystery; we shall not all sleep, but we shall all be changed, in a moment, in the twinkling of an eye, at the last trumpet; for the trumpet will sound, and the dead will be raised imperishable, and we shall be changed. For this perishable must put on the imperishable, and this mortal must put on immortality. But when this perishable will have put on the imperishable, and this mortal will have put on immortality, then will come about the saying that is written, "Death is swallowed up in victory. O death, where is your victory? O death, where is your sting?" The sting of death is sin, and the power of sin is the law; but thanks be to God, who gives us the victory through our Lord Jesus Christ.

Therefore, my beloved brethren, be steadfast, immovable, always abounding in the work of the Lord, knowing that your toil is not in vain in the Lord. (15:50-58)

Someone has written,

There is a preacher of the old school but he speaks as boldly as ever. He is not popular, though the world is his parish and he travels every part of the globe and speaks in every language. He visits the poor, calls upon the rich, preaches to people of every religion and no religion, and the subject of his sermon is always the same. He is an eloquent preacher, often stirring feelings which no other preacher could, and bringing tears to eyes that never weep. His arguments none are able to refute, nor is there any heart that has remained unmoved by the force of this appeals. He shatters life with his message. Most people hate him; everyone fears him. His name? Death. Every tombstone is his pulpit, every newspaper prints his text, and someday every one of you will be his sermon.

Thomas Gray wrote, "The boast of heraldry, the pomp of power and all that beauty and all that wealth e'er gave await alike the inevitable hour. The paths of glory lead but to the grave." As far as human power, beauty, wealth, and glory are concerned, that truth applies to Christians as much as to any others. But the hope of the Christian is not in such things, which he knows will end at the grave. The hope of the Christian is expressed by the epitaph Benjamin Franklin wrote for himself, engraved on his tombstone in the cemetery of Christ's Church in Philadelphia: "The body of Franklin, printer, like the cover of an old book, its contents torn out and stripped of its lettering and gilding, lies here food for worms. But the work will not be lost, for it will appear once more in a new and more elegant edition, revised and corrected by the Author."

That is the hope of the Christian and the message of 1 Corinthians 15. To the skeptics of every age, as to the skeptics in Corinth, the Holy Spirit through Paul gives a rebuke for denying the resurrection of the body (15:12, 35) and proclaims, "But now Christ has been raised from the dead, the first fruits of those who are asleep. For since by a man came death, by a man also came the resurrection of the dead. For as in Adam all die, so also in Christ all shall be made alive" (vv. 20-22).

In this longest chapter of the letter, the apostle has given the evidence for Christ's resurrection (vv. 1-11), the implications of denying bodily resurrection (vv. 12-19), the plan (vv. 20-28) and incentives (vv. 29-34) of resurrection, and a description and explanation of our resurrection bodies (vv. 35-49). In concluding this passage he proclaims the marvelous victory that resurrection will bring for those who are Christ's.

Paul's concluding "victory song" has been put to music in such masterpieces as Handel's *Messiah* and Brahms's *Requiem,* and in many ways it is more appropriate to be sung than preached. Praising God in anticipation of resurrection, the apostle proclaims the great transformation, the great triumph, and the great thanksgiving that the raising of God's saints will bring, and then gives a great exhortation for holy living until that day comes.

THE GREAT TRANSFORMATION

Now I say this, brethren, that flesh and blood cannot inherit the kingdom of God; nor does the perishable inherit the imperishable. Behold, I tell you a mystery; we shall not all sleep, but we shall all be changed, in a moment, in the twinkling of an eye, at the last trumpet; for the trumpet will sound, and

the dead will be raised imperishable, and we shall be changed. For this perishable must put on the imperishable, and this mortal must put on immortality. (15:50-53)

Paul reminds his readers again that the resurrection body will not be **flesh and blood,** which, though wonderfully suited for earth, is not at all suited for heaven and therefore **cannot inherit the kingdom of God. The kingdom of God** is not used here either in its universal sense, referring to God's ruling the universe, or in its spiritual sense, referring to His ruling in the human heart, but in its consummate sense, embodying both and referring to the eternal state, to heaven. "Just as we have borne the image of the earthy, we shall also bear the image of the heavenly" (v. 49).

Even Christ's own earthly body was "flesh and blood" (Heb. 2:14) and had to be transformed before He could return to the Father. The human body is renewed every seven years, but that does not prevent its aging, deterioration, and eventual death. The human body is **perishable.** It is not suited for and cannot **inherit the imperishable.** It must be made different in order to inherit heaven, and it *will be* made different. "It is sown a perishable body, it is raised an imperishable body; it is sown in dishonor, it is raised in glory; it is sown in weakness, it is raised in power; it is sown a natural body, it is raised a spiritual body" (1 Cor. 15:42-44). Like the seed that is planted, it continues its identity, but in a radically and wonderfully different form.

But what about believers who are living when Christ returns? Anticipating that question, Paul continues, **Behold, I tell you a mystery; we shall not all sleep.** As pointed out several times before, in the New Testament **mystery** always refers to that which had before been hidden and unknown but which is now revealed. The apostle now reveals that Christians who are alive when the Lord returns will not have to die (**sleep**) in order for their bodies to be changed. Those "who are alive and remain shall be caught up together with them in the clouds to meet the Lord in the air, and thus we shall always be with the Lord" (1 Thess. 4:17). As believers are resurrected or caught up they **shall all be changed.** Whether believers die or are raptured, their bodies will be changed from the perishable to the imperishable, from the natural to the spiritual. Since the perishable cannot inherit the imperishable, Enoch and Elijah must have been changed in the same way that raptured believers will be changed. In any case, **all** believers will be equally equipped for heaven (cf. Phil. 3:20-21).

Both for the resurrected and for the raptured the change will be **in a moment, in the twinkling of an eye.** It will not be a process, a supernatural metamorphosis. It will be an instantaneous recreation from one form to the other, from the earthy to the heavenly. **Moment** is from *atomos,* from which we get the word *atom,* and denotes that which cannot be cut, or divided, the smallest conceivable quantity. In the smallest possible amount of time our perishable bodies will be made imperishable. To further emphasize and illustrate the speed of the change, Paul says that it will occur **in the twinkling of an eye.** *Rhipē* (**twinkling**) literally means to hurl, and was used to refer to any rapid movement. The **eye** can move much faster than any other visible part of our bodies, and Paul's point was that the change will be extremely fast, instantaneous.

This change will occur **at the last trumpet.** I do not think that this **trumpet** necessarily will be the **last** heavenly trumpet ever to be sounded. It will, however, be the last as far as living Christians are concerned, for it will **sound** the end of the church age, when all believers will be removed from the earth. "For the Lord Himself will descend from heaven with a shout, with the voice of the archangel, and with the trumpet of God; and the dead in Christ shall rise first. Then we who are alive and remain shall be caught up together with them in the clouds to meet the Lord in the air, and thus we shall always be with the Lord" (1 Thess. 4:16-17). By that trumpet God will summon all of His people to Himself (cf. Ex. 19:16; Isa. 27:13).

During the Civil War a group of soldiers had to spend a winter night without tents in an open field. During the night it snowed several inches, and at dawn the chaplain reported a strange sight. The snow-covered soldiers looked like the mounds of new graves, and when the bugle sounded reveille a man immediately rose from each mound of snow, dramatically reminding the chaplain of this passage from 1 Corinthians.

Speaking of the coming resurrection day, Jesus said, "I will come again, and receive you to Myself; that where I am, there you may be also" (John 14:3). As He ascended to heaven the angels told the onlooking disciples, "This Jesus, who has been taken up from you into heaven, will come in just the same way as you have watched Him go into heaven" (Acts 1:11). With Paul, every believer should be "looking for the blessed hope and the appearing of the glory of our great God and Savior, Christ Jesus" (Titus 2:13).

Because earthly, natural bodies cannot occupy the eternal kingdom, such a day and such a moment has to be, **for this perishable** [that which is subject to decay] **must put on the imperishable, and this mortal must put on immortality.** The word translated **put on** was commonly used of putting on clothing, and pictures our redeemed spirits being dressed redeemed bodies (cf. 2 Cor. 5:1-5).

The Great Triumph

But when this perishable will have put on the imperishable, and this mortal will have put on immortality, then will come about the saying that is written, "Death is swallowed up in victory. O death, where is your victory? O death, where is your sting?" The sting of death is sin, and the power of sin is the law. (15:54-56)

Christ's resurrection broke the power of death for those who believe in Him, and death is no longer master over them because "death no longer is master over Him" (Rom. 6:9). But death is still the enemy of man. Even for Christians it violates our dominion of God's creation, it breaks love relationships, it disrupts families, and causes great grief in the loss of those dear to us. We no longer need fear death, but it still invades and torments us while we are mortal.

But one day, when Christ returns, the **perishable** that "*must* put on the imperishable" (v. 53) **will have put on the imperishable**, and the mortal that "*must* put on immortality" **will have put on immortality**. Then will come the great triumph that Isaiah predicted, when **death is swallowed up in victory**. The Isaiah text reads, "He [the Lord of Hosts] will swallow up death for all time" (Isa. 25:8; cf. v. 6). When the great transformation comes, the great victory will come.

The well-known commentator R. C. H. Lenski writes,

> Death is not merely destroyed so that it cannot do further harm, while all of the harm which it has wrought on God's children remains. No, the tornado is not merely checked so that no additional homes are wrecked, while those that were wrecked still lie in ruin. . . . Death and all of its apparent victories are undone for God's children. What looks like a victory for death and like a defeat for us when our bodies die and decay shall be utterly reversed so that death dies in absolute defeat and our bodies live again in absolute victory.

Quoting another prophet (Hos. 13:14), Paul taunts death: **O death, where is your victory? O death, where is your sting?** To continue with that metaphor, Paul implies that **death** left its **sting** in Christ, as a bee leaves its stinger in its victim. Christ bore the whole of death's sting in order that we would have to bear none of it.

To make his point, the apostle reminds his readers that **the sting of death is sin**. The harm in death is caused by sin; in fact, death itself is caused by sin. "Therefore, just as through one man sin entered into the world, and death through sin, and so death spread to all men, because all sinned" (Rom 5:12). Only where there is sin can death deal a fatal blow. Where sin has been removed death can only interrupt the earthly life and usher in the heavenly. That is what Christ has done for those who trust in Him. Our "sins are forgiven for His name's sake" (1 John 2:12). Death is not gone, but its sting, sin, is gone. "For if by the transgression of the one, death reigned through the one, much more those who receive the abundance of grace and of the gift of righteousness will reign in life through the One, Jesus Christ" (Rom. 5:17).

It is not, of course, that Christians no longer sin, but that the sins we commit are already covered by Christ's atoning death, so that sin's effect is not permanently fatal. "The blood of Jesus His Son cleanses us from all sin" (1 John 1:7). But for those who do not believe, death's sting tragically remains forever.

Paul continues to explain the sequence leading to death by mentioning that **the power of sin is the law**. God's law reveals God's standards, and when they are broken they reveal man's sin. If there were no law, obviously there could be no transgression. "Where there is no law neither is there violation" (Rom. 4:15). But men die because they break that law.

What about those who do not know God's law, who have never even heard of, much less read, His Word? Paul tells us in Romans that when "Gentiles who do not have the Law do instinctively the things of the Law, these, not having the Law, are a law to themselves, in that they show the work of the Law written in their hearts, their conscience bearing witness, and their thoughts alternately accusing or else defending them" (2:14-15). Anyone, therefore, who goes against his conscience goes against God's law just as surely as anyone who knowingly breaks one of the Ten Commandments. That is the reason men are doomed to die (Rom. 3:23; 6:23).

THE GREAT THANKSGIVING

But thanks be to God, who gives us the victory through our Lord Jesus Christ. (15:57)

Because of Jesus' perfect obedience to the law (Rom. 5:19) and the satisfaction He made for its victims, those who trust in Him "are not under law, but under grace," having "been released from the Law" (Rom.6:14; 7:6). Jesus has both fulfilled the law and fulfilled righteousness. Because His life was sinless and therefore fulfilled the law, His death conquered sin.

Paul gives thanks to the One who will give us the great transformation of our bodies and who has made the great triumph over sin and death. That which we could never do for ourselves **God** has done for us **through our Lord Jesus Christ.** We cannot live sinlessly and thereby fulfill the law, nor can we remove sin once we have committed it, or remove its consequence, which is death. But on our behalf Jesus Christ lived a sinless life, fulfilling the law; removed our sin by Himself paying the penalty for it, satisfying God with a perfect sacrifice; and conquered death by being raised from the dead. All of that great **victory** He accomplished for us and **gives** to **us.** "Christ redeemed us from the curse of the Law, having become a curse for us" (Gal. 3:13). He took our curse and our condemnation and gives us victory in their place.

How can we do anything but thank and praise God for what He has done for us? He has promised us an imperishable, glorious, powerful, and spiritual body for one that is perishable, dishonorable, weak, and natural. He promises us the heavenly in exchange for the earthly, the immortal in exchange for the mortal. We know these promises are assured because He has already given us victory over sin and death.

For Christians death has no more power (Heb. 2:14-15), because God has taken away our sin. For Christians death is but the passing of our spirits from this life to the next, the leaving of earth and going to be with Christ. Paul had only one reason for wanting to remain on earth: to continue his ministry for Christ on behalf of others. But for his own benefit and joy he had but one desire: "to depart and be with Christ, for that is very much better" (Phil. 1:23-24).

In Christ's victory over death, death's sting is removed; it is declawed, defanged, disarmed, destroyed. "And death and Hades were thrown into the lake of fire, . . . and He shall wipe away every tear from their eyes; and there shall no longer be any death; there shall no longer be any mourning, or crying, or pain" (Rev. 20:14; 21:4).

THE GREAT EXHORTATION

Therefore, my beloved brethren, be steadfast, immovable, always abounding

in the work of the Lord, knowing that your toil is not in vain in the Lord.
(15:58)

If we really believe and if we are truly thankful that our resurrection is sure,
that we will be transformed from the perishable, dishonorable, weak, natural, mortal,
and earthy to the imperishable, glorious, powerful, spiritual, immortal, and
heavenly—we should **therefore** prove our assurance and our thankfulness by being
steadfast, immovable [negative] and **always abounding** [positive] **in the work of**
the Lord.

Hedraios (**steadfast**) literally refers to being seated, and therefore to being
settled and firmly situated. *Ametakinētos* (**immovable**) carries the same basic idea but
with more intensity. It denotes being totally immobile and motionless. Obviously Paul
is talking about our being moved *away from* God's will, not to our being moved *within*
it. Within His will we are to be **always abounding in the work of the Lord.** But we
should not move a hairbreadth away from His will, continually being careful not to be
"tossed here and there by waves, and carried about by every wind of doctrine, by the
trickery of men, by craftiness in deceitful scheming" (Eph. 4:14).

Gordon Clark gives a helpful paraphrase of this verse: "Therefore we should
mortify emotion, be steadfast, unchangeable, not erratic and scatterbrained, easily
discouraged, and should multiply our good works in the knowledge that the Lord will
make them profitable."

If our confident hope in the resurrection wavers, we are sure to abandon
ourselves to the ways and standards of the world. If there are no eternal ramifications
or consequences of what we do in this life, the motivation for selfless service and holy
living is gone.

On the other hand, when our hope in the resurrection is clear and certain we
will have great motivation to be **abounding in the work of the Lord.** *Perisseuō*
(**abounding**) carries the idea of exceeding the requirements, of overflowing or
overdoing. In Ephesians 1:7-8 the word is used of God's *lavishing* on us "the riches of
His grace." Because God has so abundantly overdone Himself for us who deserve
nothing from Him, we should determine to overdo ourselves (if that were possible) in
service to Him, to whom we owe everything.

What a word Paul gives to the countless Christians who work and pray and
give and suffer as little as they can! How can we be satisfied with the trivial,
insignificant, short-lived things of the world? How can we "take it easy" when so many
around us are dead spiritually and so many fellow believers are in need of edification,
encouragement, and help of every sort? When can a Christian say, "I've served my
time, I've done my part; let others do the work now"?

Reasonable rest is important and necessary. But if we err, Paul is saying, it
should be on the side of doing more work for the Lord, not less. Leisure and relaxation
are two great modern idols, to which many Christians seem quite willing to bow
down. In proper proportion recreation and diversions can help restore our energy and
increase our effectiveness. But they also can easily become ends in themselves,

demanding more and more of our attention, concern, time, and energy. More than one believer has relaxed and hobbied himself completely out of **the work of the Lord.**

Some of God's most faithful and fruitful saints have lived to old age and been active and productive in His service to the end. Many others, however, have seen their lives shortened for the very reason that they were **abounding,** overflowing and untiring, in service to Christ. Henry Martyn, the British missionary to India and Persia, determined "to burn out for God," which he did before he was thirty-five. David Brainerd, one of the earliest missionaries to American Indians, died before he was thirty. We know very little of Epaphroditus, except that he was a "brother and fellow worker and fellow soldier" of Paul's who "came close to death for the work of Christ, risking his life" (Phil. 2:25, 30). He became so lost in godly service that he literally became sick unto death because of it.

Until the Lord returns there are souls to reach and ministries of every sort to be accomplished. Every Christian should work uncompromisingly as the Lord has gifted and leads. Our money, time, energy, talents, gifts, bodies, minds, and spirits should be invested in nothing that does not in some way contribute to **the work of the Lord.** Our praise and thanksgiving must be given hands and feet. James tells us, "For just as the body without the spirit is dead, so also faith without works is dead" (James 2:26).

Our work for the Lord, if it is truly for Him and done in His power, cannot fail to accomplish what He wants accomplished. Every good work believers do in this life has eternal benefits that the Lord Himself guarantees. "Behold, I am coming quickly," Jesus says, "and My reward is with Me, to render to every man according to what he has done" (Rev. 22:12). We have God's own promise that our **toil** [labor to the point of exhaustion] **is not in vain in the Lord.**

Concerning the
Collection (16:1-4)

46

Now concerning the collection for the saints, as I directed the churches of Galatia, so do you also. On the first day of every week let each one of you put aside and save, as he may prosper, that no collections be made when I come. And when I arrive, whomever you may approve, I shall send them with letters to carry your gift to Jerusalem; and if it is fitting for me to go also, they will go with me. (16:1-4)

With chapter 16 Paul makes a radical change from the doctrinal to the practical. After discussing the resurrection in great detail (all of chapter 15), he ends the letter with several exhortations in regard to giving, doing the Lord's work, faithful living, and love within the Christian fellowship. He brings us rather abruptly from the future life back to the present life.

Yet the life to come is far from unrelated to living here and now. Whenever God gives us a glimpse of the end times or of heaven it is always for the purpose of helping us live more faithfully on earth. After Peter gives a sobering picture of the last days he says, "Therefore, beloved, since you look for these things, be diligent to be found by Him in peace, spotless and blameless" (2 Pet. 3:14; cf. v. 11).

What lies ahead in resurrection glory lays great responsibility on the present. If we truly believe that we are going to leave this world and that our bodies one day will be transformed and perfectly united with our spirits to live all eternity with God, our concern should be to lay up treasures in heaven while we are on earth (Matt. 6:20).

The first practical issue of Christian living Paul discusses in chapter 16 is that of giving. In verses 1-4 he presents the purpose, the principles, the protection, and the perspective of Christian giving.

The Purpose of Giving

Now concerning the collection for the saints, as I directed the churches of Galatia, so do you also. (16:1)

The fact that Paul speaks of **the collection** indicates that his readers already knew of it. The offering probably was mentioned in the letter the Corinthians had written to him (7:1) and to which 1 Corinthians was the reply. The **collection** was **for the saints,** in particular the saints in Jerusalem (v. 3). For the same collection Paul had, over the period of a year or more, solicited contributions from **the churches of Galatia** as well as from those in "Macedonia and Achaia . . . for the poor among the saints in Jerusalem" (Rom. 15:26; cf. 2 Cor. 8:1-5). The collection was made during Paul's third missionary journey, to be presented to the Jerusalem church when he returned there (Acts 24:17).

Extreme poverty was common in ancient times, as it still is in many parts of the world. In spite of its religious and strategic importance, in New Testament times Jerusalem was a poor city. Because it was the religious center for Jews, it was often overpopulated, especially during times of the special feasts and celebrations. Its resources were continually strained, and it was maintained to a large extent by gifts of wealthy nonresident Jews who lived throughout the Roman world. To make matters worse, some years earlier there had been a severe famine (Acts 11:28), from which the people were still suffering.

Because the Christians in Jerusalem had been persecuted for many years, their economic plight was made even more serious. Many of them were put out of their own homes, stripped of possessions, prevented from getting any but the most menial of jobs, and even imprisoned (Acts 8:1-3; 1 Thess. 2:14). Though most of the believers in Jerusalem were Jews, few, if any, of them benefited from the welfare distributions of the synagogues. Because many of the early Jewish converts to Christianity were pilgrims (cf. Acts 2:5), it is likely that some of them chose to stay in Jerusalem in order to be a part of the Christian fellowship there. Despite the fact that believers shared everything they had with those in need, even to the point of "selling their property and possessions" (Acts 2:44-45; 4:34), their resources obviously did not last indefinitely.

Besides meeting the economic needs of the Jerusalem believers, Paul also wanted the collection to express the spiritual oneness of the church. The believers in Jerusalem were predominantly Jews, and most of the believers in the churches contributing to the collection were Gentiles. "Salvation is from the Jews" (John 4:22), being first given to and through the Jewish people. The Gentiles, therefore, had a special indebtedness to the Jews. Writing about this same **collection,** Paul tells the Romans, "For if the Gentiles have shared in their [the Jews'] spiritual things, they are indebted to minister to them also in material things" (Rom. 15:27). Gentiles giving an offering to Jews would help strengthen the spiritual bond between the two groups (cf. Eph. 2:11-18). Giving and receiving in love always form a bond between the giver and receiver. You cannot share gifts without sharing fellowship. The association between Christians' economic sharing and personal sharing is so close in Paul's mind that three times he uses the term *koinōnia* (usually translated "fellowship") to represent offerings (Rom. 15:26; 2 Cor. 8:4; 9:13).

The primary purpose of giving, as taught in the New Testament, is for the support of the **saints,** the church. A Christian's first obligation is to support fellow believers, individually and collectively. The church's first financial responsibility is to invest in its own life and its own people (cf. 2 Cor. 8:1-5; 9:12-15; Phil. 4:14-16).

Obviously that is not the only economic obligation we have. The parable of the Good Samaritan makes it clear that we should minister personally and financially to *anyone* in need, regardless of religion, culture, or circumstances (Luke 10:25-37). Paul also teaches that we should "do good to all men" (Gal. 6:10). But in the same verse he goes on to say, "And especially to those who are of the household of the faith" (cf. 1 John 3:17). In 2 Corinthians 9:13 the apostle calls for a generous distribution "to all." Support of the poor and needy in the world in the name of the Lord is a high-priority Christian activity by scriptural standards.

It is not simply that one local church supports its own membership and work, as did the first Christians in Jerusalem, but that all churches support other believers and churches as there is need. As he had on other occasions (Acts 11:29-30; cf. Gal. 2:10), Paul promoted a collection in one group of churches to help meet the needs of another church or group of churches.

THE PRINCIPLES OF GIVING

On the first day of every week let each one of you put aside and save, as he may prosper, that no collections be made when I come. (16:2)

In this verse Paul states or implies a number of principles concerning Christian giving, including the period, the participants, the place, and the proportion. These principles form a good basis for Christian giving in any age.

THE PERIOD

The first principle is that the most appropriate period for giving is weekly, **on the first day of every week.** This not only convinces us that the church met on Sunday, but that its worship included regular giving of money. Giving should not be spasmodic, done only when we feel generous or "as the Spirit leads." The Spirit may, of course, lead us to give at special times and in special ways. But His primary leading in giving, as in everything else, is through Scripture, and Scripture here mentions giving **every week.** Paul is not prescribing a legalistic requirement of parceling out our money so that we can be sure to have something to put in the offering plate every Sunday, even if we are paid monthly. The point is that giving is part of worship and fellowship, and, even when we have nothing to give on a particular Sunday, we should be sensitive to the needs of the church and to our part in meeting them. Sunday giving appears as a mandated element of worship, part of the duty of a New Covenant priest offering up "spiritual sacrifices" to God (1 Pet. 2:5).

Our giving should not be based on periodic emotional appeals or feelings, or on bonus income, but on regular, willing, and grateful commitment of our possessions to the Lord, to His people, and to His work. That forces every believer each week to consider the stewardship and sacrifice of giving. Weekly giving raises sensitivity to money, so that giving is seen as an ongoing, regular spiritual responsibility.

THE PARTICIPANTS

Each one of you is all-inclusive. No Christian is excepted or excused. We are stewards of whatever the Lord has given us, no matter how little it may be in economic terms. As Jesus observed different people putting their offerings in the Temple treasury, He did not discourage the widow from putting in her "two small copper coins, which amount to a cent," nor did He chide Temple officials for accepting money from someone so destitute. His reaction was to use her generosity as a model of spiritual giving. "Truly I say to you, this poor widow put in more than all the contributors to the treasury; for they all put in out of their surplus, but she, out of her poverty, put in all she owned, all she had to live on" (Mark 12:41-44).

Our generosity to the Lord's work is best determined by what we give when we have little. A person who is well off financially can afford to give much without affecting his life-style or well-being. A person who is poor, however, must give up something for himself in order to give something to others. Jesus said that if we are not generous when we have little to give, we will not be generous when we have much. The dollar amount of our giving may increase, but our generosity will not. "He who is faithful in a very little thing is faithful also in much; and he who is unrighteous in a very little thing is unrighteous also in much" (Luke 16:10).

Speaking of the churches of Macedonia, Paul wrote, "In a great ordeal of affliction their abundance of joy and their deep poverty overflowed in the wealth of their liberality" (2 Cor. 8:2). The reason for their generosity was that "they first gave themselves to the Lord and to us by the will of God" (v. 5). They gave out of love for God and for His servants. Generosity is impossible apart from our love of God and of His people. But *with* such love, generosity not only is possible but inevitable.

THE PLACE

Just as giving is primarily *for* the church, it is also primarily *to* and *through* the church. That Paul shows giving to be a part of worship seems clear from **the first day**

of every week. In the New Testament church the regular day for worship was Sunday, the first day of the week. Much of the early preaching and witnessing was to Jews and by Jews, and therefore was done on Saturday, the Sabbath (Acts 13:14; 17:2). But the first postresurrection service was held on Easter evening, when the risen Lord appeared to His frightened and disheartened disciples. "When therefore it was evening, on that day, the first day of the week, and when the doors were shut where the disciples were, for fear of the Jews, Jesus came and stood in their midst, and said to them, 'Peace be with you.' . . . The disciples therefore rejoiced when they saw the Lord" (John 20:19-20). Jesus' next appearance was "after eight days" (and therefore on another Sunday), when Thomas was with them (v. 26). Consequently, though many Jewish believers continued to worship in the synagogue and in the Temple on the Sabbath, the normal time for Christians to worship together as Christians came to be Sunday (Acts 20:7). The Sabbath was set aside in favor of resurrection day. By the time John wrote the book of Revelation (in the last decade of the first century), **the first day of the week** was referred to as "the Lord's day" (Rev. 1:10).

In the first account of Christian giving, immediately after Pentecost, when the church was new and unorganized, converts simply shared directly with each other as needs arose (Acts 2:44-45). Shortly after that time, however, believers began bringing gifts to the apostles for them to distribute (4:35, 37; 5:2). The basic pattern, therefore, was to bring offerings to the church, to be disbursed as the leaders saw fit.

A more literal translation of **each one of you put aside and save** would be "each one of you by himself lay up, or store up." The noun form of *thēsaurizō* (from which we get *thesaurus,* a collection, or treasury, of words), rendered here as **put aside and save,** represents a storehouse, treasury, chest, or the like where valuables are stored. It also sometimes was used metaphorically of the treasure itself (Matt. 2:11; 19:21; Mark 10:21; Luke 6:45). In both the pagan and Jewish cultures of New Testament times, treasuries were associated with religious temples. The treasuries in many Greek temples not only were repositories of gifts to the temple itself but served as banks in which citizens kept their personal money and other valuables for safekeeping. Paul's use of a verb form of this term for treasury suggests that the putting aside was to be in the church, in some sort of repository designated for the offerings. It was to be put there by **each one,** "by himself," on his own initiative. The church had a treasury, a place for safekeeping and dispensing the offerings.

If Paul were here referring to Christians' storing their offerings privately at home, what he says at the end of the verse, **that no collections be made when I come,** would not make sense. If the gifts were stored at home, the first thing to be done when Paul arrived would have been to have a collection in order to bring the funds together. Along with teaching regular giving, Paul's purpose in giving the instruction was to have the offering ready to be taken to Jerusalem with as little delay as possible.

The first day of the week is the day of worship, and how believers handle their money is inextricably related to the depth of their worship. Whether we put money in the offering plate every Sunday or not, weekly worship should remind us of our continual stewardship of the possessions the Lord has entrusted to us. If we do not give properly we cannot worship properly. Jesus said, "He who is faithful in a very little thing is faithful also in much; and he who is unrighteous in a very little thing is unrighteous also in much. If therefore you have not been faithful in the use of unrighteous mammon, who will entrust the true riches to you?" (Luke 16:10-11).

Many men who were superb preachers, good administrators, and faithful pastors, are out of the ministry now because they were personally irresponsible with money. Because they were untrustworthy with material things, the Lord could no longer trust them with the care of His people, who are infinitely more valuable.

Nothing in Scripture indicates that all of our giving to the Lord's work has to be given first to the church leaders. Part of that which we set aside may be accumulated at home or in a special account to meet the emergency or private needs of others whom we have opportunity to help in the Lord's name. In that way we are prepared to help immediately and directly when there is no time to go through the church or when a person does not want his need known by any others. But the primary place of giving is the church, to support God's people, God's leaders, and God's ministry. Placing our gifts into the hands of godly men for wise use is best.

THE PROPORTION

Paul's exhortation here is completely discretionary, for a Christian to give **as he may prosper.** There is much difference of opinion among Christians as to how much of our income should be given to the Lord's work. A common traditional answer has been 10 percent, based on misunderstanding the nature and purpose of the Old Testament tithe.

The practice of giving a tithe was common in many ancient cultures. Abraham gave a tithe of his possessions to Melchizedek, who was "a priest of God Most High" (Gen. 14:18-20). Jacob promised to give a tenth of all he had if God would protect and prosper him (Gen. 28:20-22). But in neither case did God require such a percentage, or any amount at all. Both Abraham's and Jacob's offerings were entirely voluntary, and apparently singular. There is no indication from Scripture that any of God's people regularly gave 10 percent before the time of Moses. The only giving amount specifically prescribed by God in the book of Genesis pertained to the famine in Egypt. Through Joseph's interpretation of Pharaoh's dream, God commanded that a fifth, that is, 20 percent, of all grain produced in the seven abundant years be set aside for surviving during the seven lean years (Gen. 41:34-35). That amount, however, though prescribed by God, was not a religious offering but was a form of governmental welfare tax, to be used for the people's own benefit during the coming famine.

In the Mosaic law 10 percent is prescribed for the first time by God. "Thus all the tithe of the land, of the seed of the land or of the fruit of the tree, is the Lord's; it is holy to the Lord" (Lev. 27:30). That tithe was "to the sons of Levi, . . . for an inheritance, in return for their service which they perform, the service of the tent of meeting" (Num. 18:21). From those tithes of the people, the Levites were in turn to give a tithe, "a tithe of the tithe" (v. 26). The tithes, burnt offerings, sacrifices, contributions, votive and freewill offerings, and the first-born of animals mentioned in Deuteronomy 14 were a second 10 percent, to be used to support the national feasts and holidays. Each third year another 10 percent was to be given for use in supporting "the Levite, . . . the alien, the orphan and the widow" (Deut. 14:28-29). As you study those and related texts carefully it becomes evident that the amount paid annually to the theocracy of Israel was approximately 23 percent, and that it essentially was a tax, used for the operation of Israel's government. It never involved freewill, spontaneous giving to the Lord. The condemnation of Malachi 3:8-10 is for failure to pay the required taxes to support the priests who ran the nation.

The basic principle for voluntary giving in the Old Testament is reflected in Proverbs: "Honor the Lord from your wealth, and from the first of all your produce; so your barns will be filled with plenty, and your vats will overflow with new wine" (3:9-10). The idea was to give to the Lord generously and to give to the Lord first. Again we are told, "There is one who scatters, yet increases all the more, and there is one who withholds what is justly due, but it results only in want" (Prov. 11:24). In other words, if you want to increase your money, share it generously; if you want to lose your money, hoard it.

To raise money to build the Tabernacle, the Lord told Moses, "Tell the sons of Israel to raise a contribution for Me; from every man whose heart moves him you shall raise My contribution" (Ex. 25:1-2; cf. 35:5, 21). The standard was heart-directed generosity, based on thankfulness to the Lord for what He had done and given. Based on that principle the gifts for the building of the Tabernacle were so great that Moses had to tell the people to stop giving (36:6)! Required giving was taxation; freewill giving was to be from the heart, with the amount left up to the worshiper. David had the key idea when he said that he would not give God that which cost him nothing (2 Sam. 24:24).

A Christian's giving corresponds to that in ancient Israel. We are required to give taxes to support the government under which we live (Rom. 13:6), just as the Israelites were to give tithes to support the divinely ordained system under which they lived (Matt. 17:24-27; 22:15-21). And we are to give to the Lord whatever we purpose in our hearts, "not grudgingly or under compulsion; for God loves a cheerful giver" (2 Cor. 9:7), just as the Israelites gave out of their hearts to the Lord. The Lord has *always* loved a cheerful and sacrificial giver.

No amount or percentage is ever required in the New Testament. Rather, each believer is to give from his heart. "Give," Jesus said, "and it will be given to you; good measure, pressed down, shaken together, running over, they will pour into your lap. For by your standard of measure it will be measured to you in return" (Luke 6:38). Paul expressed the same principle as, "He who sows sparingly shall also reap sparingly; and he who sows bountifully shall also reap bountifully" (2 Cor. 9:6). The benefits of our willing, cheerful giving to the Lord will produce both spiritual and material blessing. "And God is able to make all grace abound to you, that always having all sufficiency in everything, you may have an abundance for every good deed" (v. 8).

THE PROTECTION IN GIVING

And when I arrive, whomever you may approve, I shall send them with letters to carry your gift to Jerusalem. (16:3)

Those who give to the Lord's work have a right to expect that their gifts are used legitimately and wisely. Paul instructed the Corinthian church to appoint several respected men, **whomever you may approve,** who would be sent by Paul with **letters** of approval and explanation to the saints in **Jerusalem.**

It is incumbent on every church to entrust its property and funds into the hands of godly and responsible men. The gifts of the early Christians were first entrusted to the apostles (Acts 4:35). As their responsibilities grew, however, the apostles needed to be relieved of the job of disbursing funds for such things as feeding the poor widows. They therefore advised "the congregation of the disciples" to "select from among you, brethren, seven men of good reputation, full of the Spirit and of wisdom, whom we may put in charge of this task" (Acts 6:2-3). The qualifications were not financial or commercial but moral and spiritual. God's funds should only be put in the hands of a church's most godly men, who will prayerfully and in the energy of the Holy Spirit supervise its use, as priests who present the offerings of the people of God.

THE PERSPECTIVE OF GIVING

And if it is fitting for me to go also, they will go with me. (16:4)

I believe Paul's point here is that he would accompany the gift to Jerusalem only if it turned out to be an offering that would indicate true generosity and that he would not be embarrassed to be associated with. He was encouraging the Corinthians to give freely from their hearts in an outpouring of love and concern.

God made all of His creation to give. He made the sun, the moon, the stars, the clouds, the earth, the plants to give. And He also designed His supreme creation, man, to give. But fallen man is the most reluctant giver in all of God's creation.

One of the surest signs of a recreated person, a saved and redeemed person, is willingness to give. The Athenian statesman Aristides wrote the following of Christians living in the second century:

> They walk in humility and kindness, and falsehood is not found among them and they love one another. They despise not the widow and they grieve not the orphan. He that hath, distributeth liberally to him that hath not. If they see a stranger, they bring him under their roof and they rejoice over him as if he were their brother. For they call themselves brethren, not after the flesh but after the Spirit and in God. But when one of their poor passes away from the world and any of them see him, then he provides for his burial according to his ability. And if they hear that any of their number is in prison or oppressed for the name of their Messiah, all of them provide for his needs.

And if it is possible that he may be delivered, they deliver him. And if there is among them a man that is poor and needy and they have not an abundance of necessity, they will fast two or three days that they may supply the needy with his necessary food.

"But whoever has the world's goods, and beholds his brother in need and closes his heart against him, how does the love of God abide in him?" (1 John 3:17).

Doing the Lord's Work in the Lord's Way (16:5-12)

But I shall come to you after I go through Macedonia, for I am going through Macedonia; and perhaps I shall stay with you, or even spend the winter, that you may send me on my way wherever I may go. For I do not wish to see you now just in passing; for I hope to remain with you for some time, if the Lord permits. But I shall remain in Ephesus until Pentecost; for a wide door for effective service has opened to me, and there are many adversaries.

Now if Timothy comes, see that he is with you without cause to be afraid; for he is doing the Lord's work, as I also am. Let no one therefore despise him. But send him on his way in peace, so that he may come to me; for I expect him with the brethren. But concerning Apollos our brother, I encouraged him greatly to come to you with the brethren; and it was not at all his desire to come now, but he will come when he has opportunity. (16:5-12)

This passage near the close of the letter does not explicitly teach or exhort, except for the advice about receiving Timothy (v. 11). It is more in the form of explanation. Yet we can learn a great deal from these eight verses. The things Paul speaks about here have to do with the work of the Lord, in which all Christians should be abounding (15:58) as were Paul and Timothy (16:10).

The work of the Lord consists basically of two things: evangelizing and edifying, the two outstanding marks of Jesus' own ministry. "The Son of Man has come to seek and to save that which was lost" (Luke 19:10). Throughout the three years of His ministry Jesus also carefully taught His disciples. Until just before His ascension He continued teaching them "the things concerning the kingdom of God" (Acts 1:3). He preached the gospel to those who did not know Him and He taught those who did. Throughout His ministry He alternated between preaching to the lost and teaching the saved. Those two tasks are the heart of the Great Commission: "Go therefore and make disciples of all the nations, baptizing them in the name of the Father and the Son and the Holy Spirit [evangelism], teaching them to observe all that I commanded you [edification]" (Matt. 28:19-20).

As Paul made clear at the end of the previous chapter, when we truly do the work of the Lord our "toil is not in vain" (1 Cor. 15:58). It will not be empty, useless, or unproductive. But the "toil" (*kopos*) Paul is speaking of is not merely keeping busy; it is arduous work. G. Campbell Morgan comments: "Paul has in mind the kind of toil that has in it the red blood of sacrifice, the kind of toil that wearies and weakens along the way."

There can easily be a lot of activity without much work of the Lord genuinely being done. When the work we do is of little importance, is done in the flesh, or is done halfheartedly, it will never be fruitful for the Lord. That sort of work, though in the Lord's name, *is* "in vain."

A building must be constructed according to the architect's plans and the required building codes. Before it can be used it must pass inspection to see that the codes were followed. The church's work for the Lord is done in the same way. To truly be His work, what we do must be done according to His plan and code, revealed in Scripture, and must continually be subject to the divine supervision and inspection of the Holy Spirit. We must "be diligent to present [ourselves] approved to God as [workmen] who [do] not need to be ashamed" (2 Tim. 2:15). Doing the Lord's work in the Lord's way is building "with gold, silver, precious stones" (1 Cor. 3:12). It is that sort of dedicated, spiritual service to the Lord of which Paul speaks in this passage, allowing us to see a number of implied principles that lay behind properly doing the Lord's work.

VISION

But I shall come to you after I go through Macedonia, for I am going through Macedonia. (16:5)

The Lord's worker must have a vision for the future. The Christian who is motivated and consumed by God's love will see needs that are not yet filled and opportunities that are not yet met. He cannot help planning ahead, looking for more ways to serve and for more doors to open.

At the end of a three-year stay in Ephesus, Paul wrote this epistle and probably gave it to Timothy to deliver (16:10). The apostle originally had planned to follow

Timothy a short while later (4:19), visiting Corinth both on the way to and from Macedonia (2 Cor. 1:15-16). But he had to change his plans and decided to visit Corinth later, **after I go through Macedonia.** He had to change his plan, but he *had* a plan to change. Even while he was busy in Ephesus, he was planning the next steps in his ministry—what he would do in Macedonia, Corinth, and then Jerusalem.

The Lord's faithful worker plans and strategizes, he looks ahead with a sense· of vision and expectancy. One writer has suggested that Paul was haunted by distant regions, that the apostle never saw a ship at anchor but he wished to board it to carry the good news to the people across the water, and that he never saw a mountain range but he wanted to cross it to build up the saints. As far as his own welfare and satisfaction were concerned the apostle had "learned to be content in whatever circumstances" he found himself (Phil. 4:11). But he was not content with resting on what he had already accomplished. He always saw more work waiting to be done, more souls waiting to be saved, more believers waiting to be edified and encouraged.

Several years after he wrote 1 Corinthians, Paul wrote the letter to the church at Rome. Near the end of the letter he mentioned twice that, after he visited Rome, he planned to go to Spain (Rom. 15:24, 28). Spain was then a flourishing and influential province of the Roman empire, having produced three emperors and the famous philosopher-statesman Seneca. But as far as we know the gospel had not yet reached Spain, and Paul was anxious to preach there. He wrote the letter to Rome while he was in Corinth completing the collection mentioned in 1 Corinthians 16:1-4. Again we see that, while faithfully working where he was, he nevertheless was planning and preparing for what he would do next. Like a general poring over a map to determine where the next battle should be fought, Paul constantly surveyed the lands about him to see where to begin his next effort for the Lord.

When Nehemiah approached King Artaxerxes for permission to go to Jerusalem, he had a specific purpose and plan in mind. Nehemiah already had prayed earnestly and penitently that God would allow him to do this work and that He would open the king's heart to give permission. He then explained to the king the city's great need for its walls and its gates to be rebuilt. When Nehemiah's initial request was granted, he made additional pleas in order to secure the timber and other materials he knew he would need (Neh. 1:1–2:8). Because of vision and careful planning his great success as the rebuilder of Jerusalem began long before he left Persia.

While he was working as a cobbler in England, William Carey was moved by the great spiritual needs of other parts of the world. He placed a world map in front of his workbench, and, as he worked, he thought, prayed, and wept about what needed to be done and how the Lord could use him to meet those needs. When he finally arrived in India, his first mission assignment, he was ready to begin work. He not only was used directly to make outstanding contributions through teaching, preaching, translation, and printing of Christian literature, but helped prepare the way for every missionary who has served there since. Because he had prayed, planned, and prepared, he was ready when the opportunity came.

We may only guess at the number of works the Lord has for His people to do but for whom there are few with a vision and readiness. In fact, our true willingness to work for the Lord can be measured by what we are doing at the present to analyze needs and to prepare—even if we do not know exactly what or where the work might be.

And perhaps I shall stay with you, or even spend the winter, that you may send me on my way wherever I may go. (16:6)

While we ought to have vision, and plan ahead about what we will be doing and how, we also must be flexible. Our plans should always be subject to the Lord's revision. The future does not always come together as we think it will. Our original understanding of God's will for us may not have been entirely right or complete, or His plans for us may change. In any case, we should always qualify our intentions as James advises: "If the Lord wills, we shall live and also do this or that" (James 4:15).

Our spiritual gifts and talents, as well as our desires as prompted by the Holy Spirit, may give us clues as to the type of work the Lord has for us to do, but He may want us to use our gifts in ways that we have not imagined. If we are rigidly convinced in advance about what God wants us to do, we can become insensitive to His leading when the call to a specific ministry comes. Our vision, no matter how sincere and how carefully thought out, is not infallible. Inflexibility can be a great barrier both to knowing and doing the Lord's work. Flexibility is not a sign of weakness but of humility.

Though Paul had a good purpose in mind and a strong personal desire to visit Corinth after "going through Macedonia" (v. 5), he went on to say that **perhaps** he would **stay with** the believers there, **or even spend the winter.** Both **perhaps** and **even,** along with **wherever** and "if the Lord permits" (v. 7), express Paul's concern that his own plans and thinking not become presumptuous and inflexible, usurping the Lord's prerogative to change them as He saw fit (cf. Prov. 16:9).

The apostle was not fickle or indecisive, as the Corinthians later accused him of being, but realistic and humble. He was realistic because he knew that no one can be "captain of his own fate and master of his own destiny." There are far too many things in life that are completely out of our control. He was humble because he knew that God is sovereign and has the absolute power and right to change any person's plans whenever and however He chooses. "Therefore, I was not vacillating when I intended to do this, was I?" he later explained. "Or that which I purpose, do I purpose according to the flesh, that with me there should be yes, yes and no, no at the same time?" (2 Cor. 1:17). We are not always able to go where we want to go or do what we want to do, no matter how sincere, selfless, and spiritual our motives may be. Apostles were no exception.

Modifying the trip to Corinth was not the first time God had adjusted Paul's plans. On his second missionary journey Paul planned to "visit the brethren in every city in which we proclaimed the word of the Lord, and see how they are" (Acts 15:36).

They were able to visit most of the places as planned, but the Holy Spirit specifically forbade them "to speak the word in Asia" or "to go into Bithynia" (16:6-7). It was the Lord's will for Paul and Silas, with their new companion, Timothy, to revisit *some* of the churches on the original schedule, but before all of them could be visited, God sent the group to a completely new field, Macedonia (vv. 9-10), where they became the first to preach the gospel in Europe.

All of his life, David Livingstone wanted to be a missionary to China. Even in old age he longed to have the opportunity to go there and minister. But God sent him instead to Africa, where he worked and died opening up that great continent to mission work, much as Carey had done in India. He never went to the place where he personally wanted to go, but he served willingly, unreservedly, and fruitfully where God put him. He had a great vision for China, but because he wanted, above all else, to do the Lord's will, he was flexible. He was willing clay in the Potter's hands (Rom. 9:21), to be molded and remolded in whatever ways God pleased.

Wherever Paul was to **go**, he wanted the support of the Corinthians. **That you may send me on my way** implies their equipping and encouraging him on the mission, whatever God had in mind.

THOROUGHNESS IN PRESENT SERVICE

For I do not wish to see you now just in passing; for I hope to remain with you for some time, if the Lord permits. But I shall remain in Ephesus until Pentecost. (16:7-8)

Doing the Lord's work in the Lord's way also demands thoroughness in work we presently are doing. If Paul were to accomplish anything worthwhile during his next stay in Corinth, he knew he would have to visit them more than **just in passing**. He therefore hoped to **remain** with them **for some time, if the Lord permits**. He had a strong commitment to thoroughness. Superficiality and temporariness had no part in his ministry. He wanted everything he did to be sound and permanent, worthwhile and lasting.

The Great Commission cannot be fulfilled with anything less than thoroughness. Evangelism, making "disciples of all the nations," is only the beginning. To go on and teach new converts "to observe all that [Jesus] commanded" (Matt. 28:19-20) is a long and demanding process. It cannot be done quickly, carelessly, or superficially.

Paul had spent a year and a half establishing and pastoring the church at Corinth. He knew that the letter he now was writing would only begin to help solve the serious problems the Corinthians were having. If possible, he wanted at least to "spend the winter" (v. 6) with them before he went on to Jerusalem.

Paul wanted to teach every Christian everything he could at every opportunity he had. "And we proclaim Him, admonishing every man and teaching every man with all wisdom, that we may present every man complete in Christ. And for this purpose also I labor, striving according to His power, which mightily works within me" (Col. 1:28-29). To the Thessalonians he wrote, "We night and day keep praying most earnestly that we may see your face, and may complete what is lacking in your faith" (1 Thess. 3:10). To the Ephesian elders who met him at Miletus he was able to say, "I did not shrink from declaring to you the whole purpose of God" (Acts 20:27).

Thoroughness does not depend solely on the length of time we spend at a particular place doing a particular ministry. The earthly ministry of the Lord Himself lasted only three years, but at the end of that brief time Jesus could say, "I glorified Thee on the earth, having accomplished the work which Thou hast given Me to do" (John 17:4). Paul spent about three years at Ephesus, less than a total of two years in Corinth, and only weeks in Thessalonica. But the time he spent in each place was characterized by thoroughness, by using to the fullest advantage the time he had. He always followed his own advice. What he said to the Ephesians, he no doubt had said many times to himself: "Therefore be careful how you walk, not as unwise men, but as wise, making the most of your time" (Eph. 5:16).

Paul spoke of some believers in the Thessalonian church as "doing no work at all, but acting like busybodies" (2 Thess. 3:11). The Greek has a play on words, which could be translated, "not busy workers but busybodies." These particular busybodies were, probably among other things, spreading fantastic speculations about Christ's return (cf. 2:1-5). Not only were they misleading and confusing other church members, but they were financially sponging off them as well. They had given up productive work of every sort, and certainly were not doing the work of the Lord, despite the theological air of their activities.

Even with work that we know is the Lord's, we should never take on a ministry that we are not willing to thoroughly prepare for and work at. We should not attempt to give a message or teach a lesson that is not carefully based in Scripture and thoroughly prayed about. We should not seek to disciple a person to whom we are not willing to give the necessary time. Good purposes, intentions, and plans are worthless if they are not faithfully executed.

Because he still had necessary work to do there, Paul intended to **remain in Ephesus until Pentecost.** He could not go on to something else until he had done all the Lord wanted him to do where he was.

Almost every day I receive letters or phone calls from churches or Christian organizations requesting names of prospective pastors or other workers. Invariably they specify that they want someone with a proven record, someone who has been successful in the work he has been doing. Only the person who is "faithful in a very little thing is faithful also in much" (Luke 16:10). To that person the Lord says, "Well done, good and faithful slave; you were faithful with a few things, I will put you in charge of many things" (Matt. 25:23). Only the Christian who is doing his present work for the Lord thoroughly and faithfully can expect his ministry to grow and be extended, even into the kingdom of our Lord. The scope of eternal service to God in heaven will be determined by the strength and dedication of service rendered here and now, as the parable of the talents teaches (Matt. 25:14-30).

We should not expect the Lord to open doors of greater ministry in time or eternity if we have not entered doors He has already opened for us. Because he had faithfully entered the door God opened for preaching to the Gentiles (Acts 14:27) and the door He had opened to Troas (2 Cor. 2:12) and other places, Paul had a right to ask his Colossian brothers to pray that God would open still more doors, so that he could continue to "speak forth the mystery of Christ" (Col. 4:3). The opening and closing of doors for ministry is entirely God's doing (Rev. 3:7). Our job is to enter the doors, and only the doors, He opens to us.

A young seminary student who was a dear friend to me discovered that, because of an inoperable brain tumor, he had from six months to perhaps two years to live. While a student at UCLA he had started a number of Bible studies, which were remarkably successful. Students he discipled began leading other Bible studies and discipling other students. Some of those he led to the Lord went on to seminary, as he did. After learning of his illness he continued to minister, working for the Lord in whatever ways he could. He had many visions and plans for a future in missions, and, though terminally ill, he never ceased to be faithful and thorough in the work he had at hand. He died before graduating from seminary and was given his degree post-humously. Today, his young widow has taken up her husband's desire for reaching a lost world and has gone to the mission field alone.

Stephen and Philip started out as deacons, doing the practical, mundane work of feeding the widows in the Jerusalem church in order to relieve the apostles for "prayer, and to the ministry of the word" (Acts 6:2-5). Starting as waiters, they both became outstanding evangelists. Not only did Stephen's and Philip's doing that "lesser" work allow the apostles to increase their ministry, but it also prepared those two deacons themselves for preaching ministries of their own (see Acts 6:8–8:40). Stephen's powerful, Spirit-filled preaching and his martyr's death are almost certain to have been used of the Lord to soften the heart and lead to the conversion of Paul himself (see 8:1). Philip evangelized much of Samaria and, through witnessing to the Ethiopian eunuch, indirectly was responsible for taking the gospel into Africa.

Becoming a faithful servant of the Lord does not begin with some great opportunity, but with doing the best possible work for Him in the routine things. If we do not give God our best where we are, there is no assurance we will give Him our best anywhere else. The only opportunity we can be sure of having is the one we have now.

ACCEPTANCE OF OPPOSITION AS A CHALLENGE

For a wide door for effective service has opened to me, and there are many adversaries. (16:9)

A fourth necessary principle for doing the Lord's work in the Lord's way is accepting opposition as a challenge rather than as a hindrance. In the present age there is no such thing as an authentic ministry without problems and opposition of some sort. Satan will see to it. A work that has little opposition from the antagonistic system of Satan is one that is doing little work for the Lord. G. Campbell Morgan said, "If you have no opposition in the place you serve, you're serving in the wrong place."

Paul was not intimidated by opposition. He seemed even to flourish on it, perhaps because he realized that the devil's greatest opposition is to the Lord's greatest work. The fact that there were **many adversaries** of the gospel in Ephesus (cf. Eph. 6:12) simply meant that **a wide door for effective service had opened.**

He was not indifferent to the harm that Satan could do to God's people, and consequently was determined to "remain in Ephesus until Pentecost" (v. 8) in order to help fight the **adversaries.** Ephesus had a great system of organized idolatry, centered in the famous temple of Diana, or Artemis. Ritual prostitution and sexual perversion not only were tolerated but were promoted in the name of religion. In addition, there were certain Jewish exorcists who went around claiming to cast out evil spirits in Jesus' name (Acts 19:13-14). The city was full of occult practitioners of every sort (vv. 17-19). Paganism, idolatry, occultism, demonism, superstition, sexual vice, racism, religious animosity—of pagans against Christians, Jews against Christians, and of pagans and Jews against each other—were common and considered normal. Probably no New Testament church had more direct opposition than the one at Ephesus.

To Paul great opposition presented great opportunity. When he arrived in Ephesus, he began his work by straightening out the theology of some new believers (Acts 19:1-7). Then he proceeded to preach in the synagogue for three months and in the school of Tyrannus for two years (vv. 8-10). He performed miracles, cast out evil spirits, and rebuked false exorcists (vv. 11-19).

Of his experience in Ephesus Paul later wrote, "We do not want you to be unaware, brethren, of our affliction which came to us in Asia [the Roman province in which Ephesus was located], that we were burdened excessively, beyond our strength, so that we despaired even of life; indeed, we had the sentence of death within ourselves in order that we should not trust in ourselves, but in God who raises the dead; who delivered us from so great a peril of death, and will deliver us, He on whom we have set our hope" (2 Cor. 1:8-10).

It was not that Paul considered opposition as of no consequence or concern. He was far from naive. He did not underestimate or discount the strength or potential danger of his **adversaries.** Almost daily he personally and directly felt pain and torment from opposition. "We are afflicted in every way, but not crushed; perplexed, but not despairing; persecuted, but not forsaken; struck down, but not destroyed; always carrying about in the body the dying of Jesus, that the life of Jesus also may be manifested in our body. For we who live are constantly being delivered over to death for Jesus' sake, that the life of Jesus also may be manifested in our mortal flesh" (2 Cor. 4:8-11).

In spite of fierce opposition—in fact, partly because of it and through it— "the word of the Lord was growing mightily and prevailing" in Ephesus (Acts 19:20). It was after that experience that Paul wrote the letter of 1 Corinthians and determined to visit Corinth (which was in Achaia) on his way to Jerusalem (v. 21).

He was not quite through in Ephesus, however. Apparently some new opportunities or problems developed, which he describes as **a wide door for effective service.** He was still needed for a while, and would not leave until he was sure that it was the Lord's will for him to minister somewhere else. He had made a great investment there and wanted to secure it.

When we are looking for a place to serve the Lord, we should look for a place with problems, for a church that is discouraged, for a group in our own congregation that needs to have a better understanding of God's Word, for people who have never heard God's Word or have heard it only in a perverted or unbalanced form. That is where the Lord can truly use us.

While John Paton was a university student in Scotland, God called him to missionary work in the New Hebrides. After graduation he and his bride sailed to the southwest Pacific and began work among the savage cannibals on the island of Tanna. His wife and infant son died a few months later, and Paton slept on their graves for several nights to prevent the cannibals from digging up the bodies and eating them. After almost four years of faithful work he left without seeing a single convert. Many years later his son by another marriage resumed work on Tanna and eventually saw the entire island come to Christ. When the elder Paton revisited the island, the chief of the former cannibals asked the missionary who the great army was that had surrounded his hut every night when he first came among them. God's angels had protected him. Because of his faithful work and that of his son, when he left the New Hebrides for the last time, after ministering on another island as well, it is reported that he said with tearful eyes, "I don't know of one native on these islands who has not made a profession of faith in Jesus Christ."

TEAM SPIRIT

Now if Timothy comes, see that he is with you without cause to be afraid; for he is doing the Lord's work, as I also am. Let no one therefore despise him. But send him on his way in peace, so that he may come to me; for I expect him with the brethren. (16:10-11)

Paul was a team worker. Though he was an apostle and was privileged to receive great revelations from the Lord, he always worked closely with other Christians in whatever he did. He was never an ecclesiastical superstar, lording it over those "below" him.

Paul had sent **Timothy** and Erastus to Macedonia (Acts 19:22), and Timothy was to go on down to Corinth, perhaps carrying this epistle, to remind the Corinthians of Paul's "ways which are in Christ" (1 Cor. 4:17). The apostle was concerned that Timothy might be ignored or mistreated. The Corinthians were proud, self-sufficient, and strong-willed. If they had so strongly resisted Paul's authority, they likely would pay much less attention to Timothy.

Paul admonished the Corinthians not to give **Timothy** any **cause to be afraid.** Timothy was God's servant and a trusted and respected fellow worker of Paul's. **He is doing the Lord's work, as I also am.** The Corinthians were to treat him with respect and were not to intimidate or frustrate his work among them. Paul was an apostle and was Timothy's father in the faith, yet he considered his young friend to be the Lord's faithful worker, **as I also am.** They were equal in the faith, and because Timothy was doing **the Lord's work,** he was worthy of honor and respect, just as was Paul. No one was to **despise him,** that is, to think little of him. On the contrary, he was to be sent back to Paul **in peace . . . with the** [appointed] **brethren,** not alone. He wanted all servants of the Lord treated as he was.

Even when Paul was imprisoned and a group of leaders in the Philippian church was maligning the apostle and striving for self-glory, he refused to be resentful or jealous. His great concern was "that in every way, whether in pretense or in truth, Christ is proclaimed; and in this I rejoice, yes, and I will rejoice" (Phil. 1:15-18).

In the reports of the missionary journeys in the book of Acts, we read of Paul and Barnabas, Paul and Silas, Paul and Luke, Paul and Aristarchus, Paul and Mark, Paul and Timothy. Except when prevented by being in prison, Paul always had a joint ministry. In the book of Romans, Paul's deepest and most theological letter, he devotes the last chapter to commending a long list of co-workers, twenty-four individuals and two entire households, in the work of the Lord. Both as a believer and as a leader Paul closely identified himself with other Christians. He was not ashamed to call the worldly and carnal Corinthian believers His brethren (1 Cor. 1:10; 2:1; 3:1; etc.) or to call the young and timid Timothy a minister of **the Lord's work, as I also am.** He ranked Timothy with himself because of the glory of the work.

Paul not only acknowledged his dependence on the Lord but also his dependence on other Christians. In no way did he think of himself as self-sufficient. Epaphroditus was to Paul "my brother and fellow worker and fellow soldier, who is also your messenger and minister to my need" (Phil. 2:25). John Mark, in whom Paul once was greatly disappointed (Acts 15:37-39), later became a beloved friend whom Paul considered especially "useful to me for service" (2 Tim. 4:11). Even the runaway slave Onesimus, whom Paul had won to Christ while in prison, became "useful both to you [Philemon, the slave's owner] and to me [Paul]." He was so dear that Paul told Philemon that in sending Onesimus he was "sending my very heart, whom I wished to keep with me, that in your behalf he might minister to me in my imprisonment for the gospel" (Philem. 12-13).

God calls some people to be leaders and others to serve leaders. Sometimes those who serve leaders do that throughout their lives. Often, however, they are being prepared by God to be leaders themselves. But whatever the roles of the workers, when the Lord's work is done in the Lord's way, it will always be done with a spirit of unity, teamwork, and mutual dependence.

SENSITIVITY TO THE SPIRIT'S LEADING OF OTHERS

But concerning Apollos our brother, I encouraged him greatly to come to you with the brethren; and it was not at all his desire to come now, but he will come when he has opportunity. (16:12)

The last principle we see in this passage for doing the Lord's work in the Lord's way is that of being sensitive to the Holy Spirit's leading of other believers.

Paul had a strong feeling that **Apollos** (see Acts 18:24-28) should accompany the other **brethren**, Timothy and Erastus, to Corinth. In fact Paul **encouraged him greatly**. In his own mind the apostle was convinced that that was the right thing for Apollos to do. Apollos had leadership qualities that Timothy lacked, and seemed to be just the right person to complete the team. Paul, along with some of the Corinthians, thought that Apollos was just what Corinth needed. Apollos, however, was convinced that the Lord wanted him to stay in Ephesus for a while longer, just as Paul was convinced that he (Paul) should stay (v. 8). So when Apollos objected (**it was not at all his desire to come now**) Paul respected his convictions. He knew that even an apostle was not a mediator between God and other Christians. God may use many different persons to show us His will, but His basic leading is always direct.

When the right time would come, **when he has opportunity**, Apollos would go to Corinth if the Lord so led. In the meanwhile, he would continue to serve where the Lord wanted him now. He doubtlessly had great trust in Paul's wisdom and judgment, but his first trust was in the Lord Himself and in the Lord's direct guidance. With that trust Paul would be the last to interfere.

It is absolutely essential that God's workers work as a team. That is what unity is all about. If we are one in Christ, we are one in each other. And if all the true work of the church is the Lord's work, then we have to work together in Him because we are one in Him. It goes without saying that the Captain and Play-Caller of the team is the Holy Spirit. This text gives much insight into the Spirit's subjective leading.

Principles for Powerful Living

48

(16:13-14)

Be on the alert, stand firm in the faith, act like men, be strong. Let all that you do be done in love. (16:13-14)

The greater part of 1 Corinthians is in the form of rebuke and correction. The first fourteen chapters deal primarily with errant behavior, and chapter 15 deals with errant theology. Even chapter 13, the beautiful treatise on love, was given to correct the lovelessness that so characterized the Corinthian church. But the rebuke and correction were themselves given out of deep love. Paul was steeped in the love of God, and his rebuke, like the Lord's own rebuke of His children, was always given in love. "Those whom the Lord loves He disciplines, and He scourges every son whom He receives" (Heb. 12:6).

In 1 Corinthians 16:13-14 Paul gives five final imperatives, five last commands, to the Corinthians. They are to be alert, firm, mature, strong, and loving. These commands are, in many ways, the positive side of what in earlier chapters the apostle had told the Corinthians *not* to be. Each command can serve as a point of departure for reviewing the epistle.

Be Alert

Paul's first command to the Corinthians was **be on the alert**, which comes from one word, *grēgoreō*, which can mean "to watch," "be awake," "be vigilant," and, figuratively, "be alive" (as in 1 Thess. 5:10, where "awake or asleep" refers to being alive or dead). The term is used some 22 times in the New Testament, often in reference to Christians' being spiritually awake and alert, as opposed to being spiritually indifferent and listless.

The Corinthians seemed normally to be in a spiritual and moral stupor, and sometimes even were in a physical stupor—as when they became drunk at the Lord's Table (1 Cor. 11:21). They were not **alert** in any worthwhile way. They allowed their previous pagan ideas and habits to come back into their lives and destroy their faithfulness to the Lord and their fellowship with each other. They substituted human wisdom for God's Word (1:18–2:16); they were factious (1:10-17; 3:9; etc.), immoral (5:1-13), litigious (6:1-8); they had confused and perverted ideas about marriage, divorce, and celibacy (7:1-40); they were self-indulgent (10:1-13) and indifferent to the welfare of others (10:23-33); they misunderstood and misused their spiritual gifts (12–14); and, above all, they were unloving, exemplifying all the things that love is not (13:1-6).

In the New Testament we are told of at least six important things we are to watch out for, to be on the **alert** for. First, we are to be on the alert against Satan. "Be of sober spirit, be on the alert. Your adversary, the devil, prowls about like a roaring lion, seeking someone to devour. But resist him, firm in your faith" (1 Pet. 5:8-9). We should learn Satan's strategies, which though subtle are basically identifiable in three areas: "the lust of the flesh and the lust of the eyes and the boastful pride of life" (1 John 2:16).

Second, we must be on the alert for temptation. "Keep watching and praying," Jesus said, "that you may not come into temptation" (Mark 14:38). If we are not watching and seeking the Lord's help in prayer, we often will not even notice temptation when it comes. When our spiritual eyes are shut or sleepy, we can fall more easily into sin.

Third, we must watch for apathy and indifference. The very nature of those sins makes them hard to notice. By definition, a person who is apathetic and indifferent is insensitive and therefore cannot be alert. The church at Sardis assumed that it had spiritual life because it had "a name that [it was] alive," but it was so indifferent to the Lord's will that it did not realize it was "dead." "Wake up, and strengthen the things that remain, which were about to die," the Lord told them, "for I have not found your deeds completed in the sight of My God. Remember therefore what you have received and heard; and keep it, and repent. If therefore you will not wake up, I will come like a thief, and you will not know at what hour I will come upon you" (Rev. 3:1-3).

Christians cannot disregard the Lord's Word with impunity. To neglect Scripture is to disregard it and treat it as if it means nothing. Before long we cannot remember what we have received and heard, and the Lord's way becomes more and more vague and indefinite. When His Word is indefinite to us we become indifferent to it, and we need to begin to "keep it, and repent." If we do not, God will chasten us in love—at a time, and perhaps in a way, that we do not expect.

Fourth, Christians should be alert for false teachers, about whom the New Testament gives many warnings. "There will also be false teachers among you, who will secretly introduce destructive heresies, even denying the Master who bought them" (2 Pet. 2:1). Many people, even in the church, actually will invite false teachers into their midst. "They will accumulate for themselves teachers in accordance to their own desires," because they become dissatisfied with "the truth, and will turn aside to myths." We are therefore to "be sober in all things," Paul warns, being on the alert for any teaching that does not square with Scripture (2 Tim. 4:3-5).

The first four alerts are negative, indicating things we are continually to watch for in order to avoid, because they will harm us. But the New Testament also gives us some positive things to watch for, some things that will strengthen and help us. As already mentioned above, Jesus tells us to watch and pray in order to escape temptation (Mark 14:38). Prayer strengthens us *in* God's way just as it protects us *against* Satan's way. Prayer is not simply a random ritual in which faithful Christians are to participate dutifully. It is the heartbeat of spiritual life. "With all prayer and petition pray at all times in the Spirit, and with this in view, be on the alert with all perseverance" (Eph. 6:18).

Christians should also be watching for the Lord's return. The two great motives we have for living faithfully for Christ are remembering what He did for us on the cross and looking forward to His coming again. "Therefore be on the alert, for you do not know which day your Lord is coming" (Matt. 24:42; cf. 25:13). "But the day of the Lord will come like a thief," Peter says; therefore "what sort of people ought you to be in holy conduct and godliness, looking for and hastening the coming of the day of God" (2 Pet. 3:10-12).

BE FIRM

Another principle for powerful living is standing **firm in the faith.** As the great theologian Charles Hodge reminded us, we should not consider every point of doctrine an open question. The Corinthians, like many of the Ephesians, were being "carried about by every wind of doctrine" (Eph. 4:14). They would not take a firm stand on many things. Little was certain and absolute; much was relative and tentative.

The **faith** of which Paul speaks here is not the faith of trusting but the faith of truth, the content of the gospel. It is "the faith which was once for all delivered to the saints" (Jude 3), "the gospel which I preached to you, which also you received, in which also you stand" (1 Cor. 15:1). It is the faith in which we are to "fight the good fight" (1 Tim. 6:12). Paul told the Philippians that he expected to hear that they were "standing firm in one spirit, with one mind striving together for the faith of the gospel" (Phil. 1:27). Doctrine is in view here.

Satan cannot take saving faith away from us, but he can, and often does, obscure the content of our faith, the sound doctrines of God's Word. If we do not hold fast to right interpretations of Scripture, we are certain to slip into wrong thinking, wrong belief, and wrong behavior. Many of the Corinthians apparently had come to look on the truth of God itself as foolishness, being corrupted by the influence of their unbelieving friends and neighbors (1 Cor. 1:18-21). Human philosophy and wisdom had all but obliterated their view of God's Word. By trying to combine human wisdom and God's wisdom they had undermined the uniqueness and the authority of God's revealed truth. Paul warned them, "Let no man deceive himself. If any man among you thinks that he is wise in this age, let him become foolish that he may become wise. For the wisdom of this world is foolishness before God" (1 Cor. 3:18-19). Like many professed Christians today, they considered Scripture to be but a human commentary on views of God that existed at the time of writing. If God's truth can be known at all, they believed, it is only through the filter of man's knowledge and wisdom.

The Corinthians not only were not standing firm in their view of Scripture but also had slipped terribly in their view of the Lord Jesus Christ. Paganism had so strongly reentered their thinking that some of them, claiming to speak "by the Spirit of God," were calling Jesus "accursed" (12:3). Because they had not stood firm in God's Word, they were corrupted and perverted to the extent of attacking the gospel at its heart, by renouncing Christ and calling Him accursed. They were "denying the Master who bought them" (2 Pet. 2:1).

The apostle therefore commands that they *must* **stand firm in the faith.** They must, as he commanded the Thessalonians, "stand firm and hold to the traditions which you were taught" (2 Thess. 2:15). If we are to be firm in the faith, we must be well taught in the Word, looking at everything and judging everything by God's truth and standards. We should pray for ourselves and for the church today as Epaphras prayed for the Colossians, that we "may stand perfect and fully assured in all the will of God" (Col. 4:12).

Be Mature

A third principle for powerful Christian living is being mature, which Paul expresses here as **act like men.** The basic idea is that of mature courage. The mature person has a sense of control, confidence, and courage that the immature or childish person does not have. Again we see that Paul's command is for the Corinthians to be the opposite of what they normally were. They were characterized by anything but maturity.

Paul already had pleaded with them, "Brethren, do not be children in your thinking; yet in evil be babes, but in your thinking be mature" (14:20). The Corinthians needed to grow up. Even when he pastored among them the apostle was not able to talk to them "as to spiritual men, but as to men of flesh, as to babes in Christ. I gave you milk to drink, not solid food; for you were not yet able to receive it." Since he had left Corinth they still had not matured. "Indeed, even now," he continues, "you are not yet able" (1 Cor. 3:1-2). He has to threaten them with discipline, just as a parent must do with a stubborn child. "What do you desire? Shall I come to you with a rod . . . ?" (4:21).

Maturity is one of the marks of love (1 Cor. 13:11), a virtue in which the

Corinthians were especially deficient. Love strives for maturity in all good things—in doctrine, in spiritual insight, in emotional stability and control, in personal relationships, in moral purity, and in all the fruit of the Spirit (Gal. 5:22-23). Above all we should "grow in the grace and knowledge of our Lord and Savior Jesus Christ" (2 Pet. 3:18), "until we all attain to the unity of the faith, and of the knowledge of the Son of God, to a mature man, to the measure of the stature which belongs to the fulness of Christ. . . . But speaking the truth in love, we are to grow up in all aspects into Him who is the head, even Christ" (Eph. 4:13, 15).

How does a believer grow and mature? By longing "for the pure milk of the word, that by it [we] grow in respect to salvation" (1 Pet. 2:2). The Bible provides spiritual and moral nourishment. "All Scripture is inspired by God and profitable for teaching, for reproof, for correction, for training in righteousness; that the man of God may be adequate, equipped for every good work" (2 Tim. 3:16-17).

BE STRONG

Be strong is Paul's fourth imperative for Christian living. As here, the Greek term (*krataioō*) is frequently used in the New Testament to denote inner, spiritual growth. The verb is in the passive voice, and literally means "be strengthened." We cannot strengthen ourselves; that is the Lord's work. Our part is to submit ourselves to Him in order that He *can* strengthen us. We can only "be strong in the Lord, and in the strength of His might" (Eph. 6:10), and "be strong in the grace that is in Christ Jesus" (2 Tim. 2:1).

Only a strong spirit can successfully battle and overcome the flesh. Again, that is where the Corinthians were weak. "For you are still fleshly," Paul told them. "For since there is jealousy and strife among you, are you not fleshly, and are you not walking like mere men?" (1 Cor. 3:3). Yet they had deceived themselves into thinking they were wise and strong. "If any man among you thinks he is wise in this age, let him become foolish that he may become wise" (3:18). The apostle says of them sarcastically, "We are fools for Christ's sake, but you are prudent in Christ; we are weak, but you are strong" (4:10). Because of their spiritual weakness they even despised and profaned the most sacred of things, including the Lord's Supper—for which desecration many of them became "weak and sick, and a number sleep," that is, had died (11:30).

The person who thinks he is strong in himself is in the greatest danger of falling (10:12). At one time in his ministry Paul faced that very danger. He had been "caught up into Paradise, and heard inexpressible words, which a man is not permitted to speak. . . . And because of the surpassing greatness of the revelations, for this reason, to keep me from exalting myself, there was given me a thorn in the flesh, a messenger of Satan to buffet me—to keep me from exalting myself!" The lesson the apostle learned directly from the Lord was, "'My grace is sufficient for you, for power is perfected in weakness.' Most gladly, therefore, I will rather boast about my weaknesses, that the power of Christ may dwell in me" (2 Cor. 12:4, 7, 9).

We can no more be spiritually strong than we can be physically strong

475

without self-discipline. "Everyone who competes in the games exercises self-control in all things. They then do it to receive a perishable wreath, but we an imperishable" (1 Cor. 9:25). Spiritual strength comes from self-sacrifice, self-denial, and self-discipline.

We grow in strength as we use our strength. As we "walk in a manner worthy of the Lord, to please Him in all respects, bearing fruit in every good work and increasing in the knowledge of God," we thereby become "strengthened with all power, according to His glorious might" (Col. 1:10-11).

The supreme source of all spiritual strength, of course, is Christ Himself. "I can do all things through Him who strengthens me," Paul declared (Phil. 4:13). "I thank Christ Jesus our Lord, who has strengthened me, because He considered me faithful, putting me into service" (1 Tim. 1:12). I can imagine that Paul often remembered Psalm 27:14—"Wait for the Lord; be strong, and let your heart take courage; yes, wait for the Lord."

As we wait for the Lord, yielding our spirits to His Spirit, we become "strengthened with power through His Spirit in the inner man" (Eph. 3:16).

BE LOVING

The fifth principle for powerful living is the most comprehensive, and without it the others could make us crusty, militant, and hard. So Paul says, **Let all that you do be done in love.** Love complements and balances everything else. It is the beautiful, softening principle. It keeps our firmness from becoming hardness and our strength from becoming domineering. It keeps our maturity gentle and considerate. It keeps our right doctrine from becoming obstinate dogmatism and our right living from becoming smug self-righteousness.

Love is what the Corinthians needed most, and is what believers of all ages have needed most. "Above all," Peter says, "keep fervent in your love for one another, because love covers a multitude of sins" (1 Pet. 4:8). Love, like spiritual strength, comes from the Lord. "Beloved, let us love one another, for love is from God; and every one who loves is born of God and knows God" (1 John 4:7). We are able to love one another "because He first loved us" (v. 19).

Marks of Love in the Fellowship (16:15-24)

49

Now I urge you, brethren (you know the household of Stephanas, that they were the first fruits of Achaia, and that they have devoted themselves for ministry to the saints), that you also be in subjection to such men and to everyone who helps in the work and labors. And I rejoice over the coming of Stephanas and Fortunatus and Achaicus; because they have supplied what was lacking on your part. For they have refreshed my spirit and yours. Therefore acknowledge such men.

The churches of Asia greet you. Aquila and Prisca greet you heartily in the Lord, with the church that is in their house. All the brethren greet you. Greet one another with a holy kiss.

The greeting is in my own hand—Paul. If anyone does not love the Lord, let him be accursed. Maranatha. The grace of the Lord Jesus be with you. My love be with you all in Christ Jesus. Amen. (16:15-24)

In many ways, verses 15-24 flow out of and illustrate the command of verse 14: "Let all that you do be done in love." Paul's closing words are not simply niceties that Paul threw in at the end of his letter as a matter of custom or courtesy. As much as any part of Scripture they are part of God's Word and are given to us for a divine purpose.

In these ten verses, either directly or indirectly, Paul is talking about love in the fellowship of the church. Because the Corinthians' greatest need was for all-pervasive love, that was Paul's last appeal to them. The passage is introduced by the command for them to love (v. 14) and concludes with the assurance that they themselves are loved (v. 24).

Under the surface of Paul's closing greetings, we see reflected seven marks of love in the Christian fellowship: evangelism, service to each other, submission to godly believers, companionship, respect for faithful workers, hospitality, and affection. Thus these apparently "loose ends" have a harmonious theme, as Paul demonstrates the attitude of love he desires the Corinthians to have.

EVANGELISM

Now I urge you, brethren (you know the household of Stephanas, that they were the first fruits of Achaia, . . .) (16:15a)

The members of the household of Stephanas not only were among the first converts in Corinth but were among **the first fruits** of Paul's evangelistic work in all of **Achaia**, the southern province of Greece, in which Athens and Corinth were located.

Though most of the Athenians to whom Paul had preached were skeptical and rejected the gospel, a few had believed (Acts 17:34). From Athens the apostle went to Corinth, where he spent the first few weeks witnessing primarily to Jews. But "when they resisted and blasphemed, he shook out his garments and said to them, 'Your blood be upon your own heads! I am clean. From now on I shall go to the Gentiles'" (18:6). A few Jews, such as Crispus (v. 8), trusted in Christ, but most of the Corinthian converts were Gentiles, among whom were **Stephanas** and his **household.** Whether to Jew or Gentile, Paul never stopped evangelizing, because love never stops reaching out to those who are lost.

Stephanas was one of the few persons in Corinth whom Paul baptized personally (1 Cor. 1:16). He was visiting Paul in Ephesus at the time this letter was written (16:17) and probably, along with Fortunatus and Achaicus, delivered the letter from Corinth mentioned in 7:1. His **household** would have included not only his family but all of his servants and slaves as well.

The **first fruits** were the part of a crop that was planted first and therefore ripened and was harvested first. Its appearance was a sign to the farmer that the remainder of the crop would also soon be ready to harvest. The conversion of Stephanas and his household was a sign that God was ready to reap an even greater harvest of souls in Corinth and the rest of **Achaia**. The believers to whom Paul wrote this letter were all a part of that harvest.

Through evangelism the early church expressed its love. Because of the Thessalonians' "work of faith and labor of love and steadfastness of hope in our Lord Jesus Christ, . . . the word of the Lord [had] sounded forth from [them], not only in

Macedonia and Achaia, but also in every place [their] faith toward God [had] gone forth" (1 Thess. 1:3, 8). Though Paul had ministered among them for only "three Sabbaths" (Acts 17:2), that church's testimony became known all over the Roman world. If we love in the way God loves, and in which Paul loved and the early church loved, we too will reach out with the gospel to those who do not know Christ.

The love in which we live and witness is ours only because God has given it to us (1 John 4:19). Paul loved because Christ's love controlled him (2 Cor. 5:14). Evangelizing love, or any other manifestation of Christian love, cannot be generated by the flesh, by our humanness. It is the work of the Spirit to produce and direct our love, and, through it, to bear fruit for God.

Before his conversion Paul had been the chief Jewish persecutor of the church. After his conversion he himself became the target of Jewish persecution. While he was still in Damascus "the Jews plotted together to do away with him. . . . And they were also watching the gates day and night so that they might put him to death" (Acts 9:23-24). It must have been hard, therefore, for Paul to have convinced anyone that he loved unbelieving Jews. When he wanted to convince the Roman church of that love he gave an extended affirmation: "I am telling the truth in Christ, I am not lying, my conscience bearing me witness in the Holy Spirit" (Rom. 9:1). He then went on to declare, "I have great sorrow and unceasing grief in my heart. For I could wish that I myself were accursed, separated from Christ for the sake of my brethren, my kinsmen according to the flesh" (vv. 2-3). That was evangelistic love at its highest.

Someone has said, "Evangelism is the sob of God. Evangelism is the anguished cry of Christ over a doomed Jerusalem. Evangelism is the call of Moses: 'O this people have sinned, yet now if Thou wilt, forgive them; if not, blot me, I pray Thee, out of the book Thou hast written.' Evangelism is the heartbroken cry of Paul: 'I could wish myself accursed.' Evangelism is the cry of John Knox: 'Give me Scotland for Christ or I die.' Evangelism is the weeping in the night of the parents of an unsaved child." We need to ask God for that kind of love.

We often give up too easily when those to whom we witness resist the gospel, and in so doing we betray the thinness of our love.

SERVICE TO EACH OTHER

they have devoted themselves for ministry to the saints. (16:15b)

A second mark of love is seen in the care that Stephanas and his household had for fellow believers. **They have devoted themselves for ministry to the saints.**

The basic meaning of *tassō* (**devoted**) is "to set in order." Frequently it means to set, appoint, assign, ordain, or designate a specific person or group of persons to a specific work or office. It is used in Romans 13:1 to indicate that human governments are "*established*" by God." In Acts 13:48 it is used to teach that everyone who believes in Jesus Christ is "*appointed*" to eternal life."

Devoted themselves is in an intense form in the Greek, emphasizing that Stephanas and his household served entirely on their own initiative. It is perfectly appropriate for a church to assign ministries and responsibilities to its members, just as the early church did in Jerusalem. In order that they could devote themselves more to prayer and preaching the Word of God, the apostles instructed the Jerusalem church to appoint some qualified men as deacons to supervise the feeding of needy widows in the congregation (Acts 6:2-4).

But Stephanas and his family and servants did not wait to be appointed. They appointed themselves to the **ministry** of service to fellow believers. They spontaneously assigned themselves to help meet any need they saw among **the saints.** Their service was self-motivated and self-assigned. Though it was sometimes necessary for the early church to assign tasks, as with the appointment of deacons mentioned above, most work was done and still is done by those who simply see a need and meet it.

William Barclay writes, "In the early church willing and spontaneous service was the beginning of official office. A man became a leader of the church not so much by any man-made appointment as because his life and work marked him out as one whom all men must respect. All those who share the work and toil of the gospel command respect, not because they have been appointed by a man to an office but because they are doing the work of Christ."

Ministry is from *diakonia,* which means "service." The one who does such work is a *diakonos,* from which we get the English *deacon.* The term originally was used of table waiters and various other kinds of household servants. The duty of the first Christian deacons was literally to serve tables (Acts 6:2), but the words soon came to be associated with any service to or for the church, and therefore are often translated "ministry" and "minister," respectively. The basic idea in both words always had to do with humble, submissive, personal service, not simply with an office or a particular function.

First Corinthians 12:5 speaks of the "ministries" (*diakonia*) of using our spiritual gifts. Acts 11:29 ("relief") and 2 Corinthians 8:4 ("support") speak of the *diakonia* of giving financially (cf. Rom. 15:31). The first deacons were appointed to "serve [*diakoneō*] tables" (Acts 6:2) so that the apostles could devote themselves "to the ministry [*diakonia*] of the word" (v. 4). Onesiphorus gave Paul great encouragement. "He often refreshed me and was not ashamed of my chains," while performing the "services he rendered [*diakonia*] at Ephesus" (2 Tim. 1:16, 18). Jesus said, "If anyone serves [*diakoneō*] Me, let him follow Me; and where I am, there shall My servant [*diakonos*] also be; if anyone serves [*diakoneō*] Me, the Father will honor him" (John 12:26). What Paul said to Archippus could be said to all of us: "Take heed to the ministry which you have received in the Lord, that you may fulfill it" (Col. 4:17). Every Christian is called by His Lord to serve, and one of the surest ways we can serve Christ is to serve **the saints** in His behalf (Matt. 25:34-40).

One expressive translation of *tassō* (**devoted**) is "addicted," as it is rendered in the King James Version. The Stephanas household had "addicted themselves to the ministry of the saints." They were the type of perpetually serving believers whom the writer of Hebrews praises: "For God is not unjust so as to forget your work and the love which you have shown toward His name, in having ministered and in still ministering to the saints" (Heb. 6:10).

Drug addiction has three primary characteristics. First of all it involves a strong habit, an overpowering desire and compulsion to take a given drug. Second, it involves a growing tolerance to the drug, so that, in order to maintain the desired effect, larger and larger doses must be taken. The third characteristic is dependence, the state in which the addicted person *must* have the drug in order to function.

Because of its association with narcotic drugs, the term *addiction* today has an unfavorable connotation. But it is appropriate to the type of service Paul is talking about here. The apostle himself was addicted to the Lord's work and strongly encouraged all believers to be like him. Paul did the Lord's work habitually, out of a powerful, driving compulsion. The more he ministered the more he felt compelled to minister. His tolerance for godly work caused him never to be satisfied with what he was doing, much less with what he had done. He became dependent on the Lord's work in order to function. He could not live normally if he were not engaged in some needed service for His Lord, for the Lord's people, or for the unsaved. I am sure that, had he tried to "take it easy" and relax for any length of time, he would have had severe "withdrawal symptoms." He was not a workaholic, compelled to work for work's sake. He was addicted to ministry for love's sake.

Submission

That you also be in subjection to such men and to everyone who helps in the work and labors. (16:16)

A third mark of love in Christian fellowship is submission. We are to submit ourselves not only to the appointed leaders in the church but to all those who faithfully do the Lord's work. *All* godly people are to be respected and submitted to.

Proper submission is a key theme of Spirit-filled living. All believers are to submit to each other (Eph. 5:21). Wives are to submit to their husbands (Eph. 5:22). Children are to submit to their parents (Eph. 6:1-3). Believers are to submit to government laws and ordinances (Rom. 13:1; 1 Pet. 2:13). Younger men are to submit to older men (1 Pet. 5:5*a*). *Every* believer is to be submissive in the ways God has ordained. In the matter of submission, our primary concern should not be about whom we should be *over* but whom we should be *under.* Humility will prevent the submitting person from becoming burdened, and the person submitted to from becoming overbearing. "All of you clothe yourselves with humility toward one another, for God is opposed to the proud, but gives grace to the humble" (1 Pet. 5:5*b*). When we are humble, God's grace gives us graciousness in our leading and graciousness in our following.

Speaking of those who belong to Him, Jesus said, "Whoever wishes to become great among you shall be your servant, and whoever wishes to be first among you shall be your slave; just as the Son of Man did not come to be served, but to serve, and to give His life a ransom for many" (Matt. 20:26-28). In our relationships to other believers, our first concern should be for how we can properly submit.

Practically, that means that we should find a godly man or woman who is addicted to the Lord's will and the Lord's work and make that person our pattern for Christian living. As we submit, learn, grow, and mature, our own life will become one that others can emulate. Paul could say to the Corinthians, "Be imitators of me, just as I also am of Christ" (1 Cor. 11:1; cf. 4:16). To the Thessalonians he could say, "For our gospel did not come to you in word only, but also in power and in the Holy Spirit and with full conviction; just as you know what kind of men we proved to be among you for your sake. You also became imitators of us and of the Lord, having received the word in much tribulation with the joy of the Holy Spirit" (1 Thess. 1:5-6). The writer of Hebrews says, "Remember those who led you, who spoke the word of God to you; and considering the result of their conduct, imitate their faith" (Heb. 13:7). That is the cycle of discipleship the Lord intends for His church. "A pupil is not above his teacher; but everyone, after he has been fully trained, will be like his teacher" (Luke 6:40).

Paul wanted the selfish, unsubmissive Corinthians to submit to his model, just as he continually submitted to Christ's model. We are all called to submit ourselves to those who have proved their own submission to Christ. Who is that person to whom we should submit? It is anyone who faithfully portrays and proclaims the Word of God or serves in His ministry, **everyone who helps in the work and labors.**

Christ's people are not to fight for their own rights, privileges, and respect, but are to seek out and follow those to whom they can submit in Christ, who can be their teachers and examples. True love brings true submission. True submission would, by itself, save countless conflicts, squabbles, and hard and hurt feelings within God's family. It would make His children both happier and more productive in their Father's work.

Companionship

And I rejoice over the coming of Stephanas and Fortunatus and Achaicus; because they have supplied what was lacking on your part. For they have refreshed my spirit and yours. (16:17-18a)

Another wonderful mark of loving fellowship is companionship. Companionship is not something we directly do or give. It is the by-product of other things, things as simple as standing with a friend who is in trouble or sitting with someone who is sick, or as complex as mutual ministry. The main ingredient of companionship is togetherness; it cannot be experienced from a distance or secondhand.

Paul was grateful that his three friends **Stephanas and Fortunatus and Achaicus** had come from Corinth to be with him. They had ministered to the apostle in specific ways. They had **supplied what was lacking** on the **part** of their fellow Corinthians. But more than that they genuinely befriended Paul, by being with him, by encouraging him, and by identifying with His ministry. In so doing they **refreshed** Paul's **spirit** and the spirit of the Corinthian church that had sent them.

One of the finest compliments we can be paid is for our Christian friends to say that we are refreshing to be around. That is a mark of true companionship, just as companionship is a mark of true love. Companionship builds up God's family. Companionship can help heal our wounds even before our friends know we hurt; it can comfort us even when those around us are not aware of our sorrow; it can encourage us even when we ourselves hardly realize that we are discouraged.

Companionship is also a preventive. Just being with loving Christian friends can keep us from getting hurt, from falling into sin, or from losing heart. One of the surest ways we can get into spiritual trouble is by neglecting fellowship with other believers. The Corinthians had violated fellowship with their factions, their lawsuits, their sexual sins, their proud abuse of gifts, and their desecration of the supreme Christian fellowship, the Lord's Table.

God not only has made us for Himself but has made us for each other. What the three friends from Corinth did for Paul is what Jesus promises to do for His followers. Paul used the same Greek word (*anapauō*, **refreshed**) in this passage that Jesus used in promising "rest" to those who believe in Him: "Come unto Me, all who are weary and heavy-laden, and I will give you rest" (Matt. 11:28). Paul's friends helped the hard-pressed apostle find rest and refreshment. They helped lighten his burdens just by being with him. Because they came from a church that was not known for love or companionship, those three men doubtlessly gave Paul a special spiritual boost. "Like cold water to a weary soul, so is good news from a distant land" (Prov. 25:25). **Stephanas and Fortunatus and Achaicus** were themselves Paul's good news from Corinth, cold water to his weary **spirit.**

God can comfort us directly, but He often chooses to comfort us through others. "God, who comforts the depressed, comforted us by the coming of Titus" (2 Cor. 7:6). Near the end of his life, which he had given selflessly in serving and encouraging others, Paul was himself in special need of encouragement and help. He asked Timothy to "make every effort to come to [him] soon" and to bring along Mark, "for he is useful to me for service." Demas had forsaken the apostle, and Tychicus had been sent to Ephesus. Only Luke remained, and, dear and helpful as that friend was, Paul felt the need for more companionship (2 Tim. 4:9-12).

The kind of companionship those men offered refreshes everyone involved. The coming of the three friends from Corinth not only refreshed Paul but also had refreshed the Corinthians, **my spirit and yours.** When Titus personally reported to Paul the good news of the Corinthian church's change of heart and repentance of rebelliousness, Paul wrote to tell the church of his joy that now they too were refreshing others with their fellowship: "For this reason we have been comforted. And besides our comfort, we rejoiced even much more for the joy of Titus, because his spirit has been refreshed by you all" (2 Cor. 7:13).

RESPECT FOR FAITHFUL WORKERS

Therefore acknowledge such men. (16:18*b*)

The Corinthians are instructed to **acknowledge such men** as Stephanas, Fortunatus, and Achaicus (v. 15). *Epiginōskō* (**acknowledge**) signifies recognition of something for what it really is. In 14:37 Paul uses the term to tell the Corinthians to "recognize that the things which I write to you are the Lord's commandment." Now he tells them to recognize faithful, godly workers for what they are.

Paul is not speaking of setting up ornate plaques or statues inscribed with the persons' names. He is simply calling for respect and appreciation, which sometimes will be public and sometimes private. Proper appreciation of deserving persons in the church not only is not wrong but is pleasing to the Lord.

Typically, the Corinthians were neither respectful nor appreciative. Each member was too concerned about his own prestige and recognition. They were much more inclined to criticize each other than to praise each other. They were quick to claim, "'I am of Paul,' and, 'I of Apollos,' and, 'I of Cephas,' and, 'I of Christ'" (1 Cor. 1:12), but they used those names in pride, not in appreciation. Paul was not respected by many of the Corinthians, who had "become arrogant, as though [he] were not coming" back to correct them in person (4:18). Some, apparently, had questioned his apostleship and his authority to teach them or to be supported by them (9:1-6). At least four times in this letter Paul says or implies that the Corinthians were arrogant (4:6, 18; 8:1; 13:4).

The Corinthian church had members who were like Diotrephes, a leader John describes as one "who loves to be first among them [and] does not accept what we say" (3 John 9). Diotrephes was even jealous of the gentle, loving apostle John. He not only ridiculed and maligned John himself but also the representatives John had sent on his behalf (v. 10). Such a leader is not godly, no matter how humanly talented and capable he may be, and should not be imitated (v. 11). Demetrius, on the other hand, had "received a good testimony from everyone, and from the truth itself" (v. 12). He is the sort of Christian we should imitate, respect, and support, "that we may be fellow workers with the truth" (v. 8).

In God's pattern for church leadership, godly persons rise to the top by virtue of their godliness—their right belief, right living, and loving care for others. Such persons we are to **acknowledge,** respect, and imitate. When we choose leaders simply because of their money, prestige, education, influence, or talents we follow the world's standards rather than God's. God's standards for leadership are purity and maturity. When the church follows and respects godly and mature believers, the body of Christ is strengthened in fellowship, service, and love.

Epaphroditus was the sort of godly person to be emulated and acknowledged. "Therefore receive him in the Lord with all joy," Paul tells the Philippians, "and hold men like him in high regard" (Phil. 2:29). Epaphroditus was the epitome of the unselfish, sacrificial servant. He had served Paul in behalf of the Philippian church, just as Stephanas, Fortunatus, and Achaicus has served him in behalf of the Corinthian church. He had, in fact, almost literally worked himself to death. "He came close to death for the work of Christ, risking his life" (v. 30).

The word *paraboleuomai,* translated "risking" in the verse just quoted, means "to throw away, to abandon, to roll the dice, to put everything on the line." In the early church certain groups of faithful Christians who were continually out on the front lines of witnessing and service were called Parabolani, "The Riskers." Among other things, they exposed themselves to deadly diseases by caring for the sick and burying the dead. Their lives were always on the line in behalf of the Lord's work.

When we find someone who is faithful to the Word of God and who gives his life to the work of Jesus Christ, we should do our utmost to imitate that person. And we should give him or her our greatest respect. When that is done, Christ's church will function as an organism, a living body, not just as an organization.

Those worthy of honor do not seek it. What makes them honorable is their humility before the Lord in their service for Him. But though they do not desire honor, those they teach and serve should desire to give them honor. To give such honor is pleasing to God. "Appreciate those who diligently labor among you, and have charge over you in the Lord and give you instruction, and . . . esteem them very highly in love because of their work" (1 Thess. 5:12-13). Writing to Timothy, Paul says, "Let the elders who rule well be considered worthy of double honor, especially those who work hard at preaching and teaching" (1 Tim. 5:17).

God's design for the church is simple. The godly are to be in leadership. They rule, they teach, they admonish, they set the example. They are chosen because they are especially submissive to the Lord. The rest of the church therefore is to submit to them, in respect, honor, and love. They are accountable to the Lord for their leadership, and the rest are accountable to the Lord for submitting to and respecting that leadership. "Obey your leaders, and submit to them; for they keep watch over your souls, as those who will give an account. Let them do this with joy and not with grief, for this would be unprofitable for you" (Heb. 13:17). If we do not follow and honor those who have rightful leadership in the church, we not only frustrate and inhibit their fruitfulness but our own as well. We cannot properly serve the Lord if we do not properly respect godly leaders.

Hospitality

The churches of Asia greet you. Aquila and Prisca greet you heartily in the Lord, with the church that is in their house. All the brethren greet you. (16:19-20a)

As implied in these verses, love always produces hospitality, love for strangers. Paul did not make idle comments, much less stretch the truth, in order to impress his readers. It was not that **the churches of Asia** necessarily had sent formal greetings to the church in Corinth, but he is passing on genuine salutations. Those churches were honestly concerned for their fellow believers in Corinth, and their leaders had asked Paul to greet them when he had opportunity. Most of those involved were strangers to each other, but the love expressed was no less genuine because of that.

When God's people are committed to pure doctrine and pure living, they are bonded together in love—as individuals and as congregations—even when separated by great distances and by great differences in culture and circumstances. The spirit of hospitality exists among loving Christians even when there is no direct opportunity to be hospitable. We can support our brethren in the Lord by prayer and encouragement even if we never have the opportunity to have them in our homes.

Aquila and Prisca, or Priscilla, had become good friends of Paul's when he stayed at their house during his first ministry in Corinth (Acts 18:1-3). It is possible that he stayed with them the entire year and a half. They were fellow tentmakers, highly respected by the apostle, and valuable to his ministry. They accompanied Paul to Ephesus and, shortly after arriving, demonstrated their thorough understanding of the gospel by taking the gifted Apollos aside and explaining "to him the way of God more accurately" (Acts 18:18-19, 24-26). We know from our present text that they also established a congregation **in their** own **house.**

In the early church the homes of believers were used for almost every type of Christian activity—for eating together (Acts 2:46); for teaching and preaching (5:42); for preevangelism and evangelism (10:23, 27-48); for worship and preaching (20:7); and for witnessing and discussion (28:23). Often the home of a believer was the regular meeting place for worship and fellowship. It was in behalf of the house church of **Aquila and Prisca, . . . with the church that is in their house,** that Paul sent greetings to Corinth.

When Christians traveled from place to place in New Testament times they could expect, almost without exception, to be entertained with great care and love by fellow Christians. There were no strangers among believers (Acts 2:42-46). Hospitality was second nature, a matter of course, a natural outgrowth of their love for Christ and for all who belonged to Him. Every Christian home today should be an open, transparent, and loving haven for those who need hospitality.

From the earliest times (see Acts 6:1) the church had large numbers of widows. Those who qualified to be on a church's official list of widows had to be over sixty years old and have a reputation for doing good works, being a good mother, and "showing hospitality to strangers." Paul goes on to illustrate the sort of hospitality he had in mind. A qualifying widow must have done such things as "washed the saints' feet," "assisted those in distress," and "devoted herself to every good work" (1 Tim. 5:9-10). Hospitality is not an incidental or optional virtue for Christians.

The outstanding mark of the Good Samaritan was hospitality. Both directly and indirectly he did everything in his power to assist the man who was beaten and robbed. Because "he felt compassion," he "came to him, and bandaged up his wounds, pouring oil and wine on them; and he put him on his own beast, and brought him to an inn, and took care of him. And on the next day he took out two denarii and gave them to the innkeeper and said, 'Take care of him; and whatever more you spend, when I return, I will repay you'" (Luke 10:33-35). The supreme mark of being a Christian neighbor is hospitality; and hospitality is a notable mark of Christian love.

AFFECTION

Greet one another with a holy kiss. (16:20b)

Finally, love in the fellowship will be marked by outward, visible signs of affection.

In Scripture, kissing in a romantic sense between a man and a woman is referred to only twice, in Proverbs (7:13) and in the Song of Solomon (4:11). Every other reference has to do with the expression of affection between men and men, and women and women. The kiss was given on the cheek or forehead and represented essentially what a hug or a warm embrace represents today. Because of our greater personal isolation and insulation today, such demonstrated affection between persons of the same sex is sadly uncommon.

And, even though in the early church the practice of the **holy kiss** was a beautiful, pure, and meaningful expression of brotherly love (cf. Rom. 16:16; 2 Cor. 13:12; 1 Thess. 5:26; 1 Pet. 5:14), it came in later centuries to be abused. It was practiced so indiscriminately, for example, that a church council in the 6th century outlawed the kissing of dead bodies.

Paul was speaking of the genuine and spontaneous expression of brotherly or sisterly love, which in that day often was expressed by a kiss. A warm, affectionate handshake or an arm around the shoulder can express the same affection. In most of the church today the danger is in showing too little affection rather than too much.

One of the dangers of large churches is that they easily allow strangers to remain strangers. A shy person is often not noticed, and some Christians, unfortunately, do not *want* to get involved in the fellowship. But where there is genuine love, Christians will find ways to make friends with strangers and to show affection to Christian brothers and sisters.

CLOSING COMMENTS

The greeting is in my own hand—Paul. If anyone does not love the Lord, let him be accursed. Maranatha. The grace of the Lord Jesus be with you. My love be with you all in Christ Jesus. Amen. (16:21-24)

The main part of the letter, which had been dictated to a scribe, was signed in his **own hand** and finished by **Paul** himself. The closing remarks are a short postscript, perhaps given in his own handwriting to clearly establish the letter's authenticity.

The ending is in two distinct parts: a stern warning and an affectionate affirmation of love.

The warning is against **anyone** who **does not love the Lord**. Such a person proves beyond doubt that he does not belong to the Lord and therefore does not belong in the fellowship of God's people. The term for **love** that Paul uses here is *phileō,* which means "to have tender affection." It is not as strong a word as *agapē* (supreme love), and is never commanded to be given to God. An implication of this verse, however, is that such minimal affection is an element of the love that is acceptable to God. When Jesus asked Peter the third time if he loved Him, He used *phileō.* When Peter again answered yes, Jesus accepted that love. Peter did not claim *agapē,* but even his kind affection evidenced his trust in Jesus. Paul's choice of words in this passage flowed fom his emphasis on affection.

If a person does not **love the Lord** with tender affection, then he obviously has no supreme love for Him, and thus no part in Him at all. Such a person "does not abide in the teaching of Christ, does not have God," and should not be received into Christian fellowship (2 John 9-10). He should not even be greeted, because to do is to participate "in his evil deeds" (v. 11). He should be considered **accursed** (*anathema*), devoted to destruction.

The two seemingly inconsistent parts of Paul's closing words are related to the same truth, the theme of the epistle itself: **love.** The warning is against those whose lack of love for the Lord proves their lostness. The gracious affection is expressed to those who, with Paul, *do* love the Lord and each other.

I believe that in this context **maranatha,** an Aramaic term meaning "Our Lord, come," is Paul's appeal for the Lord to come and take away those who are **accursed,** the nominal, false Christians who are always such a great threat to the true church. The idea is, "God, come and remove them" before they cause more harm. **Maranatha** thus contains an implied invitation to those lost church members to receive Christ before God takes them away and the opportunity for salvation is forever gone.

The apostle closes with words of **grace** and **love** for those who love the Lord. Those two words summarize Paul's message to the Corinthian believers and the Lord's message to all believers.

Bibliography

Barclay, William. *The Letters to the Corinthians*. Philadelphia: Westminster, 1956.

Clark, Gordon H. *First Corinthians*. Nutley, N.J.: Presbyterian and Reformed, 1975.

Godet, F. L. *The First Epistle to the Corinthians*. Grand Rapids: Zondervan, 1971.

Grosheide, F. W. *The First Epistle to the Corinthians*. The New International Commentary on the New Testament. Grand Rapids: Eerdmans, 1953.

Hodge, Charles. *An Exposition of the First Epistle to the Corinthians*. Grand Rapids: Eerdmans, 1974.

Lenski, R. C. H. *The Interpretation of St. Paul's First and Second Epistles to the Corinthians*. Minneapolis: Augsburg, 1963.

Morgan, G. Campbell. *The Corinthian Letters of Paul*. Old Tappan, N.J.: Revell, 1946.

Morris, Leon. *The First Epistle of Paul to the Corinthians*. The Tyndale New Testament Commentaries. London: The Tyndale Press, 1958.

Robertson, A. T., and Plummer, Alfred. *A Critical and Exegetical Commentary on the First Epistle of St. Paul to the Corinthians*. Edinburgh: T. & T. Clark, 1914.

Indexes

Index of Greek Words

Index of Hebrew Words

Index of Scripture

Index of Subjects

Moody Press, a ministry of the Moody Bible Institute, is designed for education, evangelization, and edification. If we may assist you in knowing more about Christ and the Christian life, please write us without obligation: Moody Press, c/o MLM, Chicago, Illinois 60610